CAMBRIDGE SOUTH ASIAN STUDIES

RULERS, TOWNSMEN AND BAZAARS

CAMBRIDGE SOUTH ASIAN STUDIES

These monographs are published by the Syndics of Cambridge University Press in association with the Cambridge University Centre for South Asian Studies. The following books have been published in this series:

RULERS, TOWNSMEN AND BAZAARS

NORTH INDIAN SOCIETY
IN THE AGE OF BRITISH EXPANSION,
1770–1870

C. A. BAYLY

Smuts Reader in Commonwealth Studies
University of Cambridge

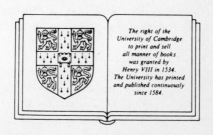

The right of the
University of Cambridge
to print and sell
all manner of books
was granted by
Henry VIII in 1534.
The University has printed
and published continuously
since 1584.

CAMBRIDGE UNIVERSITY PRESS

CAMBRIDGE
NEW YORK   NEW ROCHELLE
MELBOURNE   SYDNEY

Published by the Press Syndicate of the University of Cambridge
The Pitt Building, Trumpington Street, Cambridge CB2 1RP
32 East 57th Street, New York, NY 10022, USA
10 Stamford Road, Oakleigh, Melbourne 3166, Australia

First published 1983

First paperback edition 1988

Printed in Great Britain by
Redwood Burn Limited, Trowbridge, Wiltshire

Library of Congress catalogue card number: 82–4420

British Library Cataloguing in Publication Data
Bayly, C. A.
Rulers, townsmen and bazaars: North Indian society
in the age of British expansion, 1770–1870.
(Cambridge South Asian studies series; 28)
1. India – History – British occupation, 1765–1947
I. Title
954   DS475.1

ISBN 0 521 22932 4 hard covers
ISBN 0 521 31054 7 paperback

CONTENTS

MAPS

PREFACE

Since the Middle Ages European travellers have been fascinated by the bustle and colour of the oriental bazaar. Often they contrasted the sophistication of trade and the wealth of cities with what they took to be the barbarism and decadence of the rulers of the east. This book too grew out of a fascination with the rich pattern of commercial life still to be found in the tangled lanes of brass-smiths' stalls and ancient merchant houses which lie behind the water-front of the city of Benares. The original purpose was to put side by side the 'inner history' of merchant people which emerged from their own legends, family papers and account books with the impersonal records of the colonial customs houses in order to create the social history of an old-style Indian business community. The notion was typical of the 1960s when small-scale studies of community, village or 'caste' seemed to point the way forward, and when the vogue for business history had set the ghost of Max Weber walking again.

Some fragments of that original work have been preserved in this book, especially in chapters 4, 10 and 11. But during the 1970s the scope of the study broadened considerably. By the light of day the treasure of the old account books and family histories dimmed only slightly. But these evocative fragments required a much firmer backing in standard archival and secondary sources if they were to be used to address the major questions of Indian social history. More important, the value of local and community studies for historiography seemed to be diminishing. Often the most important questions seemed to revolve around the relationship between the small community – family, village or 'caste' – and the wider world of government, business and the agrarian economy. Of course, the day when a 'total history' of India in the French style can be attempted remains distant. The basic demographic and price data is only now being assembled for the period between 1750 and 1850, while the study of changing 'popular mentalities' looks dauntingly difficult in the Indian context.

This book, therefore, is a compromise. An attempt has been made to set the detailed studies of towns, bazaars, merchants and service people against the background of crucial developments in the political economy of pre-colonial and early colonial north India. But many important questions have necessarily been neglected or only lightly touched upon. In particular, the book is not intended as economic history. Though there is much discussion here of trade and merchants, the concern is with the patterns of social and political relations which derive from economic activity and not with economic development or with volumes of trade and production as such. Instead, the book is concerned to give depth to studies of the social organisation, ideology and politics of the 'Indian middle classes' of the later nineteenth century by tracing some of their indigenous origins in the society of the eighteenth-century successor states to the Mughal dominion and also in the conflicts and accommodations of early colonial rule. Above all the aim has been to put together types of history and periods of history which have normally been studied in self-contained compartments. Agrarian, commercial, 'colonial', even religious history appears in these pages, and it is hoped that the different levels of argument are mutually enriching.

A full list of acknowledgements would need to refer to a very large number of individual scholars working on South Asian history and most librarians and archivists who hold materials on nineteenth-century north India. But some special debts must be recorded. The United Kingdom Social Science Research Council generously supported an initial period of archival and field work on which the study is based. The Cambridge Centre of South Asian Studies under its Director Mr B. H. Farmer have long provided financial and moral support, as have the Master and Fellows of St Catharine's College, Cambridge. Librarians and archivists at the UP Central Records Office, Allahabad, the National Archives of India, New Delhi, and the India Office Library, London, have efficiently satisfied voracious demands for files and volumes.

In India I could not have achieved anything without the disinterested help of descendants of the members of the nineteenth-century business community. Dr Girish Chandra and the late Sri Kumud Chandra of Benares gave up a great deal of their time without complaint. Sri Ram Krishna, Sri Devi Narayan, Dr Anand Krishna (Benares); Mr G. P. Tandon, Sri Harimohan Das and Sri Beni Prasad Tandon (Allahabad); Professor R. S. Sharma (Agra); and descendants of the family firm Chunna Mal Saligram (Delhi), answered ignorant questions and produced dusty documents from their cupboards with grace. Two particular friends in India were Mrs R. Gandhi who provided sustenance and a convivial home base, and Sri Satyapal who instructed me greatly from his own considerable knowledge of Indian social history.

The academic debts are numerous and would fill many *bahi khatas*. Among many people who have helped form my ideas in Cambridge or at Cambridge seminars, Christopher Baker, Sugata Bose, Simon Commander, Satish Mishra, Farhan Nizami and David Washbrook have made valuable comments on parts of the text. John Harrison of the School of Oriental and African Studies, London, provided moral and material support in Britain and India. I profited from discussions at two seminars in the United States, one held at the University of Pennsylvania under the auspices of the United States SSRC, and the other at the University of California, Santa Cruz under the auspices of its Pacific Affairs Center, where parts of chapters were presented. As will become apparent, I have also relied heavily on the publications of Richard Barnett, Bernard Cohn, Thomas Metcalf and Asiya Siddiqi. Many others have helped create a climate conducive to research, but I must mention particularly my late friends and mentors Jack Gallagher and Eric Stokes; everyone in the field has benefited from the high standards of scholarship and humanity which they set. It is especially sad that Eric Stokes did not live to see this volume completed. He would have recognised many of his own ideas here, albeit mangled and devoid of his literary flair. His critique would have been gentle but penetrating.

Finally, my wife Susan has taken too much time off her own scholarly work in attempts to improve this text and the state of mind of its author. To her the volume is dedicated.

St Catharine's College, Cambridge,
October 1981

ABBREVIATIONS

AAR	*Asiatick Annual Register*
Agent	Agent to the Governor General, Benares
App	Appendix
AR	*Asiatic(k) Researches*
BCJ	Bengal (Criminal) Judicial Proceedings, India Office Library
Bd	Board of Commissioners (Board of Revenue)
CGC	Collector of Government Customs
Collr	Collector of District
Commr	Commissioner of Division
Cons.	Consultation
COR	*Calendar of Oriental Records* (UP Central Records Office, Allahabad)
CPC	*Calendar of Persian Correspondence* (National Archives of India, New Delhi)
CPR	Conquered and Ceded Provinces Revenue and Revenue (Customs) Proceedings, India Office Library, London
DG	*District Gazetteers of the United Provinces* (48 vols., Allahabad, 1903–11)
DR	'Duncan Records' (Settlement and Miscellaneous), UP Central Records Office, Allahabad
For. Pol.	Foreign Political Department, National Archives of India
For. Sec.	Foreign Secret Department, National Archives of India
GG	Governor General
IA	*Indian Antiquary*
IESHR	*Indian Economic and Social History Review*
IHC	Indian Historical Congress
IOL	India Office Library and Records, London
JASB	*Journal of the Asiatic Society of Bengal*
Judl	Judicial Correspondence
Magt.	Magistrate (of District)
NAI	National Archives of India, New Delhi
NWP	North-Western Provinces
NWPCJ	North-Western Provinces (Criminal) Judicial Proceedings, India Office Library

OG	*Gazetteer of the Province of Oudh* (3 vols., Lucknow, 1876–8)
PP	*Parliamentary Papers*
PR	Proceedings of the Resident (later Agent to the Governor General, Benares) UP Central Records Office, Allahabad
Supdt	Superintendent of Police (North-Western Provinces)
SR	*Settlement Report* (of District)
UP	United Provinces of Agra and Oudh
UPR	Uttar Pradesh Central Records Office, Allahabad
ZC	*Zillah Court Decisions, North-Western Provinces* (Agra, 1839–65)

NOTE ON THE USE OF INDIAN WORDS

In general, I have used the more accurate of the 'Anglo-Indian' transliteration of Hindustani words which are found, for instance, in the *District Gazetteers* of the early decades of this century. I have avoided both 'corrupt' eighteenth-century forms and more scientific modern transliterations with diacritical marks on the grounds that these would tend to greater confusion in historical exposition. There are some exceptions: 'Cawnpore' becomes 'Kanpur', for instance, because the former is a 'corrupt' survival. Also some eighteenth-century forms of Indian names have been retained when it is unclear what the original might have been, e.g. 'Beechuck', 'Munee Royder', etc.

NOTE ON GEOGRAPHY

The administrative divisions of Gangetic north India went through many changes between 1770 and 1870. The semi-independent Mughal province of Awadh expanded in the years 1720 to 1775 to incorporate other political entities, shown on Map 2, which had once been parts of the provinces of Allahabad, Delhi, etc. In particular the rulers of Awadh annexed some of the lands lying between the rivers Ganges and Jamna, the 'Doab'. In 1801 a large area of Awadh situated in the Doab and Rohilkhand was ceded to the British. It was added to districts conquered from the Marathas in 1803–4 around Delhi and Agra to form the 'Conquered and Ceded Provinces' of the British Bengal Presidency. The term 'Western Provinces' and later 'North-Western Provinces' came into gradual use to describe this area and the adjoining Benares Division; these were the 'North-Western Provinces' of the Bengal Presidency. After 1833 the Lieutenant-Governorship of the North-Western Provinces, composed of a series of Divisions headed by Commissioners regulating a series of Districts headed by Collectors and Magistrates took on the form it was to retain throughout the rest of the British period. These changes can be traced in detail in Imtiaz Husain, *Land Revenue Policy in North India* (Delhi, 1967), pp. 3–5. In 1856 the remaining 'Reserved Dominions' of the ruler of Awadh were annexed to become the British Province of Oudh under a Chief Commissioner. In 1901 the two provinces were amalgamated to become the United

Provinces of Agra and Oudh. On Independence this became the Indian state of Uttar Pradesh. I have also used the term 'Hindustan' to designate the cultural area covered by this book. This was an Indo-Persian geographical term which distinguished the area from the Punjab, the Deccan, and Bengal and Bihar.

Introduction

The valley of the river Ganges was the main axis of Britain's Asian empire. Along its length ran Kim's Grand Trunk Road which linked British Bengal with the capital cities of Mughal India and pointed northward to the high regions of Central Asia. Down the river in the course of the nineteenth century were transported huge quantities of cotton, opium and indigo bound for China and Europe to balance the books of Britain's whole oriental trade. By 1880 a railway ran along the river bank speeding Lancashire goods to their mass market in the interior but also bringing the angry young men of Bengal into contact with the conservative leaders of the Hindu and Muslim heartland.

British rule and British commerce had slowly crept up the great valley from maritime Bengal between 1757 and 1856.[1] Awadh (Oudh) was the major state of the area and home domain of the Vazir of the failing Mughal empire. In 1764 the British defeated its ruler and forced on him a tributary alliance which bound Awadh to pay a large annual subsidy. At the same time, the East India Company took over control of the kingdom of Benares and became protector of that great Hindu pilgrimage place. In 1801 the Awadh ruler was forced to cede to the Company a large part of his territory along the rivers Ganges and Jamna in order to discharge his tributary obligations. During the next six years war again spread across north and central India, allowing the British to conquer or coerce a further range of small states lying around Delhi, the old imperial capital. Thus by 1808, the British had established dominance over the heartland of Mughal India. But it was not until 1856 that the Victorian desire for orderly administration and bigger revenues impelled them to swallow the last 'reserved dominions' of the Awadh ruler. This final annexation provided one of the main grievances fuelling the great rebellion which broke out throughout north India in the following year.

For the British, the lands bordering the river Ganges were the most

---

[1] P. Basu, *Oudh and the East India Company, 1785–1801* (Lucknow, 1943); C. C. Davies, *Warren Hastings and Oudh* (London, 1939); C. U. A. Aitchison, *Collections of Treaties, Engagements and Sunnuds Relating to India and Neighbouring Countries* (Calcutta, 1929–33), II, 55–147, esp. pp. 57, 100–3.

populous and the most troublesome of their Indian empire. They threw up in successive generations the Rebellion of 1857, the Hindu revivalist campaigns of the 1890s, the Muslim movements of 1919–21 and in the 1930s and 1940s mass rural nationalism. But though this study concerns the period when the British were establishing their administrative and commercial system between Calcutta and Delhi, it focuses on Indian society. The aim is to trace the fate of Indian towns, merchants and service people during the period of transition between the heyday of the last indigenous states and the establishment of the mature colonial system after 1857. In doing so, the book highlights the way in which conditions in Indian society determined the emergence and form of British India.

The context of historical writing in which the book is set has been established for many years. The founders of the Indian empire in the reign of George III were well aware of the extent to which their creation rested on the compliance and aid of Indian rulers, merchants and administrators. Even though the late Victorians tended to see 'native' society as a static backdrop to British exploits, Sir John Seeley in the 1880s warned his audience against the chauvinistic belief that Britain had conquered India in any simple sense. The East India Company, he said, had merely taken advantage of the disturbed conditions after the end of the Mughal empire in 1707, and that was mainly by dint of the support of important groups of Indians.[2] This change of perspective was slow in establishing itself. The history of non-European peoples was held back for a generation by the imperial bluster of the interwar years. But after 1945 Indian history was drawn along in the train of the vast amount of scholarly writing on Asia and Africa which insisted that imperialism was created as much by events and interests in the non-European world as by the driving force of industrialisation and national conflict in Europe itself. In the words of Ronald Robinson:

The central mechanisms of imperialism may be found in the systems of collaboration set up in preindustrial societies which succeeded, or failed, in meshing the incoming processes of European expansion into indigenous social politics and evolving a balance between the two.[3]

So pervasive, even cliché-ridden has become this insistence on the indigenous component in European expansion that a reaction against it seems inevitable. Recent writers have turned back to Europe seeking there the dynamism which drove the west to create the modern world system. Asians and Africans are again in danger of dropping out of the

[2] J. R. Seeley, *The Expansion of England* (London, 1880).
[3] R. E. Robinson, 'Non-European foundations of European Imperialism', in R. Owen and B. Sutcliffe (eds), *Studies in the Theory of Imperialism* (London, 1972), p. 120.

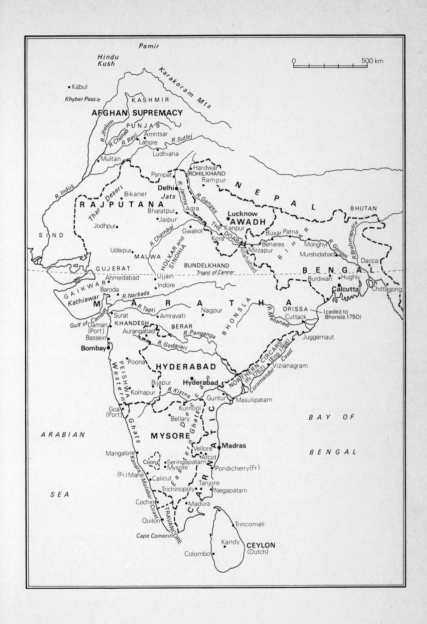

Map 1   India about 1785

picture, while terms like 'peripheral' and 'semi-peripheral zones' have replaced the evocative 'Dark Continents' of the Victorians in contemporary debate.

On closer inspection, though, the historians' retreat to Europe is premature. The junction between Robinson's 'processes of European expansion' and 'indigenous social politics' has only been sketchily made for large areas of the colonial world. It lies more in the realms of wishful thinking than in demonstrated fact. This is notably true of India which was the most populous and sophisticated of Europe's formal colonial domains. Undeniably, important advances have been made. Furber,[4] Bhattacharya[5] and Marshall[6] have all demonstrated how closely the expansion of Company trade and private European trade was linked to existing patterns of credit and marketing in Bengal. Om Prakash[7] and Ashin Das Gupta[8] have shown European traders at work against the background of the commerce and politics of the east and west coasts. Most recently, K. N. Chaudhuri[9] has accomplished a detailed reconstruction of India's textile industry. Yet once one moves inland, or passes into the second half of the eighteenth century, the trail runs cold. Little is known about inland trade routes and markets, and even less about the relationship between them and the politics and agrarian society of the post-Mughal states. Overall it remains difficult to understand the direction of social change in the later eighteenth century and how it might have related to the expansion of the colonial power.

Why is this? The most charitable explanation lies in the political complexity of pre-colonial India and in the technical problems of using indigenous sources. Regional differences appear to be so great that scholars have hesitated to generalise beyond their special areas of expertise. But certain quirks of Indian historical writing must also take part of the blame. The most impressive of Indian historiographies remains the work on the Mughal period produced by scholars associated with Aligarh University. In their studies, we find a coherent view of the evolution of pre-colonial state and society. It is possible to see how the form of the nobility moulded the cities and trade routes of the Mughal

---

[4] H. Furber, *Rival Empires of Trade in the Orient* (Minneapolis, 1976).

[5] S. Bhattacharya, *The East India Company and the Economy of Bengal from 1704 to 1740* (London, 1954).

[6] P. J. Marshall, *East Indian Fortunes. The British in Bengal in the Eighteenth Century* (Oxford, 1976).

[7] Om Prakash, 'Bullion for goods. International trade and the economy of early 18th century Bengal', *IESHR*, xii (1976), 159–87.

[8] Ashin Das Gupta, *Malabar in Asian Trade 1740–1800* (Cambridge, 1967); *Indian Merchants and the Decline of Surat 1700–50* (Wiesbaden, 1979).

[9] K. N. Chaudhuri, *The Trading World of Asia and the English East India Company 1660–1760* (Cambridge, 1978), pp. 237–62.

empire;[10] how technology and relations of production in the countryside limited the thrust of deeper economic transformation;[11] and, more controversially, how conflict between state, landlord and peasant irrevocably weakened the Mughal polity and set the scene for its demise in the eighteenth century.[12] Yet until very recently the interest of the Aligarh historians died with the Emperor Aurangzeb in 1707.

Historical writing on the following century is rather fragmented. Outside the coastal regions, debate has focused on the successor states to the Mughal regime. How did the political elites of these 'decentralised' regimes establish their legitimacy?[13] How did the regional court centres deal with the petty rulers of the locality?[14] How did these states husband their revenue resources and resist European penetration? Such questions are the starting point for the analysis of towns, merchants and service gentry in the following chapters. But in changing the vantage point, we are also suggesting that previous writing has been too preoccupied with the state at the expense of the corporate groups which constituted it. Despite the myth of Oriental Despotism, India of the eighteenth century was not like post-Reformation Europe where the state was the unchallenged political form. Rulers could only incorporate powerful groups in their realms by alienating resources and honours to them. This meant that social classes formed which could operate outside the state or in the interstices between many small states.[15]

Quite apart from war and famine, eighteenth-century rulers were at the mercy of powerful interests which provided the tools for state-building. They depended on the support or at least the acquiescence of autonomous bodies of mercenary soldiers, Indian and foreign merchants or revenue entrepreneurs, families of administrative 'gentry', and mobile bands of specialist peasant farmers. Such groups straddled several petty kingdoms and were able to redirect their service

[10] Irfan Habib, *The Agrarian System of Mughal India 1556–1707* (London, 1963); H. K. Naqvi, *Urban Centres and Industries in Upper India 1556–1803* (Bombay, 1968).

[11] I. Habib, 'Potentialities of capitalistic development in the economy of Mughal India', *Journal of Economic History*, xxix (1969), 32–78.

[12] Habib, *Agrarian System*, pp. 316–51; cf. M. N. Pearson, 'Shivaji and the decline of the Mughal Empire', *Journal of Asian Studies*, xxxv (1976), 221–35.

[13] Richard B. Barnett, *North India between Empires. Awadh, the Mughals and the British 1720–1801* (Berkeley, 1980).

[14] Bernard S. Cohn, 'Political systems in eighteenth century India: the Banaras region', *Journal of the American Oriental Society*, lxxxii (1962), 312–19.

[15] For the structure of Hindu polities see B. Stein, *Peasant State and Society in Medieval South Indian History* (Delhi, 1980); articles by A. Appadurai and C. Breckenridge, in *IESHR*, xiv (1977); N. Dirks, 'Structure and meaning of political relations in a South Indian little kingdom', *Contributions to Indian Sociology*, new series, xiii (1979); for rulers and 'other groups', M. N. Pearson, *Merchants and Rulers in Gujarat* (Berkeley, 1976); H. Spodek, 'Rulers, merchants and other groups in the city states of Saurashtra', *Comparative Studies in Society and History*, xvi (1974).

between one and another, enhancing their own economic security and sense of identity in the process. Between the revenue-based state and the mass of agrarian society, then, there existed a range of intermediate entities with strong internal organisation from which were recruited, ultimately, the Indian middle class.[16] The incoming colonial power and European traders succeeded when they were able to cajole, entice or manipulate these intermediate groups. British conquest often meant no more than the slow drift to the East India Company of soldiers, merchants and administrators, leaving the Indian rulers with nothing more than a husk of royal grandeur. The 'social politics' of pre-colonial India will become much clearer when the relationship between state, commerce and peasant society is understood.

The contrast with historical writing on other parts of the colonial world is interesting. In most areas, we have a much more precise impression of the social groups which constituted the indigenous states and how they impeded or expedited European expansion. The historiography of the Far East, for instance, has already taken on the comfortable, rounded contours which seem characteristic of European history. In China, beneath the formal political groupings of the imperial court, the regional magnates of the later nineteenth century and the warlords of the twentieth, the Confucian service gentry was slowly consolidating its grip over rural society.[17] Relations between gentry and imperial court provided the context for China's encounter with the western world. In the 1830s and 1840s, 'corrupt' gentry and local merchants allowed the British to peddle their opium into the interior of the country. Later the intransigence of 'patriotic' gentry hastened the disastrous clash between the empire and the western powers. It was the descendants of these Confucian gentry and the aspiring merchant class which brought down the Chinese empire in 1912 and determined the form of the nationalist and warlord regimes of the present century.[18]

For Japan, again, there exists a plausible social history. The evolution of the *samurai* from a warrior caste to a class of urban landlords and administrators can be set against the background of the formation of the Tokugawa state. The rise of rural market towns, agricultural development and the growth of the silk industry fit into a pattern which

---

[16] The use of the word class here is intended to convey a sense of 'status group'. All such 'intermediary groups' offered 'service' to the state, but they differed widely in their relationship to the processes of production.

[17] E. g., Chung-li Chang, *The Chinese Gentry. Studies in their Role in Nineteenth Century Chinese Society* (Seattle, 1955); H. Beattie, *Land and Lineage in China. A Study of Tung cheng County, Anhwei in the Ming and Ching Dynasties* (Cambridge, 1979).

[18] Philip A. Kuhn, *Rebellion and its enemies in Late Imperial China. Militarization and Social Structure, 1796–1854* (Cambridge, Mass., 1970).

helps explain Japan's striking economic successes after 1870.[19]

Islamic north Africa had much in common with Muslim India. In Egypt too, the evolution of intermediate groups between state and society is well documented and illuminates the history of the colonial encounter. In this case the background to the modernisation of the state and European penetration is provided by the consolidation of the landholding *sheikhs*.[20] This was a class of village office holders and rural moneylenders with connections among the army officers and intelligentsia of the towns. It was elements among the village *sheikhs* whose disenchantment with the policies of the Khedivate and support for the Arabist rebellion of 1882 helped pull the British into Egypt. Again at the end of the Great War, disturbances among these substantial people of the villages and small towns spelled the end of formal colonial rule.[21]

In each of these traditions of historical writing there are detailed speculations about relations between the state, traders, rural gentry and agrarian society. It is possible to pinpoint areas of change and also to show how these determined the pace and form of European penetration. In each case also it is possible to link the pre-colonial world with the 'new elites' or 'middle classes' of the nationalist period. Thus modernised *samurai* and rural merchants provided the entrepreneurs for Japan's leap forward. The sons of village *sheikhs* went into the army and filled the administration of post-colonial Egypt. In China the gentry gave rise to the nationalist urban intelligentsia and perpetuated its power through the 'bullies and local tyrants' of Mao's rural China in the 1920s and 1930s.

This perspective too is missing in Indian history. A few authors have been able to show how the ideologies and institutions of pre-colonial India contributed to the formation of the middle class of the modern period. But overall the picture remains curiously antiquated. In most studies, western education or the export trades of the late nineteenth century, or a structure of politics imposed by the colonial authorities, is credited with the transformation of Indian institutions which are seen as 'traditional', or at best, passive.

This book provides some of the missing perspectives. It deals with an important part, but only one part of the subcontinent. The treatment of the eighteenth century is hypothetical; that of the nineteenth century partial. Yet a study of the intermediate groups which were consolidating

[19] T. C. Smith, *The Agrarian Origins of Modern Japan* (Stanford, 1959).
[20] Gabriel Baer, *A History of Landownership in Egypt* 1800–1950 (London, 1962); *Studies in the Social History of Modern Egypt* (London, 1969), pp. 3–61.
[21] P. J. Vatikiotis, *The Modern History of Egypt* (London, 1969).

themselves between state and the peasantry seems vital. Through an examination of merchants, towns and service gentry, it is possible to view in detail some of the ligaments which tied the state to agrarian society, and to show how these were modified in the colonial period.

The book contains three levels of analysis. One group of chapters[22] traces in general terms the relationship between rulers, commerce and the market-centred parts of the countryside as it developed between about 1770 and 1870. We argue that in much of north India the 'decentralisation' of political power during the eighteenth century encouraged the further growth of a rooted service gentry and a homogeneous merchant class operating around small town centres. In the early colonial period, British government deflected these changes with a cost-cutting, centralising policy which had seriously eroded the bases of the 'eighteenth-century' political economy by the 1830s and 1840s. After the 1857 Rebellion, the state became more active again and society was galvanised by the canals, railways and new export trades. But the institutions of the merchant class and the service gentry persisted across the divide of the mid-century. The form of the state changed once again; the corporate institutions of merchant class and gentry were modified, but they remained the basis of the commerce and political life of the later colonial period.

The second level of the argument concerns the social history of the towns.[23] It shows how the development of merchant bodies and pressures on the service gentry contributed to conflicting forms of urban solidarity. From these solidarities developed both nationalism and the religious communalism of the later nineteenth century.

The third level[24] of the argument is a view of the north Indian merchant family and trading institutions from the inside. The aim is to show how economic organisation was inseparable from the family firm's identity as a body of pious and credit-worthy Hindus. Thus the corporate identities of the later commercial middle classes were, at base, formed around conceptions of religion and credit.

The history of these urban, mercantile and service people was moulded by three broad influences. First, external trade to Bengal, Europe or China speeded the growth of commercial production in the countryside and pushed the towns through cycles of boom and slump. After 1780 opportunities for export outside India increased rapidly, though even in the mid-eighteenth century trade remained more buoyant than has sometimes been assumed.

Secondly, urban and mercantile society responded to the deeper

---

[22] Below, chs. 2, 5, 7, 12.   [23] Below, chs. 3, 8, 9.   [24] Below, chs. 10, 11.

trends in the peasant economy which surrounded it. Unfortunately, little is known about population, productivity or even agricultural technology before 1850. On the surface, the years 1740–1800 appear to constitute an era of desolation, while rapid growth in both population and cultivated acreage seems to have occurred in the early nineteenth century. In fact, agricultural activity in north India may not have fallen off greatly between 1700 and 1780. There is evidence of a significant expansion in the east of the Ganges valley during the century. Here the overall trend of slow increase in population and acreage which had established itself in the early years of the Mughals was not seriously interrupted. Commercialisation associated with this growth converged with the stimulus to cash-crop production and market foundation which was provided by the pre-colonial states. Most important, not until after 1860 is there any clear evidence to suggest that agricultural production per head had reached a ceiling or that any substantial part of the region was facing a 'Malthusian crisis' of over-population and land shortage.

Thirdly, the political order created patterns of consumption, protection and revenue extraction which bound together townsmen and rural bazaars. The form of the regimes of 1740–1800 provides an essential background for the study of the merchants, gentry and townsmen which occupies much of this book. But even before turning to the varieties of pre-colonial regime in the Great Valley, it is necessary to consider some features of their famous predecessor, the Mughal dominion. The memory of the Great Emperors hung over north India in the eighteenth and nineteenth centuries as the name and institutions of Imperial Rome dominated Christendom in the European Middle Ages.

The Mughals and their successors

Generations of Europeans regarded the Mughals as a magnificent predatory horde. Mughal rulers seemed to be operating a vast system of plunder which frustrated the development of a landed gentry or a secure mercantile society in South Asia.[25] The historians of Aligarh University have laboured to correct this tenacious view. As they point out, the state's right to tax did not extinguish other rights over land, least of all that of occupancy cultivation.[26] The Mughal military elite (the

---

[25] The notion is not yet dead, see e.g., Perry Anderson, *Lineages of the Absolute State* (London, 1975), pp. 462–95; but for a more recent view, F. Perlin, 'Of White Whale and Countrymen in the eighteenth century Maratha Deccan. Extended class relations, rights and the problem of rural economy in the old regime', *Journal of Peasant Studies*, v (1978) 172–213.

[26] B. R. Grover, 'Nature of land rights in Mughal India', *IESHR*, i (1963), 1–23.

mansabdars) had some features of the classic bureaucracy.[27] The Mughal
state encouraged free peasant agriculture[28] and provided some of the
conditions for the application of capital to agriculture and trade.[29] Even
if it is hazardous to search around for the beginnings of 'modernity',
Athar Ali has drawn attention to tendencies which the empire at its
height (*c.* 1580–1700) had in common with contemporary European
monarchies: an attempt at centralised government, a reformed coinage,
and a concept of royal legitimacy which distinguished it from earlier
sultanates.[30]

Outwardly, Mughal rule was a huge system of household government
reinforced by an overwhelming but unwieldy military power. One can
easily overestimate its control, especially in the outlying areas. But the
empire was more than a mere umbrella raised over virtually autonomous
local groups. It was more like a grid of imperial towns, roads and
markets which pressed heavily on society and modified it, though only
at certain points. The system depended on the ability of the Mughal
state to appropriate in cash as much as 40 per cent of the value of the
total agricultural product.[31] A sophisticated money and produce market
must have existed to make this possible, and men who recognised the
supremacy of the emperor must have had influence in small towns and
bazaars. What held the empire together? Military power was the
ultimate sanction, but like the medieval cannon the Mughal main force
was a cumbersome and hazardous weapon to point at an adversary. The
imperial supremacy also survived because it offered advantages to the
soldiers and merchants who served it. Imperial service provided a career
open to the talents. During the seventeenth century, increasing
numbers of Hindu families were recruited to high office.[32] At a humbler
level much of the surplus which was extracted from the villages by the
Mughals seeped back into the localities as collection costs; gentry and
merchants profited from this. Finally, the emperor's judges and
administrators acted as a final court of appeal in disputes between local
elites. This adjudication satisfied the need felt by Hindus for a high king
to 'maintain religion and the order of the castes'. At the same time,
Mughal officials provided the Muslim population with grand protectors
of the faith. Interest and awe combined to form the cement of empire.

[27] M. Athar Ali, *The Mughal Nobility under Aurangzeb* (Bombay, 1968); *A Dictionary of
Mughal Mansabdars* (Delhi, forthcoming), 1, introduction.
[28] S. Nurul Hasan, *Thoughts on Agrarian Relations in Mughal India* (Delhi, 1973), p. 19.
[29] Habib, 'Potentialities', pp. 40–55.
[30] M. Athar Ali, 'Towards a reinterpretation of the Mughal Empire', *Journal of the Royal
Asiatic Society* (1978), pp. 38–49.
[31] Shireen Moosvi, 'The zamindars' share in the peasant surplus in the Mughal Empire.
Evidence of Ain-i-Akbari statistics', *IESHR*, xv (1978), 359–75.
[32] Athar Ali, *Mansabdars*, 1, introduction.

The problems endemic in this system had appeared long before they became critical in the early 1700s. The rulers required a constant expansion of revenue by conquest or agricultural growth to satisfy the aspirations of the nobility and official classes. If they could not provide office, honour and land-grants, then its own servants began to lose the will to play the Delhi game. These magnates found other, parochial ways of satisfying their urge to become kings or landed gentry, independent of the emperor or even in opposition to him. But if the centre attempted to raise more revenue from tightly administered areas, or extend its area of control, it only compounded its problems. Peasants were forced to flee to the lands of 'refractory' landholders, and coalitions of zamindars and unsettled people from the fringes of agricultural society built up against the Mughal peace.

If the Mughal state failed, it was not so much because of any barbarous deficiencies in its nobility or administration. The problem was that in the longer term it did not secure the obligation of its subjects, and so lacked the resources to carry on its course of military expansion. Some historians have emphasised the cultural differences between the Mughal aristocracy and rural Hindu notables.[33] Others have concentrated on the tensions which were engendered by the conflict over resources between state, landholder and peasant. But these are really two sides of the same coin. The empire could only survive if it penetrated further beneath the level of the *pargana* administration and into the tight clan-like brotherhood of peasant farmers in the lands away from the great roads and the country towns. Penetration required not only the coercive force of the state, but also an ideology which justified the appropriation of growing quantities of revenue.

The eighteenth century saw attempts to resolve these problems. The form of states derives in part from the conscious stratagems and needs of ruling groups. Though one should not underestimate the importance of chance, climatic disaster or outside attack, regional and local rulers of the period devised policies to overcome the difficulties of cash flow and political legitimacy which had defeated the later emperors. First, the dissolution of continental hegemony allowed the Mughal aristocracy, and ruling groups who had been at odds with it, to build up more compact domains in core areas of agricultural prosperity. Warrior–landholders who had been in intermittent revolt against Mughal suzerainty were able to retain a larger proportion of the land-revenues. Alongside them, powerful Hindu clan leaders made good their claim to be treated as kings. They moved from the status of 'refractory' bucolic

---

[33] J. F. Richards, *Mughal Administration in Golconda* (Oxford, 1975); 'The imperial crisis in the Deccan', *Journal of Asian Studies*, xxxv (1976), 237–56.

zamindars as they had been under the Mughals to the dignity of raja and maharaja. With smaller domains and roots among the peasant castes whose blood and assumptions they shared, these new princelings could strive for a closer hold on the loyalties and resources of their subjects than had been possible for most Mughal commanders.

However, the political changes of the century added up to more than a strengthening of local power-holders in the face of a weakening imperial presence. The fluid politics of the period also benefited some of the great Muslim military and administrative families who had served the Mughals at the centre. In part, the 'decline' of the empire represented these grandees' realisation that the game of imperial domination over the whole subcontinent was not worth the candle. The imperial lords slowly 'withdrew to their own domains', building up over the course of the generation between 1720 and 1750 more secure power bases in Hyderabad,[34] Bengal[35] and Awadh.[36] These 'successor states' to the Mughal hegemony presided over a redistribution of agrarian resources which favoured local gentry and magnates. But they also adapted more successfully to the cultural assumptions of their rural and Hindu subjects than had the empire in its later, more rigid persona. Awadh, Hyderabad and Bengal remain formally Muslim states, but honours and resources were spread among a diverse ruling group, so that the nawabs themselves took on many of the attributes of classic Hindu kingship and presided over a syncretic culture.[37]

In this sense also the form of the eighteenth-century regimes was an attempt to resolve the problem of legitimate rule and political obligation which had plagued the later empire. Aurangzeb had departed from the latitudinarian religious stance of his predecessors and insisted on a more full-blooded Islamic policy among his high officials. But in Gangetic north India where less than 15 per cent of the population were Muslims, and were concentrated in the cities, this was a hazardous move. Local conflicts over Hindu and Muslim practice became confounded with the tension between centre and periphery over the destination of revenue and resources.[38]

[34] K. Leonard, 'The Hyderabad political system and its participants', *Journal of Asian Studies*, xxx (1971), 569–82.

[35] P. Calkins, 'The formation of a regionally orientated ruling group in Bengal 1700–40', *Journal of Asian Studies*, xxix (1970), 799–806.

[36] Barnett, *North India*; cf. M. N. Pearson, 'Political participation in Mughal India', *IESHR*, ix (1972), 113–31.

[37] Richard B. Barnett, 'Muslim dominance. Ethnicity and redistribution in early modern India', unpub. MSS; K. Leonard, 'The Deccan synthesis in old Hyderabad', *Journal of the Pakistan Historical Society*, xxi (1973), 205–18.

[38] S. A. A. Rizvi, *Shah Wali-Allah and his Times* (Canberra, 1980), pp. 80–107; Muhammad Mustaidd Khan, *Maasir-i-Alamgiri*, tr. H. M. Elliott and J. Dowson, *The History of India told by its own Historians*, VII (London, 1877), 185–9.

By contrast, the regimes which emerged after 1740 were all remarkably eclectic in their social policy. The symbolism of the Mughal empire and Mughal 'blood' remained significant enough to be invoked by the fiercest Hindu opponents of Delhi such as the Marathas.[39] On the other hand, the staunchly Muslim invaders from the northern hills (Rohilla and Bangash Afghans) were prepared to participate in types of ritual redistribution which was characteristic of Hindu kingship. Any rigidity which Aurangzeb or his Hindu and Sikh enemies had tried to introduce into the ideology of the state was quickly softened in the century's fierce battles for honour and resources. While Aurangzeb's empire foundered when it failed to mollify and placate the 'pot black' notables of Hindu central India,[40] the situation was quite different one hundred years later. In the 1780s, the highest lieutenant of the failing empire had bestowed its most exalted military rank on a 'naked' Hindu ascetic;[41] its Lord Protector in Delhi, Najaf Khan, was a jovial barrack-room butt for the city's silver-hungry soldiery.[42]

Of course, these new local and regional powers did not emerge at a very auspicious time. Much of their energy was spent in internecine warfare over marcher areas. They were threatened by powerful external enemies while political change had unsettled the itinerant groups on the fringes of the arable. But it is possible to make out through the dust and cordite some interesting developments in the use of state power during the eighteenth century. Wherever possible rulers attempted to gain a closer grasp on the resources of agriculture by divesting of their revenue rights old communities which had dominated their bailiwicks since the days of the Emperor Akbar or before.[43] This tilted the balance of local power even where it did not wholly dispossess the old notables. But in some cases, these rulers succeeded in driving peasant farmers off the land, or in-filling rural society with colonies of more complaisant dependants and small fortress towns. This again was a technique designed to solve the problem of agricultural labour supply which had plagued the Mughal aristocracy at the end of the previous century. Even where the regional rulers did not bring in as much revenue as their Mughal predecessors had claimed a century earlier, their

---

[39] Barnett, *North India*, p. 243.
[40] Richards, *Mughal Administration*, p. 66.
[41] J. N. Sarkar and Nirod Bhusan Roy, *A History of the Dasnami Naga Sanyasis* (Allahabad, 1959), p. 179.
[42] Antoine Polier, 'A view of the present situation of the Emperor Shah Alaum and his territories around Delhi', 28 July 1775, in Pratul C. Gupta (ed.), *Shah Alam II and his Court* (Calcutta, 1947), p. 99.
[43] Bernard S. Cohn, 'Structural change in Indian rural society 1596–1885', in R. E. Frykenberg (ed.), *Land Control and Social Structure in Indian History* (Madison, Wisconsin, 1969), pp. 89–114.

administrations were more streamlined.[44]

Contemporary jeremiahs and colonial historians saw little more in the eighteenth-century regimes than a remorseless drive for dominance and silver, softened sometimes by the service of True Religion. But the logic of warfare on the peripheries of these compact, smaller dominions was an effort to conserve and enhance the resources of the good agricultural tracts which formed their cores. The slow diffusion through India of new military techniques had raised the cost of statehood and intensified the pressure for revenue.[45] It seems that the old Mughal strategy based on cavalry and defensive fortresses was becoming obsolete. Better ordnance was available from European and Persian sources. Heavy cavalry was at the mercy of the musket fire which could be laid down by European-drilled infantry. The Mughal method of granting revenue 'assignments' to men who raised their own military contingents had also become outdated. What rulers needed now were highly trained permanent forces based on central barracks. These soldiers had to be rewarded with monthly cash wages, and mercenary armies, Indian and European, were becoming common. Yet all this was happening at a time when money was scarce. Not only did the successor regimes have to be on guard against their rivals, but after 1764, the defeat of the Nawab of Awadh by the East India Company obliged the north Indian rulers to provide a huge tribute for their new protectors.[46]

Too little is known about bullion flows in eighteenth-century India or about the relationship between internal trade and the buoyant European trade of the coastal provinces to do more than speculate on these matters.[47] But what does seem clear is that political conditions encouraged states to become more commercial and bureaucratic at the same time as they exalted the importance of the professional soldier. Rulers had already taken to 'farming out' their land-revenues to the highest bidder in the days of the later Mughals.[48] Everywhere this system was extended in the following century. These changes benefited

[44] Stewart Gordon, 'The slow conquest. Administrative integration of Malwa into the Maratha Empire 1720–60', *Modern Asian Studies*, xi (1978), 1–40.

[45] Advances in cannon production in India had shifted the military balance against Mughal-style defensive points and increased the need for centralised bodies of pack-animals; the proliferation of European-trained musketry also made regular drilling of infantry men essential.

[46] Barnett, *North India*, pp. 88–91; G. S. Sardesai, *New History of the Mahrattas* (Bombay, 1948), pp. 137–73.

[47] But see, P. J. Marshall, 'Economic and political expansion. The case of Oudh', *Modern Asian Studies*, ix (1975), 466–82; K. P. Mishra, *Banaras in Transition 1740–95* (Delhi, 1975), pp. 190–210.

[48] W. H. Moreland, *From Akbar to Aurangzeb. A Study in Indian Economic History* (new edn, Delhi, 1972), pp. 235, 239–40, 249; N. A. Siddiqi, *Land Revenue Administration under the Later Mughals 1700–1750* (Bombay, 1970), p. 2.

and consolidated the intermediate classes of society – townsmen, traders, service gentry – who commanded the skills of the market and the pen.

Varieties of eighteenth-century regimes in the Ganges valley

So far an attempt has been made to draw out from the limited secondary literature some tendencies which seem to be common to many regimes of the area: the search for cash and a local base, the foundation of new towns and an attempt through patronage to grow closer to the power-holders in agrarian society. But it is important not to lose sight of regional variations. Eighteenth-century ruling groups differed in culture and organisation. These differences created patterns in commerce, in the incidence of towns and markets or in the organisation of agrarian production which persisted into the colonial period and form the subject matter of this study. To take only one example, the greater density of market towns in the west of the region (Rohilkhand and Meerut Divisions, as they became) was one precondition for the more dynamic agriculture and artisan production which existed there well before the coming of the British canals and railways in the mid-nineteenth century. This early urbanisation was consolidated by the settlement in the region after 1720 of town-dwelling Muslim warriors from the north-west.[49]

Most of the regional and local powers which will be encountered in the following chapters gained autonomy between 1735 and 1762.[50] Aurangzeb's attempt to revive the Mughal empire had foundered through over-expansion before 1700. Faction plagued the ruling elite in Delhi in the 1710s and 1720s. But the seismic shocks to the old structure came in the late 1730s when the revenues of the rich provinces to the south of the capital were rapidly drained away into Maratha pockets. The weakness of the empire was cruelly displayed in 1739 when it was defeated by a Persian invasion under Nadir Shah, and contemptuously confirmed by the Afghans under Ahmed Shah who created a power vacuum in the great plains with their defeat of the Marathas in 1761. Between these two dates, the viceroys of the old Mughal provinces of Bengal, Awadh and Hyderabad surreptitiously diverted the centre's revenue to their own purposes and set themselves up as virtually independent monarchs. During the same period, two further regimes were carved out to the north and east of Delhi by Afghan military

---

[49] Iqbal Hussain, 'Pattern of Afghan settlements in India in the 17th century', mimeo. paper, Department of History, Aligarh Muslim University.
[50] Zahiruddin Malik, *The Reign of Muhammad Shah 1719–48* (London, 1977).

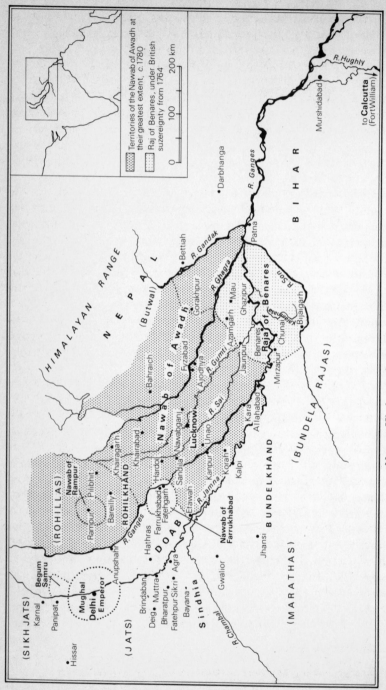

Map 2   Hindustan about 1785: towns and kingdoms

adventurers who had once served the empire as mercenary soldiers. These became the principalities of Rohilkhand and Farrukhabad. There were significant distinctions in organisation and culture between these first two categories of Muslim successor state: the independent Mughal satrapy or province, and the new conquest state. But first a political form more typical of the century must be considered. This represented the determination of the local Hindu landholders of the east of the region to stand forth as rajas in their own territories.

Resurgent Hindu kingdoms in the east

By far the most general political change which affected the whole of eastern India from Allahabad to Bengal in the eighteenth century was the consolidation of Hindu states associated with the two great categories of Hindu agrarian caste status in the region – the Rajputs and 'military' or Bhumihar Brahmins. The related process, the weakening of Mughal suzerainty, has received some attention. But since Mughal rule in eastern India had always been rather superficial, these local changes deserve greater emphasis. The rise of the dynasty of Gautam Bhumihar Brahmins who first became revenue contractors for Awadh and then maharajas of Benares between 1739 and 1760 was explored by Wilton Oldham,[51] and more recently by Bernard Cohn.[52] But these events which broke through the surface of the old administrative histories were merely the tip of a slow process of settlement which set the main features of land-control in modern times from the borders of Awadh to Bengal. In several ways these populous clans of warrior–cultivators deepened and extended their local sway. First, they completed the process of warring-down remaining pockets of resistance among aboriginal, tribal and nomadic peoples who inhabited the jungle and fringe paddy lands, pushing cultivation into the forest zones north and south of the great plains. Secondly, over wide areas they appear to have reduced earlier, lower caste cultivators to a greater degree of agrarian dependence. Thirdly, they benefited from the decline of superior Mughal administrative and fiscal control. These consolidations occurred in three great swathes. In the marcher areas of north and south Awadh (often under the nominal control of the Lucknow rulers), the Rajput clan leaders carved out areas of control over men and resources which later became the great baronies (*taluqdaris*) of nineteenth-century Awadh.[53]

[51] W. Oldham, *Historical and Statistical Memoir of the Ghazeepoor District* (Allahabad, 1870).
[52] Cohn, 'Structural change', in Frykenberg (ed.), *Land Control*, pp. 53–69.
[53] T. R. Metcalf, *Land, Landlords and the British Raj* (Berkeley, 1979), pp. 3–16; C. A. Elliott, *The Chronicles of Oonao* (Allahabad, 1862).

South of Awadh in the fertile riverain rice growing area of Benares, Gorakhpur and Bihar and on to the fringes of Bengal, it was the 'military' or Bhumihar Brahmins who strengthened their sway.[54] South again in the hilly borders of central India, it was the Baghel, Bundela and Gaharwar Rajputs who most conspicuously gained from the decline of Mughal control and the expansion of the arable.[55]

What brought success to these Hindu princelings was the strong clan organisation upon which they rested. There were perhaps as many as 100,000 Bhumihar Brahmin clansmen[56] backing the power of the Benares rajas in what later became the districts of Benares, Gorakhpur and Azamgarh. This proved a decisive advantage when the dynasty faced its rival and nominal suzerain, the Nawab of Awadh, in the 1750s and 1760s. It was the capacity of the Benares ruler to mount an exhausting guerilla war against the Awadh camp using his Bhumihar clan levies which forced the Nawab to withdraw his main force.[57] To the east again, it was the presence of more than 200,000 militant and closely organised Bhumihar Brahmins which allowed the lineages of Hatwa and Bettiah in Bihar to consolidate themselves as virtually independent rulers.[58] Efforts by the Muslim central power to crush them, or use immigrant Hindu soldiers of their own to do so, slackened after the Maratha invasions of Bengal in the 1730s, and the strengthening of their caste-fellows in Benares in the following decade.

The rise of the Rajput notables to the north and south of the Bhumihars proceeded along similar lines. The process is only preserved in legend sometimes embellished by the Gothic imaginations of the nineteenth-century British ethnographers. From A.D. 1200 onward, small Rajput bands moving from the western centres of Muslim power infiltrated and colonised the richer parts of the eastern Gangetic plain. No great *volkerwanderung* occurred. But constant petty clashes and strategic alliances with the indigenous population, mixed undoubtedly with marriage across the still lax boundaries of caste, accompanied the emergence of Rajput dominance. In their relations with the central

---

[54] M. A. Sherring, *Hindu Tribes and Castes as Represented in Benares* (London, 1872); pp. 39–40; Oldham, *Memoir*, pp. 67–70; J. N. Bhattacharya, *Hindu Castes and Sects* (Calcutta, 1896), p. 22.

[55] E.g. the rise of Rewah and Bara *rajs*, see R. Temple, 'Report on the Moquddumee Biswahdaree Settlement of Pergunnah Barah, Zillah Allahabad', 9 Sept. 1850, in *Selections from the Records of the Government of the North-Western Provinces* (Agra, 1856), xxvii, art. 15, pp. 400–1; M. S. A. Rao, 'Rewari Kingdom and the Mughal Empire', in R. G. Fox (ed.), *Realm and Region in Traditional India* (Delhi, 1977), pp. 79–89.

[56] Calculated from Sherring, *Hindu Tribes*, p. 40 and projected backwards in line with the assumed rate of growth for the general population, below, pp. 88–90.

[57] *Ibid.*, pp. 44–6, cf. Khairuddin Khan, *Tuhfa-i-Taza (Balwantnamah)*, tr. F. Curwen (Allahabad, 1875), pp. 19–33.

[58] S. G. Misra, *History of Bihar* (Delhi, 1970), pp. 19–51.

Muslim powers (first the Mughals and later the rulers of Awadh) the clan leaders switched constantly between acquiescence and defiance. Colonisations were often carried out with the licence of Mughal provincial commanders and the recognition of the overlords helped select out from clan leaders men who could assume the dignity and title of raja. Yet often the expansion of Rajput power occurred in the context of fierce struggles with the overlords over the size of the land revenue that was to be paid. Around Lucknow and Fyzabad the Nawabs of Awadh achieved a degree of control which thwarted the political ambitions of the great Rajput notables. But away from the centre, under Nawabi licence or not, the process of colonisation and clearing went on much as it had for several centuries.

What was the meaning of the word *raj*, kingdom, to these societies of warriors and cultivators? Eighteenth- and early nineteenth-century Hindi genealogies and poems on the duties of kings suggest only a limited set of functions: warfare, the service of the gods, and arbitration between clansmen and castes. In the genealogy of the rajas of Baraon,[59] we see the zamindars of Shankargarh fortified by their Bhumihar kinsmen and Kurmi servants gradually conquer surrounding villages generation by generation, sometimes expelling their previous lords, more often reducing them to the status of subordinate holders. The king's duty in these early Hindi poems is conquest and the provision of booty and fiefs for his men. Donations to Brahmins and holy men enhanced the honour of his rule. The construction of temples to both Shaivite and Vaishnavite deities at petty market centres settled the sacred and commercial geography of the kingdom.[60] At one and the same time, the *raj* was a 'vast machine for sacrifice'[61] and a tool of perpetual warfare.[62] The king maintained both these aspects by granting away assignments of revenue or the perquisites of lordship to those who served him in worship (the Brahmins and ascetics); in warfare (his clan heads and mercenary aides); and in kingly display and gift-giving (merchant provisioners, jewellers and artisans).

These movements of colonisation in the east of the central Ganges valley were slow processes. The well-watered rice lands could support a large population. Even in the eighteenth century they escaped the worst

---

[59] E.g., Pandit Bindeswari Prasad Pande, *Baraon ka Rais ka Itihas* (A history of the family of the Lord of Baraon) compiled *c*. 1820 by Pt Brahma Datta Acharya, resident of Panasa (Allahabad, 1895).

[60] E.g., Mulchand, 'Mirzapur shrines', *North Indian Notes and Queries*, iii (1893), 112–13; interviews, Benares, 1973–4.

[61] A. M. Hocart, *Caste. A Comparative Study* (London, 1950), pp. 68ff.

[62] E.g., the *Chatraprakasa* of Lali Kavi, *c*. 1720 (?); exploits of a Bundela chief, MSS Hin. B1, B63, IOL.

of war and famine. Away from the centres of Muslim rule, Hindu
ritualism and the influence of Brahmins also remained strong. All these
features gave rise in the east to a relatively stable agrarian order. A spirit
of close distinction in caste rank helped to maintain a stratified agrarian
system in which forms of landlordism, tenancy, under-tenancy and
landlessness had already become common.[63] Here local merchants and
moneylenders extended their influence as clients of an emerging landed
aristocracy. Markets and trade were heavily taxed and controlled by the
elites, constricted, as it were, within the form of the neo-traditional
Hindu kingdom.

Social movements into kingdoms: Jats, Marathas and Sikhs in the west

The consolidation of Hindu kingdoms in eastern India between Awadh
and Bengal was the product of many slow wars of attrition against earlier
land-controlling groups and agents of the emperor or the Nawab of
Awadh. But the formation of states adjoining the Ganges valley to the
west by Sikhs, Jats and Marathas was the culmination of more abrupt
social changes. By the end of the eighteenth century, most of the
constellation of kingdoms which had emerged from the invasion of these
warlike groups had also taken on some features of the classic Hindu
kingdom (though supported by Mughal revenue practices). In origin,
however, the strength of Maratha, Jat and Sikh warbands derived from
their social inclusiveness – their capacity to incorporate pioneer peasant
castes, miscellaneous military adventurers and groups on the fringes of
settled agriculture.

Throughout the late eighteenth century, the Marathas remained a
presence on the borders of Hindustan. Their great invasions of the
heartland of Mughal India in the 1730s and 1740s were less significant
than the close dominion which they established over its marcher
provinces after 1740. Malwa, for instance, was reduced to a stable
revenue-paying area between 1740 and 1760. Despite their defeat by the
Afghans and Indian Muslims in 1761, the Marathas slowly established a
firmer base in central India. Between 1780 and 1806 they dominated
most of the western region of Hindustan which included the old
imperial cities of Delhi and Agra.

The Maratha movement had emerged after 1670, as a revolt of petty
gentry in the sparse upland areas of western India against the dominance
of Muslim revenue-takers. From the beginning the Marathas had a

---

[63] William Tennant, *Indian Recreations, Consisting Chiefly of Strictures on the Domestic and Rural Economy of the Mahommedans and Hindoos* (2nd edn, London, 1802), II, 330–50; Mishra, *Banaras*, pp. 15–80.

plebeian character; a Mughal chronicler noted 'most of the men in the Maratha army are unendowed with illustrious birth, and husbandmen, carpenters and shopkeepers abound among their soldiery'.[64] The rise of the Marathas was a social movement which allowed men of the ordinary peasant society of western India to take on the trappings of ritual status which had been the pride of the warrior nobility of Rajasthan. Some of their leading families were even descendants of herdsmen (Kolis or Gaolis) who used predatory warfare to carve out revenue fiefs in areas of settled agriculture.[65] One of their most famous generals, Tukoji Rao Holkar, was only a generation away from a grazing and nomadic background.[66]

Sikhism, the second great expansive movement of the period, had similar features. Originating as a typical Hindu revitalisation movement in the tradition of the Nath Yogis, and appealing particularly to the urban commercial castes of the Punjab, Sikhism had by the beginning of the seventeenth century spread its appeal to one of the great peasant castes of central and western India, the Jats.[67] The Jats also seem to have had pastoralist origins, and were perhaps not greatly different from Gujars, Bhattis and similar groups who retained their nomadic style of life as late as 1800. The military community of the Sikh Khalsa founded in 1699 suited their warlike and itinerant qualities. During the next century, they dominated the twelve great warbands (*misls*) which spelt doom to the old Mughal aristocracy of the Punjab and spilled over into the plains of Hindustan.[68]

Thus Sikhism as a social movement also represented an outlet for the energies of aspiring social groups, especially village service communities and artisans, and for pioneer peasant warriors on the fringes of settled society. There is evidence, for instance, that some of the most important Sikh leaders came from the dry western fringes of the Punjab adjoining the Rajasthan Desert,[69] though later Sikh expansion consisted in the politic conversion of older established Jat magnates who dominated the agricultural lands north of Delhi.[70] In the east Punjab, Sikh leaders

---

[64] Satish Chandra, 'Social background to the rise of the Maratha movement during the 17th century in India', *IESHR*, x (1973), 209–18.

[65] See, e.g., R. Jenkins, *Report on the Territories of the Rajah of Nagpore* (Calcutta, 1827), p. 40.

[66] Sir John Malcolm, *A Memoir of Central India including Malwa and Adjoining Provinces* (London, 1824), I, 142.

[67] W. H. McCleod, *The Evolution of the Sikh Community* (Oxford, 1976).

[68] Indu Banga, *The Agrarian System of the Sikhs. Late Eighteenth and Early Nineteenth Century* (Delhi, 1978).

[69] P. M. Van Den Dungen, 'Changes in status and occupation in nineteenth century Panjab', in D. A. Low (ed.), *Soundings in South Asian Studies* (London, 1968), p. 70.

[70] Polier, ed. Gupta, 'View of the present situation', p. 100.

rapidly dug themselves in as small princelings. They established their own mints and darbars and submerged their origins as men of pastoralist, liquor distiller or blacksmith caste. But even in the days of the centralised kingdom founded by Ranjit Singh after he unified the Punjab in 1799, the populist *arriviste* aspect of Sikh society persisted. While Ranjit avoided calling the general council of Sikh war leaders (the *Gurumatta*) after 1805, aspects of 'aristocratic republicanism' persisted in the Punjab and the aspiring monarch was always careful to invoke the name of the Guru and the military brotherhood of the Khalsa.[71]

These features, a set of religious beliefs which tended to depress if not to eliminate hierarchy, the capacity to assimilate pioneer peasants and families from poorer areas, and the mobility within the society of low caste entrepreneurs and specialist groups, were evident once again among the non-Sikh Jats who established their dominance south and east of Delhi after 1710.[72] Men characterised by early eighteenth-century Mughal records as plunderers and bandits preying on the imperial lines of communications had by the end of the century spawned a range of petty states linked by marriage alliance and religious practice. The Jats appear to have moved into the Gangetic valley in two great waves:[73] one in the seventeenth and one in the eighteenth century. In some places, as Stokes has pointed out, persons called Jats accounted for 70–80 per cent of the total population. They were clearly not a caste in the sense that the Gautam Bhumihars were a caste. Instead they were a wide category of warrior–cultivators who had absorbed many outsiders into their ranks. This was a society where Brahmins were few and male Jats married into the whole range of lower agricultural and entrepreneurial castes.[74] A kind of tribal nationalism animated them rather than a nice calculation of caste difference expressed within the context of a Brahminical Hindu state.[75]

Large tracts in the western areas which felt the impact of Jat, Maratha and Sikh were dry and dependent on artificial irrigation. Their commerce and agriculture were moulded by natural conditions which

---

[71] Cf. Banga, *Sikhs*, pp. 29–33.

[72] Ram Pande, *Bharatpur up to 1826. A Social and Political History* (Delhi, 1970), introduction and pp. 1–35; M. C. Pradhan, *The Political System of the Jats of Northern India* (Bombay, 1966); for earlier reference see, e.g., Shiv Das Lakhnavi, *Shahnamah Munnawar Kalam*, tr. Syed Hasan Aksari (Patna, 1980), p. 21.

[73] Sherring, *Hindu Tribes*, 235; Ghulam Husain Khan Tabatabai, *Seir Mutaqharin*, tr. Haji Mustafa (Calcutta, 1789), III, 233.

[74] E. T. Stokes, *The Peasant and the Raj. Studies in Agrarian Society and Peasant Rebellion in Colonial India* (Cambridge, 1978), pp. 69–70, 82; F. W. Growse, *Mathura. A District Memoir* (1882, Delhi repr. 1979), pp. 8–9.

[75] J. Lushington, 'On the marriage customs of the Jats of Bhurtpore', *Journal of the Asiatic Society of Bengal*, xi (1833), 283–9.

supported a sparser population; and the land was too poor to afford a substantial agricultural surplus for any settled aristocracy. But the form of pre-colonial society and the history of the regimes of the region were also formative influences on agriculture and trade. Here colonising peasant farmers such as the Jats supported by mobile and flexible merchant communities were not constricted within a settled agrarian system as they were further east. Politics and war had encouraged population to migrate from the area or to cluster in defensible urban centres. At the same time, these centres, whether the embattled small towns of Muslim gentry or lineage centres built up by the emerging Jat states, provided an excellent set of strong points where merchants could be enticed to settle by trade-hungry notables.

This more flexible, 'contractual' society where political power was creating new patterns of urbanisation and agrarian settlement had much in common also with the lands of Rohilkhand, Farrukhabad and the Saharanpur Division which lay to the north. Here another variety of state – which we have called the 'Muslim conquest state' – was predominant. Seeking defence and an urban way of life, the new Afghan state-builders constructed an unusually dense pattern of town centres which stimulated the production of cash crops in the area. Not only did the mercenary gentry consume large quantities of meat, rice, sugar and tobacco, but they deliberately encouraged exports for more distant markets in the hope of bettering their land-revenue assignments. In this area capital and the independent peasant farmer already had more bargaining power before the onset of colonial rule. A later description of one of the great market centres of Rohilkhand, for instance, notes how its founder in the 1750s exerted himself to attract trade by 'reducing exactions, canvassing the men of capital (*sahukars*), and protecting traders'.[76] Indeed, the roots of the 'dynamism' of the western Gangetic plain, as of the Punjab, in comparison with the east and Bengal, are already found in pre-colonial society.

The Muslim conquest state

This third, distinctive type of domain with its military and urban ethic had characteristics in common with some of the medieval Islamic states of West Asia. The most celebrated examples in north India were the Afghan warrior leaders who established a series of petty sultanates in the towns north and east of Delhi between 1720 and 1750. The Bangash

---

[76] 'Report on a project for a railway in Rohilcund', *Selections from the Records of the Government of the North-Western Provinces* (Agra, 1846), pt xxii, art, i, p. 3; Cf. Altaf Ali Brelvi, 'Nawab Dunde Khan', *Proceedings of Indian Historical Congress*, 1941 (Delhi, 1941), pp. 428–9.

Nawabs of Farrukhabad and the Rohilla mercenaries of what became known as Rohilkhand appropriated a series of revenue fiefs while their erstwhile Mughal masters were distracted by Persian and Maratha invasions.[77] The states they founded differed in a number of ways from both the new Hindu dominions and breakaway satrapies of the empire, such as Awadh. They did not spring from dominant land-controlling clans in local society. Rohilla tribesmen in the north-western tract may never have exceeded 50,000[78] newcomers in a local population of more than one million. The Farrukhabad Bangash were still thinner on the ground even when they had imported colonists from the northern hills. The tactic of these adventurers had been to defeat the local Rajput brotherhoods, to occupy their lineage centres and convert them into typical fortified Muslim *qasbah* towns, where revenue collection could be maintained. They offered nominal allegiance to the Mughals and took pride in using symbols of legitimacy with which they had been endowed.

Unlike the Hindu rajas of the lower Ganges or the great Maratha and Jat movements, these Muslim conquerors were not supported by powerful bodies of clansmen among the cultivating communities who could in turn command deference from subordinate villagers. They took various measures to buttress this weaker political position. First, they tried to raise their status within north Indian Muslim life and the Mughal diplomatic system. A later chronicle of the Rohilla rulers tries to establish for them an heroic genealogy going back beyond the time of the Prophet to Abraham.[79] Rohillas sought to throw off the stigma of base origins by marriage with gentry families of Pathan origin. As early as 1770, Robert Orme noted that a Rohilla considered such a marriage 'an advance to his credit and always wishes to gain the appellation of Pathan'.[80] This drive for tribal respectability went hand in hand with a desire to inherit the symbolic virtue of the Mughal hegemony at the very time that its revenue obligations were being dismantled. The dream of the aristocratic Rohilla was revealed in an exchange with the Nawab of Awadh in 1794. Their support for the Nawab, they said, was dependent on pay for themselves, advances for their bodies of horse, pay for their sons, relatives, elephants and palankins, 'a place for my home and jaghir [revenue assignment], respectable connections, a Dewan and Vakil

[77] Mustajab Khan Bahadur, *Gulistan-i-Rehmat*, tr. C. Elliott, *The Life of Hafiz ool-Moolk* (London, 1831).
[78] J. Strachey, *Hastings and the Rohilla War* (Oxford, 1892), p. 29.
[79] Mustajab Khan, *Gulistan*, tr. Elliott, pp. 14–20.
[80] Orme MSS, India, xvi, p. 4659, IOL; M. Athar Ali, *The Mughal Nobility under Aurangzeb* (Delhi, 1966), p. 21.

[ambassador] to the Vazir'.[81]

Next, they sought to consolidate their position in local society. The Rohillas developed close links of patronage and fealty with the local Hindu warrior caste, the Rajputs, and they were successful to the extent that they could always count on bodies of Rajput troops in conflict with their enemies. Rohillas and Bangash also brought in large numbers of dependent merchant people, skilled cultivators and bodies of warrior colonists to strengthen their supporters in agricultural society. The Bangash Nawabs went even further and tried to create a military caste directly dependent on themselves, rather like the characteristic 'slave castes' of medieval Muslim societies.[82]

Mughal satrapies

The final category of late eighteenth-century state was the transformed province (*subah*) of the old empire itself. Often termed 'successor states', these units have been the object of much study.[83] Broadly, they represented a shift of power from the centre to the local agents of the empire. In the case of Bengal, Hyderabad and Awadh, the sequence appears to have been much the same. The emperor, seeking stability of revenue in the face of mounting internal and external pressure, despatched a powerful Mughal noble to rectify the finances and raise the revenue yield of his outer provinces. In each case, the notable or his descendants amalgamated the office of revenue manager (*diwan*) and military governor (*subahdar*) to create a new office of greater power which became hereditary within his own family. Tighter revenue management created a new class of local fiscal notables who became in time an hereditary nobility contributing to the upkeep of a new central army, which in each case was being organised along European principles before the mid-century.

The key point in the emergence of such successor states was the crisis of 1739–43 associated with the invasion of Nadir Shah. It was at this point that Murshid Quli Khan's Bengal, Asaf Jah's Hyderabad and Burhun-ul Mulk's Awadh ceased to pay their customary tribute to Delhi and enhanced their capacity for local economic integration and military expenditure. The events in Delhi and its hinterland have remained obscure both because of a lack of documents and a lack of research; but

---

[81] Enclosure in translation of letter of the Rampur Newswriter at Bareilly, 13 Oct. 1794, Home Misc. Series, 448, IOL.

[82] Cf. J. F. Richards, 'The formulation of imperial authority under Akbar and Jahangir', in J. F. Richards (ed.), *Kingship and Authority in South Asia* (Madison, Wisconsin, 1980), pp. 252–85.

[83] Barnett, *North India*, pp. 240–52.

whatever its remaining charisma, the imperial centre by 1761 had also become an extenuated satrapy displaying many similar features of political organisation. The failed dynast here was the Mughal general, Mirza Najaf Khan, who fought a brilliant rearguard action on behalf of the Mughal name between 1771 and 1783, and appeared for a few years to be emerging as a state-builder himself.[84] Like the rulers of Awadh or Hyderabad, Najaf was able to marry the imperial offices of commander and revenue manager. Like them, he seized rich territories as his personal fief. Like them he built up an army based on his personal supporters and strengthened with some European officers. But this fourth potential successor state – a kind of Timurid 'Isle de France' – was overwhelmed by impecuniousness and the press of its enemies.[85]

The guiding principle of all the Mughal successor states was to enhance yields by reducing intermediary powers to subjugation and by building up the largest area of *khalisa* (crown) land. But as political societies they could best be described as plural. As we have seen, the Hindu kingdoms were built on a broad base of armed peasant support; the Muslim conquest states relied on the strength and cohesion of the ruling military clan, but the nawabs of Awadh, Bengal and Hyderabad and even Najaf Khan of Delhi were, like the Mughals before them, 'entrepreneurs in power' attaching support by the manipulation of kinship ties, by direct patronage and favour of personal dependants and eunuchs, or by cash grants and pensions. The Awadh and Bengal dynasties sometimes faced opposition from members of the old Mughal nobility, from Sunni Muslim learned men or from groups of local power-holders with old rights over land. Their style of government and kingship therefore was attuned to bringing in a wide range of Hindu warrior and administrative groups. The nawabs of Awadh recruited the Tilangana Rajput and Gosain mercenaries of ascetic martial brotherhoods;[86] the nawabs of Bengal became dependent on the great Hindu banking houses;[87] the Hyderabad rulers slowly transformed themselves from a military warband to a bureaucratic, revenue-farming state run through the good offices of clerical dynasties from north India.[88] The culture of these independent Mughal provinces was eclectic, even Hindu, and certainly a sharp retreat from the orthodox

[84] Polier, ed. Gupta, 'Present situation', p. 95.
[85] T. G. P. Spear, *The Twilight of the Mughuls* (Cambridge, 1951), ch. 2; *Seir Mutaqarin*, III, 219, 253–6.
[86] Barnett, *North India*, p. 135.
[87] Calkins, 'Regional elite', *JAS*, 1970; J. H. Little, *History of the House of Jagatseth* (repr. Calcutta, 1971).
[88] K. Leonard, *The Kayasths of Hyderabad. The Social History of an Indian Caste* (Berkeley, 1978).

Islamic style of government favoured by Aurangzeb in the last years of
Mughal power. Hindu festivals, pilgrimage centres and sacred interests
benefited from this relaxed policy.[89]

The new power

Before leaving the eighteenth-century state, some mention must be
made of the East India Company. In 1764 at the battle of Buxar, the
Company defeated the Nawab of Awadh and secured from him the
payment of a massive annual tribute (more than Rs. 50 lakhs) and the
revenues of the province of Benares whose rulers now became vassals of
the British. Hereafter the Company, which had by now consolidated its
power in Bengal, was increasingly active on the north Indian scene. In
1774, the British intervened with the Nawab's forces in the conquest of
Rohilkhand whose warrior rulers were expelled or reduced to
pensioners, with the exception of Rampur.[90] In 1781, Warren Hastings
suppressed a revolt by the ruler of Benares, Cheyt Singh, who was
expelled and replaced by a new raja more or less directly under the
control of the British Resident. Changes to the judicial and fiscal
administration of Benares territories culminated in the introduction
there after 1793 of a Permanent Settlement of land-revenue similar to
that in Bengal under the direction of Jonathan Duncan, one of the most
famous of eighteenth-century British civil officers.[91]

Next, the return of the Mughal emperor from exile in Kara near
Allahabad to Delhi in 1772 encouraged the British to take a deeper
interest in imperial affairs. They could not afford to allow the nominal
authority of the emperor to be monopolised by any one power,
particularly after the Maratha chieftain Mahaji Sindhia took Delhi in
1784. Problems arose in collecting the Awadh tribute regularly as the
Nawab's administration became more and more decentralised. These
culminated in the cession to the Company of much of Gangetic Awadh
in 1801. At the same time, the British took the opportunity of the second
Maratha war (1802–6) to drive towards Delhi and Agra in order to create
a north-western buffer for their rich revenue-bearing and trading
provinces of Bengal and the mid-Ganges.

Such military alarums and excursions were accompanied by a slow
penetration of British private traders and an extension of the covert

[89] See below, pp. 131, 139.
[90] J. Strachey, *Hastings and the Rohilla War;* S. A. Brelvi, *Life of Hafiz Rehmat Khan*, tr.
       M. H. Khan (Karachi, 1976).
[91] For the implementation of the Permanent Settlement, see A. Shakespear, *Selections from
       the Duncan Records*, 2 vols. (Benares, 1873), Mishra, *Banaras*, ch. 2; Duncan Records,
       Settlement Volumes, UP Central Record Office, Allahabad.

trading concerns of East India Company officials. The Company secured a near monopoly of the procurement of fine cloths in the great piece goods mart of Tanda in Awadh and dominated the rising trades with Calcutta. Private merchants operated from the towns of Fatehgarh (in the Farrukhabad territories) and at Kanpur in Awadh.[92] Here British forces were stationed under the subsidiary alliance system which bound Indian rulers to pay for a force of Company troops to be stationed on their territories 'for their own protection'.

It is easy both to overestimate and to underestimate the European presence in north India during these years. Neither in Bengal nor in upper India did the Company or private European traders secure direct control of the great bulk trades in grain, salt, sugar, spices and coarse cloth. But there are two further points to be made. First, European political influence formed an important set of restraints by which indigenous changes were limited. For instance, the Company held back the flow of bullion into Bengal by sea after 1750, with deflationary consequences for its commerce.[93] After 1770, it was powerful enough to restrain the flow of two highly valuable commodities, opium and salt, into Bengal by land. At the same time its political officers intervened at crucial stages in the development of north Indian regimes to head off rivals or to favour the powerful commercial magnates with which it had business links. Secondly, important changes within the patterns of north Indian trade reflected reorientations of the whole South and East Asian seaborne economy in which British commerce was gradually becoming dominant. It would be difficult to say that the Indian economy was in any sense capitalist in form even as late as 1900. But the influence of the world economy became increasingly significant after 1784, consolidating some types of internal change at the expense of others.

The unsettled powers

All the dominions so far mentioned had some of the features commonly associated with states, even in the western definition. They controlled recognisable territories, even though territorial control may have been less important to Indian rulers than an income and the honour of

---

[92] See, e.g. N. K. Sinha, *The Economic History of Bengal from Plassey to the Permanent Settlement*, I (Calcutta, 1965), 114; Address from the merchants of Farrukhabad for the prosperity of W. Hastings, Home Public Cons., Aug, 1788, 7, NAI; P. J. Marshall, 'Economic and political expansion: the case of Oudh', *Modern Asian Studies*, ix (1975), 465–82.

[93] K. K. Datta, 'Currency and banking in Bengal and Bihar during the years of transition 1756–83', *Bengal Past and Present*, lxviii (1949), 53.

kingship. They also possessed agencies for revenue collection and justice. But large areas of north India in the eighteenth century were still controlled by powers which cannot easily be described as states. The decline of Mughal hegemony also benefited huge bands of herdsmen, 'plunderers' and other wandering groups. Sometimes these loose federations had war leaders or titular heads. But the control of such notables did not reach down into the villages, camps or herds which were their basic units. The life of these wandering groups was well adjusted to the drier, less populous lands to the north and west of Delhi. A good example are the Bhatti herdsmen of what is now Hariana.[94] These herdsmen–maurauders were based on small pockets of good agricultural land along the rivers of their homelands (the Tiptu and Beas rivers). But for most of the year, Bhatti bands fanned out into the surrounding territories exacting protection rent in the form of cattle and gold, and selling these in distant markets. They were seen as enemies of settled agriculture and settled government, but they still played a part in the local economy of the settled areas by providing them with animals, milk, clarified butter and forest produce.[95]

Much of central north India was periodically under the control of such groups, and they must have accounted for a very large percentage of the animal power of the region during the later eighteenth century. Perhaps their most famous representatives were the fabled bands of Banjara pack-bullock traders who carried much of north India's grain and salt from area to area.[96] They also operated as plunderers and ran baggage trains for the great armies of the century. The ambiguity of the position of Banjaras is brought out in a remark once made by a Mughal commander to their leaders: 'I do not mind if you burn my crops and poison my wells, so long as you feed my armies.' Another group with similar features were the Gosain corporations of Hindu ascetics and mercenaries who also emerged as some of the most powerful trading people of the century. When the British encountered them on one leg of their great nomadic cycles of pilgrimage and trade on the borders of Bengal, they were seen as marauders and robbers. But in upper India, as we shall see, they helped maintain the urban economy and the growing external trade. Even the great bands of 'irregular horse' or 'fierce banditti' who roamed central India and became known to the British as Pindaris, fall into this category of wandering or unsettled powers. They

[94] William Francklin, *Military Memoir of Mr George Thomas* (Calcutta, 1803), pp. 165–8.
[95] For the ideological dimension see, D. Shulman, 'On South Indian bandits and kings', *IESHR*, xviii (1980), 283–306.
[96] Banjaras are described by all the early travellers; for references, see W. Irvine, *The Army of the Great Moghuls* (repr. Delhi, 1962), pp. 242ff; also R. V. Russell, *Tribes and Castes of Central India* (Calcutta, 1903), 11, 162–72.

were made up of individual warbands which coalesced as mercenary armies; they lived by moving loot from one area to another. But they also benefited the agricultural stability of their own homelands by injecting cash and cattle into them.

It is easy for us to assume that the state was the only political organisation in pre-colonial Indian society, and that the peasant family farm was wholly predominant as an economic form. But in this period the state was only one of the political formations which existed, and a large part of the population subsisted through petty carrying, plunder and pastoralism. The land-revenue based state and settled agriculture did not occupy the whole of the social and geographical space of the area, and there were large tracts where they were both on the defensive. It is the triumph of the state, both Indian and British, over its competitors, and the settlement of the agrarian and commercial economy which forms one of the themes of this book. Yet this triumph could not have occurred without the simultaneous expansion of indigenous merchant firms and bureaucratic lineages.

Merchants and agrarian society

Beneath the surface of the settled states of the eighteenth century, providing basic services for powers in the process of becoming principalities and linking in with the loose federations of wanderers, were three key groups. First there were the organisations of Indian traders and bankers who moved goods, grain and cash between the petty regimes. Secondly, were the lineages of administrative and military personnel drawn largely from Muslim families but also from Hindu clerical castes who had mastered the use of the pen and the intricate system of Indo-Persian revenue management and court ritual. Thirdly, there were the networks of religious organisations which linked the shrines and schools of Indian Islam and the temples and pilgrimage centres of the Hindu population. All these groups contributed to the emergence of the regional and local regimes, but they also maintained a degree of independence and influence in relation to them. After the decline of the empire, no state could hope to control networks of resources and skills which spread over the whole of north India, let alone the whole subcontinent. The fate of these groups during the transition from Indian to British rule is of great importance. They were the oil of the Indian state system, but their adherence or quiescence was crucial also to the emergence of British India. Here it will be useful to introduce the merchants, the focus of this study, and to anticipate some of the arguments about their evolution between 1770 and 1830.

By 1750 most professional traders and merchants in north India were part of a homogeneous business culture. This involved, for instance, using standard double-entry merchant accounts[97] and participation in communities of trust which were reinforced with sanctions deriving from caste and Hindu or Jain religious precepts. A few Muslim trading communities still straddled the north Indian plains in 1750, but these 'Mughal' and 'Afghan' networks had weakened by 1800.[98] The only strong Muslim trading presence was represented by the annual descent into the plains of Kabuli Afghan moneylenders who lent to peasants on extremely high rates of interest and were not closely tied into the day-to-day working of agricultural and state finance. Knowledge about markets and trade was complicated and arcane so that certain caste groups, and certain groups of extended families within these caste groups, could dominate the more profitable lines of trade and moneylending over many generations. Most of the merchant magnates of our area were either men of the Khattri caste originally from the Punjab, Agarwals whose traditional home was reputedly further east, or tough Oswal and Maheshwari families who had been drifting out of the dry lands of Rajasthan for many generations. There were also a few powerful families of Gujerati trading people of Brahmin and mercantile caste in the towns of our area. In the sixteenth and seventeenth centuries, their forebears had dominated India's foreign trade and many of its internal routes also.[99] But their star was definitely on the wane as the Mughal empire, which had provided protection for their ventures, fragmented into smaller kingdoms.

In the localities, a rather more heterogeneous group of local merchant castes controlled trade and shared control of local markets with landowners and princes. Usually these families were also drawn from the broad mercantile caste order (the Vaishyas), but a few families of lower caste entrepreneurs of liquor distiller (Kalwar) or oil presser (Teli) caste also accumulated capital and social prestige. 'Professional' merchants and moneylenders were not, of course, the only people who lent money or brought goods to markets in eighteenth-century India. Almost anyone with money and a cart or bullock to spare – landed magnate and rich cultivator alike – did so from time to time. But it was

---

[97] The best account remains L. C. Jain, *Indigenous Banking in India* (London, 1929); see also T. Timberg, *The Marwaris. From Traders to Industrialists* (Delhi, 1978).

[98] Though see the petitions from Kabuli and other Afghan trading groups, Proceedings of the Resident of Benares (PR), 1 Dec. 1787, UPR; Pathan gentry in the west of the region also often combined moneylending with military service.

[99] Das Gupta, *Surat*; S. Chaudhuri, *Trade and Commercial Organisation in Bengal 1650–1720* (Calcutta, 1975), pp. 98, 223; some Gujerati traders seem to have escaped the decline on northern arterial routes by moving south to Hyderabad, Mysore and Madras.

unusual for people of the standard agricultural caste groups to acquire sufficient market know-how or to allay suspicion of the 'bazaar people' sufficiently to set up as long distance traders.

There was considerable specialisation among merchant people and this often overlapped with the social distinctions of caste. Money dealers (*sarrafs*), jewellers (*jouhuris*) and cloth dealers (*bazazas*) performed separate functions,[100] especially at the retail level of trade. There was also a considerable gap in status and wealth between the village grocer (*bania*), the rural merchant of the small town (*mahajan*) and the big merchant prince of the city (*sahukar*).[101] In our period, the local market networks and those of the big cities remained loosely linked in many parts of the country. Farmers and village artisans disposed of their surplus produce in small periodic markets, and the produce of the wider world reached them by way of itinerant merchants and irregular religious fairs.

Yet over several centuries, forces had been working which ultimately created a more unified merchant class out of the loose merchant 'order' of former times. Slow population growth in the Gangetic valley and the steady expansion of arable into jungle and grazing tracts had increased the volume of agricultural surplus moving along the trade routes. But the consolidation of states demanding regular cash payments of land revenue provided a more immediate stimulus to commercialisation and the growth of markets. During the eighteenth century the linking together of markets and merchant communities continued. There was, as we shall see, a significant degeneration of high arable farming in some areas in the wake of the decline of the Mughal peace. But the insatiable demand of Mughal successor regimes for ready cash pushed on the process of consolidation in the more stable tracts, and there were unmistakable signs that the influence of powerful merchant families was on the increase.

By the 1780s, then, some of the main features of the agrarian order of the central Ganges valley had already emerged. In the rice-growing, better watered east of the region, the dominance of warrior–landholders of the Rajput and military or Bhumihar Brahmin castes was already established. Population here was already quite dense, reaching perhaps 450 persons to the square mile in Benares and parts of southern

---

[100] The best contemporary description of styles of traders and merchants is to be found in the works of Hamilton Buchanan, especially his papers edited by M. Martin, *The History, Antiquities, Topography and Statistics of Eastern India* (London, 1838), 1, 366–79.

[101] C. A. Bayly, 'Indian merchants in a "traditional" setting, Benares 1780–1820', in A. Hopkins and C. Dewey (eds), *The Imperial Impact* (London, 1978), pp. 151–73.

Awadh;[102] holdings were already quite small. In some areas, close-knit bodies of high caste clansmen cultivated the land directly, or closely superintended cultivation. Elsewhere, forms of relationship which resembled *rentier* landlordism had also emerged. Magnates of this sort derived extra power from customal perquisites paid by ordinary cultivators, village artisans and local merchants. They were often the men who collected and paid revenue to the regional overlords. Day labourers drawn from lower castes (especially Chamars and Pasis) also made up a large percentage of the population. These people sometimes had small plots of land on the fringes of villages, or kept herds of goats and pigs. But whether they retained links of hereditary service with the elites of the village or simply formed a pool of free labour, to all intents and purposes they can be regarded as landless.[103]

To the west of the region, in the drier wheat-producing lands stretching from Benares up towards the Punjab and Rajasthan, conditions were more fluid. Here a process of state-building and agricultural colonisation was still going on with the Jat caste category, the beloved 'sturdy peasants' of the later colonial officers, strengthening their hold. Large areas, however, remained herding and nomadic territories. Away from the Muslim towns some rich agricultural lands had declined with the evaporation of the Mughal hegemony. Population was apparently less dense here. Even before the great famine of 1783, there were many tracts where population was probably well under 200 per square mile.[104] A rough estimate might put the total population of what was to become the United Provinces at 20 million in the last twenty years of the eighteenth century, and at least 85 per cent of these people lived in villages or country towns of under 5,000 people. But this is not to say that they were all 'peasants' in the conventional sense. Quite apart from the landless labourers there was also a large population of people engaged in services of one sort or another for rural or urban elites – artisans, carriers, soldiers, religious specialists, petty merchants, and so on. As we shall see, these people directly felt the effects of the political changes of the period.

The scene has been set with a discussion of the features and varieties of the pre-colonial regimes which existed in the Ganges valley. These states formed and moulded the commerce and towns of the period just as they

---

[102] Cf. 'On the population of Bengal', *Asiatick Annual Register*, iv (1802), 41; see below, pp. 188–90.

[103] For a comprehensive listing of materials, see B. R. Grover, 'An integrated pattern of commercial life in the rural society of north India during the 17th and 18th centuries', *Proceedings of the Indian Historical Records Commission*, xxxvii (1966), 121–53.

[104] Based on magistrates' reports, 1814, Home Misc., vol. 776, IOL.

modified areas of the surrounding agrarian economy. The following chapters describe in more detail the links between political power, trade and agriculture, with two questions in mind. First, how can we reconcile the deeply rooted view of the century as a period of chaos with the evidence of stability and even growth which arises from much of the documentation now available? Secondly, did the movements of men and resources across the countryside, which were a consequence of its political flux, represent simply a shuffling of the old cards? Or were there perceptible changes in the social order which pointed towards the consolidation of new groups and new relationships between agriculture, commerce and political power? The evidence drawn from the east of the region on the eve of British rule does not support the view that society had undergone, or was about to undergo any major transformation. Nor does the secondary material on which we have relied for an understanding of the situation in the tracts nearer Delhi. But significant change was taking place. At one level, the slow imposition of a cash revenue demand and the long-term growth of trade in the Ganges valley had made money an essential feature of agrarian politics. At another level, the requirements of post-Mughal regimes for cash and legitimacy had strengthened the influence of corporations of merchants, gentry and service people which had been consolidating themselves between state and agrarian society. These classes were more than a 'new elite'. They were bearers of a locally rooted culture which was emerging beneath the centralised pattern of Mughal India. This new culture was built up through the institutions of the market, of the ascetic 'monastery', and of the Vaishnavite temple, on the one hand. On the other, it coalesced around the Sufi saint's shrine and the tradition of gentry literacy in Persian. First, however, it is important to look in abstract at the relations between the eighteenth-century state and agrarian society in order to understand how towns and gentry could survive in what appears to be a period of dizzying change.

1

Prologue: War and society in eighteenth-century India

Fairly recently the historiography of eighteenth-century India resembled that of the European Dark Ages before Henri Pirenne or the Thirty Years' War before the intervention of the economic historians. The picture was derived from the melancholy tales of contemporary European travellers to upper India and reinforced by the self-congratulation of later amateur historians among Indian officials who told of anarchic conditions and the decline of cultivation. It was embellished with the quatrains of those Indian writers who bewailed the decline of past glories with the bitterness of the unemployed scholar, the small literary elite of Mughal India mourning the passing of the old Delhi, 'city famed throughout the World, where dwelt the chosen spirits of the age'.[1] With the emergence of nationalism, the Black Legend of the eighteenth century was enlisted in the service of imperial ideology. H. M. Elliot, for instance, berated those young Indians who wished to return to 'that dark period' of independence, 'when the bare utterance of their ridiculous fantasies would have been attended not with silence and contempt but with the severer discipline of molten lead or impalement'.[2] Yet even the nationalist writers of the early years of the present century were ambivalent about the immediate pre-colonial past. Most condemned its leaders for the betrayal of the Indian nation; some were doubtful about the advantage of rule by Muslim potentates. Hermann Goetz was one of the few historians who saw anything admirable about the century. But the cultural renaissance in the miniature painting, music and architecture of the period was, for him, but the sweetness of decay in the body politic.[3]

A more varied and interesting picture has now emerged from closer archival work. As in other dark ages, the darkness of eighteenth-century India was in large part the shadow cast by the massive historiographies of earlier and later periods. New analyses of the political systems of the period have led to the view that the conflict which contemporaries saw

---

[1] See, e.g., *Zikr-i-Mir*, tr. Ralph Russell and Khurshidul Islam, *Three Mughal Poets. Mir, Sauda, Mir Hasan* (London, 1969), p. 35.

[2] P. Hardy, *Historians of Medieval India* (London, 1959), p. 8.

[3] H. Goetz, *The Crisis of Indian Civilisation in the Eighteenth and Early Nineteenth Centuries* (Calcutta, 1938), pp. 5–8.

signalled the emergence of powerful 'successor states' which gained a closer control over rural resources and inherited the political style of the Mughal empire. Studies of the regional principalities of Bengal, Hyderabad and Awadh suggest that the turbulent events of the century heralded not the final dissolution of the Mughal polity as much as the emergence of regional dynastic rulers who initiated new cycles of growth and regeneration. Some are tempted to go further and claim that the cries of alarm and despair issuing from the elite were no more serious than those to be heard in seventeenth-century Istanbul or early nineteenth-century China. They were witness to a cyclical realignment rather than the collapse of a political culture. Indeed the Mughal empire did not fall, it was simply swallowed by a larger political organism.[4]

These new approaches have the great advantage of deriving from Indian sources and have helped to dispel many distortions inherent in European judgements of Indian affairs. For instance, the annual conflicts over the size of a territory's annual land-revenue between a regional authority and local magnates can be seen as a kind of ritualised political bargaining rather than an irrevocable slide into anarchy. So, too, in time, the feared danegeld (*chauth*) which the Marathas levied from their conquered territories was often transformed into a revenue system as detailed and even more efficient than that of the Mughals themselves. A start can also be made in revaluing the social movements of the period. To the rulers of Delhi and Agra, the Jat warriors who pressed into their territories from the south-west were rebels and bandits; to the incoming British, they were a stubborn source of resistance poised across a main artery of defence and trade up and down the Gangetic plain. But if the Jats are looked on as a social rather than as a political phenomenon, they appear more as one of the last great movements of pioneer peasant colonists which have periodically revitalised the agriculture of South Asia.

Nevertheless, there are some anomalies and omissions in the emerging consensus which stresses the positive aspects of political change and the continuities and balance within kingdoms. Most of the material so far available has come from the provinces of Bengal, Awadh, Benares and Hyderabad. Yet these were dominions which even contemporary European observers recognised to be areas of relative stability. They were the satrapies of the old empire which gradually seceded from Delhi rather than those which openly revolted against it. How do we reconcile the evidence of stability and economic health in these areas with the picture of declining towns and falling rents which

---

[4] J. C. Heesterman, 'Was there an Indian reaction? Western expansion in Indian perspective', in H. Wesseling (ed.), *Expansion and Reaction* (Leiden, 1978), pp. 31–58.

still emerges unmistakably from the once rich hinterland within 200 miles of Delhi and Agra? If contemporary conflict was on a relatively small scale, what was the cause of local agrarian dislocation? Indeed, what in more general terms was the relationship between political, commercial and agrarian change in late eighteenth-century north India?

Part of the problem is the tendency of the older works to describe these changes in terms of a general pathology which attributed all signs of decline to 'native misgovernment'. For the changes observed could be of quite different origins. The effects of warfare, population scarcity or internal migration; the redistribution of capital, and periodic cycles of bad seasons: all these have been lumped together to portray an undifferentiated Time of Troubles. But the economic background has been almost as shadowy in some of the more recent works which set out to rewrite the political history of the century. Here we find valuable discussions of the relations between the rulers of the successor states and their chief landholders and bureaucrats, but the agrarian system remains in an economic vacuum, except in the work of Irfan Habib and some of his younger colleagues. Eastern Rajasthan is beginning to come into focus,[5] but the economic performance of much of the Ganges valley between 1740 and 1810, and its relation to political change, remains an open question. This section, then, presents some preliminary hypotheses about the effects of war and political change on north Indian society. The discussion will concentrate on the movement of resources – capital, labour and skills – across the landscape. We shall stress the flexibility and adaptability of the contemporary political economy and show how the withdrawal of resources from some areas was often matched by their reinvestment elsewhere. By emphasising the interconnection between economic and political change, it becomes easier to reconcile the picture of stability and commercial growth in some areas with the evidence of decline in others.

Yet if political change could rapidly redistribute labour and capital across the countryside, some cherished generalisations about Indian peasant economy immediately become suspect. The first assumption is the lineal descendant of Sir Charles Metcalfe's famous statement about the continuity of 'village republics' unaffected by the clash of dynasties and the din of turmoil among the ruling groups. This view holds that the state in India was little more than a machine for extracting tribute from entrenched local communities, and that surface political changes hardly affected the conduct of rural life. The second is that the basic unit of

[5] Dilbagh Singh, 'Ijarah system in eastern Rajasthan 1750–1800', *Proceedings of the Rajasthan History Congress*, vi (1973), 60–9; and his Jawaharlal Nehru University Ph.D. thesis which is soon to be published.

agriculture, the peasant farm working largely with family labour, made its own production decisions in isolation from the interference of outside elites, excepting demands for rent or revenue. The third assumption is the truism that north India was an 'agrarian society'. This has obscured the fact that a very large percentage of people derived income from temporary non-agricultural employment (weaving, military service, portering, and so on) which was directly responsive to the expenditure and location of the elites.

This chapter begins by considering in abstract three basic links between the state, commerce and agrarian society, and then goes on to analyse the effect of war in view of these links. The first link in the eighteenth-century political economy was the connection between the peasant household and the land-controllers, traders and other magnates who made up elites outside village society. We will find a wide range of relationships – from the 'free' family farm at one extreme to virtual slavery at the other. The second link was the expenditure and employment offered by regional and local elites which bound together ruler, artisan and cultivator in systems of trade and redistribution. Such expenditure might be rapidly displaced from one centre to another in the course of political change which was not anarchic but rather represented a relatively orderly movement of resources and client communities. The third link bound these local economies and kingdoms together at a wider regional, or even continental, level. It was the close tie between the direction of the flows of land-revenue and the flows of trade in precious articles. This ensured that political change or shifts in the tributary relations of regimes would quickly give rise to shifts in patterns of trade which sometimes created the appearance of commercial and agrarian disruption.

Agrarian patronage

The basic unit of the north Indian economy throughout recent centuries was indeed the peasant 'family farm'. The family's hereditary connection with its land guaranteed survival and security. It provided social standing, a pledge for credit in times of need and a form of investment in times of plenty. Family heads were generally the people who made decisions about the mix of crops, the purchase and use of animals and the time of harvest. The size of the cultivated area was adjusted to the number of labouring hands within the family from generation to generation. Yet if the peasant farm was the indivisible atom of agrarian structure, the way in which these atoms were bonded together by economic, political and cultural forces outside the family differed significantly from area to area. Over much of the Ganges valley, the peasant farm worked only within the constraint of the brotherhood or clan organisation of peasant families of similar caste and economic status. Here the family's access to land, labour and honour was determined by its status within the wider lineage; its freedom of economic action was limited mainly by the need to provide for cash payments to be made by the brotherhood to the clan head, *chaudhuri* or raja, or to the outside rent-taker who periodically 'issued from a nearby mud-walled fortress to collect the revenue'.[6] Otherwise this class had many of the characteristics of the 'free peasant' of medieval Europe and often approximated to the category called *khudkasht* or 'self-cultivating' farmer in late Mughal revenue manuals.[7] This pattern was widespread in the Delhi and Agra regions, while the great military colonisation movements of Jat, Rajput and Bhumihar Brahmin which were so much a feature of the century added new waves of free peasants to the southern and western marches of Hindustan.

However, in many parts of north India there existed side by side with this pattern other styles of agrarian relations in which the peasant family farm was more closely moulded by outside forces. Here the role of the elites in providing the basic resources of grain, cash, tools and land which allowed the family to reproduce itself was so great that the autonomy of the family farm was severely reduced even in matters of agricultural production. Groups of dependent cultivators of this sort would often have fallen into the category called *paikasht* by the revenue manuals or 'tenants at will' by the early British authorities. But our category extends to include local customary relations that were recorded by neither, and forms of dependence – among market gardening castes, for instance – where the cultivators were prized and wealthy but tied directly to the fortunes and investments of the ruling elite. Cultivators of this sort provided a shifting population of agrarian servants and specialists whose movement in response to political change could rapidly transform an area from high cultivation to wilderness, or vice versa.

At one end of the spectrum of patronage and dependence there were examples of near-serfdom in which low caste cultivators had been converted into a labour reserve by conquest, social abasement or a ruler's edicts. In the Benares region, for instance, agrarian dependence amounted to slavery in several areas, though this word is rarely associated with north Indian agriculture. In the 1780s throughout the

6 Tom G. Kessinger, *Vilayatpur 1848–1968* (Berkeley, 1978), p. 26.
7 Satish Chandra, 'Village society in northern India during the eighteenth century', in *Essays in Honour of Professor S. C. Sarkar* (Delhi, 1976), pp. 252–6.

Agauri Barhar and Bijaigarh tracts where the rich arable fringed the jungle, 'the ploughmen and labourers were all of that class called Laks, that is bondsmen or slaves, liable to be sold as other slaves, and with seemingly this single distinction in their favour, that their castes are not affected by their bondage'.[8] This pattern persisted into recent times when *lakis* or ploughmen remained a kind of near-hereditary personal servant for landowning families in the area.[9] Yet examples of slavery and blanket injunctions against the cultivation or ownership of land by low castes were rare throughout much of the country. They were most common where an aboriginal or tribal population came into contact with the settled agriculture of the plains, or where it had been recently subdued by incoming colonists.

Yet it is difficult to dismiss as exceptional the many instances of severe agrarian dependence among farmers of higher caste in the great plains. Quite often, landlords or moneylenders owned and distributed the stock, tools and seed of the cultivator. In Bengal and Benares, 'share-cropping' often implied no more sharing than a basic subsistence for the cultivator. The landlord kept seed and stock between the harvests.[10] In the cotton-growing areas, even before the onset of colonial rule and the great expansion of the raw cotton trade, moneylenders and substantial zamindars dictated production decisions as important as the timing of the harvest.

One reason why the widespread intervention of the elites in agriculture has been missed is that we have come to accept too rigidly the distinction between revenue management and agricultural production. Simply engaging to pay the revenue to an outside ruler did not, of course, imply that the engager would become involved in production in the village. Nor did the purchase of land-rights imply the dispossession of earlier cultivators. But elite groups could, and did, seek to penetrate into agricultural production and management through control of the revenue system. The form of the revenue and rental

---

8 Benares Revenue Report, para. 61, Resident to Governor General (GG), 25 Nov. 1790, Duncan Records 16, UPR, published in G. N. Saletore (ed.), *U.P. State Records Series. Banaras Affairs*, I (Allahabad, 1955), 212.

9 Interviews, Benares District, Jan.–Mar. 1973; tied house 'servants' are mentioned in a number of eighteenth- and early nineteenth-century documents concerning Awadh small towns, see, e.g. deposition 5 Ramzan 1217 A.H. (30 Dec. 1802), UPR, publ. in B. P. Saxena (ed.), *U.P. State Records Series. Calendar of Oriental Records*, I (Allahabad, 1955), 28–9; for Benares, K. P. Mishra, *Banaras*, p. 75; Rohilkhand, Resident Delhi to Magistrate Saharanpur, 10 July 1808, Saharanpur Collectorate, vol. 178, UPR; eastern Awadh, Montgomery Martin (ed.), *The History, Antiquities, Topography and Statistics of Eastern India* (London, 1838), II, 427; A. K. Chattopadhyay, *Slavery in the Bengal Presidency* (London, 1977).

10 H. T. Colebrooke and A. Lambert, *Remarks on the Husbandry and Internal Commerce of Bengal* (Calcutta, 1804); Tennant, *Recreations*, I, 85.

demand itself had considerable implications for production. There were basically three systems in operation. First, there could be an assessment of the standing crop where the magnate entered into an agreement that a certain quantity of the crop would be delivered to him (*kankot* collection). Secondly, there might be an actual physical division of the threshed crop between the villagers and the magnates' agents (*batai*); and thirdly, there were fixed or fluctuating cash payments (*jama*). The Emperor Aurangzeb sagely observed that cash collection was best, for crop sharing led to landlord oppression (*batai lutai*), and assessment of the standing crop put too much power into the hands of 'unscrupulous underlings'. But even cash rental constrained the economy of the family farm to varying degrees. It generally increased the cultivator's dependence on local moneylenders and men who had access to markets for finer crops. These had to be cultivated in order to procure the silver and copper coins with which to pay the revenue. All three systems provided points of entry by which determined renters or grantees could bend the domestic economy of the village to their advantage. In the grain-rent system, the landlord could acquire the best seed or make sure the peasant farmers parted with a larger and larger proportion of the seed and thus become dependent for advances on him. Alternatively, the magnate might try to invade the village by appropriating the perquisites of the village headman.

New agrarian dependencies of these sorts appear to have developed between 1600 and 1800 as the military and service elites of the old empire dispersed to regional centres and gained greater control over local society. Let us take the case of Amroha, in the north of the Moradabad District, which lies about eighty miles from Delhi, in the heartland of Islamic state-building in northern India. Here from before 1500, a military and service gentry of Sayyid families had been establishing itself through the patronage or complaisance of the Mughal and later Rohilla Afghan conquerors of the tract. Service under the Mughals had secured revenue-free grants of land. But the Sayyids' aim was to be more than simple revenue assignees. They resolved 'to assume absolute possession of the villages ... divested the headmen of all authority and assumed to themselves the direct management'.[11] Since the headman families retained social influence which was useful to the Sayyids, they were given a share in the produce and retained as a body of pensioners-*cum*-managers at the pleasure of their new masters. Village management appears to have led on to direct control of village resources, grain and stock. In the mid-nineteenth century, revenue officers were

[11] E. Alexander, *Final Report on the Settlement of the Moradabad District, 1879* (Allahabad, 1881), p. 25.

still inveighing against the old *batai* system under which the Sayyid landlords of the tract appropriated all 'save a bare subsistence' from the cultivators, and invaded the villages for several months a year with bullock teams, armed retainers and weighmen to secure the best portion of the crop.[12]

Other, deeper forms of agrarian dependence were common in adjoining areas north-east of Delhi in the late eighteenth century. Early British reports refer, for instance, to the ploughman (*hali*) system, in which a large proportion of the Hindu cultivators had been reduced to direct dependence on the Rohilla conquerors of the tract. The ploughmen were housed, clothed and even fed on a daily basis by the families of their patrons who also provided them with the seed, tools and animals with which to cultivate. The patronage connection was so strong that when the Rohilla gentry were driven out of the southern part of their territory by the forces of the Nawab of Awadh and the East India Company in 1774, a very large number of cultivating families 'retired with them',[13] leaving a chronic shortage of agricultural labour in the area. The dependent cultivators here retained few of the features of the free family farm. They were more like personal servants on the lands of their warrior masters – and the key unit of agriculture seems to have been the 'great household' of the gentry. This helps to explain some inconsistencies in treatment of Rohilla society by contemporary observers. In the British period it was common to treat the Rohillas as 'useless drones on the soil'. But Forster, writing in the 1780s, praises them for being among the few Muslim conquerors in India who had played a direct role in stimulating the agricultural prosperity of their fiefs.[14] Barlow noted their 'encouragement' of rice cultivation for the Delhi market in the 1780s.[15]

The link between revenue management and intervention in the

---

[12] *Ibid.*, p. 29, later evidence suggests that *muafi* (revenue-free) holders among the gentry had direct agricultural management in the *qasbah* townships proper in addition to the right to engage for government revenue. But in the countryside proper they held only revenue rights with agricultural management in the hands of predominantly Hindu zamindars, see, e.g., Saharanpur Report, 1839, para. 46, *Reports of the Settlements under Regulation IX of 1833* (Benares, 1862), I, 112; cf. Stokes, *Peasant and Raj*, p. 55. Much of the best agricultural land was situated in *qasbahs* or dependent groves. In addition gentry gradually assimilated *muafi* rights to their own zamindari home farm during the seventeenth and eighteenth centuries, see below, pp. 349–54.

[13] Collector, Moradabad to Board of Commissioners, 10 March 1808, CPR, 30 March 1808, 97/29, IOL; early nineteenth-century accounts suggest that predominantly Chamar *halis* may have accounted for about 12% of the agricultural population of Rohilkhand.

[14] George Forster, *A Journey from Bengal to England through the Northern Parts of India, Kashmir, Afghanistan and Persia* (London, 1798), I, 137.

[15] R. Barlow, Report on trade in Awadh, Foreign Secret Department Cons. 6 June 1787, 59, p. 37, NAI.

agricultural process was also blurred in the production of several of the high value market crops where the initial outlay on tools, seed or labour was high. Magnates owned sugar presses in many of the villages of Rohilkhand and indirectly controlled the quantities of cane which local farmers could produce profitably. In Bundelkhand before 1800, agents of city merchants and large landholders owned the crop of cotton produced by the poorer cultivators and determined when it was to be cut by reference to the local speculative market in cotton futures.[16] In a different way, gentry and landholders also intervened in the production of the valuable fruit and vegetable crops. It was the Muslim service gentry of the small towns and large villages of Awadh who planted and supervised the growth of mango, guava and other fruit trees planted around their home market towns.[17] Groves played an important part in the rural economy of some districts where they accounted for as much as 5 per cent of the total cultivated acreage and provided a significant source of income for the landholders.[18] Specialist market-gardener and fruiterer castes (Malis, Kacchis and Koeris) were given leases of groves,[19] but the gentry retained an interest in improvement and marketing.

This is also true of the agricultural settlements and colonies which were being planted to increase the cultivated area and revenue in the last half of the eighteenth century. Here the role of forces outside the family farm varied from case to case. Sometimes the merchants, revenue-farmers, landlords or entrepreneurs who induced colonies of specialist farmers to settle took an active part only in the first few years of the colony when they provided capital, tools and protection. Thereafter the colonists might succeed in gaining and maintaining forms of quasi-proprietary right over the land they cultivated and even liberating themselves from dependence on the men of credit for capital. But in poorer areas a veritable serfdom developed with elites controlling the labour time and resources of the peasant family. In the *savak* ('pupil') system of northern Awadh (an area which was being rapidly cleared) the patron-landlords who provided advances to the peasant families

---

[16] Commercial Resident at Etawah to Board of Trade, 28 June 1803, Bengal Commercial Procs., 1 Aug. 1805, Range 156, vol. 66, IOL.

[17] The impact of the 'service gentry' in their localities can be traced in the Persian records of Awadh, UPR, Allahabad, esp. the Mallawan and Sandila Papers; e.g. Mallawan 44, declaration made by Sayyid Muhammad Ali, *c.* A.D. 1740, which records the construction in Mallawan by *kazi* and *muhtasib* Abdul Razzaq of 'houses, wells, masjids'; he also 'populated a new purah [quarter], purchased many gardens and obtained *madad-i-maash* grants', tr. Saxena (ed.) *Oriental Records*, I, 19–20, cf. II, 88–90.

[18] Habib, 'Potentialities', p. 21.

[19] Mishra, *Banaras*, p. 78.

rewarded them with as little as one-sixth of the crop and also monopolised the labour of the husbandmen's wives and children for a large part of the year.[20] Most commentators believed that this system arose from the reduction of families of 'free peasants' to the status of bondsmen during periods of famine or political disturbance, and it appears to have been consolidated after 1750. A different method of providing tied labour was used to the south-east where Buchanan reported in 1811 that there existed a bar on members of lower castes becoming self-cultivating *(khudkasht)* proprietors of arable land.[21] This custom had the effect, of course, of maintaining a large body of landless families for use as hired labour in the fields. When the British attempted to abolish the disability, there were immediate complaints of labour shortage from the landlords of the area.

Agrarian dependence did not always result from straightforward distress. Cultivators might actually opt to abandon the free peasant farm and work as dependent labourers for lords or peasant magnates at a considerable distance. This also increased the fluidity and movement of the agrarian economy, and made it responsive to changes among the elites. In the 1780s in the middle Gangetic plain, 'peasant cultivating on half produce is still worse paid than an agricultural labourer hired by the day'.[22] In contemporary Malwa, John Malcolm reckoned that a combination of political change and famine had converted a 'great proportion' of its husbandmen into 'Sookwasee' cultivators or 'seekers of protection' who moved from place to place cultivating where they were offered the best rates, for one, two or three years.[23] Movement of this sort was a consequence of pressure on the family farm, but it should not be regarded as a symptom of social disintegration. Cultivators were, after all, responding positively to stress by selling their labour to buy subsistence and protection. Malcolm and other writers noted that mobility of field labour was also a consequence of the 'competition that now exists for cultivators'. In a situation where population was sparse even in rich tracts, mobile labourers evidently held a strong bargaining position in regard to the elites. This advantage they often forfeited in the nineteenth century with the general rise in population.

More widespread than the direct involvement of trading people in agriculture was the system of 'advances' by which they provided artisans and specialist cultivators with working capital on account. While advances were specifically designed to 'contract out' work to the family

---

[20] *Gazetteer of the Province of Oudh*, i (Allahabad, 1877), 145; iii (Allahabad, 1878), 580–1; for the settlement of specialist cultivators by gentry, *ibid.*, i, 123, ii, 206, 218–19, 252.
[21] Martin, *Eastern India*, II, 235–6.   [22] Tennant, *Recreations*, II, 348.
[23] Malcolm, *Central India*, II, 27.

firm or family farm, they nevertheless moulded and restricted the production decisions of these units. We find, for instance, merchants in the cotton tracts determining when the crop should be harvested. Elsewhere, receiving advances led artisans and cultivators into debt-bondage, so that relations of production became like those between serf and master.

The system was widespread. In eastern Awadh up to 100,000 weavers were supported on an estimated Rs. 10–12 lakhs of advances from merchants based upon Lucknow and Fyzabad, and increasingly from agents of the East India Company.[24] Such an inflow of cash encouraged local specialisation of production in the villages and galvanised the cotton trade from the Doab and Central India. To the east, merchant-moneylenders in Azamgarh secured sugar supplies by advances and became petty sugar factory owners (*khandsaris*).[25] In the west, cotton and indigo were both procured through the same system. The rationale varied. Among more prosperous artisans and cultivators the object of giving advances was restrictive, allowing the merchant 'to engross the labour of the cultivator'. But in poor or unstable tracts such as the Doab, advances were necessary simply to provide cultivators with the cash to buy seed, tools and wage labour for weeding.

Once again the 'advance' system was a fragile one for local society and closely dependent on the fortunes of political power and mercantile security. The withdrawal of advances could lead to the collapse of large areas of high farming or artisan production. This appears to have happened, for instance, in the environs of Mau in Awadh in the 1770s and in the Firozabad subdivision of Agra in the 1790s. But equally the system could reconstitute itself in another area with great speed. Here then was another link between the elites and agrarian society which helps explain the peculiar fluidity of the economy.

Composition of the rural elites

What was the composition of the elite groups who were maintaining, even increasing, their hold over the peasant family farm in many areas of north India? A number of different elements are recognisable. First there were the great revenue-farmers and bureaucrats who clustered around the courts of the successor states. Here we have men such as Mehendi Ali Khan, Raja Tikait Rai and Almas Ali Khan and their retinues who settled colonies of cultivators in order to enhance the

---

[24] Barlow, 'Awadh Report', pp. 12–15.
[25] Shahid Amin, 'Sugarcane cultivation in Gorakhpur, U.P., c. 1890–1940' (unpubl. Oxford D.Phil. dissertation, 1978), ch. 1.

revenue capacity of their fiefs. Next there were the local officials of the Awadh court or expansionist local rajas who had gained from the regional rulers the right to clear and settle on outlying tracts for a stipulated and rising rate of revenue. This was a particularly lucrative way to use capital. In the long-settled areas, revenue-farmers had to deal with entrenched and recalcitrant zamindars and frequently fell into arrears with their bankers and disfavour at court. But in frontier areas where the land was being opened up, the initial outlay on the clearing lease would soon be recouped, leaving good profits. Also the new colonists might be expected to be less troublesome than established cultivators.

In the north-west, the masters of the peasant families were generally Muslim military or service gentry who had seized or been rewarded with the right of engagement for revenue over blocks of villages. These families founded or settled in small towns (*qasbahs*) which became centres of thriving cash and garden crop cultivation. Not 'improving landlords' in the western sense, they were nevertheless more than simple rent-takers. Mercenary warfare or government service was peculiarly hazardous. It was in the interest of the gentry to build up their base areas and gain a closer control over agrarian resources. They put in wells, tanks and groves; they built mosques, large houses, and fixed markets where local trade could be taxed. All this had a considerable effect on the ecology of their home settlements.

The growing importance of urban and rural men of trade and capital after 1770 will be discussed at length in later sections, but here we should note the developments which were bringing people of the mercantile classes into closer connection with the management of agriculture in some parts of north India. The progressive monetisation of rent and the resort to farming out the land-revenue by many of the regional rulers was one major force for change. In areas where peasant family farming was generally predominant such as Malwa or the Jat territories, the emergence of regional states which demanded punctual payment of cash revenue had begun to propel trader–moneylenders into agricultural management at village level. In eastern Rajasthan, Dilbagh Singh has found local moneylenders who were used by the state to make cash advances to cultivators during times of distress, taking over and managing farms when their original owners failed.[26] Malcolm noted similar instances in Malwa where 'The richest bankers mix in the petty revenue details of the smallest village: the advance they make for seed to cultivators who cannot afford to keep a store of grain is considered less a loan, than a subscription of a certain portion of stock for a share in the

[26] Dilbagh Singh, 'Ijarah system'.

profit.'[27] In the Benares region where commercial growth had gone much further, we shall see bankers and traders playing a clandestine part in village revenue matters. But it is an intermediate category of big local merchant or commercial peasant which is found most often in direct management of hired labourers, large stocks of grain and draught animals. Such rich marketing peasants were not lacking south of the Jamna either: 'Many of this class in Central India, notwithstanding changes and oppressions, arrive at very considerable wealth and employ as many as forty or fifty ploughs.'[28] For an emerging group of rural commercial husbandmen, investment in stock and the labour of the rural poor was an obvious use of commercial wealth. But for long-distance traders and urban bankers, a stake in the revenue system or agrarian production was more hazardous. It was a question of weighing up the possibility of trading loss or expropriation against the possibility of complete impotence in a hostile rural environment.

What were the forces which determined the distribution of different styles of agrarian relations across the north Indian countryside? In the west of the region the classic free peasant farm style of agriculture coincided with the areas of Jat dominance in the east Punjab and the western parts of the Meerut and Agra Divisions. In the east it was found in riverine south Awadh and parts of the Benares Division where the clan brotherhoods of Rajputs and Bhumihars had grown in numbers and become direct farming communities. Even in these tracts a high proportion of the population must have been field labourers who spent time working on the holdings of the higher caste peasant families, but it can still be said that the 'free' peasant farm set the style of the agrarian economy in these areas. By contrast, agrarian dependence on gentry and moneylenders was more in evidence in eastern Rohilkhand, the areas of new settlement to the north and south of the Ganges valley, and in the environs of the markets and cities founded by new magnates.

Satish Chandra[29] follows remarks made by Sir John Malcolm and W. W. Hunter in suggesting that the supply of land was the crucial factor in determining the degree of dependence. Where cultivable waste was plentiful, it was much more difficult to reduce the status of cultivators. Certainly some forms of near-servitude were encountered in the more densely settled eastern districts. Yet Rohilkhand, Malwa and north Awadh appear to have been very thinly populated by nineteenth-century standards, and here the bondsman (*sukavasi*, *savak* or *hali*) systems were widespread. Another explanation is that here it was a devastating series of scarcities (particularly those of 1781 to 1788) which

[27] Malcolm, *Central India*, II, 38.   [28] *Ibid.*, p. 26.
[29] Satish Chandra, 'Village society', in *S. C. Sarkar*, pp. 253–5.

shifted the balance against the free peasants. But both these suggestions attribute the balance of social relations to demography, climate or ecology. Political changes must also be considered. In Malwa, political flux resulting from repeated Maratha incursions had forced the peasantry to 'sell' much of the independence expressed in the relationship with their hereditary land in order to 'buy' protection. In Rohilkhand it may have been the heavy revenue demand imposed by the Rohilla rulers and the deliberate extirpation of the rights of intermediate zamindars after 1740 which reduced a large part of the peasantry to bondsman status. Peasant farmers had to grow valuable cash crops such as sugar cane and rice in order to find cash for the enhanced revenue demand. In turn the cultivation of these crops forced them to turn for capital to the elites who took closer control of production.

For a convincing explanation of the incidence of various forms of agrarian dependence, we had best turn to a combination of demographic, climatic and political forces. In Benares, for instance, it was the concurrence of the 1784–8 scarcities with the enhanced revenue demands of the Raja and his agents which reduced many of the regional specialist cultivators to a lower status.

It unfortunately happened that during the famine aforesaid a great proportion of the Kurmis, Kacchis and Koeris were in this district as well as in others supplanted by Brahmans ... and it is according to this unfavourable mutation amongst the cultivators ... together with the diminution of cultivation occasioned of the season and partly from there being no effectual control to check the undue exactions of the aumils [revenue-farmers], that may, I think, be fairly attributed the rapid declension which had taken place in the revenue funds of this country.[30]

These 'undue exactions' were in part, at least, a response to the unremitting financial pressure of the East India Company for the punctual payment of tribute by the Benares *Raj*.

Ideology and dominance

The political elites maintained agrarian dependence and supplies of labour through the use of force and the 'sale' of protection. But force had to be seen to be legitimate, and here notions of patronage and redistribution, common in both the Hindu and Indo-Muslim styles of government, become important. Religion and the ideology of caste were not simply masks for the material interests of dominant groups. After all, land-controllers wished to acquire resources principally in order to

---

[30] Revenue Administration Report, Taluka Jaloopoor, Resident to GG, 25 Nov. 1790, Proceedings of the Resident of Benares, UPR.

fulfil roles as gentlemen or pious kings. These were set forth in classical literature and popular codes of conduct transmitted across generations. But it seems undeniable that these dominant ideologies were constantly being adjusted to work in fluid local societies which operated by different codes and sought to protect their own resources. As the introduction showed, there were many traditions of kingship and in the eighteenth century some were found more appropriate than others by local rulers.

The overriding need of the expanding groups of pioneer peasant warriors such as the Jats, Sikhs or Marathas was to attract skills, labour and political and moral support from whatever quarter. Those parts of their traditions which emphasised brotherhood and downgraded the importance of caste hierarchy and the role of Brahmins were therefore most appropriate. But later, when Jat and Sikh magnates were building more stable kingdoms, hierarchy and caste distance re-established itself. Similar varieties in the ideology of agrarian relations are encountered among formally Muslim states. As we have seen, in eastern Awadh there were areas where both Hindu and Muslim gentry enforced a rigid injunction against the holding of land by lower castes. This had the effect of creating a large labour pool of lower caste people who could work on gentry lands. On Begum Samru's lands near Delhi, severe methods of forced cultivation were employed and the estate management kept the upper hand by exploiting the caste rivalry between Jat and Taga cultivators.[31] But it was the benign notions of royal patronage and incorporation into local systems of redistribution which were more widely appropriate to the workings of the successor states. Almas Ali Khan, the great Awadh revenue contractor, referred to his Kurmi and Kacchi cultivators as 'children' and carefully succoured the new colonies which he planted in the west of the Awadh territory.[32]

Relations of this sort were strengthened by cultural links between master and servants. Hindu agriculturalists widely venerated the Muslim shrines associated with the small town headquarters of the gentry, while in some areas there had grown up a much closer assimilation between husbandmen and their Muslim patrons. Among the Kurmis of Chunar and Jaunpur, for instance, who had been settled on their lands in recent times, Hindu families adopted the Muslim practice of cross-cousin marriage and burial; some even introduced the Islamic crescent symbol into their domestic and caste regalia.[33] Over

[31] W. Forbes, *Settlement Report of the District of Meerut (1865–70)* (Allahabad, 1874), p. 5.
[32] W. H. Sleeman, *A Journey through the Kingdom of Oude in 1849–50* (London, 1858), I, 321–3.
[33] Interviews, Benares, Mirzapur Districts, 1973–4; cf. W. Crooke, *Tribes and Castes of the North-Western Provinces and Oudh* (Calcutta, 1896), II, 350.

much of north India, there was a premium on seeking liaisons between groups of different caste status and religion rather than on creating the exclusive caste bodies which have sometimes seemed to be the pattern for pre-colonial society. The aspect of Hindu caste practice which was most appropriate to the flexible political economy was the *jajmani* system – the sets of ritualised relations of service between different occupational groups expressed in the allocation of shares in the produce of the land. We are used to seeing this operate mainly at the level of the village. But in this period whole kingdoms – even kingdoms with a formally Islamic constitution – can be seen as extended sets of *jajmani* relations.[34] Thus, in creating their new dominion, the Nawabs of Farrukhabad first brought in their kinsmen from the northern mountains,[35] then created a large 'college' of direct dependants or *chelas* (pupils) who functioned as a quasi-caste, and finally planted colonies of skilled cultivators and craftsmen throughout their domains. Not one, but several ideologies, therefore, supported the fabric of this kingdom. At the centre was the Afghan idea of the patrilineal clan and the notion of a body of direct personal retainers dependent on the will of the Sultan characteristic of the 'slave dynasties' of the Middle East.[36] But in the surrounding rural society, the Nawabs worked more as Hindu rajas, linking in cultivators and merchants through the concession of favoured rates of land-revenue and urban taxation, and by dealing with their judicial problems through caste headmen.

Two general points emerge from this. The first is that Hindu and Islamic social theory were flexible enough to accommodate many varieties of political practice in the eighteenth century. Even among the 'republican' Sikhs or Jats the notion of hierarchy persisted,[37] but during this period it was very much in the background. Any set of ideas which helped attract political support, skills or capital was advantageous. Conversely, the potential of the ideology of caste to create distance between groups was minimised in practice. So while it is true that the classical traditions set boundaries which most rulers were unlikely to overstep, in practice the interpretation of ideology was highly responsive to economic and political conditions.

[34] Cf. A. M. Hocart, *Caste. A Comparative Study* (London, 1950), p. 68: 'The King's state is reproduced in miniature by his vassals. A farmer has his court, consisting of the personages most essential to the ritual, and so present even in the smallest community, the barber, the washerman, the drummers, and so forth.'

[35] W. Irvine, 'The Bangash Nawabs of Farrukhabad', *Journal of the Asiatic Society of Bengal*, xlvii (1878), 340ff.

[36] The 'slave caste' phenomenon was more widespread than is generally known, take, e.g., the case of Yakub Khan, founder of the Koil mosque, whose dependants became a separate 'caste' inhabiting a *mohulla* of Aligarh.

[37] Polier, ed. Gupta, 'Present situation', p. 26.

Secondly, emerging classes and dominions were most secure when they adjusted themselves to the theories of 'sharing' and redistribution which were prevalent among the mass of the Hindu and Muslim population. But the converse of this is that we should not assume that significant social change was absent simply because the idiom in which social relations was expressed remained unchanged. After all, in most societies new elites and new classes adopt the conservative styles of thought of the old order. In our case, for instance, local gentry and the new merchant notables continued to operate within the *jajmani* system and to hold 'shares' in royal perquisites and festivals. The theoretical interpretation of their place in society was not modified, but their control over resources appears to have increased markedly.

Military expenditure and the 'intermediate economy'

The first important link in the political economy of this period, then, was agrarian dependency created by the penetration of political elites into village society and agricultural management. But the other side of this dependency was massive local expenditure by the elites on warfare and display. These disbursements provided employment for members of peasant families and for a great range of service communities outside agriculture. We have already modified the notion that the free peasant family farm was the norm throughout northern India. Similarly, the truism that this was an overwhelmingly agrarian society conceals as much as it reveals. At this period the boundaries between peasant agriculture and non-agricultural employment seem more blurred than they were later. At least four out of ten people in the total population could be viewed as non-agriculturalists. This emerges from the materials on which Colebrooke, Lambert[38] and Jonathan Duncan[39] based their estimates of the 1790s; and it is also supported by the early nineteenth-century enumerations in Bengal and Gorakhpur made by Hamilton Buchanan.[40]

The non-peasant category included village servants, ritual specialists, artisans and very large numbers of regular and irregular soldiers with their dependents. The non-cultivating or semi-cultivating population

[38] Colebrooke and Lambert, *Husbandry*, pp. 5–9; cf. 'On the population of Bengal', *Asiatick Annual Register*, iv (1802), 41.

[39] Mishra, *Banaras*, pp. 64, 68; cf. Arshad Ali Azmi, 'Position of agriculture in the economy of Awadh during the Nawabi regime', *Indian Historical Congress 1967* (Delhi, 1968), pp. 82–5, though these estimates, which give a massive 55% of the population as 'non-agriculturalists', seem exaggerated.

[40] Martin, *Eastern India*, lists Buchanan's occupational estimates at the end of each district chapter.

was swelled by 'travelling groups' – Gosain trading 'ascetics', mercenary and robber bands, and the famous itinerant Banjaras. There was also much overlapping between artisan, pastoral and agrarian activity. People moved out of spinning and weaving in response to the seasons and markets outside the villages. The great carrier Banjara bands roaming the countryside at the end of the eighteenth century were partly made up of peasant families which became carriers and merchants temporarily because a poor season or a passing army had raised prices in some distant district. The balance between pastoral and stock-breeding and growing food grains was also different from what it was to become after 1850 when population growth and rapid communications had greatly raised the relative price of grain. Colebrooke and Tennant[41] recorded that in some areas families took leases for cultivation only in order to gain the much more valuable perquisites of communal grazing rights. Whereas the family might only break even on grain cultivation, the return on milk or clarified butter production, or on breeding for carriage, was said to be as much as 35 per cent, per annum.[42] Buchanan was still able to make a distinction between predominantly 'arable' and predominantly 'pastoral' districts in the heart of the Ganges valley,[43] while in the north-west of the region near Delhi, the social and economic balance did not finally pass from grazing to food grain cultivation until the middle of the nineteenth century.[44] This lucrative production of milk and *ghi* implies the existence of a substantial, if elusive, market system and a large class of purchasers who may well have consumed more milk-based products than did their descendants in the following century.

Eighteenth-century north India possessed what might be called an 'intermediate economy'. It functioned not at the level of the bazaar of the large town, nor in the village periodic mart (*hath*) where peasants exchanged petty commodities amongst themselves, but in the fixed gentry seat (*qasbah*) and the small regulated market (*ganj*). Its products were medium quality cloths, specialist fruit and vegetables and milk products; its services, provisioning and carrying for local magnates and moving armies; its motive force was the distribution of local political power expressed in revenue assignments.

Any account of historical change within this intermediate economy must remain highly speculative. It was not a new development. Expenditure by the Mughal nobility had been large in proportion to north India's agricultural production as early as the time of Akbar. Though the mechanism remains obscure, at least 40 per cent of the crop

41 Tennant, *Recreations*, II, 351.   42 *Ibid.*, p. 352.
43 Martin, *Eastern India*, II, 567.   44 Stokes, *Peasant and Raj*, p. 233.

must have been marketed to pay the central government land-revenue. Shireen Moosvi's ingenious studies have suggested that expenditure by the zamindars on their establishments may have been equal to a further 30 per cent of the revenue.[45] Evidently this was an agrarian society in which elite groups had achieved a remarkable control over the movement of the agricultural surplus.

The 'decentralisation of power' after 1770 was accompanied by a further displacement of resources and of elite demand to a large number of small centres. Peasants continued to pay their revenue in cash, but the provinces nevertheless ceased to remit large tributary flows to the centre between 1730 and 1750. Awadh in the 1770s was collecting little more than half the revenue-demand of the high Mughal period, and Richard Barnett has demonstrated that a large 30–40 per cent of what was collected 'leaked back' into the local society as 'expenses' in some areas.[46] There were local declines in cultivated area during the century; but much of the overall 30–50 per cent shortfall on the Mughal revenue figure must simply have represented appropriation by zamindars and service gentry.

Around Delhi it was the petty chiefs and headmen of the Jat and Sikh villages who benefited. In Moosvi's calculation, the Hariana–Hissar area was closely administered in high Mughal times with the expenditure of zamindars amounting to a mere 10 per cent of state revenue. But in the 1820s British officials beginning to administer the area noted that the village zamindars of the tract were actually taking more in the form of perquisites than the total state revenue, while the vast and lucrative herds of the Gujar and Bhatti pastoralists virtually escaped taxation.[47] The Mughals, of course, had 'transferred' much of their revenue back into the localities in the form of grants of revenue assignments (*jagir* and *madad-i-maash*). But in the second half of the seventeenth century, more and more of the empire's resources had been directed outside the region on costly warfare in the Deccan and Punjab. *A priori* the discontinuation of revenue payments to the centre after 1730 and the rise of new regional consumer cities such as Benares, Lucknow and Fyzabad suggest that a greater proportion of the agricultural surplus was being spent locally.

The economic effects of military spending and political decentralisation in Hindustan are clear. About a quarter of a million men or 1–1.5 per cent of the total population of the area in the last

45 S. Moosvi, 'Zamindars' share', *IESHR*, xv (1978), 359–75.
46 Barnett, *North India*, ch. 6.
47 T. Fortescue, *'Report on the revenue system of the Delhi territories', Selections from Punjab Government Records, Delhi Residency and Agency*, I (Lahore, 1911), pp. 115–16.

quarter of the century were full-time, fully equipped soldiers. To this we must add the large numbers of 'husbandmen' who augmented their income by participation in the regional armies or the zamindari levies. In the insecure conditions of the time it is probable that such irregular troops accounted for at least as high a percentage as the 4–5 per cent of the population that they are estimated to have represented during Akbar's time. But this is only to count the soldiers themselves. The regular troops appear to have supported between five and seven direct dependents each. For instance, the 20,000 troops who marched with the Nawab of Awadh on his campaigns of 1782 were accompanied by a further 150,000 camp-followers.[48] This accords well with British statements that from five to ten dependents were normal for Indian armies in cantonments or in the field.[49] All in all, we might suppose that from 15 to 20 per cent of north India's total population was partly dependent on expenditure of armies.

More significant yet was the high expenditure per head of the sophisticated forces with the drilled musketry and cannon which had become essential for political survival. Awadh in the 1750s was maintaining upwards of 50,000 regular troops on the large stipend of Rs. 25 per month[50] and a 'gentleman trooper' may have received as much as Rs. 80.[51] Rather later, a Rohilla mercenary states that it cost at least Rs. 25 per month to support himself, his horse and his attendant.[52] The volume of treasure or plunder needed to maintain such forces was very great. Lord Lake, for instance, found Rs. 2 lakhs in Agra for the payment of the Maratha forces there in 1803.[53] But Rs 6 lakhs had already been paid out for three months' service to a force of no more than 2,000 men. These figures are not out of line with estimates for the Company's own Indian troops. The average pay and allowances for an infantryman at this time amounted to about Rs. 100 per annum; that of a cavalryman about Rs. 200.[54] With other expenditures, the annual purchasing power of 1,000 infantrymen may have amounted to Rs. 150,000 and for cavalry about Rs. 300,000. Later estimates suggest that

48 Tennant, *Recreations*, II, 356, 366, *passim*.
49 Madan Paul Singh, *The Indian Army under the East India Company* (Delhi, 1976), p. 135, n. 35.
50 Barnett, *North India*, p. 33.
51 Irvine, 'Bangash Nawabs', *JASB*, xlvii (1878), 264 for career and stipends of Bahadur Ali, trooper in the Awadh army; cf. *Seir*, III, 283 which mentions Shujah's corps of distressed Delhi gentlemen, paid Rs. 15 per month.
52 Capt. E. Cunningham to Committee at Bareilly, 10 Apr. 1816, BCJ, 25 Oct. 1816, 132/46, IOL.
53 M. Martin (ed.), *Despatches, Minutes and Correspondence of the Marquis Wellesley, K.G.* (London, 1837), III, 414.
54 Singh, *Indian Army*, pp. 98–100.

soldiers may have been able to keep up to 30 per cent of their pay. But even then, 5,000 cavalry and infantry – the force of a small Jat raja – may have generated an annual demand for goods and services worth Rs. 6 lakhs and 'hoarding' or 'investment' worth a further Rs. 3 lakhs per annum.

The presence of such large military forces stimulated local economic activity. British commentators were hot in condemnation of the various tolls and cesses which were levied by local soldiery. Tennant, however, marvelled at the high level of military expenditure under the old regime in Bengal and Benares, and recorded that 'Many of the poorer classes subsist by providing them with food, clothing and furniture'.[55] He went on to observe that the disbanding of these forces and the reduction of zamindari influence under the British Permanent Settlement of 1793 had put an end to as many as 12,000 rural bazaars.[56] This is powerful testimony to the importance of political power in forming and maintaining local patterns of trade and marketing.

Military incomes bulked large against the background of trade and consumption in the ordinary periodic market or small fixed market (*ganj*). By comparison, the total demand generated by peasant families and by the mass of the urban population was tiny. The average field labourer at the end of the century was supposed to earn about Rs. 30 per annum,[57] while the disposable income of a peasant farmer and family was put at Rs. 8–10 per annum. This seems compatible with an annual expenditure of Rs. 5 on cloth and a few *paisa* on salt, spices, alcohol and 'rites de passage'. Demand of this sort was large in bulk but could easily be supplied by redistribution within the villages and periodic trade through *haths*. This was the situation observed by Buchanan in Gorakhpur at the beginning of the colonial period where a few 'wretched' periodic marts supplied a 'trifling' trade of a few hundred rupees per annum worth of surplus grain, salt and spices. Under these circumstances, there was little incentive for stocking, for permanent shops, or for capital accumulation. The local market was often divorced from the financial institutions connected with revenue collection. We find instances of this in the fringe areas during the next century.[58] Zamindars would sell their grain to Banjaras and itinerant dealers who would take it to distant markets. This income would suffice to pay the revenue and would be used later in the year for buying back grain from

---

[55] Tennant, *Recreations*, I, 264.
[56] Colebrooke and Lambert, *Husbandry*, p. 48.
[57] Tennant, *Recreations*, II, 345, 348.
[58] Take, e.g., the detailed case of the local bazaar of Dhiri in Dehra Dun during the early nineteenth century, Asst Commr Dehra Dun to Government, 10 Dec. 1828, BCJ 17 Mar. 1829, 139/39, IOL.

other itinerant dealers at higher prices. Local markets here performed few stocking or credit functions and acted merely for petty commodity exchange. But a substantial local military detachment could change all this. So large was the demand of the average soldier that a grain market with credit facilities and a rapid circulation of coin became practicable. War itself was not even essential. It was simply that the expenditure of the elites was so much greater than the average that their presence could revolutionise a local economy. Buchanan's figures imply that even in 'pacified' Patna District in 1810, eighty wealthy families of about 100 persons each spent nearly Rs. 900,000 while 30,000 poorer and smaller families of the tract spent only Rs. 600,000 per annum.[59]

Most regional centres developed or enhanced the production of war *matériel*. As late as 1830, all large villages in Awadh produced their own saltpetre and towns manufactured swords and matchlocks.[60] We hear of the fine sword and buckler industries of the Afghan Rohilla towns,[61] the bow and arrow manufactures of Jhansi and the cannon foundries put up by the Marathas around Agra.[62] In Lucknow there is contemporary evidence of the social mobility engendered by the local residence of a large army. Boot-makers,[63] liquor distillers and, above all, prostitutes grew rich on the large military incomes. Many of these groups appear to have been of rural origin. In the city there was a famous group of courtesans known as 'lime-pickers' in deference to their hereditary occupation.[64]

Military expenditure also increased the flow of coin and agricultural credit in small centres. The expansion or creation of mints must have acted as a local economic stimulus. Mughal regional mints such as those at Murshidabad or Lucknow continued production.[65] But many smaller mints appeared in the Jat, Bundela and Rohilla territories in the 1730s and 1740s and in the Sikh lands after the invasion of Ahmed Shah Durrani. Even the Irish adventurer, George Thomas, minted his own

59 F. Buchanan, *An Account of the Districts of Bihar and Patna in 1811–12* (Patna, 1937), II, Table 7.
60 D. Butter, *An Outline of the Topography and Statistics of the Southern Districts of Oudh* (Calcutta, 1839), p. 38.
61 Farrukhabad Magistrate's Report, 1814 , Home Misc. 776, IOL.
62 Thomas Twining, *Travels in India One Hundred Years Ago* (new edn, London, 1893), p. 212.
63 Case of the family of the Nazir of Fatehgarh, Commr Farrukhabad to Govt, 14 Aug. 1830, BCJ, 15 Sept. 1830, 139/62, IOL.
64 Faiz Baksh, *Faizabad*, II, 10.
65 R. Burn,' Mint towns of the Mughal emperors', *JASB*, lxxiii (1904), 84–107; see also, *JASB*, lxvi (1897), 261–84; the following towns appear to have begun production of the Mughal style coinage after 1730: *subah* Awadh, Aonla, Bareilly, Benares, Bharatpur, Farrukhabad, Kalpi, Kunch, Mathura, Moradabad, Najibabad, Panipat and Saharanpur, among others.

coins at his headquarters of 'Georgegunj' in the 1790s.[66] Here the notion of kingship entered directly into the economic process. Royalty required the minting of coins which was an essential part of the ritual of the darbar. New issues were made to celebrate royal births or marriages. But we know from later instances that the presence of a convenient mint greatly improved the supply of credit. Merchants could easily transform plate and mixed rupees into local coin, and this made possible the dispersion of hoards by peasants who wished to build wells or purchase animals.

There is clear evidence of a considerable increase in the number of towns at which minting occurred in the years 1756–1805. The vast majority of these were the headquarters of newly 'independent' regional and local rulers who continued to produce coins in the name of Emperor Shah Alam II. Rohilkhand, Bundelkhand and the Jat territories were notable for clusters of new mint towns of this sort. But there were also a very large number of small states which came into production with coins which were not the Mughal pattern.[67] The Marathas and Sikh chieftains both minted coin which must have affected circulation in Hindustan.

Kingship and consumption

Warfare and defence was more than an activity of the state in India, it was the legitimate pursuit of kings – one justification of the state in both Hindu and Indo-Persian political thought. In the same way, display and sumptuary expenditure was not a frivolous misappropriation of the peasant surplus as it seemed to the puritanical utilitarians of the 1820s and 1830s. Traffic in the material tokens of royal status was the outward mark by which rulers were recognised – the circulating life-blood of the traditional kingdom which nourished the princely, commercial and agrarian economies.[68] But even the words 'luxury trade' and 'sumptuary expenditure' are dangerous and anachronistic. They imply an antithetical 'useful' or 'necessary' trade. In fact, though, it is very difficult to locate many trades outside the locality in pre-colonial India which answer to this description. Even the medium- and long-distance trade in items such as grain and salt was a reflection of taste rather than need. Fine Arrah rice, best wheat or split peas (*channa dal*) for rulers and for feasts made up a high proportion of what was transported between districts in all but scarcity years. Salt is a necessity in the

---

66 Francklin, *George Thomas*, p. 65.
67 E.g., 'statement of each description of currency in circulation in the northern district of Moradabad', 19 Aug. 1832, India Mint Procs, 9 Oct. 1832, NAI.
68 Cf. Dirks, 'Structure and meaning of political relations', *Contributions to Indian Sociology*, new series, xiii (1979), 173–5.

tropics, but the pure salts of the Lahore hills and the Sambher Lake were luxuries, and it was political pressure which forbade the production of ordinary pan salts throughout much of north India. These trades responded to supply and demand; they were thoroughly 'capitalised', yet the incidence and timing of the demand which gave rise to them was determined by aristocratic ranking and political change.

Here cultural history is relevant. The composition of aristocratic demand in India is a largely unexplored field. It represents an important line of connection between the realms of the economic historian and the historian of ideas. In particular it is important to consider the specifics of the origin and direction of royal demand in India. In most societies, kings are great spenders; Lucknow only seems unique if we forget its contemporary, Versailles. Nevertheless patterns of consumption in Indian courts and armies had unique features and varied distinctly according to the type and outlook of the ruling groups. These variations shaped the form of local economies as surely as climate.

It is curious that Indian historians and anthropologists have had so little to say about the social origins of demand when so much has been written about the impact of values on entrepreneurship and other aspects of supply. In part, this reflects a lack of attention in European historiography; in part the assumption that demand and hence the articles of trade are givens. It is Max Weber and not his contemporary Werner Sombart whose views on the impact of values on economic activity has received continuing attention in Indian studies. Yet both sought to explain the origins of 'capitalism' in sociological terms, only Weber's emphasis on entrepreneurs proved more contentious than Sombart's investigation of the origins of demand. Sombart developed a complicated sociological theory of the 'luxury' which according to him made possible the beginnings of capitalist accumulation in Europe.[69] He claims that in the west luxury consumption was a product of 'sensuality' which arose from the secularisation of love at the end of the European Middle Ages and the rising role of women in society. This is not irrelevant to the case of north India. To be sure, expenditure on harems and courtesans was one aspect of luxury in north India reaching its apogee in the seedy magnificence of late Nawabi Lucknow – the 'whore city'. But to understand the volume as much as the quality of luxury consumption in Indian courts, it is necessary to appreciate the importance of ritual display. At heart, the rationale of caste – as opposed to the economic factors which maintained it – was that the order of castes

[69] W. Sombart, *Capitalism and Luxury* (Ann Arbor, 1967); for consumption and culture, see, A. Leix, 'Periods of civilisation and the development of dress in India', *CIBA Review*, xxvi (1940), 1282–92; M. Crawford, *Philosophy in Clothing* (New York, 1940).

represented a 'great machine for sacrifice'. The king's role as chief gift-giver and receiver was a reflection of his ancient status as sacrificer-in-chief and preserver of the order of castes. The complex proliferation of service communities and functionaries required to fulfil the kingly style of life was more than 'conspicuous consumption'; it reflected the conscious ritualisation of everyday life. Even a role such as court jeweller had an added dimension of meaning in the Hindu context. For jewels were elaborate royal and family emblems which had special roles in ritual. In the same way, court dyers were guardians of colour schemes for the saris of royal women, each one of which was appropriate to different castes and festal events. In the widest sense, royal expenditure was an expression of legitimate rule. Kings were expected to spend a certain part of their income, often as high as 30 per cent, on festivals and ritual feasting. Seventy years after his death, the Hindu merchants of Lucknow were still reciting a quatrain in honour of the generosity, indeed kingliness, of Nawab Asaf-ud Daulah.[70] The Company in its time was celebrated only for the construction of jails and courthouses.

The adaptation by Muslim rulers to their Hindu environment partly explains the ritualisation of court life among them. But magnificence also served other functions in late Mughal politics. Succession was often in doubt in the successor states; and indeed, the precise degree of legitimacy and authority held by these new regimes in relation to the imperial family was equally questionable. But there was a vagueness at the heart of the Indo-Muslim conception of sovereignty and the inheritance of power which derived both from the limited role of the Sultan in classical Islam and from the fluidity of inheritance laws. Muslim rulers tended therefore to emerge from a large body of affines and favourites connected with a dead ruler's harem and concubines. The contender for power had to assert himself by piety, by valour and above all, by display and gift-giving. Pomp, ceremony, and armies of supporters (*shaun aur shaukat*) were themselves passports to legitimate power.

Against this background, trade goods in north India had a specific cultural value and use (as well as a more general money value) which was unique to its polity. To understand the composition, geographical distribution and creation of trade, we need to consider social organisation as well as economic laws. For instance, the Kashmir shawl had become a universal symbol of aristocracy in the Indo-Persian world.

---

[70] Abdul Halim Sharar, *Guzishta Lucknow. Mashriqi Tamaddun ka Akhiri Namunah*, tr. E. S. Harcourt and Fakhir Hussain, *The Last Phase of an Oriental Culture* (London, 1969), p. 47; George, Viscount Valentia, *Voyages and Travels to India, Ceylon, the Red Sea, Abyssinia and Egypt* (London, 1809), I, 156.

Muslim emperors had developed special institutions for the reception, grading and storing of shawls[71] which were closely tied into the diplomatic and tribute systems of the Iranian and Indian empires.[72] In the courts of north India, the shawl remained a widely used form of honorific currency. In Lucknow in the 1770s, the great lord Jahandar Shah gave shawls regularly to his servants and supporters, and 'in like measure their honour was increased'.[73] Members of the royal family were to distribute vast numbers of shawls and brocaded work in the course of festivals, marriages and other auspicious events in Benares. Amongst Afghans and other warrior groups, horses and weapons similarly developed a social meaning over and above their utilitarian value in warfare. Swords and daggers were a mark of coming of age for Afghan youths, and this in part explains the astonishing proliferation of metal workers in Rohilkhand and other north-western towns.[74] Fine Arab stallions and elephants also had a symbolic value. When the Nawab of Awadh ravaged Rohilkhand in 1774, he plundered 400 elephants and 3,000 fine horses from Bareilly and Pilibhit alone;[75] these animals played no part in the war. Like other Afghans, the Rohillas' luxuries consisted of 'fine horses, splendid trappings, rich attire and above all many retainers'.[76] The conspicuous consumption of followers also fulfilled a function in absorbing labour and providing employment outside the agrarian economy. This was itself a mark of royalty, as a Lucknow grandee explained:

People of independent means like cock-fighting and matching partridges, larks and amandavas. My fancy is the care of men. The reason of my entertaining persons on recommendations is, I myself like [employing] men, and gain them in every way.[77]

We have suggested that the importance of consumption by the elites was enhanced by the low level of demand from the mass of the

---

[71] Abul Fazl Allami, *Ain-i Akbari*, tr. H. Blochman, I (Calcutta 1873), 91; S. B. Panly, *The Shawl: its Context and Construction* (Yale University Art Gallery, 1975).

[72] About 1800, 'A large proportion of the Cashmere revenue is transmitted to the capital Lahore in shawl goods', W. Hamilton, *The East India Gazetteer containing particular descriptions of the Empires, Principalities, etc., of Hindostan and the Adjacent Countries*, I (London, 1815), 251.

[73] Faiz Baksh, *Faizabad*, II, 66, 71.

[74] Judge Moradabad to Committee at Bareilly, 30 July 1816, BCJ, 25 Oct. 1816, 132/47, IOL.

[75] 'List of plunder taken by Suja-ud Dowlah in the Rohilla country in the campaigns of 1774', 'Rohilla files', box E, Macpherson Papers, Centre of South Asian Studies, Cambridge.

[76] N. Campbell, 'Itinerary from Yezd to Herat and from Herat to Cabul via Candahar' in G. W. Forrest (ed.), *Selections from the Travels and Journals preserved in the Bombay Secretariat* (Bombay, 1906), p. 14.

[77] Faiz Baksh, *Faizabad*, II, 57.

population. This was, in part, a reflection of simple poverty, in part the limitation of needs in a tropical society where elaborate clothing and building was often unnecessary. In part, however, the sharp distinction between ordinary and luxury demand was a consequence of the influence of cultural models on patterns of consumption. The expensive and expansive kingly style of behaviour was only one of several styles. By comparison, priestly, merchant and peasant styles emphasised frugality. Brahmins shunned display because the giving and taking of gifts might involve them in undesirable social relations. Merchant patterns of behaviour stressed the husbanding of resources. They were the 'loins of the state', and domestic onanism was as undesirable as personal. Jain and Vaishnava Agarwal texts and traditions established a pattern which was consciously antithetical to the kingly. 'Luxurious carriage', clothing and housing, or the maintenance of large bodies of servants was frowned upon.[78] Even amongst the great peasant castes – the Jats, Kunbis and Kurmis – a strongly ascetic and parsimonious style was prevalent. Hoarding and the purchase of animals switched effective demand away from artisan wares and personal services.

It is, of course, easy to find innumerable exceptions to these statements. 'Expensive' merchants and regal Brahmins were found in all communities. But this is not the point. Neither the economic nor the social historian of India can take consumption as given. Trade, like artisan production, was also a 'moment in culture'. Even wealthy conquest groups such as the Marathas continued for a considerable time to retain limited and ascetic patterns of consumption which altered the composition of demand in local economies and hence altered patterns of trade. A marvelling Muslim chronicler noted of the houses of the Poona Maratha and Brahmin elite that they 'are as poor as those of mahajans [bankers], having neither gardens nor stables'.[79] A British Resident expanded the observation:

The Moghuls, magnificent and ostentatious, required every article of luxury – towns and cities grew out of this spirit. The Brahmins and Marattas, less refined and more parsimonious are averse from and ignorant of these costly modes of expense. Hence those towns and cities, deprived of their cause of existence are mouldering fast into ruin and the wealthier inhabitants have sunk under or fled from, the rapacity of their new masters.[80]

[78] For the influence of Jain precepts on business and luxury, see Banarsi Das, *Ardha-Kathanak*, ed. and tr. R. C. Sharma, *Indica*, vii (1970), 105–20, and below pp. 380–5.
[79] 'An account of the productions of the Mahratta countries translated from a Persian Manuscript' (it seems to be Mir Ghulam Ali Khan, *Khizana-i Amirah*, c. 1762–3), *Asiatic Annual Register*, v (1803), 34.
[80] C. Malet, Resident Poona to GG, 8 Aug. 1788, *Banaras Affairs*, I (Allahabad, 1959), 143.

Yet amongst all the great military peasant conquerors of the late eighteenth century, the 'spirit of ostentation' ultimately reestablished itself. The occasion for the emergence of new luxury consumption was not necessarily a simple increase in disposable income through plunder or efficient revenue administration. It was not until the 1770s and 1780s that a real consumer class developed amongst the Marathas, and later still amongst the Sikhs. Palace-building and luxury was financed by the dispersal of hoards which had been built up in more parsimonious and insecure days. For consumption was also a product of social change. It signalled the assimilation of newly settled warriors into a kingly style of gift-giving and their acquiescence in the still powerful culture of Mughal court ritual.

Writing in the 1830s, Sleeman perceived striking differences in patterns of consumption and investment within north India. Unlike many later observers, he recognised that Hindu temples and Muslim 'collegiate endowments' might be beneficial to the economy since they were often associated with irrigation tanks and channels of 'public utility' or with groves of trees. The mass of small wells, tanks and temples could have a cumulative effect on agriculture not dissimilar to that produced by south Indian temple complexes. In the central Indian district of Jabbalpur, for instance, he counted private investment in works of 'public and religious utility' at about Rs. 86 lakhs which included 2,288 tanks, 1,560 wells lined with brick, 360 Hindu temples and 22 mosques. The impact on the agriculture and employment of a population which in 1829 amounted to as little as 500,000 must have been considerable; much of this investment was made in the eighteenth century.[81]

However, public and aristocratic expenditure, he thought, was not evenly spread over the countryside. It was associated with the centres of Muslim rule and with Hindu kingdoms which encouraged a settled, Brahminical style of life rather than with aggressive, mobile warrior states. Thus 'there are few temples anywhere to be seen in the territories of these Jat chiefs' and 'the countries under their dominion are less richly ornamented than those of their neighbours'. For as a rule, 'That portion of India where a greater part of the revenue goes to the priesthood, will generally be much more studded with works of ornament and utility than that in which the greater part goes to the soldiery.'[82] Sleeman even saw this distinction within the Maratha territories; the domains of the Maratha chiefs were of much poorer

[81] W. Sleeman, *Rambles and Recollections of an Indian Official* (ed. V. Smith, repr. Karachi, 1973), p. 446 and n. 2.
[82] *Ibid.*, p. 380.

appearance than the lands around Poona where Brahmins had usurped the power of the Marathas, spending on wells, tanks and temples. The point is well taken. Ecological conditions determined the incidence of state and aristocratic investment in public works to a great extent. But the political culture of the successor states varied greatly; and this in itself acted as an independent force.

Armed forces, aristocracies and the merchants they attracted provided indirect sources of credit and employment for the agrarian economies which they dominated. In addition many states directly stimulated agriculture through revenue remissions (*takkavi*) and the low revenue rates allowed on newly opened land.[83] Eighteenth-century regimes were often criticised by the British for extortion. But the other side of the coin was the speedy 'recycling' of resources back into trade and farming. This link between revenue receipts and expenditure on trade and agricultural products also imposed patterns of regional integration on the immediate pre-colonial economy.

The link between trade and revenue

Expenditure on warfare and courtly 'luxuries' was central to the society and politics of the eighteenth-century kingdom. But often only in 'luxury trade' was capital accumulated fast enough or in large enough quantities to support substantial payments of revenue or tribute in money. It is for this reason that so many of the courtly or zamindari financiers began as jewellers or traders in fine cloths. Most of the luxury items which were in demand – especially shawls, horses, elephants, silks or muslins – were not available locally and the long-distance trade which came about as a result could only be supported by complementary flows of revenue or bullion. Thus revenue-payment, elite consumption and trade of this sort came to be intertwined in a manner which had a distinct impact on the agrarian economy.

The extent to which revenue demand 'primes the pump' for trade has long been recognised. Peasant farmers and zamindars needed to sell more of their crops on the market in order to get cash to pay the revenue or rent. But to an equal extent, trade 'primed the pump' for the revenue demand. The flow of coin from one area to another dried up unless trade gave to the periphery the coin with which to pay the centre. The most celebrated trade route in pre-colonial India was the great commerce between the Mughal heartland of Delhi and Agra, and the seaports on the east and west coasts which were tied into international maritime trade. The export of fine grains and muslins from Bengal and of Gujerati

[83] Dilbagh Singh, 'Ijarah System'.

silks and spices to north India gave rise to those great overland caravans upon which early European travellers continually commented.[84] But there was an intimate connection between these flows of commerce and the countervailing flows of bullion to the imperial treasuries at the centre. In effect, Bengal and Gujerat had to sell more of their goods to the centre in order to 'buy back' the bullion which was flowing there as tribute. Otherwise a continual outflow of bullion would soon have made it impossible for the outlying provinces to pay the revenue at all.

Now this system of interchange might break down on two counts. First the Bengalis or Gujeratis could stop paying revenue to the centre, in which case the centre would not have resources with which to buy goods from the periphery. Secondly, the people at the centre could become unable to buy goods from the periphery. If this occurred, then the Bengalis or Gujeratis would have to stop paying revenue unless a massive alternative source of bullion could be found, which was out of the question.

Both of these situations came about after the decline of Delhi and they were mutually reinforcing. The rise of the Marathas and Jats in the 1730s and 1740s had cut off revenue and rents coming into Delhi from Malwa and what is now the Hariana area, and this forced the Mughal elites of the heartland to curtail some of their expenditure on the products of the periphery. But since the demand from the Mughal court itself accounted for a very large part of Bengal's trade with north India in fine cloth and fine rice, the decline of this market set off a chain reaction of trading crises which affected not only the Delhi area itself but the whole downriver trading system. Charles Hamilton analysed the decline in the 1780s. Before 1740, he said, the Bengal tribute had been remitted to Delhi through bankers' bills taken out on Delhi, Agra or Lahore by the Bengal merchants,

for the payment of which sufficient funds were there supplied in the sale and consumption of the rich manufactures of Bengal; in fact, if it had not been so, no tribute could ever have been remitted; and when the depredations of Nadir Shah and a variety of other circumstances, contributed by impoverishing the court, to stop the vent there for these commodities in this quarter, the stoppage of the tribute was a necessary and inevitable consequence, *independent of any actual defection on the part of the Nabobs of Bengal*; as it was utterly impossible that the same or indeed any considerable sum could ever be continued to be transferred in cash, from a country of which gold and silver forms no part of the natural products.[my italics][85]

[84] H. K. Naqvi, *Urban Centres and Industries in Upper India 1556–1803* (London, 1968), pp. 37–64.

[85] C. Hamilton, *An Historical Relation of the Origin, Progress and Final Dissolution of the Government of the Rohilla Afghans in the Northern Provinces of Hindustan* (London, 1787), p. 169.

The local decline of the Mughal aristocracy of north India potentially affected, therefore, the economies of all the major towns, bulking and financial centres which lay on the arterial route between Lahore and Murshidabad. As we shall see, some of these centres were revitalised by new, cross-country trades, but at the very least the breakdown of the tie between revenue and trade disrupted flows of bullion and produce worth Rs. 100 lakhs a year. This was massively greater than the initial shortfall which resulted from the depredations of Marathas, Jats or Sikhs, and since the effects were felt immediately on the money supply, it was of much greater significance than the Persian or Afghan looting of the Delhi treasury.

The breakdown of administrative and political relations between the Mughal centre and their viceroys in Bengal combined with these economic consequences to have a dramatic effect on the arterial route. There appears to have been a large decline in traffic down the rivers Ganges and Jamna. In Akbar's time, the number of boatmen plying the mid and lower Ganges appears to have been substantially more than 300,000, but by the 1780s the estimate was a mere 30,000 despite the growth of European trade and the Maratha trade through Mirzapur in the meantime.[86] Between Allahabad and Lahore, the decline on the Grand Trunk Road and the rivers appears to have been greater. Mercantile interest in trade in this direction was so much reduced that the Jamna was allowed to silt up downriver from Agra at some time between 1770 and 1800, and the substantial transit town of Kora-Jehanabad virtually disappeared from the map during the same period. Once again, this decline of large and small towns had subtle rural consequences. Always a relatively unstable zone for climatic and geological reasons, the middle Doab above Allahabad was deprived of much of the investment which had previously been made by the Mughal small town gentry and the merchants who had serviced the through route. Maps and reports of the 1770s report everywhere the collapse of irrigation channels, tanks and wells coupled with the disappearance of cash-crop production. Deprived of toll and bazaar duties, local elites who had earlier been held in check by Mughal judicial officers quartered on the small towns turned instead to brigandage on the roads and plunder which further damaged the ailing trade routes.

Some of the indirect effects of the drying-up of revenue and trade flows between Delhi and the major provincial centres were even more fundamental and difficult to assess. Observers in the Delhi region and Punjab, and even in Benares, after 1770 reported a great 'want of specie' or money famine. Scattered evidence from the Punjab suggests that

86 Tennant, *Recreations*, I, 51.

quite a thriving agricultural economy continued to exist regardless of the shortage of coin. Barter and cowrie shells replaced it for ordinary transactions among the peasantry. Yet it is evident that where money was virtually the only general medium of circulation, the effects on longer-distance trade must have been considerable. This seems consonant with some pieces of evidence from the region towards the end of the century. Here we find prices considerably higher than they were in Bengal. Moreover, travellers like Abdul Kader (1797) report a paradoxical situation where a thriving peasant economy dominated by local Sikh chieftains subsisted alongside towns and trade routes which were in full decline.[87]

What was true of the most celebrated trade routes of Mughal India was also true of a large part of interdistrict trade and the small towns and traders who subsisted on it. Let us take the case of the outlying district of Gorakhpur which paid its revenue at points in the century either to the Nawab of Awadh at Lucknow or to the Maharaja of Benares. Here again trade supported revenue-payments and revenue supported trade.

Azeemghur and Mahole are principally supplied with specie from Benares as the agents of the bankers of that province discharge a great part of the revenue of the principal Malguzars [revenue-engagers], and those agents also purchase sugar, the produce of which is considerable in those districts, and likewise piece goods, etc.[88]

Other traders gained much of their livelihood by importing small quantities of bullion into the outlying districts. They could get a good rate of exchange with local rupees because there were periodic famines of the coins in which the revenue had to be paid. It is of course true that a 'natural economy' of pure exchange without the intervention of the revenue element existed where rare products of different areas were exchanged. Punjabi rock salt, Gwalior iron or the hill products of the *tarai* would have been in demand regardless of the operations of revenue demand. Yet these systems were closely intertwined. If not exactly a house of cards, Indian polities and trading systems were delicately arranged sets of dominoes. Each unit was virtually indestructible, but once the line was jolted, political and trading crises followed each other in rapid succession.

Yet the close relationship between trade and the power – even the morale – of the ruling group, had another side also. The logic of the tie between revenue and trade was quickly reaffirmed. If a revenue-bearing

[87] Abul Kader Khan, 'Route between Delhi and Cabul', 1797, *AAR*, viii (1806), 46–57.
[88] Collr Gorakhpur to H. Wellesley, 9 May 1802, Gorakhpur Revenue 3, UPR, published G. N. Saletore (ed.), *Selections from English Records. Henry Wellesley's Correspondence (1801–1803)* (Allahabad, 1955), p. 22.

area passed from the suzerainty of Delhi to that of the Nawabs of Farrukhabad or the Rohillas, then a complementary flow of goods must soon arise. The case of Rohilkhand illustrates this well. During the high Mughal period, this rich area north-east of the capital had been able to 'buy back' its coin from the capital by means of a regular trade in valuable cash crops such as tobacco and sugar. During the rise of the Rohillas, the trade to the south diminished, partly no doubt, because the Rohillas ceased revenue payment to Delhi. Instead Bareilly and the other Rohilla towns exchanged revenue for local agricultural goods during a period of great prosperity and local urban growth. When after 1774, the Nawab of Awadh held the country, a reduced revenue was sent to Lucknow. It was partly balanced by the payments made to Rohilla captains in the Nawab's service, but in order to balance the outflow of treasure, Rohilkhand sent sugar, indigo and shawls from further west to Lucknow, so that the axis of the region's trade shifted once again.

It was not only the Indian states, but the British themselves who engineered these rapid realignments of trade and revenue in the second half of the century. After 1764 the Awadh tribute to the British of more than Rs. 70 lakhs per year had to be covered by reciprocal trade and services. In the first place, British expenditure on their own contingents, and Awadh sepoys in British service tended to redistribute coin back to Awadh residents again. Secondly, much of the tribute money was in effect ploughed back into Awadh in the form of advances made to the Company's weavers working in Awadh at Tanda and Aliabad.[89] But it was not long before relative price differentials had stimulated demand for Awadh goods in Calcutta.[90] This took the form of an expansion of private trade in cloth, saltpetre and shawls and the shortfall was made up by regular shipments by Benares bankers of gold, silver and copper to the Lucknow mints. Again a whole range of small peasant marts sprang into action as they took on the role of bulking points on the rising route. In a sense, then, the commerce, urban development and specialist agricultural production which had once existed along the route between Delhi and Mughal Bengal was replicated along the link between Lucknow and Calcutta via Benares and Patna.

These three links in the political economy – agrarian patronage, elite consumption and the nexus between revenue and trade – created a flexible and adaptable set of relationships which were capable of sharp geographical realignment. Many of the apparent testimonies of decline

89 Barlow's Report on Awadh Trade.
90 Twining, *Travels*, p. 212; Forster, *Journey*, I, 99 and note.

and anarchy after 1740 reflected nothing more than the jerking of these relationships into new productive patterns. But it would be wrong to discard a picture of men locked into a cycle of political and economic degeneration and replace it with one of easy and painless adaptation, a sort of social kaleidoscope which could be shaken with little effect. For not only were north Indians of the eighteenth century afflicted by warfare, but their responses to it were conditioned in part by the potential of the agricultural regions where they lived.

Society and war

In the following chapters we shall be concerned with the consequences for agrarian and urban society of warfare and rapid political change. But it is as well to begin by establishing some basic distinctions between the different types of armed conflict which have seemed to add up to such a dismal picture of the century.

First and most spectacular were the great external invaders of Mughal India: Nadir Shah of Persia (1739), Ahmed Shah Durrani from Afghanistan (1758–62), and his less celebrated successor Zeman Shah (1797–9). The incursions of all these rulers brought about immediate financial panic and agrarian disruption. In 1739, the credit networks of the great pan-Indian bankers, the Jagat Seths, rolled back as the Shah advanced.[91] In 1759 the news of Ahmed Shah's invasion pushed up the rate of bullock hire between Benares and Patna by 500 per cent, and in 1761 'the zamindars raised their heads in revolt and blocked all the roads'[92] as soon as the Afghans renewed their challenge to Mughal rule. These shocks severely damaged the morale of the ruling group, but it should not be assumed that the economic effects of invasion were of themselves profound or long-lasting. The Jagat Seths had a correspondent in Agra again within a short time of the Durrani invasion. Another great pan-Indian commercial house, Arjunji Nathji Tiwari of Surat which had been serving the cross-country route since the 1720s emerged unscathed from the mid-century political crises. Its agents were once again moving lakhs of rupees from Bengal overland to Surat and Bombay before the mid-1770s, though they had prudently avoided the Seths' close connection with the imperial house and Delhi.[93]

[91] A. Das Gupta, 'Trade and politics in eighteenth century India', in D. Richards (ed.), *Islam and the Trade of Asia* (Philadelphia, 1970), p. 184.
[92] Sheikh Murtaza Hussain, *c.* 1783–5, tr. W. Irvine, 'Ahmad Shah Abdali and Imad-ul-Mulk', *Indian Antiquary*, xxvi (1907), p. 13.
[93] Deposition of Aret Ram Tiwari, 10 Jan. 1788, PR; Arjunji Nathji to GG, 7 Sept. 1788, *Calendar of Persian Correspondence* (Delhi, 1924 to date), v, 1079; Das Gupta, 'Trade and politics', in Richards, *Islam*, p. 184; M. J. Mehta, 'Indian bankers in the late 18th and early 19th centuries. A case study of Travadi Shrikrishna Arjunji Nathji, unpubl. paper, IHC, 1979.

All these invaders came to India to enhance their military prestige and for bullion which they secured in vast quantities. Thus Ahmed Shah Durrani appears to have taken from India nearly 40 crores[94] of rupees in the course of his three invasions. But the effects of this should not be exaggerated. Basically, all that the Persians or Afghans were doing was to move large stores of immobilised specie from treasure hoards in India to treasure hoards in their own countries. Since they did not establish a local presence, they were not in a position to exercise any more permanent lien on resources in the Indian economy. Because much of the treasure abstracted was not in circulation, and the trade between north India and Afghanistan and Iran was limited, there was unlikely to be any longer-term effect on prices or commerce. At best, we might imagine that the nobles of Delhi and Agra withheld some of their consumption and expenditure on construction in order to rebuild their treasure stores, and that this acted as a sharp local deflation. In fact, the capacity of the invaders to defeat the Indian armies was no indication of their economic strength in regard to the local population. North Indian mercenaries, camp-followers and travelling grain merchants took a prominent part in the campaign with the result that much of the plundered booty must have been redistributed to other parts of the countryside. Indeed, as a Muslim observer wrote, 'except gold and silver nothing was carried away'.[95] This meant again that other goods including stores of value, such as grain, animals, jewellery and cloths were destined to fall back into the hands of the Indian population. In the 1761 campaign, Rohilla mercenaries fighting with the Afghans each procured thirty to forty buffaloes:

The plundered goods, such as jewels and clothes, they loaded upon these buffaloes and established a market of their own within the camp, where they sold all these things at low prices. Cloth goods worth ten Rupees they sold for one Rupee and those worth one Rupee for eighty *tankah*.[96]

Even the physical destruction of the population can be exaggerated. However horrific the details of the slaughter perpetrated by Nadir or the Durranis, it was local and specific. It was a minor bloodletting compared, for instance, with the Mongol invasions of thirteenth-century Iran. Not more than 50,000 people appear to have died in the most celebrated holocausts, Nadir's massacre at Delhi[97] and Ahmed Shah's extermination of the Brahmins and ascetics of Muttra, though the plagues afterwards were greater killers. These were calculated acts of political and religious terror conceived against the background of

94 J. N. Sarkar, *The Fall of the Mughal Empire* (Calcutta, 1950), II, 280–90.
95 Murtaza Hussain, tr. Irvine, *IA*, xxvi (1907), 60.   96 *Ibid.*
97 W. Irvine, *The Later Moghuls*, ed. J. Sarkar (Calcutta, 1922), II, 375ff.

local hatred. In Muttra, the Muslim soldiers had the patience to insert the tails of dead cattle into the mouths of the slain Hindu holy men. Cities recovered quickly from this sort of sharp and temporary destruction. In Muttra in 1761, 'Everywhere in lane and bazaar lay the headless trunks of the slain and the whole city was burning.'[98] Yet within twenty-five years it was said to be 'remarkably well-built and flourishing'.[99] Only where persistent local economic decline and political flux existed were acts of military violence likely to destroy urban or rural societies. True, the histories of merchant families record their flight at the time of the 'Nadirshahi' or 'during the disturbances of the Durrani', but large-scale migration only took place where local economies had become unviable for other reasons.

The second main source of armed conflict in post-Mughal north India was connected with the emergence of new powers which were trying to establish for themselves a place in the weakening Mughal state system. This type of 'state-building' went through similar phases whether in the case of the great regional movements of Jats, Sikhs or Marathas or that of the rise of some petty local adventurer to power in Malwa or the northern hills. In either case the aspirant needed recognition from the Mughal ruler and also the compliance of trader–bankers who would advance money for the tribute or land-revenue. But the establishment of a dominance over the key people in a locality took time and had a more powerful effect on local economy and society than the more spectacular interventions of foreign invaders. Returning year by year to exact tribute, nazrana or chauth, Jats, Marathas, Sikhs and others could exercise a permanent lien on the movement of money and goods in the economy. Writing from Delhi to Bilgram in 1776, Major Polier made this very distinction.[100] Nadir Shah, he said, had been significant more because he exposed the weakness of central authority than because of the economic consequences of his raid. However, it was the 'incessant demands' of the Rohilla mercenaries for bullion, animals and wood, not the 'rapid attacks' of the Persians, which most damaged city and region. Regular forced loans and exactions acted as a kind of taxation on the local economy, discouraging consumption and investment and depressing the income of artisans and service people. In time, an actual disinvestment occurred: the greater wealth and security of the territories ruled by the insurgents encouraged capital and skills to migrate there.

Endemic local warfare of this sort and the collapse of local aristocracies had effects which were inimical to agricultural production.

---

[98] Murtaza Hussain, IA, xxvi (1907), 62.　　[99] Twining, Travels, p. 212.
[100] Extracts from letters of Maj. Polier at Delhi to Col. Ironside at Bilgram, 22 May 1776, AAR, I (1979), 34–55.

The village unit and the family farm might survive, but its relationship to the outside world might be dramatically altered. Peasant farmers living on effective lines of communication near major centres grew high quality crops for a number of reasons. But the acquisition of cash in order to pay a cash revenue was a major incentive. The slow impoverishment of urban and small town elites not only deprived such producers of agricultural investment and a market, but also freed them from the pressure of land-revenue. The revenue demands of incoming Jats or Marathas did not necessarily maintain the pressure. In the early days, the insurgents only collected a small part of the Mughal revenue and their levies often took the form of seizures of grain and animals.

In time, however, warfare and political disturbance did have a direct effect on agricultural production in afflicted areas. Cultivation was driven back from the roads by the passage of marauding armies who sometimes deliberately destroyed walls and irrigation tanks. A route report of about 1769 remarks, 'when you move away from the roads, the countryside gives a remarkable impression of plenty and cultivation',[101] but this must have created further transport difficulties and curtailed the fragile market economy. More important, warfare withdrew both men and animals from agriculture. Recruitment into armies, the consolidation of population around defensive centres in the west of the region,[102] and the general migration of cultivators to places of local security contributed to a patchy and local decline in the cultivated area. Draught animals determined the extent of cultivation even more than human labour, and there is scattered evidence of a great dearth of animal power in north central India. The extent of the problem is difficult to assess. But in 1807 the colonial authorities in Saharanpur District, long a centre of armed conflict, connected the paucity of cultivation in this once rich tract with the long history of animal shortage. Every year 10,000–15,000 bullocks had been hired to armies by merchants who found that they could make 25 per cent more profit this way than they could make in ordinary agricultural production.[103] These local scarcities must have been enhanced by the annual abstraction of large numbers of animals by Sikh, Maratha and Pindari bands. Not only did bullocks and horses fetch high prices in Deccan and Punjab markets where the invaders took them, but the decline of the money economy in some of the ravaged areas meant that levies of animals were the most practicable way in which warbands could 'tax' the conquered population.

101 Ensign Davy, 'Observations on the Delhi road from Corah Jehanabad to Atawah' (*c.* 1769), Orme 6, IOL.
102 W. Crooke, *The North-Western Provinces of India* (London, 1897) p. 40.
103 Collr Saharanpur to Bd, 3 Oct. 1807, CPR, 22 Dec. 1807, 91/18, IOL.

As in the Wars of the Roses, or the Thirty Years' War, the incidence of armed conflict in eighteenth-century India was much more limited than might appear. It seems peculiar that the periodic incursions of relatively small armies could in themselves cause the widespread devastation that many contemporary sources chronicle in what was a tough and adaptable rural economy. Yet locally endemic warfare could lead to the draining away of key resources for agricultural production. We glimpse almost the exact opposite of Ester Boserup's conditions of agricultural intensification.[104] Falling population, and animal power limited the need for double cropping. The low price of food grains and decline of transport encouraged a shift back to extensive cultivation methods and pastoralism. The practice of leaving land uncultivated in very long 'leas' which was roundly condemned by the censorious Revd Tennant, seems a perfectly rational response to conditions of this sort.[105] But a political element must be added to Ester Boserup's model-in-reverse. The political decline of consuming aristocracies not only denied peasant farmers a market for produce but often removed from them the need to pay revenue in cash at all.

Nevertheless, these were two-sided crises. Many of the unfavourable circumstances to which we have referred logically require at least a more or less equivalent intensification in some other sector of the economy or geographical area. Marathas, Jats or Rohilla mercenaries fighting with the Durranis were raiding in order to build up the stocks of bullion or animals in their own territories. Merchants who hired out bullocks for armies and farmers who moved their resources into pastoralism were evidently continuing to accumulate capital which might be used for trade or agricultural investment elsewhere. Migrating populations helped to open up old fallows or virgin land and establish artisan industries in other parts of the country. If the level of hoards increased to act as a depressant on the local economies of some regions, the pressure of elites for revenue and conspicuous expenditure by soldiers and courtiers broke down hoards elsewhere.

This chapter has set out some of the links between state and society which made the commercial economy and large areas of its agricultural production particularly responsive to political change. The merchants and farmers who responded to these pressures invested their capital and labour in areas where they could secure protection and avoid risks, rather than where the returns were highest. Yet some tracts of the great plains were naturally more favoured than others, and it was here that

104 Ester Boserup, *The Conditions of Agricultural Growth* (Chicago, 1965).
105 Tennant, *Recreations*, II, 16.

stable polities had the greatest chance to develop. The concentration of men, capital and political skills in these core areas will form the theme of the next chapter. Here the relationship between commerce and political power took on new characteristics, giving rise to expansive forces which had begun to recolonise the declining areas even before the onset of British rule.

2

Agriculture, ecology and politics

In one of the most famous passages of Indian historical writing, Sir Charles Metcalfe described village communities as 'little republics' unaltered by the clash and fall of dynasties above them: 'Hindoo, Patan, Moghul Mahratta, Sik, English, all are masters in turn; but the village communities remain the same'.[1] Metcalfe's description may hold for the tracts north-west of Delhi, or for some of the tightly knit clan areas of eastern Awadh, but there were large parts of the plains of north India where it does not apply, or must be severely qualified. Here, in the environs of cities and small towns, or in newly settled areas, the political world directly impinged on the peasant family farm and the conduct of agriculture. The link between land-revenue and trade; the direct dependence of labourers and cultivators on aristocrats and merchants for credit or protection; the importance of aristocratic consumption for employment and production in the countryside – all these welded state to agrarian society. When the state moved the base of its operations, or was captured by warriors from outside, productive forces of labour and capital could also be jerked into new geographical alignments. So the agricultural and commercial decline of one area was often matched by the expansion of cultivation and trade in another.

In this chapter we go on to define more exactly these areas of growth and decline by reference not only to political circumstances but also to ecology and climate. Some naturally well-endowed territories were able to come through the worst political troubles in a state of high cultivation and relative prosperity. But in other cases, the strength of the ruling groups or the expertise of the local cultivators appears to have been more significant. Some tracts were perhaps so good or so bad that human endeavour or conflict could do little to alter their performance within the existing limits of technology. But much of the country lay in a precarious balance between volatile climate and sparse human inputs. This could be upset by a combination of political flux and short-term changes in patterns of rainfall. It is important to avoid both ecological and political determinism. The strength of states and aristocracies was not simply a function of the agricultural stability of their domains. But

[1] Kessinger, *Vilayatpur*, pp. 24–34.

equally the formation of states has often been treated as if the agricultural product on which they subsisted was a constant. In fact, rulers were as pathetically dependent on the pattern of rainfall as the poorest cultivator. And peasants and merchants were not mere pawns on the political chess-board. They responded also to deeper changes in the volume and distribution of agricultural resources.

A more precise map of areas of stability or agricultural decline proves useful in a number of ways. First, it provides a key to the politics of the successor states of the Mughal empire. The stronger of these were often based upon (or tried to seize) areas of stable or expanding agriculture. In turn, the insatiable drive of their rulers and aristocrats for cash revenue pushed forward the frontiers of the commercial economy there. But the trade routes, towns and commercial facilities which grew up to serve and integrate these islands of agricultural stability also provided the network along which the East India Company was to move its own resources and ultimately create again a wider revenue and commercial system. Finally, the ghost of these conditions was to haunt the mercantile and agrarian world of Hindustan into the nineteenth century. For instance, the unstable, less-populous lands of the west had much more room for agricultural expansion. They were also provided with a whole range of petty market centres which grew out of older fortress towns. In the east, on the other hand, relative agrarian and political stability had allowed larger populations and more complex states to survive. Population had less room for expansion before it encountered the ceiling of falling per capita productivity;[2] commerce was limited by its constriction within the institutions of the small Rajput and Bhumihar states.

Sources and their limitations

Map 3 is an attempt to chart regional agricultural performance between 1780 and 1800. It is put together from a number of different types of evidence, none of which is very specific in itself. Areas of 'stability' or 'growth' are those described as 'double-cropped', or 'highly productive' by the first British administrators and for which there is also earlier evidence of productivity from eighteenth-century travellers, revenue figures, or the route maps compiled by European and Indian servants of the Company. Areas marked in 'decline' are those where evidence of declining revenue yields is supported by the statements of official sources and travellers that a once rich agriculture was now desolated. Tracts unmarked represent poor but stable areas and also those about which no comment is recorded. At first glance, it is clear that both

[2] Cf. Stokes, *Peasant and Raj*, pp. 228–42.

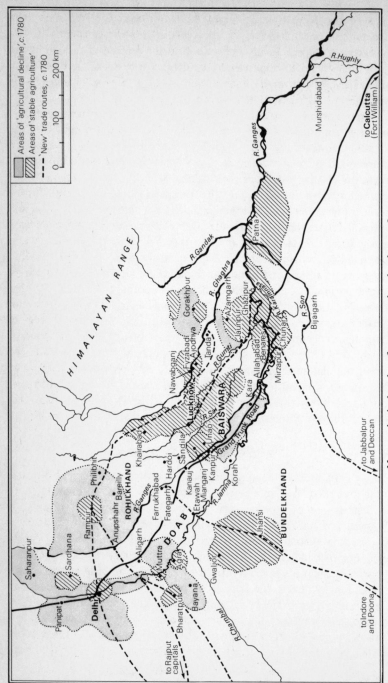

Map 3   Agricultural performance and trade, about 1785

Areas of 'agricultural decline' c.1780
Areas of 'stable agriculture'
New trade routes, c.1780

0   100   200 km

HIMALAYAN RANGE

Saharanpur
Panipat
Sardhana
Rampur
Philibhit
Anupshahr
Bareilly
ROHILKHAND
Aligarh
Delhi
Farrukhabad
Fategarh
Muttra
Agra
Bayana
Bharatpur
Gwalior
Jhansi
BUNDELKHAND
R. Chambal
R. Jamna
Korah
Kanpur
Etawah
Mianganj
Kanauj
Hardoi
DOAB
Sandila
Khairabad
Nawabganj
R. Ganges
LUCKNOW
BAISWARA
R. Sai
R. Gumti
Grand Trunk Road
Kara
Allahabad
Benares
Mirzapur
Chunar
R. Son
Bijaigarh
Ghazipur
Jaunpur
Azamgarh
Tanda
Faizabad
Ajodhya
Gorakhpur
R. Ghaghra
R. Gandak
R. Ganges
Buxar
Patna
R. Hughly
Murshidabad
to Calcutta
(Fort William)

to Rajput capitals
to Indore and Poona
to Jabbalpur and Deccan

'growth' and 'decline' are quite local phenomena and that they are often contiguous, if not balanced. A ring of outer agricultural tracts around Delhi and Agra accounts for much of the decline, and this itself is an indication of the importance of political change in the agrarian balance. Let us first consider the sources and then go on to account for the agricultural performance of specific areas.

The figures for revenue collection or assessment might be expected to give some general indication of the fate of agricultural production in the medium or long term. But comparisons between pre-1720, late eighteenth-century and early nineteenth-century figures are hazardous.[3] First, of course, differences might reflect an actual increase in agricultural production as a result of the expansion of the spring or *rabi* crop which generally required artificial irrigation; or conversely, a fall in revenue figures might represent the decline of an area through depopulation or starvation of capital. But more often than not, substantial variations represented technical changes. Sources are often vague as to whether figures represented actual or potential collections by the state, or the sums for which they were leased to revenue farmers. Similarly, the boundaries of revenue units were changed over the decades. Finally, a collapse of the revenue yield of a territory might represent a political change. For instance, a powerful local elite might have intercepted and appropriated a flow of revenue which previously went to regional or central government, and there is no reason to assume that local agriculture or trade was much affected.

The revenue figures, then, can only be used as an indication of social change if they are backed up with some contemporary evidence. Maratha and Mughal figures collected by British officials for the territories 'west of the Jumna' show this well. If we take the Rewari subdivision of the Jat state of Bharatpur, for instance, we find that the notional revenue recorded in the *Ain-i-Akbari* and Aurangzeb's manuals of the 1690s was actually used as the basis of a revenue farm of Rs. 3 lakhs in 1781, which indicates that it must have been at least as productive at this time. But in 1803, it was said to be only 'capable' of producing Rs. 140,000 because Maratha 'depredations' had driven much of the population off to Delhi.[4] It might be added that the area suffered very badly from the famines of 1784 and 1793. Conversely, the large rise in the revenue of Muttra subdivision from Rs. 28,895 in the

---

[3] Revenue Statements on Cession, Home Misc. 583, IOL; C.T. Metcalfe, 'Memorandum of Hindostan west of the Jumna, 1804', *Parliamentary Papers, 1806*, xvi, 497–500; cf. extracts from *Chahar-Gulshan*, tr. J. Sarkar, *India of Aurangzib (Topography, Statistics and Records)* (Calcutta, 1901).

[4] 'Account of the Revenues of the Countries now forming the British Territories West of the Jumna taken from different Authorities', *PP*, 1806, xvi.

Ain to Rs. 63,070 under the government of Najaf Khan in the 1770s represents both technical and economic change. Boundaries had been changed substantially in the two centuries which separated these figures. At the same time, the protection and investment offered by Najaf Khan's military commanders in the 1760s and 1770s appears to have maintained the agricultural advances in the jungle tracts which surrounded this prestigious Hindu centre.[5]

If the revenue figures are hazardous, the evidence provided by contemporary Indian and European writers must be treated with equal circumspection. The Muslim poets of Delhi and Agra wove a literary motif out of decline and rarely noted the bustling bazaars behind the decaying palaces. But even here there are significant differences of emphasis. The *Seir* depicts 'sinking of rents and decrease of husbandry'.[6] But the Delhi poet Sauda noted that the 'great lords' were not now receiving rent even from those lands near the capital which were 'producing two good harvests a year'[7] – an indication that he was aware of the prosperity being enjoyed by Jat and Rohilla 'upstarts' and other 'wicked men'.

The diaries and memoirs of European travellers in upper India are an invaluable source, but they are also partial. Many wrote with the conscious or unconscious intention of disparaging Indian regimes to the advantage of the Company. Others, notably Colebrooke and Tennant, entered into a denunciation of Indian 'domestic and rural economy' which assimilated to the picture of political decline attacks on techniques such as shallow ploughing,[8] long-fallow and the upkeep of large numbers of poorly nourished cattle.[9] Many of these practices seem quite rational in the context of contemporary conditions and more recent agronomic ideas. Again, it is worth noting that many of the most widely used travellers' journeys were made during, or in the direct aftermath of, the terrible famines of 1781–4 and 1802–4 when the countryside was in a particularly bad condition.

A final and most useful type of source are the various civil and military route maps prepared by servants of the Company,[10] which can

[5] Muttra was in 'flourishing condition' in the 1770s owing to the residence there of 'principal Moghuls in Nuzeeph Khan's service', MSS 'The Province of Agra', *c.* 1780, A. Dalrymple, *Oriental Repertory* (London, 1808), I, 314.

[6] *Seir*, II, 552.   [7] Sauda, *Kulliyat*, cited in Russell and Islam, *Three Mughal Poets*, p. 65.

[8] Tennant, *Recreations*, II, 12; Crooke, *North-Western Provinces*, p. 333.

[9] Tennant, *Recreations*, II, 11–12, 16.

[10] Collected notably in Orme 334 and xvi, IOL; cf. E. A. Molony, 'Rainfall, irrigation and the subsoil water resources of the Gangetic Plain in the United Provinces', *Agricultural Journal of India*, xii (1917), 84–9; W. H. Moreland, *The Agriculture of the United Provinces* (Allahabad, 1910); NWP Revenue and Agriculture Procs., 12 Dec. 1868, 438/58, IOL.

be used in conjunction with later revenue surveys. Such accounts only record 'cultivation' in the broadest sense, and that near the roads. But they do provide some good evidence on the location of wells, irrigation tanks and groves of trees which represent the attempts of governors and gentry to stabilise conditions along their roads and near their settlements. One point that arises from comparing the route maps with later geographical surveys is that the large areas of desolation mentioned by travellers often coincide with waterlogged soil, plains of salt-efflorescence (*usar*), tracts with poor subsoil and places where the water table is far below the surface. This may seem obvious, but it was not so for contemporaries, and it is often their account of the primacy of political impediments to cultivation which has prevailed. Forster, Tennant and later travellers, for instance, all made a point of claiming that the moment one left the rich Benares territories which were protected by the Company and passed into Nawabi Awadh, cultivation declined disastrously because of the 'rapacity of the amils'.[11] This is an important crux in the creation of the Black Legend of the eighteenth century. It was repeated by other observers and put alongside Sleeman's picture of the Province at a much later stage of its development by the editors of the *Oudh Gazetteer* in 1877. But the area west of Gopiganj was naturally poor and remained so into the next century. It was covered with broad plains of saline *usar* which were transformed into infertile ravines nearer the river. A mere thirty miles on Forster came to Allahabad, which was also under the control of the Nawab's *amils* and he found this 'flourishing . . . and in a much better state than I had been led to believe.'[12]

Another example will serve to strengthen the point. The decline of Agra and the lands around it are mentioned in many accounts. The travellers depict desolate scrub and the attacks of robber bands. A British route map of 1801 describes the relative wealth of the Gangetic lands of the Nawab of Farrukhabad (under British protection, of course) and notes the desolation as the road leaves his territory on the way to Agra.[13] What is not mentioned is that here the water table plunges far below the surface of the land, making artificial irrigation virtually impossible because of its high cost. Much of the northern part of the subdivision of Firozabad continued in poor cultivation in the next century also. But the land to the south of the city of Agra which few travellers visited was apparently in high cultivation in the 1790s and

---

[11] Tennant, *Recreations*, II, 175, cf. Revenue Survey Maps 1831–6, Map Room, IOL; *DG Allahabad, DG Mirzapur, DG Benares;* Route from Benares to Jhusi, *c.* 1770, Orme 334 (7), IOL.

[12] Forster, *Journey*, I, 78.

[13] 'Route of Col. Collins Embassy to Scindia', Dec. 1801, *AAR*, v (1803), 100–2.

benefited from the continuing pull of the urban market and from its credit facilities. The travellers of the 1780s and 1790s saw desolation; the officials of 1810 saw a 'rich, commercial and prosperous city', set in a region which was fully cropped.[14] But it is unlikely that the agricultural transformation was so dramatic.

Areas of 'natural' and 'artificial' surplus

What makes the case of Agra so instructive is that tracts which were naturally 'desolate' were quite closely associated with tracts which had gone out of cultivation through the decline of markets or lack of credit (Bayana or south Firozabad). But just as there were areas which remained unsuitable for cultivation in the absence of population pressure and advanced agricultural technology, so there were areas which remained in high cultivation throughout the century. These 'surplus areas' were key points in the political economy. They tended to receive population, skills and capital from less stable areas, and control of them was a prime objective for aspiring magnates and warbands. In a sense, of course, there were no 'natural' surplus areas; strong rulers and determined cultivators could make even the most unhospitable tracts relatively populous and successful. But certain combinations of natural conditions made the maintenance of complex agriculture easier when investment was scarce and technology limited.

What was needed was a combination of easily tilled soil with good natural drainage and irrigation.[15] Extremely stiff soils, however rich, were an impediment to Indian cultivators because their light ploughs and hoes could not break them up. Where lands like this came under cultivation, the replacement cost of tools was so great that much less capital was available for investment elsewhere – in irrigation or clearing, for instance. Stiff or stony soil also made the construction of *kaccha* or temporary wells very difficult. On the other hand, very light soils grew a smaller range of crops and were quite unstable. The only feasible form of irrigation in areas of light soil was from stone (*pakka*) wells, but a stone well cost about Rs. 100 which was more than five times the supposed annual expenditure of the family of a middling cultivator.[16] This was obviously out of the question for most peasant families and represented a considerable outlay even for a moneylender or landlord. The optimum soil type was therefore a rich, moderately heavy loam, which would retain some moisture and yet could be tilled.

Natural irrigation was the second condition affecting the distribution

[14] Note by Magistrate Agra, 3 July 1819, Agra Customs 5, UPR.
[15] *Oudh Gazetteer*, III, 173.   [16] Tennant, *Recreations*, II, 345–8.

of surplus areas. If the level for ground-water was too near the surface – under fifteen feet or so – there was a danger that the ground would remain waterlogged for large periods of the year and would turn into boggy or unproductive *usar* tracts. For this reason much of the fertile land close to the rivers and streams of Awadh remained uncultivated. On the other hand, if the water level was too low – say, forty feet or more – the cost of well irrigation would be prohibitive. In these conditions, very few soils could be expected to bear a spring or *rabi* crop. Yet the spring crop was a key condition for the emergence of a strong landed aristocracy, for it was out of the proceeds of this harvest that the peasant generally paid rent or revenue.

The ideal combination of moderately light and fertile soil with a high but not too high water table was rarely met with in the north Indian plains. The river system of the region ensured that thirty- or forty-foot water tables would be the exception rather than the rule, while much of the soil was either too heavy or too light. Some favoured areas did, however, exist. The so-called *Khadir* area north of Delhi was such a tract.[17] Here the spring water was fifteen to twenty feet beneath the surface and a peasant could easily dig out a rough well. The importance of basic agricultural conditions is illustrated by the fact that the *Khadir* areas remained in high cultivation throughout the second half of the eighteenth century, though the tract lay in the political cockpit of India and was trampled by most of the great armies which passed this way on the road to Delhi.[18] The point was that here cultivation could be resumed without a great expense of capital. A similar area was the rich, loamy soil of the central part of Awadh known as Baiswara (which falls mainly in the District of Rai Bareilly). The route maps make it clear that cultivation here was particularly impressive and they show tightly packed villages.[19] This area produced some of the greatest of the Rajput lineages of Awadh and at the height of their power, the nawabs of Awadh maintained a close interest in the collection of its revenue.[20] A third area was Farrukhabad, south of the Ganges. Two or three miles inland from the river where the water table rose to the surface again and the soil remained alluvial and rich were some of the best lands of the whole of northern India. It was in Farrukhabad where 'there is a well in

17 Francklin, *George Thomas*, pp. 92–3; D. Ibbetson, *Karnal Settlement Report 1872–80* (Allahabad, 1883), I, 36–7; Stokes, *Peasant and Raj*, p. 17.
18 'Nerilah to Soneput', Abul Kader Khan, 'Route between Delhi and Cabul', *AAR*, viii (1806), 46–57.
19 Route from Allahabad to Fyzabad, Orme 334, IOL.
20 *Oudh Gazetteer*, III, 173–6; Barnett, *North India*, pp. 56, 184, 186; the Mughals were aware of the importance of good natural irrigation in Awadh, *Ain-i-Akbari*, II, tr. H. S. Jarrett (Calcutta, 1891), p. 171; cf. C. A. Elliott, *The Chronicles of Oonao, a district in Oudh* (Allahabad, 1862), pp. 74–7.

every house'[21] that Muhammad Khan, the Pathan adventurer, decided to found his new dynasty in the 1720s.

There were other areas of good natural irrigation. The surveys and travellers' accounts confirm, for instance, the exceptional richness of the alluvial tracts along the river Ganges between Chunar and Benares and down towards Buxar.[22] Here we find closely packed rice fields watered from irrigation channels and dominated by mud-fortresses. These territories had much in common with contemporary Bengal. Given adequate but not extreme density of population and a minimum attention to the maintenance of irrigation facilities, the land would remain perpetually rich. It is not surprising that these tracts had, like Bengal, high populations and a reputation as one of the most fertile parts of the whole subcontinent. Good natural irrigation was also available where streams could be dammed to produce ponds to water the winter crops.[23] Northern Rohilkhand, particularly Rampur, benefited from the spring torrents which rushed down into the plains from the foothills of the Himalayas.[24] Fyzullah Khan's task in rebuilding the shattered Rohilla power in Rampur after 1774 was made infinitely easier by his control of these splendid lands which could grow difficult crops, such as sugar cane and tobacco, without too much extra expense on irrigation.[25]

Finally, among the areas of 'natural' surplus must be mentioned the famous 'black earth' areas of central India and in particular Bundelkhand. These soils retained moisture throughout the winter months, so that irrigation for the *rabi* harvest was unnecessary and there was hardly a well in the whole tract. Once again the economy of water underlay some of the surprising political configurations of the period. Control of these moist, rich soils was a decisive advantage when capital for investment was in such short supply. In the 1770s and 1780s when the Ganges–Jamna Doab was in decline, or at best stagnating agriculturally, travellers spoke of the wealth and power of the great Raja Hindeput of Bundelkhand.[26] From the nineteenth-century point of view, Bundelkhand seems an unlikely candidate for political eminence. By this time, the railways and canals had given the plains an initiative once again, and climatic change had dried up Bundelkhand. But in the

[21] Irvine, *JASB*, xlvii (1878), 277. [22] Route from Chunar to Benares, Orme 334, IOL.
[23] *Khulasat-t Tawarikh*, tr. Sarkar, *India of Aurangzib*, p. 34.
[24] See, collectors' reports in 'Report of Commissioners of Revenue 1808' and 'Reports of the Commissioners 1818', *Selections from Revenue Records, North-Western Provinces 1818–20* (Calcutta, 1866); for Rohilkhand, see p. 44.
[25] For the ecology of Rampur, NWP Revenue and Agriculture Procs., 26 Jan. 1867, 438/ 57, IOL; for Farrukhabad, H. F. Evans, *Final Report of the Settlement of the Farukhabad District* (Allahabad, 1875), p. 38.
[26] Remarks on 'Bogelcund' (Baghelkhand) by Col. Ironside, *c.* 1775, *AAR*, iii (1803), 95–6.

Mughal period, this had been a rich area with a major export trade in sugar and had been assigned in *jagir* to powerful Mughal officials. In 1808 about two-thirds of the total cultivated area was said to be entirely independent of weather conditions,[27] and Bundelkhand went on to play a major role in the cotton boom of the 1820s.

Artificial surplus or 'nodal' areas

In the 'natural' surplus areas, man improved on nature. Princes established votive tanks and artificial irrigation ponds. The good returns from a relatively predictable harvest made possible further investment in irrigation, tools and clearing. But not all the rich tracts marked on Map 3 were particularly well-endowed in soil types and 'natural' irrigation. There is also another category where relative prosperity was ensured by strong rulers and the persistence of long-distance trade routes which attracted population and agricultural credit. These tracts remained in high cultivation in the face of poorer natural conditions. The immediate environs of the great Mughal towns were typical cases. The route maps of the 1760s and 1790s as well as the first reports of British collectors make it clear that Agra, Allahabad and Delhi were all three surrounded on every side by 5–10 miles of high cultivation which supported two crops a year.[28] Invading armies or scarcity years only temporarily broke this pattern. The urban population was attenuated but did not collapse. Mughal irrigation wells, supplemented in the case of Agra by those put in by the Marathas and their French advisers,[29] kept the agriculture in relatively good condition. The District of Agra in 1803, for instance, was

in a more advanced state of cultivation than the country in general; the population is not supposed to be deficient, the right of property in the lands is not in many cases disputed, and the zamindars are not presented to be so entirely destitute of capital as they appear to be in other places.[30]

The presence of an urban market had helped to maintain the income of landholders, while access to a more secure food supply had held up the urban population and its demand. In the environs of Allahabad also a dense population double-cropped an area which was not notably fertile or endowed with natural irrigation. Here also regular levies by armed Nawabi retainers were taking place in the 1790s, but in itself this did not

[27] *Revenue Records 1818–20*, pp. 35–6.
[28] Route from Allahabad to Fyzabad, Orme 334; Allahabad Commrs. Revenue Records, vol. I, Commrs. Office, Allahabad.
[29] 'Note on the decrease in the number of wells in the Agra Division', *Selections from the Records of the Government N.W. Provinces* (Agra, 1854), pt XVIII, art. 23, p. 345.
[30] Collr of Agra 1808, *Revenue Records 1818–20*, p. 40.

drive away population. Tennant notes paradoxically that peasants here were displaying improved living standards by the purchase of cloth upper garments, which they had not generally worn in earlier days.[31]

In these nodal areas much of the land was already fully cultivated. The potential improvement in the next century was much less than in the areas which had gone out of cultivation altogether or in the natural surplus areas which could continue to support further population or small advances in cultivation. A later settlement officer put the situation well: 'There seems then somewhat of a balance as regards Agra between the advantages of nature, and of invested improvement if the word may be used to represent the advantages of capital, prices and tenantry.'[32] He contrasted Agra with southern Rohilkhand which had greater natural advantages but had suffered from a flight of capital and population since the mid-1770s. The other great centres of Muslim central or regional government almost always bore a similar face. So, too, did the lands immediately along the roads which connected the main cities of the more stable successor states. The Nawabs of Awadh peppered the roads between Fyzabad, Lucknow and Allahabad with fortresses, *sarais* and fixed markets.

Unstable areas

If we now turn to areas of 'decline' on Map 3 and compare them with later geological and climatic reports, it becomes clear that they have much in common with these areas of artificial surplus held in balance by inputs of credit and irrigation. The difference is that they were more distant from major town centres or trade routes and might therefore be expected to suffer from political flux or conflict. But before we go on to present some hypotheses about the process of decline in specific areas, it is necessary to indicate that ecology and climatic changes worked to worsen the instability deriving from cycles of kingship and conquest.

South and west of the river Jamna, for instance, rainfall had always been scarce; from 1400 onward, Agra had been viewed as an oven lying on the fringes of the Rajasthan Desert. But there may have been ecological change also. There is evidence that the level of the water table south of the city suffered a serious fall between 1600 and 1800 and that the prosperity of Agra's 'home farm' had once been much greater.[33] The abandonment of Akbar's capital of Fatehpur Sikri may have been part of a much more general affliction. Visiting Agra about 1750, the Jesuit

---

[31] Tennant, *Recreations*, II, 280.

[32] *Reports of the Revenue Settlements of the North Western Provinces of the Bengal Presidency under Regulation IX of 1833* (Benares, 1862), II, pt i, 189.

[33] 'Report on the decrease of the number of wells'; the 'gullying' of the river Jamna may have been the prime longer-term factor in the lowering of the water table in the region.

Tieffenthaler noted that even 'the wells within the city of Agra are very foul and it was necessary to bring water from a great distance on the backs of buffaloes'.[34] Early British officials pointed out that many of the Mughal masonry wells of Agra and its environs were now no longer adequate to reach the spring level. The origin of the decline in irrigation seems to have been changes in the course of the Jamna which resulted from 'gullying'. The river's movement tended to depress the spring levels and create large areas of unstable land along the river banks. Cycles of low rainfall such as those of the 1780s and 1830s rendered more and more wells unsuitable. Maratha and French efforts held the position stable in the 1790s, but the 'lack of a superior monied class' such as there had been in the *muafi* holders of Akbar's and Aurangzeb's time condemned Agra's agriculture to long-term relative decline.

Little is known about the climatic changes of north India in recent centuries, but it seems possible that the region was becoming drier. An observer in the early nineteenth century mentions the 'unremitting advance'[35] of the hot summer wind (the *lu*) in recent decades, and places in the foothills which had been summer residences for Mughal notables were completely unusable by the 1830s.[36] There may have been a general climatic change related to the end of the so-called Little Ice Age of 1400–1600; but more likely, the expansion of the dry areas of the Rajasthan Desert was connected with a general deforestation of the Delhi–Agra area that occurred during the high Mughal period.[37] There was already a shortage of firewood in the capital in the seventeenth century, and the eighteenth-century armies are known to have cut down vast quantities of timber. Again, it seems possible that the light, loamy soils around Delhi and Agra went through cycles of exhaustion. Heavy cropping and defective manuring practices certainly conspired to reduce the yields in these areas during the cotton boom of the 1820s, and it is possible that this had happened earlier.

More important in tipping these areas out of balance than local changes in climate and ecology was the impact of general periods of weather instability. Cultivators and merchants have always built up stocks of grain and bullion against the bad season which according to local legend is bound to come 'once in every ten years'.[38] A series of

[34] J. Tieffenthaler in J. Bernouilli, *Description Historique et géographique de l'Inde* (Berlin, 1786), I, 162.

[35] D. Butter, *Southern Districts of Oudh*, p. 48.

[36] J. H. Batten, 'A few notes on the subject of the Kumaon and Rohilcund Turaee', *JASB*, xiii (1844), 894.

[37] Habib, *Agrarian System*, p. 56.

[38] T. Fortescue, 'Report on the Revenue Systems of the Delhi Territories', *Punjab Government Records*, I, *Delhi Residency and Agency 1801–51* (Lahore, 1911), 112.

years of too heavy or too light rainfall, however, put great strain on these strategies for survival. Quite apart from mortality, the migration of cultivators and their animals, and the merchant's desire to rebuild his own stocks, made it difficult to get agricultural operations moving again in the absence of positive aid from men of capital. The crucial second harvest (*rabi*) when the market crops were grown was particularly vulnerable because continuing investment was needed to keep irrigation systems working.

The idea of cycles of weather instability is clumsier but more accurate than scarcities. It has been observed that bad seasons have tended to come in clusters in north India, with drought followed by flood in a malevolent chorus. The 1680s, the 1830s, 1860s and 1890s were such periods. So, too, were the years from 1770 to 1790. Large areas of the province received exceptional rainfall in 1770–1, when the east of Awadh 'became like a sea'.[39] From 1779 to 1783, rainfall was short before the cataclysm of the 1783 famine.[40] This is borne out both by fragmentary series for grain prices and by contemporary accounts. Again in the year 1788 there was a serious shortfall of rain which led to rioting and panic measures in the city of Benares.[41] North India scarcely had time to recover from this series of disasters when the years 1799–1803 brought a further round of scarcities.[42] These were caused in part by the shortage of bullock power which resulted from renewed warfare. In such a precarious position, the less stable areas were crucially dependent on the continuing investment of money and labour power by the ruling groups. The withdrawal of this support could easily bring about a final cycle of degeneration in which political and natural problems reinforced each other.

The pathology of decline in its later stages

In the last chapter, we showed how volatile Indian trading systems might be in times of political change and how this volatility might in turn affect the performance of agricultural society. This section takes some unstable areas and examines how they fared in the last thirty years of the eighteenth century when they were gripped by a cumulative

---

[39] G. Harper to (illegible), 19 July 1770, Orme 69, IOL.
[40] *Oudh Gazetteer*, II, 327–8; S. Roy, 'A rare document on Delhi wheat prices 1763–1835', *IESHR*, ix (1972), 91–100. The series suggests that the famine itself was preceded by three scarcity seasons, and this is borne out by contemporary sources including the price data in the Benares Resident's and 'Duncan' Records, UPR.
[41] 18 Nov. 1788, PR; C. E. R. Girdlestone, *Report on Past Famines in the North-Western Provinces* (Allahabad, 1868), p. 8.
[42] Girdlestone, *Past Famines*, pp. 12–13; *DG Bulandshahr*, p. 48.

political and agrarian crisis. These areas are the lands fanning out one
hundred miles around Delhi (with the exception of the moist *Khadir*
tracts); the areas of Bayana and Hindaun which lay outside the central
circle of the Agra District; and the central Doab between Korah-
Jehanabad and Etawah. All these tracts, though productive, relied
heavily on irrigation and other inputs provided by the elites. Hariana,
north of Delhi, for instance, is 'very uncertain in its produce from the
depth of the water under the surface rendering irrigation by wells
impracticable'.[43] Formerly, the tract had depended on the 'intelligence
and liberality of some of the former Princes of the Mahomedan throne,
from the visible remains of their mighty works, in conducting streams
from the principal rivers or *nalahs* through the different quarters of the
country'. Up to 1730, large quantities of grain and fruits from
Saharanpur and Meerut had been sold on the Delhi market and sugar
was exported to the south and west into the Punjab. Polier remarked in
1776 that 'many towns which at present bring in 20,000 Rupees of
revenue afforded at that time to bring in a lac of Rupees or more
yearly'.[44] Both east and west of the Jamna there was much evidence of
former 'abundance, population security, wealth and happiness'.

What form did the final decline take here? The effect of political flux
cannot be doubted, but it was not so much rapine and pillage as the
withdrawal of capital and supervision. The decline of the two great
Mughal canals of Zabita Khan and Ali Mardan Khan perhaps took as
many as 500 square miles of territory out of direct cultivation.[45] These
canals had been available for the use of local farmers who were able to
take cuttings for the payment of fees to the superintendent of the canal.
The elites benefited indirectly, but it is said that the water dues which
amounted to nearly two lakhs of Rupees annually before 1730 were paid
back directly into maintenance work. The canals also had other
beneficial effects. The presence of large bodies of water tended to raise
the level of ground-water throughout the territory, making irrigation
wells feasible and encouraging the growth of trees which lessened the
danger of soil erosion. Before 1740, the superintendence of the canals
had been in the hands of the Persian noble Saadat Khan who later
became the first Nawab of Awadh. When factional conflict caused him
to retire to the more secure base of Fyzabad the canals began to collapse,
though several later magnates including Ahmed Shah Durrani
attempted to repair them. Here the moral and political decay of the old
ruling class had initiated the cycle of ecological decline. But it is

[43] Fortescue, 'Delhi Report', p. 100.
[44] Polier to Ironside, 22 May 1776, *AAR*, i (1799), 34–5.
[45] Fortescue, 'Delhi Report', pp. 101–4; Revenue Maps 1833, IOL.

important to remember that decline in the immediate environs of Delhi was offset to some extent by a matching rise in investment by the same nobles and courtiers in the neighbourhood of Fyzabad.

Between 1740 and 1760 further unfavourable forces came into operation in the region around Delhi and Agra. The decline of the local market for sugar, tobacco and indigo was matched by a decline in foreign demand for indigo which had been slackening since the turn of the century and had come to a stop before 1750.[46] By this time, moreover, the snapping of the revenue–trade link between Bengal and the Mughal capitals was already having damaging effects on the small towns between Korah and Etawah. But the run-down had only just begun at this time. An early British report noted that 'Seharunpore produced a large revenue even after the decline of Delhi and the diminution of its resources cannot be attributed entirely to any external circumstance'.[47] In fact, it is the effects of the cycle of scarcity culminating in the 1783 famine which appear to have been decisive. For a neighbouring *pargana* of Hariana, we have figures which show a drop in revenue produce from Rs. 150,000 in 1770 to a mere Rs. 7,000 per annum for several years after the 1783 famine (the 'Chalisa'). The revenue had only climbed to one-third of its original yield after twenty years of British rule.[48]

The most devastating effect of the famine periods was that they led to medium- and long-term emigration out of the unstable areas of capital, stock and labour. The accompanying sharp mortality among children and old people would not necessarily have had a severe effect on agricultural production. During the course of bad seasons, there was a tendency for population to drift from the unstable to the surplus areas. So the difference between the agricultural performance of the surplus areas and the rest of the plains increased rather than diminished and more lands in the unstable areas went out of cultivation. The farmers and ruling groups of the surplus areas had the resources to offer protection to migrant families of the castes which specialised in agricultural production. There is evidence, for instance, that the Kurmis, Kacchis and others who fled from the Delhi region or the central Doab were the same ones who were being settled in eastern Awadh or Unao after 1783.

When we piece together the fragmentary materials for population density in the last decades of the eighteenth and the first decades of the nineteenth centuries, therefore, we find marked disparities between regions which appear to have been much greater than they were after

46 Sarkar, *India of Aurangzib*, pp. 94–5; Naqvi, *Urban Centres*, p. 61.
47 Polier to Ironside, 22 May 1776.   48 Fortescue, 'Delhi Report', p. 112.

1840. An extrapolation backward of the inspired guesses at population of the early revenue officials and topographers have at least a greater degree of accuracy than the remarks that an area was 'well' or 'sparsely' populated. What seems almost certain is that there was a very dramatic drop in population as one moved from the well-watered rice-growing areas of Bengal, Benares and eastern Awadh into the Doab and the Delhi territories. An estimate of the density of Benares population in the 1790s put it at about the same as Bengal's, or 260–290 per square mile. In 1870 the population density in the old Benares Raj was about 510–610 per square mile.[49] This seems broadly consistent with Morris D. Morris's estimated all-India population increase for the early nineteenth century of well under one per cent per annum.[50] Extrapolating backward from 1815 and 1830 assessments for the western areas, we seem to get very much lower populations. Early guesses by collectors point in the same direction. In 1808, for instance, the density in Saharanpur was reckoned to be about 119 per square mile;[51] and this was after there had been considerable migration back into the territory from the hills and western Awadh. Meerut may have had a density of about 130 per square mile at the same period while the figure appears to have moved up to about 160 for Rampur,[52] a rich tract which benefited as we have seen from the strong rule of the Rohilla Fyzullah Khan. In the middle Doab districts of Kanpur, Aligarh and Fatehpur the figure may have been about 110 to the square mile.[53] For Rohilkhand the only contemporary guess we have is that the total population was about one million Hindus and 200,000 Muslims in the 1770s. For what it is worth, this would have given a figure of under one hundred people per square mile, *before* the disasters of Nawabi government and the 1780s famine cycle.

These low figures of population density for the western territories amount to a distinct under-population and are quite consistent with the repeated contention of early British revenue officials that there was a general lack of agricultural labour. At the same time, they make it clear that relatively small population movements connected with political change or scarcities might have quite a disproportionate effect on specialised agriculture which required a large labour force. Agricultural society did not happily bounce back from the effects of the 1783 famine.

---

[49] *DG Benares*, p. 24.
[50] M. D. Morris, 'The population of All-India, 1880–1951', *IESHR*, xi (1974), 309–13.
[51] Saharanpur Magistrate's Report, Home Misc. 776, IOL; cf. *Revenue Records 1818–20*, p. 43; *Settlements under Act IX 1833*, II, i, 189.
[52] Moradabad Magistrate's Report, Home Misc. 776, IOL; cf. for Farrukhabad, *AAR*, vii (1808), 42.
[53] Kanpur Magistrate's Report, 1814, Home Misc. 776, IOL.

Depopulation was still in evidence in the middle Doab in the 1830s.[54] The scale of the disaster was such that population and resources did not recover for a generation or more. Michele McAlpin believes that local mortalities of up to 30 per cent were feasible for the 1870s and 1880s when communications were considerably better.[55] With this in mind, it is not possible to discount the evidence of Captain Williamson of Kanpur who reckoned in 1783 that 60 per cent of the population of the middle Doab had died in the famine.[56] His more accurate assessment, based on figures of local charity, suggests that 200,000 starving people converged on Kanpur alone in search of relief, and large-scale emigration into Awadh is mentioned by other observers. Disease followed famine.

It was the effects of the 1783 famine that Tennant assimilated into his picture of domestic and political decay in the Indian states. There were, he said, extensive wastes even within reach of the city of Kanpur. These, 'given population could be rendered productive by the labour of a single season'.[57] Of Rohilkhand in 1798 he noted 'from the quantity of land under crop, the population of Rohilcund must be very small. Not the hundredth acre is in cultivation.'[58] This cumulative decline in the cultivated acreage appears to have had further consequences. Suddenly leaving land fallow led to the spread of parasitic grasses which made it twice as difficult and costly to bring the land under cultivation once again. Waving plains of high, dense grass in areas which had been recently cultivated are mentioned by some travellers and military surveyors. Also reported are the 'depredations' of wild animals which damaged crops and very quickly multiplied in the absence of human population.[59] Both parasitic grasses and destruction by animals are well-known consequences of later and more local cycles of agricultural degeneration in north India, and they both substantially reduced the cultivator's capacity to recover his balance in the aftermath of scarcity.

Yet what set apart these more general crises of the late eighteenth century was the way in which ecological change had immediate consequences in the political sphere which further exacerbated the precarious struggle of labour and capital to get agriculture moving again. There was a close connection between the growth of 'banditry'

[54] Magistrate Agra to Commissioner, 13 Jan. 1834, Agra Revenue 7, UPR; Fortescue, 'Delhi Report', p. 111.
[55] M. B. McAlpin, 'Dearth, famine and changes in risk. A preliminary investigation of the changing impact of crop failures in Bombay Presidency', 'Risk' conference, Univ. Pennsylvania, 1977.
[56] 'Capt. Williamson's account of the Famine of 1783', in Magt. Farrukhabad to Commr Agra, 8 Feb. 1838, NWP Criminal Judicial Procs., July 1833, 231/49, IOL.
[57] Tennant, *Recreations*, II, 363, 371.
[58] *Ibid.*, p. 381.   [59] *Ibid.* p. 383.

and local decline. This is not surprising. Mercenaries and tribal people such as the Bhattis, Mewatis, and the corporations of mercenary adventurers known as Pindaris had to turn to outside looting and plunder when rent extracted from their home territories was no longer sufficient to maintain their style of life. At the same time, there has always been a strong connection between cycles of bad seasons and outbreaks of theft and robbery amongst low castes and people on the tribal fringes of Hindu society. It is between 1783 and 1805 that the reports of robbery and violence on the roads of the Delhi–Agra region reach a peak, and it is reasonable to assume that the general agricultural decline after the 1783 famine was one of the main causes of this intensification.[60] Both 'gentlemen' highwaymen (Pindaris) and lowly robbers (Gujars) receive mention, and it is from this period that the rise of *kazaki* is dated. This word, cognate with Cossack, means highway robbery by bodies of irregular horse. Roads had always been dangerous around Delhi and Agra even at the height of the Mughal empire, but the intensification of violence removed the last incentive from a farmer who might wish to sell his goods at a local market – the possibility of profit.

In these declining areas, the displacement of specialist labour and elite investment was compounded by the emigration of merchant families which had provided credit for agricultural operations. The reduction of caravan trade through the towns of Mahim, Karnal and Panipat to Delhi after the 1760s, for instance, pushed their agricultural environs further into decline. In this region, *pakka* (brick) wells of up to eighty feet depth had been necessary to realise the wealth of the soil. The inhabitants of the rich commercial town of Panipat had put in as many as fifty such wells.[61] But the cumulative political and economic crisis of the 1780s forced many of the Agarwal and Khattri merchant families into emigration towards the stable lands of the east. The distant echoes of this diaspora can be heard in the family and caste histories of the merchant families of eastern Hindustan. It was also a critical period for Agra. The great famine in Hindustan, when 'a world of men have died of hunger', increased the plundering by local military commanders. During the poor year of 1788, Agra's merchant community fled in large numbers to Bharatpur in the west and Allahabad and Benares in the east. Mirza Ismail Beg, the imperial commander, followed a forced loan of two lakhs of Rupees with a demand for the same amount in the form of a cess on shops and houses. So 'the shops of the merchants and money

---

[60] J. N. Sarkar (ed.), *Persian Records of Maratha History*, 1, *Delhi Affairs (1761–88)* (Bombay, 1953) 113, 117–18, 125; cf. letter to Poona, 1 May 1783; Twining, *Travels*, p. 182.

[61] Francklin, *George Thomas*, pp. 87–8.

changers are closed; one cannot get a draft (*hundi*) for one Rupee'.[62]

Yet two considerations mitigate this picture. Agra remained a nodal area where trade and military activity continued; during the 1790s as a Maratha headquarters it regained some of its prosperity. Secondly, Agra and Karnal–Panipat's loss in capital, skills and labour favoured trade and agriculture in more stable regions such as the Jat kingdoms, eastern Awadh and Benares.[63]

The parallel pattern of growth

While the west and the Delhi area faced widespread agricultural decline after 1740 Benares and the east fared much better, benefiting from good natural irrigation. During the sixteenth and seventeenth centuries, the area had seen a fast expansion of its cultivated acreage. Sinha's figures suggest that there may have been a five to sevenfold growth[64] between 1589 and 1720 along the northern and southern fringes where land was being opened up on clearing leases. Around the cities of Jaunpur, Benares and Chunar, there also appears to have been a significant expansion connected with the pull of urban markets. The number of seventeenth-century wells and tanks in the neighbourhood of Benares suggests that two crops a year had become standard here. Yet there was also expansion in the unstable areas of the lower Doab between Fatehpur and Allahabad where Sinha finds a $2\frac{1}{2}$ to $3\frac{1}{2}$-fold expansion of cultivation. Here the impact of military and commercial activity along the Grand Trunk Road must have been considerable. Large numbers of market villages served growing administrative centres such as Etawah and Korah-Jehanabad, while Mughal notables and local rajas put in tanks, wells and groves.

During the following century much sharper differences in agricultural performance began to appear. Rapid clearing continued on the fringes, especially in north-east Awadh and in the jungles of what is now the Mirzapur District. The nodal areas of transport and communications around the cities of Allahabad and Benares continued to stay in high cultivation, and there was almost certainly an intensification between Benares and Mirzapur. But the unstable areas of the lower Doab suffered as badly as parts of the western districts and for similar reasons. The disruption of the military and commercial traffic of the high Mughal empire led to a decline in the *qasbah* towns and small markets which, in turn, affected agriculture and drove cultivation back

---

[62] Letter, 27 *Rabi*, year 29 (6 Jan. 1788), *Persian Records*, I, 202.
[63] Khattri, Agarwal family histories, Agra, Allahabad, Benares; S. Bhandari, *Agrawal Jati ka Itihas* (Bhanpura, Indore, 1938), II, *passim*.
[64] S. N. Sinha, *Subah of Allahabad under the Great Mughals* (Delhi, 1974), pp. 145–9.

from the Grand Trunk Road. Agriculture here was in the same precarious balance, and the withdrawal of capital and regional political authority precipitated a fall-off.

The differences between the naturally stable and the unstable areas showed up clearly. The route maps and reports of the Duncan Records delineate tracts of exceptionally fine cultivation in the Chunar region, on the fertile patches along the Sai and Ghagra in Awadh and in Unao, with its light, fertile loams. Here urban decline was unlikely to affect agriculture, and urban growth could only enhance it. For instance, in the well-irrigated and fertile Jaunpur District agriculture remained 'remarkably fine and flourishing'[65] even after the travails of the 1780s when Jaunpur city and Macchlishahr, the old Islamic centres of the district, were in very rapid decline.

The stability of agriculture in the surplus areas was enhanced by the fact that they often helped sustain the strongest political orders. Fertile Baiswara became the crown lands of the Awadh dynasty and received its most energetic and trusted officials. Balwant Singh of Benares managed to survive his long-drawn-out battles with the Nawabs in part because of the strength of his support amongst the matchlockmen of the Bhumihar lineage heads, but partly because he could not be dislodged for long from the fertile revenue-bearing lands along the banks of the Ganges. Naturally, therefore, it was to these territories that merchant capital and the skilful agriculturalists came for refuge when the cumulative political and agrarian crises of the unstable areas drove them to flight. Each climacteric of drought and conflict from the 1680s onward favoured the stable areas to the disadvantage of the unstable. Thus, the Kunbis 'are found in great numbers in the country about Chunar. They come from Jainagar and other places to the east.'[66] In the Ahraura region, Kurmis and Kacchis claim to have settled during the eighteenth century, elaborating a legend that they were descendants of Maratha soldiers defeated by the Afghans at the battle of Panipat in 1761.[67] Where a ruler underwrote the cost of settlement of an immigrant group, the distances travelled could be very great. Warren Hastings's deputy at Patna, Lala Shitab Rai, brought market gardeners from as far away as Delhi and Lahore.[68] But much larger migrations could occur over several hundred miles. In 1789, the rich lands of the Jaunpur District were in high cultivation 'through the means principally of new Ryots [peasant farmers] who have fled into these districts from the oppressions of the Nabob Vizier's neighbouring Amil of Azamgarh . . . who have already

---

[65] Report on Jaunpore, 1 July 1793, PR.
[66] Sherring, *Hindu Castes*, pp. 325–6, 335.
[67] Interviews, family histories, Benares District, 1973–4.   [68] *Seir*, II, 441.

brought a great proportion of the fallow land into cultivation'.[69]

Large migrations over a hundred miles or more are also recorded along the fringes of the northern hills. The crises of 1770–1800 in Rohilkhand and Saharanpur drove many families up into the high lands of Kumaon, where they opened up much new land. When conditions deteriorated here after the Gurkha conquests at the beginning of the following century, they moved down into the plains again in numbers which may have amounted to as many as 200,000.[70] Further east there was considerable depopulation in Gorakhpur, but a matching growth of cultivation in the hill kingdom of Butwal. In the same way, Bhattis from Hariana settled in northern Rohilkhand or Awadh,[71] and large numbers of cultivators from the Doab were driven across the Ganges by the famine and wars of the 1780s.

Despite the evidence from Mughal records produced by Irfan Habib, the importance of internal migration in the economic history of pre-colonial India has yet to be recognised.[72] We still tend to think in terms of the tiny fields and settled populations of the late nineteenth century, and while this may be an accurate picture of the surplus areas in the eighteenth century, the movement of population between unstable areas appears to have been much greater. This is not to suggest that there were no pains and penalties involved in distress migration. Poorer lands were sometimes opened up, and the cost of clearing scrub diminished scarce resources which could have been used elsewhere. But this was not always the case. Some of the settlement was on 'fallow' land; that is to say, it did not involve clearing virgin jungle, but merely bringing under the plough land which had been uncultivated for up to five years. It is also well known that the productivity per acre of 'lea' and 'fallow' was often higher than that of regularly cropped land, so that internal migration did not inevitably lead to a drastic decline in the total volume of produce. In the same way the flight or migration of merchant families in an economy like that of north India could bring substantial and immediate benefits to the places where they settled. What were in short supply were merchant skills and capital. We have several examples of merchants transforming their assets into pearls or jewellery for the purposes of migration, and newcomers with the right caste and commercial connections could start up flourishing businesses with startling speed.

Yet while the influx of new men and capital helped maintain or even

[69] Benares Revenue Report 1790, para. 81, Resident to GG, 25 Nov. 1790, PR.
[70] Batten, 'Notes on Kumaon', *JASB*, xii (1844), 897.
[71] Francklin, *George Thomas*, p. 167.
[72] See Habib, *Agrarian System*, pp. 6–7; cf. A. Yang, 'Peasants on the move: a study of internal migration in India', *Journal of Interdisciplinary History*, x (1979), 37–58.

extend agriculture and trade in the stable areas, this can only have provided an increment to existing growth. The route maps of the 1760s for Baiswara, Unao and the interior of the Benares domains show a populous countryside dominated by large numbers of small fortresses provided with a well or tank.[73] Unlike Benares proper or Mirzapur, urban influences seem decidedly limited. To understand agricultural growth, it must be related to the political economy of the great agricultural clans of Bhumihars or Rajputs.

We have some very detailed conjectures of how 'democratic' lineages of 'free peasants' expanded under the influence of war and the impact of the Muslim central states to give rise to more complex political systems with rajas at their heads.[74] Let us try to introduce an economic dimension into this political world. A turning point in Richard Fox's elaborate theory of political change among the Rajput clans is when the geographical expansion of the lineage slows down because the available waste land has been settled and the clan has already come into conflict with adjoining Rajput groups. In Fox's view, the need for internal control and war leadership against outsiders encouraged the emergence of the raja above the bodies of free kinsmen. We can speculate that this was the phase when agricultural intensification on the already settled lands began. Cadet lines of the dominant clan had now to be rewarded with lordship rights in the settled lands rather than new lands on the diminishing clan frontier. Population grew on the settled rich lands near the rivers, putting pressure on the family farms to increase production by more intensive cropping. The rise of the raja saw the growth of the village which had served as centre for the lineage to something more than just a point for ritual exchange within the *jajmani* system. Population growth among the artisan families meant that more artisans could participate in interdistrict exchange. Villages began to specialise in weaving, brass-making or weapons. With more frequent and more sophisticated conflict, it became necessary to group larger bodies of armed men around permanent mud-fortresses and there was a more concentrated demand for services. Conquest of other tribal groups led to an inflow of further dependants, cattle and bullion. Some of this was invested in wells, tanks and embankments maintained by the community which dammed the plentiful water into the irrigation ponds for which Awadh is famous.

A second turning point in Fox's picture of the political cycle of the Rajput lineage is the intervention of a stronger outside political force represented by the Delhi emperors or in later times by the nawab of

---

[73] Route from Fyzabad to Lucknow, *c.* 1770, Orme 334, IOL.
[74] Richard G. Fox, *Kin, Clan, Raja and Rule* (Berkeley, 1969).

Awadh. The political consequences included the strengthening of the raja's position as a political intermediary for the central power and also the creation of basic units of 'administration' out of the 'clans' of the Rajput tribe. What would be the economic consequences of this subordination? In the first place, the rich territories of the central lineage would now be subject to two demands for revenue. They had to pay both the revenue of the central state and the lordship and local dues (*malikana*) of the raja. This forced the peasant farm to intensify its agricultural efforts by growing more valuable crops to gain the extra coin with which to pay the rulers. At the same time, the raja and the top lineages were more clearly separated off from the rest of the tribe who were now pressed closer to the soil and became something like cultivating owner-occupiers. The forging of new revenue links implied, as we have shown, the growth of trade which linked the clan area through the gentry *qasbahs* to Lucknow, or Benares and the long-distance trade.

This picture is, of course, a stereotype, but it suggests how agriculture could intensify as the result of rural political and demographic change. One need not suppose that all economic change in rural India must have been the result of the imposition of a cash revenue-demand from urban centres on a 'natural' village economy.

The final section of the chapter shows how the fragmentary evidence from Awadh and the more substantial record of the Benares territories supports this two-stage process of 'commercialisation'. The first stage sees the creation of a significant local merchant community within the bounds of the clan area and petty raj; the second sees it linked in through the mechanisms of land-revenue and luxury trade to the wider world of the towns and long-distance trader. Decentralised pre-colonial polities could provide the conditions for agricultural expansion in stable areas, as surely as their conflicts could drive away resources in unstable ones.

Traders, gentry and *ganjs*: agricultural growth in the east

A good example of agricultural intensification is to be found in the land of the Bais Rajputs ('Baiswara') which lies in the present-day Districts of Rai Bareilly and Unao. Here an exceptionally powerful set of local kingships emerged from the time of the legendary Raja Tilok Chand in the thirteenth century, sometimes in conflict with and sometimes in cooperation with the Muslim central authorities. The lineage centres associated with them show signs of rapid growth and expansion in the early years of the eighteenth century. Legend and 'agricultural archaeology' gives us a picture of well- and tank-building by its rajas and

aristocrats between 1730 and 1780. The conquest of Baiswara by the
nawabs in the 1740s linked the local economies into Lucknow
commercial life and imposed a new set of *qasbah* towns on the lineage
centres and saw the further growth of artisan industry.

Butter's reports from the 1830s help to fill in the context of change.
By then the Bais gave evidence of several generations of increased
prosperity. They were 'the best dressed and housed people of southern
Oudh', and the whole area between Baiswara and Fyzabad was
'prosperous and well-cultivated'.[75] The growth of the money economy
and a settled aristocracy had given rise not only to rich local
moneylenders who had held lakhs of Rupees apiece, but also to wide
trading connections which had grown up from within the local
economy. In this case the merchants were the Bais Rajputs themselves,
which was unusual. A prohibition against military service outside the
clan had encouraged them to turn towards trade. By 1790 Bais had
established depots for cloth and luxury trade from places as far east as
Calcutta, as far west as Jaipur and as far north as Kashmir. They
brought in goods as varied as 'elephants from Tipperah and shawls from
Cashmere'. Local trade here reached outward to link up with the long-
distance networks run by the traditional commercial communities.
Commercial earnings were remitted rather as earnings from mercenary
service were remitted in more typical Rajput communities. The
entrepreneurs 'visit their native district once in every five years, leaving
an experienced relative in charge'.[76] These commercial institutions
naturally linked up with the monetary system imposed by the demand
for cash revenue. In the 1830s, there remained many Brahmin and other
moneylenders with capital very substantial even by the standards of the
major towns. These made a profit of 50 per cent every six months 'by
making advances to the zamindars' for revenue purposes and taking
grain in return. Here agricultural intensification had given rise to a
pattern of substantial villages each with their large moneylenders who
lived alongside and serviced the lineage elites. This would not normally
be considered urban growth, but except for the actual concentration of
settlements it had much in common with the town growth which could
be seen in the peripheral *mohullas* of the major cities. Substantial artisan
communities of weavers and brass-makers participated in production
which was directed not at the major centres, nor constrained within the
limits of the village *jajmani* system, but served the clan aristocracy
scattered over Baiswara.

What were the economic and social consequences of the second stage
of intensification – the imposition of cash revenue and closer control by

[75] Butter, *Southern Districts*, pp. 39–42.   [76] *Ibid.*, p. 41.

an outside ruler? First, it extended and developed the opportunities for local moneylenders and traders to link up with the trade and revenue flows of the larger society. Let us take the case of Hirderam (Hirday Ram), the Brahmin banker of Unao.[77] Hirderam had grown powerful as moneylender and trader within the domains of Unao's largest Hindu raja, but his influence was vulnerable and constricted by the dominance of the Rajput aristocracy. About 1770 he fled to the protection of the local nawabi officials and began to trade in Awadh cotton and cloth which he imported from Mirzapur for sale to the *qasbah* gentry around the centres of Muslim government. Then he moved into an extremely lucrative appointment as treasurer to the nawabi governor of Baiswara, which meant, in effect, controlling the whole cash flow from there to Lucknow. A major source of profit was the commission he took from the Baiswara zamindars in exchanging local rupees – the symbol of their now curtailed economic autarchy – into the Lucknow Rupees in which the nawab's revenue had to be paid. Later, one part of the family moved into the British station of Kanpur which retained strong commercial links with Awadh, while the other built up for itself a large landed estate in the districts of Baiswara.[78]

Peasant farming, however, was also affected by the political vicissitudes of the regional government of Awadh. Most representative of its impact were the settlement in Awadh of groups of specialist cultivators, and the very rapid proliferation of fixed rural markets called *ganjs*. Reference is made to the establishment of forty-two such *ganjs* in trans-Ganges Awadh between 1750 and 1819; the sources are the 1877 *Oudh Gazetteer*, contemporary references in maps and travellers' accounts. Much of the activity was concentrated along the arterial routes which connected the major centres of Awadh. These places came into existence as break-of-bulk or provisioning points associated with movements of the military or the court under the first three nawabs. Some began as hunting lodges designed by the ruler; others were founded by magnates of the court, such as Tikait Rai and Mehendi Ali Khan. Another group were the foundations in areas which were being brought under the plough by the great marcher lords who had received clearing rights from the nawabs. *Ganjs* here played a key role in extending the money economy into the fringes of the Himalayan foothills. But most of the *ganjs* appear to have been constructed by the great Awadh revenue-farmers who founded them with a view to the rapid expansion of the productive capacity of their territories. Pre-eminent among these was Mian Almas Ali Khan who in the 1780s and 1790s directly controlled more revenue than his master, the Nawab

[77] Elliott, *Chronicles of Oonao*, pp. 135–43.   [78] *Ibid.*, I, 123.

himself. Almas peppered his power base of Unao and Etawah with new fixed markets centred on his own headquarters of Mianganj where he settled Kurmi cultivators and opened indigo factories with the aid of Armenian and local capitalists.[79]

A fixed bazaar or *ganj* indicates a higher level of economic activity than the biweekly peasant markets or *haths*. Some wholesale traders, a number of commission agents, permanent moneylenders and permanent buildings were the least requirements. The foundation of a *ganj* did not itself create trade. It was, however, an acknowledgement of the existence of trade in sufficient bulk for a magnate to wish to tax and protect it. The foundation of a *ganj* was also a crucial act of political economy. It asserted the founder's right to arbitrate disputes between merchants and appoint headmen – in short, to act as a 'little king'. It facilitated his independent collection of revenue and his capacity to transform agrarian wealth into commercial or military resources throughout the year without reference to the agents of the central ruler. The flowering of *ganjs* represents two stages in the history of Awadh. First, it reflected the growth of a strong central power under the first two Nawabs who founded many of the roadside *ganjs*. Secondly, it went ahead during the 'decentralisation' of power under Asaf-ud Daulah, the fourth Nawab, who deliberately allowed his local revenue-farmers to engross more of the total revenue in order to fight off British pressure for enhanced tribute. This decentralisation had the consequence of rolling outward the boundaries of the intermediate economy which developed around the fixed markets.

In the settled areas, the new *ganjs* centralised trade, but also stimulated it by encouraging economies of scale amongst traders and providing more ready access to credit for peasant farmers. *Ganjs* which were founded in marginal areas had a more significant effect. Peasant farmers rarely like to overnight at market and in eighteenth-century conditions the maximum distance a man might have been prepared to travel with a bullock load of grain was, say, seven miles. If we take a low contemporary estimate of a population density of 200 per square mile and a radius of seven miles in all directions from a centre, then the foundation of a single new *ganj* could create or improve market access for as many as 15,000 people. Fixed markets, unlike periodic *haths*, encouraged merchants to store, so that both merchant and farmer would be able to predict prices more accurately. Most of the new *ganjs* were in fact provided with *sarais* or inns where merchants could rest and store

[79] *Ibid.*, II, 496; for a contemporary account of Mianganj, see George, Viscount Valentia, *Voyages and Travels in India, Ceylon, the Red Sea, Abyssinia and Egypt* (London, 1809), I, 182–3.

goods. We can glimpse the importance of new fixed markets in the case of Nawabganj – one of the many foundations with this name – which was established across the Ghagra river opposite Fyzabad. Visiting it in the first decade of the nineteenth century, Buchanan writes:

Nawabgunj was founded by Suja ud Doulah, and its situation was judiciously chosen on the edge of the country subject to inundation, and opposite to Fyzabad, his capital city. It served therefore as a mart, where all the farmers from the northern parts of his country might bring their grain, and dispose of it to the merchants of Fyzabad. . . . The trade is still carried on with great spirit.[80]

Uncultivated areas within fifty or a hundred miles of major cities were brought under cultivation especially quickly. A typical case was the present-day Gonda District which adjoined Nawabganj. This was the *jagir* of Asaf's mother, the Bahu Begum, who created a number of secondary marts, providing centres for the hamlet-clearing type of settlement which characterised this area. In 1793 the territory was worth Rs. 8 lakhs per annum in revenue, but by the 1830s it had risen to nearly Rs. 60 lakhs.[81]

Politics brought these new fixed markets into existence and also continued to intervene in their workings. Merchants paid regular transit and market duties on produce, amounting to about 40 per cent of their gross profits. But at the same time all the mercantile and artisan communities resident in the *ganjs* were subject to taxation called *prajawat*, a lordship due derived from the word *praja*, 'a subject'. Since this was a political tax on persons rather than a tax on trade, it was adjusted like other capitations in indigenous polities to the dignity and importance of the group or family involved.[82] And this generally meant that the richest and most powerful paid the smallest levies – a situation which the incoming British found difficult to grasp when they attempted to consolidate these payments into a single 'ground rent' determined by the assumed commercial value of the market sectors different communities occupied.

In the eastern markets of old-established Hindu rulers, rates of *prajawat* and other taxes were fixed by custom and related closely to the *jajmani* shares of various village service communities. But in new markets and in the westerly districts where magnates had more difficulty in attracting merchants and artisans to settle in their domains,

---

80 Martin, *Eastern India*, II, 382; W. Hoey, *A Monograph on the Trade and Manufactures of Upper India* (Lucknow, 1879), pp. 152–3; *DG Gonda*, p. 233.

81 *Ibid.*

82 Collr Kanpur to Board, 24 May 1804, CPR, 12 June 1804, 90/42, IOL; the redistributive notions implicit in Indian customs duties are well exemplified in Khairuddin Hussain, 'Tarikh-i-Jaunpur', tr. anon., Add. MSS 3866, p. 57, Cambridge University Library; Wilson, *Glossary*, p. 423.

market rates and levies were often the consequence of an implicit bargain between revenue-farmers and the local commercial community. The chroniclers allege that Hafiz Rehmat Khan Rohilla waived all dues and duties in his domains in order to attract merchant wealth. And even in parts of eastern Rohilkhand dominated by Awadh after 1774, affluent merchants often paid rates 25 per cent to 30 per cent less than the poorer bazaar traders and hucksters, 'the aumils being sensible that the continuance of their own authority depended in great measure upon the influence of the several persons of respectability and consequence'.[83] Merchant wealth was here, as in the larger cities, an independent force and one not wholly 'encompassed' by political power as the ideological formulation has it. Yet when we write of 'capitalism', commercialisation or the expansion of market relations during the century, it is important to bear in mind the extent to which trade was moulded by the condition of local politics.

Eighteenth-century settlements of Kurmi, Kacchi and Koeri cultivators were also numerous in northern and western Awadh. On the fringes of cultivation, these castes were given special rental rates for bringing areas of jungle under the plough. In the first five years, for instance, the rent might be only half of what was common for soil of the same type. The revenue benefits to the entrepreneur or official who planted the colony were very great. Customal rent-rates for Kurmis and their like were from 30 to 80 per cent higher than those paid by other castes once a colony was established.[84] British officers later attributed these differentials to 'caste prejudices' amongst the higher rural castes against touching the plough. Yet the main reason for the superior productivity of the gardener castes was their manuring practice. Whereas the majority of cultivators manured only the lands immediately around the village and used these lands for growing food grains, Kurmis avoided using animal dung for fuel and manured the poorer lands farther from the village (the *manjha*). They were able, therefore, to grow valuable market crops such as potatoes, melons and tobacco immediately around the village, sow fine grains in the *manjha*, and restrict the poor millet subsistence crops to the periphery. A network of *ganjs* and Kurmi or Kacchi settlements could transform a local economy within a year or two.

It was suggested earlier that the decline of the *qasbah* town elites in the

---

[83] 'Gunjes and markets in Rohilcund', note by actg Commercial Agent, Farrukhabad, 19 Feb. 1803, CPR, 15 Nov. 1803, 97/38, IOL.

[84] Crooke, *Tribes and Castes*, III, 355–7; the concentration of Kurmis shows a marked correlation with areas of eighteenth-century state-building; Imtiaz Hussain, *Land Revenue Policy in Northern India* (Delhi, 1967), pp. 163–4; Evans, *Farrukhabad Settlement Report*, p. 25.

western districts had a direct effect on the agricultural lands immediately surrounding them. If not 'managers', the Islamic gentry were at least investors in and catalysts to the local economy. The redistribution of the gentry to northern and eastern Awadh after the decline of Delhi and Agra had, therefore, economic consequences. An excellent example is the development along the Nawab's road from Lucknow to Fyzabad which can be traced in route maps and contemporary accounts. The congregation of soldiers and courtiers on the roads within fifty miles of both these centres resulted in a considerable expansion of the intermediate economy. In the 1770s, Munshi Faiz Baksh mistook the town of Mumtazganj, four miles from Fyzabad, for the great city itself, 'so immense was the throng of merchants, vendors, and artisans of all kinds'.[85] A later official confirmed the impression. The road west from Fyzabad is 'marked by numerous mosques, bazaars, sarais and an astonishing number of wells which are now in a dilapidated condition'.[86] Mangalsi, Rudauli and Raunahi, three major Muslim *qasbahs* which had been given a great boost as the seats of Shuja's nobility, fronted the road. All of these appear surrounded by tightly packed cultivation in the Orme maps.[87] The alluvial tract along the banks of the Ghagra was a natural surplus area which would have flourished in the absence of much irrigation, but seven or eight miles further out, the soil declines. Here the sandy subsoil makes *pakka* well irrigation essential so that without the sustained investment of the Nawabi notables the tract could never have been fertile or populous. Merchants also left their mark on the locality. The Jain temple at Raunahi-ki-Sarai was erected by merchants with Calcutta connections between 1780 and 1810, and completed a complex of wells, fixed bazaars and storerooms at this break-of-bulk point.

More direct evidence of the rural effects of the growth of the cities of Nawabi Awadh also exists. Peasants formed a reserve army for the early Nawabs. Service groups, like palankin bearers, watchmen and courtesans were drawn from the surrounding countryside. Asaf's great monuments in the city of Lucknow were said to have employed 40,000 people from the district during the horror of the 1783 famine,[88] while the father of the great nineteenth-century magnate, Darshan Singh, was a Kurmi from the hinterland[89] who drifted into the city in search of service. The pattern indeed is very similar to the picture of secondary economic growth created by service for the political elites which had

[85] Faiz Baksh, *Faizabad*, II, 8.
[86] *DG Fyzabad*, pp. 249–50; for general growth of Awadh revenues, see, Elliott, *Chronicles of Oonao*, p. 74.
[87] Route from Fyzabad to Lucknow, *c*. 1770, Orme 334, IOL.
[88] *Oudh Gazetteer*, II, 328.   [89] *Ibid.*, p. 79.

once vitalised the small towns of the Grand Trunk Road before the Mughal decline.

Moving to the south and east, the Benares kingdom appears to have provided a similar framework for the expansion of an integrated regional economy. Stable and rich clan areas were later linked by longer-distance trade and revenue demands. The *parganas* of Bhadohi and Kuchesar were to form the Raja of Benares' personal domains in the next century and were considered to be the home of his lineage. Neither of them was particularly 'productive' in the 1720s according to Sinha's figures,[90] but by the 1780s, the Orme maps and Duncan records reveal them to be in a high state of cultivation.[91] In Kuchesar, there is evidence of the building of embankments and irrigation tanks throughout the second half of the century by the cadets of the dominant Bhumihar lineage. We know that Balwant Singh secured Bhadohi from the Nawab in 1751 for his direct kinsmen. Here a low, preferential revenue-demand allowed cultivators to sink a large number of masonry wells and support a concentrated population. Only after 1795 did the Raja seek to increase his take from the prosperity of his kinsmen by pushing up the revenue.

On the basis of a secure patrimonial tract, the Raja's lineage then sought to branch outward and gain a closer control over the rich alluvial lands near Chunar and the banks of the Ganges. The whole new area was tied together by a network of marts controlled or protected by the Benares lineage. The *Balwantnamah* records that it was Balwant Singh who decided to encourage the growth of the town of Mirzapur as a typical river *ghat* market,[92] but one which could help increase the productivity of the riverain tracts. Ahraura, Chunar and Ramnagar (which became the seat of his palace) provided convenient points for the downriver grain trade which supplied the Raja's rapidly increasing armed forces.

The economic consequences of the rise of the successor states was most clearly in evidence where war *matériel* was concerned. Balwant Singh and his successor, Cheyt Singh, encouraged the development of one of the most celebrated horse markets in north India, the Dadri Fair,[93] held on the banks of the Ganges in Ballia District, which also became a celebrated Vaishnavite festival. Zamindars bred horses to help them pay their enhanced revenue, while the rulers needed large numbers of horses for their own armies now that the horse trade with

[90] Sinha, *Subah of Allahabad*, p. 147.
[91] Route from Benares to Jhusi, Orme 334, IOL; cf. *DG Benares, DG Mirzapur, DG Allahabad*.
[92] Sherring, *Tribes and Castes*, p. 370; Khairuddin Khan, *Balwantnamah*, tr. Curwen, p. 33; cf. 'Plaint of Kullender Gir Mohant', vol. 33, p. 527, Duncan Records, UPR.
[93] Note on Dadri Fair, BCJ, 19 July 1804, 129/7 IOL.

Afghanistan and central Asia was in turmoil. Stone from the Chunar stone *mahals* also served two purposes. It yielded an excellent regular income for the Raja who was assured that the rich merchants and priests of his cities would continue to build houses and temples. But it also provided stone for the general fortification of his territory which culminated in the construction of the great riverside palace at Ramnagar.

Benares was one of the fastest growing cities during the years 1750–90. It became the subcontinent's inland commercial capital after the decline of Murshidabad and the collapse of the Jagat Seths in Bengal in 1757. It received immigrant merchant capital from the whole of north India and stood astride the growing trade route from Bengal to the Maratha territories. Yet this was also a city which benefited from the sustained agricultural performance of the rich and stable tracts which surrounded it. In this growth, it was less the urban merchants who counted than a shadowy group of substantial rural men of capital which provided a link between the village economy and the towns. As in Baiswara, the emergence of a strong centralising regime served to intensify an autonomous growth in the countryside.

The figure who made this link – as important for trade as for the security of the land revenue – was the large agricultural shopkeeper (*bakkal* or *grihasta beopari*) or the commercial farmer (sometimes called *malik*). In the Benares records of 1786–92, we come across nineteen families or groups of men who had a combination of interests strung over a number of villages and small towns. These are the 'rural capitalists' recorded in Duncan's reports on interest rates in the region,[94] and their descendants appear in Cohn's analysis of property mutations in the same region in the 1820s and 1830s.[95] Based on large market towns, these men lent money to cultivators and provided them with capital and seed. The growth of Benares and other cities gave them the opportunity to market their grain, sugar and oil, from distances of up to fifty or sixty miles. In fact, these merchants continued to bring in grain from the interior districts despite the punitive tolls which zamindars levied on them until these were abolished by Jonathan Duncan in 1787. They must have made a considerable profit on the trade in order to be able to bear cumulative charges of up to 10 per cent of the market price of the commodity.

The majority of the families which could be put into this category of commercial farmer would not have been classed among the traditional merchant castes, but were drawn from artisan or even cultivating

94 Reports on rural interest rates, Benares, 4 July 1789, PR.
95 Cohn, 'Structural change', in Frykenberg, *Land Control*, pp. 73–5.

communities. The distilling caste, Kalwars, were particularly in evidence. They were found trading in grain and cloth from a number of small centres[96] and bringing pack-bullocks into Benares loaded with grain.[97] One group of Kalwars became farmers of the Chunar stone monopoly and controlled the cartmen and boat crews who brought in the stone for the spectacular physical expansion of Benares, Chunar and Mirzapur in the last quarter of the century. Dia Kalwar was farmer of the alcohol customs in Mirzapur and became a power in the fast growing city from his rural base in the adjoining subdivision of Kantit.[98] Oil men (Telis), market gardeners (Malis), and Kurmi agriculturalists, appear in the court cases as moneylenders and small town traders in and around Benares during the same period. One rural commercial magnate of this sort was Balchand Teli of the small town of Ghazipur who 'used to lend his bullocks and send them everywhere' and traded in oil and grain throughout the north of the Benares Raj.[99] The inventory of the property of the four sons of Sheo Dayal trading in partnership in four villages, twenty miles outside Benares,[100] gives a good indication of the range of interests of such firms:

Debts due by *assamis* (tenants)	Rs. 2,500
Jewels in pawn to Roy Ruttun	2,500
Jewels and ready money in house [in] Durga [?] Das	3,000
Balance on building house	2,700
Ferry boat at the *ghat*	75
Gold and silver at several places in pawn	500
In the Kinari [gold brocade] shop	1,600
Due from the iron burrao [?]	45
House in Kulwalee village	200
5 maunds brass utensils	400
Buffaloes [kept by Ahir and Goala tenants]	400
Cows	300
Bullocks for burden	200

These brothers hired cowherds to look after their herds: one witness deposed that they were owed a further Rs. 5,000 – 10,000 by debtors in various villages.

Precisely how widespread these rural commercial magnates were will

---

[96] Appeal of Ramsahay, 23 Mar. 1789, PR.

[97] 26 Oct. 1787, PR; grain was brought to Benares from as far as Nawabganj, Jaunpur, Nerwada (Azamgarh) and Gunjgaon (Jaunpur), 17 June 1788, PR; cotton travelled over even greater distances from Amraoti and Nagpur for the consumption of Benares and its weaving villages.

[98] Petition of Mirzapur Kalwars, 4 Mar. 1790, PR.

[99] Case of Balchand, 8 June 1793, PR; cf. *Beechuck Kulwar* v. *Meherban*, vol. 37, DR, pp. 14–162, UPR.

[100] *Sheo Dayal* v. *Ram Prasad*, Raja's Court, 5 June 1784, PR.

remain unclear. However, in the relatively undeveloped district of
Gorakhpur, less than a generation later, Hamilton Buchanan reported
that 30 per cent of the rural commercial families also owned some type of
operational holding and were directly involved in agriculture.[101] In the
district of Patna which resembled Benares more closely, he described a
category of merchant husbandmen (*grihasta beoparies*) who look very
similar to these Benares people:

Some traders among them ... possess a considerable stock in carriage cattle,
with a little money to enable them to trade from one market place to another. It
is also supposed, that a good many of the Koeris especially, who cultivate land
watered from wells, have money, partly lent out at interest, partly secreted; but
there are very few said to have above 1,000 rupees and 5,000 is said to be the
utmost extent which any one possesses.[102]

All these developments suggest again a pattern of commercial
development which arose within the agricultural society and then linked
up with growing urban demand produced by the emergence of the new
kingdoms. The rise of lower caste agrarian entrepreneurs has often been
seen as a feature of the nineteenth century and the British modernisation
of the economy. But some striking gains already appear to have been
made during the period of the Mughal successor states, for there is
evidence for similar changes in Bengal and the Punjab.

The growth of market relations?

Before moving on to the related problem of eighteenth-century urban
growth and decline, we will review the evidence for commercialisation
in this relatively prosperous and stable part of eastern Hindustan on the
eve of British rule. Commercialisation implies a market in factors of
production, 'land', labour and capital and also the existence of a produce
market for commodities. An integrated produce market clearly existed
in the hinterland of Benares at this period. River trade was well
developed and land transport between intermediate markets and *ganjs*
seems to have been surprisingly rapid. On the other hand, produce in
transit was taxed both by zamindars in the village of origin and by a large
number of magnates *en route*. Produce marketed included bulky
commodities such as timber, stone, wood, and basic food grains as well
as high value commodities. There is also some evidence of local
specialisation. The Jaunpur and Bhadohi *parganas* produced grain;
Azamgarh and the east already produced sugar; and Benares cotton for
everyday use was imported from the south so that its small crop of

---

[101] Martin, *Eastern India*, II, 408–10.
[102] *Ibid.*, I, 300, cf. *ibid.*, p. 165.

higher value cotton would be used for quality handicrafts. Production of vegetables, opium and indigo was also specialised, intensive and profitable, though cultivators seem almost exclusively to have been drawn from caste groups traditionally associated with these commodities.

Merchant capital was applied directly to agricultural production to an extent which was small but significant; government functions, monopolies and revenues were also farmed out to men of capital from both mercantile and landed backgrounds. This practice seems to have been on the increase under the Bhumihar rulers. Substantial 'private' investment in agriculture by magnates and traders took the form of construction of wells, tanks and groves. The supply of draught animals seems to have been put on a commercial footing in some areas, with substantial men hiring teams out for money. Rental and revenue-payment in kind were rapidly disappearing as farmers and notables pressed hard for cash. Yet there is little sign of the emergence of 'competition rents', except in the city and its immediate environs. Even here, *prajawat* was often customary, and throughout the great agricultural tracts, caste and the pitch of the land-revenue appear to have dominated rental rates. The Bhumihar rajas' state, with its expanding urban and service population and almost desperate desire to increase its control over cash resources, provided quite a favourable ground for the growth of market transactions of all sorts. There is no question of a massive shift in social relations. But the impression is of an open society with men of low inherited status rising to power and men of wealth invading the realm of kingly prerogative. This theme will be explored further in chapter 4 which shows how the trading and banking corporations of the Benares area had achieved considerable, if covert, political power within the state.

Conclusion

Even informed guesses at quantitative changes in the agricultural economy of the Ganges valley over the eighteenth century must await much more work. But the sketchy evidence available does suggest that there was no massive decline in overall production even though there was considerable physical movement of resources. Revenue figures adjusted for political circumstances, the estimates of trade discussed in later chapters, and the evidence of market foundation, all suggest that the 'decline in rents' bewailed by the chroniclers was a limited and local phenomenon.

There are some general considerations which have a bearing on this.

The movement of agricultural labour and capital clearly meant the abandonment of fixed stocks such as houses, wells, tanks and roads in the declining areas. But it is probable that Indian agriculture could adjust to this without too great a fall in production. The areas to which people migrated were often 'old fallows' so that the costs of opening them up were not as great as for virgin land. In the context of limited manuring techniques, movement from over-cropped areas round the old Mughal capitals may also have permitted medium-term increases in productivity per acre to offset losses. Obviously, the need for protection weighed heavily with farmers and merchants during the century; they were not making simple calculations of commercial profitability when they moved investments of labour and capital from one area to another. But Habib's work has left little doubt that this was also true in the Mughal period, so that this in itself need not be an argument for decline. Overall, then, growth and decline between 1730 and 1800 may have more nearly balanced out than has usually been appreciated.

On the other hand, there is strong evidence for economic growth and social change in the more stable core areas of the successor states. Awadh and Benares (and to a lesser extent the principalities of the west) had probably sustained commercialisation, local agricultural and artisan specialisation and a growth of urban populations since the late seventeenth century. The new regimes provided a more secure context for commerce, while their problems of cash flow nudged merchants and commercial farmers into a more significant social position. These tracts were also stimulated by the immigration of labour, capital and consuming aristocracies from the unstable areas.

Finally, it is important to stress that the areas of stable farming which we have been discussing were themselves in the process of slow expansion, despite the vicissitudes of war and famine. In Awadh and Benares, *ganj* foundation went ahead in both the jungle fringes and around the towns. In the west, the islands of agricultural wealth based on Farrukhabad, Rampur, the Jat kingdoms, and even Agra were all showing signs of expansion in the 1790s. Politics and relatively high population density both dictated this outward expansion. Rulers preferred new colonies which were more amenable to taxation; villagers would colonise empty tracts given the slightest improvement in security; the structure of the merchant family firm encouraged the foundation of new branch agencies run by enterprising younger sons.

Links between the stable areas also existed. As new aristocracies established themselves, they required the fine cloth goods, salt and spices which rulers expected to consume. But the so-called luxury trade which this created helped settle and revitalise the unstable tracts through which it flowed to the new centres of growth. Under the disturbed surface of the politics of the last decades of the century was forming a new pattern of stability. Agricultural production, trade and revenue provided the framework on which new empires could be reared. The British were lucky enough to inherit this opportunity.

3

Stability and change in towns and cities, 1770–1810

The previous two chapters have shown how the organisation of the north Indian regimes of the late eighteenth century and the patterns of consumption of their warrior aristocracies moulded significant areas of the agrarian economy. This chapter moves on to consider the towns, or rather the urban networks, of the period. Here the relationship between political power and flows of revenue and trade which lay at the heart of the new kingdoms can be examined in more detail. These towns have received little attention from historians. The evidence is sparse, and city life has seemed a dismal wreck of Mughal splendour, or a lost era before the arrival of the 'modern', colonial city. Yet there are several reasons why cities are worth study. First, it was between 1740 and 1810 that the dominant urban landholding and trading groups, which were to persist through until the 1930s and 1940s, established themselves. Secondly, it was the vitality of commercial links and their close interweaving with political power which made it possible for European commerce and government to function in the risky world of the north Indian plains. Lastly, the organisations of trade, religion and local defence which emerged or strengthened themselves at this time continued to evolve during the colonial period. Ultimately, some of them provided a direct link forward to the cultural and political associations of the later nineteenth century. Thus the issue which concerns us here is how towns and cities weathered the eighteenth century and the conditions which contributed to economic and geographical stability or change. First, however, some basic information must be provided.

The word town can be applied to a number of different levels in the hierarchy of central places in India.[1] The lowest level of this hierarchy was the humble periodic market of the peasant household (the *hath*) which had no urban features at all. Markets of this sort were regularly spaced across the countryside. But near-contemporary estimates suggest that most may have done little more than a few hundred rupees worth of business each year.[2] They were, after all, only the monetised

[1] R. Fox, 'Rajput "clans" and rurban centres in North India', in Fox (ed.), *Urban India. Society Space and Image* (Duke, North Carolina, 1970), pp. 167–85.
[2] For Gorakhpur, Martin, *Eastern India*, II, 574, cf. map opp. p. 291; for centres in Bareilly, CPR, 1 Oct. 1803, IOL.

tip of a large volume of exchanges within villages, or between neighbouring villages, which was conducted not through the market but through the *jajmani* system of ritual patronage. Above the level of the *hath* were the types of small fixed market centres discussed in the previous chapter: the *ganj* founded by the agents of regional political authority, and the fortress lineage-centre of the local zamindar or petty ruler. Rennell's maps of about 1770[3] and the route plans from which he drew them, suggest that these fixed markets were also regularly placed in the interior, where they functioned as primary bulking centres in the district grain and cotton trades, for instance. But there was also a marked congregation along major routes and navigable rivers. The Doab, with the Grand Trunk Road and the Ganges–Jamna boat traffic, was thickly clustered with fixed markets, as was the Fyzabad–Lucknow–Khairabad road in Awadh.

A congregation of fixed markets sometimes became, in effect, a small town. But the most obvious bottom rung of the urban hierarchy proper was the country town or *qasbah* which generally supported a population of more than 3,000. What distinguished such places, however, was not so much their population size as their social, legal and economic status. *Qasbahs* were the residence of gentry who served as soldiers or administrators for the regional states. Sometimes these were Hindu families of the warrior castes, but very often pedigree Muslim lineages. Land rights in country towns differed from those in the surrounding country. There was likely to be a concentration of revenue-free grants (*madad-i maash, waqf, inam*) for charitable purposes or as rewards for services. Most *qasbahs*[4] also supported bodies of artisans paying varieties of ground-rent and 'professional' tax. Technically, *qasbahs* were also supposed to provide the services of the Islamic judicial official called the *kazi*, and to have a mosque with its own *imam*. But these functions had often disappeared with the decline of the Mughals. As for Hindu worship in these small centres, it was more likely to be directed to the great gods of the Hindu pantheon than to the country deities and spirits who took precedence at the smaller places.

Above a population of 10,000, we can properly speak of cities. In 1770 there were sixty larger centres in our area, and they served many different functions.[5] But broadly, these can be classified into three groups. First, cities acted as retail centres and bulking points for their

[3] James Rennell, *Memoir of a Map of Hindostan* (2nd edn, London, 1792).

[4] H. H. Wilson, *Glossary of Judicial and Revenue Terms* (1855, new edn, Delhi, 1968), 'qasbah'; *Oudh Gazetteer*, ii, 312.

[5] The base used here is Rennell's 'A Map of Oude and Allahabad', used in conjunction with route maps, travellers' accounts and backward projections of British *chaukidari* statistics, 1814–20, see below p. 304.

immediate hinterlands which served areas with a radius of from fifteen
to twenty miles around them. Many goods in the villages were provided
along networks of small-scale carriers and through periodic religious
fairs. But salt, spices, fine grains and special iron goods seem to have
passed down the hierarchy in classic fashion. These local functions
were, of course, tied in with the working of the revenue system.
Secondly, larger towns were generally transit points for the longer-
distance, high value trades which is why so many brokers and merchants
congregated there. Generally they supported their own artisan
communities which produced for this level of trade. Thirdly, the last
group of functions was grouped around the service of regional rulers or
their great lieutenants and patterns of religious observance which drew
pilgrims and devotees from the whole region or subcontinent. The
stability of the large towns depended on how well they were able to
combine these roles, but the loss of one did not necessarily mean the
collapse of the others.

What was happening to urban populations in the late eighteenth
century? It is exceptionally difficult to say, given the lack of
documentation and the biases of contemporary accounts. But an
analysis of 180 substantial places based upon maps, descriptions, later
histories and scattered contemporary information makes the broad
patterns clear at least. First, as is well known, the three great cities of
Delhi, Agra and Lahore lost the primacy which they had jointly held in
the west of the Gangetic plain. In 1700, these places had all supported
populations of at least 400,000.[6] By 1800, two places with populations of
about 200,000 (Benares and Lucknow) had achieved a comparable
degree of dominance in their own regions, while the three imperial cities
had stabilised with populations around the 100,000 mark. The number
of cities in the next group, say from about 10,000 to about 100,000, does
not appear to have changed very much between 1730 and 1800. There
was, however, a good deal of movement between them. Jat and Rohilla
conquests in the west and the consolidation of the commercial economy
in the east brought into being a number of towns in this class.

The number of Mughal centres which declined absolutely was not
great. Only Korah-Jehanabad and Kara-Shahzadpur, which were both
in the lower Doab, fall into this category. Kara was already on the
decline in the later years of Akbar when Allahabad became the
provincial capital. The interruption of the river traffic above Allahabad
and the collapse of Mughal control on the Grand Trunk Road in the
mid-eighteenth century had reduced its proud Sayyid families to

[6] H. K. Naqvi, 'Progress of urbanisation in the United Provinces 1550–1800', *Journal of
the Economic History of the Orient*, x (1968), 81–101; *Urban Centres*, Ch. 1.

'beggary' by Tieffenthaler's time (*c.* 1755).[7] Korah, once a 'rich and populous city' and *sarai* station on the great through road, suffered a similar fate. In route maps of 1770, it occupied a large ground area,[8] and there was some building going on as late as this time. But unlike Jaunpur in the east or Aligarh and the Muslim *qasbahs* of Hariana in the west, it never stabilised at a lower level of population, and had virtually disappeared from the map by 1830. What happened in the case of these places was unusual. They had lost their political functions and their role in transit trade. But there had simultaneously been a sharp decline in the agricultural performance of the unstable lower Doab, as the previous chapter showed. No adequate surplus of revenue or produce remained to support them. By contrast, Jaunpur in the east lost its political function and saw the decline of its specialist artisans. As the centre of a rich hinterland, however, it managed to survive through the end-of-century crisis with a population of about 30,000.[9]

Turning to the lower reaches of the hierarchy of urban centres, it seems likely that the loss or decline of *ganjs* and *qasbahs* in the areas of decline in the west was at least balanced by the foundation of many small centres in the east. Indeed, even in the west the search for protection tended to gather people in to the remaining centres. So it could well be that the percentage of the population inhabiting places with distinct urban characteristics was larger at the end of the century than at the beginning, though there had been displacement of population from the largest into medium-sized and small places. A rough estimate might put about 15 per cent of the population in this class, about 7 per cent in towns with a population of over 5,000 and 3 per cent in cities of over 10,000.

What can be said about the towns' occupational structure? A variety of early eighteenth-century censuses exist for the towns of Hindustan, and their percentages seem to be compatible with those of S. P. Gupta for places in eastern Rajasthan in the 1740s.[10] They show merchants, traders and brokers accounting for about 30 per cent of the registered population, which bears out the importance of transit trade for them. Another 20 per cent is accounted for by artisans, with weavers as the largest single group; a further 20 per cent can be attributed to 'services' of all sorts, including personal servants in the modified *jajmani* system

---

[7] Tieffenthaler in Bernouilli, *Description*, I, 233–4; A. Deare, *A Tour through the Upper Provinces of Hindustan* (London, 1823), pp. 233–4; Forster, *Journey*, I, 91; Fida Hussain Obeidi, 'Tarikh-i-Kara', MSS Mohulla Bazaar, Kara, and interviews, 1973.

[8] Route Maps of the Lower Doab, Orme 6, 334 and xvi, IOL; *DG Fatehpur* p. 252.

[9] 15 Mar. 1788, PR, cf. *chaukidari* statistics, Mirzapur Judicial, vol. 28, UPR.

[10] Satya Prasad Gupta, 'Evidence for urban population and its composition from 17th–18th century Rajasthan', mimeo, n.d. History Department, Aligarh Univ.

which existed in the towns, and people involved in transport.

In view of the structure of the economy, we would not expect any major change between the mid-eighteenth and mid-nineteenth century. What was more important was the change in geographical distribution of urban and mercantile occupations, and relative changes in the incomes of different groups. But two classes of people certainly did bulk larger in the eighteenth-century cities than those of the 1830s. First, there was the soldiery. The figures for soldiers given in chapter 1 relate to well-equipped standing armies who were usually located in or near the major towns. Thus Cheyt Singh's personal forces at Ramnagar or Rajghat in Benares in 1780 must have amounted to 10 per cent of the city's population,[11] while Maratha forces in Agra in the late 1790s probably represented at least 7 per cent of its diminished population.[12] This is exclusive of the large numbers of military artisans and camp-followers engaged by the forces. A second group of people who do not appear as a category in either contemporary or later enumerations were the indigent or 'seekers of protection' who are mentioned by the incoming British, especially in the western towns. Maintaining themselves by periodic labour, charity or scavenging, these people must have accounted for a high proportion of town-dwellers. In 1813–14 when commerce had begun to pick up, 44 per cent of the total households in the provinces' larger towns were officially classified as too poor to pay the rigorously managed British police tax.[13] Some of these were evidently indigent artisans, but others were the detritus of war and local agricultural collapse in the west.

The cities of the Ganges valley are unique for their variety and antiquity. In the north-west where Muslims accounted for up to 45 per cent of their population, volatile Muslim state-builders lorded over and cajoled merchant and artisan dynasties of Punjabi origin. Standing on the Red Fort one can almost smell the bracing dry winds of Central Asia. In the south-west, the Muslim presence was already dwindling before our period. Hindu traders and warlords of Rajasthan and the Deccan plateau had annexed its cities into their orbit. In the rice-growing lands of the east, cities were deeply embedded in the slower-moving rhythms of the neo-traditional Hindu kingdoms, but an advancing European presence was beginning to swell and transform their trade. Yet the fate of all these cities depended upon a few basic conditions: the stability of

---

[11] W. Hastings, *A Narrative of the Insurrection at Banaris* (Calcutta, 1782), pp. 43–5; I have under-estimated the 1780 city population at about 150,000.

[12] *Wellesley Despatches*, III, 399–400; a garrison of *c.* 7,000 compared with a city population of *c.* 60,000–90,000.

[13] Mirzapur Judicial, vol. 28, *chaukidari* statistics; Bayly, 'Town-building in north India, 1780–1830', *Modern Asian Studies*, ix (1975), 500.

their ruling groups, the role of religious practice in maintaining population and services, and the adaptability of their merchants and artisans. The following section discusses the political and administrative element in the cities in order to throw more light on the working of the pre-colonial regimes.

Ruling groups on the move

Analysis of the administrative and aristocratic element of the Indian city has not proceeded very far since Max Weber. His peripatetic, court-and-camp model of the city was itself drawn from a tradition which went back to Bernier and Manucci.[14] They saw in the Mughal city a Central Asian horde temporarily immobilised in wattle and daub. The idea of the city as a slightly more permanent form of military encampment whose physical movement was determined by military and political fortune has much to recommend it. But the pattern of town-building will become clearer and richer once the meaning of the city within contemporary Indian politics is appreciated. The movement of ruling groups between one centre and another was often a physical expression of their social organisation and conceptions of the nature of legitimate power. Problems of legitimacy and changes of rank among regional ruling groups gave rise to an intrinsic urban fluidity, but on the other hand, the continuing significance of Mughal authority and the charisma of Mughal centres provided a degree of stability.

An analysis of the darbar and the links formed around it is one key to the nature of the city. No neat formula, such as 'patrimonialism', 'feudalism' or the heritage of the Central Asian Khanate seems adequate to describe the complexity of relations within the darbar. What was most striking was the fluidity of ties. The nizam or nawab was, like the Mughal before him, an 'entrepreneur in political power'. Like the entrepreneur, he dealt in different coin. Some relationships were based on military fealty and land control (*jaidad* or *jagir*); others were bonded by common tribe or 'homeland' (*qam*); yet others arose simply from fate or chance; a Lucknow dancing-girl was later to complain that the British had substituted 'administration' for 'favour', that the handsome favourite could no longer become ruler. The patrimonial aspect of the ruler's power was also constrained by the religious context. A ruler needed to be legitimate in the eyes of the powerful Islamic elites of writers, jurists and service communities. He had to offer them patronage and also sustain the life of the community of the faithful. More subtly, no regime could hope to become a dynasty unless it

14 See, e.g., F. Braudel, *Capitalism and Material Life 1400–1800* (London, 1973), p. 410.

adjusted itself to the predilections of the mass of its Hindu subjects.

Awadh provides some good examples of dynastic town-building. It was not chance that Awadh's first semi-independent ruler, Saadat Khan, abandoned the old provincial capitals and 'pitched his tent' near the ancient Hindu city of Ajodyha, the *haveli khas* (headquarters) and cultural capital of the region. Saadat Khan quickly constructed for himself the elements of the city of Fyzabad from the social relationships at hand. Round his modest 'bungalow' he built a bastion and a wall which enclosed the key groups in the continuation of his lineage – his dependent eunuchs, his harem and his stables. At a greater distance were located the Mughal nobles who kept open his connection with the Delhi court, the merchants who provisioned his military bazaar, and his troops.

The history of the cities of Awadh emphasises once again the peripatetic nature of the administrative part of the Indian city. The historian of Fyzabad noted wryly that its founder Saadat Khan had 'little fancy for masonry'. Yet it was not only military and prudential concerns which contributed to this air of impermanency. There was an indeterminacy at the very heart of the Indo-Muslim concept of sovereignty. No single attribute, whether royal blood, military prowess, or primogeniture, clearly marked out the succession of a Muslim ruler. The successor simply emerged from the complex of relations of blood and favour which surrounded his predecessor's court and harem. Power had to be asserted; it was not transferred. The dead ruler's wives and brothers might make a bid for part of the patrimony, just as they might try for a partition of the ordinary joint-family. A ruler marked himself out by the power of his clients and the pomp with which he ruled. Essential for him was a 'place' – a darbar, a city – where he was completely dominant and where he could exercise his authority without the rivalry of the shades of the dead or the envious living.

The need of rulers to found new cities around them is splendidly exemplified by the constant flux of urban material from Lucknow to Fyzabad between 1740 and 1800. Shuja-ud Daulah, the third Nawab, moved his military and political establishment back to Lucknow until his disastrous war with the English Company in 1763–4. After this he heeded the 'friendly advice'[15] of the Farrukhabad ruler, Ahmed Khan Bangash, that

> if he now recovered the government of the province, not to trust the Mughals, but to make use of his own dependents and eunuchs and make Faizabad his capital.[16]

[15] Sharar, *Last Phase*, p. 30.   [16] Faiz Baksh, *Faizabad*, II, 4.

The Nawab went to Fyzabad and restructured the centre of the city in keeping with the new political order. He 'built anew and on a grander scale the walls of Burhan-ul Mulk [Saadat Khan]'s old citadel and raised the house of the Mughals'. Then he settled numbers of his own retainers and eunuchs immediately around the central enclosure, circling the whole with a number of cantonments containing over 100,000 troops fitted with British ordnance and muskets. Finally, he established a massive grain market to serve the whole complex.[17]

The next cycle began with the accession of Shuja's son, Asaf-ud Daulah.[18] The new ruler found it difficult to establish his personal authority in Fyzabad where the city was dominated by the vast households of the two famous Begums of Awadh, respectively the wife and sister of his father. At the mercy of favourites and plots emanating from their darbars, Asaf decided to remove his court again to Lucknow, and 'all the equipments and surroundings of his wealth and grandeur were by degrees transferred to Lucknow ... and everything connected with government and the state gathered there'.[19] The force of administrative fiat in town-building was sharply instanced by the case of one Mirza Nadir Ali who was summarily executed for not removing himself from Fyzabad to Lucknow with sufficient speed, despite the plea that he could not find carriage.[20] Yet while a large sector of the urban population simply moved off from Fyzabad, it did not wholly collapse, any more than Lucknow had done when its rival was pre-eminent. The courtly and aristocratic consumption declined dramatically along with the merchants who had supplied it, but the city continued to perform local revenue and agricultural functions besides remaining residence of the now diminished households of the Begums and their supporters.

Cities were even more important in the establishment of power and legitimate rule by the humbler martial families who rose to power. Rulers such as the Bangash Nawabs of Farrukhabad needed not only to establish a position in the Mughal diplomatic system, but also to maintain themselves against old comrades and clansmen who resented their claim to the rights of sultan. The rise of Farrukhabad was particularly significant because this new foundation was to become the key centre for British commercial and political expansion in the upper

---

[17] *Ibid.*

[18] Barnett, *North India*, pp. 43–4; A. L. Srivastava, *The First Two Nawabs of Awadh* (Delhi, 1943).

[19] Faiz Baksh, *Faizabad*, II, 34; R. Llewellyn-Jones, 'The city of Lucknow before 1856', in K. Ballhatchet and J. B. Harrison (eds), *The City in South Asia. Pre-Modern and Modern* (London, 1980), pp. 88–128.

[20] Faiz Baksh, *Faizabad*, II, 83.

Ganges valley. The Pathan warriors from whom emerged Muhammad Khan, its founder, had inhabited a number of large villages on the right bank of the Ganges to the north of the ancient city of Kanauj.[21] Fighting on behalf of the Mughals against the Hindu rajas of central India, these Hindustani Pathans maintained a strong corporate form of organisation which was reinforced by the regular arrival of recruits and brides from the northern hills of their home tribes. Reward in the empire's service was one quarter of all plunder and protection money taken in campaigns; the Pathans maintained a secure fund for the upkeep of the widows of men killed in action. An exceptional war leader like Muhammad Khan was awarded a further *jagir* in central India. Like other successful mercenaries and service people, he founded his own 'place' and fortress at the village of Kaimganj.[22] But while he lived among his own clansmen and the haughty brotherhoods of other Pathan tribes who thought themselves superior, Muhammad Khan was simply first among equals:

The Pathans would not allow him to ride an elephant through the streets for fear of their womens' privacy being infringed. Afridis, Toyas and Khazadas [other Pathan tribes] were numerous but the Bangash were very few. If the Nawab did pass by, the Afridi boys threw clay pellets at him.[23]

In the 1710s, therefore, Muhammad Khan made the crucial leap between the status of tribal warlord and that of sultan and Mughal noble. He founded the city of Farrukhabad to be the seat of his own court, the repository of his women and wealth; and he took steps to counteract the equality of tribalism by founding his own tribe. But while the search for the status of sultan required an act of town-building, it was the resources of the land and the availability of water which determined where the new city should be. Muhammad Khan chose one of the most fertile and densely peopled parts of the Ganges river-bank for his new capital. Here the subsoil was firm and water was close to the surface of the land; there was a saying that 'at Farrukhabad there is a well in every house'.

The political ambitions of Muhammad Khan and his successors determined the plan of settlement within the new town and throughout the surrounding countryside. Quite soon after the building began, the Nawab set about founding a quasi-caste of warriors and administrators

---

[21] For the social background to this movement see Iqbal Hussain, 'Agrarian change in Farrukhabad District, late 18th and first half of 19th century – a study of a local collection of documents', mimeo. paper, n.d., History Department, Aligarh Univ.

[22] Irvine, *JASB*, xlvii (1878), 276; these articles are based on Sayyid Waliullah, 'Tarikh-i-Farrukhabad', written about 1830:

[23] *Ibid.*, p. 277.

who would be entirely dependent on himself and counter the envy of the non-Bangash Pathans. These 'sons of the state' (*tifl-i-sarkar*), or 'disciples' (*chelas*) as they later came to be called, were children taken from Muslim and Rajput families, or the offspring of various concubines. They were brought up in one of the ruler's many harems and fed, equipped and married at his command. Before Muhammad Khan's death, the original plan of keeping the various tribes and castes separate had broken down, and they formed a homogeneous group of nearly 4,000.[24] Thus Muhammad Khan had founded his own Muslim tribe or caste, but to increase his independence further, he also encouraged large colonies of Bangash and other client communities to come from the northern hills to Farrukhabad, where they were settled.

As time went on, the *chelas* were settled with their own women, households and treasuries on the fringes of the new city. Inside this defensive circle were planted the colonies of Bangash and merchant communities like the Soods who were encouraged to settle by the award of privileges and exemption from taxation. At the centre of the city stood the symbols of the Nawab's sultanate – his audience hall, his private establishment of women, his stables and treasuries. In the following century, the small size of the urban divisions of Farrukhabad still attested to their origin as the great houses of the *chelas*, and the chief men of the 'quarters' were often descendants of the original grantee.[25]

Once again, the organisation of the city reflected the social structure of the ruling elites. But Muhammad Khan also had to make sure that none of his own followers had learned his teaching too well. He could not allow anyone who had taken a temporary lien of a grant of land-revenue to perpetuate his own power by the foundation of a local stronghold and market where resources could gradually be built up independently of the dynasty. The *chelas* and other officers of state were, therefore, forbidden to construct *ganjs* of stone, and the mud-brick market centres where they were allowed to collect their revenue had to escheat to the state on the death of the founder. There was one significant exception to this. Nawab Yaqut Khan, prime minister (*diwan*) and eunuch, was allowed the privilege of building in stone like the Nawab himself. He founded no less than eleven major markets in Farrukhabad and Etah Districts before 1750. Of him the Nawab remarked 'that he could never have children, and that it did not much matter what buildings he left to revert to the state on his death'.[26]

A degree of flux between central places was intrinsic to the Indian social order. It did not derive from any particularly morbid

[24] *Ibid.*, p. 341.   [25] Interviews, family histories, Farrukhabad, 1973.
[26] Irvine, *JASB*, xlvii (1878), 231.

characteristics of pre-colonial political life, but simply reflected the working out of conflicts of authority. The case of the Rohilla towns north-east of Delhi is particularly relevant here. This was among the most urban regions of India, with between 15 and 20 per cent of the population living in towns or distinctly urban *qasbahs*. But it was also an area where European observers tended to confuse the intrinsic shifting of urban material associated with the culture and politics of the Rohilla leadership with the effects of the real economic decline which accompanied the Nawab of Awadh's conquest and spoliation of the area in 1774.

Rohillas were an invading warrior 'slave caste' with an established urban form of life which responded to their need for protection as much as to a predilection for towns. They had something in common with the Mamelukes or other Middle Eastern ruling groups. Looked down upon by other established Pathan families, the Rohillas were a mixture of pedigree Pathan families who had fallen on hard times, converted Hindus, and soldier adventurers from the north-western mountains. They were in the process of developing a tribal identity which expressed real or fictive kinship and newly forged marriage alliances. Like other Afghans, they were full of the pride of ancestry, tracing their genealogies back to Abraham. The aim of the Afghan chief was to establish himself as a prince within the Mughal diplomatic system and 'live of his own' on a *jagir* which was appropriate to his standing and guaranteed the honour of his sons and dependents. The revenue-grant they sought was not so much a delimited fiefdom as an urban fortress centre which commanded the labour and tribute of a designated number of surrounding villages. It resembled the head towns and dependencies (*cabaceras* and *sujetos*) established by the Spanish conquistadores in New Spain. Again, a specifically urban centre was required where all the physical adjuncts of the sultan could be assembled: a darbar hall and a hall for settling disputes, a well-fortified palace and harem, and a treasury. Ali Muhammad, the first notable Rohilla leader, went about securing these objectives in a systematic fashion. In the early 1740s, when Delhi was still distracted by the invasion of Nadir Shah,[27] he seized the Kutheir Rajput stronghold of Aonla.[28] Then seeking to establish a recognised place with the Mughals, he sent an ambassador (*vakil*) to the Emperor requesting a charter and 'promising ... at the same time punctually to remit the tribute to His Majesty'.[29] Ali Muhammad was shortly rewarded with the title of Nawab and the high

[27] Mustajab Khan, 'Gulistan-i-Rehmat', tr. Elliott, *Life of Hafeez-ool Moolk*, pp. 12–13.
[28] Tieffenthaler in Bernouilli (ed.), *Description*, I, 140.
[29] Mustajab Khan, 'Gulistan', p. 16.

dignity of carrying his own drums, though revenue-payments soon lapsed.

Within a few years the Rohillas had made a bid for control of the whole territory of the Rajputs of Kutheir. Ali Muhammad quickly placed his revenue-collectors in the other conquered Rajput headquarters such as Moradabad, Sambhal and Shahjahanpur. But he 'did not take possession of the town of Bareilly till sometime afterward when having obtained a sunnud [charter] from the king he was proclaimed hakim [sole ruler] of Kutheir'.[30] For while Aonla represented the fortress home of Ali Muhammad's lineage within India, his legitimate power within the Mughal polity could best be expressed at Bareilly which had long been the centre of Mughal fiscal and diplomatic activity in the region. There followed one of the periodic shifts of wealth, followers and military resources from one town to the other as Bareilly grew and Aonla declined once again to a local strong point. Later in the century, William Tennant used the 'melancholy decay' of Aonla as an example of the irrevocable decline of contemporary India,[31] but what had really happened was the systematic movement of urban material from one centre to another as an expression of changing political status.

The next phase of Rohilla history saw the death of Ali Muhammad and the rise of his uncle Hafiz Rehmat Khan as the regent to his sons. Between 1750 and 1770, therefore, there followed a further general dispersion of Rohilla warbands under the leadership of Ali Muhammad's family to other town centres in the area.[32] First, his six sons were assigned sizeable revenue grants and sent off to create miniature Bareillys in their own domains. Next as the power of Rehmat Khan grew, his own town of Pilibhit was adorned with its own large darbar hall, mosque and generous harem.[33] The shifting political pattern was reflected in the size of the grant and the number of mounted warrior nobles or *rissaldars* sent to attend the chief personages of the state. Finally, after the Rohilla defeat by the British and the Nawab of Awadh in 1774, the whole Rohilla political structure was dissolved with a consequent decline in the size of its royal towns. One son alone, Fyzullah Khan, was allowed the rich and stable lands of Rampur in grant and created there an Indian state which survived until 1947. But at least half the Rohilla military nobility were banished to the west side of the Ganges. The tight, town-based tribal structure of the Rohillas was not to re-establish itself until the early days of British rule, but many of

---

[30] *Ibid.*, p. 18. [31] Tennant, *Recreations*, II, 293; Forster, *Journey*, I, 112.
[32] Hamilton, *Origin and Progress of Rohillas*, pp. 116–17.
[33] Mustajab Khan, 'Gulistan', p. 47.

its features persisted into the mid-nineteenth century. One Rohilla subdivision remained known as the 'Rohillas of the Twelve Towns', an indication of the close connection between urban and genealogical history.[34] Within the cities, too, tribal subdivisions were reflected in the organisation of individual quarters where lineage elders continued to hold juridical power until the 1830s or 1840s.

On the face of it, the court-and-camp theory of Indian cities works well for Rohilkhand. But some qualifications must be added. The shifting pattern of town centres was a product not merely of instability and conflict, but of certain features of the social organisation of the Rohilla ruling group. Evidently, the size of an urban population and economy determined, within very broad bounds, the dignity of the prince to whom it could be assigned in *jagir*. But political overlordship could itself, to a considerable extent, modify the commercial and agricultural base. The settlement of Fyzullah Khan and 10,000 troopers on Rampur set up new agrarian dependencies and new commercial links that soon increased its revenue-bearing capacity from Rs. 5 lakhs per annum to Rs. 30 lakhs.[35] What we see then is a mutual adaptation between the grades of the Rohilla social order and the economic resources of the regional economies; ecology and society moulded each other.

Other eighteenth-century systems of towns showed similar features. The military fortunes of the Jat and Rajput kingdoms during the course of the century pushed some towns into prominence and damaged others. Changes in the long-distance trade routes which traversed these territories also affected the fortunes of their bazaars. Yet the social organisation of Jat and Rajput lineages also contributed a deeper set of eddies and flows between the small towns of Jatwara and Rajasthan which denied any one of them an absolute pre-eminence. Both Rajputs and aspirant Jats ranked their dominant lineages in terms of notions of purity and seniority which were quite independent of the immediate political and military standing of the small states. Since the most powerful lineages always sought to marry into those of the highest ritual standing and since marriage alliances involved the alienation of land grants from one to the other, there was a continual tension between political power and ritual rank. This continuously redistributed resources from larger military centres to the smaller but prestigious centres of the senior lineages and helped maintain the dispersed pattern

---

[34] K. Lachman Singh, *Historical and Statistical Memoir of Zillah Bulandshahar* (Allahabad, 1874), pp. 118, 192.
[35] W. Hamilton, *Gazetteer*, p. 698; Forster, *Journey*, I, 218.

of towns which was characteristic of medieval Rajasthan.[36]

Nevertheless, against all this fluidity, two features of the eighteenth-century political scene provided some degree of continuity and stability. It is now recognised that even during the years of its greatest political disarray, the principles of imperial supremacy and the ranking of powers and principalities within the Mughal diplomatic system remained significant as a theory of imperial rule. The *barakat* or charisma of the imperial title, the gradual emergence of the concept of Timurid royal blood, and the idea of the need for Delhi as a symbolic centre remained powerful. This was recognised by the poor Muslims of Benares who gave arms to a holy man when he produced an imperial charter. It was recognised by the Marathas who prized imperial titles and encouraged Shah Alam to seek their protection in his imperial city after 1772. It was recognised even by the British who made elaborate arrangements for the reception of the imperial prince Jahandar Shah in Benares,[37] and plotted for thirty years to neutralise the influence of the Marathas over the Delhi court. In all the major north Indian cities, including Hindu and British Benares, the honour of imperial blood and titles caused rulers to make assignments of revenue for the pensions of fleeing dignitaries. Indeed, large *mohullas* and whole communities of moneylenders and purveyors grew up around the exiled Jahandar Shah in Benares[38] and the exiled High Steward of the Empire in Lucknow.[39]

Cities survived in part because they had long been the centre of imperial official business and therefore continued to be the natural centres for diplomatic activity and the places where the great bankers, skilled in the empire's fiscal business, survived in straitened circumstances. It was to cities such as Allahabad or Bareilly that aspiring adventurers came to receive imperial titles and establish their mints. Above all, this was true of Delhi which continued to receive inflows of subsidy and diplomatic gifts (*nazar*) even when the earlier vast flows of revenue were staunched after 1740. Delhi in decline was as powerful a shadow as imperial Rome had been for barbarian Europe, and any power with aspirations to a continental role had to maintain a presence there. Consequently, the heart of the city continued to beat even during

---

[36] Cf. Henri Stern, 'Power in traditional India: territory, caste and kinship in Rajasthan', in R. Fox (ed.), *Realm and region*, pp. 52–78; cf. the cases of *jagir* fission through inheritance recorded in Lachman Singh, *Bulandshahar*, p. 130.

[37] Correspondence with Jahandar Shah, 5 May 1788, PR.

[38] Viz. the *mohulla* of Shivala in Benares, see Agency Files (Persian) on the pensions of the Mughal descendants, UPR; correspondence with local moneylenders, Ratnakar Collection.

[39] Sharar, *Last Phase*, pp. 30–5.

the terrible decades of the 1760s and 1780s.

Successful courtiers and traders continued to construct mosques, temples, grandiose private houses and public wells in Delhi. For the central walled city, we have a remarkably comprehensive list of noteworthy buildings compiled by the Archaeological Survey of India in its *List of Hindu and Muhammadan Monuments of Delhi*.[40] This can be supplemented with material from the gazetteers and from Sir Sayyid Ahmed Khan's later work, *Asar-us Sanadid*.[41] On the basis of inscriptions and recorded custom, it was possible to date a large percentage of ruins and surviving structures and gain an impression of the number of building-starts for the various decades of Delhi's history. The list suggests that there was a general decline in major building projects after 1740, but by no means a total cessation. It is noteworthy that the number of monuments and large houses started in the period 1780–1800 was scarcely less than in the period 1800–20 when security was supposed to have returned to the city. There was clearly much wealth still around; but in whose hands?

A recognisable group of new structures was established by members of the imperial family, despite their penury during the 1780s, and by major Mughal officials and rulers of the 'successor states'. For instance, a whole complex of buildings, maintained and enhanced during the 1760s and 1770s, was put in by Muhammad Khan Bangash of Farrukhabad.[42] The representatives of new, non-Muslim powers were even more in evidence. Maratha supremacy was recorded in stone between 1783 and 1803, as was the growing power of the East India Company and its local supporters. Notable among this class was the great house called 'Chhata Shahji' built by Nawab Shadi Khan who was the agent of the Marathas at Delhi through whom the emperor's allowance to them was paid.[43] Shadi Khan was also the city's superintendent of weights and measures (*muhtasib*) and gained from the continuing buoyancy of the city as a terminus of the trade to Central Asia. He built a bridge on the proceeds of toll receipts and moneylending. By contrast, the large and imposing house of Bhowani Shankar was established by a wealthy Khattri who was for a time a local

[40] *Archaeologial Survey of India: Muhammadan and Hindu Monuments of Delhi*, 1, *Shahjahanabad* (Delhi, 1910); cf. W: Francklin, 'An account of the present state of Delhi', *Asiatick Researches*, iv (1795), 425, 'the modern city of Shah Jehanabad is rebuilt and contains many good houses chiefly of brick'.

[41] Sayyid Ahmed Khan, 'Asar-us-Sanadid', tr. in part, Garcin du Tassy *Journal Asiatique*, 5e série, xv, xvi, xviii (1869), see esp. xviii, 89–93.

[42] *Monuments*, 1, 4 for the origin of this connection see Nawab Durga Quli Khan Bahadur, 'Muraqqai-i-Dihli', *c*. 1740, Hindi trs. Dr Muhammad Umer, *Muhammad Shah Rangole ki Dilli* (Bharat Prakashan Mandir, Aligarh, 1970), esp. pp. 17–23.

[43] *Monuments* 1, 303.

agent of the British, while another agent built a large religious building (*imambara*) during the same period.[44]

Another feature to put against the fluidity of ruling groups in the cities was the persistence in outlying quarters of resident military and official gentry. Local families of this sort controlled land-rights and bazaars in larger cities in the same way as their relatives controlled the smaller country towns. In most cases, some members of such families were permanently in the service of regional rulers, and moved from place to place alongside their masters. But from the beginning of the previous century, gentry families had shown an increasing tendency to build up pockets of local power and wealth in settled spots. They were loath to abandon these simply because a great magnate moved his base of operations elsewhere. Sometimes these families were also tied into networks of patronage and land-control associated with the tombs of saints or with mosques. Thus, for instance, we find suburban villages such as Dariabad, Niwan, Rasulpur and Osmanpur situated around Allahabad.[45] These remained the home places of Pathan 'gentlemen' even in the bad years at the end of the century, when the Emperor and Nawab of Awadh had deserted the place. In Lucknow, a powerful family of Sheikhzadas similarly continued to preserve their influence in the suburban quarters of the Nawab's own city.[46] Just as regional rulers had carefully to sustain relations with the commercial men of the bazaars by favourable rates of taxation, so also they needed to mollify the suburban gentry by appointing their members to local public office (usually to be *kazi* or *kotwal*) or by enhancing their grants of revenue-free land. Such resident gentry provided another species of ballast for the volatile urban economies of these years.

Religion and social organisation outside the village

The political order was reflected in the towns and cities. They rose and fell as a consequence of conflicts between competing regimes and local agricultural decline. But much of the fluidity of urban life responded to the flexible organisation of the ruling groups and their notion of the role of cities in the assertion or maintenance of legitimate rule. Here, the 'instability' of the hierarchy of centres did not imply the disruption of urban societies for military, merchant and service families were organised so that they could adapt to rapid movement. Religious practice showed similar features. In general, it served to maintain the

[44] *Ibid.*, pp. 364, 366.
[45] Interviews, family histories, Dariabad, Niwan, Allahabad District, 1968, 1972.
[46] Sharar, *Last Phase*, pp. 37–44.

level of urbanisation and continuity in town centres. But it is important to take account of forms of local instability which were sometimes wrongly assimilated into the picture of general decline.

The number of people who subsisted mainly on income from religious office was large. If we extrapolate backward from the mid-nineteenth-century figures,[47] then as much as 5 per cent of the population of the area were domestic or temple priests and members of the Muslim learned classes. Religious mendicants of all sorts accounted for a further 5 per cent as late as 1880, and the percentage was certainly greater a century earlier when it was swelled by the success of the Gosains as traders and soldiers. The Atal Nagar Akhara alone was supposed to have had 300,000 members 'during the time of the Delhi Badshahs [Emperors]', and Gosain armies of men such as Umrao Giri and Himmat Bahadur sometimes reached 50,000 or more.[48] Withdrawal from the world (*sannyas*) was also a stage of the Hindu cycle of life. Pious merchants often handed over their businesses to a successor in middle age and took to a wandering life. But the role of ascetics and religious men in the community was naturally greatest in centres such as Allahabad, Benares, Muttra and Gaya, which had a reputation as holy places. There were more than 40,000 Brahmins living on charity in Benares city alone about 1810 accounting for 17–20 per cent of the population.[49]

In the cult centres, the more elevated ritual specialists such as river priests and hereditary temple priests formed close-knit bodies inhabiting separate residential areas. Alongside them should be mentioned the lower specialist castes which played a vital and exclusive part in the major rites of passage. Barbers (Nais) were prominent in the ritual organisation of the high castes, and also acted as diplomatists between the small eighteenth-century courts, achieving considerable social advancement in the Benares area. Doms and Mahabrahmins washed the dead and officiated at burials and their services were required by most Hindu communities. Later figures suggest that these inferior ritual servants may have accounted for a further 2–3 per cent of the total population. Of course, this ritual service economy cannot easily be separated from other occupations. Gosains became the largest property owners in Benares,[50] Mirzapur, Nagpur and Ujjain by 1750,

---

[47] Crooke, *North Western Provinces*, p. 205.   [48] Sarkar, *Dasnamis*, p. 89.

[49] House Census of Benares, *c.* 1799, Valentia, *Voyages*, I, App. I, 462–4, shows just under 20% of all houses occupied by Brahmins 'living on charity'. The overall figures of population given by this census are hopelessly exaggerated but the classification of houses by occupations seems more reliable, based as it is on *phatakhbandi* returns.

[50] *Ibid.*, shows 10,000 permanently resident Gosains (and Bairagis) joined by 35,000 pupils at various auspicious times. There was considerable *math* building in the city between 1760 and 1800, see, e.g., the '*arzi* of Narrow Punt', DR, vol. 49, p. 45 (1788). The census records 500 *maths*, but eighteenth-century property deeds in the hands of

and the Chaube Brahmins of Muttra[51] who officiated at the Vaishnavite shrines also became moneylenders in the villages around the holy city. Nevertheless, patterns of worship were a considerable influence on the region's economic geography.

In addition to the fixed population of religious specialists, the pilgrim population was a major influence on the organisation of the economy through markets, bazaars and fairs, providing significant extra income for rulers who collected pilgrim dues. In the year 1786, as many as 170,000 Maratha pilgrims elected to increase their merit by travelling to Allahabad in an opulent armed convoy.[52] Auspicious bathing days at Allahabad, Benares, Gaya and Hardwar continued to attract pilgrims in numbers more than 100,000 strong during the festivals at the end of the eighteenth century, despite the troubled political conditions. The economic consequences of pilgrimage can be assessed in more detail in the cases of Allahabad and Hardwar. The direct takings of river priests alone at Allahabad during the bad year of 1786 were said to amount to Rs. 17,000.[53] This was equivalent perhaps to the total annual income of about 350 urban households, or 2,500 people at a time when the city's population may have been as low as 20,000. The propensity of the ascetic orders to hoard was high, but such inflows of wealth generated demand for goods and services. At the very least, corporate religious bodies invested in substantial building during the late eighteenth century. In Benares, there was said to be one 'chooltrie' or religious rest house for every ten houses in 1816;[54] the construction of religious buildings was a major influence on the flourishing trade in dressed stone which was itself controlled by the ascetic orders.

The Hardwar fair, by contrast, was not associated with any major town, but provided substantial benefits to the surrounding villages. All pilgrims were required to pay a tax to the local Brahmins and to the village headmen. This was exclusive of the duties levied on the goods brought for sale at the fair. Another way in which the inhabitants enriched themselves was

by raising the price of grain, and articles of provision though upon balance this is not much against the visitors who bringing along with them the production of their respective countries, dispose of their goods to advantage at Hurdwar.[55]

Chaukhambha and Dassaswamedh families suggest that a large proportion of house property was in addition owned by them.
51 F. S. Growse, *Mathura. A District Memoir* (1882, new edn Delhi, 1979), pp. 9–10.
52 Tennant, *Recreations*, II, 247; Mrs N. Kindersley, *Letters from the Island of Teneriffe, Brazil, the Cape of Good Hope and the East Indies* (London, 1777), p. 261.
53 Tennant, *Recreations*, II, 247; Forster, *Journey*, I, 79.
54 Benares Collectorate Records, Misc., vol. 8, pp. 154–7, UPR; cf. Hamilton, *Gazetteer*, p. 147.
55 Francklin, *George Thomas*, p. 43.

These periodic religious fairs were linked to smaller festivals in the countryside associated with the shrines of particular saints and the worship of local deities. Armed Gosain bands and Banjara travellers were the most usual merchant groups to appear at these informal markets which helped tie together the intermediate economy. Demand for medium-range cloths, jewellery, bangles, spices and weapons in the economies of the local rajs was 'bunched'. It coincided with the marriage, *holi* festival and campaigning seasons, so that the networks of rural festivals held in the spring and late autumn were particularly appropriate for satisfying it. The existence of these intermittent and obscure flows of goods helps explain how trade and credit relations managed to continue between areas which were not politically linked.

Pilgrim income and ritual movement also helped maintain the broader unity of the Indian economy when flows of revenue between Bengal and north India and between north and western India had dried up. Pilgrims in Gujerat, Maharashtra and Bengal took from their local bankers credit notes which were cashed on the Benares bankers. This, in turn, facilitated some trade and bullion movement between the regions. In the same way, the flow of goods generated by the Hardwar fair made possible *hundi* transactions between Bengal and north-west India, or even Central Asia, when direct trade had ceased to flow in its earlier volumes. In 1815, Rs. 150,000, or between 5 and 10 per cent of Benares transactions with its best trading partners, the Maratha dominions to the south, was accounted for by the provision of cash for the pilgrims.[56] But this was after the massive overland trade in raw cotton had developed, so that in the years 1740–80, the importance of fiscal transactions with the pilgrims was probably even greater. Certainly any trader or institution wanting to provide cash at Nagpur or Poona did well to wait for a heavy seasonal pilgrim demand at Benares.[57] In 1789 the British Resident in the city urged 'the propriety of taking advantage of the present want of specie by the Shroffs [money-dealers] at Benares, to discharge the demand of the pilgrims to procure their bills, if wanted, at a more reasonable rate than for some time past'.[58]

The geography of religious practice also affected the distribution of artisan communities. Pilgrims to the Ganges customarily brought back sacred water to their homelands in brass vessels, and small brass figurines procured in Benares or Bindachal formed one of the few items of 'luxury' which country people regularly bought from town artisans. These objects had ritual value, but they also formed an object of

[56] R. Jenkins, *Report on the Territories of the Rajah of Nagpore* (Calcutta, 1827), p. 99.
[57] Resident to GG, 4 April 1789, PR.
[58] Resident Poona to Govt Bombay, 20 Feb. 1789, PR.

investment for peasant families which were unable to afford gold and silver. Such demand supported metalworkers in the bazaars of the ritual centres and also helped maintain a large trade in brass and copper between Bengal and north India. The volume of this trade is difficult to calculate for the late eighteenth century, but between 1820 and 1830 it was the second largest export trade from Bengal to the north after gold and silver, and certainly outstripped Bengal spices and European imports in value.

In general, patterns of pilgrimage and worship formed an important resource for the urban Muslim population of poor artisans who were particularly at risk from the decline of the Mughal nobility. For instance, Tajganj in Agra (the bazaar of the Taj Mahal) was one of the city's only flourishing suburban markets when the British annexed the city in 1801.[59] Its population of 3,000 compared starkly with the desolation of the bazaars stretching northward from the Red Fort which had been the residential areas of the old nobility. In Allahabad, the area around the shrine of Prince Khusru and the great mosque continued to support a reduced economic life even when the retreat of the emperor from the city in 1771 had dealt the nearby Muslim *mohullas* a heavy blow. All over north India, the mosque and saint's tomb provided work for petty craftsmen who made rosewater, cheap prayer hats or rugs and mementos. Inn keepers (*bhatiyaras*) who lived near shrines fared better than those who had relied on the passage of imperial notables down the main routeways.

Revenue-free grants for religious purposes in the heart of the Muslim quarters of the cities and small towns helped bind together vulnerable urban communities. Income from charitable alienations became crucial for secular families of the Muslim elite. The line of pupil and teacher in a religious college or of spiritual guide and follower in a Sufi shrine may have persisted. But many secular descendants of the original grantee by the Muslim law of inheritance came to share in the income of the grant. To them were added shopkeepers and artisans paying small quit-rents who became dependent on the continuation of revenue privilege and pilgrimage. Most religious foundations also gave financial aid to the local community like the monasteries of medieval Europe. They maintained regular distribution of food and alms for the poor which accompanied prayers for the souls of the deceased (*Fatehas*). In Islam, the concept of charity was a wide one. Since the whole of civil society was deemed to be a support for the religious life of the community, many secular or public buildings were regarded as worthy of religious grants from the state and nobility. *Caravansarais*, alms houses for

[59] Agra Collectorate Files 5, UPR.

visiting pilgrims, bridges which brought the faithful to prayer and aqueducts which carried water essential for their ritual purity were all the 'proper objects of *waqfs*'.

The observation that shrine centres gave stability to towns and central places may appear paradoxical in context of the flexible, *ad hoc* character of Hindu worship. Shrines appear overnight at crossroads; major gods become assimilated into minor folk deities; the sanctity of individual teachers gives rise to sudden explosions of faith which enhance one ritual centre at the expense of another. There is indeed an intrinsic instability in Hindu religious practice.[60] Worshipper and donor families might abruptly change their view of the hierarchy of divine manifestations and as one particular deity grew in estimation, a portion of the family's total worship and offering would be directed away from one of the deities which had been favoured in the past. The hierarchy itself was unstable and so were the shrines and specialists dependent upon it.[61] For instance, Shiva seems to have regained ascendancy over Vishnu in the devotions of the Maratha Holkar family after 1760 so that donations in the great Vaishnavite heartland around Muttra took less of the dynasty's resources after this date.[62] Nevertheless, deities were arranged in a hierarchy and worship was redirected among them, rarely simply switched from one to another. Shrine centres moved in wealth and fame within this hierarchy in sympathy with collective religious observance. But while individual shrines might rise or fall, clusters of shrines could not disappear entirely in the manner in which some Catholic shrines disappeared in Reformed Europe.

As in the case of movement and change in royal centres, European observers found it difficult to separate intrinsic fluidity of this sort from their assumptions about the 'instability of oriental fortunes'. Such instability no doubt existed, but it could never root up a well-established pattern of worship. The fluctuations in royal patronage around the great centres of the worship of Radha and Krishna near Muttra illustrate this well. During the seventeenth century, it had been the Rajput kings and the high Hindu officials of the Mughal court who had poured wealth into Krishna's land of Braj. In the following century the aspiring Jat chieftains took over the patronage and repair of many of the local temples. The association between their royal power and the Krishna cult reached its fullest exposition in the *chhatas* or mausolea of the Jat

[60] See, Lawrence A. Babb, *The Divine Hierarchy. Popular Hinduism in Central India* (New York, 1975).

[61] Other religious buildings survived and developed between 1780 and 1810. Daraganj traders constructed the Naga Vasuki Temple and *ghat*, K. N. Khattri, 'On serpent worship', *IA*, ii (1873), 124; interviews, Daraganj, 1968, 1973.

[62] R. V. Tullu, 'Mahesvara in Malwa', *IA*, iv (1875), 346.

rulers of Bharatpur.[63] Here paintings of the warlike careers of the dynasts are mixed with representations of the games of Krishna amongst the milkmaids. But while the area as a whole continued to attract piety, individual shrines could only be maintained if they had attracted a sufficiently wide circle of devotees. Dependence on one or two great families was dangerous. The fate of the town of Barsana, near Muttra, exemplified this. In the years 1740–70 Barsana expanded considerably through the efforts of three families. The head of one family was chief financial officer of Bharatpur; another made a fortune in the service of the Nawabs of Awadh; the third, that of Rup Ram, Katari Brahmin and Vaishnavite devotee, became family priest of the Rajas of Bharatpur and the Maratha dynasties of Nagpur and Gwalior. Rup Ram's fame and wealth enabled him to build further temple complexes and large covered markets in his native town. It was 'enriched by these princes with the most lavish donations, the whole of which he Rup Ram appears to have expended on the embellishment of Barsana and other sacred places within the limits of Braj'.[64]

Barsana's equally rapid decline followed the defeat of the Jat forces by the imperial army in 1774. The elimination of Jat influence damaged their clients. Rup Ram's office as family priest did not descend to other members of his family, and in the orotund phrases of F. B. Growse,

A hamlet became in one day the centre of a princely court crowded with magnificent buildings, and again, ere the architect had well completed his design, sunk with its founders into utter ruin and desolation.[65]

Nevertheless the association of the Braj area as a whole with the cults of Radha and Krishna was firmly rooted and Barsana retained a reduced place in the local cycle of pilgrimages. A final and remarkable phase in its saga occurred in the early days of British rule when a Bengali holy man secured from local landholders and the decayed descendants of Rup Ram, massive grants of land which he devoted to constructing temples and dwelling houses in the nearby holy cities of Gobardhan and Muttra.

Islamic shrines also suffered from an intrinsic instability, quite apart from the shocks of political change in the outside world. Like secular property, alienations for religious purposes[66] reflected the indeterminacy of Muslim inheritance laws. Grants made to a Sufi saint or other holy man remained the joint trust of his descendants who as

---

[63] Growse, *Mathura*, pp. 306–7.

[64] Growse, 'Braj Mandala', *IA*, i (1872), 67.   [65] *Ibid.*, p. 312.

[66] The extent of revenue-free land for religious purposes and office-holding in the Ceded and Conquered Provinces in 1815 amounted to the equivalent of the whole cultivated acreage of a moderate sized district, *Selections from Revenue Records 1818–20*, p. 348, cited Stokes, *Peasant and Raj*, p. 54.

managers (*mutwallis*) enjoyed the usufruct of the lands. But in these complex and often polygynous Muslim joint-families, the definition of the boundaries of the property-owning group was often vague and internecine faction endemic. Thus the descendants of the great saint of Fatehpur Sikri near Agra, Sheikh Salim Chishti, suffered debilitating conflict throughout much of the late eighteenth and early nineteenth centuries.[67] The problem at issue was the status of the offspring of the two wives of one of the saint's successors. Here the intervention of the political authority, itself unstable, only served to deepen uncertainty. Local custom pointed to one conclusion; the Delhi emperors contributed charters favouring another. Sindhia's Agra deputy, Hessing, was no more successful than his British successors in arbitrating the dispute, and the zamindars of Agra took the opportunity of stopping payments to the large body of people who were directly or indirectly dependent on the alienation.

Confusion about the status of religious grants and about the exact role of the ruler in relation to them added a further source of conflict and instability. Grants made by the emperors (*altamgah inam*) were traditionally reaffirmed at the beginning of each reign, but local magnates took the excuse of a lapse in renewal to suppress them. According to Islamic law, grants for religious purposes were permanent and inalienable. But there was sufficient disagreement among jurists on the definition of 'religious purposes' for rulers to resume the lands of minor shrines without impairing their own legitimacy in Muslim eyes. It might be argued, for instance, that grants could be resumed if the pupil–teacher succession had died out or the managers had misused the funds. When Shia Muslims came to power in Awadh with the rise of the Nawabi, they displayed less solicitude for the Sunni trusts, mosques and schools which had been established by the Mughal emperors. Likewise, the new Hindu rulers of the eastern districts and the Jat territories sometimes let earlier Muslim grants relapse.

This had serious consequences for the sections of the urban community which relied on them for income. One of the most notorious examples was the decline of Jaunpur, once a great city of Islamic learning – 'the Isfahan of India'. Even at its height Jaunpur had been a city of service rather than a centre of trade and artisan production. It had attracted large numbers of Muslim literati, Sufi teachers and students of theology and jurisprudence.[68] Many of its leading families lived on

---

[67] Local Agents Agra to Board of Revenue, 17 Sep. 1813, *PP*, 1849, xli, 383–417. Original correspondence, *mahzars*, etc. are preserved in 'Fatehpur Sikri' file, Agra Revenue Records, UPR.

[68] Khairuddin Khan, 'Tarikh-i-Jaunpur', pp. 25–7.

grants of land and the proceeds of bazaars alienated to them in trust (*madad-i maash*) by the rulers.[69] The artisans produced fine vessels, turbans, books and rosewater for the local elites, but did not acquire a continental reputation like those of Dacca or Ahmedabad. Once the Awadh rulers began to seize or revoke the ancient grants, Jaunpur and its service communities fell into an irreversible decline. Khairuddin Hussain of Allahabad, the local historian, wrote about 1810,

in the time of Mohamed Shah [c. 1730] the jageers and pensions allowed to the dervishes and jageerdars were confiscated by Nawab Saadut Khan. Only a few mouzahs in the neighbourhood of Jaunpore for the necessary expenditures of musjids [mosques], of monasteries and of foreign students who came thither for attaining knowledge were left in the name of Hossein Shawh and Hussun Shahw the [Shia *imams*].[70]

Jaunpur's decline tells us much about the nature of the Indian Islamic city as a moral and social collectivity. During its decay it did not suffer looting on a large scale, and the men who sequestered the revenue-free grants on which it subsisted were Awadh nobles, local Rajput chieftains – even its own residents. The city had depended on the reputation of the Mughal rulers and the honouring of his grants by men of local power. Upkeep of the buildings, mosques, public baths and the famous bridge over the river Gomti had been ensured by the delicate balance of interests between the Muslim judicial officers of the city (the *kazi* and *mufti*) and the heads of the various guilds and quarters. A small tax on the various guilds and trades was instituted to recompense the judicial authorities for expenditure on public buildings. Simple acts like the annual whitewashing of public religious structures by local residents were symbolic civic actions. It is not surprising that once the whitewashing of the community Idgah mosque was discontinued, Id prayers ceased soon afterwards, and within a few years the whole structure fell into dilapidation.[71] The Hindus of the city had participated to some degree in this moral community. Many of the Muslim buildings were on the site of previous Hindu temples and wells, and these still attracted veneration in the catholic traditions of the Awadh area.

Jaunpur was the most noted example of such decline, but the effect of the resumption of religious grants was seen in many towns. Of the famous Khusru shrine in Allahabad, George Forster remarked in 1783,

---

69 Report of Karimullah, Resident to Govt, 1 May 1788, PR.
70 Khairuddin Khan, 'Tarikh-i-Jaunpur', p. 32.
71 The ultimate consequences of the resumptions are described in Magistrate Jaunpur to Superintendent of Police Western Provinces, 15 Jan. 1817, BCJ, 31 Aug. 1817, 138/6, IOL.

'No fund being established for supporting this monument it cannot long survive the numerous edifices, now scattered in ruins throughout the environs of Allahabad.'[72] However, there were definite limits to the degree to which rulers were able or willing to impair religious centres. Resumptions could only be made on a large scale if charity, the outward expression of Muslim faith, was forthcoming elsewhere. Muslim nawabs and even Hindu rulers had to heed the opinions of the learned men. Thus the rulers of Awadh carried out sequestrations of *waqf* in the eastern districts but at the same time, they embarked upon major enterprises of sacred building and created new revenue-free grants in Lucknow, Fyzabad and elsewhere. All that happened was that the direction of religious patronage and the urbanisation which it created was moved geographically and tended to benefit the Shia rather than the Sunni branch of the faith. This process was completed in 1818 when the nawab became King of Awadh and the learned men of the Shia persuasion were established as a council for religious decisions throughout the dominion.

We can begin to understand the strength of tradition in religious practice if we turn to some of the smaller Muslim shrines. Robinson has traced the relationship between the shrine at Bansa in Barabanki District and the learned men of the Firangi Mahal religious seminary in Lucknow. When in the seventeenth century the fame of the great teacher Qutbuddin attracted the patronage of the Mughal court, the seminary also began to draw in young men from the learned and holy families of the many small towns which were associated with early Muslim rule in Awadh. A particular connection grew up between Firangi Mahal and Bansa.[73] The town became a venerated spot for the Lucknow theologians and attracted fame and sustenance in turn. At the beginning of the eighteenth century, the decline of the central power and the rise of an indifferent if not hostile Shia power in Lucknow resulted in the termination of court patronage for the Firangi Mahal connection. There was some initial distress, but the reputation of the Lucknow seminary was now so well established throughout India that it could survive this blow. Firangi Mahal continued to draw in Muslim students from all parts of India and members of the dominant family were retained as scholars and administrators as far afield as Mysore and Hyderabad. In turn, the lustre of the Lucknow family maintained that of the smaller shrine at Bansa.

Despite serious local instability, then, religious practice and religious centres were not closely tied to the wheels of political power. The

[72] Forster, *Journey*, I, 83.
[73] F. C. R. Robinson, 'The ulama of Firangi Mahal and their *adab*', unpubl. MSS.

explanation for this is to be found at several levels. First, the ideal separation of kingly and priestly roles in Brahminical thought and the limited role of the sultan in classical Islam provided wide ideological justification for the separation of sacred and royal centres. The priest or Muslim learned man did not need the nawab or raja to perform their ritual roles – in contrast to societies where kings headed churches or administered cults. At another level, popular religion tended to absorb into itself the great shrines and give them vitality long after the great political patron had moved off. Sects and forms of devotion were not exclusive, so that the rise of new deities and cults did not mean the immediate dispossession of earlier sacred corporations. If anything, the Hindu sacred bodies and the Islamic learned men became more important as the wealth and power of the rulers ebbed.

In the case of Islam, the emergence of the successor states displaced the practitioners of the high tradition to new centres without utterly impoverishing the old. Learned men of the Sufi orders and doctors in Muslim law and jurisprudence moved out in numbers from Delhi and Agra to Awadh, Hyderabad, Bhopal and the Rohilla capitals. Scholars from circles like those of Munshi Faiz Baksh of Fyzabad needed patrons now that the flow of charity was drying up at the centre. Yet the new would-be sultans rising in the stead of the old empire were also predisposed to support religion and learning. The continuity of the scholarly tradition is borne out by an analysis of the religious and scholarly treatises in Persian preserved, for instance, in the Allahabad Records Room. This contains a large number of transcriptions of classics, or new works, written at Lucknow, Fyzabad, Patna or Rohilkhand, in the last quarter of the eighteenth century.[74] It was at this time also that the nucleus of the great library at Rampur was built up. The piety of the new rulers was perhaps most brilliantly displayed, however, in the religious monuments of Lucknow. The Bara Imambara, built by more than 20,000 labourers and masons during the height of the great famine of 1783, was both a display of Islamic (specifically Shia) devotion and a demonstration of the ruler's care for his people during the times of their distress. Yet devotional life and the economic activity which it sustained had not ceased in Delhi or Agra. On the contrary, the great Chishti shrine of Nizamuddin Auliya at Delhi grew in fame over the century and the Taj Mahal continued to attract devotees.

High Brahminical Hinduism received an even stronger impulse during these years, despite the flowering of local and popular cults. The consciousness of Vedic revival which characterised the colonial period

---

[74] *An Alphabetical Index of Persian, Arabic and Urdu Manuscripts in the State Archives of Uttar Pradesh* (Allahabad, 1968).

awaited the researches of the European Orientalists and the new Indian literati. Yet during the eighteenth century we already glimpse a distinct growth of patronage and institutions. The long-term effects of the shock of Aurangzeb's attempt to re-establish an Islamic state on the basis of *sharia* law may have heightened the sense of Hindu identity. But political conditions were also favourable with the rise of new Hindu powers in Benares, Maharashtra and the Jat territories. A spectacular example of the significance of Hindu devotion in town-building are the 170 temples established by the Rajas of Bhadawar in their dominions between 1720 and 1740;[75] and throughout the western region Jat royal patronage did something to compensate for the ravages of the Afghans, and the earlier ravages of the Jats themselves in Agra and the Muslim *qasbah* towns.

Social movements such as the rise of the Sikhs, Marathas or Jats were associated in their early stages with devotional movements which generally eschewed the older cult centres. But as these movements transformed themselves into more stable polities, there was a shift towards orthodox religious practice and an enhanced role for the Brahmins and holy cities. In the course of their rise, for instance, the Marathas came to emulate more and more the life-style of the kingly Kshattriya princes, especially the ancient dynasties of Rajasthan, who had long come to Benares[76] and Gaya in Bihar to perform oblations to the shades of their ancestors in the rituals called *shraddha*.[77] Growing numbers of genealogist Brahmins (called *pandas*) who inhabited the riversides of the holy cities attended to their spiritual requirements. Brass plates and books in possession of one of the oldest *panda* families in Benares demonstrate how pilgrimage could enhance the wealth of a city. Every generation grants of the income of Rajasthani villages had been made to the priestly family, and records of this practice go back as far as 1686. The family of Brijendranath Phattakh served and recorded the pilgrimages, generation by generation, of nine princes of Rajasthan including the rulers of Alwar and Udaipur.[78] The family took the title of

75 A. Führer, *The Monuments, Antiquities and Inscriptions in the North-Western Provinces and Oudh: Archaeological Survey of India*, II (Allahabad, 1891), 69; cf. *ibid.*, pp. 78–9, 84–9, for examples of late eighteenth-century religious building.

76 For growing Maratha involvement with Benares, *IA*, xxiv (1931), 297 on the seventeenth-century Deccani Brahmin immigration; Moti Chandra, *Kashi ka Itihas* (Bombay, 1962), ch. 5; *DG Benares*, p. 237.

77 C. Bayly, 'Death rituals and society in Hindu North India since 1600', in J. Whaley (ed.), *Mirrors of Mortality. The Social History of Death* (London, 1981), pp. 154–86; L. P. Vidyarthi, *The Sacred Complex in Hindu Banaras* (Delhi, 1978).

78 *Khatas* and brass plates in possession of Shri G. N. Phattakh, Manikarnika Ghat, Banaras, and *pandas'* book covering period *c.* 1665–1840 in possession of Shri Devi Narayan, Sakshi Binayak; see especially copper plates dated *Sambat* 1715, 1737 and 1899, *pandas'* book, p. 239 (opposite date 1788 *Sambat*).

'Rajguru' or Royal Preceptor. The security which accompanied the high years of the Mughal empire may have popularised the practice of doing *shraddha* at Benares which was conveniently situated on the river yet discreetly removed from the centre of Muslim influence. Some of the *panda* books record the oblations of men closely connected with the households of the Delhi nobles who signed their names in the Persian script.

These patterns were not disrupted during the eighteenth century. On the contrary, the claim of the Maratha princes for a royal status on the lines of that of the great Rajput dynasties encouraged them also to seek merit by association with the holy places and to come to Benares, Allahabad, Jagannath and Gaya in greater numbers. After 1680 the Marathas appear to have replaced the Rajputs as major donors at all these centres. By the mid-nineteenth century, the majority of temples in Benares were foundations of 'natives of the Deccan' within the previous 150 years.[79] The tradition was strongly developed by the houses of Sindhia and Holkar which ruled the dominant Maratha states. Both of these houses built huge stone bathing wharves (*ghats*) in Benares and established 'colleges' of dependent Brahmins there. The Maratha immigrants in Benares accounted for about 30,000 people[80] by the end of the century and included traders[81] (Naik and Sipahi Nagar bankers), Deccani Brahmins and the retainers of the many noblemen who temporarily or permanently resided in the city. In this case, patterns of royal behaviour which were common to all India helped maintain the pre-eminence of the old pilgrimage centres. But this tendency was reinforced by the rise to power of Chitpavan Brahmins in the Maratha polities after 1750. For the orthodox Brahmins of Poona and Nagpur, Benares as the centre of the highly Brahminical cult of Shaivism was peculiarly illustrious.

So far we have been dealing with major centres, but the role of religious practice was equally significant for the income and geographical distribution of smaller towns and large villages. In rural India where the income generated by local demand was so small, the income from spending on pilgrim services, like that derived from the presence of a military force, could raise local production and trade. Hardwar's village elders prospered by increasing the price of grain. Even more striking was the case of the Muttra region which was the subject of painstaking research by one of its Victorian Collectors, F. B. Growse. Muttra and its environs were identified with the 'Braj

---

[79] *DG Benares*, p. 237.
[80] Agent to GG to Govt, 4 July 1817, PR.
[81] V. D. Vyasa, *Vanshvali Vadnagara Sipahi Nagar Kashi Nivasi* (Benares, 1938).

Mandala' of Hindu legend where Krishna sported with the Gopis or cowherds and met his consort, Radha. In the fifteenth and sixteenth centuries, the Radha–Krishna cult of Vaishnavite devotionalism received a great spur in northern India.[82] A literary tradition associated with the poems of the *Bhaktamala* was woven around the beauty of Radha's 'sylvan abode' near Muttra.[83] Art and poetry carried the fame of Braj to a popular level. The social appeal of the populist works of Caitanya and his followers in Bengal along with the art of the Kangra hills and Rajasthan which depict the romance of Radha and Krishna spread a predisposition to pilgrimage to a much wider audience. Muttra became a place of pilgrimage, and before 1750 the region had seen what is best described as a reinvention of religious tradition. Earlier cults and deities were displaced or subordinated to shrines of Radha and Krishna and a complex sacred geography was developed around their legends. Twelve sacred groves or *upbans* and twelve woods or *bans* were designated. These became points on a popular pilgrimage route – the Banjatra or 'forest pilgrimage'. A major festival called the Raslila had grown up around Barsana, legendary home of Radha, which was served by a class of specialist Brahmins called Rasdharis. Even the names of villages in the area were slowly adapted to conform with the symbols of the Cow, Milk and Milkmaids.

The population of villages adjoining the pilgrimage places appears to have increased. Growse gives the example of the village Sanket (meaning 'meeting') which was located half-way between the reputed residences of Radha and Krishna. It became a holy spot because it was identified with the place where the holy couple met. Now clearly, the villages and towns of the Banjatra existed before the rise of the cult. Most were ancient agricultural market centres and fortified settlements commanding routeways. Their importance arose from being the centres of the clan groups which had dominated the area. But beyond this a reputation for sanctity depended very much on the shrewdness of the priests of the individual village shrines. These patterns cannot be fitted into the neat mechanisms of orthodox central-place theory.

The environs of the town of Muttra became an important resort for Bengali pilgrims. Mendicants established *maths* where newly rich members of the Calcutta business classes and zamindars, such as the Raja of Manipur from the extreme east of Bengal, spent large sums on charity. A close relationship also developed between the Radha–Krishna cult and the dominant landed people of eastern Hindustan. As

---

[82] Growse, 'Braj Mandala', *IA*, i (1872), 66–9.
[83] Growse, *Mathura*, ch. 10; cf. Kanhaiya Lal, *Vanayatra* (Delhi, 1866), Hin. Tract 1537, IOL.

elsewhere, the nobles of Rajasthan appear to have been among the first donor groups in the large temples of the region, and they developed strong links with the leaders of the Vaishnavite sects. The famous Maharaja Man Singh of Jaipur, for instance, founded the great temple at the celebrated town of Gobardhan (which means 'gift of a cow'). But later it was the aspiring Jats and Marathas who took over as major donors. Despite the ups and downs of individual shrines, the inhabitants of Braj generally benefited from the fame of their homeland. Receipts from pilgrimage aided the rise to prominence of the Chaube Brahmins who became one of the region's big trading and moneylending groups.

The rise of the great fair and market town of Kotwa in Barabanki District in Awadh also gives us another case of ritual town-building. This became the centre of the Satnami sect,[84] a quasi-monotheistic brotherhood of devotees which abjured the use of idols. It was founded by the reformer Jagjivan Das in the early eighteenth century. Jagjivan Das was a teacher who attracted much veneration from the poorer and lower caste people of Awadh, and his sect was reminiscent of the early days of Sikhism or the faith of Kabir, the weaver. Jagjivan Das spent much of his life in the town of Sardana where he was born, but later went on retreat to the village of Kotwa. Lands here were given to him by the Nawab of Awadh who was building up links with Hindu religious movements and institutions. As the centre of a *math* and of Satnami worship, Kotwa quickly overtook rival market villages and became the site of one of Awadh's largest fairs where the village service castes exchanged their surplus produce.

Sects, towns and traders

If religious practice and the services it generated were important for the survival of the embattled towns, 'sectarian' patterns of belief were even more important for the organisation of the merchant communities. Chapter 4 will show how merchant trading and religious organisation could be bound together to provide the basis of a virtual corporate self-government; chapter 9 will demonstrate how religious practice related to the economic activities of the 'family firm'. Here, however, it is important to mention how tightly knit communities organised throughout India could redistribute resources from relatively stable areas to less fortunate ones.

The concept of sect in Indian religion raises problems of definition.

[84] B. H. Badley, 'Jagjivan Das the Hindu reformer', *IA*, viii (1879), 289.

What is meant here are devotional groups with some degree of corporate organisation. This would include ascetic orders devoted to the service of the great gods of the Hindu pantheon and also sects such as Jainism which would be regarded as outside the mainstream of Hindu belief. Both types had a distaste for close involvement with the agents of local political power, which helps explain their relative success during the eighteenth century. One such group were the urban and mercantile devotees of the earlier non-military form of Sikhism, called Nanakpanthis after Guru Nanak, founder of the Sikh religion. Between 1500 and 1700 Khattri merchant families of this persuasion had scattered down the Ganges valley as far as Murshidabad and Calcutta. These people remained active in the trade of the Punjab because the new Sikh regimes tended to favour them at the expense of other Hindu or Muslim trading groups. Their success was reflected in the vitality of Nanakpanthi religious and devotional life in north Indian cities such as Benares and Patna. Here were constructed communal assembly halls (*sangiths*) and sacred institutions such as the so-called Sikh 'college' at Patna.[85] Locally settled Udasi holy men and ascetic bodies emergent out of the related tradition of the Nath Yogis received donations and support, and in Benares the community seems to have been expanding through the practice of adoption within the Khattri merchant body.[86]

This community also illustrates very clearly the importance of all-India networks of devotion and religion. The institution of Nirmali Fakhirs (called Akhara) which had branches throughout north India received large sums from trading Khattris established in Hyderabad. This far-flung diaspora had occurred when Asaf Jah and other Mughal notables had decided to abandon Delhi and concentrate on the foundation of a virtually independent regime in south India. One Chandu Lal Khattri achieved enormous wealth and fame as chief financial officer of the Hyderabad government[87] and presented the Nirmali Fakhirs of north India with 'some lakhs of Rupees' which enabled them to build up their establishments in the major northern pilgrimage centres. But the Akhara was not dependent on the patronage of the courts and magnates alone. Ordinary pilgrims and devotees contributed to the institution through collections made by Nanakpanthi laymen in the conclaves which existed throughout Hindustan.

Expenses of the whole body of Fakhirs which contains several thousand

85 C. Wilkins, 'The Seeks and their college at Patna', Mar. 1781, repr. in Ganda Singh (ed.), *Early European Accounts of the Sikhs* (Calcutta, 1962), pp. 71–3.
86 *Ganga Bye* v. *the Mother of Jwalanath*, 3 Aug. 1792, PR; H. H. Wilson, 'Sketch of the religious sects of the Hindoos', *AR*, xvii (1832), 232–5.
87 Leonard, *Kayasths of Hyderabad*, p. 50n.

members, dispersed all over Hindustan, are defrayed from the proceeds at the Allahabad and Haridwar fairs.[88]

Here then, private, self-regulating bodies of pious merchants and government officials acted independently of the rulers to maintain the ritual function of cities.

Another 'heterodox' sect which grew and flourished during the eighteenth century were the Lingayats or Vira Shaivites. Though based in Mysore, the Lingayats maintained a major institution (*math*) in Benares. From contemporary records, we can see the institution expand during the years 1707 to 1780 at the very time when north India was supposed to have been in the throes of anarchy and famine.[89] It purchased more urban property in Benares, having already established itself in Gaya and Allahabad.[90] Donors were drawn from all quarters. The Benares dynasty confirmed revenue-free grants made originally by Mughal rulers, but at the same time a continuous flow of offerings from the Lingayat pilgrims who visited Benares from south India provided resources which were not directly tied to the fate of the Benares rulers. The Jangambari Math and its offshoots in the other sacred cities quickly tied themselves into the local economy. By the turn of the nineteenth century, the Lingayats had emerged as major moneylenders and property-owners in the hamlets around Madanpura in Benares and were creditors to the Muslim weavers who lived in the vicinity.[91]

Jains were another sect which had an impact on town and commercial life quite out of proportion to their numbers – a mere 3–5 per cent in the towns of the west, dwindling to under 1 per cent in the east. Tod's Jain clerk estimated that Jain businessmen commanded half of the total commercial wealth which circulated between Rajasthan and the Bay of Bengal.[92] Though this was probably an exaggeration, the expenditure of Jain merchant families on temples, bazaars and dwelling houses made a significant contribution to depressed urban economies. Jains expended

88 K. N. Khattri, 'Khattris', *IA*, ii (1873), 26.
89 *Dhanpatras, firmans* and other grants to the 'Jangambari' Math, Madanpura, Benares are preserved in the Library of the High Court, Allahabad. A number were issued by Akbar, Jahangir and Aurangzeb, but the majority of documents date from after 1740. They were translated along with the wills of the abbots (since *c.* 1820) as exhibits in first appeal no. 58 of 1934, High Court of Allahabad, Civil Side in *Sri Jagat Guru Sri Mahant Mallik Arjun (plf. appellant)* v. *Nishikant Banerji and others (defdt respondents)*.
90 *Parwana* of Muhammad Shah, *Jamadi-ul-awal, San 30* (1748); cf. grant of Maharaja Bhawa Singh Deva to the 'body of fakhirs'; and deed of relinquishment of property in Allahabad to the 'fakhirs', *Rabi-ul-awal*, 1096 A. H., 'Paper Book' of the case on film in author's possession, pp. 397–413.
91 Evidence of Ramzani and Tahir, weavers, re application of Siva Ling Jangam, Benares Magistrate's Court, Dec. 1802, 'Paper Book', p. 413.
92 James Tod, *Annals and Antiquities of Rajasthan or the Central and Western Rajput States of India*, ed. W. Crooke (London, 1920), II, 603–4.

over 25 lakhs of Rupees on religious buildings and public facilities in
Delhi alone between 1790 and 1820,[93] and this must have supported a
large population of masons and day labourers who would otherwise have
suffered from the decline of Mughal building in the capital. Again, the
hierarchy of Jain communities was largely independent of political
authority. In Rajasthan, the commercial laity maintained reasonably
good relations with the Hindu kings,[94] but generally it was the tycoon
merchant families such as the Jagat Seths which fulfilled the role of royal
patrons at their sacred places. There were sixteen of these sacred places
for the Digambara Jains and each was associated with the seat of one of
their high priests.[95] Most were commercial towns – Delhi, Sonepat,
Ajmer, Jaipur and Gwalior. One assumes that these places had been
sanctified by association with Jain teachers who had gathered to
minister to the trading people on ancient trade routes. But once
established, these central Jain communities took on a significance of
their own in the ritual and social life of the sect which tended to preserve
them even when wealth had moved off to new centres. Lucknow never
replaced Delhi as a devotional centre, and it was Delhi which continued
to receive lavish donations and temples even when the imperial house
was overshadowed in importance by the Awadh rulers.

Nearer to the mainline of Hinduism stood the great Shaivite and
Vaishnavite ascetic orders, usually called Gosains, Bairagis or simply
Sannyasis. These also helped create stability along trade routes between
the major centres, even though their raiding tactics in Bengal frightened
contemporary British observers. The ascetic institutions possessed an
advantage at a premium in the eighteenth century: they were able to
provide their own protection regardless of established political
authority. This came in two forms. First, there was the Gosains' sheer
military power which they sold to other magnates such as the Nawab of
Awadh, and used to protect their own trade routes and revenue grants.
Secondly, their capacity to protect, in part, derived from their status as
holy men 'divorced from the world'. Like the Palli Brahmins of
Rajasthan, they were able to trade in areas where members of the
professional merchant castes were unable to go. Fear of physical and
spiritual retribution together had a salutary effect. The ascetic orders
had been influential in the Mughal period, but their position was

---

[93] *Monuments*, I, 36 (Isri Das Temple); 278 (Jain Panchayati Temple); 282, 296, 301
(temples built by Harsukh Rai, Jain *divan* of Bharatpur); 333 ('Urdu' temple erected for
Jains in the imperial army, but repaired and extended in the 1790s); interviews and
family histories, Delhi 1974, suggest that Jains and Agarwals from Mahim and nearby
towns came to Delhi in great numbers, 1750–1800, possibly in search of protection.
[94] Wilson, 'Religious sects', *AR*, xvii (1832), 275–92.
[95] H. Buhler, 'Digambara Jains', *IA*, VII (1878), 28.

enhanced in the eighteenth century when their military skills were in demand and when they could count on a constant stream of recruits from broken families of the war-torn tracts.

J. N. Sarkar and B. S. Cohn[96] have both pointed to the commercial advantages of the ascetic sects. Their armed pilgrimage cycle from the Hardwar fair through the main towns of the Gangetic plain to Bengal and Jagganath-Puri provide a 'ready-made trading network'. Using a combination of military and commercial power, they could link up areas of supply and demand in the stable and productive zones and provide their own protection on the difficult routes between them. Their corporate savings and investment habits enabled them to form and direct the uses of capital with great efficiency. By the 1780s, the ascetic sects seem to have been the dominant moneylending and property-owning group in Allahabad, Benares and Mirzapur. Their networks also linked across country to Nagpur, Ujjain and Poona where they had begun to buy property and build houses. Their capacity to link up the productive economy of Bengal with the high demand areas of Maharashtra proved lucrative indeed. At first the trade was pre-eminently in 'luxury' items such as silk which was controlled by the great Nagpuri Math of Dasnami Naga ascetics at Benares.[97] But later the growth of the cross-country trade in cotton allowed the *maths* to move into the fastest growing area of trade in eastern India.[98] Their privileged social status in Hindu society provided the ascetics with unique advantages. They received dispensations from full customs rates in some kingdoms, since it was illogical to take from holy men if the justification of rule was to protect *dharma*; it was also dangerous. Since they were also technically estranged from caste, class and worldly wealth, Gosains were often regarded as suitable people for arbitrations or for witnessing commercial documents.[99] In Mirzapur in particular, they soon became accepted leaders of the merchant community.[100]

The economic role of temples in south India has long been recognised, but the importance of patterns of pilgrimage and religious practice in tying the Indian economy together at a wider level has not been appreciated. This was especially significant during a period when political decentralisation had tended to disturb existing interregional patterns of trade. And it was significant too because groups of religious

[96] B. S. Cohn, 'The role of the Gosains in the economy of 18th and 19th century Upper India', *IESHR*, i (1964), 175–82; D. H. A. Kolff, 'Sanyasi traders', *IESHR*, viii (1971), 213–18.

[97] Interviews, Nagpuri Math, Benares, 1974.

[98] Mishra, *Banaras*, pp. 80–110.

[99] 'Examination of the Khurdea', 27 Jan. 1792, PR.

[100] *Roop and Saroop Poori* v. *Badli Gir and Laulji*, Mirzapur Court, 3 April 1791, PR.

specialists and earnings from pilgrimage reached right down to the villages. Despite local instability, the desire of new rulers to serve their gods in monumental stone, the continued vitality of the priestly hierarchy, and the independent world of the sectaries, gave considerable stability to this edifice of devotion and piety. The next section goes on to consider the role of artisan production and trade in determining the fate of towns. The link between revenue and trade ensured that trading patterns would be more responsive to political change than religious practice. But not all levels of trade and production were equally affected.

Artisans, traders and urban stability

The textile industry was a major component of artisan production and probably accounted for between 20 and 30 per cent of the total artisan population of towns and villages. Perhaps 60,000 specialist weavers and dependants lived in the Benares region, 250,000 in Awadh, 200,000 in Rohilkhand and 30,000 in the lower Doab.[101] There were three levels of activity. Production of the highest quality was designed for royal and aristocratic consumption and for export by the East India Company. It was centred on a few illustrious centres: in Bengal, Dacca, Murshidabad and Lakhimpur; Benares was famous for saris and brocaded work, and there were spots of high quality work in the Awadh weaving belt around Tanda, in Rohilkhand and the lower Doab. In eastern India at least, this sector seems to have been resilient between 1750 and 1810. Its stability helped maintain overall urban populations. Next, there was a medium level of production supplying the local military, gentry and small royal courts. Some of the prestigious centres produced lower quality cloth for this market. But these less specialist weavers were also present in the region's large towns, congregating where there was a well-paid army such as in Awadh or Rohilkhand. This was the level of demand which was most likely to be fluid and unstable during the eighteenth century. Finally, there were the village weavers who made up the yarn produced by women in the villages and sold variable quantities of surplus produce through peasant markets or *haths*. A source of 1835 implies that, even then, 90 per cent of India's raw cotton production was used locally for consumption of this sort[102], and the massive total of village weavers recorded in the early censuses bears this out.

[101] Naqvi, *Urban Centres*, pp. 134–238; Barlow's Report on Awadh, 1787; Martin, *Eastern India*; Chaudhuri, *Trading World of Asia*, p. 244; Valentia, *Voyages*, i, App. 1; H. Wellesley's Reports on the Doab and Rohilkhand, June 1802, Board's Collections, 2803, IOL.

[102] Anon., *The Cotton Trade of India* (London, 1839), pp. 86–7, IOL.

Weaving and spinning in the villages was dominated by the conditions of the peasant economy around it. Eighteenth-century estimates suggest that every peasant family bought or acquired through barter three basic garments every two years, meaning that as many as fifteen million garments might have been produced for mass consumption in our region in a good year during the 1790s. Besides the effects of good or bad seasons, there is some evidence of more general changes in this level of demand. For instance, Tennant and Buchanan both observed that peasants in the Allahabad region had taken to wearing upper cloths in 'recent years'. The Benares region was also importing raw cotton from central India in the 1780s because its own production was devoted to fine goods and insufficient for the production of quilts and domestic cloths which were in growing demand.[103] This is certainly the type of mass consumption which would have been elastic to changes in income if some areas of the peasant economy were relatively prosperous. Supply factors may also have changed. The acreage under cotton in the Doab and central India appears to have expanded quite rapidly after 1760, and especially after 1783 when it became profitable to ship the region's raw cotton to Bengal. One by-product of this was the growth of new weaving centres for coarse cloths in places where the raw material was plentiful and cheap.[104] Mau and Chanderi near Jhansi were places which rose to prominence as cloth producers on the back of the raw cotton boom.

The intermediate level of the cloth economy was more responsive to political change because it produced for the local elite market. Two sets of forces were working on these weaving populations. The pressures of local community worked for geographical stability; the community provided marriage, professional aid and spiritual security. Weavers had settled in particular spots because they gave easy access to communications, water and cheap food, and it was hazardous to abandon such advantages. But the physical movement or dispersion of the warrior and gentry groups who provided markets and the merchants who provided cash advances might force migration upon weavers. The offer of protection by the new regional rulers sometimes counterbalanced the loss of traditional markets and the disruption of social life. The rulers of Farrukhabad, for instance, made a policy of attracting weavers from disturbed regions of the east Punjab and Delhi territories. One testimony to this is the existence in suburban Farrukhabad of a large Sood Mohulla, inhabited by members of this

---

[103] J. Duncan's Report on cotton in Benares, *c.* 1789, in *Reports*, pp. 368–9.
[104] K. N. Chaudhuri, 'The structure of the Indian textile industry in the seventeenth and eighteenth centuries', *IESHR*, xi (1974), 127–83.

specialist weaving and dyeing community which originated in the Punjab. In the same way, the rulers of Benares brought in weavers from as far away as Gujerat in order to expand their production of fine silks and brocades.[105] Still, the weaving populations remained immobile and great economic pressures had to be put on them before they were prepared to abandon their villages. Conditions for the marketing of middle-range goods in Rohilkhand declined considerably after 1774. But the weaving population of the territory remained as high as 200,000 in 1800, and the weavers' 'impoverishment' and 'idleness' caused the incoming British some well-grounded apprehensions about the consequences for public order.[106]

The most specialised high quality weaving communities remained in a strong position throughout the century. Certainly they were affected by the decline of the old consuming aristocracies; thus Barlow noted in 1786:

The Oudh manufactures were formerly held in great estimation at the markets of Delhi and Agra, but since the decline of those cities, the demand for them has fallen in proportion.[107]

Nevertheless, the decline of the old capitals did not signify the complete collapse of demand. Besides the rapid growth of Lucknow and Fyzabad, there was also, he noted, a 'very strong demand' for Awadh cloths in Farrukhabad, the Maratha territories and even distant Rajasthan. So strong was this demand from the 'western merchants' indeed that the East India Company found it necessary to use its political power in the Lucknow court to secure a monopoly on the production of the Awadh weavers at Tanda and Aliabad.

The persistence of this demand, and the townships which it supported, reflected once again the cultural dimension of consumption. The high quality trade was maintained by notions of aristocracy and kingship. There continued to be forms of dress which were appropriate for attendance at any kind of darbar or audience whether it was in the imperial capital or in the smallest *qasbah* where local notables 'sat with' a virtually powerless Mughal official. In the short run, the incursions and ethos of the Marathas, Jats or Sikhs had disrupted both supply and demand. But by the 1770s and 1780s, the Maratha aristocracy was becoming domesticated into the Mughal pattern of rule and was itself

---

[105] Interview, Sri Prehlad Das, Benares, April 1972; C. Malet to GG, 8 Aug. 1788, repr. Saletore (ed.), *Banaras Affairs*, I, 142; for Gujeratis at Muttra see, Growse, *Mathura*, pp. 192–3.

[106] Wellesley's Report on Trade in Rohilkhand, 16 June 1802, Bds Collns 2803, pp. 6–8, IOL.

[107] Barlow, Awadh Report 1787, App. I.

becoming a consuming class. Just as Sindhia assumed the titles of Mughal rank, so his nobles and courtiers were falling into 'moghly' forms of display as many miniature paintings testify. Their consumption buoyed up production of cloth and specialist artisan products from the Gangetic area and compensated, in part, for the decline of the western cities. This is the conclusion that must be drawn from the figures of Benares exports and imports supplied to the British at the end of the century. K. P. Mishra's study of the area shows that the trade into the Maratha territories was the most valuable transacted by the merchants of the city in the 1780s.[108] The 'Nagpuri' Gosains of Benares who worked the southern route were noted as traders in silk, while weavers in nearby Azamgarh produced fine quality turbans for export to the Maratha rulers among whom the cocked turban was becoming a distinguishing mark of high nobility. This bustle of trading activity to the south also spurred the little riverain mart of Mirzapur into growth some fifteen years before it became a major centre of European enterprise in the mid-Ganges.[109]

In many parts of India, the political flux was leading towards the re-establishment of stable regimes which were minor recreations of the Mughal polity adapted to deeper Hindu patterns of royalty. Outwardly, aristocracy was expressed in the form of architecture and life-styles and dress drawn from the Mughal example. The demand for these physical symbols of legitimate power may have slackened from time to time, but it was never extinguished. Indeed, conspicuous 'moghly' consumption reached its peak during the Pax Britannica itself. Even the 'plebeian' Jats and Marathas ultimately adopted this style, and those rulers who moved closest into the orbit of the dying star of Mughal power – Sindhia and the Jats of Bharatpur – were the most conspicuous. Jat rajas took marble and masons from Agra and constructed in the great darbar hall at Deig one of eighteenth-century India's finest monuments. Malet even noted change in Poona at the 'parsimonious' heart of Maratha Brahminism,

Poonah [in the 1780s] is still a large village to which people of all denominations and professions are now beginning to resort from the other ruined parts of Hindustan, particularly from the ruined Moghul cities. Its reputation for security since the abortive [British] expeditions from Bombay has greatly tended to promote its increase in population as the wealthier Brahmans in consequence began to employ some part of their hidden riches in building,

---

[108] Mishra, *Banaras*, ch. 5.
[109] F. Fowke to W. Hastings, 7 Mar. 1776, Foreign Department Sec. Cons., 3 Apr. 1776, i, NAI.

which circumstance necessarily gives employment to a great number and great variety of artifacers as the wants attendant on large buildings are endless.[110]

The view from the producers' end tallies with this. High quality products of Dacca and Murshidabad are a good example. This valuable trade, worth Rs. 50 lakhs in the 1720s, had been largely accounted for by a few huge purchasers, notably the Mughal court and the Jagat Seths. It was not easy to make up a deficiency from this quarter with sales to a number of small centres. Yet both cities weathered the eighteenth century rather well; their demise came in the first decades of the nineteenth. Ghosal's careful calculations revealed an apparent leap in total production at Dacca in the 1780s which was reversed by 1792. But overall, 'the falling off in total output was not very considerable and amounted to only 15 to 20 per cent'.[111] The fall in the 1790s could be attributed largely to the outbreak of the Revolutionary Wars in Europe. Ghosal was left with the puzzle that 'the decline of the indigenous courts and the old aristocracy of north India did not bring much quantitative loss to the manufacturers'.[112] This is resolved when we remember that the consuming aristocracies were to a large extent redistributed across the countryside and did not decline completely. The wearing of fine Bengal muslins remained a symbol of aristocracy in the new centres; indeed, Ghosal's own figures reveal heavy north Indian demand from the 'Afghan and Turani nobility' (i.e. the Rohillas), quite apart from Marathas and Jats.

The relative stability of the 'quality' weaving population of the great towns can therefore be explained. Since they were used to export to noble consumers over a long distance, a relative shift in trade routes would be of little importance. True, insurance and transport charges might rise to new heights, as they did during the 1790s, but to the consuming classes payment of such a premium was much less costly than the local settlement of large communities of skilled weavers who would need advances for the tools of their trade. There were plenty of later examples of the failure of such transplanted communities. Ranjit Singh never really succeeded in shifting Kashmir shawl production to his new capital, and British attempts to get carpet factories going at Delhi and in eastern Benares met with little success. The artisans most likely to move with their warrior masters were those without a

---

110 Malet to GG, 8 Aug. 1788, *Banaras Affairs*, I, 144; see also the large map-drawing of Poona, *c.* 1785, suggesting rapid development of the city with sixteen large temples, Maratha, Mughal, French and English palaces, A. Dalrymple, *Oriental Repertory* (London, 1808), I, facing p. 600.
111 H. Ghosal, *The Economic Transition in the Bengal Presidency* (Calcutta, 1961), p. 24.
112 *Ibid.*

continental reputation who depended on immediate local sale, and those highly specialised people who were tied into the patronage and ritual systems of the great households. It was the jewellers who made marriage jewellery, the dyers who made the particular colours for festive turbans or saris, or the skilled cooks and workers in silver and gold who moved from Delhi or Agra to Lucknow and Hyderabad.

Let us now move on to the forces which affected the stability of mercantile and commercial organisation above the village level. The scattered figures for occupations in cities for the eighteenth and early nineteenth centuries suggest that the category 'merchant' might have accounted for 20–30 per cent of the total urban population, if small brokers, moneychangers, warehouse-keepers, and so on, are included. The volume of medium- and long-distance trade over and above local retail trade and revenue functions was therefore quite crucial to the stability of urban economies. Before surveying the material on the fate of individual trades during the century, some general hypotheses will be helpful. First, local political insecurity need not have destroyed trade moving in a relatively closed economic system. Merchants found alternative routes for their goods, and it was in the interest of rulers to maximise rather than discourage the trade passing through their domains as they needed both supplies and revenue from transit dues. In addition, sophisticated insurance mechanisms existed which guaranteed the continuation of long-distance trade provided that merchants were sufficiently capitalised to bear the initial premia. Insurance rates rose to as much as 25–40 per cent towards the end of the century, as Malcolm's figures show for Central India.[113] But they only stuck at this level for relatively short periods, such as the course of the Anglo-Maratha war of 1802 and the consequent scarcities. Moreover, a moderately enhanced rate could be passed on to the consumer. Since the consumers were themselves the princes and zamindars who were levying extra 'protection rent' on the merchants, there is no reason why the trading system should not have survived with a somewhat smaller volume of goods circulating at higher prices.

Merchants might also create their own protection directly, as did the Gosains, or shift most of the costs of protection to some other group under their control like Banjaras or Palli Brahmins, who were often deeply indebted to urban money lenders. In this situation there was, of course, wastage as firms adapted to new methods, but there was no question of a catastrophic decline of trade. It is interesting that even those Company officials who were most pessimistic about the political state of India were aware of the various safety systems which merchants

[113] Malcolm, *Central India*, ii, App. IX.

had adopted. Barlow noted how Awadh traders contracted out the transport of their goods to operators called *hundiwallas*. These people bore the cost of insurance and local transit duties and were able to make longer-term bargains with local notables who might have plundered the trade routes:

> the inland trade throughout the upper parts of Hindostan is carried on in this manner, and the most valuable goods are transported with safety through countries where the merchant himself could not pass without endangering his life and property.[114]

One type of merchant who might be expected to suffer drastically in these conditions would be those unable to create their own protection, or those like the non-Khattri merchants of the Punjab who were discriminated against by the new ruling powers. Long-distance peddling traders would also find themselves in difficulties because they were unable to predict demand and might find their wares priced out of the market by accumulated levies and protection costs which they were unable to recover from the consumer. There are indeed a number of incidents reported in the literature which suggest that it was the long-distance peddlars who used to flock to the Mughal courts of north India who suffered the greatest dislocation. They echo Sauda's plaint:

> Why not become a merchant then? But if you do, you must reckon with the possibility that the wares you buy in Ispahan will not find a market in Hindustan and you will have to take them as far afield as the Deccan.[115]

Can anything useful be said about volumes of trade in the late eighteenth century? The problems are considerable. Even in the 1850s up to 30 per cent of all trade was thought to escape taxation and hence registration. Trade flows could change direction quite rapidly and give the impression of a sharp rise or decline within a single administrative unit. The game of tax evasion was widespread, particularly among merchants connected with the Europeans who could use political influence to avoid taxation. But one simple indication that the volume of trade could not have fallen catastrophically from the late Mughal period lies in the point which has already been made about the complementary relationship of trade and land-revenue. About 60–70 per cent of the Mughal revenue demand (of *c.* 1700) appears to have been collected in our period;[116] much of the shortfall was accounted for by the non-

114 Barlow, Awadh Report 1787, p. 30; Forster, *Journey*, I, 224.
115 Sauda cited Russell and Islam, *Three Mughal Poets*, pp. 62–3; Firak Gorakhpuri, *Nazir ki Bani* (Allahabad Law Journal Press, 1953), pp. 29–37; Faiz Baksh, *Faizabad*, II, 55–6.
116 R. Barnett, communication to author, 1980.

payment of local elites who continued to spend freely on trade goods. Total trade must therefore have been of a comparable order of magnitude, though one would expect it to have been redirected and fragmented. Scattered figures bear this out. Commerce in the Nawab of Awadh's 'family domains' yielded Rs. 5 lakhs in trade and transit duties in the 1770s. Nawabi duties may have averaged out to 5–7 cent of value; the trader would also pay duties to revenue-farmers and zamindars.[117] Thus interdistrict trade in dutiable items may have amounted to Rs. 120 lakhs per year, which is compatible with an estimated regional trade through the Benares dominions of Rs. 140 lakhs about a decade later. Making some large assumptions about population and the per capita value of trade, medium- and long-distance trade over Rs. 400 lakhs per annum for the whole of the later United Provinces and Delhi Territories seems possible. This again is not incompatible with Colebrooke's estimates of trade in Bengal, and with the likely per capita consumption of items such as salt, spices and cloth.[118] Two points follow. First, in commercial tracts, trade bore a relatively high ratio to consumers' income. For Benares, Kessinger[119] reckons a total trade of Rs. 240 lakhs, which can be set against a total income for the territory's inhabitants of about Rs. 40 lakhs. For Awadh, without the same flourishing river trade, Rs. 120 lakhs trade to Rs. 200 lakhs consumer income might stand as an informed guess. The second point that follows from this is that it is easy to exaggerate the impact of new export trades on the economy. The route to Calcutta was certainly vitalised. By 1815, goods worth Rs. 150 lakhs were going this way alone. But much of this trade was in commodities such as opium and indigo which had little effect on employment or local consumers' incomes. And the valuable cotton trade from Central India had already emerged within the context of the local states and Bengal artisan production for north Indian markets.

Two case studies of adaptation – grain and salt

Just as different styles of trader adapted differently to political change, so some commodities proved more adaptable than others. The salt and grain trades were the two great volume trades of the period. Salt is an essential part of the diet of the tropics, but consumer preference and

117 Barlow, Awadh Report 1787, pp. 10–11; but cf. the more than Rs. 12 lakhs recorded for the Ceded Provinces alone in 1799, Home Misc. 583, IOL.
118 Colebrooke and Lambert, *Husbandry*, p. 130.
119 T. Kessinger, 'Economy of North India', *Cambridge Economic History of India* (Cambridge, 1982), forthcoming.

politics moulded the form of the trade routes. It was the fine rock salt of the Punjab and the salt from the Sambher Lake in Rajasthan which north Indians wished to buy if they could afford it. The coarser, local salt was good enough for cattle and the poor, but richer people would only use it in scarcity years. Punjab rock salt was considered especially fine, but its price was nearly double that of other quality salts and it was only traded in small quantities. The great Sambher Lake and other deposits in Rajasthan were the main sources for the middle level of consumption, generating trade for the western merchants to the tune of about Rs. 12 lakhs per annum.[120] But here political changes became significant. Salt was pre-eminently a 'treaty trade' subject to close state control in production, distribution and marketing. Supply was regulated by the princes of Rajasthan, the petty states on the routes to the east and the general policy of the East India Company in Bengal. After 1771, 'western salt' was excluded from the Bengal market in an attempt to increase the consumption of the Company's own monopoly salt there. But while the Company disrupted the trade to the lower Ganges, the rise of consumption in Benares, Rohilkhand and Awadh increased the cross-country trade between north-east and south-west and speeded the developments of marts such as Chandausi and Hatras.

The viability of the salt trade in the face of political change was important since it was peculiarly conducive to maintaining large towns. Because of its potential for taxation, rulers tended to route it through centres where they found it easier to control. As a bulk trade, salt was also heavily dependent on transport services and robust storage. It gave rise to large concentrations of pack-bullocks and downriver boats, while creating business for commission and warehouse agents. Such a volume of transport services also stimulated other trades since merchants found it profitable to fill their boats and load their animals with commodities such as grain and sugar on their return journeys. As the most sophisticated merchant facilities were found in or near the older Gangetic cities, salt played an important part in the survival of Agra, Farrukhabad and Allahabad as major centres of transit trade during our period. While, for instance, Agra's noble quarters and *ganjs* declined following the general migration to Lucknow and Hyderabad, Belanganj market to the east continued to function as the great crossing for Rajasthan salt from the east and Rohilkhand sugar from the north. The transition was symbolised as one of the city's most famous Mughal palaces in the environs of the market and became first the tax office for the through trade and later the headquarters of one of the city's new merchant magnates whose firm was commonly known as 'Paramat

[120] Collr Customs Agra to Bd, 14 Aug. 1808, Agra Customs 1, UPR.

Kothi' – permit house – a reference to the customs permits taken on the salt that came through the city.[121] The salt trade had preceded the rise of the Mughals and it was to survive their fall.

But the salt trade also worked to tie the traders of the major towns to the dealers of the smaller centres. For salt was one of the few commodities which linked the cities to the peasant *haths* in a classic urban hierarchy. Salt was taken downriver to centres such as Allahabad and Mirzapur from which it was dispersed into the countryside by local dealers and travelling merchants with pack animals. Here, in fact, was a case of exchange between town and country which did not rely on the coercive power of the revenue system and could survive its disruption.

Grain provides us with quite another case. India's cities did, of course, support flourishing grain markets, but the food-grain trade does not appear to have promoted large urban concentrations to the extent which it did in other Asian states. While the salt and spice, or middle-range cloth trades, are relatively easy to reconstruct, the grain trade appears fitful and fragmented.[122] The reason for this was the limited extent of interregional specialisation in basic food-grains. Towns dominated compact agricultural hinterlands of ten to twenty miles radius which supplied their needs for essential food-grains. Regional trades were spasmodic. Scarcities, warfare or local gluts, promoted large flows in some years, but the grain trade responded to these exceptional demands more through the operation of Banjara carriers who could rapidly convene, deliver and disperse than through the fixed networks which established merchant houses operated in major towns.

One area with an integrated subregional grain market was Benares to which small hinterland traders brought pack-bullock loads from as far away as seventy or eighty miles. The riverine markets at Benares, Mirzapur and Ahraura acted as central places where the rice and wheat of Jaunpur and Bhadohi was exchanged for iron and other goods from the south. There were other similar self-contained trading areas. In 1801, the principality of Farrukhabad 'had no custom of exporting grain to any other foreign power'.[123] Grain was brought from local markets to the primate city and from there it was distributed throughout the state. Again, 'In times of scarcity in the Cawnpore district grain is occasionally imported from the province by the river Ganges, but the supply cannot be exhaustive, as the produce of the district is little more than adequate to the consumption of its inhabitants'.[124] Only in a few instances do we

[121] Interviews, family histories, Belangani, Agra, 1973; Agra Customs, 1–5, UPR.
[122] Naqvi, *Urban Centres and Industries*, pp. 21, 36–7, 76–7, 92.
[123] Magistrate Farrukhabad to Bd, 2 Oct. 1803, CPR, 21 Oct. 1803, 97/14, IOL.
[124] Magistrate Kanpur to Bd, 3 Oct. 1803, CPR, 21 Oct. 1803.

see evidence of a significant interregional grain trade – Rohilkhand rice and wheat was exchanged for Rajasthan produce; Gangetic grain was taken up into Bundelkhand on pack mules; Bahraich rice, once prized at the Mughal court, was fed to British and Awadh troops at Kanpur and Fatehpur. Further to the west, the Raja of Bundhi worked his principality like a vast farm and released his grain to Hindustan or Gujerat depending on where he could get the best price. And a little Bengal rice even found its way to Delhi as it had during the height of the old empire.[125] But the quantities involved do not seem to have been considerable. The absence of a strong, interregional specialisation and trade in food grains imposed definite limits on the level of urbanisation in India. The relative cost of transport and the absence of a grain-tribute system discouraged centralisation and the growth of grain transit towns like those of contemporary China or Japan. But even in this case, it is not clear that the overall volume of trade in food-grains had declined considerably from a Mughal peak. As in other trades, what had happened was a fragmentation and rerouting of traffic to newly important centres.

The reorientation of trade routes and merchant communities

The final section of this chapter turns from the volume and organisation of trade to the direction of flows of trade on the longer-distance routes between 1770 and 1800. In general, the importance of the arterial routes of the Mughal empire declined, but cross-country routes between the islands of agricultural stability and courtly consumption became more important. This helped to preserve some cities from more serious decline, and also put bodies of local merchants with strong links in the hinterland into a more powerful position in their economies. These developments are important for understanding the context within which European trade in north India expanded, as will be seen in chapter 6.

In 1720, major trade routes had converged on the imperial capitals of Delhi and Agra.[126] Luxury silks and muslins were brought from Bengal for the use of the Mughal aristocracy; so was rice from Bengal and from Bahraich on the plains beneath the Himalayas.[127] Bengal goods were re-exported from Delhi and Agra to the west coast along with indigo from the Bayana region and cloths produced in Hindustan. They were exchanged for Gujerati silk goods and spices from Western Asia.

---

[125] Resident to Govt, 11 May 1788, DR, vol. 6, UPR; Girdlestone, *Past Famines*, p. 7.
[126] Das Gupta in Richards (ed.), *Islam and the Trade of Asia*, pp. 181–95.
[127] I. Habib, *Atlas of the Mughal Empire* (Delhi, forthcoming), map 8B, 'Uttar Pradesh. Economic'.

Another spoke of trade led northward from the Mughal heartland to Lahore and on to Kabul, Iran and Central Asia. The mountains restricted this to high value, low bulk commodities, such as fruits, opium, dyes and spices; Delhi also received horses from the north. Three major trading communities stand out. The Gujeratis who had long been prominent on the sea routes in the Indian Ocean appear to have established themselves in all the Gangetic cities and to have been present even in Bengal. Punjabi Khattris from Multan were dominant on the northern leg of the trade, but also controlled the valuable horse and shawl trades. Merchants from Rajasthan had established themselves as financiers and jewellers in the Mughal capitals and moved alongside Mughal notables and governors. The great Jagat Seth family had linked its fortunes to the Mughal governors (later Nawabs) of Bengal, but one branch of the family had remained in Delhi to provide financial services at the failing heart of the Empire.[128]

The most striking feature of the major trade routes two generations later in 1780 was that they survived in spite of substantial rerouting and local decline. It seems to have been the high value, low bulk, long-distance trades which weathered the political changes best, while mass cloth exports and large-scale flows of grain between regions became more fitful. Another feature of the situation in 1780 was the importance of cross-country trade routes between the natural surplus areas and stronger polities, which criss-crossed the older, arterial routes. It is hazardous to call these routes 'new' since they generally existed in Mughal times. But the rise of Awadh, the Marathas and the Rohillas had enhanced their importance in the general scheme of medium- and long-distance trade.

The reign of Aurangzeb (1656–1707) had seen a great growth in trade down the main routeway from Delhi to Bengal where the Mughal grip was being tightened and the European companies were encouraging the expansion of the artisan economy. Dr Naqvi has shown how the towns of eastern Hindustan – Allahabad, Jaunpur and Benares[129] – benefited from this increased trade. Chapter 2 has suggested that local commercialisation, and political and religious changes were as significant as long-distance trade in this development. But there can be no doubt that by the 1780s the Benares region had become the financial and commercial crossroads for the whole subcontinent. Financial primacy had moved from Murshidabad to Benares after the decline of

---

128 *CPC*, vii, 192; viii, 159; note how the firm opened a branch at Allahabad when the Emperor established himself there in 1767, Nandlal Chatterjee, 'Shah Alam at Allahabad, 1767–9', *Journal of the U.P. Historical Society*, xii (1938), 6.

129 Naqvi, 'Progress of urbanization'.

the Jagat Seths, while Benares, Mirzapur and Ghazipur now controlled the crossing of the south-west and north-east routes which had converged on Delhi and Agra in earlier years. The great press of merchant people in these cities suggests how durable were all-India commercial connections as networks of skills and information. In Benares traders from the Punjab, working the shawl routes, remain in evidence. We hear of 'merchants of Lahaur, Multaun and the westward'[130] who traded alongside varieties of Mughal merchant and Muslims from the north-western mountains.[131]

The north-west route had always been adaptable. Its technique was the armed caravan in which smaller traders attached themselves to a caravan magnate (*rais*). These bosses were skilled in political relations with the ferocious hill potentates who controlled the routes.[132] The value of some of the goods passing on the route – gold, musk, horses, shawls – was so great that it was very difficult to choke off the trade altogether. Also, though they were of a peddling and caravan type, the northern routes were culturally significant. Along them, the Muslim aristocracies of north India, Central Asia and Iran remained in communication. This served to disseminate and maintain patterns of consumption which were economically of the greatest importance. Nishapur in Iran, for instance, was a producer of some of the finest red dyes which were used wherever the high Indo-Persian style of life survived. But Nishapur was also the home-town of some of the most prestigious of north India's political leaders, including the founder of the dynasty of Awadh. So this trade decentralised, shifted and reconverged, but never really died out. It remained important even in the following century by when it was dwarfed by the massive growth of the Gangetic route to the east. Nevertheless, during the eighteenth century there seems to have been a progressive shift to the east which had consequences for the feeder and service towns south of the mountains. Insecurity in the Punjab after 1710 moved trade east from Sialkot and Multan to Bilaspur on the Beas which was 'in its prime' about 1730.[133] Then, after the 'disturbance of the Durrani',[134] there was a further move to the east which brought the goods out from the mountains at Hardwar and distributed them from there to the growing principalities of Rohilkhand and Awadh, rather than directing them through Panipat and Delhi. The processes of state-building and the routing of trade were complementary. Najib Khan, the Rohilla, built

130 Petition of Merchants of Lahore and Multan, 4 Dec. 1787, PR.
131 Petition of Merchants of Kabul, Punjab, etc., 4 Dec. 1787, DR, vol. 12, UPR.
132 Forster, *Journey*, II, 219.
133 *Gunga Bye* v. *the Mother of Jwalanath*, Benares Adalat, 3 Aug. 1792, PR.
134 *Ibid.*, reply of Gunga Bye's *vakil*.

the entrepôt and fortress centre of Najibabad near the northern hills because 'there was already a large trade there'. But the reduced cost of protection to the merchants in breaking-bulk at Najibabad encouraged a further centralisation of trade.

Despite the decline of the northern markets of Delhi and of the great entrepôt town of Panipat, trade direct to the old capital did not cease completely. Forster encountered three large caravans moving south to Delhi between January and March 1782.[135] The route continued to mark the beginning of a chain of Indian trading settlements (mostly Punjabi Khattri) which stretched far up into Central Asia to Astrakhan and Lake Balk.[136] This trade existed in the sixteenth century, and probably before. One essential force maintained it: the enormous appetite of India for gold and silver.[137] The importance of bullion imported by the European companies by sea in opening up Indian trade with the west is generally known. More obscure is the significant trade which took Indian goods up to Bokhara and beyond in search of gold and silver which was relatively cheaper in terms of commodities than it was in India. Provided they continued to take their cut of this valuable commerce, the hill rajas were quite happy to allow it to continue. Forster's narrative makes it clear that it was 'free merchants' unattached to caravans who were in dire danger of robbery and death.[138] Men associated with the chief merchant of the caravan could, however, seek his protection. Even the Sikhs who were notorious as robbers in the northern hills actively encouraged the prosperity of entrepôts such as Amritsar and Ludhiana by their own client merchant communities.[139]

Whereas the northern mountain trades were well attuned to adapt to political decentralisation and flux, this on the face of it was not the case for the great western trade routes which moved from Agra and Delhi towards Gujerat. Tieffenthaler makes it clear that the old trade in Agra ('bayana') indigo had effectively ceased by 1750;[140] Ashin Das Gupta has traced the gradual strangling of this route up to about 1738.[141] Nor do we find evidence of a bulk trade in north Indian cotton products to the west, or the reciprocal trade in Gujerat silks and Western Asian spices after this date. The decline of tributary relations between Gujerat and the Mughal centre, which had occurred before 1730, may well have

---

135 Forster, *Journey*, I, 141, 218.
136 *Ibid.*, p. 220.
137 *Ibid.*, p. 234; for the import of bullion over this route, see, Mir Izzet Ullah, 'Travels beyond the Himalayas', from the *Oriental Quarterly*, 1825, *JRAS*, vii (1843), 339.
138 Forster, *Journey*, I, 219–83.
139 Polier, *c.* 1785, in Ganda Singh (ed.), *Early European Accounts*, pp. 87–8.
140 Tieffenthaler in Bernouilli (ed.), *Description*, I, 163.
141 Das Gupta, *Surat*, pp. 141ff.

undermined the financial rationale of bulk transactions like this. Falling world demand for Indian indigo with the development of Caribbean estates and political change in Iran and the Middle East were some of the external developments affecting the commercial links between eastern and western India. The establishment of the East India Company's monopoly in Bengal by 1770 also excluded western Indian opium from what had once been one of its largest markets. It was now funnelled to Bombay and Broach from where it was distributed all over the Near East by English and Bohra merchants.

Even so, we must not assume that the decline of these highly visible Mughal trade routes meant a dead stop to commercial exchange between the eastern and western sectors of Indian trade. In the 1770s and 1780s, Benares merchant houses such as Arjunji Nathji of Surat and the various Gopal Das houses were still able to remit up to Rs. 50 lakhs per annum in *hundis* to western India,[142] while the Benares commercial cases include a number of references to Gujerati merchants moving between Surat and Benares or Mirzapur. Connections with western Rajasthan also persisted. In 1790, we find the house 'Kehsee Teloksee' of Bikaner trying to break into the highly lucrative and prestigious business of moving East India Company funds from Bengal to Surat and Bombay.[143] Evidently transactions on this scale presuppose some kind of complementary flow of goods or services between the east and west and also the persistence of the links of mercantile honour and credit over these long distances. How did it happen? One suggestion has already been made. Western Indians continued to resort to Benares and Muttra for pilgrimage and this helped eastern India's balance of payments with the west. Secondly, it seems that the establishment of British maritime dominance in both the Arabian Sea and the Bay of Bengal had encouraged the development of direct seaborne commerce between Bengal and Gujerat which facilitated credit transactions across the subcontinent. Between about 1750 and 1783 considerable quantities of fine quality Gujerat raw cotton were being sold to the Bengal weaving towns. There seems to have been some direct trade in food-grains during scarcity seasons, such as 1788, when there was a famine in the west. Businessmen had certainly adapted to a very intermittent direct trade. Arjunji Nathji's agent in Benares, Aret Ram Tiwari, explained how a notional money of account called *auth* kept books balanced for Gujerat and Hindustani merchants trading with each other. Merchants could build up very large *auth* credit in each others' books, and adjustments of accounts were only made after long periods during which

142 For Arjunji Nathji see, *CPC*, v, 650; ix, 368, 735.
143 Notes on Kehsee Teloksee, 4 April 1789, PR.

time large consignments in direct trade occurred to balance the books.[144] All the same, there is evidence to suggest that direct commercial transactions overland did continue to operate between 1750 and 1800. Gujerati goods appeared at the Hardwar fair[145] in the early 1800s, and others filtered through via the Maratha territories and Jhansi, or the northern Rajasthan route through Bikaner which was kept open by Palli Brahmins and Banjaras.[146] Probably the big centralised trades of Mughal days had given way to a system which was much more decentralised and in which transport and risks were shared between many more participants. Smaller packets of goods and services were exchanged between the western Indian ports and the Maratha or Rajput principalities, which, in turn, transacted with western and southern Hindustan along a variety of old and new routes. Thus, Rohilla sugar was going into Rajasthan and Mewar wheat and salt was moving in large quantities through Agra.[147]

Finally, what was the situation on the ancient downriver trade route from the Mughal heartland to Bengal? The evidence suggests that there was a considerable drop in the old river trade, partly because security collapsed on the river west of Allahabad; partly because of the silting up of the Agra reach of the Jamna;[148] and partly as a consequence of the decline of Mughal consumption and the disruption of tributary relations between Bengal and the centre. After 1770, too, the Company's Bengal monopoly appears to have bitten into the trade from east to west in cloth and the trade from west to east in opium and salt. On the other hand, it is possible to make out at least five flourishing cross-country trade routes which intersected the Ganges–Jamna and the Grand Trunk Road as they moved from north to south.

The rise of these cross-country trade routes was closely connected with continued economic growth in the more stable agricultural areas and state-building in central India and Rohilkhand. Much trade arose from redirected tributary relations and the consequent link between revenue and trade, but there were also direct commodity exchange trades in which, for instance, the iron mined in central India was exchanged for Awadh cloths and saltpetre. The route which is best documented is that from Bengal via Benares and Mirzapur to Jabbalpur and the Deccan.[149] The British were interested in it because of the raw

---

144 Examination of Aret Ram Tiwari, 10 July 1788, PR.
145 Francklin, *George Thomas*, p. 41; Notes on the Hardwar Fair, Bds Collns 2947, p. 53, IOL.
146 Tod, *Rajasthan*, II, 1254–5. 147 Agra Customs 1–3, UPR.
148 Wellesley's Report, 29 May 1802, Bds Collns 2803, IOL.
149 'Report on the several roads in the District of Mirzapore', 6 July 1837, Mirzapur Judl, 84, UPR.

cotton trade which developed after 1783, and also because they had a
close eye on the income of the Raja of Benares from transit duties. K. P.
Mishra's work has shown that it was the most valuable of Benares transit
trades. As consumption in Maharashtra and Benares grew, a commerce
developed between them. The multitude of internal customs duties and
the extreme danger of the route did little to discourage it. Indeed, the
Maratha and Gosain merchants of Mirzapur went as far as to organise
vigilante patrols to protect their own merchandise.

Four other significant cross-country trade routes were in evidence.
First, there was that between Rohilkhand and Rajasthan in sugar, grain
and salt. Secondly, there was the route which linked the flourishing
Gangetic principality of Farrukhabad with the equally flourishing areas
of Maratha territory south of Jhansi.[150] A third route crossed the Ganges
near Allahabad and converged on the market of Phulpur in the north of
the district. In a sense, too, the trade in cloth and saltpetre between
eastern Awadh and Bengal[151] was a new, north–south development
compensating towns and market centres for the withering of the old
arterial route. Finally, the revival of urban life in the Punjab between
1790 and 1820 began to draw in goods from the stable areas of western
Hindustan. Farrukhabad, for instance, was exporting large quantities of
inferior Indian indigo to Lahore and even to Afghanistan, some years
before it became a major producer for the English market.[152]

In commerce as in politics and land control, local dominances were
being established which were to persist until the Partition of India in
1947. The emergence of regional court centres and the growth of the
practice of revenue-farming provided opportunities for the merchant
communities as a whole to adjust to the decline of the Mughal hegemony
and the trade routes which it supported, but there was a good deal of
dislocation as old trading groups disappeared and new ones emerged.
These distinctive groups of merchants were usually called by broad
caste names, such as 'Khattris', 'Gujerati Banias', 'Agarwals' and so on;
sometimes they were also designated by their region of origin, so that we
find 'Multanis' from the town of Multan in the Punjab or 'merchants of
Bikaner' from the famous town in Rajasthan. Descriptions have a
similar general value to terms like 'Genoese', 'Ostenders' or
'Alexandrian Jews' in European history. They should not be taken to
mean that trade was encompassed by caste, or that all members of a
particular trading caste rose in wealth or declined at the same time.[153]

150 W. Hunter, 'Narrative of a journey from Agra to Oujein', *AR*, vi (1799), 23.
151 P. Marshall, 'Economic and political expansion. The case of Oudh', *Modern Asian
Studies*, ix (1975), 465–83.
152 Farrukhabad Magistrate's Report, 27 Oct. 1814, Home Misc. 776, IOL.
153 Bayly, 'Indian merchants', in Dewey and Hopkins (eds), *Imperial Impact*, pp. 174–88.

Accepting for a moment these general descriptions, the main feature of the eighteenth century in the Ganges valley was the decline of the trading power of the Gujerati Bania and Gujerati Brahmin merchants who had dominated the great cross-country trade routes between Surat on the west coast and Murshidabad in Bengal during the days of the Mughals and their immediate predecessors. Since before the time of the Portuguese invasion of the eastern seas, Gujeratis had been among the great carrying merchants in Indian Ocean and Far Eastern trade.[154] As Mughal rule on land linked Gujerat with newly conquered Bengal, it was understandable that Gujerati families spread across country and down the Ganges–Jamna valley, benefiting from their excellent market information and large capital resources.[155] Even after 1707 the Gujeratis still held their own in the bazaars of Hindustan. They headed the general council of the traders of Benares and, until quite late, a Gujerati family was regarded as *nagarseth* or chief merchant of the city.[156] Gujerati families were also prominent in the great Vaishnavite centre of Muttra, and in the nearby imperial city of Agra where Arjunji Nathji and associated firms kept the cross-country trade route open during the bad years of the 1750s and 1760s. There are traces of the old Gujerati dominance in the riverain cities of Allahabad and Kara-Shahzadpur also. But by the middle of the century, they were on the wane. The decline of the ports of western India was accompanied by a shift in trade to the east where a new British-dominated merchant marine grew up in Hughly and Calcutta with its sights fixed firmly on the China trade. It was not Gujeratis, but the up-and-coming Bengal high castes who inherited their place in the export trades, while local merchant groups rose to prominence in the interior. At the same time, the Gujerati dominance on the inland routes was put under pressure by the atrophy of trade between Delhi and Agra and the western seaports. Gujerati families often retained prestige in the north Indian cities, but their grip on the growing areas of trade was weak. It was easier to be successful in long-distance trade if one had a firm grip on local trade, and this the Gujeratis did not have.

Other old-established networks of merchant families with contacts throughout the north and west of the old Mughal dominion were on the wane. The volume of trade and merchant institutions held up well, and even developed in some areas. But it was the communities with their feet firmly in the villages and small towns who made the adaptation with

---

154 Das Gupta, *Surat*, pp. 1–20.
155 Susil Chaudhuri, 'Bengal merchants in the second half of the seventeenth century', *Bengal Past and Present*, xc (1971), 211.
156 See, e.g., for Gujeratis at Benares, *Arzi* of Rahim Bibi, DR, vol. 36, p. 172.

least pain. The Agarwals and Umar of eastern Hindustan moved to take up the opportunities in the trading towns of the Benares domains. But often it was local groups from outside the bounds of the traditional merchant communities who established themselves as great merchants on nearly equal terms with older families in the corporate life of the commercial people. The atrophy of the old imperial routeways and the spread of money relations to the hinterland both contributed to this change. Its importance was that it welded together more firmly the monied men of town and country, helping further in the creation of a unified Indian trading class.

Conclusion

The argument so far can be summarised as follows. During the later eighteenth century, agricultural labour, capital, and the investment of the political elites were redistributed across the north Indian countryside. The local decline in the agriculture of unstable tracts was matched by the expansion of marketing and cultivation on the fringes of tracts which were less dependent on artificial irrigation to produce good crops. In such areas, agriculture and marketing may actually have become more intensive during the century. Overall, towns and cities fared better than it might appear. Some instability in them was generated by war and conquest, but much of the movement and flux reflected intrinsic features of Indian social organisation. There were also powerful forces working for continuity and stability. The search for legitimacy within the Mughal polity; the expression of piety within the caste system; and elite expenditure, which was often a physical manifestation of both of these, buoyed up trade and artisan production.

However, the eighteenth century was more than simply a new map of old social relationships. The very process of redistribution gave some groups significant social advancement. Particularly successful were those groups – gentry, warriors and merchants – who could move resources and mediate between the smaller dominions and the areas of advanced agriculture on which they were based. It is to the social organisation of the intermediate groups between state and agrarian society that we turn in the next chapter.

4

*The rise of the corporations**

Indian society is so complex that any unqualified exposition of historical trends must be superficial, and any deeper one will become enmeshed in paradox. The outstanding paradox of the eighteenth century was the coexistence of areas of local prosperity with political turbulence and agricultural decline. This at least is partly resolved by attending carefully to geography, and to different levels of power and production. But there remain the more serious difficulties of understanding the quality of the changes which were taking place. Was there simply a redistribution of men and resources between one place and another, with new actors filling old roles? Or was society undergoing a deeper transformation? With work on indigenous archives only just beginning, it is far too early to say. But in two senses, it already appears that more was going on than the time-honoured ouster of old elites by new men and the perpetual motion of dynast following dynast.

First, money had become a crucial component of agrarian relations in the more stable tracts. This does not mean that the free market was breaking down old dominances based on force or caste rank. Rather, relationships of power between man and man, village and village, were reinforced and modified by control of cash. Rulers, warriors and village headmen needed silver rupees, and this caused them to admit men of commerce to a small share of power or to step into the ring as lenders and traders themselves. In the eastern districts especially, the power of the dominant agricultural castes was supported by networks of trade and credit before the end of the eighteenth century.

*The word 'corporation' (often translating Hindi *sabha*) is used here to mean an occupational or religious organisation which transcended the bounds of 'caste' in the sense of *jati*. It would therefore include commercial or priestly associations (*sarrafas; mahajans* in the sense used in Gujerat; Brahmin *sabhas* called 'colleges' by European observers), as well as certain types of ascetic *akharas* and other *sampradayan* which integrated urban or rural society and acted as self-regulating entities *de facto*. My usage differs from that of B. Stein, *Peasant State and Society in Medieval South India* (Delhi, 1980), who applies the term to single-caste groups of rural people. The point that such groups needed to be 'incorporated' through temple ritual before their status was secure (Appadurai and Breckenridge, *IESHR*, xiii, 1976) is well taken. But my concern here is with the fact that Indian society could produce dynamic, multi-caste institutions in the context of growing monetisation and the weakening of central state power. It was this tendency which was overlooked by Max Weber and other theorists.

Secondly, beneath the flux of the regional courts and the great households of their revenue-farmers, more stable patterns of local power were slowly being precipitated between the state and agrarian society. There emerged a unified merchant class wielding covert political power, and a locally resident gentry of literate service families. The concern of this chapter is with the organisation and influence of the merchants. But the Islamic gentry provide a useful comparative example of a pre-colonial class which continued to evolve in colonial north India. Both groups, for instance, tended to benefit from the farming-out to great magnates of the government revenue – a practice which became a pervasive feature of the successor regimes.

Revenue-farmers and entrepreneurs in the agrarian system

Money slowly penetrated Indian rural society over many centuries. Even at its height, the Mughal military bureaucracy had always been uncomfortably closely tied into commercial networks and dependent on local gentry managers and chamberlains. High Mughal officials in Bengal and south India during the seventeenth century had owned ships, while 'local governors seem in practice to have been free to enter the market on their own initiative'.[1] Holders of revenue assignments posted at a great distance from their assigned lands could hardly have managed them without leaving a great deal of initiative to local men who were skilled at financial management and understood the marketing of produce.[2] Nevertheless, the breakdown of the system of state revenue assignments after 1707 gave rise to a situation in which more and more of the revenue was being farmed out to notables on the basis of cash payments. The beauty of such a system for the new regional rulers and last Mughal viceroys was that it provided a known and regular source of income without the problems of local collection. This was important at a time when rulers had to employ increasingly expensive armies requiring regular cash payments.

The farming of state revenue on one, two or three year leases appears to have become common in northern India between Rajasthan and Bengal before 1740.[3] But in Benares and Awadh, it was extended to

---

[1] Heesterman, 'Was there an Indian reaction?', in Wesseling (ed.), *Expansion*, p. 41.

[2] The change was not welcomed see, e.g., Bhimsen, *c.* 1720, 'In the present age unprofessional men having learnt the art of arithmetic have become masters of authority, and engaged in plundering the public', *Tarikh-i-Dilkasha*, tr. V. Khobrekar (Bombay, 1972), p. 232.

[3] N. A. Siddiqi, *Land Revenue Administration under the Mughals 1700–50* (Bombay, 1970), pp. 2-3; Moreland, *From Akbar to Aurangzeb*, pp. 235, 239-40, 249-54; Barnett, *North India*, pp. 169-70.

practically all the ruler's ancient taxation rights between 1740 and 1780. Local enterprise capital was involved in the form of duties on transit, toll, ferry and bazaar duties,[4] besides those on the trade in *betel* nuts,[5] dressed stone, wood and bamboo, etc.[6] The Gosain traders paid special rates on their transit goods through Benares; and even this tax was farmed out, possibly as a concession to their religious status,[7] possibly in recognition of the difficulty in collecting it from them.

The men who could mobilise capital on a scale large enough to speculate on farms of revenue or state commercial duties were the century's most obvious entrepreneurs. The greatest of them were few in number: the main revenue-farmers in Awadh in 1770 amounted to some fifteen men;[8] in Benares, around thirty-six.[9] Their manner may have echoed the high officials of Mughal times, but their social origins would not have graced the court of Aurangzeb. The two men who controlled up to 60 per cent of the Awadh revenue were respectively a eunuch of Jat origin (Almas Ali Khan) and a Hindu raja scarcely removed from his rustic background (Bhawani Singh). In Benares, too, the old Muslim revenue-farmers had been ousted by aspiring rural Brahmins connected with the raja along with assorted men of commerce.

These warrior entrepreneurs worked portfolios of revenue-farms, trading ventures, and military supplies through the mechanism of great households, like the Mughal *mansabdars* before them. Many could raise (or thought they could raise) up to five or ten lakhs of Rupees annually to finance their farms. Alongside them there were other less wealthy and prominent operators working quietly in the petty darbar halls. Some of the mercenary captains who fitted out and sold their troops to the highest bidder should really be seen as entrepreneurs. Then there were a variety of monopoly farmers, military contractors and general factotums, such as Shankar Pandit[10] and Beni Ram Pandit,[11] who worked the Benares opium and sugar monopolies respectively for both raja and English Company. Men like this were found in all the smaller states.

[4] 11 Jan. 1788, PR.   [5] 15 Jan. 1788, PR.

[6] In Muttra and Brindaban under Maratha *amils*, the claims of the state extended to 'nightsoil' collected by hereditary sweepers; under the British it became a perquisite of zamindars – a paradigm of change in the political economy, Magt. Muttra to Commr Agra, 15 Mar. 1839, NWP Judl, June 1839, 231/59.

[7] The king's duty to protect Brahmins was also commercialised, see J. Duncan's *perwana* to Mahip Narayan Singh, 11 Nov. 1788, PR.

[8] Barnett, *North India*, pp. 186–7.

[9] Mishra, *Banaras*, pp. 78–87; DR, vol. 24, 191–3, UPR.

[10] See, e.g., Magistrate Benares to Commercial Resident Ghazipur, 4 Oct. 1796, Benares Collectorate Records (rev.) 79, UPR.

[11] Note on Beni Ram Pandit, 11 May 1788, vol. 6, DR.

The revenue-farmers and enterprisers were not themselves a social class but a group of over-mighty subjects who reflected the adaptation of governments to the problems of cash flow in an uncertain economic climate. They represented a successful conjunction of agrarian might and capital, often buttressed with military force. But straddling the agrarian and commercial worlds, these colossi were vulnerable to groups better entrenched in both. Few revenue-farmers started with sufficiently detailed control over rural resources or sufficient entrée into the markets to survive the loss of government favour. Some, like Sheo Lal Dube, Bernard Cohn's archetype of a 'new man', were able to transform themselves into local magnates and survive into the British period as zamindars.[12] But many like Mir Amjad of Jaunpur failed to coerce intractable village communities, fell into arrears and disappeared from the scene;[13] or being fine-weather favourites or eunuchs, failed to father their own lineages.

More significant for the future were the social groups which subsisted beneath and even supported the revenue machinery of the regional rulers and the revenue-farmers. For Awadh, Barnett has argued that revenue-farming benefited 'local networks' of power[14] to whom much of the revenue percolated in the form of fees and expenses. One can point, for instance, to the rich commercial farmers and traders of Baiswara who were able to entrench their position under Nawabi management.[15] Similarly, the more obscure Muslim and Kayasth elites of the small towns of the Doab and western Awadh benefited as under-managers and collectors for Almas Ali Khan.[16] Within twenty years of his death, this great revenue-farmer survived only in legend, but his clients among the Kayasths of Hathgaon in Fatehpur or the Sayyids of Unao had perpetuated their influence as local gentry and service people around their small towns.[17]

[12] B. S. Cohn, 'The initial British impact on India. A case study of the Banaras region', *Journal of Asian Studies*, xix (1960), 418-31; cf. 12 Aug. 1788, PR.

[13] 11 Jan. 1788, PR.   [14] Barnett, *North India*, pp. 188-9ff.

[15] E.g., Nawabi Gorakhpur, Martin, *Eastern India*, I, 573.

[16] In Etawah, for instance, the Kunnu Prasad, Udai Charan and Lal Joda Bali families 'greatly benefited' from the rule of Almas Ali, CPR, 10 Dec. 1805, 95/37; in Bareilly the family of Chutter Bihari Lal had supplied several of his *chakladars*, CPR, 17 Feb. 1824, 95/37; in Maratha areas substantial monied men became *amils*, e.g., Purun Chand Pachcowrie, salt merchant, was *amil* of Farrah until 1802 Collr Customs Agra to Bd, 24 Mar. 1809, CPR, 12 April 1809, 97/31; cf. D. P. Divekar, 'Business community in eighteenth century Maharashtra', *Modern Asian Studies* (forthcoming); in Farrukhabad from 1770 to 1798, the Mehtab Rai Jain jeweller family had been treasurers taking a commission of 4 annas per cent on *dakhillas* and two rupees on every village within his own *jagir* and an annual pension of Rs. 750: correspondence on petition of Mehtab Rai, CPR, June 1808, 91/21, IOL.

[17] For an indication of the way in which revenue-farmers' patronage benefited service gentry, see *mahzar* under seal of Ghulam Kwais (n.d.) of Ghulam Saif and Sayyid

For Benares, Jonathan Duncan's settlement records, reflecting the working of immediate pre-colonial society, give us a more detailed view of the men of capital and local power who subsisted in fractious alliance with the revenue-farmers in the last few years before the Permanent Settlement was introduced into the tract in 1793. Here also, the revenue-farmers were more successful if they could patronise specialist low caste cultivators, but virtually impotent when they came up against powerful joint bodies of village zamindars who might throw up their cultivation if they could not get the terms they desired. Here, too, gentry under-managers (though often Brahmins and Kayasths rather than Muslims) consolidated local power under the aegis of the revenue-farmers. But what is most notable is the extent to which the revenue system was penetrated and constrained by the commercial classes at every level. Even in the parts of the Benares province where the primitive form of assessment in kind still prevailed, village traders and moneylenders played an important part, and the revenue-farmers needed to keep good relations with them in order to sell their portion of the crop for ready cash.[18] From time to time, there were conflicts between the two parties when the revenue-farmers attempted forced sales of old or bad grain for high cash prices. Cash revenue-payment by the cultivators themselves was, however, becoming the norm. This avoided conflict with the traders, and besides, revenue-farmers could not risk falling into arrears when grain prices were low and they were unable to sell their portion at a profit. Cash revenue, on the other hand, tended to put the village elite into uncomfortable dependence on the merchant–moneylenders. So in 1787, we find the zamindars of Karinda complaining that the revenue-farmers had forced a money settlement on them, 'as by reason of the low price of grain, the value of that produce in all the parts of the pergunneh was less than usual, the amil [farmer] told us to enter into cabooleats (or engagements) for a ready-money settlement'.[19]

The existence of a 'money settlement' tended to drive the tendrils of big urban moneylenders deeper into the countryside and reinforce the connection between them and the village traders and shopkeepers (*bakkals*) who had emerged from general agricultural growth. The urban

Mahomed Ali, Mallawan Papers, UPR, publ. *COR*, I, 16–17. Here Fath Ali 'with the help of his son's father in law, viz. Nadir-uz Zaman, brother of Almas Ali Khan Bahadur [revenue farmer] brought a harkarah [messenger] from Raja Jhau Lal [the Nawab's favourite, Barnett, *North India*, pp. 110, 113, 135] who compelled the aforesaid Qazi [Abdul Razzaq] to give a statement in writing to the effect that Fath Ali and none else is the owner of the property'.

[18] Petition of shopkeepers of bazaar Chunoo, 21 Nov. 1787, PR.

[19] Petition of zamindars and tenants of Achayl Roy of Perguneh Kurindeh, 11 Jan. 1788, PR.

financiers were the men who advanced money to the revenue-farmers and stood as sureties (*malzamins*), or even double-sureties for them with the rulers for punctual payment.[20] In the case of money settlements, a local agent of the banking house accompanied the agent of the revenue-farmer in making the collections from the village zamindars, for 'It was established custom that the person who issued the revenue advances had his treasurer in the pergunnehs.'[21] These local agents generally appear to have been village shopkeepers linked by trading connection, and sometimes by caste, with the big merchants of the city. For instance, the under-collectors for Sheo Lal Dube, the Jaunpur farmer, carried out money transactions 'through the banker who had the money collections of the village',[22] while in the district of Chunar, villagers had always paid their revenue through the agency of the local shopkeepers.[23]

Besides having a hand in revenue collection at village level, traders and moneylenders also controlled the transactions between the subdivisional headquarters and Benares itself. The commercial families changed local coin into Benares Sicca Rupees and avoided the dangerous business of transporting treasure across open country by drawing credit notes on their correspondents in the city. The added security given by this system encouraged the early British Residents to get the bankers to extend their branch agencies in the countryside as quickly as possible. In the case of the few commercial men who openly became revenue-farmers themselves, the advantage of being able to work through their own system of branch agencies partly outweighed the disadvantage of being involved in an area where prudent bankers did not tread. For instance, Sheo Lal Dube was able to set up local branches of his own firm 'Sheo Lal Dube Bunder Dube' for his revenue-farm of the Jaunpur District.[24]

Finally, and at the very pinnacle of the revenue system, the commercial houses made huge temporary loans against the incoming revenue to the raja himself. These promissory notes or *dakhillas* were considered as good as ready coin in the bazaar. Without them, the raja was unable to pay his troops, remit his tribute to the British, or maintain his ceremonial and religious functions in the realm. Thus, fifteen large

[20] E.g. note on Ram Dayal, 20 April 1788, DR 5, UPR.
[21] 24 Dec. 1788, PR; cf. DR 39, pp 103ff. Dube combined the role of *amil* and *mahajan* in his *parganas*.
[22] *Arzi* of *amil* of Secunderapore, 6 July 1795, PR; *amils* also attempted to settle 'turbulent villages' by persuading them to admit *mahajans* who had previously made heavy losses there, *arzi* of Kilroy, 1 Nov. 1792, PR; cf. Raja's answer to Kashmiri Mull, 17 June 1788, PR.
[23] J. Treves to Duncan, 21 June 1792; 8 July 1790, PR.
[24] Extract from Kulb Ali Khan's Account, DR 39, p. 93; Neave to Duncan, 5 May 1788, DR 14, pp. 1–3, UPR.

Lucknow and Benares banking houses handled the whole 40 lakhs of Rupees of the Benares revenue in the years 1760–80, taking on it a service fee which appears to have amounted to $2\frac{1}{2}$ per cent or more.[25] Naturally this gave them very considerable political power. In 1776 the Resident stated that the great Agarwal house of Bhaiaram provided the main obstacle to the consolidation of his influence in the principality,[26] while in 1787, Jonathan Duncan acknowledged that the bankers could 'in a great measure command the Raja and Government, itself with respect to the realization of the revenue'.[27]

In Benares commercial men appear to have made even deeper inroads into agrarian society from time to time. The machinations of the powerful British Residents evidently encouraged their connections among the Indian trading firms to take a more direct role in revenue management. But it was also in the interest of the banking houses themselves to exert closer control when there was a danger that the revenue-farmers might default. In the late 1770s, the banker Kashmiri Mull appears to have taken the revenue-farm for fourteen *parganas* of the Jaunpur and Ghazipur Districts 'in partnership' with one of the royal princes.[28] Other commercial men were also covertly engaged in direct management. But this was a dangerous business, for a banker's commercial credit might suffer if he was too openly involved in government. When asked to become a revenue-farmer, Kashmiri Mull had represented that,

My business was that of a mehajen or banker and that partnership was not my business in consequence of which the Raja taking the Ganga or Ganges and the Deity Beeshesher [Visheshwar] between us declared that this secret should not be revealed to anyone.[29]

Resistance to the involvement of 'professed bankers' in revenue matters was also found amongst the landed magnates. 'Dobey is a banker, what has he to do with public matters?'[30] complained an outraged Jaunpur Rajput as the great banker wove his net across the district. Again 'what foolish malzamin [surety] would take the balances [of a revenue-farm]?' said the disingenuous master of the Benares mint, Kaun Das, who had been involved in the revenue management of the failed farmer Kulb Ali in 1787.[31] So deeply had the control to the men of commerce penetrated

[25] 27 June, 4 Aug. 1788, PR; Benares Treasury Accounts, DR 31, UPR.
[26] Graham to Anderson, 5 Dec. 1777, cited Mishra, *Banaras*, p. 266.
[27] A. Shakespear, *Selections from the Duncan Records* (Benares, 1873), I, 34; 26 Aug. 1788, PR.
[28] *Ikranamah* of Kashi Nath, son of Kashmiri Mull, 9 Mar., 13 June 1788, PR.
[29] Answer of Kashmiri Mull, 13 June 1788, PR.
[30] S. L. Dube to Duncan, 5 Mar. 1789, PR.
[31] 28 April, 27 June 1788, 8 Sept. 1789, PR.

that Kulb Ali repaid his debts to them before he satisfied the state itself;[32] it took all the influence of Jonathan Duncan and the rising power of the East India Company to recover the money from the commercial corporations of the city.[33]

Merchants and the political economy

The key advantage possessed by the eighteenth-century commercial groups was their ability to command resources across much greater distances than the smaller states with which they dealt. The formal system of official control over the economy was impressive enough. The ruler set the daily price of commodities (*nikhas*) through his urban executive officer, the *kotwal*, and all other prices and percentages in the bazaar followed this automatically.[34] Competition was restricted by officially appointed bazaar superintendents, and in case of scarcity, a ruler might forbid the export of commodities from his territories and coerce the grain merchants into releasing their stocks. But there was a good deal of bluff in all this. In practice, local economic autarchy was impossible and the markets were run by a process of bargaining between dealers, financiers and the military rulers. It was the commercial community which decided who should or should not pass his *hundis* in the bazaar and if the merchants were subjected to unduly savage pressure to release food-grains or provide forced loans, they simply closed the bazaar or abandoned the town.[35]

Tribute, military supply, pilgrimage and trade were linked together in an all-India network which merchants, bankers and specialist carriers could manipulate to the financial disadvantage of the regional rulers.[36] Bullion – the key to political success – circulated throughout India with considerable speed. The only major external sources were Central Asia and the trickle of imports through European centres, such as Chandernagore and Calcutta.[37] But considerable quantities of hoarded bullion were spasmodically released by rulers of central and north India to finance their military and ceremonial enterprises. Thus, while 'Bengal' silver was transported as far as Jaipur and Surat when there was a heavy demand during the 1770s and 1780s, the north Indian

---

[32] 27 Jan., 26 Aug. 1788, PR.   [33] 26 Aug. 1788, PR.

[34] Ibrahim Ali Khan's Report on Markets, 18 Dec. 1788, PR, cf. *Ain*, II, tr. Jarrett, 41-3.

[35] See D. L. Curley, 'Fair grain markets and Mughal famine policy in late eighteenth century Bengal', *Calcutta Historical Journal*, ii (1977), 1-27; for an example of market closure in Malwa, Malcolm, *Central India*, II, 284.

[36] Cf. C. N. Cooke, *The Rise, Progress and Present Condition of Banking in India* (Calcutta, 1863), p. 12.

[37] See, e.g., the Representation of Kaun Das, Mintmaster, 4 Dec. 1787, PR.

bankers also brought in gold plate from Rajasthan to cover the Nawab of Awadh's subsidy to the British on a number of occasions when silver was in short supply in the east.[38] As the East India Company became more deeply involved in the financial politics of north India, we begin to see how the firms working the all-India capital and bullion markets could play off one regional ruler against another. In 1789, for instance, the Company wished to reduce the discount they were paying to the Benares bankers to provide their agent at Poona with funds. Normally, the annual demand of Maratha pilgrims for cash at the holy city would have brought down the rate a little. But this year, the 'wants of Raghojee Bhonsla' for cash for his troops was so great that the bankers were able to play Marathas off against the British and keep the rate high.[39] In the same year, the commercial houses raised the rate of discount between Benares and Surat to a high 11 per cent, claiming that this was the result of 'fluctuations' and heavy demand in Lucknow.[40] Should rulers try to tax the bullion trade to their own advantage, it would simply dry up. Later, rates for coining at the Benares mint were raised, so the financial houses redirected the bullion and plate they were bringing up from Bengal to Rajasthan and Lucknow, to the detriment of the city's money supply and credit.[41]

Religious corporations, bodies of merchants and many commercial towns had been tough and resourceful in the face of political change. Rulers needed the services provided by these institutions as the costs of warfare and petty statehood rose, and as the revenue was gradually farmed out to entrepreneurs. Long-distance traders, carriers and even bodies of pilgrims became brokers for goods and services passing between the many decentralised regimes subsisting on areas of high farming. In the Gangetic cities and large market villages, there was a solid rank of middling merchants standing between the great merchant princes and the petty hucksters of agrarian society. Some scholars have made out the lineaments of an Indian bourgeoisie amidst the bustle of north India's more prosperous bazaars.[42] But evidence that merchant capital was becoming more important in the economy does not necessarily imply that merchants were aspiring to a direct political role or that the indigenous state was undergoing fundamental change during the century. There was, of course, no question of *mahajans* or despised *bakkals* widely taking on the ceremonial or military functions of rulers.

---

[38] See, e.g., For. Sec. Cons., 27 Oct. 1777, 4, NAI; 26 Feb. 1789, PR.
[39] Resident Poona to Resident Benares, 10 Apr. 1789, PR.
[40] 5 July 1789, PR.
[41] Examination of bankers, 15 Sept. 1790; Report of Mintmaster, 1 May 1791, PR.
[42] Gautam Bhadra, 'Some aspects of the social position of merchants at Murshidabad, 1763-93', paper presented to Indian History Congress, Chandigarh, 1973.

Even the transition between merchant, revenue-farmer and zamindar was hazardous in the context of strong notions of the separation between the role of ruler and merchant.

What can be said, however, is that the covert and subtly exercised power of merchant bodies imposed limitations on what eighteenth-century rulers could do, and allowed commerce to achieve a more privileged position in regard to the military aristocracy. Contemporary European observers were aware that the bankers not only operated punitive cartels against them but exercised a delicate political influence. So strongly had the power of the banking fraternity of Bengal and Hyderabad impressed itself on the mind of Law de Lauriston, ex-Governor General of French India, that he saw them in 1777 as a key group in any future alliance of the French and Indian states against the English East India Company:

These are the people to whom the nawabs and the rajas always have recourse; whom they consult willingly about all civil, military and political operations, because to some extent all these matters enter into the sphere of the *sarkars* [bankers] because of the good or evil which such an operation could bring to the country. They appear without pretension at the darbars, but they excercise great influence there; one word of a renowned banker will carry more weight than the most eloquent speech of another, whomsoever he be, because this word holds fast to a chain which extends everywhere [tient à une chaîne qui s'extend partout].[43]

De Lauriston's most telling point was that it was the men of commerce in eastern India who had most to gain from European and specifically from English trade. It was they, therefore, who had constrained the rajas and nawabs to allow foreign commerce a much freer hand in the interior of the country than it had ever had in the days of central Mughal rule.

Contemporary opinion differed from region to region in its assessment of the political power of the commercial classes. As might be expected, it was reckoned least formidable in tracts where trade was backward or in decline. H. T. Prinsep, for instance, could caricature the 'enormously wealthy' bankers of the Maratha territories 'absolutely rolling in wealth ... occupied in the exclusive pursuit of sordid and selfish gains'.[44] But he added significantly that they might achieve influence where revenue was put out to farm or where there was a fierce

[43] Law de Lauriston, Minute 1777, *État Politique de l'Inde en 1777* (Paris, 1913, Société de l'Histoire de l'Inde Française), p. 111.

[44] H. T. Prinsep, *History of the Political and Military Transactions in India during the Administration of the Marquis of Hastings 1813–23* (London, 1825), II, 298; but cf. G. T. Kulkarni, 'Banking in the 18th century. A case study of a Poona banker', *Artha Vijnana*, xv (1973), 180–200.

factional split among the military elite. In some areas which had suffered sharp local agricultural decline, commercial networks had actually been rolled back. In the Delhi territories, for instance, commercial firms with agencies in the small agricultural towns had given advances on the revenue as they did in Benares, though sometime between 1760 and 1800 this practice had ceased as Delhi lost control over its hinterland.[45] But some well-entrenched commercial groups were difficult to uproot from a position of local political influence even against the background of the near collapse of trade. In Bareilly, for instance, the ancient house of Lacchman Das survived the decline of Mughal power and the rise of the Rohillas and even remained significant in local Hindu and city politics at the beginning of British rule.[46]

Awadh perhaps represents an example mid-way between Bengal or Benares and those tracts without strong inland trade. Here, the political situation was even more perilous for the bankers than it was in Bengal, but they were still a force to be reckoned with. In Awadh, the great revenue-farmers such as Almas Ali Khan and Bhawani Singh appear to have organised their own cash and credit transactions between Lucknow and the interior fixed markets where revenue was collected.[47] But in some areas, at least, banking houses must have enacted a role similar to that which they played in Benares. For when the Nawab ceded large tracts of his territory to the British in 1801, incoming British collectors had difficulty in guaranteeing the revenue in the Doab because, it was said, commercial houses had withdrawn their agencies when the revenue-farmers had retired to Awadh.[48] Even if their role in the revenue system was somewhat less developed, Lucknow's banking houses provided a key service for the Nawabi government in remitting the annual tribute to Calcutta every year after 1764.[49] So important was the annual tribute that the bankers gained access to the darbar and to the British Resident and began to take a close interest in court faction as they had done in Bengal, Hyderabad and Benares before. For instance, a famous Jain banker, Lala Bacchraj, who appeared as a partner of the Benares magnate Lala Kashmiri Mull in transferring tribute all over Hindustan in the 1770s and 1780s, had insinuated himself into the centre of Lucknow court faction by the 1790s. With the aid of the British Resident, he gained an influence over the treasury and 'began to

[45] Metcalfe's Orders on the Delhi Territories, *Delhi Residency and Agency*, 1, 8, 27.
[46] The 'Gulistan-i-Rehmat' records several examples of Rohilla rulers favouring merchant and banking groups in order to encourage their settlement, see above, pp. 22–3.
[47] Barnett, *North India*, pp. 172ff.
[48] Asst Collr to Collr Allahabad, 26 June 1804, CPR, 16 July 1804, 90/40, IOL.
[49] Resident Lucknow to Govt, 14 Sept. 1795, Home Misc. 448, IOL; *CPC*, viii, 30, 183, 198.

aspire to the distinction of Naib',[50] a major officer of state. Bacchraj's drive for power foundered and he ended his life in a Nawabi prison, along with most of his family.[51] But it was significant that even in this, the most powerful and most agrarian of the north Indian successor states, Indian financiers could come so near to the sources of power.

The forms of urban organisation

The political influence of trader–bankers was a common feature of late eighteenth-century regimes. But was this power wielded simply by a few great magnate families subject to the 'instability of oriental fortunes', or did it have a wider social and institutional base? There is indeed a body of opinion which might concede the political importance of individual capitalists in pre-colonial Indian politics but argues that the culture and political ideas of India made it virtually impossible for merchants and townsmen to achieve any significant degree of autonomy or corporate identity in the face of ruling landed elites. Ultimately, these ideas derive from Max Weber's brilliant generalisations on the religion and institutions of India. According to Weber, occupational specialisation based on caste fragmented Indian artisan, merchant and service populations, so inhibiting the development of mercantile trust, let alone political action. Caste restrictions made impossible the civic fraternisation out of which emerged western corporate institutions, while the 'passivity' of Hinduism denied rising groups an ideology which could validate their political independence. Thus, urban centres and states remained dominated by the 'patrimonial' regimes of warrior bureaucrats, and for Weber as for Marx, true social change awaited the impact of colonial rule. These ideas continue to influence more recent work. Trade, it has been asserted, was 'merged into and managed by caste bodies';[52] the Indian city was split into 'self-contained and mutually hostile neighbourhoods';[53] the political role of merchants was limited by their *dharma*, and they remained of low social status. Such ideas are almost circular since the richest sources relate to revenue administration and the cycle of dynasties, and there is a grave lack of

---

50 Abu Talib, *Tafzihul Ghafalin* (*History of Asafu'ddaulah Nawab Vazir of Oudh*), tr. W. Hoey (new edn, Lucknow, 1971), pp. 53, 91–5; P. Basu, *Oudh and the East India Company 1785–1801* (Lucknow, 1943), p. 110.

51 Note on the Bachraj Family, annex. N. B. Edmonstone to Resident Benares, n.d., Bihar and Benares Revenue Consultation, 1 Dec. 1818, 112/11, IOL.

52 D. R. Gadgil, *Origins of the Modern Indian Business Class; an Interim Report* (New York, 1957), pp. 25–34.

53 R. Fox, 'Pariah capitalism and traditional Indian merchants past and present', in M. Singer (ed.), *Entrepreneurship and the Modernisation of Occupational Cultures* (Duke Univ., N. C., 1973), pp. 16–34.

evidence on the behaviour and organisation of social groups outside the ruling warrior elites and the literate classes dependent on them.

However, the evidence from several parts of north India suggests not only that the economic and political importance of the great trader–bankers was enhanced in the period of the successor states but that corporations of townsmen, merchants and religious specialists had developed a new coherence and autonomy which in some cases amounted to a virtual civic self-government. These changes were not frustrated by caste fragmentation or the passivity of Hinduism: on the contrary, caste and religion provided building-blocks out of which mercantile and urban solidarities were perceptibly emerging. The influence of trading corporations over the landholding aristocracy was undoubtedly enhanced by the growing European presence in India. Merchants were adaptable to the style and requirements of the British and gained from the burgeoning of the export trades to China and Europe after 1770. But the commercialisation of politics and the rise of the corporations were by origin intrinsic changes within the economy and culture. War and political change, far from destroying towns and trade, had actually galvanised them into greater independence. To illustrate the potential for such changes, we will take the case of Rajasthan. Not only was this an area removed from direct western influence, but it was the natural habitat of the haughty Indian aristocracy.

As James Tod recognised, a century of war had not destroyed trade or production in Rajasthan; only the Pax Britannica made a desert, and

> paradoxical as it may appear, there was tenfold more activity and enterprise in the midst of that predatory warfare, which rendered India one wide arena of conflict, than in these days of universal pacification.[54]

As in eastern India, merchants had strengthened their hold on the working of the revenue system by financing the deficits of the rajas and clan leaders and also by working the *takkavi* advances given to cultivators in the villages. Contemporary with these economic changes,[55] the political status of townsmen and merchants was increasing. Political fluidity resulting from the decline of Mughal overlordship and the rise of small, local kingdoms caused what Tod called a 'neglect of legislation' during the eighteenth century.[56] Self-governing multi-caste assemblies had taken over responsibility for many

---

[54] Tod, *Rajasthan*, II, 1,110.
[55] Dilbagh Singh, 'Role of the mahajan'; S. N. and K. N. Hasan and S. P. Gupta, 'Patterns of agricultural production in the territories of Amber c. 1650–1750', *IHC 1966*, pp. 244–8.
[56] Tod, *Rajasthan*, I, 171.

aspects of administration, especially defence and the upkeep of trade routes and *sarais*. The influence of Jain merchant people had already secured them a number of special privileges or immunities which had developed around the concept of 'sanctuary' (*ashrama*). In several Rajput states, officers of the raja were excluded from the temples and living quarters of Jain merchants, and the high status they had achieved influenced the standing of other townsmen with whom they had dealings. In some cases indeed the rights and privileges of merchants and towns were set out in documents which reminded Tod of medieval European town charters.[57] Tod's analogy between the emergence of western representative institutions from feudal privilege and the potential for a kind of representative government based on Indian urban councils is fanciful. But he was sufficiently struck by these developments in Rajasthan to record a significant deviation from his usual picture of oriental feudalism. If he was not witnessing the emergence of parliaments, Tod had certainly seen subtle changes in the relations between constituent elements of the pre-colonial state.

Changes like this were taking place elsewhere in India, but the timing and context were often different. In Rajasthan, always a turbulent frontier of empire, the apparatus of Mughal urban government, with its Muslim judicial officers responsible to a governor, had never developed strong roots. The bazaar and the service quarters of the towns bargained with or submitted directly to the raja and the Hindu warriors. 'Want of legislation' would force them directly into self-organisation. But in the cities of the plains where up to 40 per cent of the population might be Muslim, the Mughal executive officer (*kotwal*) and 'registrar' (*kazi*) retained varying degrees of influence. In Rohilkhand and Awadh, which retained strong Muslim identities, the power of the Hindu urban and commercial groups was growing, but it remained encompassed by city-wide Islamic institutions. There existed formal processes of registration and arbitration by *kotwal* and *kazi* even if effective power was left to heads of the corporations.

In the more commercial south and east, however, the authority of the Mughal officials had been largely eroded before 1770 as chapter 8 will show. Here bodies of traders and service people had also attained a significant degree of independence in matters of police, defence and arbitration. In Benares and Mirzapur particularly, the word corporation can properly be used to describe trading and religious organisations. People of different caste were tied together in broader communities which received explicit recognition from the rulers. Here monetisation of revenue demand, the growth of inland trade, and of the city of

[57] *Ibid.*, 11, 606, cf. app. 645, *perwana* of Maharana Sri Raj Singh.

Benares itself had put trader–bankers into a strategic position in the new Benares dominion.[58] By the 1770s, the power of the major mercantile houses was similar to that acquired by the Jagat Seths in Bengal in the later days of the Nawabi. They could, to use again the words of the British Resident, 'command the state to a large extent in the matter of revenue'. But how was this power represented in institutions? How coherent were mercantile organisations? The mid-Ganges at least appears to have seen the emergence of powerful mercantile corporations similar to the cross-caste merchant *mahajans* of Gujerat.[59] At Mirzapur, the fastest growing town, there was a 'Dhurnam Pancham' or 'general body of the trading people' which adjudicated disputes between people of different background according to mercantile custom and also adjusted brokerage fees.[60] Royal authority was not eliminated from the town and its hinterland. The petty local raja of Kantit retained considerable prestige and formally appointed a head or *chaudhuri* of the bazaar. But his wealth and power was dwarfed by that of the leading merchant houses and the religious corporations. It was they who patrolled the gated areas of the town and it was their levies which policed the key trade route which ran south into central India. As in Rajasthan, the 'want of legislation' and the impotence of small states had forced merchants and other groups with regional interests to take up the role of adjudication and protection which had formerly been the preserve of kings.

In Benares a similar set of relationships developed around the Naupatti Sabha (Society of Nine Sharers) which illustrates how merchant interests could be articulated across the boundaries of caste.[61] This association was a body of nine leading city merchant families which had been brought together by the demand of the ruler of Awadh for a huge forced loan during one of his campaigns against Benares during the 1750s. The nine great burghers had come forward to subscribe a part of the loan and so save the holy city and its environs from sack. Political turbulence had galvanised the community into action which permanently placed the 'bankers' in a strong moral and customal relationship with the raja and the other great land-controlling magnates who had been unable to protect the city themselves. But we do have echoes of earlier cooperation for political purposes by the mercantile elite. A central mercantile organisation appears to have existed at least from the beginning of the century, and it is said that they played an

---

[58] For a more detailed discussion of Benares and Mirzapur, see Bayly, 'Indian merchants', in Dewey and Hopkins (eds), *Imperial Impact*.

[59] N. A. Thoothi, *History of the Vaishnavas of Gujerat* (London, 1928).

[60] *Roop and Saroop Poori* v. *Badli Gir and Laulji*, Mirzapur Court, 3 April 1791, PR.

[61] 'A short account of the Nouputtee Mahajans of Benares', For. Misc. 12, pt 1, NAI.

important role in helping Balwant Singh's line to power in 1739.[62] The Nawab of Awadh who nominally controlled Benares was looking to renew the revenue-farm of the Benares territories to Mir Rustam Ali. But the story goes that the bankers calculated the greatest extent of their capital in order to put up an even larger bid and stronger security for Mansa Ram, the founder of the Bhumihar dynasty. This was a ploy to reduce Muslim influence in the territory and benefit a local dynasty with whom they were on much more equal terms. Though it seems unverifiable, the story encouraged the commercial community to claim high status in regard to the raja's family and descendants.

The nine families in the Naupatti came from different backgrounds. One was Gujerati Brahmin, one Gujerati Vaishya, one Oswal Jain and the others Agarwals of various subgroups. In the beginning, there was a mix between old established Gujerati firms and relative newcomers from eastern India. All that mattered was finding enough liquid capital to finance the forced loan.[63] Later, the Naupatti became a self-perpetuating oligarchy of status which no aspiring family could enter.[64] But it did not separate itself off from other merchant people, acting instead as a holding alliance at the top of merchant society which overrode caste and sectarian boundaries. So while merchant people had different interests and statuses, the merchant community did have a distinct autonomous existence and was not irrevocably split by distinctions of ritual or residential area. On the contrary, ties of caste helped bind poorer merchants, brokers, hucksters and bazaar people into a corporate body of opinion which could make itself heard by both rajas and British residents.[65] Our image of caste is one of fragmentation, but in the pre-colonial period it might sometimes be better to use the image of the fasces in which the binding in of each individual element gives strength to the whole.

Let us set out the variety of these relationships. Direct marriage alliances were the lowest common denominator of both social and commercial life. In the course of the hundred years after 1750, the broad category of Agarwal merchants was drawn closer and closer by dozens of strategic marriages which pooled capital and skills. Rich newcomers like

<hr>

[62] According to the story current among descendants of the Naupatti bankers, Lala Gokul Das, a leading Agarwala and the Gujerati head of the corporation were the prime movers in backing Mansa Ram against the previous farmer of the Benares territories, Mir Rustam Ali; it was also said that the commercial community favoured a Hindu rather than Muslim ruler locally. I have not been able to verify this story from contemporary evidence but it was certainly part of the Naupatti's claim for high status.

[63] 'A short account of the Nouputtee'.

[64] Family histories, interviews, Sri Kumud Chandra, Dr Giresh Chandra, Benares, 1972–4.

[65] Petition of Bankers and Resident's Reply, 13 Jan. 1795, PR.

the Shah family were able to ally with more established but poorer families who headed the Purbiye (Eastern) Agarwal caste brotherhood. These links could help maintain relations over a much wider area also. Khattri merchants continued to marry their daughters to aspiring families at the other end of the great east–west trade route in the Punjab. The Dassapurwal Gujerati merchants display an even more interesting pattern. They customarily brought in poor young men from towns in Gujerat and other regions, married them to their daughters and set them up with houses and capital in Benares.[66]

Caste provided larger building-blocks than extended family groups. But these were not the tight-knit caste institutions which appear in some of the anthropological literature. Instead, they were more like loose bodies of patrons and clients drawn from broadly similar ritual groups which clustered around a few important families wielding ritual authority and economic power. Thus the famous family of Lala Kashmiri Mull was 'chief' of the city's Khattris and Saraswat Brahmins from the Punjab.[67] The cohesion of the group was enhanced by a relationship with the holy men of the local Nanakpanthi assembly who acted as *guru* (spiritual advisor) to most of the Punjabi people in the city. Like most other mercantile groups in Benares, the Khattris and their Saraswat Brahmin family priests and business partners had a caste assembly or *panchayat*. It seems to have met irregularly to deliberate on matters of morality and was, by tradition, quite separate from the multi-caste assemblies of 'respectable merchants' which adjudicated business matters.

While the mercantile population possessed a consciousness of caste and caste institutions which were more or less effective in matters of ritual, this did not preclude the formation of wider merchant organisations and bonds of trust which stretched across the boundaries of caste. In some trades, certain castes – or more properly, extended family groups – were predominant. So the Mehra Khattris dominated the cloth trade;[68] Purbiye Agarwals were strong in the grain trade,[69] Gujerati Banias in fine brocades,[70] and so on. Nevertheless, most trades were multi-caste ventures, and in their dealings with each other or with the authorities, merchants needed common institutions. Sometimes these were based on an interest in the trade of one region. Thus we find approaching the authorities in the 1780s, 'the merchants trading to Lahor, Multaun and the west', who included Gosains, Brahmins,

---

[66] Family history, papers, *panda* book, in possession of Sri Devi Narayan, Sakshi Binayak, Benares, Jan. 1973; interview Sri Govind Das Kothiwal, Mar. 1974.

[67] *Gunga Bye* v. *the Mother of Jwalanath*, 3 Aug. 1792, PR.

[68] Bayly, *Imperial Impact*, pp. 178–88.   [69] Interviews, Chaukhambha, 1973.

[70] Family histories, Sri Govind Das Kothiwal, Mar. 1974.

Khattris and 'Iraqis'; 'the merchants trading to the Duccin [Deccan] and southwards',[71] including Sipahi Nagars,[72] Maratha Brahmins and Bundelkhandi Jains, and 'the mahajans and traders ordinarily resident in Benares',[73] including Agarwals, Khattris and others. Another form of organisation was based on the particular function performed by merchants at different levels of the trading system. The wholesale commission agents (*arethias*) trading to particular regions had their own organisation and spokesmen, as did the petty bazaar lenders.

Conceptions of status and mercantile honour also overrode caste for it is evident that trade and credit relations over long distances could not have survived without them. 'Credit-worthiness', having one's *hundis* accepted in the bazaar, keeping regular commercial books, being frugal rather than 'expensive': these were the measures of respectability which are mentioned regularly in commercial cases and they are witness to a consistent mercantile 'public opinion'. At the pinnacle of merchant society stood the members of the Naupatti Sabha themselves who functioned as a final panel of arbitration among merchants on matters such as debt, the division of assets in family partitions, bankruptcy, and the status of mercantile custom on legal instruments. During this period it seems to have been unusual for litigation to go beyond these informal, local forums. Only in the few instances where family, caste or Naupatti arbitration had failed to impose a settlement would the *kotwali peon* – the runner of the city's police chief – or the ruler's courts be brought into the matter.[74] To all intents and purposes then, an *ad hoc* 'law merchant' existed. Excommunication remained the usual sanction for caste assemblies, but what were the sanctions available to this wider mercantile opinion? In a tight, face-to-face society, the failure of one's credit in the bazaar was a sentence of commercial and sometimes of physical death. But the sanctions of Hindu religion were also available. Oaths were made in Ganges water and in the name of tutelary deities, or with the witness of a Gosain who was technically above caste and kin since he was dead to the world. The ultimate sanction was to have Brahmins mutilate themselves before the door of a debtor in order to heap spiritual demerit on him (*dharna*); this was only the most dramatic instance of the role of popular religion in reinforcing mercantile trust.[75]

In Benares at this period there is tantalising evidence of social conflict

---

[71] Petition, 4 Dec. 1787, PR.

[72] Mehta Baldeo Das Vithal Das Vyasa, *Vanshwali Vadnagara Sipahi Nagar Kashi Nivasi* (Nagar Union, Benares, 1938).

[73] 18 Jan. 1788; DR Revenue, vol. 5. UPR.

[74] Representation of Ibrahim Ali Khan, 7 Mar. 1788, PR.

[75] Sir John Shore, 'On some extraordinary facts, customs and practices of the Hindoos', *AR*, lv (1795), 331; 7 Mar. 1788, PR.

based upon wealth. A witness in a case says 'it is not the custom of my caste to take the evidence of poor people at arbitrations'.[76] There is also the fact that members of the lower entrepreneurial castes (Kalwars, Telis, and Kacchis) generally appear to have arbitrated each others' disputes and did not have access to the Naupatti, though they were influenced by their mores and business style. Differences of class and status – *grand peuple* against *menu peuple* – are of course perfectly compatible with common civic or mercantile unity against outsiders. At other times, links of caste and patronage ensured that the complaints and difficulties of the poorer commercial people would reach the ears of the authorities. For instance, the merchant elite spoke up for workers in the Benares mint in 1791 when their livelihood was threatened by official action.[77] Later they fiercely resisted an attempt to bring in a limitation on suits for debt under the Bengal Regulations of 1793 on the grounds, among others, that it would damage the small lenders or *khurdeas*, who often waited for more than a generation for the payment of debts.[78]

If there were many links which bound mercantile people together irrespective of caste in all but the spheres of marriage and formal interdining, there were also subtle ties which bound together different occupations and statuses among the residents as a whole. Religious observance created solidarities here too. Gujerati and local Agarwal families joined together in the veneration of the Krishna temple of Gopal Lalji and were counted as members of the Vallabhacharya sect.[79] But the rajas of Benares and cadets of the ruling family were also closely associated with the shrine. From Mansa Ram onward, they customarily supported Gopal Lalji and other major shrines in the city and at Bindachal, the holy place of Mirzapur. As chief devotees and benefactors of shrines so closely associated with the ruling family, merchant people acquired enhanced status.

Within the city, Gosains and other ascetic orders also acted as a body of brokers between different social groups. They attracted veneration from the mass of the people and also had a close hand in the running of the merchant communities, and had even come to head them in nearby Mirzapur. Brahmins similarly acted as a force of integration. Not only did nobles and commercial notables feed or directly maintain the large

---

76 31 July 1790, PR.
77 Representation of Bhawani Das and others, 19 Apr. 1791; 'Petition of the Principal Bankers', 13 Jan. 1795, PR.
78 Petition of Naupatti and others, 1797, Agent to GG to Govt, 2 April 1798, PR.
79 *Ibid.*; for ancient links between the Agarwal headman family and the Bhumihar elite, see *mahzar*, 15 Apr. 1838 of Harrakhchand to District Court, 'Memory Book' (*Yadasht Bahi*), Chaukhambha.

Brahmin population, but the commercial houses employed Brahmins as runners and agents whenever possible to avoid problems of caste status with their clients and correspondents. The British Resident was horrified to find that it was customary among the merchants to take several paisa per Rupee on every *dakhila* or *hundi* transaction with the rulers for gifts to the Brahmins.[80] It was a further indication of the manner in which the ritual superiority of priest or ascetic could act as a unifying force in urban society.

Common residential areas also created knowledge and sympathies outside caste and between different occupational groups. Sometimes neighbourhood loyalties centred on the service of shrines, tanks or *ghats*. But local defence was also an important spur to organisation. Some quarters (*mohullas*) were, of course, single-caste residential areas. But an equally common pattern was the community of the great stone house or *haveli*. Each *haveli* was occupied by a single extended family and their dependents, and these were grouped together into gated areas which provided their own defence and police on the basis of a general levy.[81] Property documents show that many of these gated areas were multi-caste residential areas and the state, whether the raja or the decaying remnants of Mughal central authority, had little role in their organisation.

At the widest level then the links between the various elites in the cities created a sense of urban solidarity. This was no doubt weak by comparison with medieval Florence, but it provides evidence of the potential for organisation between the state and the mass of agrarian society. Cities such as Allahabad, Benares or Gaya had a special privileged status as *tirthas* or holy places. In theory, they were the property of the gods and all men could worship there. Out of their religious pre-eminence derived a sense of the 'public'.[82] In practice of course, private property existed in Benares and other holy cities. Yet the central part of the town north of the Dassasswamedh *ghat* was commonly regarded as an area of particular reverence. There was considerable concern to keep the 'holy mile' (*pakka mahal*) free from undesirable groups. These included not only the representatives of the earlier Muslim authority but even the raja and his collaterals. Apparent attempts by governments to impinge on this sacred liberty were fought vehemently by the Hindu city as a united corporation – the 'Babus [raja and collaterals], Brahmans and Mahajans of the city assembled'.[83] The

80 15 Sept. 1790, PR.
81 Police Arrangements, Benares Collr, Records, Misc. Series, vol. 8, UPR.
82 J. D. M. Derrett, *Essays in Classical and Modern Hindu Law* (Leiden, 1975), II, 25, 45.
83 Petition of Bankers and Resident's Remarks, 13 Jan. 1795, PR.

first indisputable record of an attempt by the citizens to protect the holy places was the protest in 1725 against the raising of an additional pilgrim tax, though there is an echo of a battle in 1664 over the establishment of a mosque on the site of a temple.[84] The British in turn were faced with a series of popular reactions beginning with the famous strike against the proposed house tax in 1809,[85] and stretching forward to the protest against the construction of a municipal water works on holy Ganges in 1889.[86]

The consolidation of corporate entities was a feature of other smaller cities and areas where bodies of merchants and religious men found themselves at an advantage in the face of the aspiring eighteenth-century states. Above all, it was the ascetic groups which successfully combined religion and commerce and contributed greatly to the synthesis of wealth and Hindu practice which was emerging under the surface of the Indo-Muslim state.

Ascetic orders and urban life

The last chapter emphasised how Hindu ascetic orders of Bairagis and Gosains had come to play an important role in the eighteenth-century economy. Their annual cycle of pilgrimage from the borders of the Punjab through the holy cities of the plains to Bihar and Orissa allowed them to move goods, money and military force between stable agricultural tracts. They were the largest owners of urban property in Benares, Allahabad, Mirzapur and Nagpur in the 1780s, and they also helped supply the large fairs and markets of the countryside which were often unsafe for unarmed merchants of lower status. An open and flexible organisation enabled the ascetics to pool resources and talent. They took in as novices young boys from war-torn villages, recruiting from all the higher castes.[87] It seems possible that there were as many as half a million Shaivite and Vaishnavite ascetics in north India in the last decade of the century.

For the ascetic corporations it was their religious status and organisation which provided the basic immunities out of which a separate political role could grow. As with the Jains, the concept of sanctuary and immunity from punishment at the hands of the ruler encouraged the development of a strong corporate life. From an early

84 Sarkar, *Dasnamis*, pp. 79–80; for a comparable incident in Delhi, see Shiv Das Lakhnavi, *Shahnama Munnawar Kalam*, tr. S. H. Aksari (Patna, 1980), pp. 112–15.
85 See Below, pp. 320–1.
86 Obit. Babu Bireshwar Mittra, *Tribune*, 25 July 1891. The scheme was ultimately accepted.
87 *Juggernath* v. *Hurrkeshen Gir*, 3 Feb. 1795, PR.

period, the Dasnami Naga ascetics, for instance, enjoyed the privilege of self-government under their 'abbots' and regional controllers along with relative immunity from imposts and interference by the rulers' police officials.[88] Hindu holy men achieved an even higher status during the reign of the Emperor Akbar when a clear effort was made to formulate an eclectic royal religion. But as with other corporations, it was Aurangzeb's lurch back towards a state founded on Muslim law which propelled the Dasnamis to a tougher defensive position. Tradition records a battle against Islamic revival in Benares in about 1664 when Gosains 'preserved the honour of Vishwanath's seat',[89] that is, preserved the great Viswanath temple on the Benares *ghats* from plunder. The Lingayat Math at Madanpura also preserves a tale of successful defiance to a Muslim ruler, though here it was a ghostly tiger which is supposed to have routed the interloper.[90] After 1707 the flux of political power stirred the corporations into more strenuous military activity. When the Afghans invaded southern Awadh in 1751, the Dasnamis who were gathered at Allahabad for the bathing festival offered armed resistance and saved the inner city from sack, for 'Siva gave help and thus saved the honour of the Dasnamis'.[91] Hereafter, powerful Gosain armies stalked the north Indian countryside, playing the role of Swiss mercenaries in Renaissance Europe. Though their commanders were particularly honoured by the Hindu Jats, their status in the Awadh armies was almost as high. The Nawab invested one Gosain leader with the rank of 'four hundred *hazari*', a high order of Mughal chivalry, and also with the right to raise troops without reference to himself.

During the eighteenth century, then, Gosains, Bairagis and other religious corporations came to play an important role both within states and in directing the diplomatic, commercial and military relations between them. In some localities they virtually acted as rulers in their own right. Gosain dominance at the great Hardwar fair, for instance, underlines the degree to which the corporations could take on the privileges of protection and punishment which had formerly been the preserve of Kings:

These mehunts [abbots] meet in council daily; hear and decide upon all complaints brought before them, either against individuals, or of a nature tending to disturb the public tranquillity, and the well management of this immense multitude.[92]

[88] Sarkar, *Dasnamis*, p. 79.   [89] *Ibid.*, p. 67.
[90] See pamphlet, *Kumarswami Veera Saiva Math, Kedar Ghat, Banaras* (Tirupandal, Thanjavur, 1955), p. 6.
[91] Sarkar, *Dasnamis*, p. 127.
[92] Thomas Hardwicke, 'Narrative of a journey to Sirinagar', *AR*, vi (1799), 315.

This observer, Captain Hardwicke, saw two fraudulent Marwari merchants fined and lashed by order of the council.[93] The Marathas who were nominally rulers of the area in which the fair was located allowed the Gosains almost total control of relations with the other predatory powers and were either unwilling or unable to claw back much of the huge levy which the corporations amassed from visiting merchants and pilgrims.[94] In the holy cities, too, ascetics achieved a striking degree of self-government. Contemporary Muttra, for instance, was run by a combination of the Chaube Brahmins who controlled local trade and pilgrimage and Vaishnavite monasteries (*kunjis*) which provided protection and ran longer-distance trade.[95] The heroic and costly defence of the ascetics to the invasion of Ahmed Shah Durrani in 1761 when many thousands of them were slaughtered, permanently enhanced their local importance.[96] On the fringes of other dominions as in major commercial towns, the Gosains were able to establish a near state of their own. One commander, Himmat Bahadur, carved out for himself a small kingdom in the cotton-growing tracts of Bundelkhand,[97] while the so-called Sannyasis of the east had established themselves on the borders of Bengal in the 1740s and 1750s to the discomfiture of its later British rulers.

In small Hindu states which emerged after 1740 the religious corporations also achieved important concessions and influence. In the Jat dominion of Bharatpur, for instance, Vaishnavite orders of Ramawat and Nemawat ascetics obtained considerable wealth and the honour of conferring benediction and legitimacy on the raja. Obeisance to the *mahants* of the main Bairagi temples which were set at the centre of the new town of Bharatpur was an important ritual in all the marriages and other ceremonies performed by the royal house. But the *mahants'* power also had a more tangible aspect.[98] They took a tithe in kind on all sorts of grain exported for sale in the bazaars and secured periodical grants of the whole of the raja's share of the produce of the bazaars. In addition, sect leaders received generous grants of revenue-free land or land at reduced

93 *Ibid.*, 314.
94 *Ibid.*, cf. Francklin, *George Thomas*, pp. 41–3.
95 For a general description, Growse, *Mathura*, pp. 189–90; see below, p. 321; interviews, Agra Dist., 1981.
96 Prabhu Dayal Mital, *Braj ke Dharm Sampradaiyon ka Itihas. Braj ka Sanskritik Itihas*, II (Delhi, 1968), 210–12, Muttra in 1815 retained a *panchayat* of three Brahmins and seven others, BCJ, 12 July 1816, 132/43, IOL; for a similar and apparently ancient corporation at Hardwar, NWPCJ, June 1855, 234/4, IOL.
97 Growse, *Mathura*, p. 308.
98 For the involvement of Bairagis with court politics and trade in Bharatpur see, Resident Bharatpur to Political Agent Delhi, 8 April 1831, For. Misc., Letters from Bharatpur Agency, NAI.

revenue, and an annual cess of 4 annas to Rs. 2 on all of the 1,200 villages within the bounds of the dominion. Not surprisingly, 'These mehunts become very powerful, especially when they are also *gurus*', or spiritual preceptors to the rulers.[99]

Other bodies of high status had achieved virtual independence within the smaller dominions. Bodies of river-priests at Allahabad, Hardwar, Gaya and Muttra had existed for centuries. The Mughal peace had enhanced their numbers and wealth as more people came to the great ritual centres in order to perform the ceremony of oblation (*shraddha*) for their ancestors. The priests' success depended on the development of links with lineages of rural magnates whose members would visit and endow them with lands and money generation after generation. The constant reiteration of the merits of holy places in the Puranas kept them in the popular mind of the localities and it was still possible to slip in new names and attributes as late as the eighteenth century.[100]

There were also groups of teaching holy men at some of these centres. After about 1680 communications with the Deccan improved and a large body of Deccani and western Indian teachers began to gather in Benares.[101] Their organisation of preceptors and pupils for the purpose of teaching the classical syllabuses of grammar, astronomy and the holy books were sufficiently well-developed to be regarded as 'colleges' or even as a 'university' by early European travellers. Nanakpanthi north Indians also had a 'college' in the city of Patna. These institutions with their wide and flexible contacts were in a good position to brave the political changes of the century and they emerged with enhanced moral and political authority. The new Hindu rulers of Benares, like the Marathas and Jats, lavished donations on them. They used the teaching *pandits* in arbitration and released the bathing priests from any kind of interference by the officers of the state. In Gaya, the bathing priests and pandits achieved an even higher status. On two occasions, they raised their own military forces to defend the area against marauding Marathas and Muslim mercenaries. As Buchanan noted, 'Many zemindar Brahmans and other warlike persons retiring the town with their families and effects gave great addition to the power of the priests.'[102]

Corporations and the analysis of Indian society

These subtle changes in power and status have been buried by the more dramatic political annals of Mughal decline. Yet there are parallels here

[99] J. Lushington, 'Marriage customs of Jats of Bhurtpore', *JASB*, ii (1833), 285.
[100] Bayly, 'Death ritual', in Whaley, *Mirrors of Mortality*, pp. 163–6.
[101] Motichandra, *Kashi ka Itihas*, pp. 236–48.   [102] Martin, *Eastern India*, I, 50.

with the rise to power of two much more celebrated groups of Brahmins, the Chitpavans of the Deccan and the 'Sipahi' or military Nagar Brahmins of Gujerat. By the mid-century these two castes had staged a virtual coup throughout central and western India where they held a near monopoly of high offices in the state, and their influence spread with the Maratha armies into the Ganges valley.[103] Their success had something in common with that of the corporate groups which we have been discussing. They had mastered the art of diplomacy between the decentralised polities which emerged out of the second phase of Maratha expansion. Their subcaste groupings and marriage networks expanded over a wide area which gave them leverage in a number of small dominions; at first they were able to move information between one centre and another; later, as they began to amass money and land-rights, wealth could be moved around. A key to influence with the Maratha rulers was also their Brahminical status. They could help to 'transform' peasant Kunbi leaders into kingly Marathas, while their skills of literacy were invaluable in the process of state-formation. Like the corporations, then, these two groups of Brahmin administrators were at both a moral and, as it were, a geographical advantage in dealing with contemporary rulers. One major difference was that their internal organisation was quite strictly bounded by caste. But this does not invalidate the comparison. It was Brahmins as a status group which achieved great power within the Maratha polities, symbolised by the great public feedings and distributions of charity to them (*dakshina*). Chitpavan Brahmins rose to prominence within this status group.

The intention in this section has been to take a new look at social and political change within the immediate pre-colonial polities of northern India. In doing this, we have encountered a number of changes which may seem surprising in the light of the still vital tradition of thinking about Indian society which derived from the ideas of Max Weber. This tradition insisted on the low status of merchants in India, and the domination of its cities by warrior or bureaucratic elites, which precluded the emergence of 'civic liberties':

in India – since the victory of the patrimonial kings and the Brahmans – it has been the endogamous caste with its exclusive taboos which has prevented the fusion of city dwellers into a status group enjoying social and legal equality, into a connubium sharing table community and displaying solidarity toward the outgroup. Because of the intensity of exclusive caste taboos this possibility was even more remote in India than in China.[104]

103 Cf. M. L. Patterson, 'Changing patterns of occupation among Chitpavan Brahmans', *IESHR*, vii (1970), 375–96.
104 Max Weber, *The City*, tr. and ed. D. Martindale and G. Neuwirth (New York, 1958), p. 97.

Weber's view depends on a number of assumptions and certain historical conditions. The main condition is the existence of large 'bureaucratic empires' or 'patrimonial states' which are held to prevent the emergence of strong corporate bodies. Where such states did not exist, he is prepared to accept that urban and mercantile solidarity might come into being:

To be sure in India during the period of the great salvation religions, guilds appeared with hereditary elders (*schreschths*) uniting in many cities into an association. As residues from this period there are, at present, some cities (Allahabad) with a mutual urban elder corresponding to the occidental mayor.[105]

The argument of this chapter does not directly contradict Weber since he would have acknowledged that the decline of the Mughal state may have enhanced the possibility of self-organisation among the local bodies.

This theme can be usefully applied to other periods of Indian history and to other areas. In medieval south India, for instance, self-regulating bodies of long-distance merchants appear to have had great influence within the petty states which developed in areas of high farming.[106] If the rise of merchant and religious corporations within the fragmented Mughal empire was evidence of social change, it was novel mainly by virtue of the geographical extent of the bodies of merchants, ascetics and Brahmins involved, and the broader context of commercial agriculture.

Weber's main assumption is that Hinduism and Jainism are essentially passive and therefore could never provide a basis for political action in the manner which conceptions of Roman law, and later revived Christianity did in the west. The degree to which Indian religious belief inhibited business in India has been severely qualified by Singer[107] and Morris[108] among others, and the evidence for post-Mughal north India suggests that this passivity can be exaggerated in the political sphere also. As we have seen, the concept of sanctuary (*ashrama*) and withdrawal (*sannyas*) could both, by a splendid paradox, provide the basis for self-government and self-defence. In contrast to Christianity, meekness was never a necessary concomitant of either. The Indian pilgrim's staff could readily be transformed into a symbol of force (*danda*). The view that Hindu religious duty (*dharma*) excluded merchants from political activity is also simplistic. True, merchants were unwilling to compromise their profession as 'money dealers' and

---

[105] *Ibid.*, p. 84.   [106] B. Stein, *Peasant, State and Society*, pp. 249–52.
[107] M. Singer, *When a Great Tradition Modernises* (Philadelphia, 1973).
[108] M. D. Morris, 'Values as an obstacle in growth in South Asia', *Journal of Economic History*, xxvii (1967), 588ff; but see below, ch. 10.

aristocrats were unwilling to deal openly in trade, but clandestine channels of influence and accommodation could always be found if circumstances pressed. Moreover, one of the strengths of Hinduism was its ability to adapt to change without losing its intellectual cohesion. Indian political theory as set out in classical texts and modified in the Puranas specifically allows for self-defence and self-government by subjects when the king, through moral degradation, is unable to protect them.[109] Significantly, this line of justification ran parallel to that in classical Islamic theory which restricted the power of the sultan to military protection of the body of the faithful. Evidently this implied a degree of self-organisation by society and its learned men, even if guilds and corporations acquired no *de jure* legal status.

One other qualification of Weber's view of Indian kingship must be made. In theory, it was never as monolithic as he implies. Political relations within a *raj* were founded on the assumption that there existed bonds of mutual obligation between ruler and subject. These were expressed in the form of alienations to worthy groups of parts of the ruler's sovereignty in the form of grants of revenue and other boons. The army, the priests and other important service groups could therefore be contracted into alliance with the state for the better preservation of order and religion. Where, as in the small Hindu states of eighteenth-century north India, privileged Brahmins and ascetics were also closely connected with trade and urban life, the *raj* itself evidently took on a more corporate character.

The final assumption made by Weber and reiterated unconsciously by more recent writers is that caste distinctions irreparably fragmented urban and mercantile communities. It may be true that caste did indeed prevent the emergence of common civic or corporate dining relations and tight marriage ties between elites, but this did not rule out the possibility of mercantile or even political solidarity. As we have seen, mercantile and credit organisations, conceptions of credit, local defence associations and festivals necessarily breached these caste boundaries. There seems no reason why the common table and marriage alliance should be the only basis of corporate activity as Weber assumes.

A parallel 'corporate culture': the Islamic gentry town

Chapter 3 indicated that there were other families of townsmen and service people besides Hindu trading and religious people who tenaciously held on to local power despite the shifting patterns of politics. Groups of service gentry, for instance, maintained patches of

[109] U. N. Ghoshal, *A History of Indian Political Ideas* (Oxford, 1966), pp. 425–6.

land-rights and influence in small towns and the suburban quarters of the cities, even when the great nobles (who often included some of their own members) moved away in the train of the regional rulers. Often too, it was local gentry who benefited, along with the bazaar people, from the high spending of the great revenue-farmers, while serving them as under-managers and gentleman troopers.

A large proportion of these families were Muslim and linked by blood or veneration to the famous religious institutions which subsisted on the revenue-free grants of earlier rulers. Where the rule of Muslim potentates waned, or changed its theological complexion, it was often local religious institutions, such as the 'Shahjehani' Sufi foundations of Allahabad[110] or the Firangi Mahal teaching seminary of Lucknow, which maintained the corporate life of the faithful. Despite occasional tensions, these institutions maintained amicable, if wary, relations with the Hindu religious and trading corporations, receiving honour and worship from the lower classes of both major religions in the cities.

It was in some of the smaller *qasbah* towns, however, that the Islamic service gentry were digging themselves in most successfully between 1690 and 1830, and here they had long been evolving a culture which ran parallel to, though not yet in opposition to, that of the Hindu commercial towns.[111]

The warriors and service lineages of the small Islamic township had something in common with the Hindu trading corporations as far as their mode of operation was concerned. They could both work beyond the boundaries of the smaller states, avoiding the consequences of local political or military decline by having skilled members placed in a number of regional or local court centres. But at the same time, they were also consolidating their hold over resources – credit and marketing in one case; land-rights in the other – in particular areas. In both service and market town also a definite corporate consciousness beyond family and caste had been created. What was different were the religious traditions around which these local powers and liberties coalesced.

The proliferation of mosques, schools, Muslim tombs and great gentry houses gave small gentry towns quite a different quality to the bustling Hindu bazaars. For even more than the quarters of the great Muslim towns, these *qasbah* societies played a key role in transmitting Islamic learning and providing a local Muslim leadership. Clan groups such as the Sheikhs of Kakori, the Barah Sayyids, and the Sayyids of Jansath or Kara served regional rulers as court officers and soldiers and

---

[110] C. A. Bayly, *The Local Roots of India Politics* (Oxford, 1975), pp. 79–80; interviews, Diara Shah Hajatullah, Allahabad, 1968.
[111] See below, ch. 9.

remained well entrenched in the lower levels of the British service during the early nineteenth century. Even later they were the dominant group in the associations in defence of Urdu and the district Muslim Leagues which were among the first forays of Muslims into electoral and pressure-group politics.

Like the mercantile and religious institutions of predominantly Hindu towns, this Islamic gentry was a well-rooted social group which evolved slowly from the days of the early Muslim kingdoms and continued to consolidate its power in the early colonial period. Whereas the Hindu traders and bankers had turned to good advantage their position in relation to the smaller principalities, the gentry could swim with the tide of local political fortune, selling their skills as administrators, soldiers and literati to one regime and another as the old polities fragmented, fissioned and later stabilised. It was a period of great opportunity when the pressure of an all-encompassing central state had been removed from them, but the penalties for failure were dire. The Barah Sayyids of Muzaffarnagar and Meerut, for instance, had been kingmakers of all Hindustan in the 1710s and 1720s when they virtually controlled the throne of Delhi.[112] They had used the wealth accumulated from service and warfare to dig themselves deeply into local agrarian society around their north-western *qasbah* towns. But when their star fell in the 1740s and 1750s, many Sayyid colonies were wiped out and their revenue rights forfeited to others. Only those lineages which had expanded so fast that their members had become holders of direct cultivating rights survived the storm. Others fled to the northern hills and into Awadh, to creep back to their small towns when the British provided the opportunity to investigate old claims in the 1820s.[113] However, there were many areas where the gentry remained remarkably resilient. The considerable gains made by Muslim zamindars between the time of the *Ain-i-Akbari* and the early British revenue surveys attest to the slow consolidation of these landed service communities around many of the *qasbah* towns.

As chapter 9 will show, north India was witnessing the emergence of a genuine gentry which was more than a body of rent-takers and had a distinct impact on the agriculture, ecology and society of the lands surrounding their urban bases. But how far can these societies be seen to have had corporate solidarities? In Muslim law, the *qasbah* had no formal status as a corporation though the term was applied to a place with a distinct urban status which possessed a mosque, a public bath and a judicial officer (*kazi*). It was, however, an inward sense of cohesion

---

[112] *Seir*, III, 83; *DG Muzaffarnagar* (Allahabad, 1920), pp. 163–74.
[113] *DG Muzaffarnagar*, pp. 173–4.

which was important. Tribal genealogy and association with one of the great Islamic ethnicities (*qam*), such as Iran or Turanistan, had been the original badges of status and lines of faction amongst the soldiers and administrators who served the Mughal empire.[114] But these elites often sought out a more secure base and tradition within India. As they embellished their small rural seats with mosques, wells and groves, a definite sense of pride in home (*watan*) and urban tradition began to emerge. By the 1750s writers were praising the qualities of these small semi-urban places. Early in the following century, we have Persian histories of places like Bilgram or Kakori which are described in the same format as the famous cities of Baghdad, Cairo or Isfahan. The corporate status and pride of these communities was enhanced by the residence there of families of the holy men who had been settled on revenue-free grants of land by the Mughals and later regional rulers. Thus a tradition of service, religion and Islamic learning was developed. The flavour of this developing local pride is caught by Murtaza Husain Bilgrami. Writing in the 1770s he pours scorn on a rival historian who claims to be a Sheikh of Bilgram, saying that he does not truly come from the famous town of light and learning, but from some miserable village across the river.[115]

The ideal Muslim *qasbah* society was formed by literacy, agrarian dependence and Islam. Families of Muslim service people from *ashraf* (gentry) families were bound together by tight marriage alliances, which often became cross-cousin arrangements. But people from less grand families – even converted Hindu Kayasths and Khattris – could reinforce the community by building up connections of culture and clientage with the elite. Though there always remained lines of social difference between the landholding Muslim gentry and their Hindu cultivators, and though compulsion played a considerable part in agrarian relations, gentry patronage and Hindu veneration of the shrines of Muslim holy men significantly diminished the scope for conflict and enhanced the solidarity of the *qasbah* as a society until well into the colonial period. Gentry families, both Hindu and Muslim, communed

---

[114] Even excellent modern studies have failed to grasp the importance of this locally based gentry. D. Lelyveld, *Aligarh's First Generation* (Princeton, 1978) posits a direct move on the part of the Muslim *ashraf* from centralised Mughal court faction to 'modern' professional and peer-group organisation in institutions such as Aligarh College; Iqtidar Alam Khan, in his *Middle Classes of the Mughal Empire* (Aligarh, 1975), draws attention to the importance of minor revenue officials, but not to their economic base in petty landholding; Satish Chandra, however, briefly anticipates the argument, 'Some aspects of the growth of a money economy in India during the 17th century', *IESHR*, iii (1967), 326.

[115] W. Irvine, 'Ahmad Shah Abdali', *IA*, xxxvi (1907), 10.

in Indo-Persian literary culture, while peasants and craftsmen participated in the same festivals and feast days.

The significance of Muslim *qasbah* society for this study is that it represented almost a mirror image of the Hindu commercial and Brahminical society in the large towns and spread outward into the rural market villages. Both societies witnessed the slow precipitation of economic power and cultural solidarity between the state and agrarian society. Service *qasbah* and commercial city flourished within the ambit of the great revenue-farmers, but the elites of both survived when these over-mighty subjects had passed away. Neither society excluded altogether locally resident members of the minority faith and culture. Thus Muslim weavers and artisans were uneasily bound into the corporate life of the Hindu commercial cities and Hindu cultivators often found an economic and a religious focus in the Islamic *qasbah*. Nevertheless, it was significant that two aspects of pre-colonial social change expressed themselves in such different cultural idioms. There was little as yet to set *qasbah* against merchant *mohulla*; they ran along parallel rather than antagonistic lines. For conflict, there needed to be some fundamental changes: first, the decline of the regional states and their agents which had provided a common political culture and forms of arbitration to minimise these differences: secondly, a series of changes in outlook which emphasised antagonism rather than diversity in religious practice. Yet some of the preconditions for conflict between the Hindu and Muslim leaderships of the later colonial period were present several generations earlier. These preconditions did not exist in the darbars where Hindu and Muslim soldiers fought and intrigued together, nor in agrarian society, but in the contrasting types of solidarities that had emerged between the two.

Conclusion

Earlier chapters have shown that there were great regional differences in late eighteenth-century north India, so it would be inappropriate to generalise too widely. But the evidence – especially from the Benares region – suggests that some lines of approach to the period are more viable than others. For instance, the contention that it is possible to see the 'sprouts of capitalism' arising out of India's mercantile economy in the years 1600–1800 does not seem convincing. There is no evidence of change in the 'putting out' system for artisan production which might have brought the producer's labour and tools more directly under the control of capital. The cheapness of artisan labour and the limitations imposed by the merchants' own conception of their social role made this development unlikely. 'Potentialities' for capitalist development in self-cultivating (*khudkasht*) holdings and garden crops certainly existed, as they had done in the high Mughal period. But the very geographical fluidity of elite demand and protection had ensured that these forms of production could not consolidate themselves in any single area. Fyzabad, Benares or Lucknow exhibited the same potential for capitalist development in the 1780s as the Agra or Delhi region had shown in the 1680s; but by then high farming had retreated around the old imperial capitals. Merchants and townsmen were powerful enough to protect their own interests and modify the forms of the state, but without a stronger political and legal framework they could not dissolve the dominances of rural society.

An alternative path of development was state entrepreneurship.[116] Perhaps the state monopolies and control of tools and labour pioneered by Tipu Sultan in the south or the Raja of Bundhi and Begum Samru in the north might have led to agricultural transformation had conditions been right. Certainly they were able to give a significant stimulus to local economies. These regimes, along with Farrukhabad and the Rohillas, do seem to have been groping towards a new, more active role for the state in society, based perhaps on revitalised religion, as in Mysore, or on greatly expanded systems of *jajmani* relations as in the northern principalities. But continuous warfare which was necessary for their expansion also vitiated the control of these regimes over capital and labour. The external conditions within which they sought to establish themselves – the pressure of the British and Marathas – were worse even than those faced by the more successful enlightened despots of the next generation outside India such as Mahomed Ali of Egypt.

On the other hand the notion that the structure of society in the last two centuries of pre-colonial India was undergoing no significant change is difficult to sustain. All 'structural change' must necessarily originate in relatively slight shifts in the economic organisation and ideology of societies. The consolidation of a unified merchant class and a locally based service gentry was much more than a simple change of personnel within a static society, though it is easy to miss those evolving classes for the dust thrown up by conventional political history and the concern with 'land-rights'. Both developments were associated with a more general process. This was the quite rapid commercialisation of the perquisites of kingship and local lordship which was gathering pace from the end of the Mughal period. A market was created in 'shares' to

---

[116] Asok Sen,' A pre-British economic formation in India of the late eighteenth century. Tipu Sultan's Mysore', in Barun De (ed.), *Perspectives in Social Sciences*, i, *Historical Dimensions* (Calcutta, 1977), 46–119.

rights, honours and powers which brought about a labile expansion of the money economy. The change was significant enough to push the men who dealt with silver rupees or those who recorded the 'shares' into a more important position in society. But it did not alter the form of peasant and artisan production in the short run. On the contrary, the market value of a 'share' in kingship was formed by the extent to which the purchaser could operate non-market forms of political coercion, or make use of the conceptions of rights and obligations which pervaded rural society. In this way 'commercialisation' actually blocked out the possibility of 'capitalism' which presupposes a freeing of the labour market.

The growth of a more commercial and more bureaucratic style of government also had implications for the organisation of groups between the state and agrarian society. Iqtidar Alam Khan saw an autonomous 'middle class' in the inferior revenue officials and professional servants of the Mughal nobility.[117] But the crucial change here was the rapid precipitation of members of this group as a petty rural service gentry after the empire had passed its peak. For it was landholding and the right to local dues which gave them their autonomy of regional political authority. In the same way, the weakening of state power in the eighteenth century threw traders into turmoil. Yet it also forced the corporations and towns into new defensive organisations which provided a much firmer basis for a true merchant class.

These pre-colonial origins are important for understanding the much-examined 'India middle classes' of the years after 1860. To a surprising extent, our general historical literature is still imprisoned by what is in effect a variant of the old modernisation theory. After 1830, the argument goes, English education and economic change created a new class, first in Bengal and then elsewhere. Colonial political institutions then 'moulded' or 'oppressed' that class (according to the political predilections of the historian). No one would deny that English education and new forms of communication greatly expanded the organisation and self-consciousness of intermediate people situated between state and agrarian society. But it must also be recognised that pre-colonial 'mentalities' and forms of organisation, particularly those which became stronger in the eighteenth century, were active forces in the creation of this new class and in directing its links with the colonial state and peasantry. Mukherjee has shown how the multi-caste faction (*dal*) of Bengal underpinned the organisation of the Calcutta

---

[117] Iqtidar Alam Khan, *Middle Classes*.

intelligentsia in the 1820s and 1830s.[118] In the south, as Appadurai has recently pointed out, the ancient division between 'right-' and 'left-handed' castes became a principle of conflict and its resolution for the urban life of colonial Madras.[119] Similarly, in the Punjab it could be shown that the charitable and religious donations of the Sikh state formed moral and material bases for the service and merchant people of the colonial period.

In the Ganges valley, the corporate bodies discussed in the last two chapters also continued to contribute to the organisation of urban and rural life through at least to the Great Depression of the 1930s. 'Modern' organisation – charitable trusts, political and caste associations – emerged as accretions around the core of these still vital solidarities. The specific features of such corporations also informed the relations between the elements of the later middle class. The organisation of the pre-colonial Hindu corporation and of the Muslim *dargah* or *qasbah* town, turned out to be a middle stage between the fluid relations of the Mughal court and the organisation of communal politics in the late nineteenth century. One stage did not necessarily lead on to the other. But the forces of secular nationalism and economic change in the colonial period would have needed to be vastly more powerful to dissolve the corporations into a unified class.

---

[118] S. N. Mukherjee, 'Caste, class and politics in Calcutta, 1818–38', in E. Leach and S. N. Mukherjee (eds), *Elites in South Asia* (Cambridge, 1970), pp. 33–78.

[119] A. Appadurai, 'Right and left hand castes in South India', *IESHR*, xi (1974), 216–60.

5

The growth of political stability in India, 1780–1830

Earlier chapters have suggested that much of the apparent chaos and disruption of eighteenth-century north India represented the consequences of the redistribution across the countryside of capital, labour and the expenditure of military elites. The movement of these resources was not random, however. They tended to come to rest in areas where flourishing farming was enhanced by effective regimes well rooted in local agrarian and mercantile society. In the midst of the political maelstrom, these islands of stability were slowly growing, driven forward by the consumption of town-dwelling aristocrats and by the investment of an adaptable merchant class and a rural gentry. The present chapter argues that these developments persisted under the fragile surface of early British rule. The growth of trade and the expansion of the cultivated area in the first thirty years of the nineteenth century, usually associated with the imposition of colonial peace, did not, then, signal a simple transformation of society by the force of modern government and new export trades. They were also a consequence of the maturity of the regimes, towns and corporate institutions which emerged in the eighteenth century. Conventional chronology sees unity in the Company period lasting from 1802 to 1857. But from the point of view of the political economy of the localities it makes more sense to take the period from about 1740 to about 1830 as a unity. It was not only that there was a continuity in dominant rural groups, or in methods of administration over the boundary between pre-colonial and colonial north India. It was also that existing processes of change buoyed up British commerce and government, making possible a rapid reassertion of trade and farming in areas which had suffered earlier.

The developments associated with the 'rise' of the Company and the 'decline' of the Mughals had much in common. They were cumulative changes in which shifts in politics and ideology moulded and were moulded by movements in the agrarian and commercial economies. The Mughal centre had lost its political hold on the provinces at the same time as its ability to consume their products was impaired. In places this had led to the decline of local centres which formed the basis of Mughal control in the countryside. Irruptions by pioneer peasant colonists and wandering groups further disrupted the delicate pattern of towns and communications which sustained the imperial peace. And since the existence of specialist agriculture depended on the consumption and investment of the small town elites, patches of real agricultural decline appeared in the Mughal heartland. These changes had further political consequences. Deprived of the benefits of rental income through the degeneration of high farming, groups of villages turned to robbery or to harbouring bandits from whom they derived an income. In fact, one of the most significant features of the descriptions of disorder by early travellers is the clear impression which they leave that thieves, 'banditti', and even Pindari raiders and Thugs were quite limited in the scene of their operations. A few miles of dangerous road were followed by many more where a peace of sorts reigned and levies by local landholders were regarded as legitimate transit dues rather than plunder. Real social disintegration only occurred in unstable regions when a further spin was given to the wheel of agricultural distress by a series of bad seasons.

Decline had resulted from subtle shifts in political relations and from sympathetic movements of agrarian resources. These could quite quickly be thrown into reverse. The advance of larger states, bigger towns and settled agriculture, which had been the dominant trend in the Ganges valley since about A.D. 1400, could then rapidly resume its progress. With minimum security and some likelihood of longer-term returns, it made sense for magnates to found markets and for dependent peasant farmers to open up new lands on lower rentals. The structure of the Indian family firm was also well attuned to a geographically extensive pattern of growth.

However, the advance of settled agriculture, marketing and population did not of themselves create empires. An ideology of dominion and the existence of groups of Indians ready to participate in the enterprise of empire-building were both necessary to take advantage of the favourable conjuncture of agrarian and military resources. To the great advantage of the East India Company, there were several features of the theory and practice of the successor regimes which smoothed the path to dominion. First, an ideology of empire existed largely unaffected by the political flux of the period and overlaying the many particular idioms of legitimacy by which sultans and rajas vaunted themselves. All regimes, even those like the Marathas in revolt against Delhi, continued to try to make their position legitimate within the Mughal diplomatic system. The person of the Mughal and the inheritance of Timurid blood became, if anything, more significant as the century wore on. As Cohn has argued, one reason for British success was their close attention to Indian court ritual and diplomatic usage. Their foreign religion and white faces did not exclude them from a system which was designed to incorporate outside adventurers. They used the name of the emperor, supported his family, used his charters, seals and darbar halls, in a manner which placated the urban populace. They stabilised the relationship between the emperor and his liegemen, and regraded the diplomatic system with themselves in high position.

But there was a deeper sense in which Hindu and Indo-Muslim conceptions of kingship aided British attempts first to stabilise and then to absorb the north Indian polities. Crucial here was the conception of *jaidad* or *jagir*, a holding of rights over men and resources which enabled a man to 'live of his own' in a style appropriate to a ruler. As chapter 3 showed, the Rohilla nobleman wanted above all a representative at court, an elephant, a drum, and a 'place of my own' where he could store his horses and women. The links between the outward expression of royalty and control of any particular territory were quite weak. It was feasible for these potentates to give up control of their *jagir* in return for a guaranteed pension which was not at the mercy of the seasons or rebellion. Neither militant Islam nor a strong cultural patriotism, such as existed in East Asian societies, impeded this resolution. For instance, we find Henry Wellesley congratulating himself on the ease with which the famous Farrukhabad dynasty was edged out of direct control of its rich territories. He clearly perceived the relative unimportance of territorial dominion in comparison with kingly behaviour towards dependents:

Previous to my departure from the Ceded Provinces, I had an interview with the Nabob at Furrukhabad, who expressed himself highly gratified by the arrangement which had taken place, and whose respectable appearance surrounded by the family and dependants formed a striking contrast with the state of degradation in which he appeared when the affairs of Furrukhabad were administered by his uncle the Nabob Kheramund Khan.[1]

The divorce of royalty from place and administration perhaps reached its most striking form in Calcutta in the 1850s. Here the last pensioner king of Awadh held a magnificent court full of dependants and family 'where even the shopkeepers and moneylenders in Matiya Burj were from Lucknow'. The Nawab retained the illusion that the British ships which dropped their flag as they approached Hughly Fort were saluting him in person.[2]

[1] H. Wellesley to GG, 10 Feb. 1803, para. 21, in G. Saletore (ed.), *Wellesley Correspondence*, p. 116.
[2] Sharar, *Last Phase*, p. 72.

By granting livings, farming revenues in the name of local rulers, feeding Brahmins and preserving festivals, the British were participating in that two-way pattern of tribute and alienation which was an ancient feature of royal practice in India. They were acting out a massive redistribution of resources and honours which involved a large part of its revenues. In turn, the stabilising of political relations affected commerce and agriculture. It gave a further spur to the long- and medium-distance luxury trades which tied together islands of specialist farming.

A third aid along the path to the empire was the persistence of an administrative culture which was used to dealing with large political units. The Mughal supremacy had ensured that hundreds of gentry families throughout north India were predisposed to the service of the state in regions distant from their birthplace. A whole literature and system of education kept the culture alive. Administrative treatises continued to divide India into its Mughal provinces. Geographical works described the country in terms of its streams, fruits, Muslim holy men, *qasbahs*, and the deeds of past emperors. Even in the new regional centres, the memory of wider dominions was preserved. Munshi Faiz Baksh and his fellow exiles from Delhi, themselves men from the small *qasbah* towns of Awadh, 'used to gather together every night to talk of old times, to narrate the ups and downs of others, and to pray for the stability of the Empire and the restoration of the City [Delhi]'.[3] Amongst these Muslim literati and comparable families of Hindu Kayasths and Kashmiri Brahmins were found the building-blocks of empire. With so many men (and horses) looking for service, a power like the East India Company, or greater Awadh, or the Sikh state of Ranjit Singh, which was prepared to adopt the rituals and practices of the old order would quickly attract a following.

The more service was provided, the more clients there would be. They were not always the best. The author of the *Seir* deplored the fact that the English officers were thronged with 'the low, the mean and the rapacious',[4] and families with a distinguished religious pedigree worked hard to find service with the remaining independent Muslim states. It was in the east, secured by nearly fifty years of influence that the Company had most success in attracting to itself the service lineages of the *qasbahs*. The Muslim and Kayasth families of Bihar and Benares gravitated quickly into British employment. They had little choice. Take for instance, the case of Sayyid Aminullah,[5] a native of Benares, who went to Calcutta and aided in the production of a Company legal

3 Faiz Baksh, *Faizabad*, I, intr., iii.   4 *Seir*, III, 563–5.
5 Case of Aminullah, BCJ, 2 Dec. 1817, 133/17, IOL.

code, the *Zakira-i-Wellesley*, modelled on its Mughal originals. Aminullah later took positions in the North-Western Provinces, supporting on his salary more than seventy direct dependents. The fate of these Islamic service families varied. Some scattered to Hyderabad or Bhopal; others were forced to the status of cultivating proprietors around their home towns. But enough of them made the initial adjustment to British service to provide continuity in the basic revenue administration.[6]

Other elements which worked within or linked together the indigenous states found an accommodation with the colonial power. The revenue entrepreneurs were ultimately to be replaced by the collectors and district treasurers of more settled times. But in the first stages of British administration, such magnates often smoothed the Company's way to Indian resources. Men like Beni Ram Pandit, Shanker Pandit or the famous Sheo Lal Dube helped to supply British armies, fed British cities, and coerced primary producers in the European interest. Then, of course, there were the urban corporations and mercantile organisations which will be treated in detail in the following two chapters. Before embarking upon this, however, it is important to emphasise again that the consolidation of British power in India, like the Mughal collapse before it, cannot be looked at on one plane. It was not simply a military conquest, or a function of the revival of trade, or a matter of the assumption of Mughal legitimacy by the British. The creation of political stability required changes in all these areas. The conflicts over status and resources which had preoccupied Indian rulers were partly resolved. This increased military security, urban growth and commerce. Trade redistributed credit and mercantile skills in such a way as to stimulate production for the market; this, in turn, stabilised the position of the rural elites. The decline of the Mughals had been a cyclical collapse. Political dislocation fed through trade to create agrarian crisis. The wheel had already begun to turn back in the late eighteenth century, and the British merely spun it faster.

The expansion of elite consumption

In the first thirty years of the nineteenth century, there was an

[6] Less prestigious Muslim and Kayasth families from Bihar and Benares appear to have been more successful in making the adjustment than the literati of the prestigious Muslim centres to the north and west; see, e.g., the case of Sahib Sahai and his connections among servants of Awadh revenue-farmers who made good under the patronage of H. T. Colebrooke, CPR, 5 Dec. 1817, 97/63, IOL; family history material which throws light on mobility in the early days of British rule is collected in, e.g., *Kayastha Samachar* (Allahabad), cf. Bayly, *Local Roots*, pp. 133–7; P. Carnegy, *Notes on the Races, Tribes and Castes inhabiting the Province of Oudh* (Lucknow, 1868).

expansion of the cultivated acreage and an intensification of agriculture in the less stable areas of the west Ganges region which had gone out of cultivation earlier. It was accompanied by a further extension of arable to the north and south of the Great Valley. As the early British civil servants recognised, a prime condition for this was the growth of political stability. But this term is used here in a wider sense than was common among them. For the increasing stability of regional states or provinces based on consumer towns, more rigorously extracting land-revenue, and protected by permanent centralised armies, was also a feature of areas where British influence remained, as yet, indirect. The Peace was not simply British, for in the Punjab, the Maratha states and Awadh, it marked the culmination of the struggles of the rulers of the stable tracts to suppress the revived internal frontier of the previous century. In many areas this process was distorted by the constant intervention of British influence, or frustrated by the Company's demands for revenue or tribute. But it remained in origin and form an indigenous change, pushed forward by Indian aristocrats, Islamic administrators and the expansion of a Hindu commercial class and peasantry. The emergence of more stable regimes helped to extend or repair the network of roads, trade routes and commercial towns on which the Mughal empire had rested at its height. Expanding trades in fine quality goods for landed aristocracies helped to settle frontier areas and encouraged the trickle back of merchant capital. This in turn speeded the revival of commercial farming and secured revenue collection.

The rise of Ranjit Singh's state in the Punjab after 1799 illustrates quite forcibly how the process of Indian state-formation ran parallel to the establishment of Pax Britannica and how developments in the Punjab and the North-Western Provinces were mutually reinforcing. During the late eighteenth century, Lahore, Multan and the other major towns of the Punjab had declined or stagnated more speedily than those of the Ganges basin.[7] The specialist sugar cane and wheat cultivation which had flourished between Delhi and Lahore as late as 1720 withered and died, while the disruption or shift to the east of the long-distance trade networks of the Multanis and 'Mughal' merchants reduced the volume of exchange within the region and between the Punjab and other parts of India. There appears to have been a currency famine, and the near-extirpation by the Sikh warbands of the small town Mughal elites damaged its artisan industries. The once healthy demand for Punjab cloth in Iran seems also to have dwindled soon after the death of Nadir Shah in 1741. Yet this was no more a total social catastrophe than it was

[7] Naqvi, *Urban Centres*, p. 127.

further east. Groups of Sikh Jat notables had appropriated the Mughal land-revenue, and it was only a matter of time before they, too, became a consuming class. In well-watered tracts such as the Jullundur Doab, thriving agricultural societies persisted, lorded over by Sikh notables who built small fortresses in the ruins of the Mughal towns.[8] Long-distance trade did not die out completely. The Sikhs, hungry for horses and muskets from the north and cloth and bucklers from the east, encouraged client merchant communities such as the Nanakshahi Khattris. The many small states north-west of Delhi needed coin for their local mints which could not always be procured by raiding parties, so that bullion was acquired by trade from Central Asia and from the great eastern Indian money market. Even the large cities were never in total decline. As in Agra or Delhi, bustling bazaars lay behind decaying aristocratic mansions. One centre of urban growth was the city of Amritsar, site of the Sikhs' Golden Temple.[9] Before the end of the century, it had expanded considerably on the earnings of Sikh pilgrims and as a thriving entrepôt on the route east for the much-prized Kashmir shawls.[10] Lahore itself must have had some life left in it for the besieged city was said to have been handed over to the new monarch, Ranjit Singh, by members of the Arain or market gardener caste who resented the interruption of their trade and agriculture by warfare.

The consolidation of Ranjit Singh's kingdom after his capture of Lahore in 1799 made the city the political centre for the whole of north-west India and directed there revenue which was equivalent to no less than half the revenue of the British North-Western Provinces. Trade inevitably reasserted itself,[11] while detailed revenue-demand and new centres of consumption for sugar and fine wheat gave a spur to the expansion of the acreage under the irrigated spring harvest throughout the Punjab.[12] One important aspect of the growing urban and commercial economy was Ranjit's construction of a permanent and centralised armed force based on the capital. When the American traveller Masson visited Lahore in 1820,[13] he saw the ruins of the

[8] Abdul Kader Khan, *AAR*, viii (1808), 46–57.

[9] 'Punjab in 1808', *AAR*, ix (1809), 430.

[10] A. Deare, *A Tour through the Upper Provinces of Hindostan*, p. 186; S. S. Bal, 'Amritsar in the 18th century', in K. Singh (ed.), *The City of Amritsar* (Delhi, 1978), p. 71; Collr Saharanpur to Lord Lake, 3 Nov. 1804, CPR, 29 Nov. 1805, 90/51, IOL.

[11] E.g., Ranjit Singh's moves to maximise the return on rock salt, 'Note on the Kingdom of the Punjab', *JASB*, i (1832), 147–8.

[12] Kessinger, *Vilayatpur*, ch. 1; Mohan Lal, *A Journal of a Tour through the Punjab, Afghanistan, Turkistan, Khurasan and a part of Persia* (Calcutta, 1834), pp. 10–13.

[13] C. Masson, *Narrative of Various Journeys in Balochistan, etc.*, ed. G. Hambly (Karachi, 1974), I, 410; cf, 'Memorandum on Lahore, the Sikhs and their Kingdom and Dependencies', in G. W. Forrest (ed.), *Selections from Travels and Journals preserved in the Bombay Secretariat* (Bombay, 1906), p. 168.

Mughal suburbs being cleared to make room for a massive cantonment to house between 70,000 and 100,000 troops which the ruler intended to maintain at his side. By 1825, Lahore had a population once again estimated at about 180,000, and Amritsar possibly 100,000. New buildings had been set on foot by the ruling group. Masson noted of Lahore: 'There are some exceedingly lofty and bulky mansions, well built of kiln-burnt bricks . . . many of them recently erected.' The most conspicuous of these was that of Khushial Singh, a 'renegade Brahman, elevated by Ranjit Singh from the rank of a scullion in the kitchen to that of a general'. Smaller agricultural market centres also expanded and, as in the British territories, troublesome areas on the fringes of stable cultivation were held down by the settlement of retired soldiers and efforts to induce wandering groups – Gujars, Bhattis and Banjaras – to take to agriculture.[14]

These developments helped, directly and indirectly, to create greater stability in adjoining British territories. The unadministered areas where raiding bands could find shelter were reduced by the efforts of the Sikh court as much as by the neighbouring British Board of Commissioners. Then, after 1805, came a rapid expansion of trade from Hindustan to the north and west. The merchants and artisans of Benares, for instance, were reported to be exporting more and more to Ranjit Singh's Punjab: 'The situation of that part of the country under Runjeet Singh appears to have opened a wide field for speculation, and at present Amritsar seems to be the chief emporium of goods of all kinds.'[15]

The boom in Punjab trade helped the Gangetic cities ride out the consequences of the third Anglo-Maratha war of 1818 and the beginnings of the decline of aristocratic consumption in Awadh. But the flowering of the north-west trade route, which was largely in the hands of Khattri and Saraswat Brahmin merchants,[16] was a two-way process. Another measure of the buoyancy of aristocratic consumption in the first two decades of the century is to be found in figures for the import of goods such as musk, drugs, dyes, horses and shawls, from the Punjab into Hindustan. Shawls were by far the most valuable of these imported goods: in terms of value, they represented one of the most important articles of trade in the whole region. The large revenue drawn by the British and Sikh states from customs duties on shawls also encouraged a close commercial accord between them. There was an increase of 200

[14] G. Hamilton, 'On the tax of Jhung', *Selections from the Public Correspondence of the Administration of the Affairs of the Punjab*, 1, ix (Lahore, 1853), 105–8.

[15] CGC Benares to CGC Mirzapur, 13 July 1819, Bengal and Benares Rev. Customs, July 1819, 112/28, IOL.

[16] CGC Farrukhabad to Board, 10 Apr. 1810, 97/36; Buchanan, *Patna*, II, 690.

per cent in the volume of shawl imports into the North-Western Provinces recorded by customs figures for the years 1805–25, and the values involved warn against regarding trades like this as somehow peripheral because they are inclined to be classed as luxury.[17] By the second decade of the century, an increasing volume of shawl goods and other specialist items from the north-west was passing on to Mirzapur and Calcutta where they were destined for the Indian beneficiaries of the Permanent Settlement, or for European hands now that the 'Paisley' shawl vogue was beginning. But the 'great centres of consumption'[18] remained the two nominally independent courts of Islamic north India, Awadh and Rampur. At this time, Awadh was passing through its final phase of relatively stable government under Saadat Ali Khan.[19] Rampur, which alone of the Rohilla domains had survived the turmoil of the Awadh conquest with its prosperity unimpaired, was benefiting from the rapidly rising consumption of Indian sugar, a state monopoly in the territory.[20] The new consumer aristocracies of Rampur, Lucknow and Benares therefore complemented those of the Punjab, and a brisk two-way trade had grown up.

This trade played a considerable part in revitalising the agriculture of the western districts of what had become the British North-Western Provinces. In 1800, southern Rohilkhand was in such a poor state that incoming colonial officials were unable to find people of sufficient capital to guarantee the land-revenue and to run government treasuries. Without a flow of goods it proved impossible to remit *hundis* which were essential to the government's military and revenue business. Saharanpur, depopulated and without any major towns, was the foremost example of a declining and unstable area throughout the region. By 1820, however, the towns north-east of Delhi were once again the hub of a flourishing commercial agriculture. The trade to the Punjab and Kashmir had given rise to a new merchant class in towns such as Saharanpur city, Pilibhit, Khurja and Deoband, and they, in

---

[17] T. Kessinger, 'North Indian economy', *Cambridge Economic History of India* (Cambridge, 1982), 11; statements of duties 1820–3, 31 Oct. 1823, CPR 95/11; shawls brought through the Meerut and Farrukhabad customs houses alone were worth about Rs. 12 lakhs per annum, equivalent to the value of raw cotton passing Agra and more than twice the estimates of Wellesley *et al.* of 1800–2; considerable quantities of Hindustani opium were exchanged for shawls, note by Collr Saharanpur, CPR, 22 Dec 1807, 91/18, IOL.

[18] CGC Meerut to Bd, 21 Jan. 1823, CPR, 1 Feb. 1823, 95/10, IOL.

[19] Sharar, *Last Phase*, p. 53, notes how the consumption of British troops made up for the decline in the size of Awadh; several new *mohullas* of Lucknow were founded and towns like Sultanganj grew in size.

[20] Translation of a letter from the GG's Agent at Rampur to Nawab Azimullah Khan, For. Pol. Procs, 2 June 1810, NAI.

turn, provided capital for wheat and sugar trading.[21] The importance of shawls in this revival should not be underestimated. The prosperity of Saharanpur itself was largely built upon them. In 1822, one key shawl trader of the town, Lala Bilas Rai, alone contributed Rs. 1 lakh per annum to government customs which suggests he conducted an annual trade to the value of at least Rs. 8 lakhs.[22]

The consolidation of a settled Maratha aristocracy also benefited the merchants, and through them the agriculture and revenue of Hindustan. The gradual political emasculation of the Maratha states at the hands of the British after 1783 did not affect trade or consumption until they began actively to disband the Maratha armies in the newly conquered Deccan in the 1820s. Throughout the first quarter of the nineteenth century Maratha demand remained strong. Large quantities of inlaid gold and silver work, brocades and fine cloths were exported from the Gangetic towns to Nagpur, Poona and Gwalior. Maratha princes appeared regularly as large-scale purchasers in the bazaars of Agra, Benares and Muttra.[23] Agra merchants in particular were able to export so much gold and silver brocade to the south that by 1815 they could afford to charge insurance and transport costs to Gwalior and Nagpur as low as 3–4 per cent.[24] This was in sharp contrast to the 20–30 per cent extracted during the troubled years between 1793 and 1806.[25] The north–south trade in artisan products and good quality cloths complemented the trade in pig-iron and corn between Gwalior and Farrukhabad which had survived earlier depredations.

The production of fine quality goods like this helped maintain employment in the towns in the first half of the nineteenth century. There were 3,000 workers alone producing *kalabatun* or gold thread in Agra in 1825,[26] besides substantial production of inlaid stone, leather work, indigenous medicines and sweetmeats.[27] Artisan production for aristocratic consumers may have employed as much as 25 per cent of the city's population in total, and it supported a large middle level of merchant firms. Certainly the most outstanding families of Agra's early colonial mercantile oligarchy rose to wealth on the back of the raw

---

[21] E.g., Bilas Rai, wealthy shawl merchant of Najibabad and Saharanpur, was the main 'capitalist' persuaded to invest in the opening up of waste land after 1818, Magt. Saharanpur to Commr Meerut, 23 May 1837, Saharanpur Judicial, letters issued, vol. 218, UPR.

[22] Petition of Bilas Rai, CPR, 31 May 1823, 95/10, IOL.

[23] E.g., Bengal Political Procs, 15 Sept. 1815, 97/56; 9 Apr. 1816, 97/58; Bengal and Bihar Revenue Procs, 16 June 1818, 112/11, IOL.

[24] CGC Agra to Bd, 27 Oct. 1809, CPR, 27 July 1810, 97/35, IOL.

[25] Malcolm, *Central India*, II, 93, App. ix.

[26] CGC Agra to Commr Agra, 1 Jan. 1835, Agra Customs 7, UPR.

[27] Notes on Agra industries, Collr to Commr Agra, 11 May 1850, Agra Judl, 8, UPR.

cotton trade which increased phenomenally after 1783.[28] But as far as it is possible to tell from family histories, a significant number of middle level merchants were originally involved in 'luxury' trades for the aristocracy of central India and the Deccan. The old Khattri community of Kinari Bazaar recovered after the rigours of the years 1750–90 by financing brocaded work.[29] The Gujeratis of Gopalkura were connected with the trade in inlaid marble which had once decorated the Taj Mahal and Agra's other superb Mughal monuments but which was now in demand at the Jat and Maratha darbars. The Greek Joanides family which set up in the Agra Spinning and Weaving Mills in the 1880s came to Agra in 1801 to initiate a jewellery business,[30] while the major Marwari (Maheshwari) lineages advanced money to Muslim weavers who produced fine silk for marriage saris and for the adornment of Hindu deities in temples. Sweets, especially a sickly confectionary called *petha*, became almost as important in Agra as they were in Benares, stimulating dairy and sugar production in nearby Muttra and Bharatpur.[31]

The buoyancy of courtly and elite consumption is important not only for a study of north Indian cities, but also for a general understanding of what was taking place in early colonial society. It has been argued that the revival of population in the Gangetic cities after 1800 was a consequence of the new opportunities for export to China and Europe of primary agricultural products such as indigo and cotton. Yet though it is more difficult to isolate, purely internal demand from within the Indian landed aristocracy appears to have been crucial in maintaining, if not enhancing, employment among merchants and artisans whose future had become uncertain with the decline of the Mughal elite. Packing, baling, and transporting cotton or indigo created employment also, but artisan production was by its nature more intensive and helped to maintain old-established communities united by professional pride and a sense of common identity. The motors of economic expansion in the early years of British rule were powered by indigenous patterns of consumption among the elites which had emerged from the changes of the post-Mughal era, as much as by the sharp and narrowly based demand which arose from the China and European markets. It was the dislocation of both these sources of demand in the 1830s which was to create the long crisis of early colonial society.

The growth of political stability in the Sikh and Maratha domains was

28 C. Bayly, 'Town-building in north India', *Modern Asian Studies*, ix (1975), 483–503.
29 Interviews, Agra, Jan. 1974.
30 Interviews, Mr T. Smith, Agra, Jan. 1974, family history, MSS, 'The Joanides Odyssey'.
31 Family history, interview, Sri P. C. Maheshwari, Agra, Jan. 1974.

largely independent of the colonial power, but there were also important continuities in local social and economic change within areas which were directly controlled by the British Raj. There was no 'abrupt caesura' to mark the turn of the nineteenth century. In the Jat principalities surrounding Agra, for instance, British rule provided a tightening circle of military restraint within which the earlier processes of town growth and elite formation were maturing. The three main Jat towns of Deig, Hatras and Bharatpur continued to expand between 1800 and 1830 even as their political independence was slowly extinguished. The protection offered by Raja Diaram of Hatras relentlessly drew in merchants, artisans and service people from nearby Islamic *qasbah* towns such as Koil, continuing the shift of local political and economic dominance which had begun to tilt when the Jat 'bandits' first raised their standards against Muslim overlordship in the sixteenth century. In the fortress market of Hatras buoyant growth maintained its momentum even after the great Raja had been driven from his dominions by British power in 1817. In 1830, it was 'bursting at the seams'[32] and traders who had accumulated capital in the days of Diaram's opulence began to invest their resources in the purchase of land-rights in the vicinity.[33] These traders had been attracted to Hatras partly by the Raja's protection, partly by its status as an entrepôt, and partly by the possibility of making large sums by provisioning the court with luxury items. But here the distinction between luxury and mass consumption breaks down entirely, for all adult male Jats of the highest lineages (at least 8,000 families in Bharatpur alone) were required to lay out considerable sums of money on the purchase of certain types of brocaded clothes, ornamented weapons and saris for their women.[34] Attendance at marriage festivities and other royal events held by all the minor princes of the region was incumbent on Jats of high status, for these festivities were intimately bound up with the slow modification of a society of pioneer peasants into a polity of royal Kshatriya warriors.

As the Jat polities were penned in by the British Raj, the end of external warfare pressed forward changes in Jat society which had significant economic consequences. The aristocratic warrior lineages of what became the Bharatpur, Kuchesar and Hatras Rajs separated themselves off as a town-dwelling landlord class, and the early predilections of the British for dealing with large magnates rather than

---

[32] Magt. Aligarh to Supt. Police, 1 Feb. 1820, BCJ, 4 Feb. 1820, 134/36, IOL.
[33] *Settlements under Act ix of 1833*; II, 290, cf. II, 261.
[34] For instance, the bridegroom's party of the ruler of Bharatpur consisted of 8,000 men even in 1832; the compulsory dress was shoes of embroidered velvet, pyjamas of finest *kinkhab* silk, *dhoti* of yellow silk, pearl-studded vest, silver bracelets, etc., Lushington, *JASB*, ii (1833), 283–5.

co-sharing brotherhoods of peasants in their revenue business reinforced this tendency.[35] The social egalitarianism of the ruling group was gradually eroded; the days when Jat leaders married with members of lower agricultural and artisan castes were over. Court patronage further consolidated the power of the Vaishnavite *mahants*, reducing the role of hereditary minstrels (*bhats*) and of devotional cults like that of Satya Narayan. Jat landholders and princes increasingly secluded their once free womenfolk.[36] The 'virtual nationalism'[37] of the Jats, as one observer called it, became more and more bound up with the history of the ruling dynasty and the institutions of kingship. The outward manifestations of this change were large-scale building and lavish display.

It was the merchant families of Agra and Farrukhabad which supplied the Jat rajas, bringing high quality cloths, spices and armaments from as far away as Bengal. When, for instance, the British prize agents made an inventory of the large quantities of merchandise in the captured bazaar of Hatras in 1817, they found that Rs. 16,000 of goods belonged to one house alone – that of Thakur Das Andhea of Farrukhabad.[38] Vast stores of ginger, turmeric, fine cloths, English broadcloth and copper vessels pointed to a typical pattern of aristocratic consumption and feast-giving by the ruling lineages.

One reason why the volume of demand remained so high in the Indian states was that until the late 1820s the demilitarisation of society by the colonial government had not progressed very far. Even after the third Maratha war, the Jat rajas may still have had more than 12,000 men permanently under arms. The petty Raja of Mursan alone had 1,500 regular infantry, 200 rocket men, 1,000 cavalry and thirty pieces of cannon in 1818.[39] At a conservative estimate, this small *raj* must have supported more than 15,000 auxiliaries to service a force of this size.

However, this demand from within the still vital Indian state system was inextricably linked with the workings of the colonial economy and the more mundane level of trade and agricultural finance in small bazaars. Thakur Das and the Farrukhabad merchants also appear as traders in Rajasthani salt through the mart of Hatras and as major entrepreneurs moving Agra and Muttra raw cotton down to Calcutta when the trade to China began to boom after the end of the Napoleonic Wars.

Further to the east, under the surface of the stately progress of British

35 Metcalf, *Landlords*, pp. 51–6.
36 Sherring, *Tribes and Castes*, II, 76–7.   37 Lushington, *JASB*, ii (1833), 284.
38 'List of goods found in Hatras Bazaar', BCJ, 16 Sept. 1817, IOL.
39 Magt. Agra to Govt, 7 Mar. 1817, BCJ, 21 Mar. 1817, 132/44, IOL.

arms and administration into the Doab and Awadh, there was a virtual 'expansion of Benares' whose commercial men, revenue entrepreneurs and carpetbaggers underpinned the whole Company advance. The agricultural stability of the Benares region had been reinforced by a great expansion of sugar cultivation in the region as a healthy demand for the refined product grew in the courts of the Maratha territories and in Mysore even further to the south. At the same time, Mirzapur became the great inland mart for Indian raw cotton. The buoyancy of Benares trade and agriculture spilled out into the less developed and unstable areas around it. In the north, Sheo Lal Dube, 'one of the wealthiest and craftiest inhabitants of the Honourable Company's territories', consolidated his hold on Jaunpur, extirpating wherever he could all traces of intermediate zamindari rights. His personal income in 1816 was said to have been greater than that of the total population of the ailing city of Jaunpur.[40] To the north-east, Benares capital was closely involved in the development of the Azamgarh Opium Agency and the fitful beginning of bazaar building in this small town.[41] To the west, Deokinandan Singh (one of Benares' most successful Bhumihar Brahmin enterprisers of the previous generation) and the Maharaja himself undertook the colonisation of the Allahabad and Fatehpur Districts.[42]

The early British collectors had little choice but to rely on the capital of the Benares oligarchy.[43] The majority of Lucknow Khattri firms which had handled the Nawab of Awadh's revenue in the lower Doab withdrew their branch houses in the city when the district was ceded to the British, or sank into obscurity soon afterwards. Only the Benares magnates could raise the cash necessary for the savage revenue assessment which the British laid on their new territories. Thus a large part of the Allahabad District's rights for revenue engagement passed into the hands of Deokinanadan, the Maharaja and and ex-revenue-farmer who had been a hanger-on of Almas Ali Khan. The episode, which involved the shoe-beating of recalcitrant zamindars in the fort of Allahabad, became a scandal in the early annals of British revenue management. But the consequences were not all dire. Deokinanadan, for instance, was largely responsible for the construction of 200 cotton warehouses on the Allahabad riverside at Daraganj,[44] and he imparted the first life into a city which had been stationary since the Mughal royal

40 Magt. Jaunpur to Supt. Police, 15 Jan. 1817, BCJ, 31 Jan. 1817, 138/6, IOL.
41 BCJ, 29 Jul. 1817, 133/13, IOL.   42 CPR, 1 Dec. 1807, 90/62, IOL.
43 R. Ahmuty to Collr Allahabad, 26 June 1804; Collr Allahabad to Govt, 25 June 1805, CPR, 16 June 1805, 90/49; Collr Allahabad to Govt, 18 Sept. 1805, CPR, 10 Oct. 1805, 90/50, IOL.
44 CPR, 10 Jan. 1804, 90/41; this early growth was jeopardised by the Maratha wars, Collr

family left it in 1771.[45] The rule of the Maharaja of Benares and his clients in the Trans-Jamna part of the district also saw an extension of clearing and cultivation[46] such as had taken place between 1740 and 1780 on the fringes of his own domains. These Benares magnates in fact retained that powerful combination of entrepreneurial skill and entrée into the land-revenue system which had spelled success during the previous century. Other Benares merchants established a foothold in Kanpur, while the great house of Gopal Das even acquired substantial holdings in distant Delhi before 1830.[47] As a logistical exercise, in fact, British expansion into upper India after 1800 was very much the sub-imperialism of Benares – the culmination of that process of maximising revenue and town-building which had been initiated by Mansa Ram in the 1740s.

Capitalists, armies and the stability of revenue

From the very beginnings of its direct government in Hindustan, the Company, like its Indian predecessors, relied on the expertise of indigenous trader–bankers not merely to underpin its residual trading operations but to finance its administration and, in a sense, to guarantee the whole land-revenue system. The colonial government and army aided in the creation of new branch agencies (*kothis*), provided fixed markets (*ganjs*) in the tradition of nawabs and rajas, and created a judicial system where merchant contracts achieved an unheard-of degree of sanctity. As early as 1786, Jonathan Duncan and his assistants were actively soliciting the expansion of Benares houses into outlying subdivisions, and supported them with force if necessary.[48] The British needed the Indian trader–banker even more urgently during the great military expansion of Wellesley's Governor Generalship, when they conveyed cash and provisions to the troops fighting on the inland frontiers against the Marathas and Jats. Under the protective shield of Lord Lake's army, the colonisation of north India by the Benares houses went ahead with great speed, and *hundi* transactions became possible on small towns which had previously been isolated. The following typical despatches during Lord Lake's campaign illustrate how the relationship

to Bd, 4 May 1805, vol. 13, Collr to Bd, 26 June, 4 Aug. 1813, vol. 67, Allahabad Collectorate Records (references kindly supplied by Major J. B. Harrison).

[45] Hamilton, *Gazetteer*, I, 20.

[46] R. Temple, 'Report on the Moquddummee Biswahdaree Settlement', *Selections from the Records of the Government, NWP* (Agra, 1856), XXVIII, art. xv, 400ff.

[47] See, e.g., Case 100 of 1849, Delhi, August 1849, *Zillah Court Decisions, NWP* (printed monthly by the Sudder Diwani Adalat).

[48] J. Neave to Resident Benares, 26 June 1788, PR.

worked. The Governor General's Agent at Benares writes to the Commander-in-Chief in 1804:

At the request of Munoo Lal and Baniparshad, Bankers of Benares, I beg leave to recommend to your protection their gomashta [agent] Laljee, deputed by them to establish a kothee [agency] at Kalpee and with directions to furnish you with whatever sums of money the publick service shall require . . .[49]

and later,

I comply with the sollicitations of Munoo Lal and Beniparshad Bankers of Benares in recommending to the protection of Your Excellency, Bajun Lal Nyansook, the agent and manager of their koothie [agency] established at Muttura. The firm has likewise requested me to sollicit Your Excellency to honour them with a preference on being permitted to furnish the supplies of cash which might be required for the use of the army.[50]

But the commercial agents of the army were equally important in the slow peacetime expansion of formal British power north into the Terai and Dehra Dun, west to the borders of Sikh territory and south towards Ajmer–Merwara.[51] In so many rural periodic marts, it needed only a small quickening of economic activity to lift business to the level of a permanent bazaar. A military bazaar lifted consumption sufficiently during the slack summer season to persuade itinerant traders and money lenders to set up a fixed market. Increased circulation of coin and a local market in turn encouraged local zamindars, as in the Dun in 1822, to turn more of their land over to cash crops. The civil authorities then firmly tied the area into the Gangetic economy by raising land-revenue sufficiently to compel zamindars and cultivators to maintain production at that level.

In the disturbed regions towards Delhi the incoming colonial authorities relied yet more heavily on Indian men of commerce. In Benares and the east the revenue yield had been comparatively stable. The west, on the other hand, was liable to suffer regular shortfalls in the monsoons, and did so in 1801–2 and 1804–6 when their effects were deepened by sporadic Maratha invasions and the plunder of large numbers of plough animals by the rival armies.[52] Faced with erratic revenue yields, unpaid soldiery and the needs of the Royal House whose protectors they now were, the British found themselves in a position not unlike that of 'short purse' Najaf Khan, the Mughal lord protector of a generation before.

[49] Agent to GG, Benares to Capt. Baillie, Agent to the Commander-in-Chief in Bundelkhand, 21 Jan. 1804, PR.
[50] Agent, Benares to Lord Lake, 21 June 1804, PR.
[51] 'Examination of Gobind Roy', CPR, 23 Apr. 1823, 95/10, IOL.
[52] Girdlestone, *Past Famines*, p. 12.

Chapter 3 showed, however, that even in the west there existed stable patterns of trade and credit, associated in particular with the east–west trades in grain and salt. It was to these that the British turned and also to friendly magnates like Begum Samru of Sardhana who controlled the surplus areas. In October 1806, Harsukh Rai, the Treasurer of the Delhi Residency, made the British a large loan at 12 per cent interest for the purpose of covering military arrears and the charges of the Emperor's household.[53] In December of that year 'Prem Narayan Ramjus' and 'Sewa Ram Sangam Lal', two firms associated with the salt trade, made further loans of more than Rs. 50,000 to the Deputy Paymaster General.[54] The connection continued after the end of the war. The Delhi authorities used the financial services of the Khattri networks when sending missions to the Punjab and the northern hills. Early British Delhi, especially its high society, was also floated on loans from the Indian commercial community. The later notorious connection between Sir Edward Colebrooke and the headman of the city's bankers[55] was only one example of the way in which the civilians inherited the relationship between *mahajan* and revenue-farmer until Victorian fiscal probity snapped the link.

During the late eighteenth century, the foundation of fixed rural markets and the stimulus given to local production by military expenditure had kept the rural economy moving forward in the more favoured areas. After 1800 British military expenditure maintained this stimulus and provided merchants with another avenue for capital accumulation besides the provisioning of Indian elites. The North-Western Provinces remained on the frontier of the British empire. This meant that resources raised from the local population (and indeed from Bengal and Bihar) in the form of land-revenue and customs continued to be expended in military bases throughout the region. During the Napoleonic Wars in particular, there was a rapid build-up of British military force, and this was maintained until the late 1820s. The last campaign against the Marathas was fought in 1818; against the Jat rajas in 1826, and against the princes of Rajasthan in 1828. Agra, Fatehgarh and Meerut remained active service stations and even downriver depots such as Mirzapur, Chunar and Allahabad remained substantial supply centres.

Large quantities of food, animal fodder and other supplies were raised for the military in local markets. In 1802, for instance, Mirzapur

[53] A. Seton, Resident Delhi to Accountant General, 23 Oct. 1806, For. Sec. Cons. 79, NAI.
[54] For. Sec. Cons., 18 Dec. 1806, 35–40, NAI; I am indebted for this reference to Sri Satyapal.
[55] For the Colebrooke case, see, For. Pol. Cons., 8 Jan. 1830, 2 vols., NAI.

dealers profited in a spectacular fashion when the military authorities purchased 120,000 *maunds* of food-grains and 1,000 *maunds* of *ghi* and had them sent to the troops upriver.[56] The problems of military supply kept the authorities in close contact with the local grain merchant and contracting community.[57] Special premia were given to the importers of grain from Bengal and Bihar, while river merchants benefited from massive auctions when the military over-purchased.[58] Quite contrary to the later laissez-faire philosophy which gradually withdrew official influence from the market, the military authorities intervened actively during this period to hold prices and compel the attendance of grain merchants at military bazaars during campaigns. Until as late as 1810, some of the largest grain markets in the country, including the whole town of Kanpur, were designated military bazaars, and prices at civil bazaars tended to follow them. This forced centralisation of the grain trade and similar direct intervention in the clothing and tent-making markets did at least have the effect of maintaining the level of activity in a number of up-country centres which were at risk from the flux among the Mughal consuming classes. The military contractor was therefore among the most prosperous and mobile of figures in early colonial society. From Dharm Das who became 'king' of Agra in the 1810s,[59] through Kanhaiya Lal and Ramnarain of Benares and Kanpur who 'prospered in the grain department during the late [Maratha] wars',[60] to the petty *faria* grain merchants and grocers of Mirzapur,[61] army service provided openings which did not arise in ordinary agricultural trade, still bound by the restraint of low consumer income.

The British armies, and particularly their European contingents, were great spenders. At a conservative estimate, a single battalion of European infantry might have generated demand in the local economy of Rs. 4–5 lakhs per annum, if we include purchase by the army of equipment which the individual soldier did not have to supply out of his own pocket. Fixed European barracks and other facilities also created much more building contracting work for the local community than did the more mobile and flexible Indian contingents. Even so, Indian infantry battalions may have generated about half as much expenditure as their European counterparts, though a rather lower proportion of the

56 Magt. Benares to CGC Mirzapur, 16 Aug. 1803, Judl letters issued, Mirzapur Collectorate Records, 72, UPR.
57 See, e.g., Bengal Military Cons., 19 Jan., 14 Apr. 1803, 20/43 and 44, IOL.
58 Invoice, 16 July 1804, Mirzapur Judl letters issued, 72, UPR.
59 Petition of Dharam Das, CGC Agra to Bd, 29 July 1816, Agra Customs 1, IOL.
60 Collr Kanpur to Collr Farrukhabad, 12 Mar. 1807, 90/58, IOL; cf. Agent, Benares to Govt, 15 Oct. 1803, PR.
61 Memorandum on grain sales, 16 July 1804, Mirzapur Judl letters issued, 32, UPR.

total would have been spent locally as the sepoys remitted much of their earnings to home villages in Bengal and Bihar. There were 10,000 troops in the cantonment of Kanpur in 1815 and of these, 2,500 were Europeans;[62] they maintained as many as 400 pieces of artillery. It is not surprising, then, that the nearby Indian town expanded from a population of about 5,000 in 1798 to 30,000 in 1830.[63] Kanpur, Fatehgarh and to a lesser degree Agra and Meerut became home bases for a whole new generation of military contractors drawn from the local commercial community who pushed forward the commercial penetration of the backward lands of Banda[64] to the south and the Himalayan foothills to the north. The firms at the base camps operated by sending agents with every detachment which was posted to a remote centre. As the only trade between the base and the new posting was likely to be in military stores, the client banking house was able to command the sole channel for the remittance of *hundis*, putting it in a strong position with the civil authorities and local zamindars. In several cases, petty military contracting allowed firms to become first commissariat agents and then civil treasurers. Capital accumulated appears to have found its way into the agricultural sector through the finance of zamindars who were turning over to indigo production.[65]

It was not only the elites who thrived on military spending in the environs of the great cantonments. There were also opportunities for employment for lower caste artisan and service communities. Chamar leather workers, Kahar carriers, Teli oil-men and Kalwar liquor distillers all found jobs with Europeans as cooks, stableboys, bearers and domestic servants. All these were positions which they would probably not have held under Hindu rulers, though service for Muslim soldiers may have provided similar employment under the Nawabi. Service villages grew up rapidly around the European military stations. The 1,200 residents of village Bokhapore, near the Meerut cantonments in 1817, all obtained their livelihood by 'daily labour in and near the Cantonments'.[66] There was a brisk trade in spirits and 'cheroots' for the troops,[67] while the production and repair of soldiers' garments provided employment for a small army of Muslim tailors.[68] In the same way, the vast European consumption of meat, which was large even by the

---

[62] Hamilton, *Gazetteer*, I, 256.

[63] CGC Kanpur to Bd, 27 Oct. 1807, CPR, 30 Oct. 1807, 91/11, IOL; cf. *chaukidari* statistics 1816, Mirz. Judl letters issued, 28, UPR.

[64] Collr Bundelkhand to Bd, 9 Feb. 1807, CPR, 27 Feb. 1807, 90/57, IOL.

[65] Most evidently in Farrukhabad where city *mahajans* lent more than Rs. 30 lakhs to finance indigo speculation.

[66] BCJ, 14 Mar. 1817, 133/10, IOL.

[67] Depositions, 8 July 1816 before Magt. Kanpur, BCJ, 16 Aug. 1816, 132/44, IOL.

[68] BCJ, 16 Sept. 1817, 133/14, IOL.

standards of a Muslim army, quickly fostered a new generation of commissariat meat contractors and cattle merchants.[69] The demand for meat in Meerut quickly became so great that there were fears for the survival of the herds of sheep in the nearby Moradabad District which had once provided a valuable form of wool for blankets.[70] The military stations also modified the local peasant economies for a significant distance around them. Near Kanpur, an island of relative agricultural prosperity was created in the midst of the depressed middle Doab, and the intensive fruit and tobacco cultivation which had been fostered by the Nawabs of Farrukhabad received impetus from the growth of the British station at Fatehgarh. As early as 1797, Tennant had noted how military bazaars had encouraged the production of new crops such as potatoes and tobacco around Kanpur. Walter Hamilton was more specific in 1815:

Agriculture in the neighbourhood of Cawnpoor has profited by the stimulus of the European market and high prices. Indian corn, grain, barley and wheat are cultivated; and turnips, cabbages and European vegetables are during the season in great abundance, not only in the gardens of the officers, but in the fields cultivated by the natives.[71]

The potato and the cabbage were, after all, among the most enduring and useful of colonialism's contributions to Indian life.

The British civil authorities also inherited the tradition of *ganj* foundation and close reliance on indigenous capital. As any traveller in north India will know, the euphonious 'Nawabganj' or 'Begamganj' easily became the outlandish 'Ahmutyganj', Hoganganj, McCleodganj or even Wellesleyganj. It is a nice irony that so many Regency Scotsmen and Anglo-Irishmen who as a class were beginning to affect to despise trade, created as their most permanent monument a series of mud-built markets in north India. Protection and safe places for bulk storage were an undoubted boon to the merchants who settled in these new foundations, but they were also a crucial facility for a civil officer attempting to recover his establishment costs, provision his staff or remit revenue from some distant subdivisional headquarters. On the fragile fringes of the settled economy, the revenue system remained dependent on the goodwill and investment of Indian traders. No indigenous moneylending class among the local zamindars would have been wealthy enough to sustain the demand for cash. When Hindu–Muslim conflict loomed in the 1830s at Kashipur on the fringes of the northern hills, the fragility of the revenue system became only too apparent:

[69] BCJ, 6 Oct. 1820, 134/34; BCJ, 7 Jan. 1820, 134/36, IOL.
[70] BCJ, 8 Dec. 1820, 134/45.   [71] Hamilton, *Gazetteer*, I, 256.

The cultivators and malgoozars [revenue-engagers] are entirely dependent on the advances they receive from the bunyas and mahajans of the city; if the latter are induced to leave the town as they are ready to do, the revenues of government will be considerably endangered. It is to be recollected that for three months in Mr Pidcock's time the bazaar was deserted, and the merchants with difficulty brought back through the assistance of the Rajah.[72]

So important remained the link between trade, revenue and agricultural production in the early years of British rule that a special Superintendent of Resources was appointed to collate information on the size and wealth of the Indian merchant community in order to smooth civil and military operations.[73] The Superintendent kept a close check on the number of merchants in given towns, with an estimate of their supposed holdings in corn, their individual capitalisation and numbers of river boats or bullocks. He also communicated with collectors and army commissaries about the best means to stimulate agricultural marketing. In 1818, for instance, the Collector of Ghazipur writes to the Superintendent:

The extention of agriculture and commerce, it must be allowed greatly depends upon the ready means afforded for obtaining specie. The banking establishments in this town are too inconsiderable in their extent and ability to have any influence in promoting the objects in contemplation ... what was required was an inducement to the Benares shroffs who hold bills drawn on the Benares treasury to extend their agency to Ghazeepore which in my opinion is alone wanting to put this place on a par with most of the commercial towns of India.[74]

The inducement most often offered to the Indian commercial classes was the prospect of running the treasury of the government or local court. Between 1790 and 1820, three great houses of Agarwal and Bhargava merchants from Rajasthan and Hariana respectively were allowed to gain control of the majority of government treasuries throughout the provinces.[75] The British government was effectively contracting out its fiscal business to the Indian trader. The relationship was sometimes uneasy, but before the establishment of a modern joint-stock bank as agent of the administration, it was necessary. The bankers received the honour of the title of treasurer (*khazanchi*) and a whole range of new clients among the zamindars who paid their money into the

---

[72] Asst Magt. Moradabad to Commr Rohilkhand, 31 Oct. 1833, BCJ, 10 Feb. 1834, 140/ 56, IOL.

[73] See, e.g., R. Barlow to H. Newman, Superintendent of Resources, 25 Feb. 1818, Benares Rev. Misc., 24, pp. 76–8, UPR.

[74] Collr Ghazipur to Sec. Bd of Commrs (Bihar and Benares) Benares Rev. Misc., 24, UPR.

[75] E.g. the family of Tori Ram Bhargava, CGC Allahabad to Actg CGC Allahabad, 19 Dec. 1820, CPR, 26 Dec. 1820, 94/16.

collectorates. The government bought at little cost expertise which they found valuable well into the Age of Reform of the Indian government. As late as 1832, collectors were being instructed to remit money 'through the agency of the shroffs at par or at any other advantageous rate of exchange'.[76]

As the correspondence of the Superintendent of Resources illustrates, the mutual dependence of the Company Raj and Indian capital was more than a necessity – it was a philosophy. By making possible the rise of free trade and free traders in the Indian interior, the Company could not only guarantee the revenue but could also lay the foundations of an Indian commercial middle class. The 'black capitalist' was for many officials of the Regency years what the English-educated professional man was to be for the early Victorians and the 'sturdy husbandman' or improving zamindar yet later in the century: the main agent of economic and social change in South Asia. Far from the 'fashionable abuse' of the Indian trader and banker which filled the settlement reports of the 1870s and 1880s, men such as James Tod saw the Indian commercial classes as the Medici of a coming Indian renaissance. W. H. Sleeman, writing when the bloom had already passed in the Depression of the 1830s, was perhaps even more emphatic. Looking for a time when India would 'abound in a middle class of merchants, manufacturers and agricultural capitalists', he exclaims:

There is no class of men more interested in the stability of our rule in India than this of the respectable merchants; nor is there any upon whom the welfare of our Government and that of the people more depend. Frugal, first upon principle, that they may not in their expenditure encroach on their capitals, they become so by habit; and when they advance in life they lay out their accumulated wealth in the formation of those works which shall secure for them, from generation to generation, the blessings of the people of the towns in which they have resided, and those of the country around.[77]

As yet, there was little fear that the rise of the rural moneylender would in any way derange landed society, though the 1834 Agra Settlement Report remarked with caution that 'however advantageous it may be for the improvement of cultivation and for the security of the revenue, it is far less so as regards the private interests of the zemindars' who were tempted to extravagance and heavy borrowing.

[76] Superintendent Resources to Magt. Mirzapur, 7 Jun. 1832, Mirzapur Financial 130, p. 7, UPR.
[77] W. H. Sleeman, *Rambles and Recollections* (London, 1844, repr. Karachi, 1973), pp. 409–10.

Political stability and the expansion of cultivation

Growing political stability also encouraged trade and agricultural development through the settlement of predatory and itinerant groups. Such settlement was in part a consequence of the expansion of cultivation itself; in part, it helped to confirm this expansion by reducing risks and levies on trade routes and, of course, augmenting the settled agricultural population. Wanderers had proved a threat to the stronger Indian regimes even where they provided services as essential as did the Banjaras. They were difficult to tax. They themselves looted and 'taxed' the settled agricultural and urban communities through which they travelled, and switched their allegiance from one state to another without much scruple. The aim of the eighteenth-century rulers was always to assert their own monopoly of taxation and control the movement of their subjects. To these traditional aims of the Hindu and Muslim officials who served them the British added their own particular perceptions of public order and criminality. Nomads and wanderers were seen as disorderly elements – carriers of roguery and dissidence. This stereotype was often applied to travelling groups as harmless as ironsmiths and potters who linked up local areas of production and consumption. It is not difficult to see how attitudes like this derived from experience of the great increase in social control which had taken place in contemporary England.

Several methods were adopted by the British to pacify the wanderers. Main routes were to be protected by the construction or reconstruction of regular *sarais* (hostelries) in which merchants could deposit their goods and spend the night in security.[78] Collectors reconstituted and made use of the old service community of *bhatiyaras* or 'inn-keepers' who had served the Mughal roads as servants of travellers and agents for police information.[79] By 1816 most towns and substantial villages had once again regular police officers commanding bodies of paramilitary police or hired militia (the *sebundi* corps). Censuses of houses were carried out in the bazaars to ascertain the size of corps needed and to locate the houses of persons deemed to belong to 'criminal tribes' such as Gujars and Mewatis.

The break-up of the more spectacular bands of gentry–mercenaries and robbers in Hindustan and central India before 1820 had considerable consequences for the economy. The dimension of the problem was great; in Rohilkhand alone, it was thought that there were as many as 100,000 mercenaries and 'banditti' in 1802.[80] Various

[78] Magt. Mirzapur to Govt, 13 April 1804, BCJ, 24 May 1804, 129/6, IOL.
[79] Suptdt Police Western Provinces to Govt, 18 Apr. 1819, BCJ, 1819, 133/10, IOL.
[80] Wellesley's Report on Trade, Bds Collns 2803, p. 6, IOL.

methods were used to domesticate them quite apart from the natural absorption of some into agriculture as cultivation increased. For instance, the British redirected the energies of Mewati robber–mercenaries by employing them as a kind of unofficial police force. All that happened was that the several thousand rupees in annual protection money which these bands had levied on villages in Aligarh and Etawah was now remitted to them directly from the government revenue as a form of payment for their police duties of taming and domesticating other Mewati bands.[81] The abolition of Mewati protection money further reduced merchant costs in the central Doab. Here they had taken 'gifts' of between 8 annas and 1 Rupee on every cart of produce or bullock which had passed through their territory for the best part of sixty years.[82] The Nawabs of Farrukhabad and the Marathas had both been forced to acquiesce in the arrangement.

Elsewhere the colonial authorities made use of the large zamindars to bring predatory groups under control. The many varieties of armed bandit – *Kazaks*, Budheks, Thugs, and the like – who had preyed on trade routes and harried unstable areas were themselves agents of the prosperity of the more stable areas. They had received the protection of princes and zamindars and in turn paid a proportion of their booty to them. One noted body of vagrant robbers were the Budheks[83] who had permanent homes in the Jat *rajs* of Hatras and Mursan and other hideouts far to the east on the property of notables of Gorakhpur. According to one authority:

Many of the Budhiks with whom I have conversed state that they are excited to this predatory mode of livelihood by their zemindars who keep them constantly in debt for advances made to their families and only allow them to reside on their estates on condition of their continuing to plunder.[84]

The authorities exerted pressure through the land-revenue system to force zamindars to expel the predators or settle them in agriculture. Measures such as this had a cumulative effect on cultivation and trade. In one area north of Rampur, a Mewati stated 'I was formerly a ryot [peasant], but, finding that I was not allowed to reap what I have sown, I became a robber. Under the Company's Government the case is different. I will now therefore become a ryot.'[85] Similarly, in the unstable west of Aligarh and in the territories north of Delhi, the expansion of cultivation itself helped to transform supposedly 'idle and

81 CPR, 13 May 1803, 90/38, IOL.
82 Collr Etawah to Bd, 16 July 1803, CPR, 2 Aug. 1803, 90/39, IOL.
83 Note by Suptdt Police, 30 Apr. 1816. Mirzapur Judl 38, UPR.
84 Suptdt Police Western Provinces to Magt. Aligarh, 8 Nov. 1815, BCJ, 132/39, IOL.
85 Note by Suptdt Police, NWP, 30 Apr. 1816, Mirzapur Judl, 38, UPR.

turbulent' Gujars into cultivators by providing them with a degree of security in bad seasons. Safer roads in turn brought down insurance and freight charges and encouraged cultivation at a greater distance from town centres. Rates of insurance south of Agra appear to have fallen by about 300 per cent in the years 1799–1816, while costs on the river had been reduced by attempts to stop zamindars taking 'gifts' at mooring places along its route and by the reopening of water transport above Agra and Farrukhabad.

The settlement of that most famous of the wandering groups, the Banjara carriers, follows a similar pattern. It was earlier suggested that the activities of Banjaras were essential to the economies of the islands of settled cultivation in post-Mughal India, but that they were also impediments to the recovery of unstable areas which had gone out of cultivation. However, the settlement and penning in of Banjaras to a more limited role in the economy and into certain marginal tracts was a process which had been going on since the seventeenth century or before. It gathered pace after 1800 in both British and Indian territory. Thus, in Bahraich in the Awadh Tarai, the Banjaras were finally pacified and settled by the Nawab's local official, Hakim Mehendi, in 1821.[86] The Sikh regime in Lahore appears to have taken similar measures to restrict the role of Banjaras by settling groups of retired soldiers in areas where the largest bands had once congregated.

In British territories, the Banjara role was restricted by three developments: first, they were more closely subordinated to merchant groups and to the new military commissariat department; secondly, their pasture land was gradually restricted by advancing agriculture; and finally, a series of cattle epidemics in Malwa and Rajasthan in the 1820s and 1830s broke up some of the largest bands south of the Jamna with remarkable speed.[87] Of course, this did not mean that Banjaras disappeared from the north Indian scene. The great army contractor Joti Prasad was able to assemble nearly 100,000 head of Banjara cattle from Tonk and Pilibhit in three months in 1848.[88] Indeed, there were still 60,000 people registered as Banjaras in the United Provinces in 1901. Banjaras had, however, lost their role as a semi-independent political system and as major carriers in the grain and salt trade down the great central trade routes. Their beat was now confined to the western marches between Rajasthan, Hariana and the British provinces.

The settlement of itinerant groups was particularly important on the

---

[86] Crooke, *Tribes and Castes*, I, 157.
[87] G. A. Freeling, 'Account of Perganna Mahoba, Zillah Humeerpore', *JASB*, xxviii (1859), 382.
[88] Magt. to Commr Agra, 27 June 1850, NWP Crim. Judl, March 1851, 232, 22, IOL.

fringes of the northern hills where there had been age-old conflict between peasant settlers, local rajas and the Banjaras who pastured their cattle there during the summer months. Along the whole tract from the borders of Bihar to the marches of the Punjab, the early British collectors consolidated on the 'pacification' which had already been imposed by the Nawab's officials and renters. Cultivation expanded rapidly. Gorakhpur, which had been enclosed by forest on two sides in 1803,[89] was opened up as far north as Kasia by 1820. Its trade had swelled from a 'trifling'[90] trade in sparse grain through a few *haths* to a major flow of rice down into the Benares Division over the same period, and population began an expansion which was to be rapid and sustained until well into the present century. It would be dangerous to exaggerate the extent of development over the end of the eighteenth century, however. When the self-congratulation of the early collectors is examined more carefully it appears that much of the increment in population and capital was obtained by reversing earlier flows into the prosperous territories of independent rajas who had created stable local dominions during the previous century.

John Routledge, Collector of Gorakhpur, was impressed by the wealth of the principality of Butwal which lay between his northern border and upland Nepal.

As the state of the two districts clearly evinces Gooruckpoor being almost an entire desert and Bootwul, though unhealthy, is nearly as well cultivated as Bihar or Benares. But it may now be expected that its cultivation will become considerably reduced as many of the late settled have already returned to the pergunnehs adjoining to it in this district.[91]

What Routledge and his officials were able to do was to provide sufficient incentives in the way of preferential revenue rates and protection to attract back cultivators who had taken out three-to-five year cultivation leases in Butwal and Awadh. But much earlier migrations were also reversed. The settlement pattern of a generation or two before was reconstituted through a careful examination of the old settlement papers, and villages were repeopled 'although not a hut remains and the sites of many of the villages can only be discovered by tanks and pukka wells'.[92] Along with the peasant farmers, and essential to the revival of agricultural operations, came the merchants. Many of these were agents of Benares and Mirzapur firms which had settled at

[89] Collr Gorakhpur to Bd, 3 Sept. 1804, CPR, 4 Dec. 1804, 90/44, IOL; for further details see also Gorakhpur Rev. Records 1, UPR; 'Kawaif-i-Zillah-i-Gorakhpur', Pers. MS 4540, fos. 2–4, IOL.
[90] Martin, *Eastern India*, 1, 88.
[91] Collr Gorakhpur to Govt, 14 Dec. 1802, Saletore (ed.), *Wellesley Correspondence*, p. 41.
[92] *Idem.*

Butwal town in order to tap the exotic but lucrative trade from Nepal and Tibet.

This pattern was repeated at many places along the edge of the foothills. People who had inhabited the hills north of Rohilkhand since the Awadh conquest in 1773 slowly drifted back to Kashipur, Kanth, and the rich lands adjoining the borders of Rampur. Yet this repeopling of the northern marches of Rohilkhand was at least partly attained at the expense of cultivation and trade higher up in Tehri and Gaharwal. Good land in the plains became more attractive still when the mountains were subject to increasing disruption in the wake of conquest by the Gurkhas.[93] Further to the west in Dehra Dun during the 1820s, 'Annually two or three deserted villages are brought into cultivation by people of capital . . . Lands which have lain waste for thirty to fifty years are breaking up.'[94] The Doon was partly repeopled by earlier emigrants to the north. Much of the capital for clearing and implements was provided by merchants of Saharanpur and Rohilkhand who wished to export the fine local rice to the growing towns of the plains. Nearby, in Pilibhit and Nainital, timber merchants and contractors who were responding to rising demand for commercial river craft contributed to the formation of capital for local trade and agriculture.[95]

In the first two decades of the nineteenth century, considerable progress was also made in the resettlement of unstable areas of agriculture which had suffered from the local decline of trade routes and *qasbah* centres. Merchant capital once again played a key role in this expansion. The first stage, as we have seen, was the re-establishment of military control in urban centres; the second, the consolidation of luxury consumption and the re-establishment of revenue flow, both of which increased medium-distance and local trade; the third stage was the investment of accumulated capital in the production of commodities for the rising export trade in indigo, cotton and sugar.

There is little doubt of the speed of the expansion of cultivation in the less stable areas. An observer in the Muttra–Hodal area between Agra and Delhi reckoned that the area of cultivation under cotton increased by 20–40 per cent in the ten years after the end of the Napoleonic War.[96] The production of cotton in Bah and Pinahut south of Agra appears to have risen fourfold between 1803 and 1816. In Rohilkhand, Brennan suggests that the acreage under sugar may have increased by as much as

---

[93] Commr Dehra to Govt, 10 Dec. 1828, BCJ, 17 Mar. 1829, 139/39, IOL.
[94] Report on Dehra by Isri Singh, CPR, 28 Feb. 1817, 133/9, IOL.
[95] Resdt Delhi to Magt. Saharanpur, 7 July 1808, Saharanpur Collr Rev. Records 176, IOL.
[96] CGC Delhi to Bd, 16 May 1836, NWP Customs, 7 June 1836, 221/86, IOL.

30 per cent between 1803 and 1807.[97] In Hariana, west of Delhi, which was a highly unstable but very rich tract, the flight of capital and cultivators was being steadily reversed. By 1808 two-thirds of the villages which had remained unpopulated since the 1783 famine and its accompanying political disturbances had been repeopled.[98] Even the sparse areas of the central Doab which had suffered so heavily between 1770 and 1790 appear to have been on the path to recovery.

What made the speed of this recovery possible? First, there was the redistribution of labour which had become concentrated on the more stable and protected tracts during the previous century. The penning down of marcher areas with settlements of 'close-cultivating' castes had begun gingerly under Indian magnates. Now it gathered pace. In addition to the drift of labourers down into Rohilkhand from the hills, numbers of peasant families which had become settled on the rich irrigated lands of Rampur began to fan out into neighbouring districts which had suffered from a 'severe lack of labour' at the turn of the century. In many cases this appears to have been stimulated by the re-expansion of families of Pathan notables who had withdrawn to Rampur with their ploughmen (*halis*) under Awadh rule. Similarly, across the Ganges in Muzaffarnagar and Saharanpur the famous Muslim service gentry of Barah Sayyids which had been displaced by Sikh and Rohilla action began to drift back to their ancestral homes.[99] Poverty forced many of these erstwhile notables to take directly to the plough themselves. There was no doubt an increase in the birth rate as populations became settled and as families recouped from the disasters of the mortality of 1783 and 1802–3, but an apparent growth in the density of these tracts from about 100 per square mile at the turn of the century to 190–200 per square mile in 1831 must have been considerably forwarded by the return of earlier immigrants.[100]

Almost any kind of agricultural activity in these tracts required substantial inputs of capital, tools, seed and animal power. The point was that if there was no money locally, it would be impossible for the peasant farmer to repair the damage of the periodic failures of the autumn *kharif* crop by stepping up production in the *rabi* which was dependent on artificial irrigation. In these conditions, the peasant

[97] L. Brennan, 'Social change in Rohilkhand 1801–33', *IESHR*, vii (1970), 448.

[98] T. Fortescue, Delhi Report, *Selns Punjab Records: Delhi Residency* (Lahore, 1911), I, III.

[99] Saharanpur Rev. I–5, UPR; cf. large-scale immigration from Bikaner and settlement of Battis in Hariana and other districts north of Delhi, India Rev. Colln 1832, 79–82, IOL, cited in K. L. Sachdeva, 'A study of unpublished settlement reports of Hissar District', *IHC 1967*, pp. 98–101.

[100] Saharanpur, Aligarh, Farrukhabad Reports, 1814, Home Misc. 776, IOL, cf. *Settlements under Act ix of 1833*, II, part i, 189.

family would be forced to migrate once again to areas where the crop could be guaranteed. From where then did this capital come? There is no doubt that around the Delhi–Hodal area, European firms such as George Mercer and Co. brought in substantial investment in the form of advances from Calcutta agency houses.[101] Investment may have reached Rs. 20–30 lakhs here. But throughout the breadth of the western Gangetic area, indigenous capital must have made the major contribution. What appears to have occurred is that monies accumulated in the more stable raj economies in the supply of military goods and aristocratic consumption were released into the newly cultivated cash-crop areas. This, then, was the last stage of the expansion of the pre-colonial political economy rather than the dawn of a new era of entrepreneurship. For instance, the recolonisation of Saharanpur by indigenous capital was achieved first by substantial Agarwal families who had survived in areas of stability such as Begum Samru's Sardhana. Later, small Bohra moneylenders from the Indian states of Rajasthan, especially Jodhpur, fanned out into these reviving territories north of Delhi.[102] In the middle Doab, the same pattern was repeated. Moneylenders and traders from Farrukhabad and Hatras financed the expansion of grain, sugar and indigo production in areas which had seen a fall-off during the previous century. The men who supplied the aristocratic consumption of the Jat and Bangash armies moved initially into agricultural finance and later into the status of *rentiers* as they began to pick up revenue-rights during the 1830s and 1840s.

The advantage to Indian traders of moving into these erstwhile unstable areas was clear. The resettlement of wandering and predatory groups had considerably reduced protection and insurance costs. Interest rates north of Delhi which had been as high as 30–40 per cent even for secured loans at the turn of the century[103] had come down to 15–20 per cent by 1826. Once the Agra river trade and the Grand Trunk Road had been reopened, the whole upper and middle Doab had a fine transport system based upon the Muslim fortress-town of the previous generation.[104] There was a growing export trade, and a significant

---

101 The slump at the end of the Napoleonic Wars encouraged European business to see India as a field of opportunity, see, e.g., E. W. Blunt to Bd, 15 July 1816, 97, 59, IOL.

102 Lachman Singh, *Bulandshahar*, p. 152.

103 Report on Saharanpur, 5 Aug. 1804, CPR, 29 Nov. 1805, 90/51, IOL. In view of the lack of *hundi* transactions between Saharanpur and Lucknow a loan had to be taken from Begum Samru to keep government business moving, Collr Saharanpur to Bd, 4 Oct. 1805, CPR, 15 Nov. 1805, 90/50, IOL.

104 The 10% expansion of cultivated area in Farrukhabad between 1806 and 1816 continued the substantial expansion of indigo and tobacco agriculture under the Nawabi, Farrukhabad Magts. Report, 27 Oct. 1814, Home Misc. 776, IOL.

demand from reviving urban centres such as Delhi and the Rohilla towns. The profits from trade and servicing the revenue were probably greater than those to be had in the more densely populated and settled areas from which they were expanding.

The fate of the stable areas of eighteenth-century north India in the first two generations of colonial rule is more difficult to assess. It almost seems as though their great advantages in the previous century – well-developed irrigation, stable rule, and the survival of capital – had begun to turn to disadvantages. The revenue officials had begun to speak of the pressure of population on resources in these areas quite early. Assessments of population density per square mile in Benares Division, Allahabad or the environs of Agra range between 400 and 500 by the 1830s. This is 60–100 per cent higher than the average for reviving tracts such as Saharanpur or southern Rohilkhand. In this reading, demographic constraints were taking over from political ones as the major determinant of agricultural performance. Whereas the assurance of an agrarian surplus in the eighteenth century had encouraged stable rule and enterprise, a critical point would soon be reached when population growth would begin to reduce the marginal rate of return in agriculture. Hereafter the development areas would be the lands in the west of the provinces where the man–land ratio was more favourable and where there remained plenty of land to open up with canal and well irrigation.

This argument has the merit of fitting with broader trends. It could, for instance, be applied to Bengal, which was the rich and stable area par excellence in the eighteenth century, but which by the later nineteenth century had run into agricultural depression and had given way to Punjab and western Hindustan in agricultural performance. It also fits well with developments in the 1830s. During the bad seasons of this decade, the stable regions temporarily regained some of their earlier advantages while the more productive tracts revealed once again their dangerous dependence on fickle rainfall.

Conclusion

This chapter has traced through some of the dynamic changes of the pre-colonial political order into the early period of British rule. These changes, of course, did not take place in a vacuum. The growth of European trade on the Bengal seaboard had been an indirect influence on north Indian state and society since the seventeenth century. The great inflow of silver through the hands of the European companies had facilitated the Mughal expansion.[105] It also contributed to the price inflation of the years 1650–1750 which enforced on late Mughal rulers their vigorous search for cash through such techniques as revenue-farming and *ganj*-foundation. Later, external conditions changed. From 1740 to about 1790 the inflow of precious metals into the Indian heartland was disrupted by three developments. First, the English East India Company, secure in its Bengal revenues, halted the inflow of bullion. Secondly, the Mughal revenue pump failed, starving the interior of silver. Thirdly, the Company's demands on Awadh, and by proxy on Rohilkhand and on other parts of north India, reversed the flow, pulling bullion and merchant communities towards Calcutta. The shortage of cash was a formative influence on the north Indian states of the later eighteenth century, and its effects only began to diminish slowly after 1795 when bullion flowed in once again in search of cotton, opium and indigo.

Yet just as the indirect influence of the European world economy long preceded the first appearance of British administrators in the plains of Hindustan, so changes internal to the pre-colonial economy persisted well into the Company era. Company government and private trade benefited from the final flowering of the 'decentralised' economy of the successor states. The great consumer cities – Lucknow, Benares, Fyzabad, Farrukhabad – continued to grow. Local merchant communities which had seized their first opportunities in the dissolution of the Mughal hegemony pressed home their advantage. They found new security on the great trade routes and in British revenue courts; their quid pro quo was to guarantee the British revenue system as they had guaranteed its Mughal predecessors. The integrated system of markets and revenue extraction in cash which had been in evidence in the eighteenth-century surplus areas was now extended to the unstable tracts to the west. Magnate, village leader and nomadic wanderer were all drawn more firmly into a rigid cash revenue system. But there were limits imposed to the resulting commercial economy which were as much the inheritance of Indian political forms as results of the aims of the British themselves. What was marketed were royal rights and the right to engage for state land-revenue. Control over peasant producers and inferior agents in the trading system remained weak. Colonial law proved little more effective at this level than had Mughal justice,[106] and

---

105 See, e.g., J. F. Richards, 'Mughal state finance and the pre-modern world economy', *Comparative Studies in Society and History*, xxiii (1981), 285–308; Frank Perlin, 'Some central problems concerning the proto-industrialisation thesis and pre-colonial South Asia', mimeo., Dept History, Erasmus University, Rotterdam, 1980.

106 D. A. Washbrook, 'Law, state and agrarian society in colonial India', *Modern Asian Studies*, xv (1981), 649–71.

while colonial government penetrated below the level of *pargana* administration, its workings were circumscribed and blunted. The next chapter considers the successes and frustrations of long-distance trade in early colonial north India.

6

The indigenous origins of the 'colonial economy'

Since the work of Holden Furber it has been recognised that Company servants and European private traders spun their webs of 'country trade' along existing lines of commercial activity, and above all from Calcutta northward into the ancient trade of the Ganges valley. However, these trading patterns, with the mercantile towns, markets and corporate bodies to which they gave rise, were not static systems simply acted upon by the dynamic pole of Calcutta. Like the regional states, they were also in the process of change and reorganisation. This moulded and limited the inland thrust of European seaboard commerce. By 1770, shifts in trading patterns had occurred which strengthened the links between Bengal and inland India. These new trading facilities predated any substantial European interest but provided a context of mercantile knowledge, credit and protection which aided the classic colonial trade in raw materials as it emerged in the early nineteenth century.

Before 1850, there was little metropolitan capital directly invested in India, and the number of European commercial personnel resident on the Ganges–Jamna trade routes remained less than one hundred. Despite the capital accumulation of the Calcutta agency houses, European up-country commerce continued to rely on loans from the Indian trading community, and it was generally managed by their agents and factotums. Contemporary observers and historians have always sought for signs that western capitalism was on the point of transforming India. What happened, however, was that Indian business methods, and the political context within which they were set, transformed and frustrated the feeble European impulse. Regardless of the steamboat, the agency house and the joint-stock bank, Indian commercial society proved almost as impenetrable to the westerners as its Chinese counterpart, and was much more costly to come to grips with.

For the Company and the European private traders, the most important developments in north India's pre-colonial commercial geography were the consolidation of Benares as the main money market for eastern India, and the growth of Mirzapur as the key commodity mart between Bengal, Hindustan and central India. The fortunes of

Map 4   The North-Western Provinces and Oudh, about 1870

Benares have already been traced in some detail. Its position athwart the trade routes, its status as a centre of pilgrimage, and its relatively stable hinterland laid the foundations for a growing importance. The creation of a mint there in 1734 and the decline of the Jagat Seths in Bengal after their fatal quarrel with the Nawab of Bengal in 1756 further increased the commercial significance of the up-country city. What was essential was that the Company and other Europeans could count on the presence in Benares of large sums of bullion or credit. This was required for their purchases of cloth and saltpetre in the north, or for moving government funds to the south and west. Even after the decline of the consumption of Bengal piece goods in Delhi, the upriver trade route from Bengal to

Benares seems to have persisted. Benares and Bengal records show that there were large merchant houses such as those of Vaziri Mull and Pinde Das (both Khattris) functioning on this route and using Benares as a forward base, even in the bad decades of the 1750s and 1760s.[1] In the 1770s, the Shahs and other bankers of Benares were bringing up several lakhs of Rupees per month from Murshidabad and Patna to be coined at Benares or to be sent on to Lucknow and the 'west'. We have no idea of the total of such transactions; but they do underline the fact that there was still a brisk bullion trade in inland India.[2] In the same way, demand for north Indian goods, like shawls, horses and cloth in Bengal, maintained a considerable trade even when the link with revenue-payment had been snapped after the decline of Mughal dominance.

The Europeans made heavy use of Benares commercial facilities. During the 1760s, there was temporarily a Company 'factory' there which worked closely with one of the senior members of the Naupatti Sabha, Lala Ami Chand,[3] who was also head of the city's Purbiye Agarwal community. The famous private merchant, William Bolts, and his Armenian agents, also used Benares as a base for the purchase of Awadh saltpetre and cloths.[4] Even after the Battle of Buxar (1764) when Benares no longer paid tribute to Lucknow, the city remained a good base for trading in Awadh because Lucknow bankers with *kothis* in Benares were the people who remitted the Nawab's large subsidy to the East India Company in Calcutta. During the 1770s, no Company factory existed in the city, but its presence remained strong. Most senior Company servants, including Warren Hastings, found that the purchase of diamonds from the province of Bundelkhand which lay to the south was a useful way of remitting their licit and illicit fortunes to England. In the late 1770s, they appear to have invested up to Rs. 1 lakh per annum in the market there.[5] In the jewel trade we see another connection between the reorientation of internal luxury consumption in India and the mercantile options of the European community. A famous and long-standing commercial dispute in the city during the 1770s (*Uma Das* v. *Chehta Mull*) reveals how the Europeans were able, through the offices of the Naupatti, to tap a vast network of transactions in precious

[1] *Gunga Bye* v. *the Mother of Jwalanath*, 3 Aug. 1792, PR.
[2] E.g., 7 Feb. 1791, PR; such transactions must have financed Bengal imports of north Indian goods (shawls, silk and horses) during the 1760s and 1770s, but more fully recorded are large despatches of gold and silver *from* north India to Murshidabad covering the Awadh and Benares 'tribute' to the Company, see, e.g., examination of the Benares 'shroffs', For. Sec. Cons. A, 1 Dec. 1777, NAI.
[3] W. Bolts, *Considerations on Indian Affairs* (London, 1772), III, 372, 411–25; cf. *ibid.*, II, 104.
[4] *Ibid.*, II, 104; Mishra, *Banaras*, ch. 5.
[5] P. J. Marshall, *East Indian Fortunes*, pp. 128, 221–2, 241–2.

stones which stretched from Afghanistan to Hyderabad but centred on Benares.[6] The city was the natural entrepôt because some of the greatest buyers were the Maratha chieftains who came to Benares for pilgrimage, and the sellers were often north Indians or Central Asians. The trade appears to have been dominated by Lala Kashmiri Mull of a Khattri family which had strong north-western connections and by Khub Chand, a Jain who had emerged as one of the city's major property-owners.[7]

European relations with the great trading corporations of Benares were consolidated in the late 1770s when the resident's treasury became a centre of private trade as well as direct Company dealings during the period of Fowke and Bristow.[8] Since Kashmiri Mull's house was creditor to the Maharaja, treasurer to the Company, revenue-farmer, and creditor to the residents in their capacity as private traders, this was almost inevitable. It followed the pattern of European relations with the Jagat Seths in Bengal and it was to be played out in Agra, Kanpur and Delhi. It was well into the next century before Victorian uprightness finally severed the link between public office, revenue and peculation. Throughout the 1780s and 1790s the connection became stronger as new European merchants were brought into the network. Most Calcutta traders with interests in north India were forced to work through the *kothis* of the Lucknow and Benares oligarchs. European agency houses such as Burgh's, White's, Palmer's and Alexander's occasionally had correspondents in north India, but generally they, too, made use of Indian *hundis*. In the 1790s, for instance, we find Dr Blanc, trader in silk at Mirzapur, securing payment through the *kothi* of Gopal Das.[9]

The most notable example of dependence was the manner in which the Company's own commercial interests throughout northern and western India relied on the good offices of the Hindustani banking houses. The Company commercial agents who purchased cloth and saltpetre at Patna or sugar and cloth at Ghazipur were as indebted to them for the supply of ready money as the first generation of revenue officers. The situation did not become much easier even when formal British control of the region was asserted. As late as 1796, the Ghazipur Commercial Agent was suggesting that Gopal Das *kothi* should remain

6 *Uma Das* v. *Chehta Mull*, Raja's Mulki Court, 27 Feb. 1789, PR.
7 Khub Chand is mentioned in the case *Uma Das* v. *Chehta Mull*; he also appears in many of the early property documents possessed by Chaukambha families. He was probably one of the Bundelkhandi Jains who dominated the Benares jewel trade throughout the eighteenth and nineteenth centuries, cf. DR 52, pp. 225–34, UPR.
8 7 Mar., 17 June, 4 Aug. 1788, PR; Mishra, *Banaras*, pp. 158–65.
9 Dr Blanc to Resident Benares, 19 July 1791, PR; for other examples of private European connections with the Naupatti, *CPC*, VIII (1785), 332; Sleeman, *Tour*, ed. Reeves, pp. 176–7.

the 'sole channel' for cash payments for saltpetre and indigo purchases to avoid making his own office into a kind of bank, for which he had no facilities.[10] Nor was the relationship simply between the Company Agent and the banker. In fact, the intermediate purchasing merchants through whom the Company dealt were debtors or relations of the great firms.

In several ways, the East India Company was the direct beneficiary of the fiscal relations which had been created between the Indian principalities and the capital-owning corporations. As we have seen, Indian bankers had made bridging loans to the rulers in the form of advances on the revenue (*dakhillas*) and these had been accepted almost as a currency in their own right. The British inherited this system in Benares, though during the 1770s and 1780s both Fowke and Duncan attempted to reduce their dependence.

The connection between north Indian capital and the Company was strengthened by a series of government loans issues which took place in the 1790s and early 1800s. Depending on the urgency with which the Company needed money, these were made at 5, 7 and 12 per cent per annum.[11] The loans became increasingly important as a method of funding military activity in the heyday of Cornwallis's and Wellesley's expansion, but they can also be considered as an indirect subsidy to Company trade through Calcutta since the surplus in Company treasuries in Bengal and Benares was regularly used for purchasing the annual 'investment' in cloths, salt and saltpetre. Again, the Company worked closely with Indian corporate institutions. The Resident approached the head of the Naupatti Sabha in Benares,[12] while in Lucknow an attempt was made in 1791 to tap the large supply of funds in the hands of smaller merchants. An address to one of the chief bankers specifies how less substantial men could approach their headmen with terms for delivery of cash at Calcutta and how, at a specified time, 'the headman should find out from the list of the names of *mahajans* whose *hundis* are together sufficient for the sum required by the East India Company . . . and he should collect their *hundis* and pay them the sums of the *hundis* from the Company treasury'.[13]

After the Cession, conditions for investment in government stock improved. In Farrukhabad, European merchants (who were probably indigo dealers) concerted with the head of the local bankers to persuade large numbers of merchants to put their spare cash into 5 per cent

---

10 8 Aug. 1796, PR.
11 10 July 1788, 15 Sept. 1780, PR; Agent to Govt, 8 Oct. 1804, PR.
12 10 July 1790, 8 Oct. 1804, PR.
13 *Perwana, Ramzan-ul Mubarak Hijri* 1250 (June 1791), Sri Ram Krishna Collection, Benares.

loans.[14] And this was only the official front of a vast system of loans to private traders and Company officers which went on into the 1820s and 1830s despite attempts to clamp down on it. Whether one can speak of a 'drain' of funds to Calcutta during this period remains unclear because of the complexity of the transactions in goods and services between Benares and Bengal. What is certain, however, is that the size and sophistication of the Benares capital market gave an enormous impetus to the British commercial penetration of Gangetic India.

The trade in raw cotton from the interior to Bengal also illustrates the dependence of the emerging colonial trade on Indian commercial institutions. Here again, growing internal demand in India and the emergence of new trade routes and merchant communities provided favourable conditions for a trade which helped Great Britain balance its payments with the whole of South and East Asia. The great mart for cotton was the town of Mirzapur. As chapter 3 showed, it was a river *ghat* which secured protection from the emerging Benares dynasty. In 1776

> The trade of this zemindary [Benares] has for a long time almost entirely centred at Mirzapure which has become the market of common resort for the merchants of Bengal, Behaur and those of the Deccan, and the countries situated to the west and north. This mart, before a considerable one, became much more so after the battle of Bucsar, which opening an intercourse with the English produced a traffic in Europe and China articles, and a more intimate connection and commerce with the Honourable Company's Provinces.[15]

At some point before 1776, the people of Benares were already importing central Indian cotton to use in the making of their own coarse cloths and quilts, since locally grown cotton was only used for fine handicrafts. On the other hand, the steady growth of Maratha 'luxury' demand for silks had already begun to balance the area's trade with the south. When the time came, it proved easy to expand this cotton trade for the purpose of re-export, first to the great Bengal weaving centres, and later for direct export to China. Let us follow the development in more detail.

In the late eighteenth century, Bengal was not in a position to meet the demand of its own manufacturers at Dacca and Murshidabad for medium and high quality cotton. Soaring European purchases of cloths, the mortality of the great famine of 1771, and the absolute poverty of Bengal cultivators were among the reasons given for this. Since the 1750s the balance of demand over what could be supplied from Bengal

[14] Commercial Agent, Farrukhabad to Bd, 21 Feb. 1805, CPR, 5 Mar. 1805, 90/47, IOL.
[15] Fowke to Hastings, 7 Mar. 1776. For. Sec., 3 April 1776, 1, NAI.

was made up by sea-borne imports from Surat.[16] But a minor revolution in the internal bulk trade of India occurred in 1784 when, for the first time, cotton was brought overland in quantities from central India and Bundelkhand to be passed on by river to Bengal. The development of this trade was of great significance since it spurred the growth of population in a whole range of minor marts including the towns of Kalpi, Mirzapur, Farrukhabad and Agra. The year 1784 was a turning point because Parliament in Britain had reduced the duties on tea, a move which opened the way for a vastly increased purchase of this commodity on the Canton market.[17] But the only commodity which the Chinese would take in exchange for tea in this period was raw cotton, and this was shipped to Canton in ever increasing quantities after 1784. The subsequent rise in the price of Surat cotton in Bengal made it profitable to import 'Mirzapur' (that is, Hindustani and central Indian) cotton to Bengal by land and river. The connection was so close that between 1790 and 1820 the price of cotton at Mirzapur 'depended entirely on the relative prices in China, the supposed demand in consequence, and the quantity likely to be produced in Guzerat'.[18] In 1789, the quantity of raw cotton imported from Bundelkhand and central India to Bengal was about 190,000 *maunds*, worth Rs. 20–30 lakhs. Between 1795 and 1800 this had risen to about 450,000 *maunds* and was worth about Rs. 40 lakhs. It was estimated that 38 per cent came from central India around Nagpur, and the remainder mostly from Bundelkhand.[19]

This novel and substantial trade could well be described as proto-colonial. None of the 'Mirzapur' cotton was as yet exported to China or Europe; but the constant requirement for the Company's piece goods investment in Bengal appears to have been an important component of the demand at Dacca and Murshidabad. The medium range of cloths for the European market rapidly switched from Bengali and Surat to the new raw material:

In 1782–3 the whole provision of the Company's investment was made from dessy and byratty kupas [local raw cottons]. In 1783–4 a small quantity of Mirzapore was imported and used for the first time . . . and about one-fourth of

16 'Reports on the Culture of Cotton Wool, Raw Silk and Opium, Collected and Printed by the East India Company from its own Records about 1836'; reports on the cultivation and trade in cotton, Bengal, pp. 313–14, IOL; Colebrooke and Lambert, *Husbandry*, pp. 130ff.

17 P. J. Marshall, *Problems of Empire. Britain and India, 1757–1813* (London, 1968), pp. 89–90.

18 Report on the Cotton Trade, 30 April 1802; 'Reports on Culture', p. 138.

19 Forbes Royle, *On the Culture and Commerce of Cotton in India and Elsewhere with an Account of the Experiments made by the Hon. East India Company to the Present Time* (London, 1851), p. 419.

the Company's cloths were manufactured with it. In 1786–7 and the two succeeding years about half the cloths are supposed to have been made with it.[20]

On the other hand, the dominant feature of production and trade remained courtly consumption in the Indian economy. About one half of the Dacca and Murshidabad production was still designed for north Indian rulers, while the capital employed in the raw cotton trade was raised from the great merchant houses. We know that in the 1830s the price of cotton in Mirzapur was closely determined by 'the state of the Benares money market'.[21] The annual inflow of bullion from Bengal for the use of up-country courts, merchants and farmers paid for the exports to Bengal and overseas. But Benares money was invested in cotton long before this.[22] Several branches of the Shah family and other Naupatti bankers who had risen to prominence as court financiers were active in the cotton trade from Jalaun to Mirzapur as early as 1790.[23] Besides Benares Agarwals, it was Maratha and Naik Kallea traders or the great Gosain corporations who were most prominent in cotton.[24] These groups were already in a favourable position because they had built up capital and market information in luxury trades to the Southern courts.

Closer integration of north Indian markets and merchants into Asian trade had only local effects on methods of production. In the Bundelkhand and central Indian regions which were producing Rs. 40–70 lakhs of cotton in the years 1803–35 Company and private merchants remained little more than final purchasers. They simply used their heavier capitalisation to suck the commodity out of the petty local markets and continued to rest on the networks of Indian brokers and financiers. There were exceptions, of course. To the west, in the cotton growing area around Agra and Muttra, the local economy was altered by the substantial investment of firms like Mercer and Co. Rather than work through Indian brokers 'a method is said to have been latterly introduced by the European merchants with a view to secure to themselves the large profit which is made by the middlemen, by introducing advances and making purchases direct from the labouring classes'.[25] Mercer and Co. and other European firms established 'factories' in the area where they were able to collect and process the cotton wool themselves and to operate some degree of quality control.

[20] 'Reports on Culture', p. 338.
[21] Magt. Mirzapur to Commr Benares, 1 May 1838, Mirzapur Judl, 85, UPR.
[22] Agent to GG, Benares to Govt in the Territorial Financial Dept, 2 Dec. 1818, PR.
[23] Case of adjustment of accounts by Gopal Das's *Kothi*, 27 May 1789, PR.
[24] *Ibid.*
[25] H. Newman, Superintendent of Resources to Accountant General, 18 Sept. 1812, Bengal Commercial Procs, 18 Sept. 1812, 157/57, IOL.

Few of the original customs house passes for the Agra area have survived, which makes it difficult to assess the volume of long-distance cotton trade generated by this more centralised and capitalised European production. A nine month's total for the Agra customs house shows that Mercer passed 74 per cent of all raw cotton across the customs line during the 1815–16 season. His firm accounted for 2,728 *maunds* or about Rs. 4 lakhs worth of the product, while his nearest Indian competitor, one of the Agra Agarwals, passed a mere 441 *maunds*.[26] Mercer and other Europeans had large trades out of Farrukhabad also, but all in all, it seems unlikely that they produced more on average than Rs. 5–8 lakhs per year in the 1810s and 1820s. This was modest compared with the total product which was still being purchased by Indian merchants through the usual petty commodity markets.

Other plantation crops in which European-controlled capital and management played an important part were also limited in their effects. The production of indigo in Hindustan had expanded rapidly. Following the American War of Independence Britain's policy was to wrest control of the indigo trade from the French, Spanish and Americans by promoting the cultivation of the commodity in India.[27] In 1784, the Company even set aside Rs. 2 lakhs annually for indigo advances in Bengal and Benares, and before Cession more than 100,000 acres had been brought under this crop in Awadh.[28] Thomas Twining, travelling in the Agra region in the 1790s, found a lone British indigo planter working a fortress-factory in the midst of Mewati and Gujar marauders,[29] while European and Armenian capitalists helped Almas Ali Khan to establish production at his seat of Mianganj. Yet Company policy was ambiguous. Sir John Shore, wishing to boost the infant industry in Bengal proper, slapped a heavy tax on indigo imports from the north-west in 1797. Revenue officials were also in two minds. Jonathan Duncan's Residency in Benares was punctuated by regular tussles with the indigo planters Gilchrist and Calder.[30] Duncan suspected the European merchants of interfering with zamindars and regarded Indian-produced sugar as a much better guarantee of the security of revenue.

Is it possible to estimate, even tentatively, the overall impact of European-controlled trade on the economy of Hindustan about 1800? Are we dealing with a pure colonial situation, or one in which the economy was still only marginally affected by European influence?

---

[26] Statement of Cotton Duties, 12 Feb. 1816, Agra Customs, 1, UPR.
[27] Court of Directors to GG, 3 Feb. 1796, 'Reports on Culture', 'indigo', p. 35.
[28] *Ibid.*, p. 24.   [29] Twining, *Journey*, p. 286.   [30] E.g., 12 Mar. 1794, PR

Without reliable figures of population, consumption revenue or trade, this is an impossible question to answer, but we may be able to make some estimate of the orders of magnitude. A rough estimate suggested that the total value of medium- and long-distance trade in the future United Provinces of Agra and Awadh, with the Delhi territories, might have stood at well above Rs. 400 lakhs at this time. If direct local investments by the Company and private European merchants in cloths, raw cotton, indigo, saltpetre, silks, jewels and luxury items are totalled up for Awadh and Benares, it seems unlikely that even at their greatest extent these could have amounted to more than Rs. 25 lakhs in any year before 1800.[31] As far as direct European involvement in trade is concerned, then, our view broadly supports that of Peter Marshall for Bengal – that it was quite limited in global terms even though it was concentrated in certain lucrative and expanding areas of trade.

At the same time, the indirect effects of European-dominated external trade were more considerable. British demand for Murshidabad and Dacca cloths was certainly one of the conditions which opened up the substantial Mirzapur trade route. Other areas of European demand within the Bengal economy appear also to have had a 'knock-on' effect by increasing the local demand for items such as raw cotton, saltpetre, shawls or horses which were beginning to come through from Awadh in greater numbers. However, it is difficult to avoid the conclusion that the main impact of European control in the Ganges valley at this time remained indirect, in setting limits to internal changes rather than creating them. Also, if the Company was a major influence on territories outside its formal control, it was more in its role as an Indian sovereign than as harbinger of western capitalist organisation. Three areas are important here. First, the annual subsidies and charges of up to Rs. 100 lakhs extracted from Awadh and Benares must have had a considerable effect on the direction of trade through the link between trade and revenue. Much of this was, of course, invested in Awadh products or in military activities in northern India. But the Company had at least gained a lien on resources which might have been used to greater effect elsewhere. Secondly, the decline of bullion imports into Bengal by the East India Company between 1757 and 1797 must have had consequences as yet unquantifiable on the circulation of money in the interior of the subcontinent.[32] Thirdly, monopolies extorted by the Company in Bengal, Bihar and later Benares acted to cut off profitable

[31] Kessinger, 'North Indian economy', *Cambridge Economic History*, II; Bengal Commercial Procs and Reports, etc.
[32] Bullion import through Calcutta began again in 1797, and, combined with cotton purchases in the interior, it must have begun to offset the deflationary tendencies predominant since c. 1760.

lines of trade to 'western merchants' (i.e. those from Delhi and beyond) in items such as opium and salt. All these pressures had an effect on the intensity and direction of production and flows of trade, but they were ancient economic tools of Indian government, and did not much affect its nature or organisation.

Indian merchants and the sahibs

What were the motives and conditions which led Indian merchant families to associate with European enterprises? We must abandon the deep-seated notion that the expansion of Europe was unchallenged. Colonial trade and colonial government were vulnerable in their early years, and if Indians recruited themselves into the Europeans' world, it was often on their own terms. One can point to many parts of Asia where indigenous merchants avoided close connection with the interlopers.

In many respects Indian commercial culture was unique, but there were enough points of contact between it and the European business world to make them mutually intelligible. Indians used a form of double entry book-keeping, made use of credit notes, witnessed agreements, and employed forms of brokerage which could be adapted to European requirements. In their capacity of ruler, the Europeans performed some of the roles which Indians expected of them, particularly control of the coinage and the maintenance of basic security. If anything, the loose and flexible relationship which had characterised the position of Hindu merchants in Muslim polities made accommodation easier. The merchant point of view remained 'You are the ruler, what is the concern of the *mahajan* with public matters?' and tension only arose when the European government intervened in the religious and mercantile behaviour of the traders. While merchants possessed an inner, domestic culture, they had also developed the capacity to play the game of darbar and royalty, so that the old Indo-Persian court culture provided, in north India, a neutral ground on which accommodation could be reached. Communities of Jewish, Armenian and Greek merchants sometimes acted as cultural brokers between European and Indian, while all-India firms with which the East India Company had an ancient connection also proved valuable intermediaries. In Benares, one of the residents' most important contacts in the business world was Aret Ram Tiwari, *gomashta* in the city of the firm of Arjunji Nathji which had been working with the Company in Surat since the 1750s.

Nevertheless, it seems clear that certain types of merchant family were more likely to reach accommodation earlier than others. In Bengal after 1757 the old long-distance merchant families of Mughal rule and the Nawabi declined side by side with the great cities of Dacca and Murshidabad. Here it was the *dubashes*, the upper class Hindu and Armenian agents of the Europeans, who replaced the earlier commercial families in interdistrict trade and state finance. In other words, it was literate 'men of business' who participated in European trade. It was not until the third and fourth decades of the nineteenth century that new families of local merchants, the Subarnabaniks, Sahas and Tantis who had previously occupied a lowly rung in commercial society, began to accumulate fortunes in the districts. The proximity of Calcutta and its houses of agency, along with European monopolies of many valuable trades, brought about a very rapid decline in the old merchant class. All this conspired to create a revolution in trading personnel even though the British directly controlled only a small proportion of Bengal's trade.

In the interior where the volume of exchange conducted directly by the Europeans was even smaller in volume, continuity in the commercial elite was striking. The families who became prominent in 'colonial' trade were already associated with the great corporations and the financial institutions of the large towns. The new sources of income merely confirmed the commercial structure that had grown up in the post-Mughal states. At the same time, *mahajans* of the highest status within the corporations were reluctant to become too closely involved in European trade at this time. The profits and honour to be acquired by acting as treasurers and court provisioners for rajas and nawabs remained very great. Usually it was rising families within the corporations, hungry for new wealth and dignity, who made the running with the Europeans at first. So in the Benares region it was hinterland Agarwal families, moving in from small towns such as Chunar and Jaunpur, who became heavily involved both in cotton trading and in passing Company *hundis* to the west and south. Yet since the British controlled the raja, the mints, and security on the routes to Bengal, even the old families were unable to stay aloof. Thus said the principal of the old and prestigious firm of Brij Mohan Das Kumun Das, Gujeratis of Benares and Muttra:

The truth is that I never had transactions with the Company neither did I ever frequent their durbar, till hearing of the good administration of the Residency I waited on and began to visit Mr Duncan. Thereafter I proceeded to Murshidabad – whilst there, my people knowing that the other bankers were employed in the many negotiations for the Company, my gomashta went to Baboo Ramkishen the treasurer asking to participate in these remittances.[33]

Something like this happened in the western territories also. In Delhi, the old Khattri and Jain elite associated with the Mughal court retained

[33] Examination of Brij Mohan Das, 15 Sept. 1790, PR

cordial relations with the British. But it was usually new families of lesser status within the corporations who became treasurers for the British and invested heavily in trades in which Europeans had a larger stake. Some degree of wealth and acceptability was the first requirement. But service for the British certainly provided an avenue of social mobility for middling families whose status in the markets was enhanced by passing their *hundis*.

Chapter 3 emphasised the importance of the great houses of Gosain ascetics in the trading pattern of the eighteenth century. It might be thought that the case of the Gosains contradicts the general point about the continuity of the corporations into the colonial trading and urban system. Certainly the early contacts of the British with the ascetics as raiders or traders did not endear them to the new rulers. Customs officials at Mirzapur complained of the undervaluation of the goods passed up country by the Gosains because 'their character and callings in life are so agreeable to the prejudices of the natives, whereas the reverse is the prevalent notion with us'.[34] Officials delighted in trying to undermine the Gosain reputation for honesty.

Accommodation was, however, both possible and necessary. Gosains, who had established a powerful hold on the trade in silks from the Ganges into the Maratha territories, were also in a strong position to bring the cotton out of central India to the wharves of the Ganges. Until the 1840s, Gosains remained the key inland merchants in the growing 'colonial' cotton trade, selling at Jalaun, Amraoti and Kalpi not only to the agents of the Company, but also to traders such as McKinnons and Hamilton Stopford.[35] Successive English collectors looked with a jaundiced eye upon the Gosain and Scottish mafia which ran the town of Mirzapur. As late as 1834 the Commissioner of the Division could remark on

the double influence which has been enjoyed by Syd Geer [Sidh Giri] for many years in his capacities of chief mahajan and chief Goshain or mahant in the town of Mirzapore – with the bulk of the Hindoo population his word is law, and he or rather his principal chela Pursram Gir could at any time or for any purpose procure general demonstrations of disaffection.[36]

Gosains tolerated the British with equal unwillingness, but came forward to use the commercial facilities which they offered. In 1857 the Gosain Maths of the provinces had at least Rs. 2 lakhs invested in

[34] CGC Ghazipur to CGC Mirzapur, 14 July 1815, CPR, Aug. 1815, 97/156, IOL.
[35] Lieut. Nicholls, Hyderabad Cavalry to Magt. Mirzapur, 9 Nov. 1841, Mirzapur Judl, 107; Magt. Benares to Commr 23 July 1834, Mirzapur Judl, 83; cf. same to same, 21 Nov. 1831, Mirzapur Judl, 81, UPR.
[36] Magt. Mirzapur to Commr, Benares, 2 Mar. 1834, Mirzapur Judl, 80, UPR.

government paper currency.[37] As some of the largest urban property-owners in the Gangetic and central Indian towns, and as important lower level moneylenders, ironically it was they who came the nearest of any Indian business community to the emerging bourgeoisie that European theorists from Sleeman to Marx wished to see.

The colonial trade in its first flowering

Despite the rapid growth of a very substantial export trade in agricultural raw materials from north India in the years 1790–1825, there was no transformation of the agrarian or commercial economy. The new trades simply swelled out the arteries of the old petty commodity production. The reasons for this are to be found in the structure of the peasant and petty mercantile economy, and also in the relationship between trade and established patterns of consumption among north Indian elites.

In the first place, it is noteworthy that the rapid expansion of the export of cotton, indigo and opium over the first thirty years of the new century was largely balanced not by the import of British goods, but by the import of bullion and copper for elite consumption and 'hoarding'. North India remained, as it had been throughout the Mughal period, a great purchaser of silver and copper. Writing of the Benares bankers in 1818, the Governor General's Agent recorded:

The trade carried on by the shroffs is a most regular one – besides their other paper transactions, they import bullion largely to supply merchants with means of purchasing the produce of the interior for which they get bills of exchange on Calcutta which are as they fall due invested in bullion. Upon any demand for ready money the exchange in the interior becomes very high, that is the demand for ready money becomes greater perhaps than all the bullion and money on the spot can immediately supply.[38]

He went on to observe that gold and silver transactions in India should be regarded as a trade and not merely a means of assisting the 'barter of commodities'. The demand was quite insatiable. Most merchant families used gold *mohurs* and silver plate in their everyday transactions as security for loans, while near-contemporary estimates put the average value of women's jewellery and hoarded bullion at more than Rs. 5 for every peasant family. The *sarrafs* or money dealers who dealt with this vast trade, which amounted to more than Rs. 50 lakhs annually in the 1820s, were the respected merchant banker families of

---

[37] 'List of Persons holding Government Securities in Mirzapur', Benares Commr, Post-Mutiny Basta 29 Judl, UPR.
[38] Agent Benares to Govt Territorial Financial Dept, 2 Dec. 1818, PR.

Benares, Farrukhabad and Jaipur. The bullion market remained focused on the more traditional centres with their elaborate forms of mercantile organisation and credit, and it was in this way that the colonial export trade continued to mesh into the older nexus of services connected with state banking and revenue. Indeed, 'the volume of trade at Mirzapore is largely influenced by the state of the Benares money market'.

Copper imports were most substantial also. In fact, they remained the most considerable import into the area until they were overtaken by European twist and yarn in the 1840s. Kishen Mohun Mullick, a Calcutta dealer of the 1870s, remembered: 'Most significant was the trade in this metal in earlier days which was influenced by constant speculative transactions carried on here by opulent up-country bankers of those days.'[39] Mirzapur was again the ruling mart, but the metal was then broken up into smaller lots and carried throughout north and central India. It was treated as one of the safest means of investment by 'the middle class of people in the upper Provinces, being easily convertible into cash'.[40] Demand of this sort also had an impact on employment in metal-working industries in the main centres, because a favourite means of storing copper was in the form of domestic plates and bowls. The value of copper imported into Calcutta in 1830–1 was Rs. 60 lakhs, and it seems likely that at least two-thirds of this found its way annually into the up-country markets, covering the equivalent of two-thirds of the value of the western cotton exported to Bengal. It is most significant, as we shall see in the following chapter, that the rapid decline of the copper trade after 1835 coincided with a series of crises in the export of cotton and indigo. Mullick attributed the halving of copper imports between 1830 and 1860 to the impoverished state of the 'middle class of people'.

During the cotton and indigo boom of the 1810s and 1820s the commercial institutions which had already been developed to handle the internal trade of the late eighteenth century simply adapted to the China and European trade without changing their basic structure. Before 1810 the raw cotton from Bundelkhand and central India had been bulked at Mirzapur and then sent to a spot market at Bhagwangola on the lower Ganges from which it was despatched in small lots to the local markets where weavers purchased it.[41] But even before the turn of the century, the effect of the growing Chinese market for the primary product was being felt directly at Mirzapur. Duncan had noted as early as 1788 that

---

[39] Kishen Mohun Mullick, *A Brief History of Bengal Commerce from the Year 1814 to 1870 with a Short Sketch of Indian Finance* (Calcutta, 1871), II, 14.
[40] *Ibid.*   [41] 'Reports on Culture', Dacca Report 1790, p. 352.

prices at Mirzapur sometimes rose not only because of demand from the weavers of Bengal, but because there were reports that several people were 'intending to purchase for export to China'.[42] At first, problems of supply inhibited the growth of trade in this direction. If the quantity imported down the Ganges was less than 600,000 *maunds* in any one year, prices would be too high for it to compete successfully with Surat cotton in the Canton market. After 1800, the acreage under cotton in Bundelkhand and central India rapidly increased. In 1803 the first recorded cargo of Bengal cotton was sent to China, and during the boom years of the early 1820s as much as 300,000 *maunds* was reaching Canton.[43]

At every level from the cultivator to the Cohong in Canton, this trade like sugar and indigo was constrained within economic and political institutions which were designed to minimise and even out its impact. Let us take the case of north Indian cotton.

A combination of ready advances, plentiful land, relatively large profits and internal pressures on the zamindars and cultivators combined to encourage the cultivation of cotton. Kessinger's study of similar areas in the Jullundur Doab suggests that changes in family structure within the context of the peasants' social system provided these internal pressures for cash-crop cultivation.[44] Peasants balanced the drudgery of labour against the need to employ members of the family or dependants, while possible cash returns were secondary considerations. The chart of expenses for a substantial cultivator in a good quality cotton soil near Delhi illustrates the context within which these familial imperatives might operate.[45] If labour is costed, then the return to the cultivator seems very small. But if the labour of family and dependents is taken as given free then a much higher rate of profit on cotton cultivation would appear. In these circumstances, the extent of the family's 'labour payment' would be determined largely by social considerations. A model of a maximising peasant responding to high prices on the world market is as simplistic as that of the impoverished *ryot* whose decisions to cultivate are totally circumscribed by debt bondage to landlord or moneylender. But even in the case of affluent cultivators, external pressures must be taken into account. In all the cotton growing areas, land-revenue was enhanced considerably around 1818. Cultivators needed to maintain an area under a valuable cash crop, simply to pay off the higher rates of land rent which inevitably followed.

---

[42] *Ibid.*, Benares Report 1790, p. 369.
[43] Royle, *Cotton*, p. 41.   [44] Kessinger, *Vilayatpur*, ch. 3.
[45] Expenses of cultivator, 'first quality land, unirrigated', Pulwul, Delhi, Royle, *Cotton*, p. 303.

In poorer agricultural areas such as the middle Doab and Bundelkhand, external pressures on the cultivator were more significant. Peasants here were often tenants of impoverished zamindars affected both by the high revenue rate, and by bad climatic conditions. Cultivators took loans and advances from Indian moneylenders and cotton merchants, from representatives of European firms based on Mirzapur, or from the Company's commercial agents at Kalpi (until 1834). W. Bruce, a Bundelkhand cotton merchant, surveyed local cultivation in the following terms in the mid-1840s:

> When first I came to Bundelcund, I was in the habit of making advances annually to the ryots for cotton in the months of July and August, generally at 8 Rupees per maund, upon the security of the zemindars of their villages. As long as the Government assessment was moderate, and the landed proprietors in easy circumstances, the system was profitable ... I was obliged, however, to abandon the system altogether when the Government assessment was raised. As the zemindars and ryots became impoverished, so the risks of balances increased, and rendered the speculation precarious.[46]

Thus a wide variety of pressures operated on cultivators at the local level to determine whether they responded to the world market and the China trade. These pressures related to:

(a) the internal structure of the family, its inclination to labour and its size;

(b) the initial affluence of the area which determined the extent of advances needed for seed, manure and labour for weeding;

(c) the government revenue demand which determined whether or not a landowner would stand security for his tenant's cotton production to a merchant;

(d) the price on the world market and the degree of overstocking at Mirzapur, Calcutta or Canton which tipped the merchant's own inclination for or against advances in the light of these earlier considerations. According to most observers, high market prices for cotton did not act directly as an inducement to cultivation for the middle or poorer peasant. In boom years none of the increased price ever reached the cultivator, 'being absorbed by the village Bunnier [moneylender], the dealer with the Ryutt, the more considerable trader to whom he sells, and the buyers in the great mart, in which the latter realises his return'.[47] One might add that local landholding and service elites extracted a substantial percentage in their turn.

[46] Anon., *The Cotton Trade of India* (East India Company, London, 1839), II, 64, note by W. Bruce, 28 June 1836.
[47] Royle, *Cotton*, p. 49.

After picking, the cotton was cleaned of its seeds. Sometimes cleaning was done within the family by means of the simple 'foot roller'. If the cotton was already mortgaged to a merchant, the cleaning might be done on a more elaborate hand gin (*charka*) at a nearby *hath* or primary market. Cotton cleaners would be employees of European firms or freelance labourers whose wage was generally a portion of the seed which was used to feed cattle or turned into oil. Marketing peasants, small merchants and cleaners gathered at certain places where the agents of wholesale dealers of larger firms were established. These primary marts – places such as Bah, Pinahut or Kuchowra near Agra – had the reputation of being cotton marts 'from time immemorial'. They were, in fact, swollen royal *ganjs* and markets for the local elites which had also attracted non-local cotton trade because of the services which they offered. Smaller merchants and growers could not afford to be 'out of their money' or to disrupt family labour for the length of time it would have taken to convey their goods to a city mart and cut out these local middlemen.

The customs records give us a glimpse of a very large pack-mule and bullock trade in many thousands of small consignments between growing areas and primary marts, and on to the bigger towns. A merchant, for instance, is intercepted by the Bah Customs Patrol Officer in the 1840s with 36 lbs of cotton on two donkeys coming from his home to Mauza Angoothie 'where he was in the habit of collecting the article and making up dispatches for transmission under the cover of Rowannas [customs passes] to the Agra mart'.[48] Similarly, large numbers of small consignments came into the mart of Bah 'to make up eventually one or more large consignments to Mirzapore'.[49] Bah and other places continued to act as normal exchange marts for sugar, salt and spices, but enterprising local merchants might build a closed market and warehouses especially for the sale and storage of cotton and take a percentage on the proceeds. People selling customs passes, customs patrol officers, headmen of bullock carts and other transport specialists swelled the population of these centres.

Such primary bulking marts became a distinctive type of small central place in the early colonial period, serving not only the cotton, but also the sugar and salt trades. When external trade slumped and internal trade was diverted elsewhere, they would sink again to the normal level of marketing activity appropriate to the ordinary fixed market.

There are also signs, however, of some changes in organisation in the marketing system as a result of the rapid growth of export trade. As

48 CGC Agra to Commr Agra, 31 Dec. 1847, Agra Customs, 4, UPR.
49 Bah Patrol Officer to CGC Agra, 31 Aug. 1844.

bigger dealers came into the market, more cotton was taken direct to the cities for bulking so that primary marts which were close to the major cities of Agra, Kalpi or Farrukhabad might find themselves in danger of assimilation. After the Napoleonic Wars, for instance, merchants in the Agra region began to gather in to the city's main cotton mart at Belanganj because they could be in closer contact with market information from Calcutta and Mirzapur. Some of the adjacent cotton marts 'from time immemorial' declined in importance when their brokers emigrated to the larger towns.[50]

The second link of the chain stretching between the cultivator and Calcutta was served by these secondary marts. Dealings here were almost entirely between large wholesalers and agents of downriver firms. Their function had developed well before the end of the Napoleonic Wars, and often in the context of the successor regimes:

The native speculators who reside at Farrukhabad and Cawnpore generally make their agreements with the Mahratta merchants in October for cotton, to be delivered at a fixed rate in January and February. Previous to the period of delivery the speculators dispose of the cotton to merchants who trade to Mirzapore.[51]

These merchants who 'trade to Mirzapore' were the big wholesale *mahajans* of the towns who dominated its mercantile society, and were a second and distinct group from the 'speculators'. The *mahajans* traded on their own account to a large extent, but also bulked, stored, insured and despatched goods for smaller concerns. The method was to write to the brokers (*arethias* and *dalals*) of the place to which the goods were to be despatched (usually Mirzapur), giving details of the qualities and amounts of merchandise. The brokers of Mirzapur would then answer saying that if the merchandise arrived by a certain date it would be sold to a particular Calcutta merchant at a certain rate of profit. Here the importance of timing became overwhelming. Any individual boat-owner, zamindar or customs official could exact his share of the profit by threatening to delay the consignment.[52]

Compared with the Bengali entrepreneur in Calcutta, the inland wholesale purchasers had the great advantage of being close to the source of supply. On the other hand, up-country market information was defective and the merchant was continually gambling on a large number of variables. Customs records, court cases and mercantile documents reveal the following constraints on the merchant trading to

[50] CGC Agra to Bd, 23 May 1816, CPR, 16 July 1816, 93/31, IOL.
[51] Report of T. Brown, 20 Oct. 1803, cited in Sinha, *Economic History*, III, 161; cf. Collr Bundelkhand to Bd, 13 Jan. 1808, CPR, 23 Jan. 1808, 91/18, IOL.
[52] Deposition of Ruttun Lall, 21 Jan. 1817, BCJ, 19 Aug. 1817, 133/15, IOL.

Calcutta from Agra, Kanpur or Farrukhabad:

(a)   the outturn of the crop, which entirely depended upon the monsoon and winter rains in Bundelkhand and central India;[53]

(b)   the availability of carriage to the merchants of the primary marts. If the season was bad in any part of northern India, they could well be competing for bullock carts against grain traders. In 1834, the customs authorities of Agra said that local trade down to the single bullock cart reflected 'the price of grain in Mewar and Marwar and the price of cotton in Canton'.[54] This is a graphic illustration both of the penetration into the interior of the 'world market', and also of the close link between the export trade and the internal food-grain market. During wartime the merchants faced the added hazard of requisition of their bullocks and boats by the British military authorities.[55] A long delay waiting for carriage could mean complete ruin for the merchant. This was because commodities like cotton were extremely vulnerable to the wet weather which could overtake the consignment at any time after the end of June;

(c)   the stocking situation in Mirzapur and Calcutta. Canton prices were not reflected directly in the upper India markets. Cotton (and sugar) was regularly left over in both of these marts from the previous season. Also, if the rumour was that Canton prices were likely to be very high, so-called 'speculators' entered the market, and there was a danger of 'overtrading' in the first few weeks of the season;[56]

(d)   a whole further set of conditions obtaining in the Canton market itself ultimately worked back to the primary wholesaler. These included the likely outturn of indigenous cotton in Kwantung Province and the state of political relations between the Company and the Chinese government or the Cohong;[57]

(e)   merchants also had the option of sending their goods for sale on the internal market if this seemed likely to offer better prices. The export trade was not entirely a rigid system, more a set of weighted options. Until 1834, however, the cotton merchants in Bundelkhand who wished to trade to Gorakhpur, Awadh or Nepal faced tough opposition from the Company's commercial agents

[53] Royle, *Cotton*, p. 540.
[54] Magt. Agra to Commr, 21 June, 1838, Agra Judl, 7, UPR.
[55] CGC Agra to Bd, 7 Oct. 1809, Mirzapur Judl, 7, UPR.
[56] E.g., CGC Agra to Bd, 9 Feb. 1836, NWP Revenue Customs 16 Feb. 1836, 221/85, IOL.
[57] Board of Revenue to GG, CPR, 31 Oct. 1823, 95/11, IOL.

who might outbid them and starve them of supplies.[58] Trading in Nepal, Awadh and central India remained hazardous because of local military activity and high local taxation.

In these conditions merchants based on Agra, Farrukhabad or Kanpur had two options. They could either continue to take a limited share in what had become a highly articulated or fragmented trade route, and allow a large number of intermediaries to participate in handling the commodity. This had the advantage of widely dispersing the risks. Alternatively, they could try to unify the whole marketing system from the growing area to Calcutta through emigration or the establishment of branch agencies at points down the river.[59] This maximised profit in the short run but involved the danger that firms might become over-extended and make very large losses. One of the biggest Agarwal firms of Agra, Piru Mal Ram Rikh, was supposed for instance to have made a huge loss of Rs. 100,000 on the cotton trading of a single season in 1836,[60] and almost every season produced a crop of bankruptcies.

Who were the up-country purchasers in the colonial trades? The evidence is still impressionistic, but some preliminary conclusions emerge. The first concerns the importance of European firms and their agents in several of the secondary marts in the period 1806 to 1826. The Company's commercial agents, of course, were by far the biggest purchaser of cotton from the primary merchants in Bundelkhand, but European entrepreneurs such as Bruce and later Hamilton Stopford also accounted for substantial dealings. Nevertheless, the share of Indian firms appears to have grown steadily after the crash of the agency houses in the 1830s, and it does not appear to have been until the American Civil War cotton boom that the trade was once again invaded by European 'country produce brokers'. The Indian firms which can be identified were almost all from traditional merchant communities. Some of them are known to have been recent immigrants into the towns from eastern Rajasthan and Hariana and were mainly 'Desh' Agarwals, Purbiye Khattris and Bhargavas by caste. But Farrukhabad appears to have been the base of a number of the 'great firm' Marwaris described by Timberg.[61] A notable feature of these firms was their versatility and the wide variety of commodities and services they managed. Some appear

---

[58] CGC Agra to Bd, 4 Apr. 1820, Agra Customs, 3 UPR.

[59] Sinha, *Economic History*, III, 163–4, App. E, 'Burrabazar in 1816'; cf. *Agarwal Jati, Oswal Jati*; family histories, UP, 1971–4; Bengali merchants appear to account for about half Calcutta's cotton importers at about this time; Desh Agarwals, Khattris and Chaubes from the Muttra region were also prominent.

[60] CGC Agra to Bd, 9 Feb. 1836, NWP Rev. Customs, 16 Feb. 1836, 221/85, IOL.

[61] T. Timberg, *The Marwaris. From Traders to Industrialists* (Calcutta, 1978), pp. 130–48.

first as salt and grain merchants; others were local company treasurers; most became involved in moneylending to zamindars in the towns. Safer moneylending ultimately tended to take precedence over commodity trading: the extreme instability of the external trade from north India encouraged this development.

Another question which is of importance in economic and social history is the destination of the mark-up on commodities transported from north India. The classic theories of imperialism suggest that international exporters and port-city agencies or compradores took the greater of the profits while the peasant and the inland trader secured very little. The data we have on cotton suggests that trans-continental freight charges and brokerage and warehousing charges in Europe did in fact account for the sharpest 'mark-ups'. Within India, however, the port-city brokers, warehousemen or wholesale dealers do not seem to have taken an exorbitant share of the profit. In fact, a progressive mark-up as the commodity passed through the hands of merchant intermediaries, with transport costs bulking large, seems to represent the situation more accurately.[62] It does not appear that Calcutta became rich on the proceeds of colonial trade at the expense of the inland merchants. On the contrary, the admittedly unreliable figures for per capita consumption and house assessment figures suggest that in the 1810s the population of Mirzapur was somewhat better off than that of Calcutta.[63]

A common feature of the urban societies of these entrepôt towns was their instability. In the case of Agra and Farrukhabad, an earlier courtly and political role was under pressure. The decline of the old political elites was hastened by the British revenue settlements and political changes after 1825. The presence of export trades in transit did not compensate these centres for the loss of their tributary hold on the surrounding countryside. As yet the towns served no sustained function as retail marts for the hinterland; the vast bulk of commodities and produce passed along the inferior networks of *haths* or bi-weekly markets. Brokerage fees and income derived from official and unofficial levies on long-distance trade therefore played a crucial role in sustaining these towns' ability to buy in supplies from the rural areas. Farrukhabad, for instance, which was a town of about 80,000 people in the 1830s retained few 'manufactures' and from the late 1820s its aristocratic elites were in decline. In 1826, 'Nearly the whole of its

---

[62] Royle, *Cotton*, p. 303; cf. Colebrooke and Lambert, *Husbandry*, p. 137.
[63] Town duties per head of population remained consistently higher in Mirzapur than in Calcutta between *c*. 1810 and 1833; Mirzapur's poor wage-labouring class was relatively smaller.

commercial concerns are conducted under the management of arritiers [brokers] and by their gumashtas [agents].' In other words, the vast bulk of the city's trade was wholesale entrepôt trade.[64]

The town of Mirzapur was also vulnerable to changes in external circumstances. It was sometimes called the 'Manchester of India', sustaining a notable growth of population and accumulating considerable wealth. But its economic functions remained limited and its society resembled that of an eighteenth-century *ganj* or *mandi* writ large, displaying few of the features of commercial and cultural change associated with Bombay or Calcutta. As we have seen, Mirzapur originated as a palace market for the raja of Kantit, and expanded with the growth of luxury trade to the Maratha kingdoms. Even in the eighteenth century, its mercantile corporations achieved a degree of independence and self-organisation, but it remained vulnerable to wider changes in political conditions. The mart was thought to be declining as early as 1773 because of the transit dues levied by the Maharaja of Benares.[65] Conditions improved during the regime of Jonathan Duncan when duties on the major trading groups were reduced, but political changes in the hinterland continued to bring sharp changes of fortune.

At its height after 1816, Mirzapur was primarily a forward cotton market for Calcutta. Some cotton was brought directly to the town in small consignments where it was purchased by European and Gosain wholesale dealers. The bulk was conveyed from the south by road or by boat from the secondary bulking centres like Kalpi, Agra and Farrukhabad. At Mirzapur it was sold to commission agents, or direct to representatives of the big European export houses of Calcutta. But there was a distinct lag before information from Canton or Calcutta reached the up-country marts. For instance, if a good cotton season in central India coincided with a good one in Canton province, large quantities of cotton would build up at Mirzapur and remain unsaleable until prices rose in Calcutta. In this situation, the role of the agents and brokers of Mirzapur was pivotal. The merchants depended on them to store and release commodities to the market when the time was right. Very few merchants at the secondary bulking points were prepared to trade the whole length of the river. In 1811, one Ramji Kant Kallea (a Maratha merchant), said to trade in cotton 'to the value of lakhs of Rupees per annum', brought cotton for sale in Colebrookegunj at Mirzapur.[66] The importance of the brokers is illustrated by the fact that he had cotton

64 CGC Farrukhabad to Commr Rohilkhand, 20 Oct. 1826, NWP Rev. Customs, Nov. 1826, 221/85, IOL.
65 Fowke to Hastings, 7 Mar. 1776, For. Sec., 3 Apr. 1776, 1, NAI.
66 Bd to Govt Judl Dept, CPR, 6 Mar. 1811, 97/38, IOL.

exposed for sale in the market for a year and three months before it was finally bought up by a Gosain. Even European houses of agency at Calcutta tended to deal with intermediaries, especially when the trade was stagnating in the 1840s and 1850s. Thus the Calcutta import/export house, McKillop Stewart and Co. dealt through the Mirzapur firm, Hamilton Stopford and Co.[67] Other firms based on the town provided bulking facilities such as screw houses and baling plants.[68] Insurance inevitably followed trade to Mirzapur. In the 1840s, the town contained a branch of the Asiatic River Insurance Co. of Calcutta,[69] as well as *gomashtas* of several up-country Indian houses which engaged in lucrative insurance business in addition to their own cotton and salt trading.[70] The conditions on the river below Mirzapur were sufficiently hazardous to justify extremely high rates of interest. River pirates and sudden squalls detained or sank one boat in three before 1840.[71]

Mirzapur's critical entrepôt function and considerable wealth did not reduce its sharp population fluctuations. Insecurity connected with the Maratha wars of 1803 and 1818 and the incursions of the insurgent Pindaris sapped the confidence of the transit traders.[72] Three bad seasons in the cotton growing areas from 1817 to 1819 were quickly reflected in a slump in the amount of stone being brought into Mirzapur for the construction of houses and temples.[73] Most persistent were disputes with the British authorities over the levy of internal customs duties, which affected both the internal and the external trades. In 1812, for instance, the town duties on salt were levied so rigorously that the chief merchants threatened to leave the mart altogether and retire to the nearby town of Chunar. The magistrate actually found the two headmen, Punjab Gir (Gosain) and Ramdayal Chaudhuri (Umar) on the road to Chunar with numerous followers 'with a view to establishing a gunje in that neighbourhood'.[74] Despite their economic function in the world market, the merchants were here using an ancient method of political protest against a predatory government.

The longer-term decline of Mirzapur was brought about by a

[67] Hamilton Stopford and Co. to Bd, 12 Mar. 1842, NWP Rev. Customs, 27 Mar. 1842, 223/48 IOL.
[68] Magt. Mirzapur to Asst Magt., 24 Feb. 1843, Mirzapur Judl, 87, UPR.
[69] Magt. Mirzapur to Secretary, Asiatic River Insurance, 7 Sept. 1838, Mirzapur Judl, 84, UPR.
[70] Magt. Mirzapur to Magt. Monghyr, 10 July 1844, Mirzapur Judl, 87, UPR.
[71] Some of the wealthiest *mahajans* in Mirzapur were *bimawallahs* or 'indigenous' insurers; one branch of the Shah family were prominent, Shah, *Shah Vanshawali*, 183; several Gujerati firms were also involved, interview, Sri Prehlad Das, Benares, 1974.
[72] Magt. Mirzapur to Agent Benares, 9 Apr. 1812, Mirzapur Judl, 75, UPR.
[73] Collr Benares to Bd, 16 Aug. 1819, Mirzapur Judl, 39, UPR.
[74] CGC Mirzapur to Bd (illeg.), Dec. 1811, CPR, 29 Jan. 1812, 97/42, IOL.

combination of internal and external pressures. The market for Bengal cotton in China and Europe was gradually squeezed by increased production in China itself and in the United States. At the same time, the number of intermediaries on the Central India–Ganges route compared unfavourably with the situation on the route to Bombay, and the growing reputation of 'Bengal' for bad quality tended also to discourage trade. Despite the temporary boost given by the coming of the steamboat in the early 1840s, the market was facing severe troubles by 1853:

The muhajuns of Mirzapore, finding that their arbitrary and fluctuating serista [commission] was driving the trade to Ghazeepore assembled in October last at the instance of Muhunt Persram Geer and revised their scale of deductions by reverting to the standard of 1795–6 said to have been fixed at the instance of the then judge and magistrate Mr H. J. Colebrooke. This timely measure has averted the destruction of the cotton trade.[75]

All participants in the export trades of the early nineteenth century from the substantial farmer to the merchant house at Mirzapur reacted swiftly and vigorously to international price levels in cotton. The same seems to have been true for sugar, though not for opium and indigo which reflected political considerations to a great extent. Business methods and marketing systems were also well developed insofar as poor transport allowed. But so many political and climatic hazards lay in wait on the 900-mile route between the major growing areas and Calcutta that few firms were able to commit themselves wholly to the export trade, or to any one commodity within it. There was a high failure rate amongst both European and Indian firms who tried to unify the whole system from grower to port-city exporter. For this reason, north India did not sustain the degree of specialisation and sustained monoculture that developed in contemporary Egypt. The institutions of the trade represented little more than the loose linking of earlier palace marts and merchant corporations.

The frustration of Europe

The European enterprise which linked the Ganges valley to the wider world of Asian trade was reared on a structure of indigenous institutions which had emerged from the political changes of the previous fifty years. But the same forces which made possible the rapid establishment of the new trading system also frustrated its development into the dynamic free market economy of Indian yeomen and capitalists which so many British observers sought. Failures and impediments to trade

[75] Magt. Mirzapur to Commr Benares, 21 Mar. 1853, Mirzapur Judl, 94, UPR.

had drawn the British into territorial dominion in India. And those failures and impediments were by no means banished by direct political control. Some writers still hold that the west successfully transformed the Indian economy, while European economic impetus was broken by the sophistication and impermeability of the Chinese economy.[76] But this is a trick of the light. The history of British commerce in early nineteenth-century north India was essentially one of disappointment. Some of the reasons for this lie outside the scope of this study, in Bengal, Canton and London.[77] But the considerable problems faced by traders and monopolists in the Indian interior also played their part. They illuminate once again the close connection between the nature of the Indian kingdom and the practice of Indian trade.

First, the very pattern of flows of credit and commodities within the Indian economy tended to militate against regular supply and predictable prices. Indian commerce was sophisticated and competent to handle large volumes. But supply and demand were bunched both by regular seasonal fluctuations and by the random movements of kings and armies. The problem for the Company and for private traders throughout the period was not so much in mobilising capital but in transferring resources from one area to another. The supply of coin for purchases was particularly constrained by political circumstances. Thus, for instance, as Aret Ram Tiwari of Benares explained to frustrated officials in 1788, the sudden rise in the exchange between Calcutta and Surat arose from a leap in the demand for coin on the west coast of India:[78] Colonel Goddard's expedition against the Marathas had absorbed large quantities of bullion there to pay Banjaras and contractors. On the other hand, when it was commodities that were required in western India and money in the east, the right conditions could be equally elusive. A good example of this was the sudden demand for grain which arose in 1790–1 when a severe famine in Bombay initiated a large inflow of grain from Bengal by sea and overland through Rajasthan.[79] As northern and eastern traders required *hundis* on Calcutta in order to remit their profits there, the exchange rate against the west fell by 8 to 10 per cent in the course of two months, gravely embarrassing persons who wished to move money in the opposite direction. As we have seen, the pilgrim traffic added another uncertainty to the interregional flows of money.

With the development of the cotton, indigo and opium trades

[76] Cf. Rhoads Murphey, *The Outsiders* (Ann Arbor, 1977).
[77] K. N. Chaudhuri (ed.), *Economic Development of India under the East India Company* (Cambridge, 1972), intro.; A. Tripathi, 'Indo-British trade between 1833 and 1847 and the commercial crisis of 1847–8', *Indian History Review*, I (1974), 304–19.
[78] 10 July 1788, PR.   [79] 7 Feb. 1791, PR.

between north India and Bengal after 1783, the Europeans needed more and more cash for payment in the northern markets. Here again they depended heavily on the noted propensity of the Hindustani peasant, moneylender and raja to invest in precious metals and copper. This was the 'great mode of remittance whereby the cotton and indigo of upper India are purchased for the Calcutta market':[80] But since it depended so closely on the erratic demand and variable standard of living of the up-country people, this was also an unreliable system, and added to the difficulty of predicting profits.

This bunching of the demand for coin was evident also in the course of each season. Revenue-payments were made in four tranches (*kists*) over much of the area, and these were not timed to coincide with the sale of produce from the harvest. Interest to moneylenders did, however, often become due at the same time as the revenue so speculators in bullion were in a position to reap huge profits if they could hoard precious metals and coin for release at these key times. Then its price in relation to commodities soared because 'the necessities of merchants and others compel them to purchase it at any rate for remittances to the [upper] Provinces'. This problem afflicted European no less than Indian merchants, and one of the chief aims of the pioneering proposal for a Bank of Calcutta in 1807 was to provide cheap loans at reasonable rates of interest which were to be repaid 'not on regular kists but on any intermediate period'.[81] Western-style banks took a further fifty years to replace moneylenders even for European borrowers; confidentiality and ease of access remained more important than low rates of interest. Yet the issue does underline the problems posed for European interlopers and the export trade by the close relationship between revenue and trade, which had otherwise proved an advantage in the extension of commercial networks.

Company agents and European private traders encountered equal difficulties in mobilising commodities and labour through the Indian market system. The formal acquisition of state power did not always ease these problems, and sometimes it increased them. In a situation where the theory and practice of commerce was so closely affected by the status of the participants and the aims of the local rulers who created the market, the European desire to have at one and the same time a 'free market' and a market where their own influence was predominant was bound to encounter resistance. Quite soon after their move into the Ceded Provinces, for instance, the authorities abolished all *sayer* duties in military bazaars in the hope of reducing prices to their own soldiers.

[80] Agent Benares to Govt. Territorial Financial Dept, 2 Dec. 1818, PR.
[81] 'The establishment of a Bank at Calcutta', 1807, Mirzapur Judl, 34, UPR.

But instead, prices rose sharply.[82] This was apparently because the *kotwals* of the bazaars who had once taken a percentage of the government's duties, now found it necessary to institute direct levies of their own which pressed harder on the market and eliminated the competition of many petty dealers.

Almost everywhere European purchasers had to work with the grain of the local political situation, but after conquest it became more difficult for the Europeans themselves to use political power. In pre-Cession Awadh, it had been usual for them to beat or imprison recalcitrant producers or agents, or at least to force great revenue-farmers like Almas Ali Khan to bring prices down. After 1803, however, this became hazardous. In the following year, for instance, the headman of the weavers of Etawah refused to take advances from the Company's Commercial Agent for the production of cloths. Indian merchants provided better advances. Besides, goods made for the European market did not accord well with Indian taste, and could not easily be sold off in case of a slump in external demand. Harassment by the Commercial Agent led the headman to seek an injunction against him in one of the recently established British courts, and brought about a virtual strike of weavers throughout the lower Doab.[83] There was a certain irony in the fact that the Company's role as royal arbitrator came into conflict with its role as Vaishya and trader so early in its career as territorial ruler.

Europeans came up against a similar problem in procuring labour for personal service or public works. As a series of Delhi cases in 1815–20 showed, they could never compete if they behaved as if there was a free labour market.[84] Headmen of labourers and guilds assigned their workmen according to the status and political weight of their clients. Europeans came low in this pecking order both because they were infidels and because they were regarded as poor employers, providing none of the free food and clothing which was expected from a patron. Yet if they tried to force a supply of labour through the good offices of the headman or police, the whole system might collapse, with the labourers disappearing to another part of the city. The only way for the Europeans to ensure supplies of labour was to create their own patterns of clientage. This took time but rooted them firmly in the Indian social system.

Difficulties of this sort plagued even such apparently successful

---

[82] Bd to Govt, 31 Oct. 1807, CPR, 90/64, IOL.
[83] Commercial Resdt Kanpur to Bd of Trade, 28 June 1803, Bengal Commercial Cons., 1 Aug. 1805, 156/56, IOL.
[84] Note by Delhi Commr, BCJ, 14 Feb. 1820, 134/36, IOL.

European ventures as the cotton trade. In general, the Company and European private traders purchased from the intermediary marts such as Kalpi or Amraoti, leaving dealings in the interior marts to Indian traders. But this was by no means successful. Quite apart from the peculations of the Indian merchants who mixed qualities and adulterated consignments, the inferior marts were themselves fortress centres of the local Bundela Rajput notables. Market relations were determined by political factors quite outside the purview of the Europeans. In 1803, for instance, the Etawah Company Agent's purchases were interrupted by a dispute between the Raja of Kuchowra and local merchants who boycotted the mart to avoid paying a forced loan which he was demanding from them.[85] On this and other occasions, the Agent was forced to work through local Maratha *amils* to recover any degree of influence over the situation.

In addition, of course, the condition of the trade was influenced by the local merchant's role as usurer supplying the cultivator's need for cash to pay the revenue. A few substantial cultivators brought their own produce to the market, but broadly, 'the market for cotton at the beginning of the season is entirely controuled by the village bunneas who make advances to the ryutts at exhorbitant [sic] rates of interest during the period of cultivation and sowing the lands'.[86] In turn, the commercial situation of the bania and local trader was determined by his political relations with local notables. It was a desire to circumvent the external influences in the market and to benefit themselves from the political perquisites of trade which led so many Britons – private traders as well as officials – to follow the *amils* of the previous century in founding marts. So in 1803 the Commercial Resident founded his own *ganj* at Etawah, called Welleslyganj, to which he hoped to attract cotton traders and financiers.[87]

Other problems in the cotton growing areas epitomised the dilemmas of early European commerce in Hindustan. First there were the simple practical problems arising from wayward seasons. Next, there was the problem of quality control when the cotton passed through so many hands between the cultivator and the final purchaser. Then there were prices. Prices, like supply, were influenced by political factors, but also by what observers habitually referred to as 'speculation'. Indeed, speculation in cotton bonds appears to have been a major form of

[85] Commercial Resdt Etawah to Bd of Trade, 28 June 1803, Bengal Commercial Cons., 1 Aug. 1805, 156/66, IOL.

[86] Bd of Trade to GG, 7 Oct. 1808, Bengal Commercial Cons., 21 Oct. 1808, 157/22, IOL.

[87] H. Newman to Accountant General, 18 Oct. 1812, Bengal Commercial Cons., 18 Sept. 1812, 157/57, IOL.

investment by any merchant, zamindar or artisan with money to spare in the cotton areas. In Etawah in 1807:

> Every change of weather has the effect almost daily in the sale of these bonds, but the expectation of large purchases has an immediate effect throughout the whole country; the petty markets vibrate on the larger and the dealings of the man who makes a positive sale at the covenant price of the day is influenced by the price at which the bonds are saleable.[88]

Finally, there was the problem of coin. Unless they were to pay very high premia, the Europeans needed to use ready money to purchase cotton, but this was easier said than done. Once again, local money circulating through the central Indian mints was tied up with the operations of the revenue system. Lucknavi Sicca Rupees could be made available at acceptable discounts when there was an actual transfer of goods between Lucknow and the trans-Ganges cotton tracts.[89] But this trade was small – as little as Rs. 5 lakhs annually in the 1800s and 1810s – and it was determined by the intermittent requirements of a few large zamindars. On the other hand, the commercial resident could always provide himself with money through the use of bills on British treasuries, but this would involve him in further complications by tying him into the imperial revenue system.

It was problems like these that caused successive commercial residents in Bundelkhand to rely on the use of powerful intermediaries such as the Kanpur merchants Lala Ishwari Prasad and Lala Shimbhunath who flourished in the 1820s. These men could provide money because they dealt on a provincial scale many times greater than that of the local money dealers of Kalpi. They could put their own agents into the smaller marts and isolate the Europeans from the friction of dealing with little-understood Indian financial institutions. But, as D. H. A. Kolff has shown,[90] this led to allegations of corruption, monopoly and incompetence which were the constant refrain of Anglo-Indian dealings at this period. Lala Shimbhunath became a monopolist and dealer in the political power of the commercial residency. He commanded the money and cotton markets, but in doing so he overspent the Company's money and threatened to overturn the whole local commercial structure by preferring his own connections.[91] One of the complaints of the local merchants was that the prices which the Company, through Shimbhunath, were paying were unrealistically high

---

[88] Accountant General to Bd of Trade, 15 Sept. 1812, Bengal Commercial Cons., 18 Sept. 1812, 157/57, IOL.

[89] Collr Bundelkhand to Bd, 12 May 1807, CPR, 29 May 1807, 90/59, IOL.

[90] D. H. A. Kolff, 'Economische Ontwikkeling zonder Sociale Verandering: de Katoen van Hindostan', *Tijdschrift voor Geschiedenis*, LIIIVII (1974), 545–53.

[91] E.g., Petition of Isree Bux, Bengal Commercial Cons., 23 June 1826, 159/72, IOL.

and that they drove all competition out of the market. The British were getting their commodity, but only by paying political charges which distorted the market and assuaged the political aims of Lala Shimbhunath's connection.

Kolff has suggested that one way of understanding the problems which Europeans and the export cash crop sector faced in dealing with indigenous commercial institutions is by adapting Boeke's notion of a 'dual economy'. In this theory, commercial dealings in underdeveloped economies stagnate because a modern rational and capitalistic commerce is imperfectly linked to an indigenous sector, bound by custom and non-capitalistic values. In some ways it is a useful application of the model, but the situation was more complex than this. First, one might argue that it was the very efficiency and responsiveness of local merchant society to price and opportunity which frustrated outsiders' attempts to predict prices and supply money. The problem in part was that money was a commodity in trade, not merely a medium of exchange, by virtue of its place in the land-revenue system. In part, regular, large-scale trade was frustrated by what one observer called the activity of many tiny local 'stock exchanges' where capital was moving very quickly between 'cotton bonds' and other commodity trades. This was not because local merchants were basically 'sharing' and non-capitalistic, but because they were spreading risks and maximising profits on very small margins. It was not so much merchants' cultural values (which were very real) but the operation of the family firm and the structural relationship between commerce and political power which gave local merchant society its appearance of impermeability. At the same time, the Company and Lala Shimbhunath were not working as untrammelled capitalist buyers. Not only was the European position abetted and compromised by the fact that the Company was ruler and revenue-receiver, but the big men on whom they relied were working commercial systems in which political power, reputation and family played an important part. What was happening in early nineteenth-century Hindustan can best be seen as a battle between 'little kingdoms' and 'big kingdoms' over the control and perquisites of markets. The irruption into the Indian interior of a great pan-Asian trading system in the form of the East India Company and its private fellow-travellers cannot be ignored. But the context of change remained the commercialisation of political power which had been the inheritance of the eighteenth century.

The problems of the East India Company with its monopolies can be interpreted in the same way. The royal monopoly had a long pedigree in India and was sanctioned both by the Hindu law books and by the practice of rajas and zamindars. The Company took monopolies eagerly in order to maintain its position against European and Indian rivals by 'engrossing the labour of the producer'. Between 1772 and 1840, it ran perpetual monopolies throughout the region in opium, salt and liquor, besides experimenting with one in saltpetre. On the face of it, these arrangements were successful in the sense that they brought large regular revenues to the state in addition to its income from land rent. But they should not be regarded as trades so much as a form of extra taxation on the consumer. Even where there was a direct traffic, this was generally a form of tribute remission, whether directly to England in the case of saltpetre for His Majesty's Arsenal, or through the Company factory at Canton in the case of opium. These were not enterprises in which it could be possible to calculate profit or loss in the ordinary sense.

The problems were those of the cost of superintendence and establishments. Where loose superintendence was adopted and arrangements were made with Indian producers and middlemen, smuggling was so widespread that the Company ceased to be a monopolist in any real sense and often ran up against problems of supply. At times, it was estimated that between one-third and one-half of all the salt sold in the Province had evaded government customs either because it was illicitly manufactured or illicitly imported from the Punjab and Rajasthan. Where contract was employed, it was inevitable that Indian society contrived to absorb much of the profits into itself. Zamindars and petty officials took gifts from the traders; and the traders sought to protect their position by placing relatives and clients in the offices designed to manage the trades. All these practices were considered entirely legitimate in the system of *chutki* by which persons in authority were expected to take a proportion or 'pinch' of the produce.

If more rigorous control over monopolies was introduced, this tended to reduce income because European manpower was limited. In the Benares opium *mahals*, for instance, direct control over production was vested in a Company agency. This system provided for much tighter control than prevailed in Bihar where contracts had been made with the cultivators through middlemen. But it proved impossible to expand the amount of opium produced in Benares to much more than Rs. 4 lakhs because the agents could not physically superintend more than 10,000–12,000 *bighas* of cultivation.[92] The cost of establishments rose rapidly, the tighter the control over supply envisaged. After Cession, the Company gained an unsteady control over opium production

[92] H. Ghosal, *Trade and Finance in the Bengal Presidency*, pp. 115–16.

throughout the Gangetic area, but it still faced serious and growing competition from opium production in the princely states of Rajasthan and Malwa where cultivators seem to have been directly responsive to prices on the world market and reasonably well rewarded for their produce. Ultimately, the Company was forced to open a Malwa Agency to buy up the crop and to put pressure on the local rulers to close up export routes. In the short term, this augmented the Company's gross profit:

But at the same time the enormous expenses involved in the running of the new agency led to a remarkable increase in the production cost of the article, so that the net profit to the Company during the three years 1823–4 to 1826–7 was less than half of what it had been in the preceding three years.[93]

The levelling tendencies within Indian commercial society had asserted themselves. What was happening was similar to the outcome of zamindari or ryotwari systems of management in the countryside. If the authorities gave away their right to control revenue to a set of powerful intermediaries, they would be starved of information about society and most probably fail to receive a proportional increment with the rise of productivity. This was the story of the Bengal Permanent Settlement, but in a small way, it was also the story of many up-country farms for spirits, town duties, tolls and ferries. If, on the other hand, they tried to deal more directly with the level of production as in the ryotwari system, there might be an appearance of closer control. But what would happen in fact was that the state's take from the operation would still remain low because there would be a considerable 'leakage' in the form of gifts and perquisites to its own nominal servants. The outcome for the authorities in a system of direct and indirect management was likely to be much the same, and equally unsatisfactory. The outcome for the mass of the commercial and agricultural populations was gloomy. The high cost of being part of a redistributive society constantly encouraged the authorities to redouble their exactions to the extent that production and consumption were reduced. Even in the case of a commodity like salt where the production cost was negligible, the problems which the British faced in running the monopoly of Nho salt from western Rajasthan encouraged them to sell the produce at punitively high levels.[94] In this the British commercial state behaved no differently from the Mughals and their successor regimes.

In almost any circumstances, crops such as cotton, opium and indigo were difficult staples on which to build sustained economic growth.

---

[93] *Ibid.*, p. 121.
[94] CGC Agra to Commr Agra, 5 Mar. 1832, Agra Customs, 7, UPR; he estimated that the tax on salt in Ghazipur alone represented 400% of the primary price at Bharatpur.

Cotton was peculiarly vulnerable to climatic instability and subject to great fluctuations on the world market. Indigo was expensive and uncertain, providing fewer opportunities for increased agricultural employment even than cotton. The institutional inhibitions to a more effective export performance in India do seem to have been severe even by comparison with the contemporary Nile Delta, for instance. Some impediments, such as poor land transport and low quality product, which appear to reflect straightforward lack of resources, turn out also to be susceptible to political analysis. Interruptions in transport were constantly being caused by the intervention of the military commissariat or local rajas in the small pool of draught animals. The poor quality of cotton wool was the result of damage sustained as small packets were passed from dealer to dealer in a trade still fragmented by political and cultural boundaries.

By 1825, therefore, gross demand in the north Indian economy was being affected by the trade cycles of European capitalism through the medium of the China trade.[95] But in most respects, the economy remained pre-capitalist for at least another century. That same loose texture of society which had allowed the British to penetrate the subcontinent defeated their tentative efforts to create a legal and institutional context for sustained commercial growth. Yet institutional impediments to trade were not simply those which derived from the indigenous revenue system or the tradition of taxation and gift-taking by the Indian elites. Arguably, the inclination of the colonial state to laissez-faire economics and the divorce of trade from revenue sacrificed the only substantial influence which European interests ever had over the bulk of the Indian economy. Observers in mid-century constantly compared the excellence of Dutch management in Java, where the state forced the production of cash crops through the cultivation system, with the poor record of the British Indian economy. The withdrawal of the East India Company from the cotton and cloth trades by 1834 certainly had consequences more detrimental in the short term than the much more notorious influx of British goods. The disappearance of the 'corrupt' Company official trading on his own account may not have been the victory that early Victorians claimed it was. Both developments closed off that 'leakage' from the revenue system into trade and consumption which was so characteristic of the Indian regimes and had given the trade of that 'dark period' its paradoxical local buoyancies.

[95] S. J. Commander, 'The agrarian economy of northern India, 1800–1880. Aspects of growth and stagnation in the Doab' (unpubl. Cambridge Ph.D. dissertation, 1980), ch. 5.

7

The crisis of the north Indian political economy, 1825–45

The aim of the last two chapters has been to demonstrate that the system of Indian states was not a passive victim of British expansion but that, though constrained, it continued to develop along existing lines. The buoyancy of many trades, towns, merchant communities and areas of high farming can be attributed to the continuing growth of consumption, and even investment, by the elites to which the 'successor states' of the eighteenth century had given rise. The emergence of the new pattern had been a violent and uneven process, of course. Trade and agriculture suffered during the three Maratha wars, and turbulence in the Punjab several times interrupted the process of consolidation. Rohilkhand outside Rampur took two generations to recover from the war of 1774. The British conquest also caused some immediate disruption. In the Doab, the Cession and the withdrawal of Awadh influence brought about a definite, if temporary, slump in the trade in the 'finer articles of produce', the silks and spices which had been consumed by the Nawab's luxurious soldiery.[1] Military industries also felt a chill wind. The British Peace reduced the 'excellent sword industries of Farrukhabad' and the musket-makers of Bareilly, by beginning to close off the possibilities of mercenary service to Rohilla and Rajput alike.[2] That great employer of mercenaries, Amir Khan, submitted to the British in 1817, and his domain was speedily transformed into the peaceable central Indian state of Tonk. All the same, the crucial changes were only beginning to work through as much as a generation after the British had assumed formal control of the region. The decline of the military aristocracies of the principalities within the Company's control was a slow-moving process.

For the first quarter of the century, the growth of political stability in the Punjab, the Maratha states, the Jat lands and Awadh supported the long-distance luxury economy and towns associated with it. Over these years, the Company's revenue policy was relatively indulgent to the notables within the North-Western Provinces whose local pomp and display helped to maintain employment in the intermediate economy of

[1] CGC Kanpur to Bd, 27 Oct. 1807, CPR, 30 Oct. 1807, 97/28, IOL.
[2] Farrukhabad Magistrate's Report, 27 Oct. 1814, Home Misc. 776, IOL.

military, artisan and transport services. In Awadh and even in territories under more direct British influence, magnates continued to found fixed markets which offset the centralisation of new imperial facilities on the large cities. New areas to the north and south of the Great Valley were brought within the domain of the money economy, while unstable and declining areas to the west were recolonised by merchant capitalists and marketing farmers. The rising agricultural export economy in cotton, indigo and opium combined with this buoyancy of the intermediate economy and the pressure of the heavy revenue-demand to speed up the pace of agricultural exchange. Henry Newman, Collector of Government Customs at Farrukhabad and later Superintendent of Resources, wrote of the 'great increase in the number of interior marts' in the province between 1810 and 1826.[3] As Asiya Siddiqi has shown, clear patterns of regional agricultural specialisation were becoming more apparent before 1830, with the riverain areas producing cash crops for export, and the inner districts feeding them with grain and pulses.[4]

After about 1825, however, this pattern began to fragment throughout north India. The 1830s saw a disruption of demand at both the luxury and intermediary levels of the economy. This was accompanied by decline in the rate of town growth and political turbulence in many Indian states, both independent and formally dependent. The crisis of the 1830s involved a complex set of changes which had wide repercussions throughout Indian social and economic life, but thus far, only some aspects of the transformation have received adequate coverage. That the Gangetic area and western India suffered a virtual depression which derived from acute problems of liquidity is generally accepted. The acreage under export cash crops, and especially indigo, had been kept artificially high because they were used as a channel of remittance for Indian profits and salaries to Great Britain. The collapse of some of the major European houses of agency in 1827 and 1828 brought about a general disruption in the flow of cash and credit which began in the export sector but rapidly affected internal trade also.[5] Once the bubble had burst in Bombay, a whole commercial house of cards in the west of the North-West Provinces came tumbling down. Around Farrukhabad alone, indigo houses and Indian bankers failed to the extent of Rs. 30 lakhs, the total revenue of the territory for one year. But this was only the beginning.[6]

[3] CGC Farrukhabad to Bd, 1 Nov. 1826, reprod. NWP Rev. Customs Jan. 1836, 221/85, IOL.

[4] Siddiqi, *Agrarian Change in a Northern Indian State* (Oxford, 1973), ch. 8.

[5] 'Statement of British Subjects and Other European Residents in or holding lands for the Cultivation of Indigo in the District of Farrukhabad', see esp. list of creditors of J. Mercer, BCJ, 14 Dec. 1830, 139/64.

[6] Metcalf, *Landlords*, pp. 105–35.

Eastern India was also facing a deeper if less dramatic decline in export performance which has attracted little attention. Taking the period 1830–60, agricultural produce exported from the region met increasing competition in foreign markets as other areas within and outside India began producing the cotton, indigo, opium, silks and saltpetre which had given rise to the heady but narrow growth after the end of the Napoleonic Wars. Problems of long-distance transport, quality control and supply which derived from the relative inefficiency of the peasant and petty mercantile economy of Hindustan made its products more and more uncompetitive. Only in the case of specialist products where European-controlled capital could make a quick killing (tea and jute, for instance), or where a change in tariff policy gave a massive stimulus (the sugar of eastern Hindustan, for instance), would islands of high-income commercial farming for export expand. And even here, there was no guarantee that the mass of the peasant economy would benefit very much. In the midst of these difficulties, the Gangetic area suffered in the 1830s from the sort of cycle of weather instability and problem of subsistence which was reminiscent of the 1780s and 1800s: an ancient pattern of distress on the Indian scene. Famine, migration and internal plunder revived on a small scale conditions which had been typical of the unstable areas during the last third of the previous century. Indeed, it was those areas and sections of the population which had fared worst in earlier periods which suffered most again in the 1830s. Theoretically, Indian traders and peasants should have been able to ride out such conditions of famine, and agricultural incomes should have recovered in the medium term. But in the midst of these other difficulties, recovery was not general before 1845, and some of the less favoured areas remained depressed for a generation or more.

Finally, at a deeper level, a more important transformation was occurring whose social consequences were to persist beyond the Great Rebellion itself. This could be described as a general crisis of the Indian political system. Having survived for a generation or more in uneasy symbiosis with the East India Company, the societies of the local and regional kingdoms in British territory and outside its borders were beginning perceptibly to crumble. The political leading edge of these changes was the British diplomatic offensive against the Indian states symbolised by the famous 'Policy of Lapse' and the anti-*taluqdar* settlements of the 1830s and 1840s in the North-Western Provinces. The new official generation had finally cast off the inheritance of prudence and enlightened tolerance of the Indian political order which had characterised the humbler orientalists of earlier years. The magnates and revenue entrepreneurs who had acquiesced in, or even provided conditions for the British expansion, were now regarded as extravagant parasites on a peasant economy straining to transform itself into a society of progressive yeoman farmers. But there were subtler and slower processes moving below the surface. British standardisation of the economy slowly eliminated the local taxation, local mints and 'idle consumption' which had been the hallmark of the *rajwari* societies, besides enticing away the mercantile capital which supported them. The dispersal of the armed bands and retainers of the regional states and local magnates profoundly affected the artisan and service economies, not only in the Indian states, but in the British territories themselves.

It was earlier stressed that luxury production and consumption were the life blood of the pre-colonial order and that they had a social and ritual value which cannot easily be conveyed by the glib term 'luxury'. Indian social philosophy was acted out in forms of relationship between orders of people, and gift-giving, feasting and display were the outward expressions of this philosophy. The progressive atrophy of the Indian state system which became apparent in the 1830s had deep and long-term reverberations. Indeed the rebellion of 1857 was merely one of the later indications of dislocation. Yet it seems likely that the change would have been less severe if the decline of employment – virtually the decline of social function – for soldiers, artisans and service people had not been compounded by the onset of a high laissez-faire philosophy within the Company's government. For the 1830s saw a cutback too in the meagre Company expenditure on military and civil government; a withdrawal of its embarrassed patronage of Hindu and Muslim places of worship; and a curtailment of the Company's residual trading functions. Taken together these setbacks and changes of policy represented a considerable deflation of the north Indian economy. But the word deflation cannot carry the full implications. To Indians the Company was failing to fulfil its duty as ruler, though evidently exercising with even greater determination its right to revenue. The cry was heard: '*Company ke amal men kuchh rozgar nahin*' ('under Company rule there is no employment').[7] The British were in fact facing a crisis of legitimacy which derived from their failure to follow the implications of the exercise of power within Indian society. But this decline of the princely economies not only strained relations between the foreign government and its subjects; it also changed the balance between the constituent elements of the old social order. Later chapters will show how the decline of aristocracy and gentry and the altered position of the merchant classes opened new fissures between the Hindu and Islamic corporations of town and *qasbah*. Thus it was the moral and social effects of the dislocation of the 1830s which persisted after the economy had

[7] Sleeman, *Rambles*, p. 365.

revived. Trade along the Ganges basin was considerably greater in 1850 than it had been in 1800; new consumers had arisen in the rich commercial cities to replace the failing demand of the military aristocracy. But the disruption of statuses was not so easily repaired.

Each district economy reacted in different ways to the gathering economic problems; some indeed emerged more or less unscathed. Yet there were deeper connections under the surface. For instance, the deflation of the economies of the Indian states contributed to the problems of liquidity which affected the export economy because the great Indian firms tended to operate in both. Thus the Collector of Aligarh remarked in 1832 that one of the general causes of the Depression was the 'decline of the Indian ruling powers whose seats of government had formed the principal centres for the consumption of luxury goods'.[8] In the same way, one of the contributing causes of the money and credit famine of the early 1830s was the decision to close the local mints of Farrukhabad, Saugor and Benares. This political act was a conscious attempt to reverse the decentralisation of the economy, the origins of which can be traced back to the 1730s. It had severe if temporary repercussions not only on the export traders but also for the broad agrarian economy. On the other hand, it is not fortuitous that the British decision to cut away many of the privileges and powers of Indian notables should have occurred at a time when the early growth of the colonial economy was running out of steam. While the economy was expanding, strains between the paramount power and the Indian states were reduced. But agrarian standstill or decline raised the question of who was to control the resources. 'Misgovernment' in Awadh or among the Bundela rajas seemed more acute because economic change was putting strains on the internal government of the Indian states. In turn political conflicts between the ruling groups speeded the migration of merchant capital from independent to British territory, and so helped further to undermine their regimes.

Of all the changes introduced by the British in India, the ending of the 'chaos and anarchy' of the eighteenth century was the one of which they were most proud. Yet even within the rolling passages of imperial exultation written by Tod, Sleeman or Malcolm, we find signs of doubt. Why was it that trade in Rajasthan in 1820 was less than it had been in 1770? What were the transitional consequences for the artisan and service classes, for the moral economy of north India, of the ending of warfare and the erosion of courtly Indian society?

---

[8] Collr Aligarh in Bengal Financial Letters, 38, 343ff., IOL; cited in Siddiqi, *Agrarian Change*, p. 169.

The disruption of elite consumption

Contemporary comment and figures on individual trades show that there was widespread disruption in patterns of consumption as the old military and political systems began to crumble faster in the late 1820s. This adversely affected some towns, trade routes and areas of specialist agriculture, deflecting developments which had originated since 1740. Of course this does not mean that the expenditure of elites was permanently reduced either in absolute or relative terms. 'New men', both landed and mercantile, came to compensate for the decline of sections of the aristocracy. Consumption of dutiable goods per head in Mirzapur was twice as high as that in the Rohilla centres as early as 1817, and there is later evidence of rich merchants building stone houses even during the bad days of the 1830s. Yet there was a widespread view that traders and other nouveaux riches concentrated their resources on food rather than artisan products, and that their restricted life-style created relatively little employment. Against this background the slow-down of the 1830s and early 1840s was significant. The rate of land-revenue per acre reached its highest point of the century in real terms,[9] while the value of agricultural produce fell. The embarrassment of the old military and service classes was reflected in the accelerated sale of land-rights, especially in the Doab.

Just as the consolidation of consuming aristocracies in the independent states had contributed to the stability of British territories before 1825, so after that date the reduction of their armies and great towns adversely affected the economy of the Ganges valley. During the heyday of the Maratha states the great warlords had held as many as 150,000 men poised on the southern perimeter of the Gangetic plains. Their consumption continued to maintain those north–south trade routes which had been so buoyant during the last quarter of the previous century. The disbanding of the Maratha armies acted as a considerable deflation of the urban and bazaar economy of the Deccan, and its effects can also be traced in Hindustan. In the case of Nagpur, the decline of military and court retainers after 1825 brought about a 'sudden reduction in the amount of population of the city and environs'.[10] Demand for agricultural produce was also curtailed for 'the dispersion of these hordes on the introduction by us [the British] of order and good government, necessarily diminishes the consumption of produce as of the land as of the loom'.[11] There was a sharp decline in the import of fine

[9] Commander, 'The agrarian economy', Table 4.3, p. 173.
[10] Jenkins, *Report on the Territories of the Rajah of Nagpore*, p. 100.
[11] *Ibid*. Sumit Guha has shown the significance of political change for the economy of the Deccan in his unpublished Cambridge Ph.D. dissertation, 1981, 'The agrarian economy of the Bombay Deccan, 1818–1941'.

products from Agra, Benares and Mirzapur between 1825 and 1830 because nearly 75 per cent of the fine muslins, *kinkhabs* and shawls imported had previously been purchased by the Maratha court itself, though later redistributed to soldiers and retainers.[12] The disappearance of this demand had indirect effects also. It caused the closure of mercantile *kothis* which pushed up the cost of remaining imports and thus choked off further demand. Artisan producers, wholesale traders, insurance firms and transport specialists all suffered. The decline of its southern trade was one condition restraining the urban growth of Benares and Mirzapur which had been tied to Maratha fortunes since 1700 or before. Both cities also found their Punjab commerce in difficulties in the 1830s, and were forced to depend more and more on the fickle trade in raw cotton. This had itself begun to bleed away with the opening of regular transport west to Bombay in the late 1830s.

The main impact of these changes of the 1830s on the Indian elites came from four types of measures. First, between 1803 and 1830 there appears to have been a substantial increase in the real revenue collected by the colonial government. This reduced the disposable income of the great zamindars and cut off the large variety of perquisites which had formerly filtered back into local society through the 'expenses' of the great revenue-farmers. Secondly, a large number of old princely families, such as those of Benares, Farrukhabad or Hatras, were pensioned off on allowances or fixed stipends. These began as only small proportions of the original income of the darbars, and within a generation they had generally been minutely subdivided by the laws of inheritance among numerous descendants, none of whom was wealthy enough to live in adequate style.[13] The records of the Governor General's Agent in Benares, which was a seat of many of these dispossessed princelings, reveal that by the 1830s the bulk of government pensions were being paid directly into the hands of the mercantile creditors of the aristocratic families, the thrifty *mahajans* of the Benares bazaars.[14] Thirdly, even those rulers and zamindars who retained some control over their domains were being slowly deprived of the estimated 10 per cent of income which they had formerly derived from transit duties, bazaar duties, cesses and other gifts. These were

---

12 Jenkins, *Report*, p. 101; court consumption of shawls, *kinkhabs* and muslins accounted for about 80% of all 'foreign' imports into the Deccan capitals.

13 In the west of the Province large numbers of *jagirs* for life had been granted by the incoming British officials (see For. Sec. Cons. 1804–7, NAI); these had progressively reverted to government with the death of the grantees, impoverishing many aristocratic families, e.g., the case of the relatives of the poet Ghalib, *Ghalib*, tr. and ed. R. Russell and K. Islam (London, 1969), I, 23, 67.

14 See, e.g., basta 3, files 4, 20, 44, 59; basta 6, 48; basta 12, 22; basta 18, 18, Persian files, Benares Agency, UPR; Sangam Lal papers, Sri Ramkrishna Papers, Benares.

generally assimilated into the state's own revenue as settlements of land-revenue became more meticulous. Finally, of course, military lineages lost the substantial income which they had gained from mercenary service outside their territories.

The important point about these changes was that they had a differential effect on sections of the population. Some elements of the mercenary gentry, artisan groups or old merchant communities were able to adjust to the changes and to find employment and openings for trade in the narrow and more specialised sector linked to the export economy. As Brodkin has pointed out, this was the case with some of the Rohilla gentry.[15] In Rohilkhand, the sugar boom of the 1820s saved some of the military families from decline. Landholding groups in and around Bareilly profited from rising sugar prices and some got a grip on warehousing, transport and marketing.[16] But success in this transition was dependent on some capital and physical access to nearby large markets. Many old families in Rohilla townships, such as Aonla and Pilibhit, had already declined too far. Fortified with a military tradition and a history of opposition to British rule, they were, as Bishop Heber noted in his travels, a distinct threat to colonial control in northern Hindustan.[17] By contrast, the aristocracy of Rampur, where the Nawabi itself remained a monopolist and entrepreneur in the production of sugar, generally preserved itself despite constant British pressure to cut away areas of additional income from transit and other dues.

British inroads into the political economies of the Indian states varied in intensity. There were cases like that of the central Indian state of Jalaun where the British virtually abolished the local *raj*, setting off a lengthy and costly revolt by the Bundela Rajputs which further disrupted trade and agriculture between 1842 and 1858. Here the end of the Indian state may have had some minor effects in freeing the cotton trade route from 'vexatious dues', but it also spelled further decline for the commercial and agrarian economy of Bundelkhand which was already suffering from the withdrawal of the Company's huge Rs. 40 lakhs investment in cotton. A whole network of moneylending and luxury trading houses centred on the towns of Kunch and Jalaun disappeared;[18] Bundelkhand which had prospered on its moist soils and

---

[15] E. I. Brodkin, 'Rohilkhand from conquest to revolt, 1774–1858' (unpublished Cambridge Ph.D dissertation, 1968), pp. 152–3.

[16] For Kumu Khan and other Pathan *Khandars*, CGC Bareilly to Bd, 23 Sept. 1824, CPR, 28 Sept. 1824, 95/39, IOL.

[17] R. Heber, *Narrative of a Journey through the Upper Provinces of India from Calcutta to Bombay* (London, 1829), II, 119–25.

[18] *DG Jalaun*, pp. 45, 161; P. J. White, *Final Settlement Report of Pargana Kalpi* (Allahabad, 1875), pp. 3–10; petition of Durga Prasad, head of the *mahajans* of Kalpi, NWP Crim. Judl, Jan. 1840, 231/66, IOL.

princely expenditure throughout the eighteenth century became an area of permanently depressed agriculture – a stagnant backwater of Hindustan.

A serious change of fortune also overtook the Jat states south and west of Agra which had enjoyed relative prosperity since the 1720s, with an interval of disruption during the imperial resurgence under Najaf Khan. The decline of local cotton and indigo production after 1827 affected the local elites. But it was the disappearance of 'service' which created the greatest hardship. As late as 1816, the small Jat principalities may have supported as many as 25,000 well-equipped regular soldiers. But Sleeman, who visited the tract in the 1830s, gave a vivid account of the consequences of the decline of the courts of Deig and Bharatpur. This last state was particularly hard hit. Bharatpur forces had halted the conquering army of Lord Lake in 1806, and the British were only too happy to expel the Raja and impose a severe treaty of subsidiary alliance when a violent succession dispute broke out there in 1826. Demilitarisation was particularly abrupt in Bharatpur. The Company saddled the new ruler with a large indemnity at the very point when the Darbar also lost Rs. 1 lakh of its Rs. 4 lakhs annual income when, under Regulation 16 of 1829, the British excluded Bharatpur salt from the North-Western Provinces, so curtailing customs income and closing the salt pans.[19] Trade in the territory remained stagnant until after 1850.[20] Some Bharatpur troops were replaced by Company sepoys; but most were discharged as the Darbar got deeper into financial trouble. Sleeman noted:

There was a general complaint among the people of the town of the want of 'rozgar' (employment) and its fruit, subsistence; the taking of Bharatpur had, they said, produced a sad change among them for the worst ... 'what are we to do who have nothing but our swords to depend on, now that our chief no longer wants us, and you won't take us?'[21]

This had particular force against the background of traditions of fidelity and service to rulers which was a feature of the warrior kingdoms. Ziegler, for instance, has shown that for Rajput princes the necessary power to conquer and rule was thought to derive from devotion and service to a tutelary god (*thakur*). Service performed by lesser rulers and warriors for the greater had become an act of religious devotion in itself. It ensured them their own lesser sovereignties, and either salvation

---

[19] Political Agent Bharatpur to Resident Delhi, 20 July 1831, Delhi Agency Correspondence, NAI; the number of regular troops appears to have been reduced from *c*. 15, 000 to less than 5,000; Pande, *Jats of Bharatpur*, p. 179.

[20] *Rajputana Gazetteer*, I (Calcutta, 1879), 168–9.

[21] Sleeman, *Rambles*, p. 364.

through death on the field or material reward for fidelity.[22] But besides acting as a profound shock to the values and subsistence of soldiers, retrenchment also disrupted the networks of merchant people and artisans. These had also been incorporated into the principalities by systems of household provisioning which were held to be varieties of 'service.'

Sleeman noted that the political upheaval affected not only the military aristocracy but also the shopkeepers and merchants 'who provided these troops with clothes, food and furniture, which they can no longer afford to pay for'. The manufacturing, trading and commercial industry that provided them with comforts was thrown out of employment, and 'the whole frame of society becomes, for a time, deranged by the local diminution in the demand for the services of men and the produce of their industry'.[23] In a situation where occupational boundaries remained strong, and physical mobility had become less easy, there was little question of such men moving into employment in the cotton towns. Instead, they tended to become bandits, drifting labourers or religious mendicants, fostering an 'unquiet transition spirit' calculated to give anxiety to settled government. Thus it was often the nature of pre-colonial military arrangements which determined the fate of the soldiery in the colonial period. Where soldiers had been supported on grants of rental income made under one of the large numbers of 'military tenure' loosely called *jaidad* they were more easily absorbed back into agricultural society as managers or even cultivators. But eighteenth-century armies in the north had also included large numbers of freelance mercenaries who had no toehold in agrarian society, as well as persons of high dignity who would not touch the rent-roll, let alone the plough. It was such men whose indigence swelled the numbers of genteel poor in the towns and unquiet wanderers in the countryside.

The practical, rationalistic policy of the enthusiastic empire builders of the 1830s and 1840s was also reflected in the famous anti-*taluqdari* settlements of Thomason and Bird. These sought to deprive the little kings of the locality of a large proportion of their revenue-engaging rights, and put in their stead a variety of village magnates who were perceived as 'ancient owners of the soil'. In some areas the *taluqdars* fought back with success, using links with sympathetic British officials, the power of the courts, and their own local pre-eminence. Yet as Metcalf shows,[24] these settlements did substantially alter the social map of the

---

[22] Norman P. Ziegler, 'Some notes on Rajput loyalties during the Mughal period,' in J. Richards (ed.), *Kingship and Authority in South Asia* (Madison, Wisconsin, 1980), p. 34.

[23] Sleeman, *Rambles*, p. 365.   [24] Metcalf, *Landlords*, pp. 94–8.

Gangetic valley, and especially its western tracts. The landlords and large owners of Agra, Etawah and Mainpuri Districts were permanently weakened. Over a period of twenty years, many notables spent large sums in fighting law suits. Some permanently lost a large part of their income. The Raja of Mainpuri, for instance, found his income reduced from Rs. 80,000 per year to Rs. 30,000, and in the upper Doab the great majority of notables were heavily in debt by the late 1840s.

These administrative changes coincided with the collapse of the indigo boom and the scarcities of the 1830s so that in the short run no prosperous and viable village landlord element emerged to fill the landlords' local economic role.[25] When finally the pace of agricultural production, population growth and trade began to pick up after 1842, the landed collateral given by the notables to their moneylenders during the crisis began to acquire extra value. Moneylenders foreclosed on debts and revenue rights came onto the market in a great rush. Contemporary settlement officers regarded these large holders as no more than a burden on agricultural production, and later commentators have queried the effects of the transfer of rights over land through auction sales. Nevertheless, the notables and their consumption had a significant local economic role, and their disappearance entailed dislocation and even agricultural decline.

In the Trans-Jamna tracts of the Allahabad and Mirzapur Districts, the Maharaja of Benares and the Rajas of Bara, Meja and Daiya had all, despite their 'fraudulent' land transactions during the first settlements, put a great deal of capital into improvements, clearing and petty town-building in the first years of the century.[26] After 1830 this development came to a halt. Heavy assessment and inadequate capital resources continued to plague the area until the 1880s.[27] Several intermediate market centres such as Khairagarh and Shankargarh lost their vitality in the same way as similar places in Awadh ceased to be centres of

---

[25] Any significant decline in 'aristocratic' consumption should certainly have fed through into the price depression as it did in the Deccan from 1820 to 1840. But NWP prices are unrevealing because of (i) great regional variation, and (ii) the impact of 'external' factors – export demand within and outside India, fluctuations in bullion inflows, the severe famines of 1833–4 and 1837–8. But the decline in fine-grain price series, 1826–33 (see Siddiqi, *Agrarian Change*, pp. 188–93, Commander, 'The agrarian economy', Roy, *IESHR* (1972), 91–100, Agra Judl, etc., UPR) probably reflects demand as well as purely monetary factors; several contemporaries considered so. There is also much local evidence of the dislocation of consumption causing price falls from 1820 onwards, e.g., the decline of non-food-grain prices in Agra 1816–36, *Agra Settlement Report 1880*, pp. 33, 77; the slowdown in consumption of quality building materials in Benares, Chunar and Mirzapur by 'wealthy natives ... in recent years', Collr Mirzapur to Bd, 16 Aug. 1819, Mirzapur Judl, 39, UPR.
[26] R. Temple, 'Report on the Moquddamee Settlement,' *NWP Selections*, XXVIII, art. 15.
[27] Records of the Commissioner of Allahabad, Post-Mutiny, Dept. XII, basta 21.

consumption when local politics were tamed after the Mutiny.[28] In the west there were similar unhappy consequences of the anti-*taluqdar* policy. Eric Stokes has noted how the small *taluqdars* of the Aligarh region had helped put in irrigation in this unstable tract: 'not until the British had dismantled many of these smaller *taluqs* in the later 1830s and early 1840s, and the number of wells fell off alarmingly in consequence, did they come belatedly to appreciate how important the magnate role had been'.[29] On the other side, the acquisition of land-rights by the merchant community as a result of foreclosure on indebted magnates in these years was by no means an unmixed blessing for them. The immobilisation of capital and managerial problems it created formed an important turning point in the transition of a substantial number of Hindustan's merchant families from the merchants of earlier days to the 'stagnant entrepreneurs' of the later part of the century, when *rentier* income had come to replace trade and agricultural investment.

British attempts to standardise and regulate the local economy were particularly significant in the realm of fiscal policy. The closure of the Farrukhabad mint (1824) and the Benares mint (1829) contributed to the 'lack of money' which precipitated the Depression.[30] But the effect on the agricultural economy was also evident. Rural credit had always been tied up with the trade in precious metals, and purchase of silver and gold ornaments was an important form of investment for peasant families. Local mints provided a key service here. In bad seasons, or simply in the course of the purchase of seed, stock or tools for everyday use, peasants could sell their ornaments for near their intrinsic value to *sarrafs* (money dealers) who could always make a profit by having them coined in the local treasury. So there had always been 'speculators in bullion ... who carried on a thriving, and to the public a beneficial trade thro' the existence of the Farrukhabad, Benares and Saugor mints'.[31] Smaller mints in the Rajput and Jat states of Bundelkhand and Rajasthan provided a similar facility. The decline of these mints, therefore, spread 'ruin thro' the native mercantile community of upper India' and deepened the liquidity problems created by the collapse of the agency houses.[32] Poorer people in the towns and countryside felt the

28 *Oudh Gazetteer*, iii, 530.   29 Stokes, *Peasant and Raj*, p. 67.

30 The Company sought practical results such as the end of the 'imposition of the shroffs', but it was also aware of symbolic issues, especially 'the need for some emblem of British sovereignty' to assert legitimacy over the many petty sovereigns who had the right to coin, India Mint Procs, 12 Jan. 1835, NAI.

31 Commr Agra to GG, 11 Apr. 1838, NWPCJ, July 1838, 231/49, IOL.

32 Siddiqi, *Agrarian Change*, ch. 8; the Benares commercial community continued to press for the re-establishment of the Benares mint for a decade, see, e.g. Harrakhchand to Magt. Benares (Persian), 11 Oct. 1839, 'Memory Book' (*Yadasht Bahi*).

changes most severely during the bad seasons of 1833 and 1838. Official reports showed that between 1827 and 1832 grain prices had fallen in the Aligarh region compared with silver by not less than 30 per cent, while in Rohilkhand, the stoppage of the bullion trade as a result of the abolition of the Farrukhabad mint had dealt a severe blow to the once-thriving grain trade.[33] Boulderson, the Collector of Bareilly, estimated that at least 8 per cent of the price fall had resulted from the abolition of the mints. But whereas the 'shortage of specie' had put pressure on peasant families who still had to pay their revenue in silver, the absence of mint facilities had absolutely the opposite effect when silver was disgorged onto the market with a great rush in 1833 and 1838. In Agra during the later famine year, 'the value of silver ornaments is far below their intrinsic worth and no purchasers are to be found because there are no means of exporting the bullion or converting it into specie'.[34]

A whole range of changes in the late 1820s and 1830s thus represented a conscious British policy of centralising Indian society and economy. Indian states and elites came to be seen as anachronisms or parasites whose 'idle consumption' held back beneficial change. Meanwhile the vigorous adoption of laissez-faire principles withdrew the East India Company from the cotton market and encouraged the abolition of internal town and transit duties. All these measures restricted the viability of small, local centres of trade, production and consumption. However, some of the developments of these decades were not the results of conscious British policy so much as the unforeseen consequences of the new centralisation of trade on the cities of the Gangetic valley, and ultimately on Calcutta itself. The prudence of merchant and peasant farmer encouraged investment in 'safe' British provinces so that local economies were slowly leeched of labour, capital and skills which had been redistributed to the smaller centres during the Mughal decline.

Traditional economic geography assumed that any movement of capital regarded as profitable by individuals would be the optimal distribution for the economy as a whole, given the type and difficulties of transport. But in the early nineteenth century, protection and security still acted as quite arbitrary factors inhibiting such rational allocation of resources. Merchants who were highly averse to risks to their 'credit' and persons might easily decide to opt for a much lower return on capital by investing in safe British territories. When merchant

---

[33] Replies of commrs and collrs to Bd of Revenue NWP, Indian Mint Procs, 9 Oct. 1832, NAI.
[34] Commr Agra to GG, 11 Apr. 1838, NWPCJ, July 1838, 231/49; Offg. Commr Agra to GG, 31 Nov. 1838, NWPCJ, Jan. 1839, 231/58, IOL.

wealth found its way to growing British centres of commerce, this does not necessarily mean that the economy as a whole was benefiting from the decline of local economies because these new investments created faster growth. On the contrary, the local economies may well have been losers to the extent of an essentially arbitrary premium put on safety.

The flight of capital to safe havens was particularly evident in the case of Awadh, and here the pressure of British demands was itself a major reason for the new sense of insecurity. In this case the largely unreciprocated transfers of resources had begun with the huge tribute paid to the British by the nawabs after 1764. But the rule of Saadat Ali Khan (who died in 1814) had been the Indian summer of the dynasty of Awadh, now constituted a monarchy.[35] Lucknow's great palaces of saracenic baroque were then being raised, and considerable expenditure by the British residents and a growing European business community which fed the court with luxuries had offset the effects of the partial dispersal of the large army which had been maintained at Lucknow between 1740 and 1802. Up to about 1830, there was evidence of local agricultural expansion, *ganj*-construction and the emergence of viable local *taluqdari* economies in the districts.[36] But the economic foundations of Awadh and the peculiar type of late Islamic kingship which it supported were perceptibly weakening.

The cession of more than half of the nawabi territory to the British in 1802 had not only deprived the centre of massive revenues but had also tended to turn Awadh into a commercial backwater, far removed from the Gangetic economy. Many of the Lucknow families which had served as bankers to the nawab's revenue officers had withdrawn from the Ganges cities before 1810, or opted to remove themselves and as much of their capital as they could extricate into British territory. Either way the Lucknow financiers and traders lost their stake in the developing part of the region's economy.

The kingdom gave a false appearance of stability in the years 1810–30. Serious strains were building up which were ultimately to vitiate the performance of agriculture itself. Awadh had to pay the Company a heavy 'subsidy'. In order to overawe local notables and collect sufficient revenue, the ruler needed to maintain a large and expensive standing army which stood at 70,000 men and 5,000 bullock drivers in the early 1830s.[37] But much of the revenue collected appears to have found its

---

[35] S. Ahmed, *Two Kings of Awadh. Muhammad Ali Shah and Amjad Ali Shah (1837–47)* (Aligarh, 1971), pp. 91–120; J. Pemble, *The Raj, the Indian Mutiny and the Kingdom of Oudh, 1810–59* (Hassocks, Sussex, 1977).

[36] E.g., Butter, *Southern Districts*, pp. 5–7.

[37] Resdt Lucknow to GG, 29 Nov. 1837, extract from For. Sec. Dept., 27 Dec. 1837, For. Pol. Procs, 27 Dec. 1837, NAI.

way into the hands of high officials who sought to protect themselves against future dismissal and disgrace by investing it in safe havens.

Factional conflicts between ministers was deepened by intrigue between the British residents, dependants of the East India Company who resided in Awadh and members of the royal family.[38] So by the early 1830s the pressure of the fiscal machine on local society appears to have reached a critical point. Wealthy people who might have supported a high level of taxation had 'almost disappeared from the land'. Conflict at the centre had encouraged the revolt of zamindars and *taluqdars* even in the rich Crown lands such as Baiswara. In November 1832 the Resident remarked to the King that 'formerly the only part of the kingdom which was remarkable for disorder was Durshun Sing's Talook, but now ... you seem to have Durshun Sings in all directions'.[39]

Newsletters of 1832 recorded the closing of large sections of western Awadh by revolts around Mianganj, which had once been closely controlled under Almas Ali Khan. Mokhum Singh, the zamindar of Bilgram, 'plunders the bankers daily'[40] and the price of grain and other commodities rose in Lucknow as a consequence. By the autumn of 1832 the authority of royal officials in Baiswara had been permanently undermined. The court in its desperate search for new sources of revenue required the *amils'* attendance in Lucknow and extorted from them extra payments ostensibly to 'confirm' their appointments. When the officials returned to their districts and attempted to recoup their losses from the zamindars disturbances increased. Finally the court was forced to the expedient of abandoning direct management of this crucial revenue-bearing zone and farming Baiswara to a Tiwari banker.[41]

The events of this short period mark a milestone in the transition of the Baiswara region from the rich agricultural tract of the late eighteenth century to the overpopulated and relatively impoverished district of the mid-nineteenth century. Much of the very recent deterioration noted by Butter in 1838 was probably due to the depression and agricultural hardship of the era. In 1837, for instance, the 'calamitous season' was adduced as a reason why royal income was likely to decline over 'the next few years'.[42] Some deterioration also appears to have been a consequence of deforestation and the consequent drying out of the soil.

[38] Same to same, 16 Oct. 1832, For. Pol. Procs, 26 Dec. 1832, NAI.
[39] Same to same, 6 Nov. 1832, For. Pol. Procs, 3 Dec. 1832, NAI.
[40] Trans. of *akhbarats* (newsletters), enc. same to same, 3 Dec. 1832, NAI.
[41] Same to same, 16 Oct. 1832, For. Pol. Procs, 26 Dec. 1832, NAI.
[42] 'Translation of the Prime Minister's Rough Estimates of the Annual Receipts and Disbursements of the Oude Govt. for the year 1838', same to same, 29 Nov. 1837, NAI.

But as in the case of the much grander cycle of the Mughal decline itself, these ecological disasters only became critical in the context of a disruption of the links between state and agriculture. The loose, corporate nature of the successor state could not support an ever increasing revenue demand. The capacity of local merchants and magnates to finance agricultural expansion was extinguished by the blanket of state revenue demand, and Awadh began to disintegrate as a political society. Large bodies of peasant colonists settled by pre-colonial lords began to drift across the southern and eastern boundaries into British territory.[43] Merchants faced with heavier dues resorted to closure (*hartals*) and increasingly withdrew their capital from the kingdom.[44] Most seriously, the great revenue entrepreneurs moved their fortunes into safer pastures.

Large amounts of Awadh capital were withdrawn and invested in Kanpur and Farrukhabad Districts between 1830 and 1850. In one estimate, Awadh investment in Kanpur alone amounted to Rs. 15–20 lakhs in the early 1840s.[45] The beginning of the flood came in 1831 when an ex-chief minister of Awadh, Mutumad-ud Daulah, moved to Kanpur, followed in the next few years by an increasing number of merchant and notable families. The amounts of money brought into Kanpur were so great that they 'tended to a greater circulation of money in the city', and enriched the local mercantile community which had begun to invest in land-rights in the district. This inflow of Awadh capital was thought to have made it possible for an unusually heavy land-revenue to be levied on Kanpur. The figures of Lucknow residents' investment in government bonds and promissory notes, reproduced by William Hoey in the 1870s, tells a similar story. Between 1833 and 1843 nearly Rs. 48 lakhs were transferred from Awadh to Calcutta in the form of loans, and a further Rs. 48 lakhs were raised in 1854 and 1855, immediately before Cession.[46] When we consider that Hoey reckoned the total amount of money invested in Lucknow and its environs in the form of loans amounted to only Rs. 30 lakhs in the 1870s, it can be seen that this outflow represented a startling immobilisation of local capital. Hoey himself reckoned that one reason for the decline of trading and artisan production in central Awadh had been this enormous outflow of local resources. Government loans bore a low (if secure) rate of interest,

43 E.g., *akhbarat*, enc. same to same, 16 Oct. 1832, noting withdrawal of peasants and proprietors of Rampur into Company territory; for settlement of Awadh Kurmis in Allahabad see, *SR Allahabad, 1878*, p. 73.
44 Resident to GG, 16 Oct. 1832, NAI.
45 R. Montgomery, *Statistical Report of the District of Cawnpoor* (Calcutta, 1849), p. 110 and *passim*; Safi Ahmed, *Two Kings*, p. 78.
46 Hoey, *Monograph on Trade and Industry in Upper India*, pp. 43–5.

while British expenditure in Awadh in the form of sepoys' wages and residency expenses were paid for out of the Awadh subsidy – that is, out of the nawab's own pocket.

This indirect deflation of the princely economies was also evident, for instance, in Rajasthan which had proved an important trading partner for western Hindustan in the late eighteenth century. Up to 1770, peasant farmers in Jaipur and Udaipur had profited from growing demand for opium throughout India and the Middle East, while 'western merchants' had brought down Rajasthani opium to Hindustan and Bengal. After 1770, the British sought gradually to exclude Rajasthan opium from its eastern and western markets to benefit the production which they directly controlled. By the 1820s, Tod was inveighing against the Company's monopoly stranglehold which he considered was largely responsible for the mercantile decline of the princely states.[47] But it was once again the 1830s which proved the particularly bad decade. A growing exodus of Marwari businessmen from Jaipur and Shekhavati was both a cause and consequence of the commercial stagnation. There was a dramatic fall-off in trade through central Rajasthan between 1822 and 1838, and this affected the major entrepôt towns of Ajmer and Nyanagar. There were a number of causes for this. Warfare, the decline of the Rajput armies, and the opening of a new northerly route by Charun and Palli Brahmin traders played their part. So did the customs system introduced by the British when they annexed the Ajmer District in 1825. But at the same time, the Commissioner of Ajmer and the famous Fatehpuri Seths, who were the most powerful merchants of the area, complained of a general 'diminution of credit' in recent years.[48] This may have reflected the disruption of the old north Indian bullion market which had once linked the Jaipur mint with those of Benares and Farrukhabad.

Most of the developments which tended to deflate the local *rajwari* economies during the 1830s were in some ways connected. But there were also events which occurred more or less fortuitously to deepen the crisis. Luxury trades which had shown remarkable resilience even during the 1780s came under severe pressure from failures both in supply and demand. Uncertainty in foreign export markets such as Afghanistan, Iran, Central Asia and Nepal tended to trim the profits of merchants in shawl goods, horses, drugs and spices which had been the staples of the old north-western routes. In 1835–6 came a series of savage epidemics in Kashmir, compounded by political turmoil,

---

[47] Tod, *Rajasthan*, II, 128.
[48] Note by Commr Ajmer–Mewara, 8 Sept. 1839, NWP Bd Rev. Procs, 15 June 1841, 223/26, IOL.

which sent weavers fleeing down into the Punjab where the famous shawl wool was difficult to obtain. Shawl imports into the British territories were slashed by more than 75 per cent in two years, and in 1836, the Hardwar Fair, which was essentially a great shawl market, failed for the first time on record, and to the tune of about Rs. 2 lakhs.[49] The Rohilla towns which had escaped the worst of the bad seasons from 1833–4 were badly hit by the stagnation of these north-western trades.

As the authority of the Indian states was reduced and their resources widely dissipated, substantial numbers of fixed market centres in the small towns dwindled or stagnated. This is most evident in the Jat territories and Bundelkhand, but urban life in parts of Rajasthan and Awadh appears to have suffered a similar setback. British rule had already initiated some changes which curtailed that intermediate level of centres between the village *hath* and the large city which had been so buoyant in the eighteenth century.[50] The Permanent Settlement had put pressure on zamindari incomes in Bengal and Bihar in the first generation after 1793; as many as 15,000 fixed rural markets had disappeared before 1790, according to Colebrooke. In the western provinces and Benares, *ganj*-foundation by revenue officials and new markets for export cash crops had more than made up for the decline of some older *qasbahs*, though it was often a gain for the environs of the large towns at the expense of more remote tracts. After 1830, however, the local decline of small towns went ahead with some speed because income from service of the rajas tended to disappear at the same time as the export economy ran into difficulties. The new British subdivisional establishments supported by a few policemen and *peons* had nothing like the same impact on agrarian society as the *amils'* headquarters or warrior lineage centres of the earlier days. Many small centres, then, were suffering a relative decline in 'urban' population well before the coming of the railways in the 1850s assimilated a further range of their break-of-bulk functions to the large towns, and increasingly to one centre alone, Kanpur.

Geographers and development economists have noted that in India substantial centres between the large city and the village periodic market seem to be relatively few in number, that the urban hierarchy seems

---

[49] NWP Bd Rev. Procs, 7 June 1836, 221/86; cf. C. L. Datta, 'Significance of shawl wool trade in western Himalayan politics', *Bengal Past and Present*, lxxxix (1970), 23–5.

[50] This assertion is difficult to quantify; changes in *chaukidari* assessments for places with a population under 10,000 cannot be regarded as significant. But the qualitative references found in early gazetteers, settlement reports and proceedings come down heavily on the side of relative stagnation or even decay for smaller places after about 1825. The exception may be places on the few new metalled roads (e.g., the Grand Trunk Road or the road south from Mirzapur) which benefited from the slow move from pack-bullocks to carts.

rather 'flat' compared with that of other great agrarian countries. Nineteenth-century developments may well have exaggerated this phenomenon. Political organisation had always been crucial in creating and maintaining this intermediate level of small towns. In Japan, for instance, small castle towns provided a buoyant intermediate level of this sort. 'Country places' sustained by the demand of rural elites for silks and metal work were a significant indicator of Japan's rapid pre-industrial development. By contrast, British centralisation in India was partly responsible for the attenuation of this type of centre. The consequence for rural society was probably a restriction of access to markets, credit and employment outside agriculture. In Bundelkhand, Rajasthan and Awadh, mid-nineteenth-century Indians may have been more the classic peasant than their forebears a century earlier.

One theme throughout has been the importance of spending by the political authorities for employment in the intermediate economy. This gave buoyancy to small town economies and parts of agrarian society. Broadly, the deflation of this type of demand by changes in the Indian states in the 1830s and 1840s was not made up by any large-scale spending by the British authorities; this did not come until after 1860. On the contrary, the 'Age of Reform' was a period of retrenchment in civil expenditure and stagnation in military expenditure. The great expansion of the Anglo-Indian bureaucracy had not yet begun to compensate for the decline of employment in the princely economies.[51] Despite stirring pronouncements, the growth of public works programmes had hardly begun before the Rebellion of 1857, and even expenditure on the great Ganges Canal was only just beginning to grow in the last few years of Lord Dalhousie's rule.[52] One observer reckoned that total British expenditure on public works during this period over the whole Bengal Presidency was rather less than that of an average central Indian raja. In truth, the 'Age of Reform' was more an age of hiatus.

Only the British army continued to afford salaries and contracts to the people of Hindustan, and even here the great boost to town-building and employment afforded by the Bengal army between 1780 and 1825 began perceptibly to slacken. This is not to say that there were no longer fortunes to be made. Despite the creation of an army commissariat department, the military authorities still depended on Indian agencies to keep them in the field. The Sikh wars of the 1830s and 1840s threw up

---

51 E. T. Stokes, 'Bureacracy and ideology. Britain and India in the nineteenth century', *Transactions of the Royal Historical Society*, 5 ser., xxx (1980), 149–50.
52 See D. J. Howlett, 'An end to expansion. Influences on British policy in India *circa* 1830–60' (unpubl. Cambridge Ph.D. dissertation, 1981), ch. 2.

immensely wealthy grain, cloth and bullock dealers as the Maratha wars had done before. Chaube grain dealers of Agra had netted Rs. 30 lakhs in supplying the Punjab Army in 1834–5. There was also the case of Joti Prasad, the great contractor of Agra who was building up an unparalleled network of mercantile subcontractors among the Khattris and Banjaras of the western districts in the years before the second Sikh war.[53]

Yet openings of this sort were not as plentiful as they had been for people in Hindustan at the turn of the century, and spectacular examples such as Joti Prasad may be misleading. In fact, the military frontier of the British empire had rolled on into the Punjab, leaving the cities of eastern Hindustan without income from military spending, and those of the west mere sluggish supply depots. In terms of its impact on the Gangetic economy, military expenditure may have reached its peak by about 1820 and then declined progressively until 1858. The Sikh wars and concern about the security of the northern frontier countermanded the most determined stirrings towards economy. But there was an overall slowdown in the growth of military manpower in the region after 1826, while military expenditure per head of the civil population must have dropped substantially. The Bengal Army expanded from about 26,000 men in 1796 to about 140,000 men in 1826.[54] By 1857, it had boomed and slumped several times, but the overall increase was a modest 20,000 men over the 1826 figure. On the other hand, if our figures are broadly correct, at least 200,000 full-time soldiers of the armies of the Indian states must have been stood down in the Gangetic region since the beginning of the century. Sleeman was not exaggerating when he observed of the difference between British and Indian armies:

We do the soldiers' work with one-tenth of the soldiers that had before been employed in it over the territories we acquire, and turn the other nine-tenths adrift. They all sink into the lowest class of religious mendicants, or retainers; or live amongst their friends as drones upon the land.[55]

More significant even than the slackening of the pace of growth of the Bengal Army was the disposition of its forces. Those high spenders the European battalions had moved off to the Punjab; and whereas there had been five battalions in the North-Western Provinces in 1801 there was only one between Delhi and Calcutta in 1857, as the British were to find

---

[53] Jt Magt. Agra to Magt., 27 June 1850, NWPCJ, Mar. 1851, 233/22, IOL.
[54] Madan Paul Singh, *Indian Army*, pp. 57–8; J. A. B. Palmer, *The Mutiny Outbreak at Meerut* (Cambridge, 1966), p. 34.
[55] Sleeman, *Rambles*, p. 365.

to their cost. Taking account of the permanent armies of Indian rulers,[56] the number of towns or bazaars which supported more than 5,000 troops appears to have declined from sixteen in 1800 to three (Meerut, Agra and Lucknow) in 1857.

Problems in the export economy

The export trades in agricultural produce of the years 1780–1830 were moulded and constrained by existing patterns of social organisation. At the level of production the 'harvest cycle' of particular crops and the inclination of the peasant household to avoid risks imposed its own rhythm.[57] Next, the supply of credit, the level of investment and access to markets were heavily influenced by the redistributive economics of the petty kingdoms of the localities. Finally, Indian merchant society which linked these institutions to distant markets was influenced by its own conceptions of 'safety first' – its own moral economy. The interlocking of these different types of organisation produced inherent instability in the markets. But between 1827 and 1847 these local tremors were exacerbated. The role of the East India Company in eastern trade was drastically curtailed, and a series of slumps occurred in India which distantly echoed the changing tempo of the great engine of the North Atlantic economy.[58]

After 1834 the end of the Company's monopoly on the export of raw cotton to China resulted in an immediate boom but ultimate stagnation of this crucial staple of the area's export economy. The initial effect of the withdrawal of the Company from the market was beneficial to the Indian merchants who had dominated it since the collapse of George Mercer and other European entrepreneurs. The Company, anticipating its demise as a monopolist, had run down its stocks of cotton in Canton, and Bombay and Bengal houses rushed in to make up the difference, purchasing massively from their up-country Indian agents. By 1838, however, demand was slumping once again because of overstocking in Canton, and prices had fallen to under 50 per cent of their 1834 level. The modest profits that peasant farmers and interior dealers made on the trade were severely squeezed. And in such a situation, the cotton trade of the Bengal area was bound to be the major casualty. Though

---

56 The crisis in the Sikh kingdom during the 1830s and 1840s also led to the standing down of mercenary troops from Hindustan, Lieut. Nichols to Magt. Mirzapur, Mirzapur Judl, 107, UPR.
57 Commander, 'The agrarian economy', pp. 215–50.
58 For an extended discussion of the export economy see C. A. Bayly, 'The age of hiatus. The north Indian economy and society, 1830–50', in C. H. Philips and M. D. Wainwright (eds), *Indian Society and the Beginnings of Modernisation* (London 1976), pp. 83–105.

'Bengal' (i.e. Hindustan and Central Indian) cotton already had a name for poor quality, dealers had unwisely adulterated their crop in the boom years after 1834. K. M. Mullick of the Calcutta Chamber of Commerce remembered that 'All manner of adulteration found its way in screwing the bales here, which were shipped under fictitious trade marks'. So in the buyers' market which developed after 1838, export of 'Bengal' raw cotton slumped from a value of Cos. Rs. 62,63,777 to Cos. Rs. 19,26,237 in 1839–40.[59] More seriously, by the mid-1840s, growing production of indigenous Chinese and American cottons had further diminished the market for India in the Far East and the west. Attempts in the 1840s by the Court of Directors to improve the quality and types of Indian cotton met with little success. In fact the growing international disfavour in which Indian cottons were held was only forgotten in the great boom which followed after American production was dislocated by the Civil War. All the while the cotton trade of eastern India was suffering from its own particular problems. The development during the 1840s of overland carriage from the producing areas of central India to Bombay diverted trade from the route that led through Jabbalpur and Mirzapur to Calcutta. This contributed to the stagnation of Mirzapur, north India's 'Manchester' of the previous generation. Cultivators and merchants still had alternative markets open to them in Awadh and Nepal, but in general terms the continued relative decline of income from raw cotton was a serious blow to the one cash crop whose extensive form of cultivation and bulking and transport requirements had rapidly enriched some peasant farmers and merchant families.

Just as the rapid growth of cotton cultivation before 1826 had led to the 'proliferation of interior marts' and town-building at major centres, so the social effects of the relapse were unmistakable. In the years 1816 to 1825, a very large business had been done in the Agra area by Messrs George Mercer and Co., an agency house which employed one of the largest European staffs in the interior, and by a set of powerful Agra Agarwal families headed by Lala Piru Mal who had begun to dominate the cotton and salt trades shortly after 1800. By 1836, the Europeans had failed or withdrawn their capital and Piru Mal had made a loss of more than Rs. 1 lakh in a single season. The Delhi Customs Master noted that 'Since the year 1827 the whole of the cotton screw houses scattered over the country have been abandoned', while N. B. Wright, a customs patrol officer who worked south of Delhi, reckoned that the annual produce of the region had fallen from 300,000 *maunds* to a mere 22,000 *maunds* over the years 1826–36.[60] The rapid expansion of cultivation in

[59] Mullick, *Bengal Commerce*, I, 17, table.
[60] CGC Delhi to Bd, 16 May 1836, NWP Rev. Customs, 7 June 1836, 22/81, IOL.

the Muttra–Agra area by as much as 30 per cent had provided suitable soil for the cotton boom, but by the mid-1830s the general withdrawal of European capital, and adverse ecological changes caused by over-cropping, had made it virtually impossible for the local zamindars to pay the revenue.

Merchants could, of course, redirect their trade to slowly developing internal markets, but the effect of the booms and slumps of the years after 1827 was to increase the instability of the interior centres. Already in the years 1812 to 1816 a whole network of periodic markets in Bah and Pinahut divisions south of Agra had collapsed under the pressure of poor seasons and customs house exactions, throwing out of employment an estimated 30,000 people who provided labour for the petty industries which rose on the back of the cotton trade.[61] After 1826 such situations became general throughout the Agra region. Some Indian cotton merchants moved in to mop up the declining trade abandoned by Mercer and Co., but in general places like Pulwul declined. The relative over-assessment of the area provided an additional check to development of a higher level of local consumption. In 1836 Wright noted: 'I may here remark that to my personal knowledge, one European purchased nearly as much cotton in one season as all the native merchants together during the last.'[62]

The effect on the large towns was more complex. At one extreme the variation of Agra's population over the bad years after 1827 was quite remarkable. Always at the mercy of an unstable hinterland, the city seems to have lost between 10 and 30 per cent of its population to mortality and temporary emigration during the bad seasons of 1818–19 and 1833–4. During the terrible famine of 1838, the loss may have been nearer 40 per cent. The volatile nature of the cotton, grain and cattle trades on which the city had thrived accentuated this fragility. Internal traffic, for instance, was severely reduced by the 'Depression' of 1830–3. But so long as the cotton trade continued, even in recession, Agra received some very large despatches from its hinterland. It was a convenient depot for small merchants who could not afford 'to be out of their money' for the long period that would be necessary if the goods were to be bulked in Delhi or Kanpur.

Allahabad was another town which did not maintain the rapid growth which it had experienced in the immediate aftermath of Cession. By 1824 it was said that 'the town itself does not seem to have been on the increase, but rather to have suffered in size and importance'.[63] The

61 Judge Agra to CGC Agra, 11 Nov. 1816, CPR, 11 Jan. 1817, 97/59, IOL.
62 CGC Delhi to Bd, 16 May 1836.
63 'The town of Allahabad in 1824' in D. and B. Bhattacharya (eds), 'Report on the population estimates of India, 1820–30', *Census of India 1961* (Delhi, 1963).

evidence suggests a rapid growth from 1803, when Hamilton estimated the population as a mere 20,000, to about 40,000 in 1820, followed by a slow stagnation until the late 1840s. This was connected with the vicissitudes of the raw cotton trade, the decline of military spending and the gradual depletion of the weaving population which had continued to supply Nawabi troops until the 1840s. By contrast, Mirzapur and Kanpur continued to expand until the 1840s. Kanpur appears to have benefited from the decline of Farrukhabad as a major commercial centre during the Depression,[64] while Mirzapur was not really feeling the pinch until the mid-1840s. Even when the Maratha demand and cotton trades were in recession, Mirzapur still gained from the steady southward trade in sugar from the Azamgarh and Gorakhpur Divisions. As late as 1836 police arrangements in the city had to be revised to take account of the growth of those wards of the city which dealt particularly with the cotton trade. It was not until the late 1840s that complaints about the decline of the city became insistent following the rerouting of much cotton through Bombay.

Figures for north India's cities and large market towns are quite treacherous before 1870. But it seems reasonably clear that the first thirty years of the century saw population maintaining itself in the centres which had emerged during the eighteenth century, and an increment in towns which became British political centres or bulking points for the export trades. In general, the next twenty years – from 1830 to 1850 – recorded slower growth or stagnation in urban population. In fact, since there was a faster rise in total population after 1838, there may well have been a net decline of urban population over the period. This was probably concentrated in intermediate market and political centres.

For some substantial areas, however, there is absolutely no doubt that the whole commercial economy went into sharp decline. For instance, in the late 1820s, Company investment in cotton of the Bundelkhand area was still Rs. 40 lakhs per annum,[65] while private investment ran at about Rs. 18 lakhs. The inflow of money into the region came to a drastic halt in 1834 when the Company disbanded its commercial agency in Kalpi on the termination of the China trade monopoly. This move deepened the distress caused by the 1834 famine, and 20,000 starving people converged on Banda and Hamirpur.[66] Even though the

[64] CGC Farrukhabad to Dty CGC Farrukhabad, 20 Oct. 1826, NWP Rev. Customs, 29 Nov. 1836, cf. chart of 'town duties' at Allahabad and Kanpur, 1826–36, *idem*, 2 Feb. 1836, 221/85, IOL.

[65] *DG Jalaun*, p. 45.

[66] Dty Opium Agent, Bundelkhand to Govt, 23 June 1836, CGC Bundelkhand to Bd, 27 June 1842, NWP Rev. Customs, 12 July 1842, 223/49, IOL.

cultivated area picked up quite quickly after 1838, more than half of the total number of villages in the subdivisions of Kalpi, Kunch and Hamirpur were still said to be abandoned in 1842. By this date, moreover, private investment in Bundelkhand cotton had dwindled to Rs. 7 lakhs annually so that, in total, the area had suffered a loss of cash inflows amounting to Rs. 50 lakhs during a single decade. This, of course, coincided with the gradual erosion of luxury trade and courtly employment. The cumulative decline of Bundelkhand meant that whereas as late as 1842 there were agents of 52 banking houses in the town of Kunch, by 1872 there were only two shops left where *hundis* could be negotiated.[67]

After cotton, sugar had the greatest potential as a 'development crop'. Given good market conditions, demand in both the internal market and the world market was expected to increase as consumers with an improved standard of living turned to more refined varieties. European demand in 1830 was estimated at 450 million pounds per annum while the total of all East Indian sugars exported was a mere 5½ million pounds.[68] Sugar, like cotton, was a crop which favoured Indian middlemen and producers and required the development of a basic technology around collection points. Bengal sugar had received an early advantage in the English market in 1792 when the failure of West Indian sugar and the cheapness of tea resulting from the Commutation Act made it competitive for the first time despite the punitive duties levied. Nevertheless before 1836 when duties on the West and East Indies were equalised, export was discouraged by a differential duty of eight shillings per hundredweight over the West Indian produce.[69] After the equalisation, of course, exports rose rapidly, reaching a peak value of about Rs. 166 lakhs per annum in 1849, but then declining to Rs. 53 lakhs in 1858 and Rs. 9 lakhs in 1869. As with cotton and indigo, production for export went through a curve, with Indian products becoming relatively less competitive in world markets after an initial boom. Once again the major reasons were foreign competition and institutional discouragements. After 1849, the triumph of free trade principles in Britain opened its market to various plantation and slave-produced foreign sugars which had been totally excluded in earlier days. The problems of transport and petty commodity production put Indian sugars, and particularly those of eastern and western Hindustan, at a disadvantage compared with these foreign competitors.

[67] *DG Jalaun*, p. 45.
[68] J. Bell, *Review of the External Commerce of Bengal from 1824–5 to 1829–30* (Calcutta, 1830), p. 28.
[69] Mullick, *Bengal Commerce*, I, 26; Colebrooke and Lambert, *Husbandry*, pp. 120–5.

The local effects in inland India of the failure of sugar export are much more difficult to determine than those of cotton because there had always existed a much more responsive internal demand, particularly in central and southern parts of the country. When the Company withdrew its own investment in 1833, prices in the Azamgarh and Ballia Districts fell, but there does not seem to have been a great decline in the acreage under the crop.[70] Similarly, when European demand slumped in the late 1840s, sugar from the eastern region which had been temporarily siphoned off to Calcutta and Europe resumed its earlier route through Mirzapur to central India.[71] The social effects of the sugar boom were consequently more stable than those of cotton or indigo export. Around Benares the cultivated area under sugar held up relatively well in the years between the settlements of the 1840s and the 1870s, and Indian middlemen and rural *bania* families became wealthy. In the late 1830s raw sugar was manufactured in large quantities by innumerable small firms, European and Indian, whose factories were scattered over the districts of the Benares Division. Prominent were those of Dip Chand Sahu of Azamgarh.[72] It was in the 1840s also that the ancestors of the great Benares firm of Raja Sir Motichand Gupta who had previously served as *taluqdari* bankers in Ajodhya moved from their base in Azamgarh district and established themselves in Calcutta, developing a new line of business in sugar.[73] The linking in to the riverine economy of the districts of the Bihar borderlands which had proceeded slowly in the 1820s and 1830s was speeded by the development of sugar and opium at the very time when other parts of Hindustan were being knocked out of export farming. Nevertheless, it cannot be said that the momentum of growth was maintained sufficiently to alter basic conditions of the peasant economy. Merchant capital was not concentrated in large-scale investment in plant. The structure of the peasant family and regressive revenue-demand discouraged the development of a class of really substantial yeoman farmers.

Finally, mention must be made of the fate of opium and indigo production over these years. And what must be emphasised again is the extreme instability of indigo as a cash crop and the geographical limitations of the benefits to the whole Bengal area of the opium trade which passed through it. Indigo had, of course, been associated with some of the earliest signs of the recovery of commercial agriculture in the unstable parts of the upper Doab. Around Farrukhabad, large numbers of Indian banking firms and zamindars had become attached to

---

[70] *Revenue Settlements under Reg. ix, 1, 7.*
[71] *Ibid.*   [72] *Ibid.*
[73] Interview, family histories, Sri Jyoti Bhushan Gupta, Benares, April 1974.

the nets of credit required by the Bengal Houses of Agency in financing their operations up-country. The collapse of the Agency Houses and their Indian partners after 1827 revealed that indigo cultivation had been vastly overextended for institutional reasons. In the words of J. Bell, writing in 1830:

The prices in the Calcutta market ... have been kept up not so much by actual consumptive demand, as by its use as a medium of remittance, consequent on the depression of exchange, but for which the cultivation before this would have in all probability been considerably reduced.[74].

The reduction in the acreage under indigo proceeded by fits and starts through from the 1830s to the early 1900s when indigo finally succumbed to synthetic dyes. Though there were a number of booms and slumps associated with commercial crises in England in 1836 and 1847, the industry in upper India never recovered from the crash of 1827. As late as the 1870s, settlement officers noted the large numbers of ruined indigo factories scattered through the pristine countryside of the western districts, an indication of the extent to which sustained export performance might have provided conditions for rural capital formation. What survived were oases of village production associated with colonies of 'gardener castes' which had been planted by the eighteenth-century rulers. This was not negligible. In the years 1822–4, more than 35 per cent of the production of the Agra District was still directed to indigenous consumption in Delhi and Rajasthan.[75] Nevertheless, the Farrukhabad indigo houses alone failed completely, precipitating a crisis which drove more than fifty merchant houses out of the city and bankrupted many of the hinterland zamindars. The earlier closure of the Farrukhabad mint had damaged the grain and bullion trade. The slow expansion of the city which had proceeded cautiously since the 1720s came to an abrupt and permanent halt.

Opium, by contrast, was almost entirely a cash crop for export, the small quantity required for local consumption being sold by district treasurers or smuggled. When labour costs were taken into account, opium production was relatively unprofitable for the farmer.[76] Extensive cultivation of opium was therefore limited to poor or developing areas like the Ghazipur District where the government Opium Agency pumped in advances to get as much acreage under cultivation as possible. Here again, political considerations intruded into production, just as external political and commercial considerations limited the potential of opium as a development crop. The total number

[74] Bell, *External Commerce*, p. 26.
[75] CGC Agra to Bd, 5 Oct. 1824, CPR, 3 May 1825, 95/62, IOL.
[76] Colebrooke and Lambert, *Husbandry*, pp. 113–14.

of chests of Bengal and Bihar opium exported to the Far East rose from 4,200 in 1820/1 to 7,324 in 1829/30 and 64,000 in 1863/4.[77] However, from the late 1840s Indian opium was under increasing competition from the cheaper Chinese product, and the Bengal and North-Western Provinces governments were forced to protect their own revenues by artificially extending production and forcing down the prices of their own crop.[78] State intervention here certainly pushed forward the development of a number of small towns in the Gorakhpur and Ghazipur Districts and helped tie them into the Benares commercial area, but the benefits to the cultivator appear to have been limited to a small area, particularly the Padruana Tahsil of the Ghazipur District. Even here it is noteworthy that the major cultivators took the first opportunity of the coming of the railway to move into much more lucrative grain production, leaving the difficult, costly and polluting drug to their poorer neighbours.[79]

The general picture, then, for both Hindustan and Bengal was of a relatively successful early penetration of foreign markets, followed after 1830 by a stagnation or even absolute decline of agricultural exports. The commercial and agrarian benefits of capital accumulation through export were, therefore, geographically unstable. Different areas deep in Bengal and Hindustan were temporarily vitalised by foreign demand and inputs of capital, only to slump again when external conditions turned against them. Since land-revenue usually remained fixed at the higher level consonant with lucrative exports, wealth created in the boom after the Napoleonic War proved insubstantial.

A turning point for imports?

If the years 1827–40 were critical for north India's exports, did they also see a sharp increase in the flow of European imports? Bentinck's remarks on the 'bleaching bones of weavers' and the precipitous decline of weaving in the cities of Bengal after 1815 alerted official opinion to the consequences of the decline of artisan industries. But we are less concerned here with the extent of absolute 'deindustrialisation', for which the evidence remains inadequate, than with the dislocation of the old intermediate level of artisan production, for which it is more plentiful.[80]

[77] Mullick, *Bengal Commerce*, I, 40.
[78] Collr Gorakhpur to Commr Benares, 15 June 1841, NWP Rev. Procs, 2 July 1841, 223/27, IOL.
[79] *DG Ghazipur*, p. 53.
[80] Cf. A. K. Bagchi, 'Deindustrialisation in Gangetic Bihar, 1809–1901', in Barun De *et al.* (eds), *Essays in Honour of Prof. S. C. Sarkar* (Delhi, 1976), pp. 499–522; M. Vicziany, 'The deindustrialisation of India in the 19th century. A methodological critique of Amiya Kumar Bagchi', *IESHR*, xix (1979).

It was during the boom after 1815 that there were the first indications of substantial European imports. Dacca and Murshidabad in Bengal and Tanda in Awadh were all said to be in decline in the years 1810–30, though here it is difficult to separate the consequences of the ending of the Company's investment in Indian cloths from those of increased import. As far as Tanda is concerned, private European purchases and sales to the kingdom of Nepal seem to have remained buoyant until the 1840s.[81]

Much more significant than the impact of finished goods in these decades was the astonishingly rapid market penetration by European twist and yarn which completely wiped out Indian spinning before 1850, except for the production of the 'sacred thread' which continued in some areas. Imports through Calcutta rose from Rs. 1,23,145 in 1824/5, shortly after the introduction of 'mule twist' in England to Rs. 31,11,841 in 1830/1. After this, the volume and value of imports continued to expand rapidly, reaching Rs. 79,90,32 by 1840/1.[82] As early as 1813, the Collector of Benares had noted distress among the spinners of the city, who were generally poor or aged relations of the weavers;[83] while before 1836 European twist and yarn, made up in Delhi, was making inroads into the markets of the west. The significance of the decline of Indian spinning probably lies in its deleterious effect on a total income of families who were employed in both spinning and weaving, rather than a simple collapse of employment. Another commodity which rapidly moved into the north Indian market during this period was English-made iron. Here again, economies of scale had been so great that English products were competitive even in the face of much lower Indian transport and labour costs, and as semi-manufactured goods there was no problem of suitability for the final market.

Both semi-manufactured and manufactured imports seem to have leapt ahead in the 1830s. Imports of finished cloth through Calcutta increased fourfold during the decade, and qualitative evidence suggests that penetration into the Gangetic valley was quite rapid even during these poor years. On the face of it, the Depression and low consumer demand due to the scarcities ought to have suppressed demand in general, as occurred during the scarcity years of 1869–71. What may have happened, then, is that the relative rise in grain prices after 1833 increased the labour costs of Indian weavers and chintz stampers sufficiently to make European imports competitive in medium quality grades.[84] At the same time, the decade saw a general improvement in

81 *Oudh Gazetteer*, iii, 490–3.   82 Mullick, *Bengal Commerce*, I, 4, 7–11; *ibid.*, II, 3.
83 CGC Benares to Bd, 23 July 1813, CPR, July 1813, 36/97, IOL.
84 For some evidence of this, *Settlements under Regulation ix*, I, 9–10.

communications and culminated in large-scale troop movements during the Sikh war. Market networks and demand had to be created, so that inroads into the Punjab in the late 1830s saw a massive increase in demand for 'British and other goods' in the area of operations, and the countries 'west of the Sutlej', which rose from Rs. 20 to Rs. 60 lakhs over this short period.[85] Again, the end of internal customs duties speeded the growth of imports. Around Agra there was a large increase in the demand for European iron as a result of the 'freedom of trade from extortion' after 1836. Finally, the decline of aristocratic centres of consumption speeded the dispersal of old artisan communities, leaving the field open to imports.

The emphasis should fall more on the rapid pace of dislocation among artisan communities during the 1830s than on the 'deindustrialisation' of India, or the complete demise of craft production. The decline of paper-making in the lower Doab, for instance, was in part caused by the desuetude of the traditional Indian paper varieties as the *farman* (charter) was replaced by the 'proceeding', but it also reflected the growth of new paper-making industries at Serampore in Bengal.[86] Weaving communities were often relocated rather than annihilated; the weavers of *qasbah* Shahzadpur, abandoning the declining service communities of their locality, moved across the river Ganges to seek protection and patronage among the *taluqdars* of south Awadh. In the same way, Mirzapur's brassware production almost achieved factory dimension during these years as it was now receiving cheap European raw materials along the burgeoning river trade route. The decline of brassmaking in the cities of the west of the region partly reflected the growth of Mirzapur production.

The scarcity cycle of the 1830s

What exacerbated the dislocation of the 1830s to crisis point was its fortuitous conjuncture with the worst period of weather instability which the region had seen since the Chalisa famine of 1781–3. The first point to establish, however, is that both the Depression and the famines (1833–4 and 1837–8) affected different parts of the territory in different ways. The districts of the interior which had not specialised in the cultivation of export crops generally survived the crash of 1827 without too much damage, while the 'older' well-irrigated tracts of the east did not suffer so badly from drought as those parts of the west which remained almost as unstable as they had been during the late eighteenth

[85] NWP Bd Rev. Customs, 29 June 1841, 223/26, IOL.
[86] Interviews, Kara, Allahabad, 1973–4.

century. Bulandshahr District, for instance, had never been so heavily involved in indigo as some of its neighbours, and, given good river communications, it was able to prosper by exporting grain through the 1830s.[87] Allahabad and Fatehpur were also exporting grain for the first time in the late 1830s, and there were distinct signs of prosperity among the substantial village merchants of their hinterlands.[88]

The effects of the depression and scarcities also fell with different degrees of severity on various sections of the population. Substantial traders who had diversified their interests were able to profit from both. In 1837 many of the great Delhi and Kanpur salt merchants rapidly switched their riverboat capacity from salt to grain and made a killing. Quick adaptation among the largest dealers accounts for the fact that the overall volume of trade seems to have fallen off by as little as 20 per cent during the famine, while in 1839 trade was given a positive stimulus as large dealers made haste to restock their salt and grain holdings.[89] Lesser merchants, however, had much less room for manoeuvre. Primarily, they lacked sufficient capital to move rapidly from one branch of commerce to another. An officer on patrol in the Agra region in 1837 noted large droves of cattle belonging to the Banjaras of Beana returning unladen from the northern markets of Farrukhabad and Shahjahanpur.[90] Usually these traders had exchanged Rajasthan salt for Rohilkhand grain, but this year the prices were so high that they could not purchase with any hope of immediate gain in the western markets. Intermediate traders were also badly affected by the withdrawal from the salt market of two or three of the largest dealers who had switched into grain. These big dealers had previously bought salt in bulk at Bharatpur and provided the lesser dealers with salt on credit.[91] For those without much capital, in fact, the famines must only have been the culmination of a series of blows which began with the 'money famine' of 1828/9. Well before the 1833 food famines there had been a considerable fall off in the petty traffic on one or two bullocks or on headloads which had represented the contribution of smaller merchants to the commercial growth of the Agra region. Traders dealing in commodities such as brass vessels, low grade cloths and liquor which depended on the existence of a small monetary surplus in the hands of agricultural people were obviously in a bad position once silver became scarce.

87 Collr Bulandshahr to Collr Meerut, 19 June 1834, Rev. Extracts Bulandshahr, Elliot MSS Eur. D. 310, IOL.
88 *Settlements under Regulation ix*, II, 63.
89 Comparative general returns of gross and net customs receipts by stations, 1837–40, NWP Rev. Customs, 7 Aug. 1838, 222/45, and 31 July 1840, 223/5, IOL.
90 CGC Agra to Bd, 2 Jan. 1837, NWP Rev. Customs, 13 Jan. 1837, 226/16, IOL.
91 *Ibid.*

Artisans were also among the first to be hit by any form of economic slowdown. The Depression affected the market for small manufactures while restricting the supply of credit. The scarcities which followed it disrupted grain supplies to towns and temporarily destroyed the market altogether. Indeed, commentators during both famines noted that artisans who were not tied into the *jajmani* systems of 'big men' were harder hit even than the rural poor and came flocking to the relief works. Similar conditions obtained in the villages. As usual, it was the weakest who suffered most – women, children and those unable to rely on the aid of a patron. During the depression and famine years, moneylenders restricted their credit to individuals who had security of tenure on their lands, and therefore possessed some viable collateral. After 1834, moneylenders in the Agra district were even said to be very reluctant to lend to anyone who did not own irrigated land.[92] There were also sharp differences between the condition of labourers in different types of villages. During the 1838 scarcity, for instance, labourers in the parts of Kanpur District which supported large zamindari holdings received hand-outs from the zamindars who wished to keep their bands of labourers together. By contrast, labourers in areas of joint smallholding (*pattidari*) could expect little aid from their impoverished employers, and there were cases where whole communities fled to Central India.[93]

For labourers in both town and countryside, the little evidence available suggests that the 1830s were a period of decisive reverses in standards of living. In the late eighteenth century labour shortage had given them a certain advantage on the labour market which slow but steady population growth in the early colonial period gradually eroded. The decline of opportunities for service in local Indian armies and construction works by rajas and nawabs must also have affected them adversely. But during the 1830s, the relative depreciation of the copper currency against silver created a critical situation for people who were paid wages in copper and had to buy food and firewood. One indication of this is the rapid decline of government revenue from *abkari* or low class liquor shops.

The Abkarry Revenue throughout the provinces has suffered much from the scarcity of silver and consequent depreciation of the copper currency ... the Abkarry shop is supported principally by the sale of liquor to the labouring classes, who are in many instances paid their daily wages not in the fractions of a Rupee but by a certain number of pice without reference to the relative exchange. The labourer then finds that to supply his necessary daily portion of food takes all his pice and leaves him nothing wherewith to purchase the liquor of the abkar.[94]

92 Collr to Commr Agra, 15 July 1838, Agra Judl, 3, UPR.
93 Girdlestone, *Report on Past Famines*, p. 46.
94 Note, NWP Rev. Customs, 5 Jan. 1836, 221/85, IOL.

The general *abkari* statistics were distorted by local administrative arrangements, but the overall trend throughout the provinces was a sharp fall in revenue throughout the 1830s, with little evidence of recovery until the late 1840s.[95]

Labourers also felt the pressure directly. The fall in food-grain prices in the early 1830s did not compensate them for the consequences of the depreciation of the copper coinage, and besides, wholesale grain prices do not necessarily reflect actual local market conditions. One observer, for instance, noted that the price of grain purchased per *seer* in the Kydganj market at Allahabad had doubled between 1802 and 1833, though this was by no means reflected in official prices for the district.[96] Firewood, moreover, had doubled in price in less than five years, and this was a necessity of life in the cold north Indian winter. There is evidence also that the scarcities of the 1830s disrupted the system of free meals provided by employers which had once been a crucial part of a labourer's remuneration. Even the 'pinch' of salt which the petty dealer used to throw in with small retail purchases had become a thing of the past. In earlier years 'the poorer classes never bought salt but the Banyas threw a handful of salt with each "attadal" of split peas, but now it is not a handful and the saokars [*sahukars*] inform me that the Banyas do not take a ⅓ of their former quantity of salt'.[97] Indian statistics do not allow us to construct the sort of wage and price curves that have become a commonplace of European history. All the same, there is good reason to feel that the 1830s in north India did represent a 'conjunctural crisis' of the sort that significantly altered the economic standing of one section of the population in relation to others. Petty merchants, artisans and labourers appear to have fared particularly badly, and there is little reason to imagine that their position improved much before the 1850s when government and railway expenditure began to grow significantly.

In many respects, the 1830s were a faint echo of the 1780s, as far as the social conditions of the famine years were concerned. In both periods, the more stable eastern districts received large numbers of immigrants from the west and the upper Doab. Older patterns of social conflict and adjustment also reasserted themselves. Williamson's report on the 1783 famine had spoken of grain hoarding and looting bands traversing the countryside. In 1837/8 there was again widespread looting throughout the Agra and Rohilkhand Divisions by gangs of up to 1,000 men 'composed principally of half-starved people headed by some few daring

95 Statement showing the total *abkari* revenue by *pargana* and district from 1820–1 to 1840–1, NWP Rev. Customs, 12 Aug. 1842, 223/49, IOL.
96 BCJ, 17 June 1833, 140/41, IOL.
97 Patrol Officer Doab to CGC Agra, 8 Dec. 1845, NWP Rev. Customs, 30 Jan. 1846, 225/19 IOL.

or notorious villains and ... in some cases connived at by the zemindars out of enmity to the mahajuns because they discontinued their advances'.[98] In Shahjahanpur District during August 1837 there were eighty-three dacoities alone. Mewati and Rajput zamindars led their men against the towns and there was imminent danger of an attack on the grain markets of Jalalabad.[99] The Collector put landholders under heavy penalties to protect market villages with their own servants. In 1838 there was a series of savage grain riots in Delhi which was already disturbed by conflicts between European and Mughal officers in the city and rumours of political disturbance in the north-west.[100] As in the 1780s, social groups on the margins of the economy were easily pushed into internal plunder. Mewati military gentry resumed their depredations on the route between Delhi and Muttra. Further north, Gujar cattlemen turned to robbery once again as they did during every major political disturbance between the Chalisa famine and the 1857 Rebellion; and large bandit gangs which had been penned by British forces south of the Jamna erupted into the Ganges valley. For a short period the foundations of the Raj in Hindustan trembled, but as yet there was no defection from the military or police such as was to occur twenty years later.

The agricultural setback of the 1830s had begun with a 'liquidity crisis' and had been deepened by a periodic cycle of drought. Yet the vulnerability of agrarian society to these events may have been increased in some areas by a deeper exhaustion of productive forces in the countryside. In the less stable areas which had been brought under the plough so rapidly at the beginning of the nineteenth century, there was, by the 1830s, some evidence of falling yields, or 'exhaustion of the soil' as it was called at this time. N. B. Wright of Pulwul suggested that the problems of the depression had been exacerbated by the rapid pace of the earlier development. By 1827, 'most of the waste lands had been broken up and the quality of cotton considerably deteriorated from the want of new soils, and the repeated croppings from those previously broken up'.[101] According to Sleeman's informants among the peasants of the area between Delhi and Agra, their agriculture faced a general threat of 'declining fertility'. Besides the iniquity of an unbeliever's government, the main reasons given for the change was 'the want of

---

[98] Commr for Dacoity to Bd, 23 Aug. 1813, BCJ, Sept. 1837, 231/39, IOL.
[99] Collr Shahjahanpur to Commr Rohilkhand, 6 Sept. 1837, NWPCJ, June 1838, 231/48, IOL.
[100] See below, pp. 310–12.
[101] N. B. Wright, on Patrol, to Customs Master Delhi, 12 May 1836, in CGC Delhi to Bd, 16 May 1836, NWP Rev. Customs, 7 June 1836, 221/86, IOL.

those salutary fallows which the fields got under former governments when invasions and civil wars were things of common occurrence, and kept at least two-thirds of the land under waste'.[102] In the light of earlier findings, one could emphasise that the flexible nature of the pre-colonial political economy with its mobile peasants itself encouraged long leas and fallows independently of the incidence of civil war. This flexibility, however, had begun to disappear by the 1830s. The recovery of the tract from the 1783 Chalisa famine and the return of migrants had increased local population, reducing the scope for long fallows. Population per square mile may have increased from under 100 to at least 250 in the middle Doab districts during the first thirty years of the nineteenth century. But government revenue-demand also acted to keep areas under perpetual cropping. Thus in Pulwul, 'By degrees the zumindars found that the cotton no longer paid the revenue, which had been increased by its indirect means, till at last it has been discovered that the assessments are higher than the soil can possibly bear.'[103] In the absence of good manuring techniques, this was almost bound to happen since a large bush like cotton was likely to exhaust the soil much more rapidly than ordinary food crops.

Rapid expansion had other consequences which contributed to a setback in the medium term. The destruction of trees appears to have gone on very rapidly over these years, if anecdotal evidence and the price of firewood are put together. The subsequent change in local ecologies probably lies behind complaints in the 1830s of the 'rapid advance in recent years of the hot winds'[104] from the Rajasthan Desert which were now penetrating further east, drying out the soil and making the plantation of summer (*zaid*) crops more or less impossible. One can speculate also that the restriction of pasture by the spread of cultivation had reduced the large herds of cattle which Lambert and Tennant had observed in upper India in the previous generation, further limiting the supply of manure. As in other periods of rapid agricultural expansion, more was being taken out of the soil than was put into it. The significance of this apparent fall in marginal productivity on newly opened up agricultural land was heightened by the stasis which we have already noted in the areas which have been described as stable. Here in the central Agra District, or Allahabad or Baiswara, most good land had been brought under double cropping before 1800, and population density was edging over 400 per square mile. With a stagnant agricultural technology and limited capital, agriculture in these areas

---

102 Sleeman, *Rambles*, p. 413, cf. pp. 415–17.
103 N. B. Wright to Customs Master Delhi, 12 May 1836.
104 Butter, *Southern Oudh*, p. 48.

had already reached a plateau some time before the expansion outward began to lag.[105]

The recovery, 1843–57

By the mid-1840s Hindustan had generally recovered from the immediate effects of the Depression and scarcities. The cultivated area and population began a further steady expansion, as far as it is possible to determine from the poor statistics of the early censuses. Trade, down the Trunk Road and river systems at least, developed speedily with river steamers beginning to replace the slow wooden boats. But there were considerable variations in the rate of real recovery. Some areas such as Bundelkhand, Rajasthan and, possibly, south Awadh, never regained their relative prosperity. The outer, more unstable parts of several of the western districts also remained in the doldrums. The central part of Agra District, for instance, recovered rapidly; the 1839–40 harvest was only 30 per cent less than that of the year before the famine.[106] But in Bah and Pinahut, once great cotton growing regions, the devastation took a generation or more to repair. The area had lost more than 25 per cent of its population in 1838,[107] but there had also been much greater loss of cattle than in any other famine, including the Chalisa of 1783. On the other hand, some unstable areas benefited from the stimulus that scarcity gave to official and private investment in irrigation. In the north-west, the Ganges Canal began its slow creation and in forested Muttra:

The year of the great famine Samvat 1894, that is 1838 A.D. is invariably given as the date when the [forest] land began to be largely reclaimed: the immediate cause being the number of new roads then opened out for the purpose of affording employment to the starving population.[108]

The social context within which this patchy revival took place differed from the eighteenth-century pattern in some important respects. The role of courtly consumption in the economy and society was being steadily reduced. North India was beginning to resemble the classic 'colonial economy' in which exports of primary agricultural products were offset by imports of foreign manufactures, and in India's case, of bullion. The service people, artisans and mercenary soldiers

---

[105] Commander, 'The agrarian economy', pp. 281ff.

[106] Note by Collr (?) Aug. 1839, Agra Rev., 6, UPR.

[107] H. F. Evans, *Report on the Settlement of Agra District, NWP* (Allahabad, 1880), pp. 25, 32; Girdlestone, *Past Famines*, p. 39, for 'distress selling' of stock and permanent loss of capital by farmers during the famine.

[108] F. B. Growse, 'Braj Mandal', *IA*, i (1872), 66.

who had found service within the earlier princely systems were going through a period of dislocation, and, as yet, expenditure by the British government and westernised elites had failed to create a substantial alternative demand.

The position of Indian merchants in the state and agrarian society had also changed rapidly during this period of hiatus. Their links with British and Indian rulers had atrophied. Now that the great revenue systems were established features of the landscape, Indian merchants were not needed as guarantors, and district treasury bills had begun to replace the *hundi* as the basic instrument of official transactions. At the same time, the decline of the old luxury trades had eroded the merchants' role as kingly provisioners. But most seriously, the consequences of agricultural depression had been redoubled by the activities of the British courts which enforced the sale of land for debt. The huge loans which magnate families had taken during the depression years were now being realised. Commercial families often had little choice but to buy into land-rights in order to retain some benefit from the capital which had been immobilised in the form of advances to landholders. The Indian merchant moneylender has often been portrayed as a 'usurious capitalist', the carrier of an unproductive or stagnant form of entrepreneurship which did little but expertly cream off the surplus of the peasant family in the form of interest payments. But in the Indian states the usurious role of the merchant had often been offset in part by lavish royal expenditure and investment which the merchant community also helped to finance. Merchant, peasant, artisan and ruler had been part of a system in which it was not in the interest of one element to reduce any of the others to complete dependence. Many of the negative features attributed to the Indian bania in more recent times do not seem to be a product of inherent viciousness but of particular historical circumstances. In particular, his role changed in the absence of the lavish local elite expenditure and intrusive political authority which had once put limits to the consequences of his commercial ruthlessness.

The turning point of the 1830s also helps to put into new perspective other major events in the history of colonial north India. How, for instance, did it relate to that other, more widely known 'crisis', the Rebellion of 1857? The work of Stokes, Metcalf and Brodkin has provided us with splendid, detailed glimpses of the motivation of local participants in the Rebellion, and of its specific economic context. Yet it is always difficult to derive 'causes' of revolt from considerations of local circumstances alone. The actual level of land-revenue or the specific degree of penetration by moneylenders in particular areas may have been much less important than the general feeling that society was out of joint, or that the power of the infidel, the bania, or the low caste *arriviste*, was growing in some unspecified way, and ought to be diminished. Recent work has under-emphasised the wider political context of the revolt, and especially those broad, popular notions of good government and moral economy which have been so pervasive in all historic insurrections. Against this background, the Great Rebellion seems to have been a belated response to the political changes which gathered pace after 1825, and which had given such a jolt to dignities and livelihoods throughout north India without providing the lineaments of a strong new system such as emerged in Bengal and the Punjab.

The erosion of princely dignity was to prove to be an insistent theme in the ideology of the rebels. The proclamation of the rebel Nawab of Banda, for instance, bewailed the gradual impoverishment of the royal houses as pensions were reduced by inflation and subdivision so that 'the ample allowance for one person became a mere pittance for several individuals ... by which the number of attendance [sic] is also reduced'.[109] The disruption of lordships by an alien government was a fear which affected practically the whole of the old ruling classes; the proclamation of the Begum of Awadh dwelt on the fact that 'The Company professed to treat the chief of Bhurtpore as a son, and they took his territory; the chief of Lahore was carried off to London ... the Peishwa they expelled from Poonah Sitara; the Raja of Benares they imprisoned in Agra.'[110] But the disturbance was felt at a local level. Indeed the revival of the agrarian and commercial economy in the late 1840s and 1850s only heightened pressures on those notables and service people whose grievances had been submerged by the general distress of the 1830s. The sense of 'relative deprivation' became more insistent. In the Agra region where the anti-*taluqdari* settlements were particularly severe, ancient marriage patterns linking Rajputs of the British territories and those of the Indian states had been disrupted. In 1856 an officer warned pointedly: 'I believe it is not uncommon for them [the Bhadouria Rajputs] to state their expectations of eventually regaining their ancestral possession on our government giving way to some more powerful as the Muhomedan rule gave way to us.'[111]

The deflation of aristocratic consumption was also a grievance for the many fragments of the old artisan economies which had come under more severe pressure in the 1830s. In many *qasbah* towns throughout

---

[109] S. A. Rizvi and M. I. Bhargava (eds), *Freedom Struggle in Uttar Pradesh* (Lucknow, 1956–60), I, 22.

[110] Proclamation of Begum of Awadh, *ibid.*, I, 437.

[111] Collr to Commr Agra, 23 Feb. 1855, Agra Rev., 12, UPR.

the Doab and Rohilkhand, weavers, spinners and dyers proved an inflammatory element in the disturbances. Drawing on this hostility, the proclamation of the Azamgarh Maulvi denounced the import of European goods which had reduced 'every description of native artisan' to beggary. It added that under the government 'the native artisans will be exclusively employed in the services of the kings, the rajahs and the rich, and this will no doubt ensure their prosperity'.[112] The rebels even attempted to draw on resentment among the merchant classes to government monopolies and taxes, and the aspersions on their commercial honour made by 'worthless people' in the British courts. In fact where the rebels did elicit patchy support from merchant families, it was almost always from those like the Gurwala family of Delhi which had been closely tied in to the court provisioning of Indian powers. This broad context does not, of course, explain in detail why certain groups revolted and others in a similar situation did not. For this we need to fall back on detailed studies of the military situation and factional conflicts in the localities. But it is nevertheless useful to distinguish between immediate causes for rebellion and general preconditions which provided both grievances and justification for it.

Conclusion

The striking fact about the downturn of the 1830s in north India was the way in which a wide range of adverse climatic, ecological and monetary conditions converged. Yet it was, first and foremost, a crisis in the political economy. That is to say, it resulted from a disturbance of the links between state, commerce and agrarian society which had been established after 1740. The decline of princely consumption and agrarian patronage in the intermediate economy magnified the disruption caused by a political assault on the north Indian monetary system and the collapse of the false commercial economy which had remitted its Europeans' political perquisites to Britain. It was not a crisis of modernisation; it represented the impact on the Indian localities not primarily of European capitalism, but of a conquistador imperialism using Mughal methods to push for a degree of centralisation which the Mughals had never achieved. Even in those areas where 'soil exhaustion' and the end of agricultural expansion underlay these external problems, the context within which agricultural productivity began to fall was created by the pressures of the revenue system and the lack of state

---

[112] Azamgarh Proclamation, 25 Aug. 1857, repr. in R. Mukherjee, 'The Azimgurh Proclamation and some questions on the Revolt of 1857', in B. De (ed.), *Essays Presented to S. C. Sarkar*, pp. 477–98.

expenditure. Yet if this was a 'colonial crisis', it had particular features because of the very special implications of gift-giving, royal service and ritualised consumption within the Indian political economy. The only close parallel was in early colonial Java where the Dutch assault on the Hindu–Muslim polities unleashed a similar dislocation among service people and merchants who had supported their ritual and display.

In other parts of India similar disturbances took place, but less elided in time. In Bengal, the decline of the *rajwari* economies had come earlier, between 1770 and 1800, with the disbanding of the Nawabi armies and the pressures on the zamindari which accompanied the Permanent Settlement. The old service classes had already melted away, and the 1830s and 1840s saw instead the frustration of the indigenous Bengali commercial class. In the newly conquered Punjab, by contrast, the demise of the Sikh notables and their expenditure was consciously made good by the incoming British who bought acquiescence by military and civil expenditure.

8

Conflict and change in the cities, 1800–57

The next two chapters take up again the history of the north Indian city. Apart from Bombay, Calcutta and Madras, the towns of the early nineteenth century have not attracted much interest. It is only with the coming of local self-government and the political associations in the 1870s and 1880s that they have seemed worthy of attention. Yet the urban societies of the Company period are significant for several reasons. First, towns and bazaars supply evidence on what was happening in the cash-crop sector of the agrarian economy. Secondly, it is important to provide an historical perspective for the development of urban politics and association after 1870. Otherwise it is easy to fall into the trap of ascribing innovation entirely to the political impetus of the new imperial government, and to make a false antithesis between the unchanging traditional city and a dynamic western element. For, as chapter 4 showed, the corporate bodies which intervened between caste groups and the state in the Indian city had long been in the process of slow, unobtrusive development. When one strips off the varnish of western political discourse and organisation from the Young India associations of late nineteenth-century Hindustan, it is the institutions and solidarities of this developing tradition which are often discovered.

Thirdly, however, the city, like the small kingdom or the 'zamindari estate', is one of those institutions in which we can trace in detail some of the changes which dominated the history of the wider political economy. In particular there appear on a smaller stage manifestations of the problems of political authority which gathered pace in the 1830s. The decline of the city-wide institutions of the Indo-Islamic tradition and of the role of the ruler as arbiter of social equity had reverberations throughout the economic and social life of the cities, and exacerbated tensions between economic interests and social groups. The picture of the traditional Indian city as a house set against itself, divided into warring communities and quarters seems more appropriate to the hiatus of the middle of the nineteenth century than to any period before or since. This chapter will take up these broader themes by concentrating upon a number of outbreaks of disorder between 1800 and 1857. But first it is important to refer to some aspects of urban society which provided a background to all these conflicts – rapid population movement and poverty.

Taking the first half of the nineteenth century as a whole, there appears to have been a clear but not startling growth of the total population living in towns of over 5,000. The rate of urban growth may only marginally have exceeded that of the population as a whole. But this represented not so much the stagnation of a stable urban population as a sharp contention between forces pushing forward urbanisation and equally powerful ones tending to its decline.[1] On the positive side, the development of the commercial economy in the first half of the period drew into the entrepôt towns colonies of hinterland merchant people. They inhabited the new bazaars and *ganjs* which were being established by the authorities before 1830. Economies of scale encouraged the concentration of bulking, transport and insurance facilities on big towns such as Agra, Farrukhabad and Mirzapur. The horizons of petty entrepreneurial communities like liquor distillers, oil pressers and cultivators of *betel* nut were widened by the early expansion of consumption. Their immigration was maintained by the abolition of 'town duties' in 1836, which encouraged smaller dealers to sell in cities.[2] So if the typical new urban community of the eighteenth century had been the rising military gentry, in the early nineteenth century it was the

[1] For urban populations '10 years after Cession', I have taken NWP town populations from D. and B. Bhattacharya, *Report on the Population Estimates of India, 1820–30* (Delhi, 1965) and tried to adjust them against figures derived from *chaukidari* statistics for the period 1815–20 (BCJ and Mirzapur Judl, 28), and a number of other town censuses available in CPR, BCJ and private papers, IOL. The total numbers of houses have been multiplied by the relatively high number of 6 persons per house. Under- rather than over-enumeration was general because (a) persons tried to avoid *chaukidari* tax, (b) most cities were surrounded by urbanised gentry villages or cantonments not assessed, (c) town merchants lived outside city boundaries to avoid 'town duties'. Twenty-seven places with an assumed population of above 10,000 produced a total of 918,000 against a general population estimate (adjusted on W. Hamilton, *Gazetteer*, i, 412) of 13 million or 6.8–7%. Maps, descriptions and town duties material (CPR) suggest that there were another 72 places with populations between 5,000 and 10,000. Assuming an average of 6,000 in 1810, we have a total 'urban' population of 1,350,000 or 10–11%. (Another 3–4% may have lived in distinctly urban places with populations under 5,000.) Taking estimates for the same places, *c.* 1850 (NWPCJ, DG, etc.), we arrive at almost the same result on an NWP population of about 28 million, i.e. 10.8%. The population in the category of the towns over 10,000 had actually declined to 5.2% of the total while that in smaller towns had grown. Even allowing for considerable under- enumeration of the total population in the earlier estimates, urbanisation did not proceed very fast between 1810 and 1850.

[2] Mullick, *Bengal Commerce*, II, 49; not all institutional forces tended to increase city size; greater political security also encouraged small merchants and moneylenders to move out into district towns, especially in the west where trade had been more hazardous in the eighteenth century, C. Bayly, 'Age of hiatus' in Philips and Wainwright (eds), *Beginnings of Modernisation*, p. 88.

petty rural merchant group such as the Gurwala Banias of the west or the Umar of the east who were attracted by the spluttering growth of the export economy.

On the other hand, the decline of the military and royal establishments during the 'Age of Reform' contributed an almost equally sharp decline of both service and artisan communities, especially in the smaller towns. Economic historians may shrink from the 'deindustrialisation' thesis, but there is some evidence of the dispersion to the countryside of urban artisans in both the east and west of the region. More basic features of the economy and society also tended to limit the growth of towns and to increase their instability. Regional specialisation in agricultural produce had increased in the first thirty years of the century, but the shocks of the 1830s set it back, along with the growth of entrepôt towns to which it gave rise. Epidemics also kept the survival rates of town-dwellers low. Scattered figures suggest that it is possible to exaggerate the degree of endemic disease in north India's cities,[3] but great epidemics like those of 1817 and the mid-1830s carried off large numbers.[4]

Quite apart from longer-term movements associated with economic and political changes, periodic subsistence problems which resulted from bad seasons also ensured that the size of towns and the composition of their populations varied greatly from year to year. During the scarcities of 1817–18, 1833 and 1838, for instance, Agra, which had always had difficulty in guaranteeing its food supply, lost up to one-third of its total population[5] as people took up well-tested options of emigration to other cities or to the villages. In the small towns of still unstable areas like Kumaon, it was customary for heads of families to decide every season how many dependents they could afford to support. Others were sent off to live in the countryside for the duration.[6]

The limitations on the growth of Indian cities were largely economic and political, and there is little evidence to suggest that the close, exclusive organisation of trades and professions in itself inhibited urbanisation. Where the incentives to live in cities were strong enough, immigrants merely bypassed the caste and corporate organisation of the

---

3 See, e.g., Delhi computations, 'Results of an enquiry concerning the law of mortality for British India', *AR*, xx (1836), 190–3.

4 Severe epidemics were recorded in 1818–19, 1833 and 1838; they coincided with famines and periods of military activity. Basic statistics are available in BCJ and NWPCJ in the form of surgeon generals' reports on the work of dispensaries established from 'local funds'; see also *Delhi Gazette*, 17 Jan. 1838 (death from disease of 75% of population of town of Palli) and Sleeman, *Rambles*, pp. 163, 232.

5 E.g., Magt. Agra to Superintendent of Police, NWP, 30 Nov. 1817, BCJ, 27 Jan. 1818, 134/40, IOL; cf. Agra Judl, 17–19, UPR.

6 'Notes on Almorah and Srinagar', *AR*, xvi (1828), 151.

residents and created their own 'alternative' urban society in shanty towns on the city fringes. In Delhi during the 1810s and 1820s, for instance, large numbers of impoverished people of mixed caste from the thirsty and war-torn tracts of Rajasthan continued to move into the city in search of subsistence and protection. They set themselves up as a petty labour market outside the tightly organised and relatively prosperous neighbourhoods of the resident Chamar labourers who were secure in their own patronage relations with the leading families of the city.[7] In time, such communities generally established a tenuous internal organisation and a place in the *jajmani* system. But a substantial pool of free labour appears to have existed in most cities, and the decline of the aristocratic households tended to keep it replenished. Conflicts between immigrant groups and established urban communities therefore added to the many social tensions which afflicted centres suffering quite rapid dislocation of population.

Though it is almost a truism for pre-industrial cities, the great extremes of wealth and poverty in urban life must be emphasised. In the first decade of the century, as much as 47 per cent of the permanently resident urban population was exempted by the British authorities from the payment of the police tax on grounds of poverty.[8] Poverty was defined as a net household income of less than Rs. 3 per month, and contemporary discussions of the diet of jailed prisoners suggests that this was very near the cost of bare subsistence.[9] The house tax figures also suggest that the percentage of poor townsmen was highest in places such as Allahabad or Jaunpur where a large artisan population existed alongside an impoverished group of aristocratic consumers.[10] The richest cities were those such as Chunar, Mirzapur or Benares, where the population was largely mercantile and connected with cash-crop trades. This is confirmed also by figures for the rate of town duties per head which is a rough guide to consumption of goods and food other than grain. But even in commercial centres, the fluctuations of the

[7] Note by Civil Commissioner, Delhi, BCJ, 14 Feb. 1820, 134/36, IOL.

[8] Chaukidari Statistics, 1814–16, Mirzapur Judl, 28, UPR.

[9] Discussion of the revision of allowances for prisoners' food in jails, Magt. Agra to Commr, 27 Feb. 1838, Agra Judl, 7, UPR.

[10] *Chaukidari* assessments were based on supposed household income; for the poor, the system was formalised, viz. 2 annas for a merchant, 1 anna for a weaver, etc.; but above the standard rates of 3 as. an attempt was made to adjust to the relative wealth of household; bearing in mind all the many objections to the value of such figures it is still striking that Mirzapur (pop. *c.* 40,000) registered 946 households above 2 annas in 1818; comparable figure for Agra (*c.* 120,000) was 339, for Moradabad (*c.* 20,000) 144, for Meerut (*c.* 15,000) 107, Saharanpur (*c.* 20,000) 165, Bareilly (*c.* 70,000) 169, Allahabad (*c.* 20,000), 144; very high numbers of 'exemptions on grounds of poverty' were recorded at Allahabad, Jaunpur and Bareilly, Agra Chaukidari Report, 1817, BCJ, 16 Dec. 1818, 135/51, IOL.

export trades created instability in incomes for the labourers, artisans and transport specialists who subsisted on secondary employment in the cash-crop sector. Urban wealth also attracted large numbers of beggars and indigent religious men to commercial cities.

Poverty, however, was not confined to the plebeians. In many cities it was sections of the old nobility who suffered the sharpest relative decline of their fortunes over the period. They were replaced by a variety of eighteenth-century revenue entrepreneurs, officials in British service and landholders who had managed to benefit from the febrile commercial booms. Real indigence among the Mughal aristocracy of Delhi and the Pathans of some of the western towns was a source of constant comment. The transfer of urban property into the hands of moneylenders and other new men was as striking in the towns as it was in the countryside, though it has received no attention. Much Muslim property in the Chandni Chauk area of Delhi was mortgaged to merchant families before 1857, and in Agra there was hardly one substantial Muslim family of the old order left by 1840.[11] In Benares the pensions of most of the Muslim and Maratha princes who had settled in the city at the end of the previous century were in the hands of Bhumihar landlords and bania merchants before 1830.[12] Reckless and indebted younger sons of noble families living on pensions reduced to a few rupees a year joined with street gangs and provided a constant source of alarm to the authorities during this half century.[13]

The chapter now turns to a consideration of conflict and social control in the colonial towns. Of course poverty and oppression provided a constant background to urban conflict and revolt in the early nineteenth century. But material deprivation alone was not usually enough to create organised opposition to the colonial authorities, or sustained contention between different groups of townsmen. This was more often the result of some violation of the political or moral preconceptions of the population. The erosion by the colonial authorities of the power and status of the old officers and institutions of the towns, therefore, had consequences in every area of urban control. Yet this is not to suggest that eighteenth-century towns had been free of conflict. On the contrary, changes had already taken place in the relations between ruler,

---

11 'List of respectable native residents of Agra and District', Magt. Agra to Govt, 28 Feb. 1843, Agra Judl, 10, UPR; the city's *mufti* and *kazi* families are mentioned, but great dispossession of Muslim landowning families had taken place in the periods of Jat and Maratha control between 1770 and 1802.

12 Agency Records, Persian, UPR, and papers of Lala Sangam Lal, Shiwala, see below p. 423, n. 81.

13 Commr Bareilly to Govt, 3 Oct. 1829, BCJ, 8 Dec. 1829, 139/46, IOL.

town magistrate, and neighbourhood corporation before the British set out to restructure them.

Urban government under strain, 1760–1800

The chief official functionaries of the north Indian city in the late Mughal period were the *kotwal*, a chief executive and police officer, and the *kazi*, the chief registrar who was also a kind of censor of morals. These officials were associated with an individual called the *mufti* who was a less formal representative of the Muslim faithful of the city and a link with the doctors of law (*ulama*). In the ideal situation, *kazi* and *kotwal* were themselves checked and regulated by the emperor's 'grand almoner' (*sadr-i sadr*) and by the imperial spies who were supposed to exist in the main centres.[14]

Beneath the *kotwal* there were various officers of watch and ward, notably the *muhtasib* who controlled markets, market morality and weights and measures:[15] these consulted and advised the notables or *mohulladars* who were representatives and controllers of their urban neighbourhoods. The *kotwal's* duties consisted of patrolling roads, keeping a register of houses, and reporting on travellers at public resthouses. He should 'name one of every artisan guild as a guild master and another as a broker', and from them he received the graded dues which were the equivalent of the land tax. There was a strong moral, even religious, sanction to the smooth working of city life. The *kotwal* was supposed to work through the faithful and public-spirited citizens, 'engaging them in pledges of reciprocal assistance and binding them to a common participation of weal and woe'.[16]

The *kazi* was an agency for the registration of property transactions and other public undertakings, but it was unusual for him to intervene in a transaction unless called upon to do so by the representatives of the neighbourhood. As a 'censor of morals' he was supposed to enforce public righteousness only when the force of public opinion embodied in periodic religious and caste assemblies had been unable to do so. He was supposed to check on marriages and the circumcision of (Muslim) youths and register the deaths and proper burials of citizens. Public women and 'bad characters' were supposed to be confined to appropriate quarters and kept under close control by him. The *mufti* was a respected member of the local *ulama* who could seek out and express Islamic opinion. This was done by informal consultation with the teachers of religious schools and the connections of Sufi teachers and

---

[14] S. P. Sangar, *Crime and Punishment in Mughal India* (Delhi, 1967).
[15] *Seir*, II, 565.   [16] *Ain*, II, 41.

pupils centred on the landholding *dargahs* of Sufi orders (*tariqas*) which played an important role in most north Indian towns.[17]

In the central Islamic lands, the theory of urban government appears to have conflicted with its practice. The *sharia* law recognised no privileged status for one group of the faithful over another. There were no guilds and corporations with autonomous legal status which could be delegated royal power as in the cities of medieval Europe. Thus the associations of merchants, artisans and clerisy which existed in these cities were originally no more than instruments of the state through which the sultan carried out his duty of maintaining the material life of the faithful. In practice, however, the very unspecific nature of the sultan's role in society meant that local bodies acquired the status and privileges of autonomous guilds. In India the conflict was resolved in the system established by Akbar's eclectic mixture of Indian and Islamic forms of government. Hindus already had what amounted to corporations in the form of caste and occupational councils (*panchayats*, *mahajans*, *sabhas*, and so on), and these were bound to retain much autonomy since the status of caste and occupational custom was recognised in Islamic courts. It was a fundamental principle of Hindu thought that the status of different groups of subjects differed in accordance with their sanctity, even 'generic substance'. This notion, along with its corollary, the idea that the raja was one who 'maintained the balance of castes', was in effect absorbed into the norms of the Islamic government. During the heyday of the Mughal empire, the autonomy of the various segments of the city was recognised, but the ruler intervened constantly to maintain equity.

The autonomy of corporations of subjects increased over much of the country between 1600 and 1800. First, the Mughal administration and its successors were forced to leave more and more of the details of local control to powerful bodies of landholders and Hindu princely lineages. In Benares, for instance, the Bhumihar zamindars had by 1740 established the right to establish and tax their own household marts. These grew into some of the city's greatest bazaars, and were largely outside the control of the emperor's *kotwal*.[18] Powerful Muslim landholding gentry also maintained or achieved privileged status in the towns as well as the countryside. In Lucknow, for instance, the ancient Sheikhzada family held considerable power in the outlying neighbourhoods and was able on several occasions to outface the power

---

[17] E.g., Khairuddin, 'Jaunpur', pp. 57–9; Report of Ibrahim Ali Khan, 7 Mar. 1788, PR; for details of Sufi orders see, e.g., Rahman Ali, *Tazkira Ulema-i Hind* (Lucknow, 1914).

[18] E.g., Resdt to Judge Benares, 27 Apr. 1796, PR.

of the Nawabs in their own capital.[19] When we also take into account the growing power of the commercial corporations, it becomes clear that the situation at the end of the eighteenth century was a series of balances and accommodations between powerful local property-owning and mercantile bodies and the representatives of a weakening but still legitimate central authority. At most administration was like a continuous judicial enquiry, active on behalf of powerful individuals or groups when alerted, but passive at other times. This was true in areas as different as property relations, police organisation and price formation in the bazaars. Let us take some examples from the Benares area.[20]

The *kotwal* and *kazi* only appear to have intervened where other methods of control or conciliation had broken down or were in doubt. In a case of debt during the 1770s, for instance, the creditors and other people with an interest in the case behaved appropriately according to mercantile custom when they 'plundered' the defaulter's property in order to make a distribution on the basis of equity. A more formal adjudication and redistribution by 'approved *mahajans*' might follow, but only in the last instance would the *kotwal*'s authority be introduced and the case be referred to the city court. In the same way, bodies of private citizens had the right to distrain a defaulter's goods and those of the whole of his household. Only if there was a danger that he might escape would application be made for a *kotwali* guard to be stationed at the house.[21] A similar set of assumptions governed the communities' relations with the *kazi*. Deeds and transactions were only automatically registered where they related to the ruler's own rights over bazaars or houses. Other deeds were only registered in cases of conflict or doubt. This remained the case well into the nineteenth century, and the usual manner of proving property rights was by a sworn statement of the 'men of the *mohulla*' or neighbourhood. The local community also jealously guarded its right of 'vicinage', that is, pre-emption of houses within the gated area.[22] Policing in several cities was also left to the neighbourhoods, and the *kotwal*'s function was merely to arrest and imprison offenders.

This was a delicately balanced system, and even under a judicious ruler there was a problem of access to the arbitration of *kotwal* or *kazi*. But in the late eighteenth century, these offices were decaying from

[19] Sharar, *Last Phase*, pp. 37–49.
[20] Some cases were tried in the Resident's Court, or the City Adalat, but the legal forms employed were late Mughal, for background, 27 Jan. 1788, PR; Saletore (ed.), *Benares Affairs*, II, 63–138; the forms date back to the *Hedaya* Islamic code, see, V. Kennedy, 'Abstract of Muhammedan Law', *Journal of the Royal Asiatic Society*, ii (1835), 112–20.
[21] Case of Khushaly Ram Dube, 7 Mar. 1788, PR.
[22] *Arjun Giri* v. *Munoo Royder*, 1 Dec. 1790, PR.

within at the same time as their functions were reduced by the power of corporations or landed gentry. Political conflict in Delhi[23] meant that the Mughal sanction and the Mughal charter could be acquired more easily, so that the possibility of conflicts over rights and jurisdictions was enhanced. Mughal princes in exile and persons who had bought or usurped offices and jurisdictions spread discord to provincial cities. According to Ghulam Hussain,

the office of cazi is leased out, and underleased ... we see everyday faithless cazies who are ignorant of the principles of Mussulmanism, and worse in their lives than so many renegadoes and so many atheists, take leases of what they call cazie's rights and underlease them to others.[24]

Imperial *farmans* became a stock in trade for forgers, while Mughal princes in Lucknow, Benares or Patna demanded rights and perquisites simply because of their imperial blood. In some cities respect for the legitimacy of the Mughal officers had also been impaired by the religious disputes which arose after Aurangzeb's lurch back towards a harder Islamic position. Periodic conflicts over the Gyanbaffee mosque in Benares and the Sulaiman Mosque in Ajodhya appear to have become endemic before 1750. Some Muslim law officers supported their own religious community in these incidents and consequently forfeited the confidence of Hindu residents.

The moral decay of the *kotwal*'s and *kazi*'s office, notable in the cities of the east, encouraged powerful zamindars to vaunt their own power more vigorously. The princelings of the new Hindu house of Benares began to assert their jurisdiction over bazaars simply by raising a flag and beginning to collect transit duties. The raja's own *mulki* court also began to invade areas of jurisdiction that had once fallen under the purview of the emperor's officers.

Not only in villages but in the towns and renowned cities the servants, the the favourites, the dependants, nay very often, the very spies and emissaries of a zemindar, having wiggled themselves into the service of Government commit upon the inhabitants a variety of oppressions and exactions.[25]

Not least among these usurping new men were the officials of the East India Company who were gradually undermining the independence of the judiciary both inside and outside the territories which they formally controlled as diwan. Though his power was later broken, the agent of the Company's chief at its transient Benares Factory was already acting like 'kotwal, faujdar and mint master all in one', as early as 1765. With power tipping towards the magnates and the British, more and more

---

[23] Sauda, *Kulliyat*, cit. Russell and Islam, *Three Mughal Poets*, p. 61.
[24] *Seir*, II, 557.   [25] *Seir*, II, 559.

people moved over to them for protection, and older forms of control were weakened.[26] In Patna, Ghulam Hussain saw gaming shops, brothels and public houses springing up. The streets were filled with 'drunken butlers and sepoys . . . especially the servants belonging to the English'.[27]

The old Islamic elite, mindful of the *sharia* and the glories of the past, naturally saw these events in the darkest terms. To Mir these were times when 'the face of the earth and heaven has changed'. But it is possible to exaggerate the decline of the old forms of authority in the towns. In Rohilkhand and Farrukhabad and the west, for instance, the *kotwal* and *kazi*, fortified by the authority of the ruling dynasties and Sunni *ulama*, presided over forms of arbitration which were not essentially different from those of Akbar's time. The changes initiated by the British in Benares after 1782 and in the west after 1802, slowly departed from these norms, however. In the early nineteenth century there was not so much a revolution of modern administration as an erosion of older authority. The old order and its methods became outdated, but there was nothing much to replace it. The role of the ruler lost many of its moral connotations. Justice was administered; peace was kept. But the British lacked the will and the information to intervene in matters of morality and religion. The change was even reflected in the physical layout of the cities. The royal palace, located near the mosque, had usually been near the centre of the cities. The ruler appeared regularly in state, distributing charity and honours and continuously participating in the everyday ritual life of the city. The new administrative offices of the British were generally well outside the old cities. Austere bungalows with Palladian frontings reared themselves on distant hills. Khairuddin Hussain noted how the new British collectors kept themselves physically apart from the declining town of Jaunpur.[28] This, he implied, further damaged its status as a set of interlocking moral communities.

'Bind over' and rule: the British system

In the eastern districts and Bengal, the British had evolved a system of control for towns. This relied on the collector's darbar, civil courts and a downgraded *kotwal* for compromising major disputes, but leaned heavily on powerful men in the *mohullas* for the day-to-day running of urban communities. The old pan-urban law officers – the *kazi*, *mufti* and *kotwal* – gradually saw their power eroded by the Bengal Regulations and British magisterial ordinances. The judicial function of the *kazi* as

26 Bolts, *Considerations*, III, app. c, 300.
27 *Seir*, II, 565.   28 Khairuddin, 'Jaunpur', p. 3.

interpreter of Muslim *sharia* law was superseded, but men of *kazi* families were sometimes used as legal advisers to the courts in cases of Muslim law. Under Bengal Regulation 39 of 1793, which was later extended to the Conquered and Ceded Provinces, the *kazi*'s duties were confined to attestation of deeds of conveyance and superintending Muslim marriages and funerals.[29] The *kotwal* also lost his judicial power and became a subordinate, often a despised subordinate, of the district magistrate, with control of a small number of police matchlockmen.

The transition was sharper in the provinces ceded or conquered after 1801. Not only was the decline of the *kazi* and *mufti* families sometimes precipitate, but the secular, utilitarian approach of the British magistrates and law courts tended to eliminate whole areas of moral and social jurisdiction. Despite the straitened circumstances of late eighteenth-century Allahabad, city-wide adjudications on Muslim law or questions of Hindu custom continued to be held. But these were ceasing to operate as early as 1814, and 'synodical assemblies and their censures for pollution of caste, heretical conduct, debauchery, gambling etc. are fast falling into disrepute and not upheld by our institutions'.[30] The British made some symbolic gestures, such as restoring and repairing the great mosques in Allahabad and Meerut,[31] but city-wide institutions appear to have decayed quite rapidly.

On the other hand, the tight, clan-based bodies of individual quarters and the eighteenth-century corporations retained much of their vitality and independence from official intervention. The bodies of merchants, ascetic traders and powerful urban landholders who had aided the British in their rise to power saw their influence grow as the pressure of superior authority was removed from them in commercial matters. As for the guild-type organisations of the artisans and labourers, their survival depended on the play of the labour market and the predilections of the ruling power. In some areas where labour was plentiful and employment in the old services had collapsed, as in Patna[32] or Jaunpur,[33] the influence of the headman (*chaudhuri*) was quite rapidly superseded. Elsewhere, as in Benares where the Muslim weavers combined and used court action in the face of deteriorating economic conditions, magistrates displayed hostility towards guild action and price-control.[34] Often laissez-faire arguments were introduced to disparage the activities of such bodies. Yet where the labour market was not on their side, the British civil and military authorities found

29 Bengal Reg. xxxix, 1793; Wilson, *Glossary*, p. 272.
30 Report of Magt. Allahabad, 1 Sept. 1814, Home Misc. 776, IOL.
31 Petition of Kazi Hayat Baksh *et al.*, 25 Feb. 1816, BCJ, 13 Apr. 1816, 132/40, IOL.
32 Buchanan, *Patna*, II, 700.   33 15 Mar. 1788, PR.
34 CGC Benares to Bd, 23 July 1813, CPR, 13 Aug. 1813, 97/56, IOL.

themselves buttressing and perpetuating the office of *chaudhuri*. In Delhi in 1819–20, for instance, the civil authorities had issued a regulation that

craftsmen, workmen and labourers were not to be procured by direct application to the police officers, but by applications to the headman of each class or description, which headmen are endowed, appointed and authorized servants of the class [sic].[35]

The military officers complained that this interposition of the headmen had undermined their control of labourers, who now turned up after sunrise and complained about rates with which they had formerly been satisfied. It appears that the civil officers and private European citizens of Delhi could only be guaranteed labour by inheriting the system of precedence which had supplied Mughal grandees in their dealings with occupational communities. The reinforcement of old institutions was not confined to the Mughal capitals either. In Mirzapur orders were issued as late as 1833 that *kotwals* should not interfere with the provision of labour but 'refer applications to the proper chowdry who has been established by the natives to attend to the wants of the *European* [ringed] inhabitants'.[36]

It would be simplistic to say that traditional institutions and precedences were destroyed by the influence of the market and the colonial bureaucracy. But two processes appear to have been general. The first was the collapse of the wider institutions of urban control which had bound the *mohulla* and occupational corporations together. The second was the growing influence of the commercial and landholding elite of the cities as a class of notables unfettered by the power of the old rajas and the influence of the law officers. There was a perceptible shift from institutions to elites, even if the power of the elites was still buttressed by their roles in religious bodies and by caste precedence. The elites came from a number of origins. Some were notables of the merchant corporations who had worked along with public and private European capital for many years. Others were members of ex-ruling families who had compromised with the British in return for pensions and the continued control of private fiefs. Others still were the great eighteenth-century 'enterprisers' such as Sheo Lal Dube of Jaunpur, Deokinandan of Allahabad and Dharam Das of Agra. Often the establishment of British rule in the towns merely signified their capture by some great magnate who had access to both landed and commercial wealth. In Jaunpur for instance, Dube, 'one of the most

[35] Note by Civil Commr Delhi, 10 June 1819, BCJ, 14 Feb. 1820, 134/36, IOL.
[36] Magt. Mirzapur to Col. Davis, Chunar, 7 June 1833, Mirzapur Judl, 82, IOL.

artful and mischievous, as well as one of the most opulent and powerful men in our provinces', completed the decline of the old *maulvi* families of the city and established a near-monopoly of power. Besides being farmer or zamindar of almost all the land in Jaunpur District by 1816 his relations controlled the *kotwali*, the local revenue courts and the *tahsildaris*.[37] He established a mansion near the Atala mosque, the moral heart of old Jaunpur, and one official estimated that his family income was greater than the total income of all the other inhabitants of the city.

The system adopted in the early days of colonial rule, then, was a curious mixture of moral suasion, administration and neglect. The British loosened the ties which bound together corporations and neighbourhoods by weakening the power of the rulers and the law officers. Justice and taxation in some areas was effectively contracted out to powerful new magnates; in others it was left in the hands of pensioned-off maharajas or nawabs. The moral role of the headmen of occupational groups was sometimes eroded, but their administrative authority was strengthened. An important tool in this job of 'contracting' was the *ikranamah* or 'bond to keep the peace'.[38] Notables and heads of corporations were summoned to the collector's bungalow where they entered into written agreements to control riot and arrest offenders at the risk of losing large cash securities. Thereafter the European magistrate normally stepped outside the ring.

Social control and the 'market'

Some more general conclusions about social change in colonial north India flow from this. Much of the anthropological literature assumes that 'traditional' occupational and caste institutions continued in pristine form until some time, usually 'about 1900', when they were transformed by the forces of economic and political modernisation. But the evidence from the earlier period suggests that these institutions, like the network of caste relations in larger villages, had been continuously modified by the impact of the state and of the money economy. This had implications for the nature of social control in the colonial period. The 'market' and the impact of the colonial state did not undermine existing forms of social organisation, but moulded them. In particular, the 'market' for shares in the proceeds of the rights which rulers and occupational groups held in various services, continued to develop. For instance, hereditary sweepers (untouchable Chamars and Doms) who

---

[37] Second Judge Benares to Register Nizamat Adalat, 19 Dec. 1813, BCJ, 12 July 1816, 132/43, IOL.

[38] Lit. 'a compulsion to act contrary to one's own will', Wilson, *Glossary*, p. 215.

collected ordure from household latrines which opened out onto the streets held particularly important rights which were allocated as hereditary 'beats' to a particular family. The scavengers made a living by selling 'nightsoil' for manure to zamindars who lived on the fringes of the towns but they also 'received gifts of clothes, food and occasionally money at different seasons and on the occasion of births and marriages'.[39] Nightsoil 'shares' were already farmed to bidders under the Nawabi government,[40] but with the value of manure rising again at the beginning of the nineteenth century more and more scavenger families took to mortgaging their beats to outsiders. Their vital domestic position which was reinforced by the fear of pollution made it possible for them to combine against house owners to extort higher fees, and a regular system of leasing and sub-leasing grew up in these rights.

Practically every area of the service economy saw similar developments. The rituals of death and oblation in the holy centres had always been highly commercialised. But before 1850 funerary officiants and hereditary ancestral priests (*pandas*) were resorting to British courts to fight over the proceeds of these services which became increasingly subdivided between different branches of families.[41] A related phenomenon is what is best described as 'bazaar caesarism'. The British had formally abolished most types of duties on 'professions' (*prajawat*) at the beginning of their rule; they went on to abolish 'town duties' and landholders' taxes on small bazaars wherever they could. But the spirit of the eighteenth-century system survived. Descendants of the 'ancestral' owners of bazaars continued to lease and even underlease their supposedly extinguished rights to local strongmen who managed to collect large sums from the bazaar people.[42] Rights which had formerly appertained to *kotwals*, bazaar headmen and weighmen were also rented out or sold informally wherever local power could exact a rupee from dependents.

What was happening in these small corners of cities and in the most established rural *ganjs* was simply another example of the direction of change in the political economy as a whole. British rule and the opportunities for export had not really initiated a free market or

[39] Jt Magt. to Commr Agra, 26 Apr. 1839, Agra Judl, 8, UPR.
[40] Magt. Muttra to Commr Agra, 15 Mar. 1839, NWPCJ, June 1839, 231/59, IOL.
[41] Adjudications between bathing priests had formerly been private and were entered in the *khatas*, see, e.g., Phatakh *panda* book, Benares, p. 231 and *passim*; sanctions of the law courts were similarly brought to bear on cases between *ghat manjees*, note by Commr Benares, 6 Mar. 1832, Mirzapur Judl, 2, UPR: cf. 88 of 1848, Allahabad, Dec. 1848; 75 of 1849, Mirzapur, Sept. 1849, ZC.
[42] For the constant sub-letting of bazaars see Mirzapur and Benares Judl, UPR throughout, e.g., case of 'Turnbulganj' Magt. to Commr, 4 Apr. 1854, Mirzapur Judl, 95; same to same, 15 Sept. 1854, Mirzapur Judl, 96.

undermined the headman system. What occurred was that the commercialisation of 'shares' in the perquisites of authority, which had been a marked feature of the eighteenth century, was progressing at a local level. Almost every right or perquisite (including most notoriously the right to engage for revenue) was now up for sale. But what made the sale worthwhile was that *within* the 'little dominion' which was being put on the market, competition and the free market were still excluded. Here, political muscle, the authority of the headman and the rights of caste rank continued to operate to produce cash, labour or commodities. Thus while rights to engage in scavenging came on the market, it did not mean that outsiders could employ their own labour in this area without first submitting to the authority of neighbourhood leaders of the Chamars.

What explains this peculiarly limited form of commercialisation? First, of course, the colonial state and its agents had very similar requirements to its immediate predecessors. On the one hand, it required ever increasing and regular quantities of cash revenue, which encouraged the authorities to bring as many 'shares' into the cash nexus as possible. On the other hand, the need for social control and financial security predisposed district officers to deal with a few powerful individuals who could be held responsible for conflict or default.

But pressures working within Indian society pointed in the same direction. Leasing and sub-leasing of rights had the advantage of releasing aspiring individuals from direct contact with occupations which were degrading, while at the same time guaranteeing a cash income for them. Too open access to the human units of labourers or producers would undermine the value of the share and also devalue the social position of the headman by creating competition from others both inside and outside.

These considerations also help to explain the features of social mobility in nineteenth-century India. At any time from the mid-eighteenth century onwards, one can point to examples of lower caste families rising to wealth and honour within the community. Lists of works of 'public utility' maintained by magistrates in Agra and Benares mention distillers, tailors, oil-men and water carriers establishing wells, tanks, temples and public wharves.[43] But the logic of the status system and the form of commercialisation both required that this should be a flexible, but not an 'open' society. Those who had passed through the gate had a strong interest in closing it behind them. Yet by the same

[43] See, e.g., *Muhammadan and Hindu Monuments*, I; 'Abstract of Works of Public Utility constructed by Individuals at their own private cost, Zillah Agra during the year 1839', Agra Judl, 1843 vol. (number missing); cf. 20 July 1845, Agra Judl, 13, etc., UPR.

token, we cannot speak of unchanging, traditional institutions. For both the state and the market had played a part in modifying relationships which superficially seemed to be played out in the same ideology of shares and redistribution.

This also has a bearing on the nature of opposition to colonial rule in north India. In some non-western societies (East or South-east Asia or Africa, for instance), 'capitalism' and the colonial state are held to have broken down existing forms of elite control and created large problems of vagabondage, dispossession and resistance. What is most striking about the Indian case is the fragmented and temporary character of mass revolt throughout the colonial period. In general, popular resistance to the British was widespread only in the wake of resistance by the elites. The form of administration and the limitations of the market both helped to preserve colonial control. But it was not only the institutions of control in settled society which remained strong. Early nineteenth-century judicial and police records also reveal how coherent were the institutions of what was regarded as the 'criminal', alternative society. The complex and disciplined organisation of such bodies as the Thugs and Pindaris has long been part of the Anglo-Indian canon. But these were only the most striking examples. The villages around Delhi, for instance, each maintained carefully delimited 'beats' in which they, and only they, were allowed to rob.[44] Forgers, counterfeiters,[45] Gujar and Banjara bands which turned to plunder from time to time – all these had *panchayats* and forms of organisation which could closely direct their activities. By coercing or binding over the headmen of such groups, or the zamindars and moneylenders who supported them, the authorities were able to restrict 'criminality' to an acceptable level. Even the social organisation of beggars when it is fitfully revealed in the records appears to rival in ordered complexity that of the highest Brahmins.

The definition of marginal people in the Indian case is therefore by no means easy. For the early colonial period absolute destitution seems more characteristic of those caught between the tight organisation of the recognised labouring castes, on the one hand, and the 'counter society' of robbers, mendicants and wandering people, on the other. Such were the respectable beggars, the secluded ladies in Muslim families where the husband had died, the drifting destitutes from war-torn or famine-ridden tracts. Yet these pools of unorganised and uncontrolled destitution do not appear to have grown large enough for them to

---

[44] *Delhi Gazette*, 5 July 1837.
[45] 'Thana Daroga's List of Forgers, Agra District', Magt. to Commr Agra, 30 Dec. 1853, Agra Rev., 8, UPR.

constitute a distinct or turbulent social force in their own right. Death from famine or disease, absorption into the groups of robbers operating around *sarais* and *hookah* shops or into the corporations of mendicants must have constantly operated to diminish their size.[46]

The many revolts which took place in the towns and bazaars of north India during the early nineteenth century were not, initially, spontaneous eruptions of the poor. Society was too closely organised by its informal leadership for this. Dissidence almost always arose because the British had shaken this informal leadership by discontinuing accepted procedures or threatening to overturn popular expectations about the role of government.

Taxation and resistance to the colonial government

The early nineteenth century saw a number of outbreaks of urban dissidence directed against aspects of colonial rule. At three points, during the taxation protests of 1810–19, the food crises of the 1830s and the Rebellion of 1857, these assumed a serious and general form, attracting support from urban labourers and country people. The potential for organised and articulate opposition to colonial policies existed much earlier than is commonly assumed, though there was no coordinated general leadership.

These revolts took place in the commercial east of the region as well as in the more turbulent and military western districts. Indeed, some of the most serious early outbreaks occurred in Benares city which was regarded as a safe base for British north India. Cheyt Singh's revolt of 1781 against the Company had involved most of the great Bhumihar and Rajput magnates as well as a large number of townspeople. Warren Hastings had received the ambiguous support of the Naupatti bankers of the city who were themselves in dispute with the Raja, as well as the direct aid of one branch of the Bhumihar elite led by Babu Ausan Singh.[47] It was on these bases of support that the British were to build until 1860. But there were several later tremors. Vazir Ali, an exiled contender for the throne of Awadh, staged a revolt in 1799.[48] He killed the British Magistrate of Benares, but receiving little active support in the city retired into the marches of the Benares territory. Here a number of the Rajput clan chiefs who had been in almost perpetual conflict with the Benares rulers since the rise of Balwant Singh, took him under their protection. Yet even in this case, there was concern amongst the British

[46] Deposition of Gokul Brahmin, 17 Dec. 1849, Mirzapur Judl, 44, UPR.
[47] Hastings, *Narrative of Insurrection at Banaris*, pp. 12–28.
[48] Agent Benares to GG, 28 Feb. 1799, PR.

officials that Vazir Ali retained commercial relations with some of Benares' banking magnates, and rigorous enquiries were made among them.[49]

A serious outbreak of communal violence over one of Aurangzeb's 'converted' mosques occurred in 1809 and several commercial magnates defied British moves to enforce a settlement on this occasion. However, the most revealing episode was the mass protest against the newly instituted tax on houses which occurred in 1810 and 1811.[50] Act XI of 1810 provided for the imposition of a general tax on house property for the support of local police, watch and ward. It was intended to replace an earlier system of contributions by the gated areas of the city (the *phatakhbandis*) which was operated by the communities of the different *mohullas*. The response of the townsmen was sharp. A programme of petitioning and oath-taking organised by *mohullas* and occupational groups was followed by the general closure of shops and a mass picket in which as many as 30,000 people may have taken part. Working through the Raja, the family of Ausan Singh and a leading Naupatti banker, Babu Jumna Das, the local authorities managed to quieten the situation. The house tax was withdrawn and continued to be operated in its earlier form through the individual councils of each *mohulla*. But the incident became an important object lesson for Benares and other dissident towns.

There were a number of significant features in these events. First we see the reappearance of some of the complex forms of community organisation which had been active during the eighteenth century. The cross-caste organisation of professional corporations and the large, mixed-caste *mohullas* was utilised. But so were the tightly bound councils of the artisan and lower castes in which caste and occupation were more congruent: for instance, masons, ironworkers and weavers. In fact, 'every class of workmen engaged unanimously in this conspiracy', to the extent that rites for the dead at the *ghats* and all commercial transactions ceased.[51] These revolts make it clear again that the commercial and artisan groups of Indian cities were capable of joint action; and also that the plural organisation of living quarter, caste and occupation existed as part of a wider universe of political and religious notions. Again, there were significant links between the townsmen and the surrounding countryside. During the height of the protest 'several thousand Lohars, Khoonbees, and Khorees were enticed [sic] from

49 Agent Benares to Govt Pol. Dept, 24 Nov. 1812, PR.
50 BCJ, 1811, 130/27–9; these events have been analysed in R. Heitler, 'The Varanasi house tax hartal of 1810–11', *IESHR*, ix (1972), 239–57.
51 *Ibid.*, p. 245.

their village homes and collected here by this excitement'.[52] There was no question of the city being a world of its own; it was the cultural centre of most rural groups and the political centre of the dominant landholders. And finally, it appears that the main objection was not economic (though it was felt that a further tax fell hard on the impecunious Brahmins, *sannyasis* and widows who inhabited the city). Opposition was basically to the principle of direct taxation on property which was held to violate both the *sharia* and the *shastras*,[53] though some radical *ulama* of the Naqshbandi order followed Shah Abdul Aziz in considering *all* British taxation illegitimate.

Similar events occurred during 1815–17 in other urban areas when the British attempted to introduce a more general regulation for chaukidari tax. Most towns protested by means of large numbers of formal objections, the rich and powerful simply omitted themselves from the rate lists. But there were more serious outbreaks in Muttra and the Rohilkhand towns. In Muttra, the powerful organisations of Vaishnavite ascetics which had been reinforced by the violent events of the Durrani invasion withdrew cooperation from the local authorities in conjunction with some commercial people. After operating a kind of *dharna* on the magistrate and following him to Agra, representatives of the religious houses were finally prevailed upon to agree to assess themselves for a minimal tax along with the 'heads of trades'.[54] The agreement was formulated so that it in no way infringed the corporations' hard-won rights of self-government, and even exempted their representatives from punishment should the institution fail to pay.

These were not isolated incidents. The 'contumacy' of the Benares crowds of 1810 was quoted as a reason for the violence of the outbreak in Bareilly in 1816. Moreover, quite sophisticated political ideas were circulating in the province at a remarkably early date. A judge with his ear to the ground reported some of the rumours which were circulating in the Benares Bazaars in 1813. Dissidence arose from:

The Assassination of Mr Percival [the British Prime Minister] the dearth of cash which they attribute to Lord Minto's having dispatched all the money to England to pay a heavy claim of the King against the Company; the renewal of the Company's Charter; the system which will be established if the charter is not renewed; and, the probability that if the exclusive charter ceases, the Company's creditors will all be cheated out of their money.[55]

[52] *Ibid.*, p. 247.
[53] Benares Petition of 3 Jan. 1811, BCJ, June 1811, 130/29, IOL; cf. Kennedy, abstract of *Hedaya, Journal of Royal Asiatic Society*, ii (1835), 92, 109.
[54] Magt. Agra to Govt, 23 Dec. 1816, BCJ, 10 Jan. 1817; Magt. Agra to Bd, 30 Dec. 1816, BCJ, 17 Jan. 1817, 133/6, IOL.
[55] Second Judge Benares to Register Nizamat Adalat, 12 Jan. 1813, BCJ, 12 July 1816, 132/43, IOL.

This early version of the 'Drain of Wealth' theory of the Indian nationalists was confounded with rumours of trouble on the northern frontier, general opposition to the house tax, and a deep suspicion of what were seen as government attempts to interfere with the 'custom of the merchants'. According to this observer, since 1810 the Benares Hindu population had developed 'new tactics' which should be 'cudgelled out of them' rather than 'being shown that whenever they please they can cow not only the less numerous sect to whom they are hostile; but the Hakim [ruler] himself who ought to be an impartial and intrepid arbitrator between the two'.[56] These last remarks were a reference to the threatening tactics adopted by merchant and Brahmin corporations when a Muslim tried to slaughter a cow in the Aurangabad *sarai* against custom and precedent. The grumbling of Benares, however, was nowhere near as serious as events elsewhere.

Throughout the early nineteenth century, the western districts of the North-Western Provinces proved consistently more turbulent and rebellious than the east. A history of armed robbery ('dacoity') in districts such as Aligarh culminated in widespread revolt throughout the Doab and Rohilkhand during 1857. After the Rebellion, the towns of the west retained their reputation for turbulence though this more often took on the character of strife between Hindus and Muslims. Eric Stokes has explained the different regional incidence of the Revolt of 1857 in terms of the emergence in the east and the riverain tracts of 'new magnates' who had done well in the cash-crop trades and were more disposed to support the British Raj.[57] Robinson[58] has suggested that the greater incidence of Hindu–Muslim conflict in the west resulted from the rapid commercialisation of the area after 1860 which set Muslim gentry against Hindu traders. No doubt there is some force in these arguments. But it must be emphasised that the different social and political patterns of the two regions were already established very early in the nineteenth century before the impact of the new commercial growth had been registered. In fact, it was with the legacy of the Rohilla polities that the British collectors were grappling throughout the following century.

In the east Mughal institutions and the Muslim fiscal lords had already given way to new Hindu dynasts and the commercial corporations before the onset of Company rule. The British benefited from the stability created by the new magnates of the eighteenth

---

[56] *Ibid.*
[57] Stokes, *Peasant and Raj*, ch. 5.
[58] F. C. R. Robinson, 'Municipal government and Muslim separatism in the United Provinces, 1883 to 1916', *Modern Asian Studies*, vii (1973), 389–441.

century. In the west, however, they were faced with the rapid decline or dislocation of the Islamic systems of government which had still remained intact on Cession in 1802–6. These problems of understanding and working indigenous institutions were compounded by the often violent response of elements of the gentry of the west to the loss of their dominance within the states which had emerged in the previous century.

One of the most spectacular armed outbreaks against British rule between the Cession and the 1857 Rebellion took place in Rohilkhand during April 1816.[59] The ostensible cause was the method of collection of the new house tax which the British had introduced in large towns throughout the Provinces in 1814. A savage urban riot, centring on a Muslim holy man, spilled over from Bareilly to the nearby small towns, and embittered Rohilla armed gentry converged on the city from the surrounding countryside. In the conflict which took place between the insurgents and the exiguous British forces between 200 and 300 men were killed. The newly reared edifice of British rule trembled slightly, but the Provincial Battalion of Rohilla conscripts to British arms held firm, and a number of palliative measures were rapidly applied.

The interest of this event lies partly in the way in which it foreshadows the course of the 1857 Rebellion in Rohilkhand, but partly in the insight it affords into the social organisation of the Rohilla townships at a point before the changes induced by British rule had proceeded very far. This was a typical 'post-pacification revolt'. The final goad was the hated *takas* (tax) which threatened to put influence in the hands of 'mean and low' collectors. But the local decline of the Rohilla gentry was the real cause. Mercenary income was rapidly being curtailed. Warfare in west and central India was coming to an end as Amir Khan, ruler of Tonk, disbanded his large forces of Rohilla mercenaries. Openings in British employment were limited; and besides, the first campaign of Rohillas under British arms against the Nepalese Gurkhas had proved a fiasco with both the new rulers and their Pathans losing face. The Rohilla gentleman who needed at least Rs. 30 per month to support his expensive equipment, horses and servants, was caught in a vice. Service and mercenary income was becoming more unsure at the very time when heavy British land-revenue assessments were beginning to erode what little income remained from his rural grants and landholdings.[60] The pinch became excruciating in 1814 and 1815 as European war and bad harvests pushed up the price of grain to

[59] Correspondence and subsequent investigations are preserved *in extenso* in Magt. Bareilly to Govt in Judl Dept, 18–21 Apr. 1816, BCJ, 10–16 May 1816, 132/41, and 25 Oct. 1816, 132/47, IOL; see also *DG Bareilly*, p. 167.

[60] Magt. Bareilly to Govt, 18 Apr. 1816, BCJ, 10–16 May 1816, 132/41, IOL.

new heights throughout the region. Moreover, the bitterness of the Muslim gentry and their supporters converged ominously with opposition among the Hindu merchant classes to taxation and what was seen as British interference with matters of trade custom. For traders the possibilities of resistance had been illustrated by the 'resistance of the mob at Benares' in 1809 which was 'in everyone's mouth'.[61] Finally, the issue was envenomed by factions amongst the city's leading merchants and hatred of the new Hindu *kotwal* of the city widely regarded as a 'man of mean origin' who had got above himself through connection with the British rulers.

Dumbleton, the magistrate of Bareilly, attempted to have the house tax collected through the chief men of the quarters of the city. These *mohulladars* were in the main descended from the Rohilla clan leaders and other military and commercial notables whom the early Rohilla rulers had induced to settle in the city during the 1740s and 1750s. The city was bound together by a series of ancient blood and patronage relations between the headmen of the *mohullas*. At the same time, however, there existed an informal religious organisation based on the mosques of the *mohullas* and the teacher–pupil relationship of the city's major Sufi orders. When trouble broke out, both these patterns of organisation moved into opposition against the colonial authorities. First, one of the main *mohulladars*, Mahomed Isa, refused to have tax collections made in his *mohulla*, and large crowds gathered in defiance of the collectors. Mahomed Isa had recently been discharged from the service of the Nawab of Tonk, and failing to secure a pension from the British, he was in dire financial straits. Next the crowd turned for support to the ancient *mufti* of the city, Mahomed Ewaz, who presided at a mosque near the main bazaar and was also associated with a venerated saint's tomb, the Shahdana, on the outskirts of the city. The *mufti* was traditionally a leader of the local Muslim community and the law officer who expounded the law to the civil administration of a city. Popularly, *mufti* Mohamed Ewaz was the learned man who intervened with the authorities on behalf of people who had suffered some injustice. In his petition he stated that from the time of Hafiz Rehmat Khan and the Nawab of Awadh 'whenever I interceded on behalf of the people they [the rulers] consented to my request'.[62] But now even the poor were assessed for tax 'although they possess nothing but the clothes they wear [and] some indeed are in want of daily bread'. The *mufti*'s opposition to house tax had a more overtly political strand also. He is reported to have

[61] *Ibid.*
[62] Transl. of address of Mahomed Ewaz, 27 *Rabi* 1231 *Hijri*, BCJ, 25 Oct. 1816, 132/48, IOL.

regarded house tax as 'a sort of *jizya* on the Muslims and therefore an insult to Islam'.[63] The *jizya* was a tax traditionally levied by Muslim rulers on non-Muslim subjects, and the *mufti* seems to have viewed this 'Christian' tax as a symbol of the end of Muslim political dominance. For him India was no longer a land of Islam, but *dar-ul harb,* a land of war in which *jihad* (holy war) was possible.

It was when the crowds began to think that the *mufti* was in danger of arrest that the real explosion of mob anger began. A very large crowd retired to the Shahdana mosque in the outskirts and the green flag of holy war was unfurled. The British moved troops and cannon to surround the rebels.

At this stage, the revolt moved into its second phase and spilled over into the surrounding countryside. Chapter 3 showed that the Rohilla towns and townships were the creation of a unified Pathan ruling group. The strong connection between the various tribal elders continued through the bad days of Awadh rule and were reinforced by marriage and a rota system by which Pathan mercenary gentry took it in turns to fill the dwindling military positions offered by the remaining independent states. Within hours of the outbreak of Bareilly, armed bands of Pathan horsemen supported by Hindu zamindars and villagers were on their way to the scene of the trouble. As Henry Dumbleton wrote: 'Aonla, Budaon, Tissoah and every town without exception supplied its quota...'[64] These were all lineage centres of the major clans. Particularly alarming from the British point of view was the mobilising of forces in the semi-independent state of Rampur which had since 1774 been the moral centre of Rohilkhand, and in the backwoods district of Pilibhit where the Pathans had traditionally located their redoubt and final line of defence. Religious organisation continued to play an important role in the rapid spread of the movement. The contingent from the small town of Bilaspur, for instance, was headed by the chief Muslim judge (*kazi*) of the town. Yet religious and secular fears continued to reinforce each other as far as their supporters were concerned; members of the force which assembled outside Bareilly said

---

63 Siddiq Hasan, 'Tarikh-i-Qanauj', Aligarh M.U. MSS., pp. 266–9; Mahomed Yaqub, *Akmal-ut-Tawarikh* (Badaun, 1331 AH), pp. 46–7. I am indebted to Dr Iqbal Hussain Aligarh for these references; he has established that Siddiq Hasan was a close relation of Mahomed Ewaz and a member of the Naqshbandi order; and that his father was a disciple of the famous Shah Abdul Aziz of Delhi, becoming a follower of Sayyid Ahmed of Bareilly who initiated a religious war against the British in the north-western mountains (see, Rahman Ali, *Tazkira Ulema-i Hind*, Lucknow, 1914, pp. 24–5). Key members of the Rohilkhand *ulema* were thus closely related to the more militant strain of north Indian Islam.

64 Magt. Bareilly to Committee of Investigation, Bareilly, 20 Aug. 1816, BCJ, 25 Oct. 1816, 132/47, IOL.

that they had rallied to the green flag because they wanted lower land-revenue assessments and also hoped to obtain more 'appointments' from the British.

In the semi-independent principality of Rampur a group of dissident gentry 'hoisted the holy flags on the Jumma Musjeed [Friday Mosque], interchanged oaths, and declared to all persons that whoever was a true Moosolman should assemble under the flags and unite with them',[65] for a march to Bareilly. An anonymous pamphlet claimed that the *kazi* and *mufti* of the town, as well as its governor, had joined the movement initially, though later, 'with the wiliness of a Cashmerian' the governor had made a show of loyalty to the British government when the defeat of the outbreak at Bareilly became known.[66]

This pattern of gentry mobilisation had been followed when Hafiz Rehmat Khan made his stand against the Nawab of Awadh in 1774.[67] It was to be followed again during the Revolt of 1857, though on this later occasion joint action with the Hindu zamindars soon broke down.[68] However, in 1816 the rising was concerted with a Hindu commercial revolt in the centre of the old city. The principal 'Banians and muhajuns' joined the crowd at the Shahdana and one of the chief sugar merchants of the town, Kumao Mull, played a decidedly ambiguous part. What was striking was the forward role played by the well-organised and cross-caste group of commercial magnates whose resistance appeared at first to be more implacable than that of their peers at Benares six years earlier:

The Bunneans and Saokars were from the beginning particularly active in forming a band of union among themselves which should resist an individual application (for payment) and defeat every effort to divide or persuade them.[69]

Relations between the Muslim *mufti* and the Hindu bankers were close and the Muslims persuaded the Hindus that their religion was also in danger from the onset of infidel government. This solidarity should not surprise us. Communal relations in Rohilkhand had always been good. Indeed the Shahdana shrine which was the centre of resistance had

65 Agent to GG in the Ceded Provinces to Govt, 24 April 1816, For. Sec. Procs, 18 May 1816, NAI.
66 Transl. of pamphlet entitled, 'How the Afghans of Rampur took part in the Mufti's Revolt', For. Pol. Procs, 25 May 1816, NAI.
67 'The alarm of war having spread, numbers of Afghans from Mau and Farrukhabad and the inhabitants of Katehr, both subjects and strangers obeying the instinct of clanship gathered around Hafiz Rahmat ... zamindars of the Rajput tribe, who had lived in peace under his rule, came in troops to support him without summons', Sadat Yar Khan, 'Gul-i Rahmat', tr. Elliot and Dowson, *History of India*, VIII, 311.
68 See below, p. 365.
69 Bareilly Committee's Report, 25 Oct. 1816, BCJ, 25 Oct. 1816, 132/47, IOL.

been built by a Hindu Khattri governor of the town in the Mughal period. For all their Sunni intransigence, the Rohilla rulers had cultivated good relations with the Hindu commercial groups. They had insisted on the precedence of Muslim religious ceremonies but at the same time had abolished internal customs and patronised the leading merchants. The decline in communal relations in the area came later – during the 1830s.

It was only the speedy suppression of the revolt in Bareilly which prevented its spread to other, larger towns. Throughout November 1814, the inhabitants of Moradabad had held nightly meetings at mosques and at the house of one of the leading local Rohillas to concert plans against the house tax.[70] It was rumoured that the population, both Hindu and Muslim, had agreed to abandon their homes and encamp as a sort of mass picket around the magistrate's house. The constant movement of armed men between Moradabad, Rampur, Bareilly and the army of the Amir of Tonk, made it possible for local leaders to collect information readily. Moradabad, therefore, requested a stay of execution of the house tax until 'Bareilly, the chief town, had accepted taxation'.

A final element of revolt – as in all urban risings – was the participation of artisans and day labourers, especially dyers, 'weavers, shoemakers and bricklayers'.[71] From time to time, they were joined by the indigent of the bazaars, mostly of the Gujar caste. These events indicated that the British had not yet perfected their local system of control. In the early days of conquest, they had usually been able to rely on the support of the Hindu commercial groups, but official bungling and insensitivity had alienated the Company's most likely supporters. Attempts to make contact with the rebellious religious establishment through the Muslim law officers working with the British law court at Bareilly did not prove successful, and the British were thrown back on their last, military line of defence. The key differences between this outbreak and the much more serious events of 1857 were that the military did not mutiny and that the leading Pathan family, that of Hafiz Rehmat Khan, deserted the rebels after an initial flirtation. In 1857 it was to be Khan Bahadur Khan, a grandson of Hafiz Rehmat, who welded the rebels into a more lasting union. Nevertheless, the union that temporarily emerged in 1816 is interesting in that it revealed the eighteenth-century political order of the city working together against the new conquerors. The Hindu commercial groups and the Muslim

---

[70] Magt. Moradabad to Committee Bareilly, 11 June 1816, BCJ, 25 Oct. 1816.
[71] Bareilly Committee's Report; it appears that artisan protest only came about *after* *mohulladars* had opposed government collectors.

mufti were in communication. There is no sign of religious, caste or urban–rural cleavages which have so often been taken as the universal features of the Indian city. The commercial classes also took an active, political role.

The vast majority of historical revolts have involved issues of taxation. But it was the principles rather than the weight of taxation which underlay opposition to these novel British imposts.[72] Hindu and Muslim law books approved stinging taxes on moveable wealth in some cases, but houses were always held to be exempt. The levy of taxation also had a distinct ideological connotation. It was after all, an act of exchange – the exchange of coinage as tribute for protection. Men were ranked according to what they gave and received. The British concept of taxation was based on different assumptions. These related to a theory of individual obligation and civic duty and tended to the welfare and utility of the community. Simply put, an individual had an obligation to provide according to his means, whereas, in the Indian case, it was a ruler's duty to give exemptions according to a man's honour. This underlay the concern at Benares that the houses of Brahmins, *sannyasis* and widows (persons in 'perpetual mourning') should not be taxed. There was a profound objection to any system which not only released police spies into the neighbourhood communities, but which also invited people of dubious origin to assess others' status and honour as represented in exchanges with the rulers.

Everywhere people preferred various forms of indirect taxation such as 'town duties'. In many instances, these were quietly adopted over the next fifty years to take the place of the house tax. A tax on imports into cities was the most acceptable form. This was similar to what was supposed to have been the original form of taxation in India – the *chungi* or handful of grain or produce taken from the passing cart and bullock-load.[73] Here only the mercantile community would be compromised by direct contact with the lowly servants of the rulers. Another acceptable form of taxation was the impost on occupations and transactions within the bazaars of the town which could be adjusted through the headmen of the respective market or occupational group. However, both these forms clashed with the British notion of good government. Transit duties (especially those on grain) came to be regarded as undue interference in the market or 'restraint of trade'; while a tax on 'professions' as opposed to income was held to be objectionable in a

[72] Cf. J. C. Scott, *The Moral Economy of the Peasant. Rebellion and Subsistence in Southeast Asia* (New Haven, 1976).
[73] For a discussion of British and Indian taxation systems see, Commr of Saugor and Nerbudda Territories to Govt, 7 Aug. 1854, NWPCJ, Aug. 1854, 223/78, IOL.

system of administrative law which was still self-consciously reacting against feudal notions of status.

Yet some officials continued to appreciate the practical advantages of the indigenous system. T. Fortescue noted after various clumsy attempts to reform the town duties of Delhi in 1816–17:

I found in short that an astonishingly large revenue continued to be realised by a process which was extremely delicate and refined and yet easily conducted and in a manner free from irritation and discontent.[74]

These taxes were legitimate and absorbed into the system of ranking in the city. Insiders could be used to work them. The British and their Indian servants who were generally outsiders found it more or less impossible to command the same level of information. In fact, where the house tax functioned in a manner which was at all satisfactory, it was when virtual self-regulation was allowed to the *mohulla* communities, and indigenous conceptions of rank were satisfied with wholesale exemptions for men of status and religion.

Much the same was true of the town courts and police establishments. These worked best when they acknowledged their dependence on the existing informal agencies of urban control. For instance, the lowest civil courts of the towns (the courts of the principal *sadar amins*), sent commercial cases to be adjudicated by bodies of 'respectable *mahajans*', and this practice was made formal under Act IX of 1839.[75] Besides a great rush of litigation about book debts owing to moneylenders in the towns or large markets and some substantial land cases, north Indians resorted to British courts very little in the first half of the nineteenth century. Cases of reported crime were few and the number actually brought to trial infinitesimal. Magistrates and police officers frequently noted this in their reports, and concluded that the vast majority of disputes and offences must have been dealt with in their localities by informal tribunals or the adjudication of the chief men of the *mohulla*. Even if such local redress was not forthcoming, resort to the police would be likely to detract from a man's local position. The 'expense, tedium and intricacy'[76] of the British court system was well known, and in many towns large-scale businesses in forged deeds and court papers existed. People were able to protect themselves only by arranging private justice and dacoities.

Similarly, the vast mass of property transactions never came into the purview of the British administration. In the past, the *kazi* had been

74 T. Fortescue, 'Report on the Customs and Town Duties of the Delhi Territories, 1820', *Delhi Residency and Agency*, p. 134.
75 See, *Zillah Court Decisions NWP* (High Court, Allahabad, c. 1840–60).
76 Magt. to Commr Agra, 30 Dec. 1853, Agra Judl, 8, UPR.

introduced when the opinion of the neighbourhood was divided, yet royal justice could be bought as a service. Respectable people were even less likely to bring their deeds and documents to the reduced registrary of the early colonial period. Yet while the *mohulla* community appears to have remained relatively impervious to the new agencies of the colonial rulers, the pan-urban authorities represented by the old law officers and the authority of raja and nawab were gradually eroded. The decline of these authorities was an important condition for the spate of violence between communities which occurred in the early nineteenth century.

'Redistributive justice' and the grain market

According to the popular traditions which derived ultimately from the Puranas and the 'sayings of the Prophet' rulers were entitled to take huge forced loans and to tax in a manner which would now be considered inequitable since those of lower status were liable to contribute more. What they were not expected to do was to disturb those statuses by forcing people into relations of giving and receiving with government officials or neighbours of low status. Incoming British officials tried to rectify what they saw as oppression of the poor in the interests of the rich or the ritually superior. But the forms of taxation which they devised often compromised statuses and impaired their own control. There was, however, another side to the concept of the just ruler which throws light on the social strains which emerged in the early colonial cities. This was the idea that taxation ought to be matched by reciprocal disbursements in the form of periodic distributions of coin (*nisar*) or of grain in time of famine. In a sense, the success of the ruler itself was judged in terms of the degree of opulence he displayed, the amount of 'service' he created. The British had difficulty in following these standards of conduct also. Their government was notably parsimonious and obsessed with retrenchment in the later days of the Company. If they built edifices they were likely to be 'jails and courthouses' not the temples and *imambaras* of the past. Most seriously, the official mind became more and more hostile to any form of intervention in the grain market whether by public distribution or coercion of the grain traders.

During the famines of the 1780s those British officers who held executive power in Indian cities tended to follow the practice of Indian rulers. The export of grain was forbidden, bounties were given for its import, and in Benares Jonathan Duncan even attempted to intimidate the grain merchants by issuing at drumbeat regulations against hoarding.[77] But there was already some resistance to the practice of

[77] Girdlestone, *Past Famines*, p. 3.

distributing coin or grain on the grounds that it was detrimental to public order. The French editor of the *Seir* noted with horror that public distributions of grain were usually accompanied by riot and death;[78] much better, he thought, to lower the price of the commodity. But equally, the distribution of coin by local officials violated the standards of accountancy and fiscal probity which the Company strove hard to maintain. The sums in question were quite large. During the Chalisa famine, for instance, the Nawab of Awadh had given out Rs. 5,000–10,000 daily, besides employing up to 40,000 people in the construction of the great Imambara. It is true that the British in Kanpur raised Rs. 1 lakh for famine relief during this terrible year, but this was from private, not public funds. During the early nineteenth century, direct state aid was rarely forthcoming and the revenue authorities were notoriously reluctant to give substantial remission even during catastrophes such as the drought of 1833/4. The British instead insisted on the technique of 'relief works', that is to say, paying indigent people to labour with gangs constructing roads and other projects of 'public utility'. There was a strong prejudice against direct support of any sort. At points during the year 1838/9 as many as 250,000 people in the Agra Division were employed on works of utility and gained a very basic subsistence.[79] But here again the colonial authorities were in danger of compromising deeply felt notions of honour and status. High caste Hindus and *ashraf* (respectable) Muslim families were reluctant to participate in labour gangs with common workmen and peasants; in the past, it had always been possible to send a household servant to join in the scrummage for charitable distributions organised by Indian rulers. But families of high status also were distressed by the 'want of service' and the disappearance of the great grain pits which accompanied the decline of the royal economies.

Even more difficult for the colonial authorities to come to terms with were popular expectations concerning the intervention of the government in grain markets. The Indian grain trade was fragmented and poorly articulated. Grain was pumped out of the villages through a variety of mechanisms which could easily break down in times of scarcity. But it had to pass through the hands of a number of intermediate dealers before reaching the consumer.[80] In most towns, wholesale grain traders bulked the produce of many small farms which was then sold to commission agents or *arethias*. The *arethias* then sold to city retailers. There were, then, three points at which prices were formed and where the flow of grain could be interrupted in times of

[78] *Seir*, II, 438n.
[79] 'Report of Agra Relief Society', BCJ, 10 Mar. 1838, 231/47, IOL.
[80] E.g., Magt Agra to Govt, 20 May 1817, BCJ, 6 June 1817, 133/11, IOL.

crisis and conflict. In many areas also, the smooth running of the trade was further prejudiced by the fact that groups of grain dealers were divided along social as well as functional lines. So, for instance, the rural dealers who brought food to Delhi were generally Jains, while the city retailers were almost all Vaishnavite Agarwals.[81] In this situation, the officials of the ruler, above all the *kotwal*, who promulgated the reigning market prices (*nikhas*), had a clear function in keeping the flow going through intervention and even on occasions through outright coercion. It is not possible to say how far this proved productive or otherwise, but the important point is that there was an expectation of intervention by the ruler. The British faced two severe problems in fulfilling these expectations. In the first place the gradual demise of the old Muslim law officers made it difficult for them to secure adequate information or control over the grain markets. And secondly, the growing strength of laissez-faire philosophy in ruling circles at home and in Calcutta discouraged local officials from paternalist measures which they might otherwise have taken. The whole question of regulating the grain trade had been a particularly contentious one in late eighteenth-century England when the old market controls had been lifted,[82] and once they had forgone the right to tax the grain coming into the cities of the Western Provinces in 1809, most high executives were happy to encourage measures of 'free trade' when and where they could.

Local officers with their ears nearer the ground were much more likely to favour the old methods of paternalist intervention. An interesting case arose in 1817, for instance. During this year persistent reports of starvation in the cities of Agra and Farrukhabad and a messy dispute between the civil and military authorities of Agra about grain supplies[83] encouraged the Provincial Superintendent of Police to search for a means to punish what were seen as criminal acts by the grain dealers who had been accused of hoarding and forestalling the market. He called for a *fatwa* (pronouncement) of the Muslim Law officers of the Provincial Court as to whether there was a *sharia* punishment 'for a person who has collected large stores of grain with the intent of selling them at exhorbitant prices at a time of scarcity'.[84] The learned men issued a *fatwa* on 'forestalling' and 'monopolising' which they declared could be punished at the discretion of the ruler, most appropriately by flogging. The higher authorities, however, would have nothing to do with the intrusion of criminal law into the market. They rejected the

---

[81] E.g., Petition of Khwaja Hussain *et al.*, NWPCJ, Dec. 1838, 231/51, IOL.

[82] E. P. Thompson, 'The moral economy of the English crowd in the eighteenth century', *Past and Present*, 1 (1971), 89–94.

[83] Commr Agra to Govt, 20 July 1841, Agra Judl, 16, UPR.

[84] Proceedings of Suptdt Police Western Provinces, BCJ, 27 Jan. 1818, 143/40, IOL.

distinction that local officers were inclined to make between 'natural' and 'artificial' scarcities caused by hoarding. On the contrary, according to the doctrines of free trade, high prices in a bad year were beneficial because they created an atmosphere of economy and stimulated the entrepreneurial instincts of merchants who would bring grain into a scarcity area. At the most, officers should hold consultations with the major grain dealers in order to avoid conflicts which might be detrimental to public order. Even the practice of forbidding export of grain from scarcity areas, which had been a cardinal point of Indo-Muslim political economy, was discouraged.

These problems came to a head during the bad years at the end of the 1830s. It is interesting that in Delhi during 1837 and 1838 riot and tumult derived from the decision of British officers both to intervene in and to stay out of the grain market. These events, however, were more than simple crises of subsistence, for they also reflected the local impact of the general crisis of the old order which we have seen as characteristic of this decade. It was during the 1830s that the British Commissioners of Delhi attempted to sweep the remnants of Mughal authority from the city and restrict it to the area within the walls of the Red Fort.[85] One part of this campaign was to curtail the influence of the imperial court over the city *kotwal* by replacing an official of standing in Muslim eyes by one who was much more at the beck and call of the local magistracy. This policy produced racial and administrative conflict[86] which reverberated in many areas of urban life, including the grain markets.

The growth of civil disorder in Delhi during the great famine of 1837/8 reflected not only physical starvation but people's response to the actions of their rulers. The outbreak of 5 October 1837, for instance, followed the decision of the Commissioner, T. T. Metcalfe, not to force grain dealers to bring down prices.[87] He thought that this would have conflicted with the Bengal Regulations, but the population of the city believed that his decision conflicted with the duty of a just ruler. There was a general expectation that government would act. A mob of 'Purbias', refugees from the east who had come to Delhi in search of food, attacked grain merchants' boats moored on the river.[88] They were joined, first by Gujars, members of Delhi's indigenous wage-labouring class, and later by ordinary citizens of Delhi who themselves looted the looters. Popular anger was fuelled by the knowledge that grain was selling for 22–25 *seers* per Rupee in peripheral wholesale markets while it

[85] Narayani Gupta, *Delhi between Two Empires* (Delhi, 1980), pp. 10–11.
[86] *Delhi Gazette*, 27 June 1837.
[87] For an Anglo-Indian discussion of these events, *Delhi Gazette*, 8 Nov. 1837.
[88] *Delhi Gazette*, 11 Oct. 1837; Petition of Chinsukh Bustee Ram and other grain dealers, Jt Magt. to Offr Commanding Delhi, 7 Aug. 1837, NWPCJ, Aug. 1837, 231/37, IOL.

was selling for under 12 *seers* for the Rupee in the retail markets.[89] The reason was that the grain merchants were conserving stocks in the wholesale markets and in some cases only using Delhi as an entrepôt on the route to even more famished areas such as Gwalior. However, this was the point at which the ruler would have been expected to intervene to protect the subsistence of his subjects. It is interesting that even when rioting broke out, it was rumoured that the government had itself sanctioned the redistribution of grain, and the only stocks looted were those which had already been appropriated by the Gujars and 'Purbias'. Ordinary grain merchants were left untouched, as were stocks of cloth.

A problem almost exactly the opposite of Metcalfe's faced the city's joint magistrate, John Bell, when he moved to intervene much more directly in the markets during the following year. As the scarcity deepened during the winter and spring, Bell became increasingly angry with the great wholesale merchants of Delhi whom he suspected of diverting the city's adequate food stocks for the purposes of profiteering in other parts of the country. But relations between the joint magistrate, the mercantile community and many sections of public opinion were already poor.[90] He was suspected of conniving to increase direct European control of the *kotwal*'s office. He had offended one group of city merchants with a plan to break their monopoly by establishing a centre-city grain market under the aegis of one of their competitors, Ramji Mull of the Gurwala family. Now a rumour began to circulate that Bell was threatening the mercantile community and forcing them to bring the price down to 17 *seers* per Rupee, which was the price current in the surrounding country. What seems to have happened is that he had 'advised' the dealers to reduce their price.[91] But working under his protection the suspect new *kotwal* had gone further; bypassing the usual daily consultation with the merchants, he had fixed a daily price which was 25 per cent lower than the prevailing market price. The wholesalers had responded by closing down the bazaars and denying the city even the inadequate flow which it had previously received. They claimed that, bearing in mind transport and insurance charges, they would be selling at a loss if this price was maintained, and it became necessary to withdraw the order with grave loss of face to the European magistracy. Bell and his subordinates were acting in good faith. But it is evident that market intervention, which would have been perfectly usual in Indian states or even in the days of Jonathan Duncan, could only have

---

[89] *Delhi Gazette*, 11 Oct. 1837.
[90] Commr Delhi to Govt, 30 Aug. 1838, NWPCJ, Aug. 1838, 231/51, IOL.
[91] Magt. to Commr Delhi, 6 Aug. 1838 and trans. of Magt.'s *robkaree*, NWPCJ, Aug. 1838, 231/51, IOL.

exacerbated the situation when the British had abandoned the ultimate sanction which eighteenth-century regimes had operated, namely, the direct physical coercion of the merchant community.

Some early origins of communal violence

During the 1820s and 1830s, there was a series of bloody Hindu–Muslim clashes in the cities and rural bazaars of north India. These occurred at Benares (1809–15),[92] Koil (1820), Moradabad, Sambhal, Kashipur (1833),[93] Shahjahanpur (1837),[94] Bareilly, Kanpur and Allahabad (1837–52),[95] among other places. There is little basis then for the assumption made by many writers that Hindu–Muslim conflict did not occur until the creation of local representative bodies and the emergence of 'modern' politics in the post-Mutiny era. How novel these earlier outbreaks were themselves depends in turn on assumptions made about the Mughal era and the eighteenth century. Communal conflict certainly occurred before colonial rule.[96] The bitterness associated with Aurangzeb's attempt to replace temples with mosques in the eastern districts rumbled on until the 1850s. The bloody massacres of Ahmed Shah at Agra and Muttra in 1761 were calculated acts of religious savagery. The alacrity with which emergent Hindu and Sikh regimes banned the slaughter of cattle within cities suggests that this practice had always rankled with the majority communities. It is clear that the fortuitous clashing of Hindu and Muslim festivals had given rise to tension before 1800. But while it cannot be assumed that a blithe tolerance characterised relations between Hindus and Muslims in the pre-colonial period, the political context of these periodic outbreaks did change dramatically in the early nineteenth century.

Most significant was the erosion of the authority of the old law officers of the towns – the *kazi*, *mufti* and *kotwal* – which had also given rise to

92 For file of past correspondence on clashes see 'Gyanbaffee Mosque' file, bundle 50, file 97, Judl 1866, Commissioner of Benares Post-Mutiny Corr., UPR; cf. dispute at the Aurangabad *sarai*, 2nd Judge, Benares to Nizamat Adalat, 19 Dec. 1816, BCJ, 12 July 1816, 132/43, IOL.
93 Asst Magt. Moradabad to Commr Rohilkhand, 31 Oct. 1833, BCJ, Nov. 1833, 140/43, IOL.
94 Collr Shahjahanpur to Commr Rohilkhand, 19 Apr. 1838, NWPCJ, June 1838, 231/48, IOL.
95 Magt. Kanpur to Commr Allahabad, 31 Mar. 1840, NWPCJ, May 1840, 231/68, IOL; for past correspondence on Allahabad disturbances, Collr Allahabad to Commr, 2 Jan. 1882, basta 279, 45 Judl of 1882, Records of Commissioner of Allahabad, Commissioner's Bungalow, Allahabad.
96 See, e.g., Rizvi, *Shah Wali-Allah*, pp. 197–202; he mentions two sets of communal disturbances between 1725 and 1734, one of which concerned Delhi shoemakers and the other which took place against a background of conflict between local Mughal officials.

tensions in the economic management of population centres. In the past, the paths of compromise and coercion were clear: the authority of the *kotwal* derived directly from a secular ruler advised by *kazi, mufti* and Hindu headmen. The authority of all these arbitrators and enforcers was now in doubt as the European police and magistracy reduced their influence and played one off against the other. In several of these riots, the old law officers were seen taking leading parts in riots by the Muslim population against what they regarded as modifications of custom and precedence in religious practice. In Kashipur in 1833, for instance, the *kazi* of the division had to be removed. He had denounced a Muslim police officer as a heretic and threatened to pollute the town with cow-slaughter after an unpopular compromise with the Hindus over the location of a temple.[97] In Shahjahanpur, the relationship between the decline of the *kotwal* and the riots of 1837 was equally clear. As late as this the *kotwal* was a descendant of the family of Hafiz Rehmat Khan, and his police force was 'composed almost entirely of Pathans'.[98] Here as in other towns throughout Rohilkhand, Hindus had by custom desisted from acts of merry celebration during the Muslim Mohurrum festival. They did not wear red turbans, shout 'Jai! Jai!' or blow conch shells in deference to the Muslim festival of mourning. Conflict had been settled directly as the *kotwal*, as chief executive of the city, was also a member of the central Muslim ruling group. After 1815, both the old ruling family and the *kotwal* had lost influence in the city. They became representatives of only a section of the population, not of the urban order as a whole. When the *kotwal* sought to suppress uncustomary merrymaking by the Hindus during the Mohurrum of 1838, the European magistrate interpreted this as a case of 'harrasment' and pressed for a further reduction of the *kotwal*'s powers and the creation of a 'balance' between Hindus and Muslims in the *kotwali* police force.[99]

The new scope for perpetuating conflict by appeal to the magistracy and the British courts against urban notables and the law officers was extended by a subtle change in the attitude of the rulers to the nature of government and administration. In the eighteenth century, the ruler was seen as guardian of the existing system of caste ranking and social precedence. By the 1830s, however, the new breed of British district official was working on the basis of assumptions about 'equity' and 'precedent'. The aim of administration was now to balance rights, not to enforce religious and social duties. The magistrate of Shahjahanpur

[97] Commr Moradabad to Sec. Govt Judl Dept, 20 Aug. 1833, BCJ, Nov. 1833, 140/43, IOL.
[98] Report of Collr Shahjahanpur, 24 June 1837, NWPCJ, July 1837, 231/37, cf. Collr Shahjahanpur to Commr Rohilkhand, 19 Apr. 1838, NWPCJ, June 1838, 231/48, IOL.
[99] Commr Rohilkhand to Govt, NWPCJ, 22 Apr. 1837, 231/35, IOL.

grasped the change. Up to the 1830s, he said, the precedence given to the Rohilla aristocracy,

unavoidable perhaps on the accession, has been perpetuated by several official acts ... These orders which ought never to have been issued by magistrates, have now of necessity been discontinued as incompatible with the celebration of the [Hindu festival] Ramnowmee. Consequently both sects are now for the first time placed on a footing of perfect equality, as regards the performance of religious rites.[100]

This explanation of the growth of religious conflict under early colonial rule is not exhaustive, of course. It relies on the simplistic assumption that a stable set of social relations was upset by outside, colonial forces. It is in danger of ignoring the importance of social and economic changes within Indian society itself. This is not to say that these clashes can be reduced to class conflict based on economic differences. What it does mean, however, is that uneven economic and fiscal changes after 1800 had given power in the cities and bazaars to bodies of entrepreneurs and property-owners who were not well accommodated within the older relations of ranking and precedence. Since about 1800 in many cities and bazaars of the west there had been steady commercial change and a shift of economic power to mercantile groups such as the Jains of the Delhi region, Agarwal Banias around Kanpur or Chaubes in the Muttra region. These filled the vacuums left in the *qasbah* societies by the decline or withdrawal of the Islamic service people. Alongside the growth of trade and political stability since the mid-eighteenth century there had been a great expansion of pilgrimage up to the lofty mountain shrines of Baijnath and Badrinath. In towns on the pilgrimage route there was great pressure to assert Hindu ceremonial precedence and abolish the marks of inferiority which Hindus had willingly accepted under the Rohillas.

Newcomers and newly rich men in the towns who had little connection with the patronage of the earlier Muslim rulers were often unwilling to acquiesce in a continued ceremonial inferiority which their new rulers were disinclined to enforce. Thus in a town like Rewari, north of Delhi, it was the Hindu commercial community led by about 300 'wealthy and influential persons' who tried in 1838 to coerce the Muslims into giving up the slaughter of meat in the town by operating a *hartal* against them and denying them food. According to the Magistrate, the Hindu leaders here were citing examples of ancient Hindu rule, for the wealth and security of Rewari had encouraged the

100 *Ibid.*, cf. events in Delhi where changes in existing practice over processions and cow-slaughter increased tension between groups of Hindus and Muslims as well as between Sunnis and Shias, Gupta, *Delhi*, pp. 10–11.

'oppressed' (by which he meant the Hindus) to become the 'oppressors'.[101] Conversely, in Sambhal in 1820, it had been Muslim grain dealers (*jhajhas*) who had been forward in 'coercing' Hindu merchants;[102] while in Kanpur in 1840 Hindu Gurwal Banias (originally sugar merchants) exacerbated tensions by reportedly parading an offensive mock Muslim *tazia* (representation of the tomb of the Shia martyr *imams*) through the streets.[103] Even in Delhi, sporadic communal violence in the early colonial period was associated with merchant communities whose power and wealth in the city was rapidly on the increase. In 1807, for instance, 'there was tension in the city because of the demonstrations against a Jain banker who sponsored a Rathjatra procession with great fanfare'.[104] As we have suggested, hinterland Jains were filling the vacuum left by the decline of some of the older houses which had been associated with the Mughal court.

On the other hand, the stance of established commercial families during communal disputes was often mild and accommodating. The Chaudhuri family of Bareilly, for instance, whose experience of Muslim rule predated the Rohillas, was a key group in the various compromises over ceremonial precedence which were worked out in the city during the 1830s.

It would be wrong to trace an ideological energy as profound as the sense of separate communal identity simply to the changing political context, or to economic imbalances which arose from the growth of trade. The sharpened sense of community grew from a slow transformation of the symbolic value attached to religious adherence which was associated with new movements of religious teaching and the growth of 'orthodoxy' among both Hindus and Muslims. But these external developments in the economy and in government did provide the historical conditions for the emergence of 'communalism', and explain why processes of compromise were progressively eroded in the early colonial period.[105]

Social conflict in a commercial mart

In the great trading city of Mirzapur, problems of control took on a different complexion. In contrast to most other north Indian cities,

101 Magt. Gurgaon to Commr Delhi, 2 May 1838, NWPCJ, May 1838, 231/48, IOL.
102 Magt. Moradabad to Govt, 2 Nov. 1820, BCJ, 24 Nov. 1820, 134/44, IOL.
103 Magt. Kanpur to Commr, 31 Mar. 1840, NWPCJ, May 1840, 231/68, IOL.
104 Gupta, *Delhi*, p. 10.
105 Other economic conflicts which 'fed into' the sense of communal identity were those which divided weavers and merchants in weaving villages; see, e.g., the case of the weavers of Mubarikpur and Mhow in Azamgarh who were enthused by the doctrines of Sayyid Ahmed of Bareilly, *Settlements under Regulation IX*, I, 10.

there had been no dominant royal court or Muslim gentry. The influence of the commercial families dwarfed that of the local raja of Kantit before 1800. The headman and city magistrate had long been Hindus, and the system of *kotwal*, *kazi* and *mufti* had never taken root in an overwhelmingly Hindu environment. Here as nowhere else in Hindustan the influence of the great trading and ascetic corporations was predominant throughout the late eighteenth and early nineteenth centuries. The fluctuations of the export economy put great pressure on merchant and labourer in Mirzapur and similar towns. But in the absence of a discontented gentry leadership the colonial authorities maintained order, even in the crisis of 1857.

Mirzapur after 1815 gave a remarkable impression of a boom town. Population galloped ahead from about 20,000 to about 55,000 between 1800 and 1840.[106] The city's roads and *ghats* were blocked by the cotton screws, cotton bales and other commercial apparatus of the great Gosain traders, Pursram Gir and his *chela*, Sidh Gir. The growth of the town and especially of the market of Wellesleyganj put pressure on the antiquated police system,[107] and public facilities were strained to breaking point. Loads of valuable merchandise were piled up in an unprotected set of warehouses on the far bank of the river known as the Barrah.[108] A vigorous underworld developed. Merchants ranged into factions over the control of markets and commission agencies in cotton and sugar, employing as henchmen and toughs large numbers of peasants from the surrounding villages. In Mirzapur, one person in every twenty was a beggar in 1829, and there were 'many in the town ... who live by robbery'.[109] Assaulting persons after dark, it was said, 'has its origins in the constant quarrels of dallals brokers and merchants who are mostly men of very low origins who find that an appeal to the lathee [club] is the most expeditious mode of settling their commercial differences'.[110]

The Magistrate's castigation of the 'low birth' of the townspeople was evidently intended to extend to its European inhabitants too. Racial boundaries buckled under the strain of money-making to a degree unusual outside Bombay or Calcutta. In the 1830s, the European treasurer of the Bank of Upper India was involved in a range of conflicts and frauds traced to one of the leading merchant bosses, Runge Lall. At

---

106 See Mirzapur Chaukidari Statistics, espec. 'Comparative Table of the Chowkeedaree Assessments of 1834 and 1853', Magt. Mirzapur to Commr Benares, 9 Feb. 1854, Mirzapur Judl, 95, UPR.
107 Magt. Mirzapur to Suptdt Police, 26 July 1919, Mirzapur Judl, 77, UPR.
108 Magt. to Suptdt Police, 11 Jan. 1820, Mirzapur Judl, 77, UPR.
109 Magt. to Suptdt Police, 24 Feb. 1821, Mirzapur Judl, 80, UPR.
110 Magt. to H. J. Stewart, 10 Apr. 1830, Mirzapur Judl, 80, UPR.

the same time, one of the major factory owners, H. J. Stewart, skilfully adapted to indigenous commercial mores by having three of his Brahmin servants mount a ritual fast unto death (*dharna*) on a debtor who had failed in the delivery of some indigo.[111] Stewart was only restrained by the personal intervention of the Magistrate.

Most of the cities of north India provide some examples of the rapid acquisition of wealth and status by members of inferior merchant and artisan groups. In Benares men of the castes which cultivated *betel*-nut (Barhai) and pressed oil (Teli) became successful city entrepreneurs after 1750. In Agra some families of the leather worker (Chamar) caste were accepted as creditworthy merchants by mid-century. What is striking about Mirzapur was the wealth and importance achieved by a large group of local petty traders and moneylenders, the Umar. This community held a ritual position which was considered to be well below that of the traditional urban merchant castes. They seem once to have been connected with the degrading oil trade, and one of their sections was called the Til (oil) Umar.[112] Many of the merchant elites of mid-nineteenth-century Hindustan were descended from petty rural traders, but it was unusual for a large group from such origins to achieve the measure of power they acquired in Mirzapur. A dispute about local administration in 1836 revealed it forcibly:

It is to be observed that the leading houses alone have signed this petition. There are not five or six who are not reputed to be the owners of a lakh of Rupees or more. The chiefs among the Khattrees and Omers, were it considered expedient, could command each the signature of 300 of their poorer brethren.[113]

Artisan and labourer families of very low status also rose to positions of wealth and influence in Mirzapur. The rapid development of the town's brass industry made it possible for some of the household manufacturers to market their own produce, so that there were a large number of very wealthy Kasseras (brass workers) by 1860. Kalwars (liquor distillers) had achieved influence even earlier. By 1787, a number of Kalwars from the palace market of Kantit were doing extensive business in the town, and they were powerful enough to embarrass and curtail the power of the Company's Indian collector of customs. Evident also was the opulence of persons connected with transport which was a feature common to all rapidly growing marts. By 1850 there were already five large hostelries (*sarais*) in the town for the accommodation of travellers. The headmen of cameleers, bullock-cart

[111] *Ibid.*, cf. same to same, 24 Aug. 1830, Mirzapur Judl, 80, UPR.
[112] Interviews, Benares, 1973.
[113] Jt Magt. Mirzapur to Commr Benares, 6 May 1846, Mirzapur Judl, 89, UPR.

drivers, riverboat owners and people who provided armed guards for the movement of bullion were all classed among the most wealthy inhabitants.[114]

Mirzapur's cottage industries had also begun to give rise to problems of labour control which were to become common in great industrial cities like Bombay and Kanpur later in the century. It was difficult to organise free factory labour on the basis of the typical system of occupational headmen. Workers in the aniline dye (*lac*) factories, for instance, appear to have been drawn from a number of neighbourhoods and several caste groups; men and women also worked together. Cases of abuse forced the authorities to consider guaranteeing these workers the right to claim basic conditions of service. They hoped to prevent forms of employment in these incipient factories from becoming a system of legalised slavery.[115] Faced with the opposition of powerful interests among European employers, these efforts do not seem to have been very successful. Nevertheless, problems of labour relations in Mirzapur indicate that the town was beginning to experience on a minor scale some of the issues which came to the fore in Bombay, Kanpur and Calcutta much later in the century.

The environment in which this tiny working class emerged was not a capitalist city. But neither was Mirzapur merely another incarnation of the 'traditional India', dominated by landed aristocrats. Instead it represented the maturing of the eighteenth-century corporations within the context of the rapid expansion of both internal and external trade. Merchants dominated the city and played some of the roles appropriate to rulers. Their organisation was flexible, yet coherent. It was built up on the basis of individual factions and sub-castes. But under pressure there emerged a definite 'opinion of the mart' reinforced by political organisation capable of opposition. Civic feeling was less marked at Mirzapur than in Benares because many of the business people were merely agents of great houses in more established centres. But the nearby Hindu shrine of Bindachal did provide a weak moral focus for the community.[116] Mirzapur should be seen as a burgher city, an indication of the direction of social change in pre-colonial India as much as a product of colonial economic relationships. In Mirzapur and the other commercial cities of the east, the British could rely on the relationships established during the first years of their commercial expansion to take the strain in times of conflict. Social tensions existed here, but they did not imperil colonial government as did the problems

114 Memo. by Magt., 15 Sept. 1850, Mirzapur Judl, 92, UPR.
115 Jt Magt. to Sessions Judge, 15 Mar. 1853, Mirzapur Judl, 94, UPR.
116 Interviews, Allahabad and Benares, 1972–4.

of legitimacy and the frustrations of the gentry of the large towns of the west.

Conclusion

The analysis of the political economy in earlier chapters suggested that the relationship between political power, elite consumption, trade and the agrarian society established in the mid-eighteenth century had come under pressure by 1830. These pressures originated in the incompatibility of the colonial state and the Indian successor regimes to the Mughal empire. But they coincided with a period of instability in north India's long-distance and export trades. The histories of individual political units, states or towns do not, of course, all fit neatly into these broader patterns. Yet this chapter has argued that many of the conflicts between different social groups, as between the colonial authorities and the citizens of early colonial towns, do reflect the changing role of the state. The British had eroded the old forms of government and redistribution without replacing them with a new system.

By 1850 the framework of institutions and moral ideas which had been the framework for the ideal Indo-Muslim city was widely in disarray. The *kotwal* had been reduced to an inferior officer of police; the *kazi* was little more than a glorified registrar, the religious sensibilities of learned Islam no longer bore on the officers of government through the *mufti*. The disgrace of many old families during the Rebellion itself further reduced their significance. In the conquered towns of Awadh the corrosive process went ahead with even greater speed as the new collectors and commissioners drew as much as possible of the formal business of the cities into their own courts. Yet colonial institutions had not developed sufficiently fast to fill the vacuum, though some tentative beginnings had been made. From 1814 onwards, the proceeds of local police and other levies had been consolidated into funds which were allocated to works of public utility, such as the repair of bridges, roads and drainage in the cities.[117] There is little doubt that the physical fabric of many cities improved considerably. Some Indians were associated with the bodies which disbursed funds, but the sums involved were small and the greater part of the cities' economic and social life lay completely outside their purview.

Some western institutions had, of course, emerged in the towns; and efforts were made to link these up with Indian organisations and

[117] Magt. to Govt, 16 July 1836, Mirzapur Judl, 84, IOL.

aspirations. The Delhi College, for instance, represented an attempt to co-opt into the European world part of the Urdu literary and religious scene of Delhi,[118] while the Benares Sanskrit College, founded by Jonathan Duncan at the end of the eighteenth century, had some success in finding roots among the religious corporations of the eastern region.[119] Bengali immigrants in several cities also created institutions which linked the world of the new colonial intelligentsia with the older traditions. In Benares again, Jai Narayan Ghosal's school and literary productions came to play this role.[120]

The ripples of reforming British ideology reached Hindustan's towns and *qasbahs* during the 1840s and 1850s, though their impact was uneven. H. B. Tucker, Commissioner of Benares in the 1850s, was unusually active in trying to extend the provisions of the urban police system to small towns in the countryside which he felt were in need of a firmer civic constitution. But as a fiery evangelical who wished to abolish 'heathen' oaths in law courts and to encompass other measures of moral reform, he created uneasiness among the population and in official circles. At Allahabad, Tucker anticipated the reforms of the post-Mutiny era by holding a public meeting in the Khusru Bagh to elect a city council with surveillance over watch and ward and conservancy in the city. But the office of 'city panch' was 'primarily a very invidious one, and will be shirked unless honour and consideration be attached to it'.[121] Thus far, however, the imperial and local governments were uninterested in municipal organisation, and efforts to associate 'native opinion' with the state on a new footing were limited to the efforts of a few energetic and knowledgeable men such as Tucker and H. T. Prinsep, Magistrate of Benares in the 1830s.[122] Serious attempts to create a new civic structure and culture awaited three developments. First, there was the influx of a larger number of European residents and soldiers after 1858 which raised the problem of public health in a much more acute form when the ruling race was at risk. Secondly, there was the search for new sources of taxation which appealed to the financially straitened governments of the 1860s and

---

[118] Gupta, *Delhi*, pp. 7–8; C. F. Andrews, *Zakaullah of Delhi* (London, 1929); note that efforts were made to associate leading Delhi *ulama* (including 'militant' Naqshbandis) with European educational institutions.

[119] Miss R. Gabriel of the University of Virginia is working on this issue; see also DR, vol. 52, pp. 272ff., UPR.

[120] See, e.g., Agent Benares to Govt in the Pol. Dept, 12 Feb. 1819, printed Saletore (ed.), *Banaras Affairs*, II, 185.

[121] H. B. Tucker to Govt, 26 June 1854, NWPCJ, June 1854, 233/78, IOL.

[122] Take for instance Prinsep's efforts to build a large grain market at 'Halloo Ghunna' near the Trilokchandi Ghat, Magt. Benares to Govt, 10 Apr. 1830, BCJ, 27 Apr. 1830, 139/60, IOL.

1870s. Finally, the atmosphere was changed by the impetus of mid-Victorian ideas of civic virtue which represented a response to the contemporary social problems of Britain.

The decline of the old city-wide offices and the great households did not, of course, reduce mid-nineteenth-century urban society to an amalgam of competing castes and small neighbourhoods. The solidarities of economic interest and religion which we have called corporations continued to develop even though the wider urban context within which they operated had changed. The period 1800 to 1850 was by no means a bad one for the bodies of Hindu traders, ascetics and learned men, even though their political influence was circumscribed by the re-emergence of a strong imperial government in north India. Peace and fragile commercial prosperity extended the scope and numbers of Hindu pilgrimages and the great fairs connected with them. The rising value of urban property enriched traders and Gosains who had put their money in houses and bazaars during the previous century. *Rentier* income from the countryside began to flow in also. It is true that after the Depression of the 1830s many of the older houses lost their dynamism as entrepreneurs, tending to fall back instead on their activities as moneylenders and landowners. But they still continued to act as a prestigious multi-caste group at the top of Hindu commercial society. The Benares Naupatti association for its part assimilated no new families after 1800 and became an hereditary monied caucus. But it continued to arbitrate disputes and to set the tone for a large section of urban society. Rising families sought to move nearer to the Naupatti by marriage alliance if possible, or by changes of residential area or by support for the religious trusts and enterprises which were the special concern of the great bankers. In all the cities of the region, stone wharves, rest houses and wells for pilgrims and temples were built in considerable numbers by traders and urban landlords during the 1810s and 1820s. For many families of learned men and priests, the patronage of wealthy traders became as significant as that of the royal families. The relationship between commerce and learning forged through Hindu piety was to provide an important link for most of the political, social and religious organisations of the later nineteenth century. In terms of organisation as well as ideology, the new India of the 1880s was the product of a developing tradition, not a sudden burst of westernisation in the context of a cultural and social vacuum.

The early colonial period, in short, saw the further consolidation of a merchant and service class between the state and agrarian society. It was as much the product of the slow commercialisation of political power which had gathered pace in the late Mughal period as of the export trades and land market of colonial rule. Of course, in the Ganges valley this class was not so articulate or self-aware as it was in the great coastal cities of Madras, Bombay or Calcutta. But as an indication of the persistence of an indigenous social change, it was no less important because its idiom remained 'traditional'. The next chapter moves on to a different location, the small gentry town, in which another element of the later Indian middle class had been in unbroken evolution since the days of the Delhi emperors.

9

Small towns in the political economy: the qasbah *under pressure*

It was in the large towns that the impact of colonial rule was most evident, but much of the north Indian population had little experience of them. This was not so of the smaller towns of the countryside. Even predominantly 'agricultural' districts had a generous scattering of places which could by some measure be described as urban. Sitapur District in Awadh, for instance, recorded an 'urban' population of only 4 per cent at the Census of 1871. But the contemporary *Gazetteer* listed the monuments and markets of 28 'towns' whose combined population accounted for more than 13 per cent of the total. In the Muslim west of the area, the percentage population living in recognisably urban places probably topped 20 per cent.[1]

These small country towns were deeply embedded in the fabric of rural society. They were the bases of the landlords and moneylenders who moulded the form of the peasant household. They supported the local temples and saints' tombs which linked the popular religion of the villages to the formal practices of Brahminical Hinduism and orthodox Islam. In the later nineteenth century, it was in the small towns that the new politicians and leaders of religious movements built up their first rural audiences.

The fate of these small places in the early nineteenth century reflected the history of the wider economy. Peasant market places (*haths*) grew in numbers with the expansion of population and the cultivated acreage during the first thirty years of the century, but suffered a setback in some areas during the 1830s. More substantial *qasbahs* went through a bewildering variety of cycles of growth and decline in tune with the fate of the elites and trade routes on which they depended. But here also the colonial export trade and the imperial government adapted to the institutions of eighteenth-century India. Old gentry towns were swollen with large despatches of cotton and sugar, only to decline again when trade moved elsewhere.

The relations between town and country remained rather one-sided as they had been during the previous century. Peasant producers sold their

---

[1] Calculated from *Oudh Gazetteer*, iii, 373; *Sitapur District Settlement Report* (Lucknow, 1875), ch. 4.

goods to small town merchants in order to pay revenue and rent. Apart from salt and iron goods, they do not seem to have purchased directly in the *qasbahs*. However, the customs records reveal that there was much trade between the small towns in petty consignments of 'country cloth', sugar, cotton, tobacco and spices.[2] This sort of trade is easy to lose sight of, but in volume it was significant, providing much employment for marginal people and some extra income for peasant producers over and above the cash requirements for land-revenue. Where *qasbahs* grew wealthy on trade, new demand from their controllers and middlemen tipped the scales in favour of country producers who could satisfy it by bringing in surplus local production. But for some, the best days were over by 1830. The decline of military service and many local courts severely restricted the by-employment and extra demand which linked the agricultural population to their country towns. The new commercial security of British rule enriched the small town bania to the detriment of artisan and gentry.

Only one new type of country town emerged before the 1880s: the railway mart. The construction of the East India Railway to Allahabad, and later of its Awadh extension, contributed to the decline of many of the old trading towns of the Ganges–Jamna riverbank. But it also gave rise to a number of places conveniently situated for railborne trades which provided a new political context for commerce. Merchants could now predict prices in more distant markets with some confidence; the press of insurers, *hundiwallahs*, experts in transport and security who had thronged earlier marts, was reduced. On the other hand, railway rates were high, so that the dominance of the prosperous rural merchant was reinforced. There was little place for the small man who had frequented earlier marts. The hold of aristocrats and gentry was also significantly reduced. As early as 1793, the British had formally abolished 'bazaar duties' and other taxes on commerce levied by local land-controllers. But in practice, markets situated in the heart of petty rajadoms or the *qasbahs* of Islamic service gentry had remained dominated by these local lords. In the new railway marts, by contrast, trade was freed from many of these constraints. Few historians would now argue that capitalist relations of production had advanced very far in the Ganges valley before the end of the nineteenth century. But the wealthy grain merchants of the railway marts were in a position to accumulate capital on a novel scale.

The coming of the railways, then, removed some rural merchants from the domain of the aristocrat and landowner. But the railway was

<hr>

[2] See, e.g., statement of imports and exports for the towns of Aligarh District, June–July 1810, Agra Customs 13, UPR.

not, of course, transforming unchanging, traditional societies. Merchants and moneylenders had been unobtrusively acquiring a more significant role in the political economy since the end of the Mughal period. The world of merchant and gentry had already drifted apart. Predominantly 'burgher' towns like Mirzapur had emerged at the very same time as a distinct class of land-controlling gentry had been forming out of the press of revenue intermediaries. Gentry and merchant class were both products of the changes in the pre-colonial state. Yet they related to peasant production in different ways, and the institutions within which they perpetuated their political power were also different in quality. In the commercial bazaars, Hindu and Jain religion provided the solidarities out of which corporations and a sense of urban, even political identity was forged. These places were 'small Mirzapurs'; temple and bazaar went together. Later in the century, Hindu revival added pens for the protection of sacred cattle and civic platforms where religious teachers and political lecturers orated. It was from such places that many of the rural merchants and school-masters who supported the Congress movement were to originate. Very different in economic function and quality were the *qasbah* towns of the service gentry, and above all, those with a pronounced Islamic flavour. These places were the repository of aristocratic and courtly values in north India, and many were to become the seed-beds of Muslim political movements towards the end of the century.

This section provides a brief consideration of the forces which moulded the Islamic *qasbah* town and its elites over the eighteenth and nineteenth centuries.[3] As in earlier sections, the service gentry stands as a kind of control for the study of the commercial groups and commercial towns which are the focus of the study. Similar themes emerge: the creation of economic and political solidarities within the context of religious tradition; the strengthening of local identities in response to the weakness of the institutions of the state, and the emergence of

[3] There exists a considerable literature on petty urbanisation in the area, see esp. R. Fox, 'Rajput "clans" and rurban settlements in northern India', in Fox (ed.), *Urban India: Society, Space and Image* (Duke, N. C., 1968), pp. 167–85; K. N. Singh, 'The territorial basis of the medieval town and village in eastern Uttar Pradesh, India', *Annals of the Assn of American Geographers*, VIII (1968), 219–30; B. Cohn and McKim Marriott, 'Networks and centres in the integration of Indian civilisation', *Social Research*, I (1958), 1–8. My categories 'Islamic service gentry' and 'service gentry *qasbah*' refer to types; individual towns and social groups sometimes had the characteristic of more than one type. Thus a place could be both a 'Rajput lineage centre' and an 'Islamic service *qasbah*'. Similarly, some Rajput families sent members to service in the army or police, and some Brahmins on *shankallap* (gift) tenures could be considered 'service gentry' in that they obtained part of their income from state grants or stipends. But I take continuous connection with the rulers, dependence on service income and literacy to be defining features of the groups with which the following section deals.

dominances in the countryside which moulded even if they did not revolutionise the forms of production of peasant society. But the most important point is that there was a continuous evolution of institutions from the Mughal into the modern period. It is against the background of *qasbah* communities of the small towns as much as the religious schools of the cities that the 'middle class' of Muslim India emerged into the turmoil of the present century.

The development of Islamic *qasbahs*

Seven centuries of Muslim expansion had scattered small centres across north India from Punjab east to Monghyr and the fringes of Bengal and south to the Hyderabad Deccan. In the valley of the Ganges they were clustered in the upper Doab and western parts of Awadh. It was from these urban islands that families of Islamic soldiers, administrators and learned men expanded into the Hindu hinterland, becoming a virtual landed gentry by the eighteenth century. But it was the families and traditions of the saints which played the key part in founding and perpetuating the most famous *qasbahs*.

In recent centuries the moral centre of most of these towns remained the tombs of noted holy men who were popularly thought to have lived between the eighth and the eleventh centuries A.D. After the first Muslim invasions of the subcontinent there appears to have been a long period of peaceful penetration before the great Islamic sultanates began to dominate the central Ganges valley. During these years, the expansion of the mystic Sufi orders was crucial in the growth of town societies.[4] The key to this diaspora was the concept of spiritual 'territories' (*vilayats*) into which the Sufi teachers divided the known universe. Each *vilayat* was to be led into submission to the Will of God by bodies of mystics settled among them. The heads of the orders appointed subordinates (*khalifas*) for towns still dominated by Hindu rajas, and these teachers often became the nucleus of small Muslim communities.

As the Islamic governments of the Sultanate period (twelfth to fourteenth century A.D.) were established more firmly, small towns were constituted with the formal offices of *kazi* and *mufti* so that the legal

---

4 K. A. Nizami, *Some Aspects of Religion and Politics in India during the Thirteenth Century* (Delhi, 1978), p. 57; for examples of this sort of development, Syed Imdad Imam, 'The pirs or the Muhammadan saints of Bihar', *Journal of the Bihar and Orissa Research Society*, iii (1917), 341–8; S. H. Aksari, 'The Mausoleum of a saint of the Madari order, Hilsa, Bihar', *Bengal Past and Present*, lxviii (1949), 131, 44; also the whole gazetteer series, esp. *OG* which draws heavily from works such as Mhd Abdal Jalil, *Tabsirat-al Nazarain* (copy AMU Aligarh).

business of the Muslim state could be transacted in the locality. *Kazis* were drawn from the ranks of Muslim doctors of law who had links with the Sufi seminaries. This three-cornered relationship between the state, the disciplines of Muslim law and Islamic mysticism persisted through into the colonial period. The autonomous development of the schools of mystics based on hospices for meditation (*khanqas* and *dargahs*) continued to support the moral unity of the town settlements. From piety or policy the Sultans and their Mughal and Nawabi successors maintained a steady flow of endowments to the holy families descended from the original saint–missionaries. The history of Awadh towns such as Bilgram, Makanpur or Kara,[5] reflects the spread of Sufi hospices and also the accumulation of grants of revenue-free lands in places where the Muslim presence as a landholding community had once been minimal. The local Muslim lords came into contact with the Hindu cultivators both as agrarian superiors and as men of religion and power. Popular Hinduism was prepared to venerate almost any manifestation of spiritual authority, and early Islamic conquerors and teachers became the objects of cults. Such, for instance, was the case with the worship of the 'Panchon Pir' in the Benares region. In many places tombs of Sufi saints became the particular resort of Hindu men and women seeking relief from illness or wishing to obtain the intercession of the saint in their conflicts and tribulations. So while the establishments of Brahmins and Muslim doctors of law publicly stood aloof from each other, at a more popular level, *qasbah* society put out roots into the Hindu hinterland. These connections survived the Islamic revivalist movements of the seventeenth and eighteenth centuries. It was only in the later nineteenth century that Hindu regenerations and Pan-Islamic fervour began to erode this popular and eclectic local religion.

The second, parallel process in the formation of *qasbah* society was the slow growth of the power of Muslim service families as a local gentry. An important turning point here was when these locally resident Muslims began to acquire substantial areas of heritable land-rights around their small urban centres. Before the mid-seventeenth century, of course, the *qasbahs* were already flourishing centres of scholars, artisans and office holders; but their political and military life revolved around the great Muslim courts of Jaunpur or Delhi. As late as 1590, Muslims held only small patches of land as zamindars in Awadh and the Doab. In Hardoi District, for instance, where there existed a remarkable number of famous *qasbah* towns at the time of the Emperor Akbar, Muslims held only part of the town of Bilgram and perhaps fifty

---

[5] See, e.g., the collection of sixteenth, seventeenth and eighteenth centuries, *Madad-i-maash* grants for Soraon and Kara recorded in, *National Register of Private Records, Kerala . . . and U.P.* (Delhi, NAI, 1972), pp. 162–3.

villages elsewhere.[6] In 1860, however, they held as many as 1,445 in Sitapur Division; and this was rather less than the total had been in 1800. It seems that the Muslims of western Awadh had little interest in acquiring property rights until 'the latter end of Akbar's reign; and this is the reason that no deeds of mortgage or sale can be found bearing a date prior to his reign'. At this time they aimed at 'getting rent-free land granted them for life only'.[7] But from the end of Akbar's reign onward Sayyid Muslim families rapidly gained land-rights all over Awadh and also throughout the Doab. In the later eighteenth century, they probably held the proprietary right in two-thirds of the Awadh villages and made a significant contribution to the ecology of the area, as chapter 2 has shown, by irrigation investment and the cultivation of fruit groves.

Generally this expansion remained a peaceful affair. It was 'not the conquest of the invader but the slow accumulation of thrift and diplomacy exercised on a more simple people'.[8] From time to time, there were cases where the Sayyid families physically expelled earlier controllers and their tenants, especially when these were competitors also in the skills of literacy and public office. But the Muslims generally held the great advantage of monopolising the revenue and registration offices of *kazi* and *kanungo* (chief revenue surveyor) in the small towns from which they expanded. The Rajput communities, who were themselves often descendants of clients of earlier Muslim lords, were divided and fragmented in this part of north India.[9] They displayed none of the cohesion and opposition to outsiders which Cohn found among the more easterly Rajputs and Kessinger among the Jats of the Punjab. It proved easy for the Muslim clerical and military families to manipulate property deeds to their advantage.

The later Mughal empire created a climate in which the service gentry could consolidate at greater speed. The first emperors had been hostile to their servants acquiring large tracts of zamindari land or transforming their revenue assignments into control over the usufruct of land. During Aurangzeb's reign, however, the state gave tacit recognition to the growth of gentry power. A *farman* (charter) of 1690 recognised revenue-free charitable land (*madad-i-maash, aima,* etc.) to be heritable within the family of grantees.[10] During the same period, many zamindars appear also to have begun to assimilate their zamindaris to revenue-free

[6] *Oudh Gazetteer,* iii, 339.   [7] *Ibid.*

[8] A. Hartington and W. Blennerhassett, *Report of the Regular Settlement of the Hardoi District* (Allahabad, 1880), p. 63.

[9] *Ibid.,* p. 44.

[10] Muzaffar Alam, 'Some aspects of the changes in the position of *Madaad-i-maash* holders in Awadh, 1676–1772', *Indian History Congress* (1974), pp. 199–203; Sayyid Z. H. Jafri, tr. 'Two Madad-i-maash farmans of Aurangzeb', paper prepared for *IHC* 1979, mimeo. Aligarh M.U.

holdings, thus avoiding state land tax and other dues. So the balance of power moved towards the gentry and away from both the state and the free peasant proprietor. If the later emperors could not halt this process, at least they might gain advantage from the enhanced influence of a class which had a much greater investment in the continuation of empire than the rebellious Hindu clans which surrounded them.

The formation of these landed dominances was speeded by their relationship to the successor states. In the seventeenth century, the emperors had been able to benefit from the balance which existed between the interests of the high officials (*mansabdars*), the local officials (*kazi* and *kanungo*), and the predominantly Hindu clan headmen. As the Bilgram document *Sharaif-i-Usmani* shows, gentry lineages in conflict might still appeal to the emperor or nawab to resolve their differences after 1720.[11] But the central authorities had less leverage. In Rohilkhand the new Muslim military gentry dug themselves into agrarian society by coercion or force of arms. Further east, indigenous Sayyid families shielded themselves behind the revenue-farmers or the *chakladar* – a new tier in the revenue hierarchy[12] which was more amenable to local influence. Between 1780 and 1830 men from the small towns of western Awadh such as Bilgram, Sandi and Sandila dominated the office of *chakladar*. Their relatives acquired land-rights more easily; and their own salaries and perquisites were ploughed back into purchases and building in the environs of their native places.

As chapter 4 suggested, a vital feature of this petty service gentry in north India was the fact that its influence was perpetuated through institutions which drew on a specific Indo-Islamic cultural tradition. In these small towns of Awadh and the Doab, a distinct corporate tradition arose out of religion and pride of ancestry. But even for the Hindus of the service towns, this tradition was formally Persian and Islamic. Consciousness of high lineage broadened out into reverence for 'home place' (*watan*), while spiritual and marriage links between leading families created an urban, literate culture. Of course, bitter factionalism between Muslim gentry clans was a feature of many *qasbahs*; the conflict over land-rights between the Sayyids and Siddiqis of Bilgram was merely the most celebrated of these battles because it threw up an extensive written record. The tight, cross-cousin marriage alliances which were maintained by the purest gentry also ensured that 'blood' and lineage continued to be important determinants of politics and social life. However, other tendencies in society and politics aided in the creation of wider solidarities.

[11] Ghulam Hussain Siddiqi, 'Sharaif-i-Usmani', Aligarh M.U. History Department Library; I am grateful to Prof. Habib for attempting to instruct me in these matters.
[12] S. A. Rashid, *Calendar of Oriental Records*, III, introd. p. xiii.

First, gentry clans had not always been impermeable. Muslim families had often cast their marriage alliances more broadly than became the fashion for the priestly and literate elite in the nineteenth century. Moreover, the process of conversion to Islam among Hindu clerical people such as the Kayasths left residual lines of social intercourse even with rural Hindu families. More important, the operation of Mughal justice and administration had left much responsibility to the 'sense of the neighbourhood'. This was capable of overriding local factionalism. Indeed, it is important to remember that the very documents which reveal clan conflict between gentry groups are often themselves reflections of an ultimate consensus. The *mahzar* was a legal document setting forth the facts of a case for adjudication by higher authorities; it was common for both parties in a dispute and respectable local men to offer testimony that the claims and the evidence were genuine. Thus a *mahzar* of *qasbah* Hasampur of 1712 asserts the concurrence of the 'Ulemas, Jurists, Saiyads, Shaikhs and the residents' of the town in presenting evidence of a dispute.[13] Requests by the authorities to the local communities also confirmed the corporate identity of the *qasbah*. For instance, there is a document of 1796 addressed to 'the leading Saiyids, prominent Sheikhs and other inhabitants of the town of Sandilah'[14] which later refers to a meeting of the 'assembled Mussalmans' or elsewhere of the 'officers and raises [magnates]' of Sandila.[15]

How far did this sense of urban community cross the boundaries of religion? Several documents from eighteenth-century Awadh towns refer specifically to assemblies of Muslim magnates; and there are one or two incidents which can be interpreted as communal conflicts.[16] But very often the office of *kanungo* was hereditary to Hindu families. This created links between the leading families of the two religions.

Literary and religious reputations acquired by individuals also came to redound to the credit of the *qasbahs* where they had their ancestral places. *Tazkira* literature on the lives of the saints and the poets sought to glorify particular attributes passed on from pupil to teacher. The worthies of a Bilgram, Kakori or Sandila were eulogised in such works as the *Nazrut-un Nazarain* and the *Shajra-i-Taibaq*. In time, however, the small towns themselves became the object of pride and the practice of toponomy grew up. Learned service people in distant courts gloried in the title 'Bilgrami'. Thus for instance, Sayyid Wasi Ahmed Bilgrami,

---

13 *Mahzar* (c. 1712 A.D.) doc. 1235, UPR, tr. *COR*, III, 7; the tendency of the *kazi*'s office to become hereditary also strengthened *qasbah* identity in the face of rulers, see, e.g., C. Elliott, *Chronicles of Oonao* (Allahabad, 1862), p. 115
14 *Farman* 7 Rabi II, 1211 A.H. *COR*, I, 26.   15 *Ibid.*, p. 28.
16 E.g., *mahzar*, 3 Regnal Year of Farruksiyar, *COR*, III, 8–9, cf. introd., p. x.

an eighteenth-century poet of Koath in the Arrah District of Bihar, boasts of the 'purest water' of his lineage and claims relationship with the celebrated Bilgram poets Sayyid Abdul Jalil and Ghulam Ali Azad: 'My house is situated at Bilgram and belongs to the same eminent personage.'[17] In the same way, the sympathies created in mosque or religious school were reinforced through the disciplines of Sufi mysticism.

Gentry *qasbahs* under colonial rule

The first three quarters of the nineteenth century were, paradoxically, a more trying time for the elites of the Muslim small towns than the eighteenth-century flux had been. The history of each place was unique, yet a number of general changes can be isolated which affected their societies. First, and most crucial were relations with the state and other local landed groups expressed through the medium of land-rights and revenue payments.

In Awadh the hold of the Islamic gentry of the small towns over revenue-rights already appears to have weakened before the imposition of British rule in 1856. The high point had been the reign of Asaf-ud Daulah when the gentry were in full possession of the rights which they had accumulated in the service of the rising Awadh regime. In the first two decades of the nineteenth century the position remained stable, but in the reign of Wajid Ali Shah there was a definite reaction as the *qasbah* zamindars came under pressure both from the state and from the revived power of the Rajput clans of the countryside. The town of Sandi, for instance, which remained in possession of resident Sayyid families after about 1680, was resumed by the state in 1843.[18] Elsewhere, the powerful Rajput princelings who emerged during Awadh's terminal political crisis in the 1840s managed to prise away rights which had been slowly accumulated by the Sayyids in the previous century. Whole districts like Hardoi were virtually out of control of the kingdom's central authorities during these years, but it was the militant Hindu yeomanry rather than the literati and official landholders of the towns who benefited most from the flux.[19]

In the North-Western Provinces the revenue histories of the Islamic gentry were variable. The early British settlements of the land-revenue were, of course, notoriously harsh, especially in Allahabad and the

---

[17] 'Saiyid Wasi Ahmad Bilgrami: A Persian poet of Shahabad District', *Journal of Bihar and Orissa Research Society*, ii (1916), 469; for a brief discussion of the cultural role of the *qasbah*, see R. Barnett, 'Avadh', *Encyclopaedia Persica*, vol. I (Columbia, forthcoming); Mr Farhan Nizami of Wadham College, Oxford, is working on the issue.
[18] *DG Hardoi*, p. 249.   [19] Sleeman, *Tour*, I, 336; *ibid.*, II, 2; *DG Hardoi*, p. 140.

middle parts of the Doab. Much charitable land was also resumed. Where the small town elites were little more than *rentiers*, their position was obviously precarious. They found it difficult to corner any part of the proceeds of agricultural expansion because they stood so far from the actual cultivation. The 'melancholy revolution in the landed property of the country' which has earned Holt Mackenzie such sceptical attention from historians in the recent past may hold a grain of truth as far as the Sayyids, Pathans and Kayasths of the middle and lower Doab are concerned. Take the case of Namdar Khan, a resident of Dariabad, a suburban settlement of Allahabad. In 1802, now nearly ninety years of age, he petitions for the return of lands near Dariabad.[20] He had, he says, been in the military service of Awadh as early as the Battle of Buxar in 1764 and had relatives who were officials in the southern part of the district. But he had grown too old for military service and had suffered from the high revenue assessments levied by the last Awadh *amils* and then jumped up even more savagely by the British. Ultimately the seizure of his garden lands as a result of default in revenue payment had denied him the last honourable income left to a Muslim gentleman, an income of Rs. 7,000–8,000 per annum from 'mangos, jack fruits, guavas and roses' which he had marketed in the nearby city. He and his dependents had been reduced to penury and 'without your [the Governor General's] support I cannot maintain my respectability and rank'. Since they were a relatively new social group, gentry like this still had only a fragile hold on agricultural resources. Once they lost their revenue-rights, they were in a wholly different position from the 'dispossessed' among the Rajput clans of the east who had demesne land and local caste fellows to fall back on.

On the other hand, British legalism and the search for 'ancient proprietors of the soil' ensured that some at least of dispossessed eighteenth-century gentry were able to re-establish a toe-hold in the revenue system. We have noticed, for instance, how the Barah Sayyids of Muzaffarnagar and Meerut Districts were able to creep back into some of the villages from which they had earlier been ejected, once British settlement operations began. Nevertheless, almost everywhere political change, the rise of monied men or the resurgence of Hindu landholding communities put pressure on the Islamic gentry. The Settlement Officer of Sitapur remarked in the 1870s that 'As in all Kasbahs, the latter Muslims represented the greater part of the learning and intelligence of the community, but they are poor and impoverished.' Still, he hoped that a careful register of rights in groves, gardens and suburban zamindaris would give 'these respectable

---

[20] Petition of Namdar Khan, CPR, 2 Sept. 1800, 95/11, IOL.

gentlemen' some hope for the future, and that British administrative service would offer openings to them.[21]

Government employment was, in fact, the second main condition which defined the future of the *qasbahs*. In the early colonial period Awadh gentry were quite successful in retaining their hold on major appointments both within the Nawabi and outside. The Bilgramis were represented well at court, while the famous minister Mehendi Ali Khan continued to patronise this and other small centres of learning. A Bilgram man, Muhammad Khan, was also chief clerk of the Governor General in the Foreign Department during these years.[22] But the situation became more precarious everywhere towards mid-century. The abolition of Persian as an official language in 1836 closed off some openings: 'You don't need to learn Persian to be an oil seller!' ran a quatrain in the new, mordant literary language, Urdu. Then the annexation of the Kingdom of Awadh slimmed down the administration here as elsewhere, and gave new men from Bihar, Bengal and the east of the North-Western Provinces the chance to compete on equal terms with the local gentry even on their own turf. It is true that Muslims as a community remained well represented within British service and that after 1857 the *qasbah* elites did manage to adjust to an extent to the new demands. Many sought appointments in the service of refurbished Muslim regimes such as Awadh or Bhopal; others took up the challenge of an alien educational system through education at the Aligarh College. But the gross figures for provincial appointments cover over the evidence of considerable local decline amongst the old service elites of the Doab and western Awadh. For these men, 'Muslim decline' was more than a myth.[23]

Finally, the gentry were affected by the main lines of economic change which affected not only the Islamic *qasbahs*, but all the small towns of provincial India. The siting of major routes was of particular importance. One of the most obvious features of the distribution of the Awadh and Doab townships was that they mostly lay on the great Mughal roads – the trunk road from Delhi to Bengal, and the more ancient route from Kanauj to Fyzabad. After 1860, trade and administrative personnel was diverted by the coming of the railways and the decline of the Ganges–Jamna river traffic. Often trade and agricultural produce moved from declining *qasbah* to one of the new,

[21] M. L. Ferrar, *The Regular Settlement and Revived Assessment of the District of Sitapur in the Province of Oudh* (Lucknow, 1875), pp. 102, 126.

[22] *DG Hardoi*, p. 179; Haji Abbas Ali, *Historical Album of the Rajas and Taluqdars of Oudh* (Lucknow, 1880).

[23] Cf. Paul Brass, *Language, Religion and Politics in North India* (Cambridge, 1974).

bustling railway marts, denying the gentry their residual income from tolls and cesses. But even where *qasbahs* were able to benefit from the proximity of the railway lines, as in Hardoi which lay on the Lucknow–Shahjahanpur branch of the East India Railway, it was rarely the old elites who benefited. In Hardoi, several of the small towns were participating in a flourishing export trade in grain and vegetables by the 1870s. But one of the conditions of this success had been 'emancipation from the system of local cesses imposed by the landed proprietors'[24] when railway traders began to create their own free bazaars.

The fate of local industries also provided another variable. The small towns of Rohilkhand and Farrukhabad had successfully preserved their reputation for 'country cloth' and metalware, and many continued to support a substantial artisan population bringing in income from outside agriculture. In Tanda, Fyzabad and eastern Awadh, some of the old cloth centres also survived in a reduced form. Western Awadh and the Doab, however, were not so well placed. From the beginning they had fewer artisan industries, and those that existed seem to have disappeared during the hard years of the 1830s and 1860s. By the 1870s, for instance, Hardoi was importing Rs. 3 lakhs of English and country cloth from Fatehgarh, most of it for local consumption.[25]

The late nineteenth century was a poor time for the middle-sized landed estate.[26] It was a difficult time for the old service communities and it also saw serious challenges to the cultural dominance of the *qasbah* gentry. Under the patronage of commercial men and larger landholders, a revived Hinduism was taking the offensive. Within a hundred miles of Delhi, Hindu temples built in the spire form to differentiate them from mosques were still unusual before 1870. In the ancient town of Sandila in Awadh, an amicable Muslim intransigence had ensured that not a single Hindu temple was built in the town until the last quarter of the century.[27] Thereafter the reassertion of Hindu tradition was forceful. Caught between a new, interventionist European government and a revived popular Hinduism, the Muslim small town gentry sniffed decline.

For some towns, indeed, the problems of the mid-nineteenth century were simply the culmination of a slow process which had edged them out of control of economic resources. The town of Kara on the Ganges eight miles from Allahabad was a good example.[28] It had once been the

---

[24] *Settlement Report Hardoi*, p. 28; cf. *Settlement Report Sitapur*, p. 121.

[25] *SR Hardoi*, p. 28.

[26] Stokes, *Peasant and Raj*, pp. 214ff.

[27] *SR Hardoi*, p. 34.

[28] C. A. Bayly, 'The small town and Islamic gentry in north India. The case of Kara', in K. Ballhatchet and J. Harrison (eds), *The City in South Asia* (London, 1980), pp. 20–48.

provincial capital of Muslim empires in the central Ganges, but as early as 1586 it suffered the first blow when the representatives of high political authority moved to the more defensible site of Allahabad. During the Awadh and early Company periods, artisans and traders drifted off to growing market centres downriver. At the end of the eighteenth century, Kara and its environs were still producing as much as Rs. 15,000–20,000 of good quality cloths. Yet the signs of decline were already evident. Mrs Deare on her travels in 1815 noted that the earlier luxury trades had 'fallen off'. By 1816 the problems of the dyers and weavers had been increased by inflexible British duties on the raw materials the industry needed to import, so that:

The mahajuns and chintz printers of Shahjadpore [a suburb of Kara] are now migrating and establishing themselves in the Gunj of Zalim Singh on the opposite bank of the Ganges in Pergunneh Manickpore in the Domains of the Nawab Vizier.[29]

By the mid-nineteenth century, cloth production in the area had virtually ended, reflecting not so much the import of European goods as the political decline of the local elite. The histories of several Benares Agarwal families note that they emigrated to the city from Kara or nearby villages between 1820 and 1840; an indication of how fast merchant capital was bleeding away from the town during these years.

Yet before the elites of the *qasbahs* began successfully to adapt to the manufacture, Kara remained a centre of Muslim culture and of illustrious servants of government. Its total population declined over the century from about 15,000 to 2,000 but literacy remained high in the area, and local gentry managed to retain lucrative official posts both in British territory and in Indian states such as Hyderabad and Bhopal where the old scholarly traditions were still venerated. A powerful literary tradition represented by the great satirical poet, Akbar of Allahabad, continued to flourish among both Muslims and Hindus.[30] It was, in fact, out of the strong defensive traditions of this declining *qasbah* that emerged many of the first generation of Muslim political men and improving zamindars who created the Muslim League in the Allahabad area. The Urdu Defence Association was strong here as was the movement in defence of the Khilafat at the end of the First World War.[31] Like other small Muslim towns throughout north India, Kara made a disproportionate contribution to Muslim religious and political organisation in the modern era. The new academies – Aligarh College or Deoband – which equipped Muslims to face the western world, were

---

[29] CGC Allahabad to Bd, 23 Oct. 1816, CPR, 12 Nov. 1816, 97/59, IOL.
[30] Fida Hussain Obeidi, 'Tarikh-i-Kara', MSS Mohulla Bazaar, Kara.
[31] Bayly, *Local Roots*, pp. 174, 223, 255.

finishing schools for a cultural education which began in places like Kara or in the tight-knit Muslim quarters of the large cities with which they were closely linked.

Yet before the elites of the *qasbahs* began successfully to adapt to the economic pressures of British rule, they were faced with the savage shock of the 1857 Rebellion. Attempts to explain the behaviour of men under pressure and men in fear of death in terms of their social milieu are, of course, always open to question. All the same, a consideration of the role of large towns and *qasbahs* during 1857 opens up a new vista on the Rebellion besides illustrating some of the themes of the last two chapters.

The Great Rebellion in the towns

While the origins of the 1857 Rebellion are only partly to be found in the towns and rural bazaars, urban strong points provided the focus of operations for the Raj and the rebels alike. On the British side, success depended on keeping the Grand Trunk Road open as a supply route for the beleaguered garrisons which maintained a tenuous connection between the European forces in Bengal and the Punjab. Just as the towns with their Mughal strong points and client mercantile communities had provided the point of entry for British power into upper India, so in the early months of 1857 when the system of alliances with the rajas of the hinterland had collapsed, British power was rolled back once again on to this fragile network of roads and forts. As it transpired, the Trunk Road and the Ganges were controlled by the British throughout the struggle. The gunboat *Coil* was able to cruise up and down the river bombarding rebellious fortresses, while the advancing British armies were supplied with grain and stores by the boats of the great mercantile firms who had been so conspicuously benefited by British rule.

There were some critical moments, though. In May and June 1857, much of the hinterland of the Benares Division had joined the western districts in revolt. The dispossessed landholding communities who had seen their power eroded first by the rise of the Bhumihar rulers of Benares and later by the British auction sales sought to regain their position. Embittered Muslim gentry of Jaunpur, Macchlishahr and the interior towns joined them in revolt. Only Benares, where British rule had beaten off two successive revolts in 1781 and 1799, and Mirzapur, a new commercial centre, remained in their hands. Even in these cities, the bazaars were full of ominous rumours. It was crucial that the alliance with the mercantile, Rajput and Bhumihar people of Benares city held for 'the loss of Benares would have left us [the British] the whole country to reconquer almost from the gates of Calcutta'.[32] Once the British had regained the initiative here the occupation of the west proceeded much like the conquest of 1801–6. Towns and their garrisons were secured. From these, control over the big rural bazaars was reimposed, and the alliances with the landholding communities were repaired by a deft use of confiscation, hanging and revenue patronage.

Though the Rebellion is generally seen as a rural or even peasant uprising, towns and bazaars played an equally important part in the calculations of the rebels. In the west of the provinces, the wars of 1857–8 took the form of a series of skirmishes around key urban centres. Sometimes indeed it seemed to degenerate into a struggle between Islamic *qasbah* towns and the lineage centres of the interior zamindars – a replay of some of the events of the Rohilla and Bangash conquest of the local Rajputs some 120 years before. Both practical and symbolic considerations encouraged the rebel leaders of Rohilkhand and Farrukhabad to seek control of the old garrison *qasbahs*. These had been the seats of their *gaddis* (thrones) and the centres of their revenue holdings. Thus around Bareilly, the revolt became an informal levée of the Rohilla gentry from the small towns who gathered in support of Khan Bahadur Khan, descendant of the old Rohilla leader, Hafiz Rehmat Khan. This was reminiscent of the events of 1774 when the Rohillas had mobilised to face the Nawab of Awadh, and it resembled the house tax revolt of 1816. But there were crucial differences. In 1816 the British had retained control of the family of Hafiz Rehmat Khan and deprived the revolt of its ultimate legitimacy. In 1772 and 1816 Hindu landholders had fought alongside the Rohillas. But in 1857 attempts by the 'rebel' successor regime to bring in its revenue brought fighting with the Hindu chieftains which erupted into bitter communal conflict.

In 1857 we see for almost the last time the temporary re-emergence of the old forms of urban government and community control which had slowly been eroded by the European-style police and magistracy. Whether they did so as a conscious act of rebellion or merely in their role as protector of the people, the *kazi* and *mufti* families widely emerged as leaders in the Rebellion and arbitrators of its conflicts. In Bareilly the reconstituted Nawabi government was headed by a council of the Muslim law officers and mercantile leaders of the city's quarters. They concerted to put an end to cow-slaughter by Muslims which had caused such antagonism between the two communities in the 1830s. In Coil (Aligarh) the main mosque was used as a centre of organisation from

[32] Narrative of Events, Jt Magt. Jaunpur, *Freedom Struggle in Uttar Pradesh* (Lucknow, 1957), IV, 25.

which holy war was declared against the infidel. In Banda the rebellious Nawab reinstituted the post of *mufti* 'to please God and Man'.[33] But the tactic of reintroducing Islamic government was not always successful. The famous Maulvi of Fyzabad was unable to prevail against the influence of the Royal Mother and the Hindu courtiers who supported her. In Allahabad the local radical *maulvi* Liaqat Hussain established his writ amongst the artisan Muslims of the city and the petty landholders of the outer villages.[34] Immediately he installed himself with a guard of ex-*kotwali peons* in Amir Khusru's garden which had been the moral centre of the city's headless Muslim community in the eighteenth century. But the leading Shia divines of the city would not follow him, declaring that this was a political, not a religious, revolt and that Shias could only be led in holy war by a Shia *imam*.[35] Unsupported and without the stabilising force of a legitimate political authority, religious revolts of this sort tended to be divisive and impeded the rebels' cause. The authority of the rebel successor states was most obvious where the old ruling elites remained relatively intact, as in Rohilkhand or Central India. In the Gangetic cities where they had been eroded in the eighteenth century or overlaid with new networks of commercial power, revolt was scattered and fragmentary.

Commercial groups are widely thought to have been unanimous supporters of the colonial rulers during the revolt. But this is an oversimplification. Actually there are a substantial number of cases on record where commercial people gave quite strenuous support to the rebels. In Jaunpur the family of the district treasurer which had ancient links of patronage with some of the rebellious zamindars was regarded as suspect by the British.[36] In Delhi again it was the prestigious Gurwala family of Chandni Chowk which acted as financial officer of the rebel court. New men such as the Vahi Khattri family of Chunna Mal Saligram kept up a correspondence with the British and benefited by getting large tracts of central Delhi under their control during the confiscations of 1858.[37] But the commercial elite was favourable to the Mughal house at least until British forces began the siege of the city.

The commercial families who were most implacably opposed to the Rebellion were those who had least connection with the old royal courts. The families of grain and cotton traders who had prospered on the growth of the commercial economy after 1816 threw in their lot with the

33 *Ibid.*, I, 437.   34 *Ibid.*, IV, 549.
35 'Mutiny rewards', post-Mutiny basta 212, Records of the Commissioner of Allahabad, Commissioner's Bungalow, Allahabad.
36 'Mutiny rewards'; District Jaunpur, Benares Commissioner's Records, 225 Judl, 1858, UPR.
37 *Rokad Khata*, Chunna Mal Saligram, 1858–9, film in author's possession.

British almost unanimously. This was not surprising. To them the Mutiny seemed little different from the periodic waves of looting of their river boats by interior zamindars such as happened during the 1830s. So also the 'auction purchasers' amongst the small town moneylenders were adversely affected by a movement which in many areas took the form of a reassertion of ancient land-rights. It was not that capital was invariably opposed to the rebels: what mattered was the type of capital.

Yet for every merchant who threw in his lot with the British or the rebels, there were ten who hedged their bets. In many areas the mercantile corporations emerged as powerful, coherent bodies, with definite but very limited political objectives as in the eighteenth century. Their main aim was the preservation of peace and the continuation of the link between revenue and trade. In Kanpur for instance, the *mahajans* of the city led by 'Gunga Pershad tent-maker, and Jugal Kishore, jeweller, and Badri panseller and Shew Kishore khazanchee [treasurer]' concerted together and recommended to the rebel leader, Nana Sahib, the appointment of Holas Singh as *kotwal* of the city.[38] The military contractor family of Sheo Prasad Tunti Mul which, as Nana Sahib rightly charged, had 'risen under the protection of the English', initially worked with the rebel regime and only later reopened correspondence with the British as their power revived.[39] In Benares, Mirzapur, Delhi and Agra, the councils of the 'sahukars' worked with the authorities, be they British or rebel, to suppress looting and control communal outbreaks. Other old corporations played a similarly ambiguous role, seeking in general to protect their interests. The Gosain *maths* of Benares and Allahabad were at first suspected of complicity in the Rebellion, despite their holdings of government promissory notes. By contrast, the British sought to use the pilgrimage priests of Bindachal (Mirzapur) to counteract anti-British religious propaganda.[40] And the priests of the great Hanumangarhi temple at Ajodhya who had recently been in dispute with local Muslim officers openly supported the British at the beginning of the revolt.[41]

By the winter of 1857, when the British were once again on the offensive and reinforcements were already disembarking at Calcutta, the commercial community of the Gangetic cities had come out openly in support of the British. The volume of supplies going to isolated British garrisons increased rapidly, while the incoming troops had no difficulty in securing transport and credit facilities. The British

[38] *Freedom Struggle*, IV, 528–9.
[39] Recommendation of Sheo Prasad, son of Tunti Mall, Benares Commissioner's Records, 49 Revenue of 1879, UPR.
[40] *Freedom Struggle*, IV, 46.   [41] Interviews, Ajodhya, 1973.

recognised the contribution of the mercantile world and rewarded it handsomely with offices and grants of land sequestered from the rebels. Perhaps the most remarkable return to grace was that of Joti Prasad, the famous Khattri contractor of Agra, who had been prosecuted for corruption during the second Sikh war. He had supplied for several months the 5,000 Europeans and Indian Christians who had been besieged in the Agra Fort. It was freely admitted that 'Without Jooteepersad we could not have held Agra!'[42] But in other towns the story was the same. At Delhi it was the relatively humble family of Chunna Mal Saligram which prevailed over the ancient firms of the Chandni Chauk to entrench themselves as the powerful notables of the post-Mutiny period. Their first extant commercial ledger dates from 1858–61 and records massive transactions of up to Rs. 10 lakhs connected with the purchase and sale of the urban properties forfeited by the rebellious Muslim aristocracy of the city. In Allahabad and Kanpur, it was related branches of another Khattri family, the Tandons, who emerged as the most opulent of these cities' commercial landowners after 1860.

There is another side to the picture, however. The large-scale acquisitions of land by commercial men as a result of the events of 1857 brought about another substantial immobilisation of capital and skills in *rentier* land-management. Merchant families were tempted to round off their zamindaris with further purchases, and for many the comfort of a low regular return from landed property was to outweigh the larger but more uncertain returns from trade and contracting. While it is difficult to say what effect this had on the economy of the area as a whole, it certainly helped to confirm the conservative style of the late nineteenth-century business community.

The events of the Rebellion also illustrated some of the social tensions within towns and between towns and countrymen, which had lain dormant since the end of the eighteenth century. Almost everywhere the breakdown of public order was followed by attacks on the commercial quarters of the towns on the part of communities whose style of life had been cramped by the growth of colonial bureaucracy and the commercial economy. Some of these were old military groups which had not adapted well to the new peaceable ways, such as the circles of Meo and Mewati gentry who surrounded the towns of the west or the suburban Pathan villagers near Allahabad. Others like the Banjaras of Pilibhit or the Gujar 'cattle thieves' of the Moradabad Division inherited the great tradition of armed plunder which had reached its height in the 1780s. Once the British had disappeared, townsmen expected attack. In

---

[42] J. Lang, *Wanderings in India* (London, 1859), p. 192.

the summer of 1857, Banjaras were reported to be 'gathering in the woods for mischief'[43] around Bijnour, while 'Pindaris' were supposedly marching on Mirzapur. These fears reflected memories of attacks which had happened as recently as 1812; sometimes they were fully justified.

There is no reason to develop an elaborate set of proximate economic causes to explain the participation in the Rebellion of marginal groups who were constantly on the look-out for booty in peace or war. It was quite usual indeed for Gujars, Mewatis and other robber-bands, to have their own well-designated quarters of cities which constituted their own private plunder grounds. But there are some indications that the peripheral role in the commercial economy which some of these people had filled during better times predisposed them to plunder. For instance, the Gujars who looted the sugar wagons of a Hindu commercial magnate of Bulandshahr were themselves *chaukidars* or security guards in the local wholesale markets. One of the attempts made by the Bulandshahr people to buy off the Gujars centred on a proposal that they should receive 'fixed pay' in future.[44] Day labourers from marginal groups who participated in the unstable export economy were particularly vulnerable to its fluctuations; one explanation of the nature of the plundering that took place in 1857 is that such people were attempting to guarantee their own security by securing bullion, ornaments and other negotiable items. For instance, in the small town of Sekunderabad in the same district, the well-organised Gujars first defeated the stubborn defence of Muslim weavers, carpet-makers and gentry[45] and then systematically looted the bazaars:

the town was ruined and desolate, and the rebels . . . continued for two or three months digging out and carrying away the rafters and door parts and doors, and in search of ornaments, etc, ruined all the houses.[46]

In nearby Bijnour, Meos and Jats attacked the town of Chandpur, while Jats of Sawaheri looted the rich Muslim hucksters and small merchants of the place.

Fissures also opened up between different groups of townsmen. Quite widely it was the Muslim artisans and bazaar craftsmen who initiated conflict by attacking commercial men and landlords. In Najibabad, for instance, the rebel leaders secured the support of 'many Muslims including weavers and all the peddlars of Saweheri whom the Hindus had been exploiting';[47] these discontented elements all came together

43 Sayyid Ahmed Khan, 'Tarikh-i Sarkashiy Zillah Bijnaur', tr. Hafeez Malik and M. Bembo, *Sir Sayyid Ahmed Khan's History of the Bijnor Rebellion* (East Lancing, 1974), p. 16.
44 *Freedom Struggle*, v, 47.　　45 *Ibid.*, p. 41.　　46 *Ibid.*, p. 47.
47 Sayyid Ahmed, *Bijnor*, p. 74.

near Jelalabad 'under the Muhammedi flag'. At Haldaur, the Muslim cloth printers and confectioners had been at odds with Hindu landlords over house rentals. Early in 1857 they set fire to all the houses of the town in order to encourage the rebel leadership.[48] Later they were wiped out by the avenging Hindu landlords.

Even in Benares city itself where the town population remained remarkably quiet, Muslim weavers temporarily raised the green flag of holy war.[49] The proclamation of the Maulvi of Azamgarh claims that the general dislocation of the weaving and other artisan industries which resulted from the decline of the old courtly centres was regarded as a general grievance. And vengeance was often wreaked on moneylenders who were the most obvious agents of poverty. As in the 1830s, conflicts and fears over the running of the grain markets also contributed to the explosive tension of the towns. In the Awadh bazaars, the British were supposed to be distorting the grain market by hoarding and monopolising by means of the military commissariat.[50] Town-dwellers who had no easy access to food were as frightened as they had been during the earlier subsistence crises, and their natural response was to loot wealthy neighbours.

The Rebellion of 1857 uncovered many agrarian economic tensions, but basically it was a succession struggle fought out in the context of an abrupt collapse of British power. As such, it was a political crisis, and like the earlier crisis of the Indian polities, it had consequences for the way in which religious communities and castes related to each other. Where viable regimes established themselves speedily as in Delhi or Lucknow, communal tension was minimised. But in areas such as Rohilkhand or the Doab, where British rule had rapidly eroded the authority of the indigenous powers, political conflict might easily take on a religious tinge. In Bijnour, Sayyid Ahmed recorded that there had been little tension between the communities because many Hindus had continued to seek employment in the great Muslim households. As a consequence of the Rebellion, 'the tree of Hindu–Muslim aversion . . . became tall and too firmly rooted to be dug out'.[51] Once the great landed houses of the district were pitted against each other, economic and social distinctions between Hindu corporate bodies and Muslim gentry *qasbahs* proved a fertile field for the growth of real conflict between the communities. In many small towns, for instance, artisans who were

48 *Ibid.*, p. 76.
49 Benares Collectorate Records, Narrative of Events, 1857, UPR.
50 *Freedom Struggle*, I, 282; for other grievances, *Tilsim* (Firangi Mahal, Lucknow), 22 Aug. 1856, discussed Iqbal Hussain, 'Lucknow between the Annexation and the Mutiny', mimeo, n.d., Aligarh. M.U.
51 Sayyid Ahmed, *Bijnor*, p. 47.

Muslims in the main attacked Hindus who were commercial men and urban landlords in the main, and this began to give the impression of general conflict on sectarian lines. On the other side, a Hindu sect called the Bishnois were very prominent in the assaults on Muslim *qasbah* towns which occurred once the British had withdrawn. The Bishnois were a successful trading and agricultural group with very different economic interests from artisans and gentry. The particular bitterness between Bishnois and Muslims also had a cultural dimension. The Bishnois had adopted Islamic forms of dress, deportment and greeting while remaining practising Hindus, and this gave great offence to orthodox Muslims. Economic and cultural differences between the intermediate groups in society could easily reinforce each other and give rise to permanent distrust when the aristocracy was unable to play its part as arbitrator.

Conclusion: the *qasbah* and Indian society

Urban history can no longer be seen as a self-contained field of study, especially in the Indian context. However, the history of gentry *qasbah* and commercial city illustrates more general themes in the society and politics of north India.

As an urban type, for instance, the north Indian Muslim *qasbah* represents some of the features of the classic Islamic city from Algeria to Indonesia. But in important respects it deviated both from the pattern of the larger Muslim cities in India and from the classic forms discussed by Islamicists such as Massignon, Hourani, Stern and Lapidus. The *qasbahs* we have discussed had once been on the fringes of Muslim society. They originated as colonies of Sufis and gentry deliberately placed in the midst of a wholly Hindu and rural environment. Some of them were founded before regular Muslim authority had been established throughout the area; always they were on guard against the intrusions of the great Hindu land-controlling clans of the hinterland. A degree of self-organisation and a definite corporate pride and tradition were, therefore, necessary to guarantee survival. The Muslim ruling power was distant, even though men from the *qasbahs* sought service with it and the rulers occasionally made revenue-free grants to local divines.

L. Massignon's picture of the emergence of a guild-like, corporate identity for Muslim cities within the framework of the mystic brotherhoods has come in for criticism recently.[52] Guilds, it has been argued, were no more than the tools of political power used to control

---

[52] A. Hourani and S. M. Stern (eds), *Papers on Islamic History*, I, *The Islamic City* (Oxford, 1970), 13.

the urban environment, and the lack of organisation within the Muslim city reflected a wider lack of formal organisation within Muslim society as a whole. But these Indian settlements seem to have something of that corporate identity and self-organisation which Massignon described. And this was most true during periods when local power was at a premium. The corporate identity of such towns was represented not only by the links of learned men and Sufis, and by the connection of local Muslims and Hindus with the tombs of saints and warriors, but also by the very structure of the gentry itself. Marriage alliances and traditions of service and scholarship associated with the particular home town bound the Sheikh and Sayyid gentry together, but also proved strong enough to assimilate new men (some of them even Hindus). The fact that Kakori or Bilgram did not have definite municipal institutions and a definite legal corporation is immaterial. The public offices of *kazi*, *kanungo* and *mufti* were indeed derived from the ruler in theory; but in practice they became tools of local authority and independence. Neither the Islamic *qasbah* nor the Hindu commercial corporation were prone in the face of a dominant political authority.

Since the gentry *qasbah* was an important context of Muslim activity, does its history in the early nineteenth century help illuminate the question of the origin of later Muslim political separatism in north India? Some of the small towns were the scene of conflict between the two major religious communities in the 1830s, and political conflict took a religious tinge during the Rebellion of 1857 in parts of the west. But on the whole, outbreaks were limited to the larger towns before the 1890s. The conditions which led to conflict here in the first two generations of colonial rule were much slower to develop in the *qasbahs*. The British system had not disrupted local offices and statuses to the same extent, and wealthy trading communities tended to drift off to growing commercial centres rather than express their social independence within the local arena. There was less room for conflict or the reorganisation of ceremonial precedences because landed or commercial representatives of one community were dominant.

Qasbah towns then remained integrated Muslim societies while many of the trading centres were overwhelmingly Hindu in flavour. But this was itself important for the future. The two most significant social formations to emerge after the decline of the Mughal empire had been a unified merchant class and a locally resident service gentry. Large sections of both of these groups operated in sharply different economic and cultural contexts. In many areas, trade and marketing patterns had diverged quite sharply from the links of employment and patronage which sustained the service gentry.

At the same time, local organisation was related to religious traditions which, though far from being mutually hostile, were already sharply and consciously different. Recent interpretations of Muslim separatism have emphasised the importance of government policy and the creation of self-identity through the new schools and colleges of the larger cities after 1870. But in the early nineteenth century profound impediments to the emergence of a unified Indian middle class already existed. These were not recent developments but arose from the different political and economic histories of urban communities in the pre-colonial states.

The problems of service gentry under colonial rule also help to set the scene for some other themes in the history of the later colonial period. As the previous section showed, conflicts between the *qasbah* elites and the Hindu notables of the hinterland or between commercial men and artisans of the small towns added a further skein to the complex events of the Revolt of 1857. Again, in the later nineteenth century, the social and educational platforms of both the Muslim League and bodies representing Hindu clerical people from small towns (such as the various Kayastha associations) reflect the tensions of petty landholding and government service. The predicament of this half-formed Indian gentry also provides an essential background to a proper analysis of the agrarian tensions of more recent times. As late as the 1820s, *qasbahs* remained a dynamic force in many parts of the countryside, bringing employment and some investment to the surrounding rural societies. Inflation, the subdivision of holdings and diminished access to government employment after the middle of the nineteenth century changed the picture. Descriptions of agrarian conflict around the turn of the present century have often dwelt on conflicts between substantial peasant and the great *taluqdar*. Yet a very large proportion of incidents of agrarian violence in the Doab and western Awadh featured a backlash of frightened petty gentry who had only a tenuous hold on government service and the rural economy. It is only over the longer term of pre-colonial and colonial history that the evolution of these themes can be fully appreciated.

10

The merchant family

The following two chapters deepen the analysis of the intermediate groups of Indian society with a study of the behaviour and perceptions of the merchant family of the early colonial period. The aim throughout the work has been to trace the emergence over the longer term of some of the key elements which came to make up the 'middle classes' of north India in the later nineteenth century. In this way it is hoped to provide a more adequate account of the connection between India's colonial and pre-colonial history. We saw that the gloomy political reputation of the eighteenth century concealed significant developments. Though merchant capital in coastal India suffered from the disruption of international trade and the growing stranglehold of the British on the eastern sea-routes, merchant people in the interior gained from the drive of the smaller, successor states for cash revenue and the buoyant consumption by their aristocracies and their soldiery of artisan and agricultural produce. Though political flux and the waning of the power of Delhi destroyed the Mughal nobility, a locally resident and predominantly Islamic gentry continued to divert the rewards and perquisites of office to landholding and the embellishment of small towns. In their early days, British trade and administration were dependent on these emerging social groups.

During the early colonial period, gentry and merchants, like the princely regimes which they served, gained security from the expansion of trade and administration. But neither was securely established or independent enough to experience the decay of the old political order which speeded up after 1825, without some disruption. The decline of princely and military regimes affected merchant firms which were simultaneously trying to adjust to the instabilities of external trade, and many found themselves saddled with large tracts of land in settlement of debts which they were unable to manage. Service gentry found themselves competing for a declining volume of military and administrative service with a still unsteady hold on *rentier* income. The decline of the old order also had subtler effects. The new style of colonial government tended to widen fissures between corporate institutions and communities whose interests had already diverged as a result of the uneven political and economic changes of the eighteenth century. Strains between different elements of the intermediate classes were reflected in explosions of communal violence and conflicts with the colonial authorities.

Thus far, however, this has been a picture of the formation of classes largely from the outside. Much of the nature and outlook of the modern Indian business class or the erstwhile Muslim gentry can, of course, be explained by reference to the form of the state or of petty peasant commodity production. Not surprisingly, then, these Indian groups have something in common with those found in other Asian or Islamic agrarian monarchies. Chinese merchant society, for instance, was delicate and sophisticated, yet also arcane and impenetrable to Europeans.[1] Here the formal hostility of the Confucian system to trade and the instabilities of agricultural production formed family- and kin-based trading institutions which had much in common with their Indian counterparts. Again, the fact of working within a colonial state both set limits to the development of local capitalists and provided them with access to new legal forms and commercial security. This was as true of colonial Egypt or Indo-china as it was of India. But there were, and are, features of the Indian middle classes, and especially of the commercial sections, which are unique, just as there are features of the Indian peasantry which are unique. These derive ultimately from the relationship between the family firm or the family farm and the institutions of caste, marriage and religion. Even though Weber's grandiose formulation of these relationships may fall at the first fence, an account which ignores the social dimension of Hindu and Jain business life (or Islamic gentry life) is ultimately unsatisfactory, simply because it is unable to explain much of what merchants did and even more of what they appear to have thought. As this chapter will show, caste and religion, or more precisely conceptions of 'right marriage', piety and credit, were central to the basic operations of the family firm as a unit. First, however, it is necessary to take a broader view of the form of the merchant class in the early colonial period.

By the early nineteenth century, then, there existed a north Indian merchant class. By this is meant a group of entrepreneurial castes with common professional practices who were also linked together through a system of hierarchically organised markets. These Hindu and Jain commercial castes had not always exercised such a firm grip on trade even in the larger villages and cities. Mughal notables, Muslim traders from the northern hills, and Banjaras had all performed many of the

[1] A.L. McElderry, *Shanghai Old-Style Banks (Ch'ien-Chuang) 1800–1935* (Ann Arbor, 1976).

functions which the branch agencies of established commercial families came to perform later. Vast numbers of specialised, local-purpose coinages had existed, and in many regions the links between the village grain dealer (bania), the local money dealer (*sarraf*), the travelling trader (*faria*), and the great merchant of the city (*mahajan* or *sahu*) had been tenuous.

The conditions of the eighteenth century, however, encouraged greater market integration, at least in the settled areas. The farm for cash of the whole range of royal perquisites had helped to extend the branches of the large city firms to small towns and *ganjs*. The building of local polities had also widely displaced Gujeratis, 'Multanis' and Muslims from long-distance trade, replacing them with families drawn from rural commercial communities. Finally, the revival of Hindu religion in the new states provided standards of orthodox behaviour to which all who participated in the moral community of the merchant were constrained to respond.

The changes accompanying early colonial rule further consolidated the merchant class. The British needed district treasurers and commissariat purchasing agents in remote subdivisions. Members of the major commercial families hurried along new, more secure roads to fill these positions. By 1840, a standard imperial coinage and system of weights and measures had been created. In the short term the abolition of local treasuries created hardship, and the conservative corporations of Benares and Farrukhabad bitterly resisted the standardisation of weights and measures.[2] But in the longer term, commercial society became more cohesive as many levels of petty brokers and money dealers were eliminated from the market process. The role of travelling merchants, Banjaras and other middlemen was also reduced as fixed, multi-purpose markets developed around military and civil stations. In the eighteenth century, merchant capitalists had already achieved financial control over Banjara bands. Now they subordinated them altogether, hiring pack-drivers directly as virtual wage labourers.

How far did the legal and administrative systems erected by the British impinge on the moral community of the merchants? To the colonial administrators, the 'bunnea' was, unfortunately, the chief beneficiary of colonial rule. To the merchants relief at the disappearance of the arbitrary levies of indigenous governments was modified by irritation at frequent interventions in the 'custom of the merchants' in

[2] The existing system was so complex that Farrukhabad merchants expected to suffer from the change; according to Agra merchants Benares resisted out of 'self-willed ignorance and intolerance of all change', Govt NWP to Bd of Revenue, 18 Aug. 1835, Mirzapur Judl, 42, UPR.

the interests of administrative tidiness. The relationship between government and merchant remained as ambiguous as it had been before. Merchant society worked on secret, inward lines of communication and trust, though government continued to provide employment and even honour. But some changes were perceptible. As in other spheres, the British tended to create a single customary law out of many different local customs. Practices like the 'plunder' by his peers of a bankrupt merchant were gradually replaced by recognised forms of arbitration of 'respectable mahajans' initiated through the local courts.[3] The notion of individual legal responsibility was introduced, though how far it eroded joint responsibility for debts varied from community to community. Most important, the relative security of mercantile documents in arbitration before recognised courts encouraged a greater use of paper instruments of credit. By the 1830s and 1840s endorsed *hundis* had attained the status of a mercantile paper currency. A *hundi* might circulate through the hands of twenty or thirty different businesses unknown to the issuant, before it was finally cashed.[4] This use of the *hundi* in providing more extensive merchant credit was implicit in earlier business practice, but it became general in the early nineteenth century.

   The merchant corporation itself showed few outward signs of development. In Benares, the merchants of the Naupatti Sabha continued to adjudicate cases as they had done in the eighteenth century. The procedure became more formal. 'Respectable native merchants' were issued with collectorate badges[5] and held lists of 'accredited mahajans'. In Agra, a less hidebound commercial centre, a kind of trades council which operated a series of regulations set out in the western manner had come into existence.[6] 'General merchants' of an English type also began to appear in the environs of the great military stations. However, it was the continuities in Indian commercial life and

---

[3] Merchant arbitrations and caste councils continued to operate but their judgements were increasingly challenged in civil courts; 'respectable merchants' might then be asked to submit written evidence on custom, etc., see the correspondence between Lala Harrakhchand of Benares and the local courts in his 'Memory Book' (*Yadasht Bahi*), c. 1818 to 1848, in possession of Dr Kumud Chandra, Benares, e.g., Civil Court to Harrakhchand, 15 July 1838, requesting an inspection of the books of Bala Rao; cf. Persian letter from Court of the Additional Judge Benares to Harrakhchand, 17 April 1838 and reply, 21 April 1838, relating to the alleged outcasting of one Gobind Das.

[4] E.g., case 8 of 1849, Mirzapur, June 1849, *ZC*.

[5] Harrakhchand to Agency, 23 Nov. 1843, ref. circular 1196 Fasli, 'Memory Book', Chaukhambha.

[6] 'Mahajanon, sarraf, wa byoparon ke khayede ka khulasa', List of members of the Agra *Sarrafa* and working rules c. 1870 (film in author's possession); the chief firms here are those that had been accepted as heads of Agra commerce since the 1820s, esp. Piru Mall, Budh Sen, Nund Ram Chhote Lal.

the capacity of the older houses to incorporate newcomers into their moral community which was most striking.

The ideology of business practice remained cautious and conservative. From contemporary depositions and more recent family histories, it appears that merchant people had a very clear idea of dignity and status within the commercial world, and knew how to go about becoming a 'great merchant'. Different types of traders were ranked according to the fixity of their residence, the size of their capital, the respectability of their clients and the 'currency' of their credit notes within the bazaars.[7] The rank of their caste was important but it was only one consideration bearing upon their relations with the heads of the corporations. One went about raising status by coming closer and closer to the ideal of the 'respectable and professed' *mahajan*. This involved slowly moving out of trades (such as oils, liquor or leather) which were regarded as detrimental to status[8] and acquiring the reputation for soberness and respectability, possibly by acting as agent for some established concern.[9] Above all, it meant playing an active and steady part in the temple as well as the bazaar.

There were examples of social mobility in the Ganges valley during the early nineteenth century. Families of the liquor distiller (Kalwar) caste, for instance, consolidated the gains they had made in the eastern region during the late eighteenth century. In Allahabad and Benares, Kalwar families who had adopted the caste name Jaiswal and purified their domestic practice became respected members of the commercial oligarchy, participating for instance in the ritual exchanges of credit which began the business year.[10] Men from families which had once cultivated *betel* nut (Barais) also achieved wealth and respectability,[11] based no doubt, on the growing demand for luxuries like *betel* nut, snuff and tobacco in the large cities. There are also examples of men from landowning or cultivating castes establishing themselves as 'creditable' merchants and moneylenders. The Maharaja of Benares and several of the landholding Brahmin aristocracy of Benares, for instance, lent

[7] E.g., 'Summary of depositions taken in the case of the security of Nund Kishore who has offered to be responsible for the fulfilment of the contract on the part of Gungaram to farm the town duties of Agra', CGC Agra to Bd, 9 Oct. 1829, Agra Customs, 6, UPR.

[8] Martin, *Eastern India*, I, 369.

[9] *Gomashtas* or agents were paid small fees in '*gomashtagaree*'; these could be as little as Rs. 100–200 per annum in major firms (e.g., case 101 of 1849, Mirzapur, 27 July 1849, ZC). Agents were given almost unlimited trust and could enhance their own 'credit' as traders before entering into business independently.

[10] C. A. Bayly, 'Patrons and politics in northern India', *Modern Asian Studies*, vii, 3 (1973), 380–6; cf. account books of Gappoo Mall Kandheya Lal, Ranimandi, for the 1880s and 1890s.

[11] Interview and family history, Badal Ram Lakshmi Narayan, Benares, Jan. 1973.

money and maintained account books in the merchant style. There were even occasional cases of the cultivators of sugar and tobacco setting up their own shops in market towns and cutting out the various brokers and dealers who would normally have dealt with the produce.[12] All the same, the boundaries between merchants, landlords and cultivators remained quite firm, if permeable. To be a merchant, one had to submit to the discipline of the relations of the bazaar, and this involved accepting the sumptuary and religious as well as commercial practices of its inhabitants.

The following sections attempt an interpretation of aspects of the ideas and behaviour of north Indian merchant families in the early and mid-nineteenth century. Observers seeking a more vigorous spirit of entrepreneurship were inclined to describe their behaviour as 'queer'[13] or 'irrational'.[14] But it makes more sense to see the social and business practice of the merchant family firm as a special kind of economic enterprise. They sought profits, but only when subsistence and the mercantile credit which guaranteed it were already ensured. In order to ensure the continuation of credit, family firms had adopted practices and developed institutions which would be described by economists as 'risk averse'. The vagaries of climate, poor transport and the existence of a political authority which was at one and the same time weak and intrusive, encouraged close, inward-looking lines of communication and trust. Merchant society was efficient and sophisticated, but it was difficult for outsiders to penetrate. The men of the bazaar remained separate from the men who controlled land.

An analysis such as this is fraught with methodological problems. Is it, for instance, possible to describe a whole community of people as 'risk averse' as opposed to an individual firm? How can it be shown that firms were in fact forgoing profits for security when no long-term estimates of profit were available even to the firms themselves? Most seriously, what was the meaning of profit in a context where many families were directing their energies to improving their position within marriage groups or systems of sub-caste ranking, an equally vigorous form of entrepreneurship?

Historians' attempts to describe the activities of social units from the inside, linking economic practice with assumed goals and ideologies, have been hopelessly vague and imprecise from the point of view of

[12] Customs records have many examples of cultivators of indigo, sugar and tobacco becoming petty merchants, but only in high-value commodities of this sort where successful production required some prior knowledge of the working of the market.

[13] *Report of the United Provinces Provincial Banking Enquiry Committee, 1929–30* (Allahabad, 1931), IV, *evidence* (321).

[14] Jain, *Indigenous Banking in India*, p. 91.

orthodox anthropology or economics. But they have often been peculiarly enlivening and productive of debate, as witness Le Roy Ladurie's reconstruction of the moral economy of medieval herdsmen of the Pyrenees, or Kessinger's adaptation of Chayanov's 'peasant family farm' to the north Indian material. The analytical sketch which follows, therefore, is not intended to apply to all Indian merchants, or even all north Indian 'indigenous bankers' throughout the nineteenth century. It merely seeks to draw out some of the most constant themes which arise from their own documents or histories and from the comments of outsiders. This section, then, is intended to complement the earlier analysis by looking at the world of colonial north India from the vantage point of the merchant class itself.

The merchant family and its credit

From the perspective of the merchants themselves, the basis of mercantile society was the family 'firm', its credit (*sakh*) and the totality of its relations with gods and men, creditors and debtors. The 'firm' was not seen as something separate from the family; there was no commonly used word for firm as a concept, only as a location (*dukan* or *kothi*). And credit or reputation was not simply a residual category of financial benefit like 'goodwill' in a modern European firm. Without 'credit', a family could not trade or call on merchant arbitration at all. Merchant corporations kept lists of creditable merchants whose credit notes could expect rapid discount in the bazaar (*sahajog hundis*).[15] Even small dealers knew whose *hundis* were 'current' in the market and whose were not. In traditional commercial centres, the corporations imposed heavy penalties for breaches of trust in the same way that caste councils punished immorality. Sharp practice and unorthodox behaviour reflected both on the social and economic status of the group since merchant families had to be respectable marriage partners as well as trustworthy traders.

Even the word 'business' is a simplification of the term *mamle* ('concerns') which eighteenth-century merchants often used. For merchants concerns included the management of their temples, *ghats* and the ritual organisation of the bazaars which all impinged on the life of the family. Like the peasant 'family farm', the merchant family

---

15 S. Roy, *Customs and Customary Law in British India* (Calcutta, 1911), ch. XIV ('Trade Customs'), esp. p. 536; for an earlier exposition, 46 of 1853, Kanpur, 15 Aug. 1854, ZC; one type of *hundi* required endorsement, the other made out to 'bearer' often included the words 'Make sure you pay a respectable man, for you pay to any other at your own risk'. The intrusion of subjective notions of 'respectability' into *hundi* transactions enhanced the security consciousness of the old-style firms.

business was a 'special kind of economic enterprise' and one in which mercantile decisions were constantly taken with a view to their wider implications for the life of the family as a social group. In most firms, cash accounts and annual profit and loss accounts were meticulously kept, but the profitability of the business was almost impossible to calculate because many of its goals were incalculable social benefits. As in the peasant family, for instance, family members, servants and agents were rarely paid a cash wage; instead they had rights and obligations within the family economy. Many of the great houses provided accommodation and commercial space for poorer relatives and caste fellows within their own premises, and these were assessed as *prajawat* (a lordship due) which was generally customary. Like the classic peasant family, the whole household was also able to expand or restrict consumption in relation to the success of the trading season. Some families observed a rule of thumb that only ten or twenty per cent of their annual income should be expended, but during years when the family was anticipating a prestigious alliance, massive expenditures on charity, feasting and ritual were contemplated.[16] Orthodox economic reasoning might see this as 'conspicuous consumption', but from the point of view of the family it could equally be seen as 'investment' in social relationships which might have definite financial advantages in bad seasons, or at times when the family had to fall back on the resources of its peers to raise cash speedily.[17] There are problems with this, however. We should not assume that certain types of 'uneconomic' behaviour on the part of merchant families can always be explained in terms of an underlying rationality based upon the hope of future profits. In some cases, the profit-making part of a family's concerns was simply kept moving slowly in order to provide modest resources on which it could base its strategy for acquiring higher status through marriage alliance or royal office. It is common for economic historians to report that luxurious firms engaging in unwise expenditure were ousted by shrewd new men who turned their capital over more rapidly and avoided aristocractic connections. However, from the point of view of many high-status merchant families among the Khattris or Agarwals, notoriously high rates of profit were a positive mark of discredit. These new men may have achieved success in the bazaar, but the proper area of

[16] *Panchayats* for the arbitration of separations in joint-families took into account matters such as the imminence of a daughter's marriage. In one case 20% of the firm's assets are set aside for this purpose, see 199 of 1847, Saharanpur, June 1848, *ZC*; one branch of the Benares Shah family opened a special *khata* for the expenses of a daughter's marriage, beginning under date *Aghun Sudi* 10, *Sambat* 1911 (1854 A.D.), Shah Khatas (film in author's possession).

[17] Communication from Prof. Alan Heston to participants in the conference on 'Risk and Uncertainty', University of Pennsylvania, 1977.

entrepreneurship was society as a whole, and it was the cautious, pious and creditworthy who succeeded here.

This dual role of the merchant household as a profit-making enterprise and as a constellation of relationships through which honour was acquired and conferred was vividly illustrated in the standard form of account books (*bahi khatas*) which all significant families kept. Besides the daily cash book (*rokad khata*) and individual's account books (*lekha khata*), there often existed separate books dealing with a family's bullion and jewellery, urban and rural property, and daily expenses. In theory, all deposits or expenditures made by any member of the household in any domain of life could be traced here. Most books begin with salutations to various deities, lists of temple accoutrements and accounts of offerings to religious preceptors. The daily expense account (*kharach khata*) recorded constant expenditures on worship, bathing in the Ganges and gifts to Brahmins.[18] As in other highly orthodox communities, gods were considered to be integral, living members of the family, so that elaborate provisions were made in wills and trusts to see that they were clothed, fed and fanned during the hot weather. Besides the worship of family deities, most merchant families paid regular *puja* (worship) to Lakshmi, goddess of wealth, especially at Diwali and Holi festivals which were the beginning and end of the busiest part of the trading year respectively. Brahmins were also closely involved in the daily life of the business family. Many firms employed Brahmins as their agents or debt collectors, thus acquiring spiritual merit and an added religious sanction over their debtors. Among the Benares and Patna Khattris it was even common for their Saraswat Brahmin domestic priests to enter into business partnerships in the Punjab shawl and horse trades.[19]

Merchant books also reveal how different family members operated within the total economy. In one firm where the business was undivided and carried on by three brothers, their mother (always *Maji* in the accounts) appears to have been the linchpin in the purchasing of jewellery and provisions.[20] In general, access to family resources was determined by status within the family. In one case it was said that the elder brother was a spendthrift, but his sober younger brother was unable to 'say anything' because of his junior status. In undivided joint families where a senior partner had died, it was quite common for the uncle of the man's heirs to take over effective running of the business because of his greater experience.

More important even than these family relationships, however, was

18 See, e.g., the Shah *kothi*'s expense and daily books, *Sambat* 1929–33.
19 Interviews, Sri Devi Narayan; family histories, Benares, 1973.
20 Shah *kothi* expense books, *Sambat* 1929–33.

the relationship between the proprietors and their business clerks or *munims,* for it was often in their hands that the continuity and credit of the family were entrusted. Sometimes *munims* used their reputation to establish their own firms on the basis of the credit of their original employer. But *munims* often seemed to have passed on their employment to their heirs, so that an hereditary relationship grew up between the families of the principals and their clerks. *Munims* were not always of the same caste as their employers but nevertheless became an essential part of the extended household.[21] In the epidemic-ridden conditions of nineteenth-century Indian cities, it was common when adult male members of the family died to leave a *munim* as effective manager directing the business of female and minor members. Trusted retainers were necessary for the continuity of the family, and many didactic tales were in circulation to illustrate the honourable role of the *munim* in the family's credit.[22] One such has the spendthrift sons dismissing the aged *munim* on the death of their father. The business then goes from bad to worse. Finally, one evening a massive credit note for payment on sight (*darshani hundi*) arrives, running to lakhs of Rupees, which must be paid before the gun on the fortress signals nightfall if credit is to be retained. In a panic the young men beg the *munim* to return to the firm. At length he comes to the shop and mobilises his dead employer's friends among the merchants to provide cash to pay the *hundi.*

Finally, the books reveal the family acting as a system of ritualised occupational relationships within the city and its environs. For instance, dyers (*rangil*) appeared frequently in the expense books of the Agarwal firms.[23] This was because the colour of the saris of female members of these families was governed by peculiarly rigid conventions. Family priests, barbers, gold and silver workers and all sorts of artisans appear as borrowers, depositors and lenders. The hierarchy of relationships was not confined to humans either. In many of the more orthodox merchant households, cows occupied the bottom storey of the house. Their preservation and feeding was an act of religious devotion which also provided the family with milk and butter, and echoed the Vaishya scriptural occupation as cattle keepers. Men honoured the gods and the

[21] Thus the families of the connection of Sir Motichand Gupta in Benares traditionally had Gujerati *munims*, while the 'Calcuttawallah' Gujerati firm had north Indian Agarwal *munims*, interview, Sri Jyotibhushan Gupta, Feb. 1974; similar cross-caste relationships of trust bound firms' principals to *gomashtas* and *arethias*; there are cases where Hindu firms retained Muslim *arethias*, particularly in the shawl trade.

[22] Sri Ram Krishna and Sri Mathura Das of Benares provided many of these stories, interviews, 1972–4.

[23] Daily cash books of the family firm of Bhartendu Harish Chandra, *Sambat* 1942–3, in possession of Dr Kumud Chandra, Chaukambha.

sacred animals, but a reputation for piety no doubt redounded to their commercial credit. One story has the great merchant prince Kashmiri Mull visiting his rival, the austere and orthodox Manohar Das as the latter mucks out his cow sheds. 'Watch out for your shoes' cries Kashmiri Mull; 'Watch out for your accounts!' responds the other, implying a relationship between piety, frugality and mercantile success.

The merchant account books indicate how inextricably linked were the commercial and social goals of merchant families. But there was a sense in which the books themselves were a symbolic affirmation of the unity, continuity and credit of the family. Some of the older Delhi firms actually staged an annual ritual at which the old account books were worshipped as a virtual representation of the dutiful lives of the ancestors who founded the 'firm'. The idea of the long continuity of the family's substance and credit over time was reflected in other ways. In one firm, the sum total of capital passed over from one year's books to the next was entered in the name of the founder of the firm three generations before;[24] elsewhere account books which were no longer current were religiously returned year by year to the ancestral village of a family which had left it eight to ten generations before. The most crucial span of generations for the passage of credit, however, was three. According to the Shastric texts, a man was responsible for the debts of his forefathers to this extent.[25] The payment of such debts was a prior duty even to the fathering of an heir, though it was only a male heir who could guarantee his own translation to the status of an honoured ancestor after death, and to ultimate salvation, through the rites of *shraddha*. Thus, the names of firms often joined together grandfather and grandsons in a three-generation span, and the evidence suggests that such relationships of credit and debt did persist over very long periods as late as the eighteenth century. When the British tried to introduce the idea of individual competence in law and temporal limitation of liability in the Bengal Regulations of 1793, there was an immediate outcry:

In bankers' concerns it is the old established rule that the descendants are responsible for and must pay the debts of four generations, whether they have inherited of a grandfather's wealth and possessions or may have been left nothing in consequence of their poverty.... The purport of the order in the existing regulations is that if a son shall not have inherited the wealth of his father that son shall not be responsible for his father's debts. Honourable Sir, the concerns of the bankers are decreased and their incomes ruined.[26]

---

24 Books of Gappoo Mall Kandheya Lal, Ranimandi, Allahabad.
25 Raghunandan, cit. H. T. Colebrooke, *A Digest of Hindu Law on Contracts and Succession. Translated from the Original Sanscrit* (Calcutta, 1797), I, 6.
26 Representation of the Principal Bankers of Benares, 13 Jan. 1795, PR.

Liability for debts was thus conceived to be coterminous with the ritual unit which was directly involved in the oblation rite of *pitraprajna* or *shraddha*. But the consequence of failure to repay, which was deemed a sin, should also fall on the debtor's family as a whole.

In former times when any person became bancrupt [sic] and was absconding, he absconded with all his family from apprehension of his creditors, and we who were in search of him obtained intelligence of his place of residence in consequence of his family being along with him. And then indeed being embarrassed and distressed from his being accompanied by his family, he informed us that our money should be paid.[27]

But as a result of the Regulations, the petition went on, a debtor could 'sit quietly at his home with comfort and satisfaction to his women and children, with ornaments and numerous attendants'. Here again the slow introduction of elements of British commercial law had cut into areas of customary practice which derived from an almost physical notion of the passage of credit within a family.

This helps to explain the extreme reluctance to show books to outsiders which characterised the old-style firm. Their opening is always attended by a feeling of ceremony. When a man agrees to show 'my books' (never 'the firm's books') he is, as it were, discovering the credit of his ancestors. The most reluctant of all to do this were the Jains who maintained strong sanctions against the release of any information about ancestry, commercial or sexual practices, even to Brahmin families which had been associated with them for generations. When merchants claimed that their credit would suffer by showing their books in the ruler's court, they were not simply making a statement about commercial morality, but about the honour of the family. Hence it followed that the production of books in open court was considered superior evidence in a suit even to oaths made on Ganges water. The witness was making a solemn statement equivalent to a Muslim oath over the tombs of ancestors. For merchants of prestige even to be called upon to produce books in court was, therefore, a source of discredit:

in consequence of their books being there produced [in court] our concerns appear to foreign bankers to be unimportant and embarrassed.[28]

One of the features of merchant society before the middle of the nineteenth century was the devastating consequences of loss of credit. A trader who could no longer buy and sell in the market might be reduced to penury more speedily even than a peasant who lost his land. The peasant at least retained the hope of being employed as a field labourer by the new owner. But there were cases in the Benares of Jonathan

[27] *Ibid.*   [28] Representation of Bankers, 15 Sept. 1790, PR.

Duncan where great merchants who had participated in the business of state lost their credit and died of starvation.[29]

Interpretations of the behaviour of the peasant farmer in an uncertain world have stressed that his first concern was always to guarantee subsistence. Many of the seemingly irrational procedures for working land, 'hoarding' and investment seem explicable in these terms. The political and social priorities of cultivators seem to reflect what has been called the 'subsistence ethic'. The behaviour and ideals of the merchant family firm were also directed to survival first and foremost, but survival here meant above all the continuity of family credit within the wider merchant community. There is nothing to suggest that the old-style Indian merchant did not wish to make money, but questions of profit and loss had always to be set in the context of the future of the family as a whole. Like modern western business enterprises, they split up their trading operations into 'portfolios' which could be manipulated in order to avoid risks. Yet at the same time decisions in the sphere of money-making had to be adjusted to the goals of social survival and enhancement in the uncertain world of caste politics and marriage alliance.[30]

Business credit was a commodity which could slowly disappear if a family allowed its substance to be degraded by suspect behaviour or by unworthy marriage alliances. Marriage for all Indian families has been a most tricky and complicated aspect of life. The higher the caste, the higher the status and fewer the options. For Indian merchants marriage posed even greater difficulties because of their commitment to a highly orthodox and Brahminical style of life. A number of suggestions have been made as to why this was so. Some commentators have argued that the 'Brahminising' behaviour of merchant people was a reaction to their somewhat ambiguous position in caste society: that they were trying to throw off the taint of inferior, Shudra status. Others have detected an instrumental relationship between the need to preserve mercantile credit or security and rigid social mores. But whatever the origin of their style of life, aspirations to higher caste status imposed severe restraints on the more prestigious merchant families. Khattris, for instance, were divided into a number of overlapping 'clans', regional 'factions' and marriage groups.[31] These distinctions severely limited the number of

---

[29] Case of Manohar Das Rora, 26 Aug. 1788, 30 Jan. 1790, PR; governments might actually precipitate bankruptcy by declaring a firm insolvent, e.g., Mughal *shuqqa* declaring a Delhi bankruptcy, *CPC*, v, 19 Oct. 1780.

[30] I am indebted to members of the SSRC Conference on 'Risk and Uncertainty', University of Pennsylvania, 1977, for discussion of these notions.

[31] Kashi Nath, 'Khattris', *IA*, ii (1873), 27; Harnan Das Varma, *An Account of the Khattris as a Race of Ancient Kshatriyas* (Lahore, 1901), pp. 23–4.

families who could consider marriage alliances with each other. In relatively recent times, the most prestigious Khattri clans of the most prestigious subdivisions (Bahri Khattris of the Mehra, Khanna, Kapur and Seth exogamous clans) developed a further set of rules which limited even further the number of subdivisions with which they could marry. Thus the 'purest' were called the Dhaighar – 'those who could only marry with two and a half houses'.[32] These families exclude as marriage partners 'not only the father's clan but also such families of the mother's clan as are closely connected with her; and thus reduce the clans available for intermarriage to two and a half'. Elaborate exogamy to keep the clan 'pure' was characteristic of many other prestigious mercantile clans also, so that 'most Banias prohibit intermarriage, at any rate nominally, up to five degrees'. During the nineteenth century, boundaries of this sort seem to have become stronger. As the urban population grew, families developed stable sets of marriage patterns within their own localities. For instance, after 1780 , more exclusive marriage patterns became evident among the Benares Agarwals who had at one time drawn their brides from a much wider geographical area, and probably from a much larger number of subdivisions.[33] Involution as a social group went hand in hand with their metamorphosis from an open group of traders to a closed group of landowners and zamindari moneylenders.

Success as an 'entrepreneur' in marriage and social relations therefore implied a gradual narrowing of marriage circles and a gradual elimination of all practices and relationships which might endanger the purity of the family group. This tactic of withdrawal fitted well with the frugal and cautious mentality of the village or small town moneylender. But it created profound cultural tensions for those families who sought wider fields of action. Previous chapters have shown that connection with military contracting and political power offered the most rapid social advancement in north India into the colonial period. Against the background of a slow-moving, low-demand rural economy, it was state finance and revenue management which held forth the opportunities for real wealth. The conditions of the wider political economy forced merchant families to steer between the twin perils of failure in the marriage market and extinction in the commercial market. But one can recover enough of the merchant mentality from stories and random judgements of value to appreciate that failure in either sphere was a constant nightmare for them.

[32] D. Ibbetson, *Panjab Castes* (Lahore, 1916), p. 250.
[33] *Agrawal Jati*, II, *passim;* Benares Agarwal family histories in author's possession; communication from Dr Anand Krishna, Rai Kishen Das, Jan. 1974; cf. R. V. Russell and Rai Bahadur Hira Lal, *Tribes and Castes of the Central Provinces* (London, 1916), II, 115.

Two pictures of merchant behaviour can be seen in stories and legends. These might be called the 'frugal merchant' and the 'great *sahu*'. The frugal merchant avoids expense and luxury, inhabits a modest house and uses his adequate wealth to establish relations with learned men and priests; at the age of fifty or thereabouts, he is likely to leave his business to sober heirs and become a religious mendicant. This was a professional rather than a caste model of behaviour. We hear of such and such behaviour as not being suitable for a 'professed *mahajan*' or not creditable for a 'money dealer' (*sarraf*). By contrast, the 'great *sahu*' character is both admired and disapproved of. There is a pull towards establishing oneself as a magnate or little king; but it is also realised that this behaviour is ultimately destructive of mercantile credit. The 'great *sahu*' is free spending; he lives in a great palace rather than a modest mud-brick house; often he has Muslim concubines. The 'great *sahu*' has an ancient tradition. He appears for instance in Banarsi Das's poetic autobiography of the early seventeenth century, the *Ardha-Kathanak*. Here Banarsi, a middling Jain merchant of Agra, writes of the tycoon Sehbal Singh:

He [Banarsi] went to Sahu for several days, but he [Sahu] had no time for accounts. Sahu was intoxicated with prosperity. The singers sang; the *pakhvaj* was sounded constantly in his court, and it resembled that of princes. He gave in charity incessantly, and poets and bards sang his praises ... Banarsi did not know how the accounts could be settled. He attended on the Sahu for several months but the latter had no time to spend on business or the dispute. Whenever he spoke of the accounts to Sahu, he promised to settle them in the morning. But for one engrossed in carnal pleasures the Sun neither rises nor sets.[34]

In anecdotes regarding the Benares of the late eighteenth century, the figure of the 'great *sahu*' is represented by Kashmiri Mull, head of the Pacchaina Khattris. His humiliation and ouster by the Agarwal family of Gopal Das is attributed to the Khattris' magnificent life-style which is contrasted with the Agarwal's piety and frugality. In one story, Kashmiri Mull, who apes Persian manners and lives in a great Mughal-style palace, is discovered by his father smoking a *hookah* and is forced to throw it out of the window. The frugal merchant stands somewhere between the 'great *sahu*' and the despised miser figure who has no money even for Brahmins and charity. In one case, considerations of profit were allowed to override the religious objects which were part of the *mahajan*'s function; in the other, the 'great *sahu*' ignored the need for profit and honour, thus undermining his credit. The aim of merchant *dharma* was to steer a middle course between these two extremes.

[34] Banarsi Das, *Ardha-Kathanak*, ed. R. S. Sharma, *Indica*, vii (1970), 2, 114.

The one thing which could be guaranteed to draw a merchant into an uncontrollable web of demeaning social relationships was an attempt to manage land. Yet all the changes in the eighteenth- and early nineteenth-century political economy pointed in this direction. Somehow a method of indirect, covert management had to be found which did not reflect adversely on mercantile credit. Kashmiri Mull was asked by the Raja of Benares to hold the revenue-farm of Ghazipur District in 1786.

On this I replied that my business was that of a mehajin or banker and that partnership in land management was not my business, in consequence of which the Raja taking the Ganga or Ganges and the deity Beeshesher between us declared that the secret should not be revealed to anyone.[35]

The banker persuaded the Raja to keep the revenue-farm publicly in the name of one of the royal princes, so that the credit of his business house should not suffer. Throughout, the attitude of business houses to estate management remained ambiguous. In the nineteenth century, they were prepared to accept the enhanced status that being a landlord gave them in local society and the district office. But they rarely took an active part in running their zamindaris, preferring instead to leave this to an agent. The notorious inadequacies of 'moneylenders' as landlords derived in part from their reluctance to become entangled in the duties and rights which were appropriate to a 'little king'.

How did merchant families seek to avoid these grave social risks and still carry on their businesses? It was perhaps among the Jains that the code of conduct was most elaborate and rigid. According to Jain teaching, business provided the sustenance for members of the family who 'cannot afford to renounce the World at once'.[36] A balance must be held between legitimate pleasures and comforts which result from honest business, and over-indulgence which would result in lust, greed and dishonest business. There is 'always a kind of fear while enjoying or using money earned dishonestly'.[37] For the Jains, then, there were certain danger spots in a man's life when the householder, rather than holding himself in balance for future spiritual progress, could actually degenerate into a lower moral (and material) being. He is at risk from intoxication, lust, meat-eating, boisterous and unseemly behaviour; but also from the conspicuous creation or consumption of wealth which might give rise to these vices. In particular, a man should not keep a large number of vehicles, accumulate even necessary possessions in

35 Reply of Kashmiri Mull, 13 June 1788, PR.
36 Sri Samanta Bhadra Acharya, *Ratna Karanda Sravakachara*, tr. C. R. Jain (Arrah, 1917), p. 30.
37 H. Warren, *Jainism* (Arrah, 1912), pp. 77–8.

large numbers, express envy at the prosperity of others, overload his pack-animals or in anyway take part in business which risks the destruction of life.

There emerges a code of piety and restraint in which spiritual risks can be balanced out by acts of pilgrimage, meditation and vows to limit worldly possessions (called *parigraha-parinama*), 'once having fixed the measure of one's worldly possessions, grain, cash and the like'. Banarsi Das's *Ardha-Kathanak* shows how this higher teaching might actually impinge on the life of men in the bazaar. Almost all the incidents in this poetic autobiography relate to business and moral risks. The first can be overcome by knowledge of the market, restraint and listening to the advice of mercantile elders.[38] Moral degeneration can be avoided by pilgrimage, vows and meditation. To all intents and purposes, the distinction between bad moral and bad economic conduct disappears altogether. The wise merchant like Kharagsen makes a vow of restraint from the building of another house. The foolish and profligate merchant like Sehbal Singh damages his accounts, his reputation and his moral being by lust and bad management.

The ideal life-style of the Jain merchant householder was, of course, modified in practice. The famous Jagat Seth himself declared that he would be unmoved if the whole tribe of Brahmins immolated itself at his door. But participation in the moral community of the Jain merchants entailed at least an outward reverence for religious values. Moral peril and economic unreliability were seen to be closely connected. When spies were sent out to ascertain the credit of firms which had applied for the farm of government monopolies, the most damning report was that they were 'expensive people', indulging in much building and retaining many servants. Family histories and stories told in merchant schools also explain the economic fortunes of different groups largely in terms of the moral conduct of family members or the rapacity of rulers. We often hear of the young men of the family pushing expenditure beyond the 10 per cent of the annual income which is considered safe. Degenerate Muslim or European ways are acquired. The family credit collapses, there is a run on the firm, and starvation looms. The cycle begins once again when a younger son refounds the business on the basis of piety and moderation.

Similar codes of conduct were current among Hindu merchants who often found themselves in close social communion with the Jains. Once again, physical and moral 'substance' must not be endangered by contact with pollution lest marriage alliance and the continuity of the

[38] *Ardha-Kathanak, Indica*, vii (1970), 65; *ibid.*, p. 114; cf. Warren, *Jainism*, p. 30.

family be endangered.[39] There was constant pressure to withdraw from relationships or trades which might be considered harmful. Wisely perhaps, the Hindu lawgivers regarded money itself as a neutral medium, but commerce in polluting substances was avoided. Buchanan-Hamilton, for instance, noted that in Patna, wealthy and high caste traders in leather shoes were regarded as of low status.[40] Once they had acquired wealth oil-pressers, liquor distillers and traders in base metals generally tried to abandon their original staples and cut themselves off from those members of their castes who continued to trade in them. But insecurity was enhanced by the travel abroad, which was an essential part of merchants' lives and tended to make them suspect in the eyes of the most orthodox. Hindu merchants tried to avoid the public Mughal *sarais* and lodged with relatives and caste fellows. But beyond a point, travel took merchants into areas where the basic rites de passage of orthdox life could no longer be guaranteed. *Prayaschita*, the rites of purification which Hindus were supposed to undergo on return from travel before they could be received back into caste, originated as a system of security against social risks. It was an attempt to guarantee the continuance of trade, not as it later came to be seen, as a means of restricting contact between India and the rest of the world. Returning merchants were considered to be actually purged of foreign and impure substances by imbibing the products of the cow. That travel beyond the seas (the *kala pani*) necessitated purification is widely known. What is less well known is that the River Attock in the west Punjab formed the northern barrier of the 'safe' cultural area.[41] Khattri merchants moving up into Central Asia and the towns of Balk and Astrakhan where they had substantial colonies were considered to have lost caste in the same way as sea-voyagers. Even the Himalayan Terai to the north-east appears to have been regarded as a barrier in the late eighteenth century. Caste Hindus were said to regard the area with suspicion so Gosain traders who were considered 'dead to the world' dominated the trade route at this time.[42]

The area of the greatest and most pervasive social risk, however, was for Hindus, like Jains, the boundary between the inward, frugal life of the merchant and the kingly manner which involved constant giving and receiving. Merchant families might find themselves trapped in the

[39] Cf. McKim Marriott, 'Hindu transaction: diversity without dualism', in B. Kapferer (ed.), *Transaction and Meaning* (Philadelphia, 1976); this model is useful for understanding the attitudes of north Indian merchants who are cognisant of the 'religious' way of life; it seems doubtful whether it could be extended to the 'South Asian mind' in general as the article intends.

[40] Martin, *Eastern India*, I, 369.   [41] Forster, *Journey*, II, 292.

[42] E.g., Representation of Geean Gir, 7 Sept. 1791, PR.

limbo between these two styles of life, unable to command the power and respect of the ruler yet 'expensive' enough to forfeit credit in the mercantile sphere. For merchants necessarily became involved with political power. They needed to have a hand in the organisation of mints. They were forced to take leases and control market sites in order to guarantee the sale and passage of their goods without harassment. Since they were dealing with landowners and Muslim judicial officials, they needed some entrée into the Persian courtly culture. The service or succour of kings which was enjoined in the law books was constantly reiterated as a goal in merchant family histories.[43] It involved the giving and getting of political honour and tied them yet more closely into darbars. The ideal balance between merchant, king, priest and labourer could not be maintained in practice. Money was coming into a commanding place in the economy, reducing the importance of other forms of redistribution of food, land or followers through the king.

Confusion of life-styles and ideals was deepened. How, for instance, was a community like the Khattris to be ranked within the Hindu system? Under the Mughal rulers of the Punjab they had achieved political power and influence, and many 'western' Khattris had assumed a life-style which was at least externally Islamic.[44] Even the four basic sub-caste divisions into which all Khattris were grouped had supposedly come about as the result of an intervention in the community's marriage practice by early Muslim rulers. Khattri family histories also display a similar ambiguity. On the one hand, they take pride in close association with the great Muslim dynasties. On the other hand, family migration is often attributed to lust by Muslim rulers for Khattri women. The dispute as to whether Khattris were of princely (Kshatriya) or mercantile (Vaishya) stock was of consuming importance, and it rumbled on throughout the nineteenth century until it was spurred into frenzy by the British Census commissioners in 1911.[45]

Merchant people adopted various stratagems which served to reduce the danger of being caught between two conflicting models of behaviour. First, they sought anonymity, avoiding publicity when they became involved in the management of land or men. Secondly, they maintained a sharper distinction between their inward and outward styles of life. For instance, amongst the Khattris of Benares in the late eighteenth century, 'Punjabi' dialect was used in the home,[46] Persian

---

[43] See, e.g., P. N. Mullick, *History of the Vaishyas of Bengal* (Calcutta, 1902), pp. 31–3.
[44] E.g., the 'Western' Khattri families of Chipiwara, Delhi, esp. that of Munshi Raghunath Singh which appears to have had a particularly 'Islamicised' life-style, being creditor to the Mughal nobility of the area, interview, family documents, Dec. 1973.
[45] H. D. Varma, *An Account of the Khattris*.
[46] *Gunga Bye* v. *the Mother of Jwalanath*, 3 Aug. 1792, PR.

outside; Persian court dress was exchanged for the *dhoti* at home; the outward magnificence of the *haveli* palace contrasted with the severity of the inner rooms; 'Khattri' jewellery was kept separate from 'Mughal' jewellery.[47] In the nineteenth century, one often finds that the very same family which built huge Mughal-style palaces on the outskirts of cities continued to inhabit small mud-walled quarters in the old central city area.

The tension between the ascetic and self-denying and the lavish and outgoing appears also in the religious practice of merchant people. For some, indeed, lavish religious activity appears as an attempt safely to resolve this inner conflict. For, paradoxically, wealthy merchants who were noted for their restrained style of life were generally devotees of the Vaishnavite rather than of the more austere Shaivite cult.

the Vaishnava cultus, partly from the opportunities it affords for magnificent display, partly from the absence of blood-offerings, which commends it to a class deeply influenced by the Buddhistic [sic] reverence for the sanctity of life, is more popular among the rich merchants of the towns.[48]

This love of devotional display was particularly strong among some branches of the Vallabhacharya sect which was influential in Gujerat and in Hindustani towns where there had been an early Gujerati influence. Vallabhacharya had preached that fasting and asceticism had no particular merit in themselves. He exalted the service (*sewa*) of the deity and complete surrender which included the 'giving up of the body, mind and worldly belongings of the devotee'.[49] But in time, the luxury and display of the spiritual heads of the sect (the Goswamis or Maharajs) caused a reaction in favour of a simpler and more austere form of religion. The first of these movements of reform was associated with Charan Das, a Delhi teacher of the 1730s, who attracted a large following among the merchants of the commercial towns.[50] In Bombay in the 1850s, a similar internal movement of reform to purify the practices of the Maharajs merged with the zeal of the first generation of 'social reformers' and gave rise to one of the most notorious court cases of Victorian India.[51] Among the Jains also there was a similar tension between austerity and religious display. On the one hand, there were the austerities of the priestly class and the moderation of the laity; on the other hand, the dazzling images and lavish shrine building. One need

---

[47] *Ibid.*
[48] Crooke, *North Western Provinces*, p. 247.
[49] N. A. Thoothi, *The Vaishnavas of Gujerat* (London, 1935), pp. 92–7.
[50] H. H. Wilson, 'The religious sects of the Hindoos', *AR*, xvii (1832), pp. 181ff.
[51] C. Dobbin, *Urban Leadership in Western India* (London, 1972), pp. 65–70.

only think of the crores of Rupees spent on embellishing Mount Abu or Delhi by the great Jain families of the eighteenth century.[52]

In the individual's mind, the lavish expenditure no doubt reflected simple devotion to the god or teacher. But this is not incompatible with the notion that it also fulfilled a social function. Lavishness – costly, regal display in worship – was enhanced precisely because the merchant life-style discouraged other forms of conspicuous expenditure. Religious donation exalted the merchant as a substantial and pious man capable of fulfilling his role in society. It was at the same time safe, since the feeding of gods and Brahmins could only redound to his spiritual credit. In Allahabad, a merchant of the early nineteenth century was in the habit of distributing fifteen *maunds* of split peas (*dal*) daily in the bazaar and feeding many hundreds of cattle.[53] This was a similar act to the redistribution practised by rajas, and yet it was devoid of the element of risk because it was conceived of as meritorious charity, having first been given to the gods. The merchant was able to become a king by proxy.

Merchant families in many societies have been associated with particular, sectarian forms of religious practice. But the relationship between mercantile credit and exclusive forms of worship has remained obscure despite constant debate. India provides no exception here. Quite apart from the obvious examples of Jainism and Parsi Zoroastrianism, merchants were well represented among sectarian groups which grew more directly out of the Vaishnavite Hindu tradition, such as the Vallabhacharyas, Satnamis and Radhavallabs. To what extent are we justified in regarding sectarian attachment of this sort as a tactic in the maintenance of family credit? Certainly, devotion to a *guru* or a set of precepts which attracted a group of devotees from several different castes fulfilled the requirement that involuted social relations had to subsist with wider business contacts. In the late eighteenth century, for instance, the Jains were still increasing in numbers by incorporating Hindus of the merchant castes. The peculiar inwardness of Jain religious and social life might actually increase the credit of families which still had to work partly within a Hindu context. There was a great emphasis on secrecy. No doubt the austere nature of Jain domestic life also had its advantages during a century when rulers were always on the lookout for opulent merchants to mulct. In areas such as Malwa where Jains dominated commercial life, a shift across sectarian boundaries was not unusual. Malcolm recorded:

---

[52] Sayyid Ahmed Khan, *Asar-us Sanadid*, tr. Tassy, 'Description des Monuments de Delhi', *Journal Asiatique*, 5e série, xv (1869), 4.

[53] *Agrawal Jati*, II, 15, Lala Har Bilas.

The Soucars, Shroffs and Bunnias in Malwa are either of the Jain or Vishnu faith, but by far the greatest numbers are of the former, and their prevailing influence and wealth attracts many converts. Almost all the Vaisya and Sudra agents and servants they employ, if not before Jains, conform to the tenets of that sect.[54]

Other sects also gained adherents as a result of close commercial relations. For instance, Vallabhacharyas and Nanakshahi Sikhs continued to increase their numbers in the Gangetic cities during the eighteenth century. However, slow adaptation to a prevailing culture could also work in the other direction. In Bengal, the great Jagat Seth family which had once been among the chief donors of Jain temples throughout India, gradually abandoned their Jain practices and drifted back into the Vaishnavite business and landowning community which surrounded them. In the same way, 'western' Khattri merchants from the Punjab who moved down into the plains of Hindustan often came to place less emphasis on the Islamic and Punjabi part of their cultural inheritance as they were drawn into more intimate communion with the orthodox life of the banks of the Ganges.

While 'changes' of religious affiliation of this sort cannot be regarded as simple utilitarian acts, they certainly enhanced the social, and hence commercial security, of trading families isolated in a new environment. Viewed from the inside of merchant family life, these were, perhaps, not dramatic events. The family was in continuous communion with a whole range of business associates, gods and men. All that happened was that a portion of family resources and worship was redirected to deities which were honoured by neighbours and business associates. Earlier religious practices usually continued alongside the new. So among Jains in Bihar in the early nineteenth century, Brahmins and Hindu deities were venerated without embarrassment.[55] Similarly, in the case of the Nanakshahi Khattris, Hindu forms of worship were not felt to be incompatible with accepting the holiness of the Guru Granth Sahib (the Sikh holy book).[56]

Before moving on from the question of the 'credit' of the merchant family, it is worth considering it in the context of the political response of the commercial community. As we have seen, genealogies exult in connections with famous rulers both Hindu and Muslim, but over-close association with rulers might lead a family into expense and depravity. In the same way, fear of the predatory ruler was a constant refrain in the demonology of merchant people. Mughal rulers and nawabs were

---

[54] Malcolm, *Central India*, II, 160.
[55] Vaishnavite and Jain Agarwal families in Benares also regularly intermarried.
[56] *Bedamo* v. *Bowanny Singh*, Benares Adalat, 6 Jan. 1792, PR.

popularly remembered for their benevolence, but their lieutenants were accused of meddling in commercial custom. In 1813–15, unease in the bazaars of Benares and Mirzapur was heightened by the comparisons which were being made between an unpopular British judge and Todar Mull, the famous Mughal financial minister.

... the townsmen consider him to be a sort of mostaufee, which means one who takes all – some such officer as Torur Mull was under Akber – how popular their likening him to Torur Mull proves him to be may be judged by the well known quatrain which gives the date of that financier's death – 'when Torur Mull whose oppressions had overspread the World went towards hell, a whole world of people were rejoiced, 998 Hijree'.[57]

The Todar Mull legend was very general. He is supposed to have enforced the standard form of account books which was used throughout India in the eighteenth and nineteenth centuries and to have been responsible for many interventions in the business of the commercial corporations.

Many other stories related to the levy by impoverished or avaricious rulers of forced loans which were never repaid. But it is important to catch the nuances of these legends. Family histories often seemed to take pride in succouring a great king with no hope of repayment, yet still remaining rich and creditable people. The great Gurwala banking family of Delhi, for instance, claimed to have lent up to ten lakhs of Rupees to the Mughals during the early nineteenth century on an interest-free loan which was never repaid.[58] Such stories were probably exaggerated, but the mentality underlying them may help further to correct some of our notions of the anarchy of the eighteenth century and the meaning of the 'Pax Britannica'. Under indigenous regimes 'plunder' (*zulum*) was expected, and could partly be insured against. Forced loans could be seen in the light of 'protection rent'. Indeed the Hindu law books themselves sanctioned the seizure of up to one quarter of the total assets of merchants during times of famine or danger. In that pregnant metaphor, the merchants were the ruler's cattle, to be milked by him if the necessity arose.[59] 'Plunder', then, was built into the theory and practice of Indian states and their mercantile subjects. It could carry connotations of an exceptional levy or of equitable redistribution rather than the criminality and breakdown implied in the English word. In some regimes, 'plunder' took the form of a periodic readjustment in the

57 Second Judge Benares to Magt., 12 Jan. 1813, BCJ, 12 July 1816, 132/43, IOL.
58 Gurwala family history, copy in author's possession; but see *Ramji Das and Narain Das v. Agent to the King of Delhi*, 91 of 1852, Delhi, June 1852, ZC.
59 P. V. Kane, *History of Dharmasastra (Ancient and Medieval Religious and Civil Law)* (Poona, 1941), II, i, 41; cf. Hocart, *Caste*, p. 39.

context of a low fixed land-revenue and minimal customs charge. British observers noted with bewilderment that townsmen and peasants seemed to remain in contentment and that Hindu merchants could adjust to the direst forms of what they took to be oppression. Among the unwilling suppliants at the darbar of the ruler of Kandahar in the 1820s:

> there were invariably from fifty to one hundred Hindus, some of them doubtless men of respectability and wealth, and all merchants and traders who had been seized in their houses and shops and dragged before the Durbar for the purposes of extorting money. This was not an occasional or monthly but a daily occurrence.... I have seen on an occasion of a festival the Hindus of this city assembled in gardens without their walls and displaying every sign of ease and wealth in their apparel and trinkets; nor were they the less grateful than they would have been in a Hindu kingdom. The gains of these men must be enormous, or they would never provide to the exactions of their governors, and without such profit operating as an offset never would submit to the indignities they are compelled to suffer.[60]

But plunder, even social indignity, could be tolerated by a cohesive merchant group fortified by its own internal perceptions of credit. Merchants could only be forced to flee if the ruler appeared to push them below the margin of subsistence during a bad period, or if their credit which was the basis of their livelihood was threatened in any novel or discriminatory manner. It is against this background that we should place the many stories claiming that merchant families migrated from a particular city because its ruler had designs on their womenfolk or was forcing upon them some practice which was obnoxious to their religious feeling. Here it was the credit, continuity, even bodily substance of the individual family which was in jeopardy, and the danger was greater than from any forced loan which could be absorbed and discounted by the community as a whole.

These notions also provide a key to the issues which brought merchants and townsmen into conflict with early colonial rulers. Almost always there was some perceived threat to the moral economy of the merchant family. The British attempted to introduce conceptions of individual legal responsibility limited to one lifetime. Earlier, debt had been a matter of family credit over several generations. As a Persian newsletter of 1837 commented,

> the chain which bound the soucars [bankers] together in their trading relations is broken... Previously in cases of bancruptcy the whole body of the soucars would get together and award equitable reparations, but now a son could declare himself bankrupt in a civil court when his father was still in possession of lakhs.[61]

[60] G. W. Forrest, *Selections from Journals*, p. 110.
[61] 'Dishonest Sowkars', Extracts from Persian *Akhbar, Delhi Gazette*, 29 Mar. 1837.

The reorganisation of tolls, bazaar duties and urban taxation by the colonial authorities posed another subtle threat to merchant status because it overturned local indemnities and privileges. The sphere of mercantile custom was invaded in many minor but irritating forays. At one time or another, the colonial authorities demanded the production of bankers' books in court; they tried to suppress the 'plunder' of a failed merchant's stock or they attempted to make registers of bullion dealers which violated the basic tenets of mercantile secrecy. Finally, they blundered once or twice into policies which offended the religious interests of the commercial population. It is notable that the only times when Hindustan's bazaars closed down altogether during our period were when cattle, Brahmins and the purity of the River Ganges seemed under threat.

11

The merchant family as a business enterprise

Merchant credit was essential for the continuity of the family as both a social and a commercial entity. At many points in the ordinary conduct of their businesses the principals of firms needed to forgo higher profits in order to guarantee this continuity. On the birth of a daughter, for instance, it was common practice to set aside a part of the total capital in a special account which would ultimately constitute the girl's dowry. But quite apart from these regular calls made on resources for social investment, merchants had to develop strategies which would guarantee survival in the ordinary business world. Many of the patterns of behaviour which seem to characterise the family firm of nineteenth-century north India can be understood as tactics to avoid the risks of operating in a peculiarly hostile business climate.

For merchants as much as for peasant farmers unstable rainfall and the possibility of crop failure posed the greatest threat to survival. A crude assessment of the likelihood of drought could be made, of course: in the Delhi region it was said that 'every tenth year when the numbers are even, as 40, 50 etc, brings one of want and distress'.[1] Investment in jewellery, bullion and grain hoards provided some security against expected shortfalls. But such measures were not adequate for dealing with prolonged or severe scarcities, and besides there must be some doubt that merchants or farmers invariably behaved sufficiently rationally to give themselves adequate cover.[2] Trader–bankers were particularly at risk from the failure of the autumn (*kharif*) crop. The repayment of instalments on loans after the crop had been harvested provided the cash with which to finance the agricultural trade of the busy winter months. For them a failure of the spring harvest was less important since it was followed by five or six months of hot and monsoon weather when trade was sluggish.

For retail traders and smaller commodity traders who sold goods with a high price elasticity of demand, the spring harvest was, however, crucial. Peasants generally paid their land-revenue and rent from its

[1] T. Fortescue, *Delhi Residency*, I, 112.
[2] But see G. Chapman, 'Perception and regulation. A case study of farmers in Bihar', *Transactions of the Institute of British Geographers* (July 1974), pp. 71–93.

proceeds. If it was bad, then the demand for commodities such as sugar, fine salt, drugs, liquor and quality cloths for the March and April festival or marriage season would be sharply reduced.[3] The weather and the annual cycle of rituals bunched the consumption of rural families into a few months, so that a merchant's whole profit for the year might be made or lost in a week's trading. While families could do something to adjust to the probability of regular crop failure, the actual form which the scarcity would take might be uncertain from day to day. For instance, complex problems of transport might result from the death of cattle, but even in the worst famines it was by no means clear whether cattle would die or not. In 1783, enough vegetation remained to feed them, while in 1838, it died.[4] Again, the moneylender's decision to advance credit for sowing the crop in a period after a failure depended entirely on his estimate of whether rain would set in or not. If he advanced a loan, he ran the risk of losing his cash resources; if he did not, he risked losing through emigration or death the peasant farmer, who was his own best security.

Problems of demand were almost as severe. Complicated systems of storage and agency emerged to deal with them, but 'glutting' of the wholesale market was frequently given as a reason for mercantile failures during the early nineteenth century.[5] In trades such as raw cotton and indigo where export was an important part of the total trade, the reasons were clear. Merchants could estimate local supply and demand with some assurance; indeed, there had been a sophisticated market for cotton futures in north India well before the growth of the China trade.[6] But information about the likely outturn of cotton in Canton, the major export market, would only reach north Indian merchants after they had contracted to send the commodity downriver to Mirzapur and Calcutta. A glut building up in the Mirzapur market over two or three seasons would affect the prices of the internal market as well. On the other hand, if the Canton crop failed, the East India Company (until 1834) might move into the market and buy up the entire crop at ruinously high prices.[7] Indigo was an even more hazardous commodity than cotton because substantial advances had to be made to the peasant farmer before the likely outcome of the crop was known. Extensive speculative markets in cotton, indigo and opium futures

---

3 Statements of Irrecoverable Abkari Balances, NWP Rev. Procs, 13 Nov. 1839, 222/65, IOL.
4 Girdlestone, *Past Famines*, p. 37.
5 E.g., CGC Agra to Bd, 29 May, 8 June 1820, Agra Customs 4, UPR.
6 H. Newman to Accountant General, 18 Oct. 1812, Bengal Commercial Procs, 157/57, IOL.
7 CGC Agra to Bd, 4 Apr. 1820, Agra Customs 4, UPR.

added to the uncertainties of pricing and demand. Investors from outside the regular business community could suddenly enter these markets for reasons quite unconnected with the trade itself.

Despite the long-dated *hundis* and money of account (*auth*)[8] which were used by Indian bankers, mercantile credit in long-distance trading was also underdeveloped.[9] Capital supply was therefore generally identified with the supply of money. Yet the supply of money was subject to sharp fluctuations which originated outside the commercial sphere. Sudden military movements in the late eighteenth or early nineteenth century could cause 'money famines'. Unpredictable political events also jeopardised the supply of transport for trade. As late as 1826 the British Commissariat Department continued to seize pack-bullocks in the event of border wars, and the decline of the Banjara bands after 1820 increased the difficulty of finding alternative sources. Delays of this sort could be fatal. For instance, raw cotton from Central India moving by way of Jabbalpur and Mirzapur had a leeway for transport of no more than a month. If it had not reached storage by early June, then there was a strong probability that it would be ruined by rain on the roadside.[10] Sugar, salt and clarified butter were other commodities peculiarly vulnerable to transport bottlenecks.

From first to last, the commercial behaviour of the merchant family was dominated by techniques for avoiding risks. Merchants might be 'expensive' people, they might turn over capital too fast, they might participate in too heavy speculation. But this was against a weight of opinion and practice that stressed the need for caution. From early youth, children in merchant families were taught that good business involved the constant division of capital into small, manageable portfolios. One *mahajani* formula was built around the letters of the Hindi alphabet: K = *kam*, work; KH = *khana*, food; G = *garna*, to hoard (jewellery, etc); GH = *ghar*, house and so on.[11] This was taken to mean that work produced food; then a merchant should purchase jewellery which could stand as security in time of need and a dowry for daughters, followed by a house in which to carry on business. Other rhymes and jingles taught that capital should be divided into at least four portions. One portion should be hoarded as coin; one used to buy jewellery; one lent out at interest, and only one quarter invested in trade. The importance of correct book-keeping was also instilled from

---

8 For use of *auth*, CGC Agra to Bd, 23 Mar. 1809, CPR, 12 Apr. 1809, 57/31, IOL.
9 Many unresolved problems existed in commercial practice relating to *hundis* quite apart from the social judgement inherent in the notion of 'respectability' for *sahajog hundis*, see, e.g., 280 of 1855, Fatehpur, Sept. 1855, *ZC*.
10 Anon., *The Cotton Trade of India* (East India Company, London, 1839), I, 15.
11 Interview, Babu Ram Krishna, Benares, Jan. 1974.

an early age. Children were made to read *hundis* as they were received in the banking house and were taught sophisticated forms of mental arithmetic. Written manuals were available in many of the merchant *mahajani* schools which were run by retired clerks in the major commercial towns, and after 1850, the government itself encouraged a standard form of merchants' books.[12]

Correct understanding of the accounts was essential for the firm's security. Double entry book-keeping and a central daily cash book (*rokad khata*) which controlled all other subsidiary accounts made it possible for businessmen to keep track of the large number of transactions entailed in businesses with many portfolios. The system was designed not to produce figures for overall profit, but to operate a large number of checks on the immediate cash flow position of the family firm. In the flourishing business of discounting *hundis*, a further check on liabilities was kept in the form of a *nakal bahi*. This account listed advice of the arrival for discounting of future *hundis*. Obviously, the whole mercantile system was built upon the availability of rapid, accurate information from distant marts. Certain types of commercial communication were amazingly well developed. At the turn of the nineteenth century, correspondents in Aurangabad (Deccan) could get news from Panipat on the borders of the Punjab in nine days, and merchant runners regularly outpaced government sources.[13] In Awadh, a cheap and regular postal service survived into the 1830s:

It clearly appears that the native Dak post was maintained not withstanding its extremely low rates of postage by the immense number of letters sent in it. People of small means such as servants and peons could afford to keep up a constant correspondence with their relatives while mahajuns, buneas and others inter-changed letters daily with their correspondents in the different bazaars and marts of these provinces.[14]

This makes it easier to understand how highly sophisticated all-India markets in capital, bullion, jewellery and fine goods could have existed in the context of the political flux and poor land transport of the eighteenth century.

Once merchants had 'become *mahajans*' – that is to say, once they kept 'books', passed *hundis* in the bazaar and received regular commercial information – there was the matter of allocating capital between different 'portfolios'. Many business communities were

12 Anon., *Mahajanon ki Pustaka* (Agra, 1849), *Boharon ki Pustaka* (Agra, 1850), Hin. Tracts 1594, IOL.
13 J. Baillie Fraser, *Military Memoirs of Lieutenant-Colonel James Skinner* (London, 1851), I, 123.
14 Magt. Mirzapur to Offg Commr Ghazipur, 1 May 1838, Mirzapur Judl, 85, UPR.

particularly associated with one line: Mehra Khattris for cloth, Khandelwals for grains and oil seed, and so on. But very few of the larger businesses failed to diversify to some extent. This was seen to be an elementary means of enhancing family security and avoiding the risks inherent in unstable supply and demand. At the very simplest level, the rural grain trader and the small town retailer avoided specialisation and dealt with a whole range of grains, *dals* (split peas), salts and spices. This behaviour paralleled that of the peasant farmer who sowed a wide variety of crops, mixing in mustard with his grains and planting hot weather crops as an insurance against uncertain seasons. Indeed, the aversion to specialisation amongst peasants and small traders reinforced each other. Peasant commodity production was on a small scale, and it might take many journeys to individual villages to procure sufficient quantities of any single product for a large consignment. The typical form of exchange in local markets was therefore a vast number of small dealings between individual buyers and sellers. But aversion to specialisation was also seen at the other end of the scale with the great 'native' firms, agency houses and 'country produce brokers' who flourished at various points during the nineteenth century. The tendency for a larger number of smaller operators to divide their own trade between a range of different commodities was even more striking after the 1830s when people who had concentrated on one or two cash crops paid such a heavy price.

Certain groupings of trades and services were particularly favoured. Grain and salt trading, for instance, were often combined. Both required substantial transport, and these were commodities which were unlikely to encounter problems of supply or demand at the same time. Long-distance cotton traders often maintained an interest in the grain trade also. This was because losses from a bad cotton season could sometimes be recouped at the eleventh hour by buying heavily into the remaining spring crop grain.

The rapid extension of branch firms across the country is another typical feature of north Indian business. This is often seen in terms of 'enterprise', with the Marwaris 'capturing control' of moneylending in the Deccan or Khattris and Agarwals moving into the lower Ganges valley. But such behaviour can equally well be interpreted as a search for added security on the part of established concerns, rather than the entrepreneurship of new men. In the late eighteenth and early nineteenth-century, towns such as Hissar, Bhewani, Delhi and Agra were nodal points of trade, but they also lay in the centre of highly unstable climatic regions and the political 'cockpit' of India. The classic movement of the branch agencies (*kothis*) of major firms into the lower Ganges valley (Benares, Patna, Murshidabad) was a bid to minimise uncertainty by straddling several climatic and political regions. A study of twenty-three major Agarwal, Khattri, Bhargava and Maheshwari firms suggests that the urge to expand the system of *kothis* was particularly strong in the 1780s and the 1830s, which were both eras of notorious climatic harshness and political uncertainty. The migration behaviour of these firms is very similar to that of peasant farmers in the scarcities of 1783 and 1833–8 who also tended to move east into the better irrigated tracts of riverain Awadh, Benares and Bihar.

Patterns also emerge in the way in which merchant families diversified their businesses over time. Generally, they were careful only to deal in the riskiest trades or services when they had established regular income from the more secure. It would be possible to establish a hierarchy of business and services in terms of risk and profit. At the top of the hierarchy would be a trade, such as opium or other vegetable drugs, which ranked high on both counts. We are told for instance that the great Muttra merchant family of Lakshmi Chand managed to make a total loss on the opium business of the incredible sum of Rs. 17 lakhs in the late 1840s.[15] On the other hand, moderate dealers in the milder drugs could net as much as Rs. 60,000 per annum,[16] the value of a comfortable landed estate. Apart from the difficulty of cultivating these products, large unsecured advances were required for cultivators and middlemen.

At the other end of the scale, we have a commodity such as oil seeds for which the annual net return on capital might be as little as 8 per cent (comparable with a very modest return from a moneylending business, or a highly productive landed estate). Since it fulfilled a wide variety of functions in the domestic economy, the trade in oil seeds was relatively inelastic to changes in consumer income and consequently safe. In the intermediate range, we might find trades and services ranked in terms of risk and profitability as follows: on the high side, sugar, the management of government ferries, tolls and liquor duties, then cotton, salt, fine food grains; on the low side, rough cotton goods, metal utensils and regular moneylending to zamindars secured with irrigated land. The impression that emerges from family histories is that only the biggest enterprises with security in the form of a wide range of other trades and services, government bonds, land, etc., would speculate in the most risky items on a regular basis. However, small men trying to break into an urban market or failing firms whose consumption was rapidly overtaking income might venture a short period of 'speculation' in the hope of dramatically improving their capital position.

Two other variants of diversification by firms are 'horizontal

---

[15] 1 of 1851, Agra, July 1851, *ZC*.
[16] Books of Manohar Das Chunni Lal, *Sambat* 1946, Ranimandi, Allahabad.

integration' – a move towards monopoly or cartel – and 'vertical integration' – an attempt to control the whole line of production and distribution in a single commodity.[17] Both helped Indian firms to avoid risks. Regulated and spontaneous monopolies were forms of adjustment to rapid fluctuations in supply and demand. There are many examples of informal cartels of grain or salt merchants or attempted monopolies.[18] Similar groups of financial entrepreneurs attempted to fix the exchange rate on *hundi* transactions between various parts of the country.[19] Their activities were usually perceived as profiteering – the 'iron monopoly of the shroffs and banias'. But the incidence of failure amongst late eighteenth-century salt merchants and *hundi* brokers at least suggests that, as they claimed, the rate of profit was low and the risks high in these businesses. Monopoly behaviour was a way of reducing risks.

The final method of diversification to reduce risk and uncertainty is what is called 'vertical integration' in the theory of the firm. Here a big wholesale dealer attempts to minimise insecurities of supply and control demand by unifying the whole chain of production and sale from the agriculturalist to the retailer. This of course was the classic method by which the European East India Companies attempted to gain control of the Indian cloth or Indonesian spice trades. In this instance, the advantages of steadier supply and quality had to be offset against the loss of security which would otherwise have derived from intermediaries bearing the cost of transport and the initial risks. Indian merchants acted in a similar manner in certain conditions. Thus, firms dealing in indigo or sugar were forced to operate at village level in order to provide advances and engross the produce, whereas in the cotton trade, Indian wholesalers generally worked through middlemen since heavy advances were not essential in order to get the crop grown and harvested. The best examples of 'vertical integration' are to be found in the grain trade. Given very high rates of profit, grain traders bought up land-rights and required peasant farmers to repay loans or produce rent in kind. Whole systems of grain debt-bondage were developed by the trader Manik Chand of Phulpur in the Allahabad District[20] or by the Seths of Jabbalpur in Central India during the rapid price rises in the 1850s and 1870s.[21]

Diversification in western industrial firms can only partly be explained as a search for security. As output expands, 'market

[17] E. Penrose, *The Theory of the Growth of the Firm* (Oxford, 1959).
[18] E.g., CGC Delhi to Bd, 7 June, 1834, Agra Customs 2, UPR.
[19] E.g., 10 July 1788, PR.
[20] Notes by H. M. Elliot on the Trans-Ganges *pargannas* of Allahabad District, MSS Eur. F 60/A, pp. 53–5, IOL.
[21] Stokes, *Peasant and Raj*, ch. 11.

imperfections' begin to appear and the declining profitability of existing markets encourages firms to expand their range of products. But it is not necessary to assume that existing markets have become unprofitable in themselves, only that they become relatively less profitable for any new investment.[22] If it were possible to elaborate a theory of growth in the Indian family firm, security against falling profitability would bulk much larger as an explanation for diversification. In a highly uncertain climate with low consumer income, the chance of increasing sales to existing markets was rapidly exhausted. Secondly, the social and administrative costs of trading one commodity in one centre increased as the family grew and became more active in local society, with obligations as a redistributive (*jajmani*) system. Thirdly, there was such a pool of impoverished mercantile families able to work on smaller and smaller margins and overheads that a static firm would inevitably succumb to newcomers. The success during the nineteenth century of men of small capital whether Rastogis, Marwaris or the whole range of travelling merchants, against the mercantile aristocracy of Khattris and Agarwals is proof enough of this contention. The difficulties inherent in 'vertical integration' before the improvement of communications meant that the typical form of diversification in Indian family firms was across space, from town to town, and between products at the same wholesale level. This explanation is, however, incomplete. We must also take into account the social incentives to diversification. The opening of new branch agencies in downriver towns was also a response to the need to set up sons and relatives in substantial and respectable callings. In the case of the Jains, early partition and division of the family was even held to increase religious merit,[23] and as an observer noted:

It is a well known practice with the mahajuns of these provinces to establish branch banks more or less connected with their own establishment, and dependent upon the credit of the old firm for their success. At the head of these offshoots they ordinarily place their near relations, for I believe that I am not wrong in saying that the object on these occasions is as much to provide for the junior members of their families, as to secure the extension of their business.[24]

Hoards and rates of interest

The propensity to create stores of wealth and the high interest payments extracted from many classes of borrowers were other typical features of indigenous business practice. Both have been fair fields for those who wish to argue that Indian merchants were grasping monopolists or

[22] Penrose, *Firm*, ch. 7.
[23] Jain (ed.), *Ratna Karanda Sravakachara*, p. 32.
[24] 38 of 1847, Moradabad, May 1849, ZC.

'superstitious and ignorant'. Here was the other side of the contention that peasants were spendthrift and incapable of perceiving their own interests. This line of thinking has been perpetuated by a more topical animus against the rural capitalist. Looked at from the inside of the family firm, however, these were further techniques for avoiding financial risk and adjusting portfolio management to guarantee the future of the family in honourable circumstances.

'Hoarding' was another practice schooled into the children of merchant families through early teaching. It is extremely difficult to assess the percentage of capital that a respectable merchant family would deposit in this way before the 1870s when bankers' books were retained in greater numbers. Court cases from the early nineteenth century suggest that relatively small concerns in villages deposited sums as large as Rs. 1,000–3,000 in the form of bullion or jewellery.[25] Banking firms from the 1880s through to the 1930s appear to have maintained between 15 and 25 per cent of their total assets in the form of jewellery, bullion, plate and government paper, and this acted as a reserve fund only to be called into play in an emergency or in case of partition.[26] Sources such as the Banking Enquiry Commission give the impression, however, that even 'respectable' bankers were keeping a smaller and smaller percentage of their capital in reserve. The tumultuous crash of indigenous banks in the Depression of the 1930s would seem to support this contention.

It is impossible to answer the question of whether bankers hoarded because there was no productive investment elsewhere. Conditions obviously varied over time and from region to region. Yet before 1850, 'hoards' clearly served a variety of specific functions which could not be discharged otherwise in the existing state of development of financial and fiduciary instruments. 'Hoarding' was thus not one form of behaviour but many, and was opted for to discharge certain needs within the family and firm, rather than being a dump for unusable capital. We can distinguish the following types of 'hoarding':

1. Distress hoarding. This was common in the late eighteenth-century in the old imperial cities. It was a technique for survival and should not be confused with hoarding that occurred as part of the regular running of businesses.
2. The deposit of 'family' jewellery. This had ritual and social significance; it

25 ZC decisions, *passim*.
26 On the death of Lala Harrakhchand his family firm appears to have held about Rs. 10,0000 in Government promissory notes (Letter 12 June 1842 to Agent, Memory Book, Persian); the firm's total assets were probably in the region of Rs. 3 lakh at this time; on partition in 1892 Gappoo Mal Kandheya Lal held about 35% of their assets in the form of government paper, Manohar Das Kandheya Lal, *Rokad Khata, Magh Sudi* 11, *Sambat* 1950; *Leader*, 23 Mar. 1911.

was an aspect of the family's 'honour' and closely guarded from outside eyes. At the same time, it was one of the few forms of property which according to custom devolved on the wife after the death of the husband, and could therefore act as a kind of insurance for the wife under Hindu inheritance systems. A Benares case of 1783 turns around the question of whether jewellery is 'Khattri', i.e. the property of a widow, or 'Mughal', i.e. the property of the business house and therefore of the male descendants.[27]

3. The purchase of jewellery and pearls as a form of liquid moveable capital superior to money because it was universally negotiable and not subject to moneychangers' discount (*batta*) when moved from region to region. In 1786, for instance, a merchant of Meshed in Iran decided to retire to Benares and start his business there. His capital was conveyed in the form of eighty pearls.[28] High officials at the Indian courts bought jewellery for similar reasons. It was not as easy for the ruler to sequester if they lost office.

4. Gold pieces and jewellery as collateral. This was particularly important to the merchant community before they held easily transferable land-rights and when urban property remained of low value. The most usual form of deposit for this use was the gold *mohur*, the highest form of Mughal currency. A stock of gold coins appears to have been held by most firms and notables for use as collateral;[29] government bonds and land came to supplant them to some degree after 1850.

5. The family firm's basic reserve held usually in the form of silver. This was the equivalent of the peasant's 'iron chest' and grain store combined. The cash flow position of the firm whose books have been examined always appears to have been extremely tight, especially during the harvest when loans were still out and agricultural trade was speeding up. Here the silver reserve acted as an insurance against sudden demands – the appearance of a long-dated *hundi* to be discounted, for instance, which forms a recurrent nightmare in the folklore of the merchant families.

6. Finally, it is important to remember that gold and silver continued to be commodities traded in the north India of this period. The merchant provided the crucial link between the peasant family and the local Mughal mints which continued to exist in north India until they were abolished by the British, with dire consequences, between 1824 and 1829. In bad years, a vast quantity of jewellery and bullion would reach the market for minting in a short time; but even in ordinary seasons, peasants and others would sell off smaller quantities in order to buy bullocks or provide for marriages. Many moneylenders acted also as *sarrafs* or moneydealers. They kept ledger books (*khatas*) and stocks of precious metals and stones simply as part of their business enterprise.

'Hoarding' seems to shrink in importance against this background. It was not irrational, but provided many functions in the normal activity of business. At a later period when other instruments could provide these functions, merchant practice may often have lagged behind the new

---

27 *Gunga Bye* v. *the Mother of Jwalanath*, 3 Aug. 1792, PR.
28 *Ummer Das and Cheta Mull* v. *Bihari Lal*, Benares Adalat, 27 Feb. 1789, PR.
29 Jain, *Indigenous Banking*, p. 99; large loans (totalling Rs. 2 lakhs at one time) from Babu Harrakhchand to the Maharaja of Benares, were secured with gold *mohurs*, see, e.g., bond dated *Shawal* 1247 *Fasli* (1828).

opportunities to use the cash that would have been hoarded in the earlier period. But before 1850, it is difficult to see that this 'lag' existed.

The question of rates of interest raises similar issues. L. C. Jain points out that rates in rural India and in small towns during the nineteenth century were strangely static. There appears to have been a significant fall in rates as political conditions improved after 1800, but thereafter rates changed little from decade to decade. When the amount of money in the hands of lenders was greater than the demand, there was no general fall in rates, and when money was scarce rates did not rise very much either. Jain quotes figures from a UP banking firm showing that the rate of interest for 'creditable' people on the security of gold remained 7½ per cent between 1867 and 1884, when it stuck again at 9 per cent for some years.[30] Our materials show a similar pattern. Rates differed drastically between different types of borrowers, but steady overall. This is quite different from the practice of present day clearing banks where rates change with the state of the wider economy, but relatively little between borrowers. Jain states that the reason for the 'stickiness' of the rates of interest was the 'ignorance and adherence to custom of the villagers' and also the 'moneylenders' reluctance to incur unpopularity by departing from a customary rate in a land where custom has such a remarkable hold on the imagination of the people'. But if custom was so powerful, why was it that these same bankers and moneylenders operated a highly volatile exchange rate in discounting *hundis* which changed from day to day in response to the money supply and traders' demand? First, it is necessary to work out what elements go to make up an interest rate.[31]

Interest rates are thought to comprise the following elements.

1. The administrative cost of the loan which would take account of the provision of skill, the moneylender's time and his family's subsistence.
2. The opportunity cost: a premium paid to the lender for forgoing the opportunity of using his capital in an alternative manner. This is particularly important for the Indian trader–moneylender who has to meet demand for loans at the same time as he is required to finance his commodity trade.
3. Risk premium: this accounts for the risk of default by the borrower. It is determined either by a subjective judgement of the reliability of the borrower, or by the supposed market value of his collateral. But this component also takes care of the risk of a more general harvest failure which would considerably raise demand for the moneylender's loans. One might add here that one explanation for the 'stickiness' of high interest rates when money is plentiful is that, given an inelastic supply of consumables, food prices are bound to rise. The moneylender is thus securing himself any

[30] Jain, *Indigenous Banking*, p. 100.
[31] See, A. Bottomley, *Factor Pricing and Economic Growth in Underdeveloped Areas* (London, 1972).

possible rise in the cost of his own subsistence, or added insecurity of repayment should prices rise generally.

4. Monopoly rates: most development economists seem to feel that this is a very limited part of the interest rate; it certainly appears to be a derivative of the 'wicked bania' stereotype, fortified with a dash of hostility to rural capitalism. It is not at all clear that many moneylenders were in a monopoly position. According to the late nineteenth-century village census data, a very high percentage of the population had immediate access to more than one family of professional moneylenders; a wide variety of peasants and small zamindars also lent within the agricultural community.

What does seem to be the case, however, is that the risk premium paid to the moneylender reinforced existing inequalities in the control of resources. In almost all cases, a peasant with irrigated land could command interest rates more advantageous than one without access to wells, tanks or ponds. Only very substantial collateral in the form of land pledged could induce lenders to support tenants of unstable land. This, rather than a propensity of lenders to move into landholding, seems to account for the very high percentage of ownership of land-rights by banias in unstable agricultural tracts. In very bad seasons, lenders might refuse to issue loans to any farmer with unirrigated land. This was simply throwing good money after bad, for the absence of crops would make the loan irrecoverable, and besides, there would be a large demand for loans to start agricultural processes again once it had finally rained. The effect of irrigation as security was very evident, for instance, in Kanpur District during the great famine of 1837–8.

> The chances of the Rubbee in the eastern part of the District were such that the native bankers had not been averse to giving the zamindars accommodation. But in the Western Pergunnehs no one would run the risk of lending a Rupee; yet in the matter of wealth and trustworthiness, mahajuns and zemindars were on a par in the eastern and western pergunnehs.[32]

In what ways, then, did social factors impinge in the formation of interest rates? The moneylender however big or small was resident of a village or a town *mohulla*, and Epstein's work on rural service communities appears to be relevant here.[33] She defines two types of relationship between service communities and village controllers. First, there are tied customal servants who are rewarded by a fixed percentage of the harvest regardless of the outturn or the amount of labour they do. This she conceives of as a system against risk, supplying the peasant farmers with adequate labour in a good year, and labourers with the security of minimum subsistence in a bad year. Secondly, there are the 'free' service families such as the jeweller, bangle-maker, etc., who are able to raise prices according to demand or produce for markets outside

---

[32] Girdlestone, *Past Famines*, p. 46.
[33] T. S. Epstein, 'Productive efficiency and customary systems of rewards in rural South Asia', in R. Firth (ed.), *Themes in Economic Anthropology* (ASA Monograph 6, London, 1967), pp. 229–52.

the village, but have no such communal security system. The moneylender in the village or town quarter seems to stand somewhere between the two. Traditionally he was servant of the village leaders, and had often been invited into the village and offered protection in return for his skills and services. It was in his interest to lend to members of the village (or town quarter) during a bad season, simply because his own subsistence would be jeopardised if the community collapsed. At the same time, the moneylender had other outside opportunities as the nineteenth century progressed and increasingly invested his money in land or outside trade. In Delhi as early as 1820,

> The Bunneah was formerly necessitated by the sharers [village controllers] to become the banker, cash-keeper and accountant but at present he lends himself less to the interests of the sharers, being, by our system, more at liberty to employ his time and capital as he pleases.[34]

Any form of outside trade or lending inevitably built up relations and expectations with outside clients. Much of the tension between peasant and moneylender, or between the urban crowd and the grain merchant, appears to derive not from 'exploitation' but from the clashing requirements of two security systems, of two moral economies, the 'inner' and the 'outer'. During the 1838 famine, rural and urban riot had similar springs. Landlords and peasants still had no objection to selling grain to the bania at very low prices compared with those outside, but riots broke out led by the zamindar community when it was known that

> banias were withholding the usual advances, and preparing to carry off the grain necessary to the support of the village communities, and disposing of it on the market.[35]

Profiteering undoubtedly took place, but the bania needed to guarantee his own survival and maintain his credit with outside agents and buyers who were vociferously demanding supplies.

It has been suggested that irrigation was a major determinant of credit worth in villages. How significant, though, were caste and other social factors in determining rates and size of loans? The suggestion that they were of some residual importance over and above matters of risk and opportunity cost should not be rejected out of hand. Merchants and rural banias consistently designated their clients in terms of caste nomenclature in their books; and one only need look to the structure of rental differentials by caste in the villages around Benares to see controllers of land apparently applying these criteria.[36] First, however,

---

[34] T. Fortescue, *Delhi Residency*, I, 85.
[35] Commr for Dacoity to Bd, 23 Aug. 1837, BCJ, 30 Sept. 1837, 231/39, IOL.
[36] For the effect of 'caste' rental rates during scarcity, see J. Duncan to GG, 25 Nov. 1790, *Banaras Affairs*, I, 207.

it must be said that it is more or less impossible to disentangle caste from perceptions of risk. The lower castes in traditional India were seen as 'unruly' and a danger to hierarchy in the same way as women and the lower classes in early modern Europe. The idiom was pervasive, though no doubt exaggerated when lovingly recorded by the Anglo-Indian ethnographers: 'when you see a Gujar hammer him. You cannot tame a hare, or make a friend of a Gujar', 'you will get good out of an Ahir when you get butter out of sand', and conversely, 'better a solvent Kurmi than a bancrupt millionaire'.[37] In the law books there is no perception of conflict between questions of caste and questions of risk. Colebrooke's eighteenth-century Benares source states that rates of interest vary according to 'the order of the classes' (meaning *varna*) and goes on in the next few lines to lay down:

All borrowers who travel through vast forests may pay ten, and such as traverse the ocean, twenty in the hundred to lenders *of all classes*, according to circumstances, or whatever interest has been stipulated by them, as the price of risk to the lender. [my emph.][38]

Perceptions of caste status and perceptions of risk were mutually reinforcing. High rates of interest to lower castes in Benares villages at the end of the eighteenth century were expected (from Kurmis and Ahirs) because they were shifting tenants at will (*paikasht*) without landed security. Benares moneylenders charged 30 to 50 per cent monthly interest on small unsecured loans (*ugahi*) to the people of the bazaar because they were not 'respectable', and the risk of default was very high. Shopkeepers who had a fixed place of residence and members of the 'moral community' of the creditable merchants were generally also of the higher castes.

In Benares as in other north Indian towns, prosperous members of the lower castes played an important part in business in the early nineteenth century. The court cases seem to indicate, however, that the volume of transaction between them and the Khattri and Agarwal commercial elite was limited. Kalwars, Telis and Barhais are found adjudicating each others' disputes and lending to each other, but not with merchants of the higher castes. Over two or three generations, there were, of course, some conspicuous examples to the contrary. In Benares, several Barais (*betel*-leaf growers and sellers) were incorporated into the 'moral community of the creditable merchants'; they were allowed to cash *hundis* freely in the bazaar and could call on interest-free loans and arbitration from the prestigious Naupatti *mahajans*. In Agra, a family of

---

[37] H. Risley, *The People of India* (London, 1915), App. I, 'Caste in proverbs and popular sayings'.
[38] H. T. Colebrooke, *A Digest of Hindu Law*, I, 47.

leather workers (Sita Ram) had even taken its place as a powerful member of the local trade guild. Yet in all these cases, the improvement of status was a slow and patient process. It could be achieved only by incorporation into the dominant group, and not by breaking the boundaries down. A reputation for reliability and credit, lending to prestigious families on an interest-free basis, and above all, severance from the poorer and unruly members of one's erstwhile caste group by refusing marriage and interdining were necessary. Temple-building or religious charity was an essential part of the improvement of status because 'feeding the gods improves embodied rank'. The point is that so close were the conceptions of mercantile risk and low caste or social status that a low caste merchant family which was to be accepted as 'creditable' had actually to change the outsider's perception of its ritual ranking – of its generic 'substance' to employ Inden's conception[39] – before this was possible. There was no such thing as a creditworthy Kalwar family, but a Kalwar could become a creditworthy Jaiswal. It can be argued, in fact, that the apparently objective element 'risk premium' which goes to make up 'interest rate' is an empty category which is filled out by particular conceptions of rank and credit current in different cultures and localities.

On examination, the concept of 'opportunity cost' also shrinks into uncertainty. For the purposes of economic argument, it may be assumed that a moneylender wishes overall to increase the number of medium-sized loans to moderately creditable people. More loans would reduce an 'unwanted degree of leisure',[40] and hence the 'opportunity cost of his time'. But this formulation is in danger of taking economic rationality out of its social context. In three of the urban banking families studied in detail, there appeared over time a definite tendency to restrict the number of loans and to give a small number of very substantial ones to persons of great quality and credit (rajas and their widows, for instance).[41] The aim here was to acquire honour by association with great men, and in the social sphere it was a perfectly rational objective, providing the family with friends and security in high places. The 'opportunity cost' of time is also a meaningless term since it depends

[39] R. Inden, *Marriage and Rank in Bengali Society* (Berkeley, 1975), p. 91.
[40] Bottomley, *Factor Pricing*, p. 94.
[41] See *Bahi Khatas* of the Harrakhchand–Harish Chandra family, Benares, 1820–47, 1889–94; the family seems to withdraw from the multiplicity of trading operations (indigo trade, *lac* and wax trade, small-scale lending) which it operated at the beginning of the nineteenth century. By the end of the century its pattern of operation seems quite different, and its capital is lent almost exclusively to large and respectable Bhumihar landlords of eastern Bihar and the Benares region. A high status had been acquired very early by virtue of an ancient relationship with the Maharaja and prestigious Ausanganj family.

entirely on what people wanted to do with their time. In this case, the aim was to become notables (*raises*) of Benares, litterateurs, social reformers or even politicians. By contrast, families ran the risk of allowing their social and economic goals to get dangerously out of line if they concentrated on a fast turnover of capital in moneylending. One family of high caste status in Benares was regarded as distinctly inferior because, although wealthy, they lent large sums to small men in the bazaar (and, it is alleged, to prostitutes),[42] had too fast a turnover, and did not mix with respectable people. They had had difficulty in finding marriage partners for their sons and daughters in the last century. A similar mix of 'social' and 'economic' considerations appears to govern rental rates in the countryside. It may be in the interest of a land-controller to lease out as much as possible of his land to low caste Kurmi tenants who pay a high rental; but if his aim is to maintain reputation and security in the village, it may be better to lease out a large quantity to kinsmen caste fellows and Brahmins, who pay less rent. Thus, as Lipton remarks, 'The survival of caste rigidity, too, represents *inter alia* a communal sacrifice of income for security.'[43] In matters of rent and interest alike, we could well do with some such concept as the 'social opportunity cost'.

In the absence of reliable data on the long-term returns to firms working in early nineteenth-century conditions, any attempt to fit business practice into patterns is bound to be hypothetical. It seems, however, that the security of mercantile credit and the wish to avoid the risks attending heavy investment in any one 'portfolio' can help to explain some characteristics of indigenous commerce which have puzzled outside observers. But even if every firm were to operate according to its own perception of how to avoid risk, there was still no guarantee that the commercial system as a whole would have been significantly more stable. This section, then, turns to an examination of some wider mercantile institutions. It cannot be argued that the internal trade of north India was primitive, or unable to match supply to demand, which is an assumption lurking in the works of writers as diverse as W. H. Moreland and Niels Steensgaard. On the other hand, these mercantile institutions had distinct limitations. Merchant society operated on strong internal lines of communication which impeded the entrance of outsiders and limited their capacity to pool and use capital

---

42 Interviews, Chaukambha, Shivala, Benares, 1973–4; the line was not hard and fast: prestigious families also lent on a daily basis to small people, but some families were particularly associated with this type of usury.
43 M. Lipton, 'The theory of the maximising peasant', *Journal of Development Studies*, iv (1968), 332.

accumulated in society at large. Merchants' response to opportunities which involved high risks was often muted.

Mercantile institutions against risk

Markets with poor means of communication and transport have great difficulty in stabilising supply and demand, but price fluctuations would be socially disruptive to a merchant community many of whom were living close to the margin of subsistence. A primary method of avoiding risks and stabilising prices in internal trade was the wholesale market itself. K. N. Chaudhuri has shown that sophisticated wholesale markets in spices, indigo and other items in major export trades were an established feature of medieval India.[44] But wholesale markets (*mandi, gola*) in grain, spices and salt existed in major towns in the late eighteenth century. Wholesale grain dealers, for instance, located themselves on the fringes of cities and on major waterways. Here they purchased from the variety of small rural dealers, marketing peasants and itinerant Banjaras who had bought from the village markets. The wholesale dealers set daily prices which reflected supply, demand, the risk of replacement and prices in other wholesale markets. They were free to sell either to rings of retail dealers in the city, or redirect their stocks to other areas where higher prices gave sufficient margin for insurance, transport and profit.[45] The stocks held were very considerable. Wholesale dealers in the marts around Delhi in 1837 were supposed to have enough grain in stock for three years' consumption in the city.[46] In 1854 in Mirzapur 'There are about 100 grain merchants . . . who are supposed to keep always in hand a stock equal to 50–60,000 maunds of grain of different kinds.' This was at least a year's supply for the city.[47] Price formation therefore took place at two levels in the urban market, first through the wholesalers and then by the retail sellers who established a fixed daily rate in consultation with the political authorities. When grain suddenly became unavailable in urban markets, it was usually because wholesalers were not releasing stocks to retailers and were selling elsewhere. But this was an exceptional event. It was reckoned that the price of grain in Gwalior would need to rise a good 30

[44] K. N. Chaudhuri, 'Markets and traders in India during the seventeenth and eighteenth centuries', K. N. Chaudhuri and C. Dewey (eds), *Economy and Society* (Delhi, 1979), pp. 143–62.

[45] E.g., BCJ, 21 Mar. 1818, 133/44, IOL; the importance of the *arethias* in the business community is instanced by the case of Rai Khirodhar Lal of Benares who married into the Naupatti oligarchy and became creditor to the European Collector of customs. His papers are with the Chaukambha Collection, film in author's possession.

[46] *Delhi Gazette*, 8 Nov. 1837.

[47] Memorandum dated 18 Feb. 1854, Mirzapur Judl, 95, UPR.

per cent above that in Delhi before wholesalers gained a sufficient margin for export.[48] While the prudential behaviour of grain dealers might well conflict with the 'moral economy of the crowd', the serious scarcities which hit Indian cities in the century from 1750 to 1850 are not themselves evidence of the weakness or unsophistication of mercantile security systems.

The second main institution for stabilising supply and demand was the commission agent system (*arethia, arot, adhat*). The key functions of the *areth* were stockholding and match-making between buyer and seller. They also held and stored the goods of merchants until they could be advantageously released to the retail market or middlemen, and in the case of high-value commodities, such as shawls, this service could be performed over several seasons and thus make it possible for a travelling merchant to reduce considerably transaction costs. Brokerage charges would be paid by both buyer and seller, and such was the volume that the charge to both parties would be as little as one per cent in the major grain markets. In long-distance trades where major markets stood at the boundaries of several cultural areas like Mirzapur or Shikarpur, *arethias* would be conversant with the languages and customs of the different regional traders. Groups of merchants were attached to particular *arethias* so that at Mirzapur, we hear of the 'aurotheas of the Duccin [Deccan] merchants' and the 'aurotheas of the Bundelcundee merchants'.[49] Hindu merchants often lodged with their *arethias*. Even if they were not of the same caste, they would at least observe ritual proprieties and provide security in the social as well as the economic sphere. Finally, *arethias* developed skills for dealing with the local authorities, customs officials and the complex Persian-written pass system (*rawana*). Long delay at a customs post could ruin produce or frustrate a mercantile bargain, so the commission agent became a vendor of blank customs passes and in some cases infiltrated the customs system with his relatives and connections.[50]

How were *arethias* selected? Many of them were relatively poor men of low status, living on very small margins of profit. It should be mentioned, however, that many of the men we think of as big wholesale *mahajans* in the towns transacted a very large amount of business on commission, providing other smaller merchants with insurance and warehousing. In sensitive trades, such as grain or salt, the authorities appear to have had a hand in selecting and registering the chief *arethias* since they were responsible for establishing wholesale prices. But

[48] *Delhi Gazette*, 8 Nov. 1837.
[49] Bayly, 'Indian merchants' in Dewey and Hopkins (eds), *Imperial Impact*, p. 180.
[50] Correspondence, CPR, 24 July 1818, 97/38, IOL.

essentially, the system was indigenous to the merchant community. The authorities registered *arethias* once they had emerged. At a wholesale mart in north Allahabad in 1810, for instance:

Seetul opened the aurote at Foolpore from the month of Kaurtick and transacted business for the merchants who sell Juggree [unrefined sugar], etc., and besides which Seonarain Daroga of the Customs told the iron sellers to appoint Seetul as their auroteah.[51]

Another typical figure in early nineteenth-century up-country markets was the merchant middleman. Official opinion strongly felt that these were the 'ruin of the trade', and that they along with the agents of the wholesalers (*dalals*) were responsible for the crippling mark-ups on commodities between the primary mart and the Presidency. In the case of raw cotton, for instance, it might amount to sixty per cent. In opium and cotton a purely 'speculative' market also existed. Individuals would buy and sell the crop at various stages of growth and harvesting in the form of bonds of ownership. 'Every change of weather has an effect almost daily in the sale of these bonds . . . in fact the value of these bonds regulates the price from the time the cotton is sowing till the whole produce is exported.'[52] Other speculative middlemen actually contracted to deliver raw cotton to bigger merchants or the agents of the East India Company. In Kalpi during 1821, these included as unlikely entrepreneurs as 'printers of chintz and cloth, bunneahs, embroiderers, dealers in tobacco, silversmiths, shrooffs, money dealers, sellers of bhung and gunjah drugs . . . not proper persons from whom to expect regular deliveries'.[53]

Chains of middlemen such as this were a regular feature of north Indian trade during this period, and it can be argued that they had a definite function and were not merely 'parasites'. Dantwala, who defends *arethias* and *dalals* in the cotton market against their detractors who were still vociferous in the 1920s, remarks significantly that the middleman performed 'no useful function beyond shouldering the burden of price fluctuations'.[54] But this was function enough. Undoubtedly limitations on individual capital and moral or social predispositions towards the specialisation of functions between many regional or occupational groups also played their part. But like the wholesale mart or the *arethia*, chains of middlemen shared the burden of

51 CGC Allahabad to Bd, 24 July 1810, CPR, 13 May 1811, 97/35, IOL.
52 H. Newman to Accountant General, 18 Sept. 1812, Bengal Commercial Procs, 18 Oct. 1812, 157/57, IOL.
53 Petition of Isree Bux, Bengal Commercial Procs, 13 July 1826, 159/71, IOL.
54 M. L. Dantwala, *The Marketing of Raw Cotton in India* (London, 1928), p. 37.

bad seasons. The safe elimination of up-country middlemen and commission agents only became possible slowly between 1870 and 1920. By the later date, the Calcutta or Bombay firm (European or Indian) which employed agents to deal directly with the village producer had become the norm. The risks of vertical integration had by this time become significantly smaller than the uncertainties of supply and quality which had characterised the 'leap-frog' system of earlier days.

The existence of the commission agent and of sophisticated 'spot' and 'forward' markets in the internal trade of eighteenth-century India has significance of a more general nature. The writing of J. C. van Leur initiated a line of thought that 'traditional Asian trade' was mainly of a peddling variety, even when it was on quite a large scale. Uncertainties of supply and demand were increased by the lack of a system whereby buyers could continuously meet sellers, hold stock and form stable prices. Markets were therefore highly fragmented and prices would swing wildly, making it impossible for merchants to predict the state of trade with any accuracy. N. Steensgaard has recently reiterated this theme, arguing that stock-holding methods combined with the 'internalising of protection costs' represented a once-and-for-all advance in trading methods pioneered by the Dutch and English East India Companies. He admits that it is ethnocentric to call the peddling system 'primitive', but argues that the system did not encourage entrepreneurs to enter Asian trade. Moreover, 'trade on commission, if practised at all by Asian merchants is at any rate not demonstrated in the sources'.[55] The idea of a culturally defined Asian or Indian trade whose institutions are fundamentally different from those of the west is also echoed in some recent anthropological work on Bengali rural trade. A picture emerges of a market one day filled with buyers of vegetables without sellers, the next day filled with sellers without buyers. There is no doubt that peddling trade associated with these sorts of institutional problems continued into eighteenth- and nineteenth-century India. Travelling merchants, small hawkers of vegetables and the like, and even wealthy merchants speculatively bringing large consignments of valuable shawls to Indian courts all exist in the literature. However, alongside them, and more significant than them, existed the commission agent and wholesale market which were able to reduce trading risks and stabilise prices.

Indigenous insurance methods

In England, mercantile, fire and life insurance developed into specialist professions in the course of the eighteenth century. Life insurance had

[55] N. Steensgaard, *Carracks, Caravans and Companies* (Copenhagen, 1971), p. 42.

its origins in medieval peasant society where there are cases of people conveying small capital to a friend or neighbour in return for an agreement to 'care for them' in old age. The great spur to the development of specialist insurance was, however, the rapid urbanisation of the eighteenth century when nuclear families and other small households living alone in the cities and cut off from their rural kin found it necessary to protect themselves against illness or death of the supporting member.[56] It is not surprising that life insurance as such never developed independently in India. Here the extended family itself provided insurance for aged members. Urbanisation in India might indeed give rise to smaller households, as in Europe, but family authority, property and the institutions of kinship generally appear to have continued to stretch to the support and control of the separate household units.[57] In a sense, feasts to the brethren and other kin activities could be seen as investments in future security, though it seems unlikely that people perceived them in this utilitarian light. Among artisan and small merchant groups living in the towns, caste *panchayats* played a similar function in addition to arbitrating matters of ritual. The member who had honoured and supported the caste brotherhood during his lifetime could be sure at least that the brotherhood would bear the cost of his burial rites, see to the support of his widow and the marriage expenses of his daughters. Written settlements between merchants sometimes contained provisions of this sort, as did agreements on the partition of the assets of family firms.[58] But this was not so much an alternative to the 'natural insurance' of the family as a public guarantee that family benefits would be forthcoming in cases of doubt.

Even if kinship and caste organisation had not provided assurance for life and health, it seems unlikely that business could have provided an alternative. This is because a regular system of commercial insurance could only have been based on actuarial assessments of the probability of death or illness. English insurance had developed alongside public statistics,[59] but this sort of information was not forthcoming in India until the Census of 1871 began regularly to collate registers of births and deaths and other aspects of the civil condition of the population. Lack of information also inhibited the development of anything like a regular fire insurance for property. Moreover, the value of house property in

---

[56] Charles Wilson, *England's Apprenticeship, 1603–1763* (London, 1965), p. 335; cf. D. E. W. Gibb, *Lloyds of London* (London, 1957).

[57] A. M. Shah, *The Household Dimension of the Family in India* (Delhi, 1973).

[58] E.g., 199 of 1847, Saharanpur, June 1848, ZC; 'Interrogatories of Babu Harrakhchand', c. 1838, 'Memory Book'.

[59] Wilson, *England's Apprenticeship*, p. 335.

India was low until the railway era. If the contents of warehouses were to be insured, this would be done through the mechanism of mercantile insurance itself which was, by contrast, extremely well developed.

We have already alluded to the substantial risks involved in all inland transport in India before the development of the railways. The hazards included impassable roads, robbery, and in the cases of the Ganges–Jamna trade, river squalls and detention by Rajput princelings demanding tolls. While robbery was an altogether uncertain feature and sent insurance rates steeply upward, risks of ordinary loss could be estimated with reasonable precision. The East India Company, for instance, was able to reckon that it would lose about 10 per cent of its boats per annum on the three-month trip between Kalpi and Calcutta in 1828, and adjusted its internal rates for insurance accordingly.[60] Indian merchants were able to make similar calculations as a basis for insurance premia.

Most of the references we have to indigenous systems of insurance combine transport fees with insurance, since accurate knowledge of the trade route and a degree of control over pack bullocks and boats was an essential prerequisite of a viable business. In Agra in 1820, for instance, there was a large trade in gold and silver thread (*kalabatun*), and

so secretly and securely is this system carried on that the thread can be carried to Gwalior for three or four per cent, including all charges of insurance, risk of robbery and expenses of carrying it.[61]

Here the insurers actually took delivery of the goods in person and arranged for protection. Similarly, we find some of the large downriver cotton traders acting as insurers and deliverers for their smaller clients who had less information on the state of traffic downriver, lacking an extensive network of *kothis*.

At the same time there were some specialist firms trading specifically in insurance (*bimawallahs*), who were often branch family firms trading within larger constellations of kin networks who dealt in general merchandise. For the early nineteenth century, Sir John Malcolm makes a distinction for the Malwa firms between those who were insurers proper and those who engaged for the transport and payment of government duties for other merchants (*hoondah bharawallahs*).[62] The 'transport and duty' merchants appear to have speculated on individual enterprises at fixed rates and secured their business by control over the

---

60 Commercial Agent Etawah to Bd, 10 June 1827, Bengal Commercial Proc, 12 Sept. 1827, 160/12, IOL.
61 CGC Agra to Bd, 24 Mar. 1829, Agra Customs 6, UPR.
62 Malcolm, *Central India*, II, 95–6, and App. IX, 'Average rates of insurance for three periods of the last twenty-five years in Central India'.

Banjara carriers to whom they lent money and by paying off the political authorities.

Insurers, on the other hand, worked according to a fluctuating rate which was based on an actual assessment of risks over which they had no direct control. These rates varied according to the length of the route, the time of the season and guesses as to the activity of robbers. Thus, the rate of insurance on jewellery and pearls between Malwa and Jaipur rose from 6 annas per hundred to one Rupee per hundred Rupees after a major robbery. Higher premia were also paid to insurers who were known to be men of credit and would pay up quickly in the event of loss. It may seem peculiar that the rates on gold jewels and bullion were so much lower than those on cloths and general merchandise. This was because bullion was considerably more portable and easily hidden than large consignments of valuable cloths which were especially vulnerable to bandits. It is one explanation for the survival of a trans-continental money market in eighteenth-century India when long-distance commodity trade (e.g. between Surat and Agra) had almost entirely broken down.

The rates appear relatively moderate. Even those on cloths average around 6 per cent for a 300-mile overland journey during the dry season of a year of peace. This was clearly a premium which the urban consumer was able to absorb, particularly if he were an aristocrat receiving receipts from tolls on trade. The uncertainties of warfare could in fact be taken account of up to a fairly high degree of intensity by the mercantile system, and, as many observers pointed out, it was not in the interest of military leaders or 'plunderers' to cut off a trade route for any long period. All the same, indigenous insurance did have its limitations. The rates must be seen in context. For instance, UK–Italian maritime traders were insured for about one per cent during peacetime in the early eighteenth century, and for about 6 to 8 per cent during the war of 1739–48. The risk costs of the London–Livorno maritime trade were therefore almost exactly the same in peace and war as the land trade between Indore and Mirzapur some fifty years later.[63] For very big consignments, however, Indian insurers ran into considerable capital and cash flow problems. For all its bravado, the risk taken by one of the great Malwa insurers in insuring the contents of an entire bazaar against the advancing Marathas was not considered an acceptable risk by his partners.

The premium paid was twenty-four thousand, the expenses of protection and

---

[63] *Ibid.*, App. IX; cf. R. Davis, *The Rise of the English Shipping Industry in the Seventeenth and Eighteenth Century* (Newton Abbot, 1962), p. 87.

carriage incurred, fourteen thousand, and the profit ten thousand rupees. . . .
No insurer ever lived in Malwa but my brother Kewaljee, who would have dared
to undertake such an enterprise. But he had a Burrah Chattee, a great breast –
B'hot Burrah Chattee 'a very great breast!'[64]

And even in more secure times, acute problems of cash flow following
losses might force insurers out of business. Thus a Benares banker–
insurer in 1804 was remitting about Rs. 50 lakhs bullion from Calcutta to
Lucknow every year at five annas per cent (about 3 per cent). But the
loss of two lakhs in a single season was having an impact:

From the various heavy losses that have been sustained in the last five years . . .
insurance has become in great measure confined to his house, and especially
after the death of his relation Dowarka Das.[65]

In the longer term, however, the face of insurance in India was
changing. The insurer–carriers of 'great breast', who were essentially
speculators in wartime risk, were giving way to insurer–despatchers of
cash crops down the Ganges and Jamna who were able to take much
smaller premia. By the 1840s, joint-stock insurance Companies based on
Calcutta and Mirzapur were beginning to appear (Asiatic River
Insurance and Calcutta River Insurance Office). Europeans switched
over to them, and the bigger Indian enterprises were also drawn in this
direction. A merchant despatching twenty or thirty large boats down the
river every year was after all operating a basic system of insurance
against loss simply by dividing his stock up amongst them. He could
afford to pay relatively low premia. But with the advent of river boats
towing many large craft at once, the risks of total loss became
unacceptably high, and only the joint-stock insurers were able to bear
them. Railway trade also massively reduced risks in such trades as
opium, indigo or raw cotton. The railway companies were effectively
internalising much of the cost of protection within the transport costs.
Consequently, the old-style north Indian *bimawallah* had largely
disappeared along with the many varieties of merchant–broker
intermediaries quite early in the railway era.[66]

Partnership as an institution against risk

Joint-stock firms and banks had become a small but significant part of
Indian commercial life before 1850. It is therefore appropriate to
consider these organisations in comparison with indigenous forms of

64 Malcolm, *Central India*, II, 98, fn.
65 Magt. Jaunpur to Sec. Govt Judl Dept, 1 May 1804, BCJ, 24 May 1804, 129/6, IOL.
66 Hoey, *Trade and Manufactures*, pp. 27–8; interview and family history, Sri Prehlad Das,
   Benares, Jan. 1974.

partnership as structures against risk. In England, the joint-stock company was heir to the tradition of the medieval *commenda* partnership, on the one hand, and of the guild or more directly, the late medieval 'regulated company' on the other.[67] The joint-stock company was a direct product of the large capital requirements and great uncertainties involved in distant Asian and American commerce. The concept of limited liability emerges alongside it and also in the equally hazardous business of shipowning.

In the Indian case, the ideas of partnership and corporation had both existed, but the crucial juncture of these elements within the framework of limited liability appears only as a European innovation. Partnership emerges in the ancient Hindu law books, and even in the pre-Islamic period, the rights and duties of partners had been the subject of a considerable amount of textual glossing.[68] It was partnership within the extended family which remained the most usual form. For instance, an elder might set up two younger members of the family, who were not necessarily close relations, as partners in business. The young men would supply some of their own capital and this would be topped up by the more established relative. Profits would be shared annually according to a formula, say five annas, five annas, six annas per Rupee. The starting capital supplied by the senior man might be paid off slowly until the firm became an independent entity under the aegis of the other family firms.[69] This type of family partnership distributed risks in two ways. First, the elder was hazarding less of his own resources than if he were to found an offshoot of his own business directly, or to enter into partnership himself. Secondly, as a senior member of the family, he had more authority over the infant enterprise than he would have had if the partner was outside the kin group or a family agent (*gomashtah*). If the young men failed, they could always be made to discharge their debt in the form of 'labour payment' in the original firm. Once again, there were also purely social benefits from this sort of arrangement, for the elder was fulfilling his prime moral duty of arranging for the physical continuity of the family and the increase of *dharma*.

Risk-taking partnerships of two parties from different families and even from different caste groups were also known in the 'traditional' trading and banking sectors. A celebrated case was the long partnership between the great bankers of Lucknow, Lala Kashmiri Mull (a Mehra Khattri) and Lala Bacchraj (a Jain Oswal). Besides several joint ventures

[67] W. R. Scott, *The Constitution and Finances of English, Scottish and Irish Joint-Stock Companies to 1720* (Cambridge, 1910), vol. I, ch. I.

[68] See J. D. M. Derrett, *Bharuci's Commentary on the Manusmrti: the Manu-Sastra-vivarana, books 6–12* (Wiesbaden, 1975), II, 108

[69] E.g., Banarsi Das, *Ardha-Kathanak*, vii (1970), 71.

in revenue-farming, they used their capital and credit jointly in the remittance of tribute and other monies between the various regimes of late eighteenth-century north India. Throughout the period, we also encounter many examples of alliances between smaller merchants in risky trades, such as sugar, salt or grain. Some of these were once-and-for-all ventures on a particular season. But there are also longer-lived alliances where profits were regularly shared in the same proportion as the original starting capital provided by the partners. For instance, profits and losses might be divided in a proportion of 10 annas to 6 annas per Rupee[70] or one-third, one-third, one-third.[71] Partnerships could be terminated when the final accounting had taken place and both sides had issued a note of clearance (*farkati*), but the impression is that even possession of a *farkati* did not limit an ex-partner's liability for the debts of the partnership in some legal cases. Outside the formal trading or moneylending sphere, there are also examples of joint boat-owning enterprises on the Ganges or of complex partnerships in revenue management.[72]

Funds sufficient for very large ventures could be had on loan. Even respectable merchants could work on capital two-thirds of which was borrowed without incurring the risk of damage to credit, and by the late nineteenth century, the proportions had relaxed even further.[73] It seems then that the most important aspect of partnership was risk-sharing and the pooling of knowledge and experience. This was particularly evident in the case of grain-trading partnerships which were common in the west of the region. Groups of merchants would purchase grain together on a fixed share, profit and loss basis. The commodity would be stored for a year or two in a jointly held pit or *khatta*, and only released when the selling price assured a good profit.[74] Ownership of the grain was conferred by *chittis* (tickets), and these were sold on the open market as grain prices fluctuated. Similar types of business was carried on in the opium trade where we hear of *tejee mundi chittis*.[75] These enterprises are the nearest thing we have in the Indian trade to joint-stock companies whose shares are sold on the market; but there is no evidence that long periods of general trading were involved, and there is certainly no question of limited liability. The more parties were involved in businesses of this type, the more complex the organisational and potential legal and ownership problems. As S. Arasaratnam has

70 E.g., 29 of 1849, Ghazipur, Dec. 1849, *ZC*.
71 12 of 1848, Allahabad, Mar. 1848, *ZC*.
72 E.g. 52 of 1850, Allahabad, Sept. 1850, *ZC*.
73 V. Krishnan, *Indigenous Banking in South India* (Bombay, 1959), p. 20.
74 E.g., 204 of 1847, Saharanpur, Aug. 1848, *ZC*.
75 S. Roy, *Customary Law*, p. 97.

shown,[76] the East India Company sometimes encouraged Indian businessmen involved in their piece goods trade, or cotton, or money dealing, to cooperate on a recognised partnership basis, but in north India there appear to be few cases where this type of activity took place without a hint of European involvement. The case of 'forced loans' is perhaps an exception.

Many of the conditions for extensive partnership or joint-stock-like institutions did therefore exist in the 'traditional' inland trade of India. In addition, religious trusts provided an example for the separation of legal ownership and management in both Shastric and Muslim law. In the case of 'speculative' trades such as opium or cotton, a futures market existed which attracted people outside the old merchant classes who had small capital to invest. One obvious answer to the question of why joint-stock type institutions did not develop further is that there was no need. Partnerships between two merchant families were effectively junctions between much wider units of capital and skills since both partners could call on further resources from other family firms within their kinship network on an interest free (*par hath*) basis. Since the joint shipowning and *commenda* arrangements of seventeenth-century Bengal in which Mughal nobles had participated, Indians had been pushed out of the high risk and capital hungry international trade. Internal trade did not demand capital and risk-taking beyond the capacity of the merchant institutions as they already existed.

Yet Indians tried and failed to form joint-stock ventures before 1850. The key may lie in the question of authority and accountability, that is in the social or even political rather than the strictly commercial field. A conception of public accountability and enforceable legal (or custom al) sanctions must exist in society if risk-sharing, profit-sharing and limited liability is to provide the basis of an extensive partnership between large numbers of unrelated people. In the case of the family or kinship group, authority could force reparation. Even in the case of non-relations who were creditable merchants working within the ambit of a locally recognised *panchayat* system, a form of customal law could be invoked to adjust accounts and take care of the many social conditions which impinged on business arrangements (e.g. the respecting of funds put aside for marriage, temples, etc.). But outside the 'moral community of the respectable merchants' no external form of rules or sanctions could be relied on to provide security. Indeed, an involvement in public and novel forms of business could actually damage one's credit within that moral community.

[76] S. Arasaratnam, 'Indian business methods in the eighteenth century', *IESHR*, iii (1966), 85–95.

In the immediate pre-British period mercantile *panchayats* formed 'courts of first instance' in commercial matters. Once an appeal had gone before the ruler, individuals could appeal to a wide range of authorities in commercial or property cases. These included the 'custom of the caste', 'custom of the *mahajans*', arbitration by 'respectable *majahans* not of the caste', the Shastras, Muslim legal codes and (sometimes) trial by ordeal.[77] Judgement was given in accordance with locally formed ideas of equity which often took account of social factors. On default of payment or failure in business, a merchant's neighbours, for instance, had the right of the 'plunder' of his property until the city authorities were prevailed upon to adjudicate the issue and redistribute remaining assets. By 1800, the rudiments of a more codified legal system had been introduced, but its force was weak. Common Law (*Lex Mercatoria*) was never introduced into the *mofussil*, that is to say, it never became current outside the jurisdiction of the High Courts of Calcutta, Bombay and Madras. A 'Hindoo' law was also codified out of a variety of more local legal and Shastric sources, but its purview was also strictly limited. The 'customary law' and 'traditions of the merchants' could still be pleaded in 'derogation of Hindu Law', and most important, lack of knowledge of the customs of a local market was no defence for a trader who had engaged in commercial activity in it, however small (here the role of the *arethia* as a repository of local knowledge was reinforced).[78] Even in the realm of European-style financial and business institutions, external legal sanctions had little force. The principle of limited liability in joint-stock enterprises was not effectively introduced before the 1850s. Broadly, then, we can conclude that any commercial advantages which might have accrued from spreading risks outside kin, caste and local 'moral communities' of the merchants was cancelled out by the uncertainty surrounding the effectiveness of external legal sanctions.

Security and innovation

Institutions which played an important part in underpinning commercial and social security in pre-industrial business could both restrain innovation and change and also provide a base for it. What was crucial was how businessmen assessed the commercial risks and social insecurities which might arise in various types of enterprise. In the case of the early New England cotton mills, for instance, Dalzell has found that the search for investor security in order to maintain a 'patrician' life-style impelled mercantile families to invest in industrial shares because

[77] Bayly, 'Indian merchants', in Dewey and Hopkins (eds), *Imperial Impact*, pp. 182–3.
[78] Roy, *Customary Law*, ch. XVI.

these provided safer returns.[79] In the Indian case, the risks involved in many of the more lucrative internal and external trades prompted diversification outside the trading sphere into the holding of government bonds, urban and rural landholding, and later into industrial investment. But industrial investment was well down the list, and this appears to have been because risks and institutional uncertainties in nascent Indian industrial concerns made them scarcely more attractive than the run of trading enterprises.

Over time, the balance of risk and uncertainty changed. A striking feature of early nineteenth-century firms in north India, and of the biggest concerns of the late eighteenth century, was their very heavy investment in government bonds. As early as 1790, substantial sums had been raised from the indigenous money market in Calcutta, Benares, Murshidabad and Lucknow on bonds that yielded as little as 5 or 7 per cent per annum. This was considerably less than the average rates of interest on loans to 'respectable' landowners. Honourable service of government was an important motive, and the tradition of forced loans had not died out at the local level. But large sums continued to be invested and formed an important element in merchants' reserve holdings long after British rule had been firmly established. Security must have been a major factor for merchant investors. In the 1870s, Hoey pointed to the poverty of artisan and industrial enterprises in Lucknow and contrasted it with the great sums of money which local men had invested in government bonds since the turn of the century.[80] What is particularly interesting about his table is that the peak of investment seems to have coincided with the decline of political security in Awadh during the heyday of Sleeman, as chapter 7 suggested.

From the 1820s, land became increasingly significant as an alternative investment for merchants. Case studies make it clear that there were many motives for investment in land, and many situations that might eventuate in its acquisition. In some places, landholding was a tactic to secure supply in the grain trade, as we have seen. Elsewhere, merchants acquired land-rights in difficult or remote areas simply because land-rights had been collateral for zamindars who later failed.[81] Land as security became more attractive as British rule and British law courts

[79] M. Dalzell, 'Rise of the Waltham Lowell system', *Perspectives in American History*, ix (1975), 256.

[80] Hoey, *Trade and Manufactures*, pp. 43–4.

[81] Cf. B. S. Cohn, 'Structural change' in Frykenberg (ed.), *Land Control*, pp. 82–3; my material suggests that the acquisition of land-rights by business families was usually the result of lapsing collateral security and that it was quickly resold. It should be seen as a contingency of moneylending strategy, rather than an investment for its own sake. This is exemplified by the papers of Lala Sangam Lal, *mahajan*, Shivala, Benares in the early years of the nineteenth century (film in author's possession).

made the revenue-engaging right saleable on the market. During the administrative upheavals and depression of the 1830s, the first substantial acquisition of rights by commercial men occurred. After 1860, the enhanced value of agricultural produce increased the security of landed income in its own right. A regular return of 5 per cent from landholding backed now by the sanction of law and police became a viable alternative to a return of 10 per cent on less secure trading enterprises, where income was more at the mercy of seasonal factors.

Industrial investment had only reached tiny proportions in north India before 1900. Most of the capital put into industry in Kanpur was European in origin. The big Indian concerns were by no means averse to investment of any kind in 'modern' concerns. Indian joint-stock remained unreliable, but they invested in European banks like the Allahabad Bank and the Agra Savings Bank, and even became agents for them.[82] But industry remained risky. Demand for manufactured mass products was unsteady precisely for the same reasons that caused trade fluctuations – low purchasing power and climatic insecurity. Rising consumption of cheap manufactured goods could not be guaranteed even in times of rising prosperity because Indian families tended to spend additional income on food. European imports or goods manufactured by local European concerns in Kanpur had pre-empted the only mass market in which north Indians might have competed on a large scale. The case of Ahmedabad suggested that the safest returns were to be had from concerns which specialised in better quality products bought by the growing middle class.[83] But here again it was the European concerns with a tied market in the Army through the Kanpur Commissariat which captured the small north Indian market.[84]

Even granting the low level of demand for manufactured goods, there is still the question why it was European entrepreneurs rather than Indians who moved into the areas of industrial investment which promised a better return. Indian merchants, after all, had more knowledge of the internal market than Europeans who used Indian merchant outlets much of the time. Indians also quickly acquired technical knowledge, as was evident in the case of the few indigenous concerns in Kanpur which acquired European operatives. The crucial point may be the relation of would-be innovators among the Indians to the authorities and security systems within the merchant communities of different centres. Simple questions of differential rates of return on

[82] R. S. Rungta, *The Rise of Business Corporations in India 1851–1900* (Cambridge, 1970), chs. 1–2; C. N. Cooke, *Rise and Progress*, pp. 230–40.
[83] K. Gillion, *Ahmedabad. A Study in Indian Urban History* (Berkeley, 1968), pp. 92–3.
[84] See below, pp. 442–3.

investment or potential markets had to be seen in the context of gains and losses in security within the merchant community as a whole. In Ahmedabad, the one case of a 'traditional' merchant city which industrialised from inside, it was several of the leading families who controlled resources and status within the trade guilds who went into the cotton mill ventures. No small man could go it alone. But if the leaders of the community who could themselves call on a wide range of security and information made the initial move, then others would follow. By contrast, the examples of failures of joint-stock banking and other enterprises in Benares and Delhi quoted by C. N. Cooke all show men on the fringes of 'respectable' merchant society trying to mobilise resources and men whom they would not have been able to mobilise for the purposes of ordinary trade.[85] Most of the major families stayed aloof. Considerations such as this do not explain why Benares did not become another Ahmedabad, but they do provide a key to differential rates of innovation in cases where unexploited opportunities existed. Even in the late nineteenth century when joint-stock companies had come into existence in some numbers in Benares, the big financial families stayed aloof or took a small part in them. These concerns were inaugurated by professional men or outsiders. They were suspect; failures were evidenced; and open participation might harm the credit of the family. Above all, they did not meet the prudential requirements of family continuity and status. The great Khattri house of Chunna Mal Saligram, for instance, held many shares in the Delhi Cloth Mills in its early days. But the heads of the family sold them off because house property holdings in the city 'were more reliable and offered an assured rental income'.[86]

Conclusion

The last two chapters have been devoted to analysing some features of the behaviour of the merchant family firm and the institutions of trade which existed in the north Indian plains during the early and mid-nineteenth century. The focus has been much more specific than that adopted in earlier sections of the book. And while it is not possible to integrate all aspects of the history of family firms into that of the wider political economy, some themes are common to both. For instance, merchant institutions and their inward, even arcane, notions of credit developed in a situation where the political authorities were both weak

---

[85] Cooke, *Rise and Progress*, pp. 234–7; cf. Benares family histories, *Agrawal Jati*, II, *passim*, and in author's possession.
[86] Interviews, Chandni Chowk, Delhi, Jan. 1974.

and intrusive. Merchants needed, during the eighteenth century, to retain close and amicable relations with rulers who were able to foster their businesses through revenue management or abruptly to damage their credit and deny them subsistence. On the other hand, the fragmentation of authority into smaller parcels meant that public security and access to wider legal sanctions were even more unsure than they had been in Mughal times. The British Raj increased mercantile security and provided courts in which bonds and undertakings were more easily enforced. To this extent it might seem that the exceptionally cautious practices of trader–bankers were an example of institutional 'lag' – that they were still working with methods and assumptions which were more appropriate to an earlier century. Again, the very high rates of interest charged by merchants to their artisan and rural creditors might be seen as no more than 'monopoly profits'.

Possibly some merchants or cartels of merchants operated systems which were conservative and customary, and others were in fact ruthless profiteers. However, it is possible to exaggerate the degree of security which the colonial state actually imparted to the commercial economy. Custom and practice continued to vary widely from area to area and community to community; courts were intricate and uncertain; joint-stock institutions were fragile. As late as the Banking Enquiry Commission of 1929–1930, the majority of expert witnesses considered the high rates of interest taken by professional lenders justifiable in view of the difficulties of collection and enforcement in the countryside and the poorer quarters of the cities. Merchants continued to operate security systems, and the risks of new enterprise were often hard to justify in medium-term profits.

But was the style of Indian business enterprise no more than an elaborate response to purely commercial risks in the context of weak political institutions? The answer must be no. This account has shown how closely the social dangers inherent in the ambiguities and convolutions of the mercantile caste system were tied into questions about trade and profit. Credit could be damaged by social unorthodoxy as much as by getting into debt or turning over capital too fast. Caste status and ideology cannot be banished from a discussion of Indian commerce or the response of Indian entrepreneurs, even though Weber's formulation of the connection between the two is unsatisfactory. He may have underestimated the capacity of merchants to organise in the face of political authority; he may have failed to see the complexities of Indian religious practice. But his critics, too, have often missed the point. Weber was trying to explain the absence of the entrepreneurial, expansive spirit of western capitalism in India. He was not concerned with whether or not the objective conditions for capitalist growth existed. Equally, it is not really a refutation of his position to show that once external agencies had initiated industrialisation, Indian merchants adapted their social behaviour to these changed conditions. The real problem is the validity of counterfactuals in historical analysis. Weber might have rephrased his question in this way. If demand in the Indian economy had been raised (as it was, for instance, in Tokugawa Japan), would Indian commercial institutions have been able to infuse Indian society as a whole with capitalist values? And if it had not been able to do this, how important would questions of caste, rank and religion have been in impeding its response? It is unlikely that this is a question historians, economists or anthropologists will ever be able to answer. But it is important to stress that it remains a viable question. And it is also clear that the unique social situation of the pre-industrial Indian entrepreneur represented by caste and religion did, in fact, form one context within which his commercial decisions were made.

The ground is much safer when one turns to what actually did happen. The involution of mercantile society and the inwardness of the Islamic service gentry impeded the development of a unified north Indian middle class even when stronger and more aggressive governmental institutions emerged at the end of the nineteenth century. The peculiar factionalism, 'communalism' and fragmented nature of modern Indian politics which has recently been portrayed in such relentless detail can be attributed not only to the structure and aims of colonial government, but also to the development of Indian institutions over the previous two hundred years.

12

Towns, trade and society after the Great Rebellion

This study might have seemed to have greater thematic unity if it had ended with the disruption of the old order after 1830, taking the Rebellion of 1857 as its savage epilogue. We have seen that changes in the form of the state were registered in parts of the agrarian economy. They also impinged on the development of the intermediate classes of commerce and service. Some of the eighteenth-century merchant families disappeared with the kings and warriors which they had provisioned; others became firmly drawn into landed society as they rapidly accumulated zamindari rights during the 1840s. The service gentry suffered, forfeiting privileged tenure and rights to revenue in both Awadh and the British North-Western Provinces.

The 1857 Rebellion could also stand as an acceptable end-date. Several important developments became apparent in its aftermath. The railways and iron ships rapidly improved land and sea transport after 1860, bringing prices in markets in India and abroad into line. Crown government began to take a more active role in public works and pushed forward the modernisation of administration, the professions and education. More important, the small English-educated intelligentsia of northern India expanded. Before 1857 it had been based in the Delhi College, in Agra where the Sudder Revenue Court had been located, and in Benares where some Bengali educationalists and reformers had been active. After 1860 the volume of communication between Bombay, Calcutta and the interior expanded greatly.

However, there was also continuity across the divide of the mid-century. The institutions and traditions of the townsmen and intermediate classes adapted to these changes; they were not overwhelmed by them. This study comes to an end by providing a new perspective on the politics and social life of the period after 1860. Government along with expanded external trade and new ideas achieved a superficial westernisation. But the society which they modified was already moving along its own, slower paths of development. These stretched back to the pre-colonial period.

The first force behind the growth of the commercial economy and the towns in the later nineteenth century was government spending. We have seen that aristocratic consumption was a formative influence in the town economies of the pre-colonial period and that it also affected their environs through the provision of credit, protection and markets. In the course of the 1820s and 1830s government withdrew from the market and reduced its own expenditure at a time when the princely consumers were in decline. The economic and moral shock which resulted from the disruption of earlier patterns of patronage and service was as significant as any positive aspects of westernisation which the colonial government introduced. However, after the Great Rebellion, government agencies became more active again and pushed forward plans for expenditure and development which had been drawn up during the regime of Lord Dalhousie in the 1850s.

Action by the state which might now be regarded as 'development' was very limited in scope. This was no Meiji government of Japan. Recent writers have pointed out how puny were the sums spent on agricultural improvement in relationship to the total size of the land-revenue. Yet this was the period of the second colonial conquest of India, when the British military machine once more rolled through the bazaars and *qasbahs* of the mid-Ganges valley. New work for military contractors had already appeared in abundance in the Punjab after 1850 as the British tried to consolidate their hold on this new acquisition.[1] The Rebellion in the North-Western Provinces resulted in large disbursements there also. Costly new barracks sprang up in the major centres – particularly Allahabad, Meerut and Delhi: it was decided that the sepoy was now to be the 'auxiliary' of the European soldier and not vice versa.[2] In the immediate aftermath of the Revolt the number of European troops almost trebled from the 1853 strength to 61,000 and a larger proportion of them were deployed in the western districts of the NWP which had provided the greatest challenge to British supremacy. Building and military expenditure gave an immediate stimulus to wages and prices in the environs of the cantonment bazaars. In Bareilly, for instance, where only a few hundred more troops were stationed than before 1857, the civil authorities noted a rapid increase in the amount of cash circulating in the surrounding villages.[3] With rural per capita purchasing power still tiny, a change like this was registered as rapidly as in the previous century.

Expenditure on 'public works' and railways had economic effects

[1] D. J. Howlett, 'An end to expansion' (unpublished Cambridge Ph.D. dissertation, 1980), ch. 5.

[2] 'Appendix to Minutes of Evidence taken before the Commissioners appointed to enquire into the Organisation of the Indian Army', *PP* (1859), v, App. 21, p. 104.

[3] S. N. Moens, *Report on the Settlement of the Bareilly District, North-Western Provinces* (Allahabad, 1874), p. 6.

also. The famine in canal expenditure had ended in 1848 when the imperial government released funds for the great Ganges Canal. This had already cost Rs. 146 lakhs before the Rebellion. Expenditure on canals continued at a higher level after 1858. While the new canals created some unfortunate side effects, in the drier regions of the Meerut Division they had by 1870 made a 'substantial contribution to wealth and security'.[4] In the same period, military considerations had also given a boost to railway construction. The sums involved were large. The cost of putting in a mile of railway was reckoned to be between Rs. 1.5 and 2 lakhs. The distance from Buxar in Bihar to Delhi was 534 miles, while the branch line from Allahabad to Jabbalpur was a further 220 miles.[5] It is true that much of the manufactured material and even the sleepers of the railway were imported. Nevertheless, local labourers and contractors received some of this large expenditure in the form of wages and payment for bullocks, gravel and bricks. The coming of the railway had indirect effects too. Even before 1880 labourers' daily wages had risen noticeably along the line, and new agricultural bazaars had begun to spring up. The presence of government and its armies had been an important determinant of local urban and agrarian prosperity since the Mughal period. Even a small enhancement in public expenditure could therefore tip the scales towards growth.

Changes in the pattern of private expenditure also determined the form of the mid-Victorian economy. Population growth and better communications had put new wealth into the hands of grain traders. In the North-Western Provinces, the 1860s and 1870s were a period of relative prosperity for landowners before they began to feel the enhanced taxation of the new round of land-revenue settlements.[6] The administrative style of the Crown's government concentrated this wealth in the hands of professional and merchant people in larger centres. But it also gave rise to what might be called the 'colonisation of taste', which began to modify the balance of consumption and the physical appearance of north Indians and their cities. Just as the Mughal empire had rested on a network of towns and roads maintained by a constant flow of horses, cloths and other badges of honour, so the British slowly and largely unwittingly created an imperial style which also underpinned their empire's economy.

Access to the new professions and to the law courts, schools and colleges which indicated the more solid British presence after 1860

---

4 I. Stone, 'Canal irrigation and agrarian change. The experience of the Ganges Canal Tract, Muzaffarnagar District (U.P.), 1840–80', in Chaudhuri and Dewey (eds), *Economy and Society*, p. 108.
5 *Administration Report of the North-Western Provinces, 1860–1* (Allahabad, 1862), p. 124.
6 Metcalf, *Landlords*, pp. 201–16.

encouraged landowners to found urban establishments. Stone-built houses in the exclusive European civil lines and cantonments were matched first in the new service quarters of the old cities, and later in the district towns. Noting the recent appearance of large numbers of huge palaces of saracenic baroque and 'shocking travesties' of gothic buildings in his district, F. B. Growse wrote in 1875:

If the mercantile classes of society are distinguished by their conservative adherence to ancestral usage, the landed gentry who are on visiting terms with European officials cherish equally strong aspirations in the opposite direction.[7]

Even the merchant families often found it necessary to construct large, buildings of European or Mughal style on the outskirts of their cities, though piety and credit constrained them to live in the old mud-walled buildings of the bazaar.

The impact of these developments on local trade and production was considerable. The trades in dressed stone, fired brick, lime and wood received a stimulus from the rise of urban property values and rapid refurbishing of the towns and zamindari palaces after 1860. Rural labourers who had begun to inhabit shanty towns near the cities moved into private labouring work once the commissariat and railway contractors had moved off. And with these new buildings came new tastes in clothes and personal property. For the service people of the booming law courts foreign cloth replaced homespun, leather replaced cloth bags and kerosene lamps replaced the little flames of vegetable oil.

However, if government expenditure and new patterns of taste exercised a formative influence on the economy after 1860, in terms of volume the slow and patchy growth of the internal market was even more important. The main causes of change here were the growing momentum of population increase[8] and the diffusion of small technological improvements through the countryside. Early census figures for British India are, of course, notoriously unreliable. There is reason to feel that much of the apparent increase in population density between the guesses of the early 1800s and those of the 1840s reflect the physical movement of populations rather than large natural increases. But the evidence for a substantial increase in most of the Gangetic districts between 1845 and 1865 seems more plausible; it fits well with the idea that the population was increasing rapidly after the bad decade of the 1830s, and accords with qualitative evidence. The increase was probably in the region of one per cent a year over the three decades

[7] F. S. Growse, *Bulandshahr or Sketches of an Indian District. Social, Historical and Architectural* (Benares, 1884), p. 58.
[8] Commander, 'The agrarian economy', pp. 392–422; I. Klein, 'Population and agriculture in Northern India, 1872–1921', *Modern Asian Studies*, viii (1974), 191–216.

from 1840 to 1870. The growth in the labour force may well have been particularly beneficial in the western districts of the Meerut Division and Rohilkhand which still bore their eighteenth-century inheritance of relatively low population density. There was plenty of land to be reclaimed here; in the early 1880s it was reckoned that there was still 25 per cent of the cultivable acreage for the taking in Rohilkhand Division.[9] The expansion of well irrigation, the use of the Persian wheel for raising water, and the building of great canals themselves gave much of the region a buoyancy it had probably not experienced since the days of Hafiz Rehmat Khan. Distribution and marketing facilities were good, thanks to the network of Rohilla *qasbahs* and the roads that joined them. Most observers agreed that the region's prosperity was moving forward steadily on the backs of the Jat cultivators. In recent years, historians have written much on the boom in wheat export from the North-Western Provinces after 1872.[10] But the figures strongly suggest that 60 per cent of the fine grains produced were consumed locally by the richest 10 per cent of the population who were predominantly townsmen, small town traders and zamindars.[11] Other areas of rapid growth in the internal economy were the cultivation of sugar, tobacco and garden crops, all of which seem to have increased their acreage substantially in Rohilkhand and the Meerut Division.

The Doab and the eastern part of the region were less fortunate. Population here moved ahead rapidly also. But these were areas which had been relatively stable and prosperous in the eighteenth century, so that population started from a much higher base. In 1889, it was reckoned that only 13 per cent of the Benares Division was available for a notional increase in cultivation, and much of this remaining land was rather poor.[12] In districts such as Ballia and Benares 'the limit of cultivation has practically been reached already'. There was also much less scope for improvements in irrigation here, with 55 per cent of the area under wells and other sources of irrigation compared with only 25 per cent in the rest of the Province. The margins of the eastern districts were also being populated and brought under the plough with great speed. The District of Gorakhpur for instance, which had recorded the relatively low population density of 435 per square mile in 1871 had

9 *Settlement Report of the District of Meerut, 1865–70* (Allahabad, 1874), pp. 2–8.
10 P. J. Musgrave, 'An Indian rural society, the United Provinces of India 1870–1930' (unpublished Cambridge Ph.D. dissertation, 1976), ch. 4.
11 *Selections from the Records of the Government of India*, CLX, *The Wheat Production and Trade of India* (Simla, 1879), I, 159ff.
12 Orders of Government, 15 June 1889, p. (4), in F. W. Porter, *Final Report on the Survey and Revision of Records recently completed for the Benares District* (Allahabad, 1887), pp. (1)–(6).

climbed to 583 in 1881. This reflected larger natural increases as well as immigration from the already heavily populated districts to the south.

In these eastern districts, the precarious economics of sugar production gave little hope that the countryside could escape from the future of overpopulation and stagnation which had already overtaken parts of Bihar and West Bengal. Falling marginal productivity in agriculture was deepened by the lack of the energetic merchant and commercial landlord class which stimulated the economic life of many western districts. As the settlement officer remarked in 1889,

It would be difficult to find any country where the population is more closely packed, where a very considerable aggregate of wealth is more minutely and evenly distributed, and where society is more stagnant and more destitute of all apparent principles of movement or development.[13]

Thus in the absence of a programme of state development and vigorous town-based entrepreneurs, the growth areas of the eighteenth century became the stagnant tracts of the twentieth century.

The third engine of economic change in the Ganges valley after 1860 was the export trade in agricultural products. This too acted unevenly on different parts of the countryside. After 1860, cereal, cotton and sugar prices in the United Provinces and east Punjab were tied much more closely to those in Europe. The volume of export trade had advanced considerably since the 1840s. But many of the underlying features of the economy and most of its institutions remained unchanged. Instabilities in external demand, problems with factor supplies in India, and the caution of peasant household or merchant firm continued to blunt the edge of change.

The wheat trade of the western districts epitomises the underlying causes and also the limitations of commercial change. The appearance of the wheat of central and north India on the breakfast tables of Europe was a striking development. In 1871, the total value of Indian wheat exports for the English market had been a modest Rs. 23 lakhs; by 1876–7 this had risen to Rs. 180 lakhs, and by 1900, to more than Rs. 300 lakhs.[14] The exports of north and central India had been slowly advancing since the railway link to Bombay and Calcutta and the opening of the Suez Canal had completed the transport revolution. Nevertheless, changes in the political sphere gave the impetus to their rapid growth as in the 1820s. In 1873, laissez-faire pressure freed India's wheat from export duties. The contemporary worldwide fall in the ratio of silver to gold resulting from external fluctuations in the price of precious metals also helped to make India's exports cheaper, and

[13] *Ibid.*, p. (4), cf. pp. 8–9.   [14] *Ibid.*, p. 10.

cancelled out some of the still heavy transport costs. A third influence on the English market was a disturbance in supplies from Eastern Europe which had been a traditional source.[15]

It was in the broad valleys of central India that the response of India's producers and merchants was most vigorous. Large areas of Nagpur, Saugor, Jabbalpur and Hoshangabad Districts were turned over to rolling fields of corn.[16] British exporters in Bombay established agencies and later mills in many of these centres, while the great Marwari firms scattered along the ancient Central Indian trade route bought heavily into land-rights in the producing areas in order to enhance their control of the trade.[17] On a more modest scale, the Jat cultivators of east Punjab and Meerut Division turned over more of their holdings to the export crop. There was still a substantial acreage of tolerable land to bring under the plough in many of these districts, and canal irrigation had given a considerable boost to cash-cropping in areas which had once been unstable. The inheritance of the pre-colonial political economy – numerous fort-market centres where local entrepreneurs could make contact with marketing producers without the intervention of magnates – also contributed to an atmosphere of flexibility and enterprise. By 1878, Meerut Division with 1,371,103 acres under wheat was well in the lead, but Rohilkhand and some of the western districts of Awadh were also performing respectably, aided by good road transport and their histories of *qasbah* town-building.

In the wheat-boom regions, the basic unit of production remained the family cultivating holding, and this was reflected in the considerable variations in export from the Provinces in good and bad years. The cultivators' subsistence strategy ensured that the first call was to refill the small *khatas* or grain pits which clustered in the larger villages. Where commercial capital did take a direct hand in production in these districts, it was often in the poorer areas, and with meagre results. Thus the Meerut Settlement Officer marked out village differences: 'The Jat can make the earth give forth a Rupee where the bunniah with his Goojur or Chamar cultivator would with difficulty have raised 4 annas.'[18] Even settlement officers refrained from describing the peasant farmers of these areas as rich. In a good year modest profits of Rs. 7–8 per acre of wheat might have been accumulated, and revenue now pressed less fiercely on the land than it had in the early part of the century. Nevertheless, any widespread reconstitution of the family farm either by merchant capitalists or by commercial yeomen was to await later and more permanent green revolutions.

[15] *Wheat Production*, pp. 77–9.   [16] Stokes, *Peasant and Raj*, pp. 258–9.
[17] Especially the family of Seth Gokul Das of Jabbalpur.   [18] *SR Meerut*, p. 5.

Nor was there an export revolution in the wheat trade. In fact, the dominant consideration for the merchants remained the local and Indian market. One estimate of the late 1880s suggested that only between 10 and 20 per cent of production was available for export to Europe. Any sudden extra demand from abroad was therefore met chiefly by drawing on the surplus stores in stock, or by a decrease in local consumption when prices rose in Indian markets. As for the structure of the trade, it remained in the hands of the old merchant communities. Small dealers and substantial farmers brought their wheat into a whole range of petty markets from which it was taken by road, rail or water to major bulking points such as Delhi, Agra and Kanpur. Small *sarai* towns and roadside marts like Ghaziabad near Delhi went through the same hectic process of expansion as the cotton marts earlier in the century.

European firms known as 'country produce brokers' appeared in some numbers at Kanpur and Delhi as agents of Calcutta and Bombay agency houses. In Kanpur, for instance, Greek merchants were the largest dealers, while Harris Bros. and Co., had a direct link with the great British millers, McDougall.[19] But like the majority of European cotton firms, at this period they tended to work through networks of Indian merchants. In an unstable trade it was more in their interests to leave purchasing to people who had regular access to peasant markets. The difficulty of assuring supplies from a host of peasant producers and intricate chains of brokerage gave rise to a hectic speculative market in Kanpur and discouraged heavier commitment by European firms. The cries of 'poor quality' and 'bad storage conditions' which issued from Europeans were reminiscent of those of forty years before from cotton merchants. Most of all, the UP exporters continued to suffer, as they had during the days of river transport, from high internal transport costs. The railway charges from Kanpur to Calcutta accounted for as much as 25 per cent on the final costs of the commodity during the 1870s, which is extraordinary in view of the further heavy costs incurred on account of sea-transport and insurance.[20] Nor were the exporters in a position to improve performance at the level of production. English millers noted that even the direct cultivating holdings of *taluqdars*, who might hold proprietary rights over scores of villages, were too small to warrant the introduction of primitive threshing machines.[21] It is not surprising that in the longer run, north and central India were unable to sustain the volume of exports, once external conditions turned against the area again after 1910.

The wheat boom was ultimately ground to nothing by the upper millstone of high transport costs and the lower millstone of inefficient

[19] *Wheat Production*, II, 135, cf. *ibid.*, I, 185.　　[20] *Ibid.*, I, 198.　　[21] *Ibid.*, II, 135.

petty commodity production. But in the densely settled landlord tracts of the east, sustained commercial development ran up against more serious obstacles yet. A brief European presence in sugar milling in the Azamgarh District had largely vanished by 1850. But Indian moneylender–manufacturers (*khandsaris*) were themselves in trouble by 1880.[22] Beet-sugar was beginning to appear on the world market in increasing quantities and this drove prices down wherever cane sugar was produced. Already, however, the commercialisation of peasant agriculture had suffered a false dawn. In Benares and Jaunpur Districts, the acreage under sugar was reduced by half between 1840 and 1880. This labour-intensive, 'difficult' crop was abandoned for a more comfortable mix of rice, hemp and millets, which put much less pressure on the peasant producer. For 'If the sugar crop fails, the loss to the cultivator is very heavy, but if it succeeds, the gain is large, but not so large in proportion to what it used to be formerly when the price of grain was low.'[23] The rise in the relative price of grain was in part the consequence of the steady growth of population throughout the east. This also tended to push up the prices of wood and other raw materials which the petty manufacturers needed in their mills. Many of them had, therefore, moved their operations across the district borders to Gorakhpur where there was much land still available on clearing leases and where low fuel costs and revenue assessments still made sugar production viable. Here in Gorakhpur the whole cycle of parochial economic advance was played out once again; a small area boomed, limited prosperity was apparent in some villages, and local merchants and zamindars afforded sturdier houses.

The pace of change had begun to quicken after 1860. A new centralised political system was matched by a more vigorous and integrated export economy in primary products. Population growth appears to have been speeding up too. But this was no transformation. The monies disbursed by government into society were small in volume even if agriculture made some significant local advances as a consequence of canal irrigation. Exports provided only limited stimulus. It is against this background that the form of the towns, middle classes and public politics of the region can be understood. Growth and change there were, but uneven and insufficient to break the bounds of institutions as tenacious as the merchant family firm or the peasant family farm.

[22] S. Amin, 'Sugar production in Gorakhpur', ch. 2.
[23] *Benares SR*, p. 20.

The towns of the later nineteenth century – a new urban system?

The growth of the courtly cities of the eighteenth-century successor states had been stalled by the political and agrarian dislocation of the 1830s and 1840s. In many cases, this stagnation was given a brutal and destructive twist by the events of 1857 and their aftermath. Farrukhabad, for instance, had been in trouble since the abolition of its mint in 1828. Then, between 1850 and 1870, it proceeded to lose between 30 and 50 per cent of the total volume of its trade.[24] The rise of nearby Kanpur partly explains this collapse, yet in few places was the old aristocracy more completely eliminated by death and confiscation. Lucknow also suffered, though less drastically. Its royal court was in exile in Calcutta, and a large section of the remaining nobles were reduced to the status of indigent pensioners.[25] Erstwhile ladies of the Nawabi court were forced to eke out a living as humble embroiderers. Luxury trades declined as their old clients disappeared and the protective tariff barriers which had once separated Awadh from British India were swept away.[26] Lucknow remained the headquarters of the Chief Commissioner of Oudh. The *taluqdars,* the only clear beneficiaries of the British presence, maintained a tawdry nobility amongst the ruins of the Kaiserbagh, and Lucknow remained an agricultural central place for its still rich hinterland. But the mood of the city was best reflected in the elegy of Abdul Halim Sharar and those melancholy early photographs which show the once splendid royal barge beached and rotting on the banks of the Gumti and the fine monuments of Asaf-ud Daulah in full decay from the effects of cannon shot and neglect.

Smaller royal and administrative centres of the old regime also suffered. Khairabad and the towns of the Muslim gentry often went the way of Lucknow. Here as in Bundelkhand or Jatwara the railway often completed a decline which had begun with the demilitarisation of the 1830s. For instance, by the 1870s, the seven towns with a population of more than 5,000 in Unao District were

rapidly falling to decay. Their prosperity was intimately connected with the native government ... now these establishments have been removed, and the residents having lost their service, and having for the most part no property to fall back on, are sunk in the deepest poverty and wretchedness.[27]

Yet, as in earlier periods, the picture was one of redistribution and dislocation, not complete stagnation. There were already new patterns

---

[24] *Statistical, Descriptive and Historical Account of the North-Western Provinces of India,* VII, i (Allahabad, 1875–6), 249, 252–3.

[25] Arshad Ali Azmi, 'The decay of the city of Lucknow, 1840–1870', *IHC,* 1970, pp. 169–71.

[26] Hoey, *Trade and Industries,* p. 28.   [27] *Oudh Gazetteer,* iii, 530.

of urban growth. Merchants and brokers drifted off to bustling railheads, while service people congregated in Allahabad, the new capital of the Provinces. These new commercial and administrative centres registered the fastest population growth in the years 1860–80, moving the overall percentage of population in cities over 5,000 in the Provinces from about 9 to 11 per cent over the same period. Allahabad itself increased its population from 55,000 to 120,000 in the first three decades after the Rebellion as it became successively a major military cantonment, centre of government, seat of the High Court and of the Allahabad University. Old established service families moved there from Delhi, Agra, Patna and Calcutta. The great expansion of minor clerical posts in departments such as the Board of Revenue and the High Court also drew in many literate people from the small *qasbahs* of the Doab, Jaunpur and southern Awadh.[28]

Along with this administrative centralisation, there was also a redistribution of mercantile facilities throughout the Provinces. Fixed railway charges encouraged buyers and brokers to congregate at a few favoured cities, and especially in Kanpur, Fyzabad and Delhi.[29] The agents of Bombay and Calcutta firms became more numerous in these new railway cities and the drastic reduction of travelling time to the Presidencies encouraged a limited investment of European capital in the interior. Among the old entrepôt towns, Farrukhabad, Kalpi and Lucknow all lost out to some extent but Mirzapur undoubtedly suffered the worst decline. Although the opening of the cotton route from Central India to Bombay in the 1840s had already dealt the city a serious blow, it was the arrival of the East India Railway at Allahabad in 1869 which decisively altered the patterns of trade of the eastern districts. Dealers could now bulk commodities directly in the western cities, and Mirzapur lost its significance as a great exchange mart between Calcutta and the interior. Mirzapur's own trade was diverted away to cheaper channels. The famous merchant houses, European and Indian, either collapsed or followed the trade to its new centres. The branch of the Bank of Bengal was closed and 'the city fell almost to the ordinary somnolent level of other small district capitals'. Population, which had risen with such rapidity between 1760 and 1830, fell back almost as quickly, declining from 75,012 in 1853 to 71,849 in 1865, and 67,274 in 1872. This was a period when several other urban centres were growing markedly and even the smaller towns of Mirzapur District managed some modest growth.

28 Bayly, *Local Roots*, pp. 60–8.
29 Gupta, *Delhi*, pp. 164–5; Robinson, 'Municipal government', *Modern Asian Studies*, vii (1973), 397–8.

What precisely were the sectors of the town's economy and society which suffered most? In the first place, the cotton business was substantially reduced. The huge warehouses which had existed around the old fort, the 'Kot', fell into disuse.[30] In the Bundelkhandi *mohulla* of the city where the southward trading cotton and piece-goods merchants had established themselves, urban decline was most marked, 'The large houses in the Bundelkhandee Mohulla which were formerly occupied by flourishing traders and stored with piece-goods are now deserted and empty'[31] (1872). The through-trades in sugar and salt was also now carried almost exclusively by rail past the city, and the brokerage, insurance and embarkation facilities connected with them disappeared. The effect on the lower classes dependent on these trades was appreciable. In a period when the overall level of grain prices rose by 40 per cent and the wages of day labourers in the province generally kept pace with this rise, the wages of cotton pressmen and sugar cleaners in Mirzapur remained static at between one and 3 annas daily from 1840 to 1880. Storehousemen, weighmen and all varieties of petty brokers also found their position deteriorating.

The fate of Mirzapur's merchant families is more difficult to follow. There is plenty of evidence to indicate the abandonment of house property in and around the city and this suggests a rapid decline. Later references to some of the old magnate families such as that of Lallu Naik indicates that they were in 'reduced circumstances' by the 1870s.[32] While this must certainly be taken as a sign of the 'instability of oriental fortunes' we should beware of exaggerating the crash which occurred. Even as late as 1877 the magistrate could write:

Though Mirzapur is not now what it was some fifteen years ago, yet it has not lost all its importance as an emporium and consequently there is much more monetary transaction here than at most of the 2nd class treasuries. There are headquarters of several banking firms here which cash supply bills from Punjab at our treasuries or which get money orders to a considerable sum from Raipur, Bilaspur, Sholapur and Ahmad Nagar.[33]

These last three places give a clue to the location of persisting wealth within Mirzapur's local economy. They were all supply centres for the town's aniline dye factories in which as much as Rs. 31 lakhs of European, Armenian and Indian capital was still said to be invested in the 1880s.[34] Capital accumulated in transit trading had been invested in

[30] President, Municipal Council Mirzapur to Commr Benares, 31 May 1872, 132 of 1878, Benares Commissioner's Records, UPR.
[31] *Statistical Account, NWP*, XIV, 100.   [32] Benares Agency Files, vi, G, 17 of 1864.
[33] Collr Mirzapur to Bd of Rev., 15 Jan. 1877, T 6, 'Pay of Bishambhar Nath', Benares Commissioner's Records, UPR.
[34] *Statistical Account, NWP*, XIV, 100.

artisan industries on a small scale. This was no Ahmedabad where an old established mercantile oligarchy moved consciously into industrial production, but some of the town's wealth was being redeployed. Carpet weaving, the production of brass vessels and calico printing were other employments which managed to adapt successfully to the railway age and saved the town's population from an even more drastic decline.

Nevertheless, the most striking fact about Mirzapur remains its instability. Within a few years, the 'Manchester of India' had been reduced to little more than a district town. Some of the old firms collapsed; some survived as landholders in the environs or by reinvesting their wealth in artisan industries. In many cases, however, the change involved no absolute impoverishment. A large number of Mirzapur's mercantile establishments in the 1820s and 1830s had been simply branch agencies of cotton, salt and sugar trading firms based on Agra, Allahabad, Patna or Calcutta. The collapse of Mirzapur merely reflected their principals' decision to reroute trade and cut out some of the links in the chain after the coming of the railway and the decline of the river trader.

On the face of it, the redistribution of urban material across the plains which accompanied the coming of the railway and Crown government was simply the latest example of a pattern which stretched back to the Mughals and before. But there were differences. First, the stability created by fixed railway freight rates was more permanent. Secondly, this redistribution of urban population was the prelude to a limited but significant industrialisation.

The emergence of the city of Kanpur after 1860 as the major industrial centre in Hindustan marked a change in relations between Calcutta and the interior. The fluctuating and unstable type of urban centre associated with long-distance and colonial trade between 1790 and 1860 gave way to more stable towns located at strategic points on the new railway lines. The benefit to merchants bulking their goods and receiving supplies through a single centre became overwhelming, and since a much wider range of products was now traded, urban centres were less liable to the sharp fluctuations which had occurred when they had been dependent on a single cash crop. Railways also brought more stable supplies of food-grains for the towns, and this made possible the fairly rapid and uniform expansion of the urban population which took place between 1860 and 1890.[35] Kanpur did not, however, represent simply a stable agglomeration of the commercial and urban material which had been so volatile in the early nineteenth century. It was also the first offshoot of the coastal capital and industrial economy in the

[35] *Census of the North-Western Provinces* (Calcutta, 1872), I, xciii.

interior of the subcontinent. The growth of a new type of city supplying a large hinterland from its own manufactures and drawing in a much greater volume of labour and services from rural north India was a slow process which could only be seen in its early stages in 1900. Within a generation, however, the emergence of the Hariana–Delhi–Kanpur belt as a major focus of European and Indian manufacture broke the monopoly of the coastal presidencies on the industrial life of India. It is interesting that during the very period when the volume of commodity transactions between Calcutta and the interior registered such a sharp rise,[36] and when European twist and piece-goods made their severest onslaught on the Indian mass market, Calcutta's dominant role in the colonial economic system in north India was being reduced. Not only had locally produced Kanpur and Agra commodities begun to oust products brought through or from Calcutta before 1900, but a substantial volume of the area's trade had now begun to pass along the East India Railway to Bombay.[37]

Before 1857 Kanpur had been a cotton and indigo bulking city in the same class as Mirzapur, Farrukhabad and Allahabad. But it had also built on its status as a military station and the proximity of the semi-independent state of Awadh. As a turbulent frontier town where persons moving from Awadh congregated alongside émigrés from British territory, Kanpur, 'the Alsatia of the upper Doab', already had a reputation for roughness before 1857. Yet this brought considerable economic advantages. Awadh bankers, traders and government servants found Kanpur a convenient place in which to save money so that large sums were invested in house property and land-rights between 1840 and 1860. Moneylending by traders to local landholders also increased the circulation of land-rights as lapsed collateral fell into mercantile hands. By 1870 nearly a third of rights to land in the District were held by commercial families. We need not look for any striking social changes in rural society as a result of these conditions. But it seems likely that only external capital could have borne the District's extremely high revenue assessment. The presence of monied capital was thought to have marginally increased overall purchasing power and the degree of commercial farming in the area.

The industrialisation of Kanpur after 1870

While Cawnpore is the greatest manufacturing centre in India after the Presidency towns, its development is almost wholly due to European enterprise and initiative.

[36] Hoey, *Trade and Industries*, pp. 3–4.   [37] *Statistical Account, NWP*, VI, 147.

So trumpeted the 1910 *District Gazetteer*.[38] On the face of it, Kanpur seems to be a case of a city which illustrates in its own development the passage of late nineteenth-century imperialism from the age of commerce 'when cotton was king' to the 'Age of Capital' when investment, railways and manufacturing became predominant.[39] This is broadly true, yet some important qualifications need to be added. First, in Kanpur it was not private capital, either Indian (as in the case of Ahmedabad) or European (as in the case of the Calcutta jute mills), but the demands of the British Indian Army which provided the stimulus and the tied consumer market for the earliest stages of industrialisation. Secondly, Kanpur remained a distribution point for incoming goods and a bulking point for cotton grain and indigo, and in these trades substantial amounts of Indian capital were invested. Thirdly, the role of Indian capital in the major industrial enterprises was at first very limited, but the percolation of new skills and entrepreneurial initiatives amongst the Indian population had, by the turn of the century, given rise to much small-scale 'bazaar industrialisation' which imparted to the city its present distinct social and economic character.

The railway which reached Kanpur in the early 1860s put the merchant brokers of the city into a strong position to exploit the cotton boom during the American Civil War, and the rapidly increasing volume of European imports. Cotton from Bundelkhand which had been previously bulked at Kalpi or Allahabad was now brought direct to Kanpur. Mirzapur lost its earlier position as a great entrepôt mart and Farrukhabad's role as an up-country distribution point was dramatically curtailed. Proximity to Kanpur also damaged the entrepôt trade of other less important marts.

The present cheapest and most direct route between Lucknow and Calcutta is *via* Cawnpore. Hence Lucknow retailers of imported goods, cloth and iron, for instance, and retailers from all places beyond Lucknow buy in the Cawnpore market. The more direct route between Calcutta and Lucknow is via Banares but the break in railway communication at the Ganges in the last named place operates to prevent the adoption of this line.[40]

The development of the export trade through Kanpur also tended to bring 'the ordinary country produce of the Doab' to the merchants there.[41] Bulking and commission charges were lowered through the operation of economies of scale. Kanpur was also in a position to benefit

38 *DG Cawnpore*, p. 77.
39 Cf. E. J. Hobsbawm, *The Age of Capital* (London, 1975).
40 Hoey, *Trade and Industries*, p. 30.
41 *Statistical Account, NWP*, VI, 152; Har Narayan Prasad (ed.), *The Encyclopaedic Indian Directory. Cawnpore* (Cawnpore, 1919), p. 84.

from the one major new export trade which arose with the improved land and sea communication, that in grain through Calcutta.[42] This trade was extremely unstable in the 1880s and 1890s, as we have seen, but Kanpur became the great collection centre. About 30 per cent of total grain shipments came to the town from the north-west down the Ganges Canal, while another 60 per cent was brought by land from Awadh along the old road. The District itself began to export on a large scale:

the crops grown in this district [Kanpur] are more than sufficient for local consumption and are largely exported. Their value is partly re-imported in the shape of piece goods, and any balance in favour of the district is employed either in trade or in usury.[43]

Some of the major import–export firms were Indian-owned enterprises of Marwari or Awadh origin.[44] But it is important to stress in connection with Kanpur's early industrialisation that the strong European presence there in the 1860s and 1870s resulted initially from the rapid growth of commodity trading. More than 80 per cent of the European firms in Kanpur in the 1870s called themselves 'traders in country goods', 'commission agents' and 'country produce brokers.'[45] Most of these firms were offshoots of Calcutta houses of agency and their capital was raised in Calcutta, London or Scotland. The growth of the European population in India which followed the Rebellion, the steamship and the railway appears to have given rise to a spurt of investment in Indian 'country trade' such as had not occurred since the crash of the 1830s and the build-up of facilities for the commodity trade was a precondition for Kanpur's industrialisation.

The actual stimulus for manufacture came, however, from the Army and was associated with the tanning industry.[46] The Rebellion increased the number of troops in Hindustan, called for a massive re-equipment of those that were already there and gravely damaged the government's overall financial situation. The military authorities were anxious to avoid costly imports, and actively patronised the Cawnpore Tannery which was established in 1863. A Government Boot and Shoe Factory was established soon after, and went on to acquire the large army

[42] *Statistical Account, NWP,* VI, 142–3; see also. T. Prasad, *The Organisation of the Grain Trade in the North-Western Region of the United Provinces* (Allahabad, 1932).
[43] *Statistical Account, NWP,* VI, 133.
[44] E.g., the future famous industrial firm of Kamlapat Juggi Lal, or Sanwal Das, hide merchant.
[45] *Thacker's Bengal Directory* (Calcutta, 1870), 'Mofussil Directory', p. 59; *Thacker's Indian Directory* (Calcutta, 1880), pp. 571–2.
[46] A. C. Chatterjee, *Notes on the Industries of the United Provinces* (Allahabad, 1908), pp. 98–101.

contract for the whole of India. In the leather industry as also in the woollen industry, entrepreneurs had the enormous advantage of a relatively wealthy and tied internal market in the Army. But once production had got under way, manufacturers were able to branch into supplies for the still attenuated internal market in manufactured goods. The tanneries, for instance, had begun to produce leather bags, portmanteaux, leather cases and so on by 1895, while the woollen mills moved into a range of blankets and coats for civilian use. These goods were directed to resident European and also to the Indian consumers among the professional classes who had at last begun to succumb to the colonialisation of taste.

The dawning of the Age of Capital in the plains of north India is best illustrated by the case of the Kanpur spinning and weaving industries.[47] Beginning with the Elgin Mills (founded 1869), five spinning and weaving mills were established at Kanpur with a total paid-up capital of about Rs. 90 lakhs before 1900. Most of the production was directed to low quality twist and yarn for the local weavers.[48] The impact of local manufacture was already noticeable by 1900. A. C. Chatterjee thought that Kanpur production accounted for more than a third of all consumption in the province by this date,[49] and the import figures suggest that it was rapidly ousting European and Bengali twist and yarn from the market. The cotton spinning industry was also a very good example of the manner in which industrial skills might proliferate within a city once the initial breakthrough had been made. The tradition of cotton baling and pressing connected with the old entrepôt trade provided a pool of skills when the first mill was established. Later, in 1875, the Muir Mills were founded by a European former manager of the Elgin Mills, and the Cotton Mills was established by another former employee in 1882. Industrial activities finally spilled over into the Indian community when a former weaving master of the Elgin Mills interested Sheo Prasad, a wealthy trader–banker whose family had been long concerned with clothing supply for the Army in Kanpur and Allahabad. Together they founded the Victoria Mills Co. (1885). Similar proliferation took place in the tannery and leather industry. Chatterjee noted in 1907 that several hundred ex-employees of the larger factories had set themselves up to produce shoes in the Kanpur bazaar.[50] They employed a more sophisticated method of tanning and preparation than had been common with the artisan Chamars but produced a more traditional style of shoe, appropriate to the Indian market.

By 1900, then, Kanpur had already reached a critical point when it could add to its existing entrepôt functions a substantial and growing

[47] *Ibid.*, pp. 3–4.   [48] *Ibid.*, p. 4.   [49] *Ibid.*, p. 5.   [50] *Ibid.*, p. 103.

retail trade with its environs. It had begun to generate within itself the potential for future growth in a manner which the earlier bulking points and entrepôt cities had not. In turn, the rapid growth of its population (122,770 in 1872 to 197,170 in 1901) and in particular of its semi-industrial labour force (c. 27,000 male labourers in 1901) increased the demand for food and raw materials from its hinterland. The demand for vegetables and hides reached the limit of local production well before 1900, and the city had already begun to import sugar from the eastern districts for its own factories, thus reversing the previous flow of this commodity to Calcutta. Why had Kanpur been able to reach this critical mass of commercial and industrial activity in the 1880s and 1890s while Mirzapur, for instance, had failed to do so before 1860? The most convincing answer to this problem lies in patterns of consumption. The market for Indian manufactured goods was small and poor. Hoey, for instance, suggested in the 1870s that it was futile to establish industry at Lucknow because Kanpur had already pre-empted the market for any goods that were somewhat more expensive than artisan products.[51] For Kanpur, the Army and the European population had provided the crucial bridge for consumption and made possible a substantial investment of European capital from the coastal city (about £1 million was invested by 1920).[52] The balance of goods required was also significant. Mirzapur's industrial capital in the early nineteenth century had gone into highly specialised manufactures for long-distance and overseas trading. By contrast, Kanpur's metals, leather and cotton provided a number of products and encouraged the development of webs of secondary specialisation. The volume of industrial activity in Kanpur, of course, remained small before the 1940s. Only about half the sum of capital was invested in Kanpur cotton manufacture as in the cotton and weaving mills around Calcutta, while the total of capital invested in the port city was perhaps fifteen to twenty times as great, and the labour force along the banks of the Hughly was more than eight times as large.[53] But it was not insignificant. To put it in context, it is worth remembering that Kanpur's total of spinning looms alone was equivalent to nearly half the total for the whole of China in the first decade of the twentieth century. Moreover, the emergence of Wuhan as an inland manufacturing complex in China similar to Kanpur had hardly got under way before the Great Depression.[54]

[51] Hoey, *Trade and Industries*, p. 29.
[52] Chatterjee, *Notes*, p. 3; cf. *Imperial Gazetteer of India Provincial Series, Bengal*, I (Calcutta, 1909), 87–8.
[53] *Ibid.*, cf. *DG Cawnpore*, p. 262.
[54] Art, 'Cotton Manufacture', *The Encyclopaedia Britannica* (1911), xv, 292, 299.

The society of Kanpur had on a larger scale some of the features of rapid social mobility which were evident earlier in Mirzapur. Members of inferior castes (Chamars, Doms, Telis, Kalwars) had improved their position through the development of the leather, oil-seed and metal businesses. In the 1890s and 1900s, there were also a number of well-publicised cases where Brahmins became entrepreneurs in trades or industries which were commonly thought to be polluting. However, there is little evidence of the fast modernisation of traditional business methods or of westernisation. The Chamber of Commerce founded in 1893 was the preserve of Europeans for many years, and indigenous banking remained strong in the city until the 1930s.[55] Indian entrepreneurs continued to be drawn overwhelmingly from the traditional commercial classes. They were Agarwals from Lucknow and Farrukhabad,[56] Marwaris from Rajasthan[57] and Khattris who had long been connected with the town's military commissariat.[58] The mercantile practice and self-image of these businessmen continued to be orthodox and cautious. Merit was acquired through temple-building, cow-protection and other Hindu activities. What is more noteworthy perhaps was the extremely low level of public and political life in the city in the late nineteenth century. Kanpur was notorious for its lack of nationalist involvement, and the merchant class was not even drawn into large-scale cultural and religious activity as occurred elsewhere. The case of Kanpur indeed bears out the view that large-scale economic change did not necessarily imply social or political modernisation. The network of economic connections which terminated in Calcutta was in no way congruent with the political hinterland of the Indian Association and the progressive up-country political networks of Surendranath Banerjea.

There is always a temptation to opt too firmly either for an argument which stresses continuity or for one that stresses change. Before 1930, the industrialisation of Kanpur was puny by contemporary European standards though significant by Asian and indeed Russian standards. Yet the city's growth took place within an agrarian context which was being modified much more slowly. As Shahid Amin has shown in his study of sugar production in the eastern part of the Province, the raw materials brought to the mills of the new city were still procured largely through the pressures of debt and land-revenue payments and not in a

55 *U.P. Provincial Banking Enquiry Committee*, IV, 87–92.
56 *Agrawal Jati ka Itihas*, II, 75–8; 213–15; 295–8; family histories, Allahabad and Kanpur, 1968–73.
57 B. Modi, *Desh ki Itihas me Marwari Jati ka Stan* (Calcutta, 1940).
58 Especially the family of Lala Sheo Prasad Tunti Mall, see below.

free market for petty commodities.[59] We have also seen that the stimulus to industrialisation was provided by the army of the colonial state rather than by raised consumption or by a great new accumulation of mercantile capital in the interior. Even Kanpur's growing working class had been anticipated by the tiny pool of wage labour of mixed caste which had developed in Mirzapur in the 1830s. All the same, to deny the importance of the development of the city on these grounds seems to be to fall into the error of the 'westernisation' thesis: that is, to insist that the only significant changes are those that directly follow European models.

How far had other cities changed their function in the agrarian hinterland? In the first decades of British rule, the pre-colonial pattern had continued to hold. While the revenue and rental demand obliged farmers to sell produce in towns, or to men who were based in the the towns, the urban population in its turn did not sell much to the countryside. Even great trading towns such as Mirzapur do not seem to have been comparable retail marts for their environs at this time. Instead village artisans and rural traders working through networks of peasant markets supplied the great bulk of rural demand, which was limited in any case by the low income of consumers. Yet there was a slow change after 1860. Agricultural prices rose fast, while the rate of government revenue per cultivated acre appears to have been on the decline after 1850. Whether we believe in exploitative zamindars or rich peasants, it seems clear that some elements in the rural population had significantly greater disposable income, at least in those areas where population was not pressing too hard on the limits of cultivation. This is consistent with the figures which show that up to 40 per cent of the population of several districts were being supplied with imported cloth in the 1870s,[60] while village weaving was by no means totally eliminated. Shoes, iron tools, kerosene and umbrellas were other items of retail trade which were passing in greater volume from town to countryside, while the internal market for the fine grains of the west had also grown appreciably.

Urban services were also becoming more significant for rural people. The explosion of land litigation after 1860 brought the town lawyer and land agent into contact with a growing number of landlords and tenants. The accumulation of urban receipts from such services is reflected in the relative growth of income from 'professions' compared with those from

---

[59] S. Amin, 'Sugar production'.
[60] *Statistical Account, NWP*, VII, i, 255; *Selections from Records, Govt. NWP* (Allahabad, 1864) pt XL, art. iv, 'Information Regarding the Slackness of Demand for European Cotton Goods', p. 117.

'moneylending and trade' revealed in the income tax figures for the later nineteenth century. And even education was beginning to exercise an urban pull. Hardly anyone from a true peasant background went on to education in the towns before 1900. But the Muslim and Kayasth families of the *qasbahs* and some Hindu zamindars were beginning to board their children in towns such as Allahabad, Benares and Aligarh for secondary education, now that examinations had begun to replace patronage as the avenue of professional advancement.[61]

All these changes were highly significant for the future of cultural and political activity in the countryside. Teachers, lawyers and the sons of estate managers with experience of both town and country helped mobilise their relatives and dependents for religious and nationalist activity. Small town merchants, now linked more closely to the pace of the city bazaars, also played an important part in the beginning of nationalist politics in the countryside. Yet the pace of change was slow. The export economy was fitful and constrained; the growth of the internal market was limited by painfully low consumer income. The gulf between town and countryside was often breached, not by the development of common economic interests, but by links of culture and religion which had long bound the service people and corporations of the cities to the markets and temples of their hinterland. The last sections of this study, therefore, turn again to the merchants and urban corporations. From this environment were to emerge the most potent political traditions of modern Hindustan and also many of India's most successful industrialists. The powerful support which substantial peasants brought to India's anti-colonial consensus in the 1930s and 1940s was added to, and constrained by, the older alliance of commerce and petty service in the towns.

The forms of commercial life in north India changed only slowly between the days of Jonathan Duncan and the World Depression of the 1930s when many of the old firms finally went out of business. The joint-stock company made even slower progress in the Ganges valley than in Bombay or Bengal, so that the family business of the Vaishya traders remained predominant. In centres such as Kanpur or Agra where the beginnings of industry were perceptible before 1900, some families from commercial communities outside the old business world had made headway. Broadly, however, the new men were poor relations or caste fellows of the oligarchs who dominated the corporations.

After 1860, the pace of change speeded up a little. The stimulus given by government or military expenditure and by new tastes did provide

---

61 E.g., Bayly, 'Small town', in Ballhatchet and Harrison (eds), *City in South Asia*, pp. 32–3.

limited opportunities for newcomers and new lines of trade. Most important was the growth of a fringe of enterprises which lay somewhere between the old business world or trade in luxuries and agricultural produce and the world of the pen-pusher and government servant. Printing, bookselling, the commission agency for land sales – all these brought the professional man and the *mahajan* together. Europeans dominated these new skilled service trades in the 1860s and 1870s but by the end of the century, a number of Indians were involved, including some from the old business communities.[62] The growth of a 'colonial' style of consumption also created the retail shop and general store. These catered at first for the European military and civil service, but began soon to provision Indian professional men and 'modern' zamindars. Some of the new wealthy were men who had begun by hawking empty bottles, ice and cheap watches around the civil lines and cantonments.

Contracting work for the civil and military authorities remained the most important avenue for anyone trying to break into the small circle of the richest. Though many of the construction materials for the railway were imported, local labour, transport, wood and stone were required by the authorities at places such as Moghul Sarai (the Benares junction), Allahabad and Tundla (near Agra).[63] Quick fortunes were made by small town merchants at these places. The dominant families of the larger cities had all been closely involved in military contracting also. Sheo Prasad and Tunti Mull of Kanpur had played a careful game with the British and the rebels during the Mutiny to emerge as the city's chief house owners and general merchants.[64] Their relatives, the Allahabad Tandons, became contractors to the city's arsenal and serviced its growing population with bungalows and quality cloth imported from Calcutta.[65] In Agra and Delhi, Joti Prasad, another great Khattri contractor, survived as one of the heroes of the Rebellion. In addition to his extensive bullock and contracting trade, his firm ran the first fleet of hackney carriages for the European residents of Delhi.[66]

There were areas of decline also. With the destruction of the great courts of Delhi, Lucknow and Farrukhabad, the communities of Oswal jewellers took a savage blow. During the Rebellion many had lost their

[62] See, *Thacker's Indian Directory* (Calcutta, 1880–1900).

[63] E.g., family history of Lala Mina Ram Kapur from Sri Radhey Mohan, Agra, Jan. 1973.

[64] Family history from Sri Hari Mohan Das Tandon, and MSS compiled by Sri Manmohan Das Tandon, *c.* 1935, Ranimandi, Allahabad.

[65] *Ibid.*, Bayly, 'Patrons and politics', *Modern Asian Studies*, vii (1973), 368–76.

[66] *Report on the Administration of Public Affairs in the North-Western Provinces for 1855–56* (Calcutta, 1857), p. (31).

capital and though demand revived after 1858, severe problems of cash
flow hampered the industry's recovery over the next twenty years. The
end of Awadh's tariff barriers and the decline of the old consumers
similarly decimated the indigenous shoe industry and the trade in
brocaded cloth which had answered the requirements of the princely
darbars. Another industry which went down hill after 1850 was
indigenous insurance or *bima*. 'Native insurers' had once insured and
transported items such as gold, indigo and opium. But now the railways
and river steam boats provided secure forms of transport.[67] The
insuring was done in Calcutta and usually in the European style.

Another change which came over the merchant class was closer
involvement in the management of land. Many of the old mercantile
families had picked up land-rights during the 1830s depression and
again as rewards or bargains after the Rebellion. The enhanced value of
landed property with the coming of the railways encouraged further
purchases, and one can also infer that with better rural police, the
conditions of management improved. The unspectacular modification
of mercantile organisation and culture also proceeded more rapidly.

Corporations, *qasbahs* and the new politics, 1870–1920

In most historical writing the stark dichotomy between tradition and
modernity has long since been abandoned. But, curiously, it lingers on
in many treatments of the emergence of 'modern' politics in India, and
of the origin of the modern Indian middle class. Voluntary association is
thought to have come with the railway and the electric telegraph in a
simple adaptation of the methods of the Anti-Corn Law League or of
Irish nationalism. The artificers of social reform and Congress politics
alike are supposed to have been westernised outsiders, especially the
Bengal civil servants and lawyers who trickled more rapidly into north
India in the train of the Crown Government. As for the middle classes,
these were seen to evolve on the basis of English education or modern
ideology and the expansion of modern administration and overseas trade
after the Great Rebellion. Even the Cambridge historians who have
sought consciously to distance themselves from these models of the
1950s have tended to over emphasise the impact on 'local' society of new
administrative structures erected in order to give the colonial rulers a
more detailed and lucrative control over its resources. Of course, some
writes noted how the new social and political movements absorbed or
co-opted indigenous corporations, caste councils or other relationships.
But these were generally regarded as the flotsam and jetsam of

[67] Hoey, *Trade and Industries*, pp. 27–8.

traditional society, as 'arcane reformations'[68] or as impediments to the development of a 'proper' class-based society.

This study has emphasised that the relationship between market, temple and king had been in continuous development since the pre-colonial period. And it was this relationship in a new incarnation which formed the basis of many of the voluntary associations and social movements which flowered in the later nineteenth century. In all the major centres of Hindi-speaking north India the new religious and political associations had links with existing shrines, *sabhas* and commercial solidarities. In Allahabad, for instance, commercial and devotional relationships generated by the great bathing fair, the Magh Mela, contributed as much to the emergence of modern political associations as the camaraderies of the Bar Library. In 1888, at the first meeting of the Indian National Congress held in Allahabad, a spiritual descendant of the Gosain leader who had saved the city from the Rohillas in 1754 joined with the corporate bodies of the bazaars to give the westernised lawyers of the High Court Bar a stronger base.[69] In Benares, descendants of the notables of the Naupatti banking fraternity gave an impetus to Congress, the propagation of modern literary Hindi and Vaishnavite Hinduism. The same type of continuity can be discovered from the east Punjab to Jabbalpur and Indore in Central India.

The style of Hindu politics which emerged from the corporate urban life of the later nineteenth century remains vital throughout north India. The westernised radical politics of the great coastal cities, or more recently Delhi, continued to conflict with this tradition whether in the guise of the Hindu Mahasabha of the 1930s or of the Jana Sangh in the 1970s. It was into a conservative political alliance pioneered by the service people and merchants of the district towns that the leaders of the great rural yeoman castes – Jats, Rajputs, and Bhumihars – were recruited in the 1930s. When the peasant 'returned' to South Asian history after the end of the First World War, many of the political conventions had already been set.

The ideology and organisation of Muslim separatist politics also had deep roots in a developing tradition. Several writers have shown how important small zamindars were in the early Muslim League, while the *ulama* and Sufis are said to have 'come into politics' and strengthened the mass base of the Pan-Islamic movement at the end of the First World War. But a new perspective is needed here also. The Muslim service gentry who participated in the Urdu Defence Association and the

[68] Bayly, *Local Roots*, chs. 3–4.
[69] Bayly, 'Patrons and politics', pp. 368–72.

Muslim League must be set firmly against the background of their homes in *qasbahs* or the Muslim quarters of the district towns. This class of literate small zamindar had strengthened its position in the course of the seventeenth and eighteenth centuries. But after about 1830, it was coming under growing economic pressure. A strong sense of identity built around the traditions of these small rural places was progressively widened to embrace an Indian Muslim 'community' as a whole.

The early chapters of this book have argued that the commercialisation of royal power during the seventeenth and eighteenth centuries encouraged the development of a rooted service gentry and a unified merchant class. The service gentry had perpetuated its sense of identity and its economic dominance through the institutions of the rural *qasbah* town. The merchant class was formally divided by caste and function. But its common interests and values were expressed through the organisation of markets, mercantile credit and Hindu or Jain religion which transcended these divisions. Different levels of solidarity subtly interlocked with each other to create a corporate culture of great vitality which could mobilise considerable reserves of political influence. Thus caste associations often emerged in the course of the nineteenth century out of the old caste *panchayats*. This development may have been speeded by the policies of imperial government. But among specialised urban communities it owed much more to the evolution of relationships within Hindu society itself. Before the expansion of colonial trade or administration, special relationships between local caste groups had already begun to bond this apparently fissiparous society more tightly. There was, for instance, an ancient ritual tie between Khattri merchants and their Saraswat Brahmin priests. Before the end of the eighteenth century (and probably much earlier) some Brahmin families had moved into trade in their own right, and were active along with their caste patrons on the great shawl routes to the north-west. As the nineteenth century proceeded the relationship developed. Joint religious trusts between the two communities gave rise to 'caste associations' which took an interest in topics such as education and social reform. Both Allahabad and Benares had their own 'Khuttree and Saraswat Sahbas' before 1900.[70]

This was only one example of how a relationship between Brahmins and high caste merchant people developed consistently from an early period to form the basis of modern social and political organisation. And the association also worked the other way. Members of the great merchant families had always needed to participate in the public world

[70] *Hindustan,* Dec. 1888; annual report of Benares Sabha, *c.* 1910, available with Sri Devi Narayan, Benares.

of the rulers' darbars, and had employed Persian-writing clerks or ambassadors (*vakils*) to represent their interests. By 1880 the younger sons of some merchant families were themselves moving into English education and the law. As public law became more intrusive, it was to the advantage of men of commerce to have direct representation in the professions. In this way the links between the commercial and the service classes were strengthened, laying the groundwork for a more cohesive middle class opinion.

Chapter 6 pointed out how the great ascetic corporations, the Gosain *akharas*, adapted to the commercial changes of the early nineteenth century. They were much more than an exotic product of pre-colonial chaos, doomed by the onset of modernisation. Outwardly these corporations made few concessions to the late Victorian era, apart from the donning of the occasional loin cloth. But inwardly their institutions were in constant evolution. They diversified rapidly into urban property-owning after 1802. Later they capitalised on the rapidly rising value of urban property following the construction of the railways. They maintained their position as a major moneylending group not only in the cities but also in the small towns and villages where their routes of pilgrimage took them. Their *mahants* had been among the first to respond to the challenge of Christianity in the years after the Cession. At the time of the early Congress, Gosain leaders were engaged in trying to orchestrate an orthodox response to reform movements such as the Arya Samaj, and they also put in occasional appearances at meetings of the nationalist leaders.

In most cities the cross-caste institutions of the trading people remained cautious and conservative. They were prepared to use their informal organisation to express a political view when alienated by government or encouraged into activity by their nationalist contacts among the lawyers. They sometimes flirted with joint-stock banks and a few even became their treasurers. But there was no clean break between the earlier associations and later chambers of commerce. Almost everywhere westernisation was skin-deep, and these new institutions were dominated by a few great families of the dominant commercial castes whose origins can be traced back to the eighteenth century. The transition is particularly clear in Agra. Here in the 1860s and 1870s, there existed a Merchants' Association with formal rules and recorded membership which bridged the gap between the informal trade council of the past and the Chamber of Commerce which came into existence at the beginning of this century.[71] The mercantile oligarchy remained

[71] Agra 'Merchants' Book', film in author's possession; interviews Agra, 1972–4.

stable through these three phases, though newcomers from Rajasthan and from the lower castes were allowed to participate.

So far the associations of particular groups have been cited, but the communities and corporations of Hindu society had always possessed subtle links and common sympathies. This made them a recognisable social group; they were never simply the fragmented castes and contending *mohullas* of Weber's model. The strengths and the limitations of these binding institutions were also carried over into the era of public politics to form the ligaments of the emerging Indian middle class. The management of *dharamshalas* (rest houses for pilgrims), religious trusts and festivals had brought men of different caste and profession together. After 1830 the legal form of such trusts was further defined through the elaboration of a general 'Hindu Law'.[72] Some part of funds previously devoted to the building of temples or *ghats* was now expended on education and projects of civic benefit. But the management of these institutions and the community of religious assumptions lying behind them remained particularly important in linking together the 'respectable part of Hindu society'. There were two reasons for this. First, economic change was not rapid or even enough to forge stronger links of direct material interest between merchant class, service class and Hindu gentry. But secondly, in the absence of a completely effective contractual law, notions of credit, piety and commercial security were closely tied together.

No less than the English working class, the Indian middle class was 'present at its own creation'. The writers and public men of Hindustan sought consciously to adapt the institutions and ideologies which had formed the context of Hindu urban life. This is noticeable in the work of men like Harish Chandra of Benares and Balkrishna Bhatta of Allahabad who themselves came from the background of bazaar and temple. Harish Chandra, who has a good claim to be regarded as the creator of the modern Hindi novel and Hindi drama, was himself head of the Eastern (Purbiye) Agarwal *panchayat* of Benares city and a member of one of the original Naupatti families.[73] In his own style of life, Harish Chandra sought to transform the thrifty and inward-looking model of

---

72 This is a topic that will need much more research. Cross-caste or multi-caste charitable funds for the upkeep of temples, *ghats*, etc. existed before the colonial period; in the early nineteenth century there are examples of charitable trusts being deposited with committees of bankers by zamindars and wealthy men, who act in a similar way to the *mutwallis* of Muslim endowments.

73 J. Lütt, *Hindu Nationalismus in Uttar Prades, 1867–1900* (Stuttgart, 1970); Rai Kishen Das, 'Bhartendu Harish Chandra', *Saraswati*, i (1900); interviews Sri Kumud Chandra, Dr Giresh Chandra, Benares, 1972–4; R. S. McGregor, *Hindi Literature of the Nineteenth and Early Twentieth Centuries. A History of Indian Literature* (ed.) J. Gonda, VIII (Wiesbaden, 1974), 80–3.

behaviour thought appropriate by merchant people. He wanted family money to be spent openly and generously on cultural and literary ventures. For social and artistic reasons he became one of those 'expensive' people who were viewed with suspicion by the men of the bazaar. From the early 1870s, he founded a succession of societies and journals: notably the Tadiya Samaj, a Vaishnavite religious society which later became a forum for political discussion (*c.* 1873)[74] and *Harish Chandra's Magazine* (1873–85). But though Harish Chandra was prepared to disregard the ethic of the mercantile community in regard to thrift if it was in the best interests of society as a whole, he remained unyielding on the matter of meat-eating, alcohol and other forms of ritual impurity. We can see in his work, as in the writing of his contemporary Srinivas Das,[75] the transformation of the purist tenets of the Vaishya and Brahmin into the socially conscious moderation which became a feature of the much broader Indian middle class. These writers held that excess not only damaged the credit and *dharma* of the family but reflected a general social malaise which had led to Hindu India's abasement before Muslim and European conquerors. Thus Harish Chandra's first independent drama, *The Excesses of the Orthodox are no Excesses* (1873), was a farce satirising meat-eating and alcohol. His best known play *India's Plight* (1880), depicted an ailing, ageing Mother India: 'efforts on the part of westernised Indians to revive the victim prove unavailing'.[76]

The early Hindi prose writers, journalists and publicists transformed many other themes which had seemed important to the townsmen and corporations of earlier periods. Several historians, for instance, have pointed to the importance of the cow-protection movements of the 1880s and 1890s in creating a sense of Hindu community and also in bringing together townsmen and countrymen. But here it was only the scale of activity which was new. Restriction of cow slaughter had been a common concern for the Bhumihar rulers of Benares and its merchant corporations since at least 1790. Jain and Vaishnavite trading communities had long been associated with the upkeep of *gaushalas* or pounds for stray cattle. In and around the Vaishnavite centre of Muttra protection of the cattle of Krishna's homeland had been a basis for political alliance as early as the Anglo-Jat wars of 1806.[77] After 1860, this

[74] The proceedings of the Tadiya Samaj have been preserved in fragmentary form, film in author's possession; see also proceedings of Agarwal caste *panchayat*, Chaukambha.

[75] A. S. Kalsi, 'Realism in the Hindi novel in the late nineteenth and early twentieth centuries' (unpublished Cambridge Ph.D. dissertation, 1977).

[76] McGregor, *Hindi Literature*, p. 79.

[77] See, e.g. Niranjan Lal to Jaswant Rao Holkar, n.d., 1806, *PP*, 1806, XVI, 83ff; J. R. McLane, *Indian Nationalism and the Early Congress* (Princeton, 1977), ch. 9; Sandria B.

tradition was reinforced and extended in a way that provided bonds of moral interest between middle class people of different sect and occupation. And it was not only the orthodox Hindu revivalists who adapted and transformed the themes of cow-protection. The Arya Samaj whose roots in the ancient reforming traditions of Hinduism are now becoming clearer, also took it up vigorously. Their vision of a return to Vedic purity encompassed a world free of corrupted Brahminism from which the great sin of cattle murder had been banished. Cow-protection provided, therefore, a link of organisation and sentiment between the Urdu-writing Hindu service communities (particularly Kayasths and Khattris) who were strong in the Samaj and the ubiquitous communities of local Brahmins and merchants who tended to a more orthodox form of revivalism.

More important still was the case of the Hindi language itself. Above all, it had been Brahmins and merchant communities who provided continuity in the face of the inroads of Persian and Urdu. In the early and mid-nineteenth century, *mahajans* had begun to set themselves alongside the Hindu rajas as patrons of Hindi religious poetry, and some men with a commercial background had even begun composition themselves. The literary and linguistic movements of the 1880s and 1890s such as the Hindi Literary Society (Sahitya Samelan) and the Benares Society for the Advancement of Hindi (Nagri Pracharini Sabha) developed easily out of these beginnings. It is remarkable how many of the early literary men of the Hindi-speaking area were drawn from the commercial classes themselves or from parts of cities where poorer Brahmin and trading communities lived alongside pious Vaishnavite merchants.[78]

In both organisation and ideology, the urban middle class and Hindu society of the later nineteenth century possessed roots which stretched back not only to the earlier part of the century, but into the pre-colonial era. It is a foreshortened view that slices social development into eras that begin respectively in 1801 and 1858. At the same time, these findings imply that some of the conditions which fractured the life of modern north India into Hindu and Muslim camps must be dated much earlier than is commonly supposed. It was not a question of 'Two Nations' from time immemorial, or even of inevitable conflict between members of the two religions as a result of 'modernisation'. But the social formations which consolidated themselves between 1700 and 1830

Freitag, 'Sacred symbol as mobilising ideology: the north Indian search for a "Hindu" community', *Comparative Studies in Society and History*, xxii (1980), 597–625; Anand A. Yang, 'Sacred symbol and sacred space in rural India', *ibid.*, pp. 625–57.

78 Among others, Harish Chandra, Srinivas Das, Devkinandan Khattri and Balkrishna Bhatta.

– what we have called the 'merchant class' and the 'service gentry' – had tended to develop within two very different economic and cultural contexts, the Islamic *qasbah* or *mohulla* and the Hindu corporate town. While strong, indigenous states retained power, these parallel developments did not necessarily presage conflict. But from the 1830s the disintegration of the old magistracies and notabilities left broader spaces for contention.

Qasbah gentry were in the forefront of Muslim social and political movements after 1860. Great Muslim landholders gave fitful patronage to educational ventures and newspapers founded in the Muslim interest; the small group of English-educated scholars, barristers or government servants provided the skills of western discourse to Muslim political movements. But it was the petty landholders of the small towns and their scions in the district courts and subdivisional offices who provided the constituency. Their dilemma was summed up by the poet Akbar: 'Our belly keeps us working with the clerks/Our heart is with the Persians and the Turks.'[79] These small service families were prominent in the associations which formed to protect the Persian script and Urdu language from the 1870s onward. Many such men were later to become involved with the early Muslim League, especially its more radical 'Young Party' which had a less easy relationship with the British rulers.[80]

The gentry also gave sustenance to movements of religious and educational revival which became more active in these years. Lelyveld has shown that 54 per cent of the students in the new Aligarh College between 1875 and 1895 came from places 'distinctly rural, old fortresses now torn down or small market centres',[81] even though they had often passed through schools in the larger, more cosmopolitan cities. In more traditional Muslim institutions the presence of rural service people was even greater. Barbara Metcalf's study of the religious seminary at Deoband has shown how closely it was linked to the small zamindars of the western United Province and east Punjab.[82] Similarly, Robinson reveals a close connection between the older and more traditional school at Firangi Mahal in Lucknow and the surrounding small towns, particularly the shrine centres of Bansa and Mohan.[83]

[79] R. Russell and K. Islam, 'Satirical verse of Akbar Ilahabadi', *Modern Asian Studies*, viii (1974), 55.

[80] F. C. R. Robinson, *Separatism among Indian Muslims* (Cambridge, 1974), ch. 5.

[81] D. Lelyveld, *Aligarh's First Generation. Muslim Solidarity in British India* (Princeton, 1978), p. 181.

[82] B. Metcalf, 'The reformist ulama: Muslim religious leadership in India, 1860–1900' (Ph.D. dissertation, University of California, Berkeley, 1974).

[83] F. C. R. Robinson, 'The *Ulama* of Firangi Mahal and their *adab*', unpubl. MSS in author's possession.

In this case too the values and solidarities of these small communities were consciously broadened out by writers and public figures into a programme for the Muslim community as a whole. Paul Brass regarded the contention that Muslims in the area were backward under colonial rule was a 'myth'.[84] Certainly, their under-representation in the civil service, the new professions and landholding was not as dire as their leaders tried to make out. But for many of the prestigious *qasbah* communities, such as Kakori, Kara or Bilgram, decline was a reality. Steeped in a proud, defensive tradition and isolated from the Hindu commercial and service classes by history, their different material base, and often even by geography, these communities had fewer bridges to the broad stream of nationalist politics than either the peasants or the sophisticated service people of the big cities.

[84] Paul Brass, *Language, Religion and Politics in North India* (Cambridge, 1974).

Conclusions

For the Europeans who came from societies on the brink of political and industrial revolution, the pace of social change in pre-colonial Asia seemed glacially slow. And in their eyes the cycles of its politics represented little more than the degeneration of once awesome despotisms. But from the Asian standpoint, the two centuries before the heyday of European dominance in the mid-nineteenth century was a period of rapid change. It witnessed the creation of new types of states and new social classes as surely as it marked the decline of the old. Three broad forces were at work. First, coastal and inter-Asian trade were expanding rapidly. Rising European demand, partly fuelled by the distant discovery of New World silver, had caused a chain reaction in Asian commerce.[1] It enriched some Asian lords and merchants and created a new economic balance between the coastal regions and the populous interior of the continent. Secondly, the domestication of epidemic disease and relative political security triggered a widespread advance in population and cultivated acreage. This was most evident in China but it appeared also in South and West Asia, though subject here to frequent setbacks.[2] The consequent expansion of the internal market provided new opportunities for inland traders as various as the Shansi bankers of north China, the southern Chinese who spread into South-East Asia, and the Punjabi traders who linked late Mughal north India with the Central Asian Khanates. At the same time, a growing population tended to advantage landlords and office-holders serving rulers who now required a more detailed control over agrarian resources. Both groups profited from the general monetisation of the

---

[1] E.g., J. F. Richards, 'Mughal state finance and the pre-modern world economy', *Comparative Studies in Society and History*, xxiii (1981), 285–308; F. Perlin, 'Some central problems concerning the proto-industrialisation thesis and pre-colonial South Asia', mimeo., History Department, Erasmus University, Rotterdam, 1981; J. Brennig, 'Silver in seventeenth-century Surat: monetary movements and the price revolution in Mughal India', paper presented to comparative world history workshop in pre-modern monetary history, Madison, 1977; C. A. Bayly, 'Putting together the eighteenth century: trade, money and the pre-colonial political order', paper presented to Leiden workshop on comparative colonial history, 1981.
[2] W. McNeill, *Plagues and Peoples* (London, 1977).

Asian economies. Finally, new military technology spreading from European and Ottoman sources upset the political balance and galvanised the finances of eastern kingdoms. Compact despotisms fortified with Turkish-style ordnance or European musketry emerged within the ambit of the old empires. This is one feature common to powers as diverse as Mahomed Ali's Egypt, Hyder Ali's Mysore or the regional commanders of the Tung-chih restoration in mid-nineteenth-century China.

These tendencies can also be recognised in pre-British India. But they were often localised or incoherent, and have been lost amidst the annals of Mughal decline and European expansion. It will be years before the uniformities and links can be plainly seen beneath the variety of eighteenth-century society and politics. But the emerging synthesis is likely to upset our picture of the nineteenth century by predating many of the changes which were once thought to be characteristic of the colonial period. One good starting point for an analysis of the society of eighteenth-century north India is its recently reconstructed political history. In many ways, it is better to think of decentralisation or of the commercialisation of power within the Mughal polity than of anarchy. Between 1720 and 1740 Mughal magnates began to amalgamate provincial offices which had once been separate and to found new dynasties. These regimes developed closer links with rural society and favoured the petty rulers of the countryside by allowing generous perquisites and remissions. Even the Hindu and Sikh warrior states which were in open revolt against the empire retained much of the Mughal revenue machinery and continued to operate within a loose imperial system of honours and legitimacy which still centred on Delhi.

Political decentralisation encouraged the growing economic vitality of small places away from the imperial capitals. Magnates and gentry employed by the regional states founded fixed markets and settled colonies of specialist cultivators around them. While the merchants of the great Mughal towns faced disorder, local traders extended their branch agencies to secure the flows of artisan products and provided advances for the fine crops which the local aristocracies and armies needed. Religious foundations continued to flourish as pious rulers displayed their faith in eclectic religious patronage. This pattern was widespread throughout India. Islands of high farming and commercial enterprise existed around the courts and camps of all the lavish-spending contemporary nobilities. The environs of Hyderabad were settled with new colonies of farmers. The Maratha princes encouraged cash-cropping and artisan ventures around their capitals at Poona, Nagpur or Gwalior as their peasant parsimony gave way to Mughal luxury. Hyder Ali's Mysore was run like a huge estate.[3] Even in the far south the warrior *poligars* founded fort–mart centres which drew in petty local entrepreneurs and laid the foundations for later commercial enterprise.[4]

There was also another pattern which cannot be ignored. The desire to paint a more balanced picture of the 'Black Century' should not obscure the existence of large tracts where political change actually produced a serious decline in local commerce and agriculture. This decline was not necessarily the result of war itself; for the military engagements of post-Mughal India were generally small-scale affairs. Sometimes decline resulted simply from the orderly movement of aristocracies, capital or skills from one centre to another and the subsequent realignment of trade and production. Physical movement was an integral part of the eighteenth-century social order and should not be regarded as a pathological feature. Sometimes, however, these patches of decline were the consequence of banditry or warfare in areas where agriculture was fragile and heavily dependent on artificial irrigation. This was the case in the tracts north and west of Delhi. But the drier areas near Madras, for instance, were also greatly at risk from an interruption in the repair of village water tanks like that that took place after the invasions of the Mysore rulers.

The first chapters of this book tried to rectify the picture of economic collapse without retreating to a stereotype of 'Traditional India' where cultural and political norms worked in an economic vacuum. First, it was suggested, the areas of decline were quite limited in extent. Secondly, their existence actually advantaged the richer and more stable territories which preyed on them. Thirdly, the farmers, merchants and aristocrats of the stable areas were already expanding outward to colonise the waste before the imposition of the British Peace at the beginning of the nineteenth century.

Most important, however, is the subtle social change which was taking place in the stable zones even during the most war-scarred decades of the century. The 'farming' to magnates of the perquisites of kingship – the commercialisation of royal power – had been a feature of the later Mughal empire. These regional dynasts pushed the process further. The new nobility was drawn from entrepreneurs who could mobilise both military forces and capital. And even regimes of pioneer peasants such as the Marathas, Jats or Sikhs needed entrepreneurs of

[3] Asok Sen, 'A pre-British economic formation', in B. De (ed.) *Perspectives in the Social Sciences*, I (Calcutta, 1977), 46–119.

[4] B. Stein, *Peasant State and Society in South India* (Delhi, 1980); D. Ludden, 'Ecological zones and the cultural economy of irrigation in southern Tamilnadu', *South Asia*, vi (1978, 1–15; C. Baker, *An India Rural Economy, 1880–1955*, Oxford, 1984).

this sort once they had ceased to be expansive movements of plunder and protest and became settled kingdoms. However, the fortunes of these new magnates and fiscal barons themselves rested on the networks of skill and credit created by moneylenders, stewards and service gentry – people whose families had long acquaintance with the management of bazaars and revenue papers.

These groups of intermediaries between state and agrarian society demonstrated great resilience during the political flux of the eighteenth century. But they also provided the British merchants and administrators with the keys to the vast resources of inland India. Much of the book has dealt with two sections of the intermediate classes: the trading community and the service gentry.

On the face of it, the eighteenth century was a bad time for Indian commercial towns and traders. Along the coasts, the British established an unshakeable hegemony. The old oligarchies of Indian Ocean trade which dated back before the time of Vasco da Gama were strangled by piracy and internal depredation. Ancient Gujerati houses declined in Bengal and their native western India at the same time as revolt against the Mughal empire severed their internal routes. Disruption of demand in the Ottoman and Iranian empires or in the Arab lands dealt a savage blow to the west coast ports, while the decline of the Dutch and wars in the extreme south marked the passing of an age here also.

But even for international trade and the coastal economies, this picture of collapse is too stark. True, indigo and cloth exports through Surat fell off, but Malwa opium was still sold in vast quantities throughout West Asian markets.[5] Coastal trade down the length of the Gujerat and Konkan coasts remained buoyant.[6] Cloth exports from eastern India to Europe and South-East Asia were still considerable in the second half of the century.[7] The hardy overland trade to Central Asia in gold and luxury produce often managed to reroute itself in the face of political turbulence. Thus the volume of shipping in Indian ports controlled by Asians remained surprisingly large in the early years of the nineteenth century. Only on the lucrative China routes were the Europeans utterly dominant. And even in Bengal where the Company and the agency houses were building up their own exclusive society, the death-knell of international trading ventures pioneered by local men awaited the Scottish and Marwari deluge of the mid-nineteenth

---

[5] See, Bombay Commercial Proceedings and Reports, 1780–1820, IOL.
[6] S. C. Ghosh (ed.), *Journal of a Route through the Peninsula of Guzeraut in the years 1809–10* (New Delhi, n.d.).
[7] D. Washbrook, 'Some notes on market relations and the development of the economy of South India, c. 1750–1850', paper presented to Leiden workshop on comparative colonial history, 1981.

century.[8] In fact the reduction of Indian merchants to a position of dependence within the Asian trading world was not assured until after 1850 when the high-speed ship and the electric telegraph revolutionised commercial information and risks.[9]

During the eighteenth century great volumes of Indian produce continued to find their way to foreign markets albeit by different hands and through different ports than a century earlier. This helped to keep the inland trade routes moving. But there were also internal sources of commercial vitality. The vast trade of the Indian interior continued to dwarf its external trade. Of course, it is important not to exaggerate; in many areas, volumes may well have declined between 1720 and 1800. But what is striking is the rise of rich overland trade routes to compensate for the clogging of the great Mughal arteries. Indian trading institutions were well adapted to move nimbly in the wake of the new aristocratic consumers and protectors. The persistence of revenue-payment in cash – and in similar orders of magnitude to those paid in the later Mughal empire – provides the simplest and most telling evidence of the capacity of the commercial community to adjust to new political conditions.

Yet the question at issue is not simply one of the shifts of routes or the percentage rise and fall of trades. More significant was the role of commercial people in society at large. For the 'Black Century' saw the redeployment of merchant capital within India, not its destruction. Increasingly, control of land or men became ineffective without access to silver, credit and markets. The extraction of revenue from the peasantry was facilitated by the village trader. Revenue-farmers could not farm without merchants; and the dominance of the new magnates of the countryside was enforced in silver rupees as much as by the iron-shod staff. In an age of cash-hungry small states, it is not surprising that commercial people subtly extended their influence. Few aspired to the dangerous heights briefly commanded by the great Hindu merchants of Bengal, the Jagat Seths. But in many parts of the country, commercial men in cartel could 'command the state' in the matter of revenue.

This represented more than the emergence of a new elite within the politics of the successor regimes. The influence of the commercial houses straddled the realms of the petty states and linked up with new patterns of commerce in more stable parts of the countryside. It was the harbinger of a slow social change, not merely a cyclical modification in

[8] B. Kling, *Partner in Empire. Dwarkanath Tagore and the Age of Enterprise in Eastern India* (Berkeley, 1976).

[9] M. Vicziany, 'Bombay merchants and structural changes in the export community, 1850–1880', in K. Chaudhuri and C. Dewey (eds), *Economy and Society* (Delhi, 1979), pp. 163–96.

the composition of the ruling class. But at the same time, these developments did not amount to the emergence of an Indian bourgeoisie. Capital controlled by traders and revenue-farmers was becoming a junior partner in the politics of the land; kingship was being commercialised. But capital was not being applied directly in the creation of new modes of production, nor were landed magnates giving place to capitalists.

What we can see is the creation of a unified merchant class. Groups of entrepreneurs in money and credit were consolidating themselves yet more rapidly within the interstices of small, commercialised and bureaucratic monarchies. Their independence was expressed through corporate institutions and rights which were recognised by the rulers. Paradoxically, the disturbed conditions of the eighteenth century tended to increase the homogeneity and independence of these solidarities. The needs of revenue-extraction and the consumption of aristocrats in small centres pulled the great merchants of the towns into the bazaars and *ganjs*, and brought the petty traders of the localities into the cities. The decline of some of the old Muslim and Gujerati traders with their continental networks meant that local merchant groups united by culture and religion were able to control the whole hierarchy of centres from peasant market to urban entrepôt.

This was happening across the subcontinent. In many parts of the country, inferior merchant groups aggrandised themselves at the expense of the cosmopolitan oligarchs of the past. In our area it was Chaube Brahmins, Rajasthani Bohras, Agarwals and eastern Khattris who were to form the trading and urban elites of the future. In the Punjab it was the Nanakpanthi Khattris and Aroras associated with the Sikhs, who took over from their more Islamicised caste fellows. In the south, Kannada merchants and local Chettis slipped into positions occupied by the old Armenian, Jewish and Vaishya firms. However, the story did not end here. It was from the groups of local merchants whose fortunes greatly improved with the commercialisation of power in the eighteenth century that much of India's modern industrial and business class has been recruited.

It is now a truism of colonial historiography that Europeans could not have established their trade and administration in Asia or Africa without the compliance of key people in indigenous societies. This book has tried to give such an assumption greater depth and precision in the case of India. We start from the proposition that the pace of 'expansion' and the form of the colonial relationship was determined mainly by the form of the society penetrated in the years before the full force of industrialisation was brought to bear on the non-European world.

To begin with, the theory and practice of Indian states – in particular their limited notions of authority or territorial integrity – were crucial. The coastal kingdoms of the fifteenth and sixteenth centuries had put up only intermittent resistance to the Portuguese interlopers because they did not consider sea trade and the 'business of merchants' to be important matters for kings.[10] This was in sharp contrast, for instance, to the case of China where ancient notions of the subordination of foreign traders as 'tribute bearers' and the apparatus of detailed state control of trade through trade guilds (*hongs*) long frustrated the foreigners. In China, the Europeans had to launch a direct assault on a continental empire before they could prise away further commercial privileges. In India, however, the relationship between trade and power was highly ambiguous. The notion of 'farming out' rights, including rights over trade and markets, was designed to raise cash. But the redistribution of rights and duties was also an expression of the corporate nature of kingship. This created a peculiarly loose-textured political system in which a ruler could alienate much of his revenue and control without affecting his status as a king. So in India merchant corporations could quietly service and encourage European interlopers with impunity. Yet since trade required protection, the Europeans were forced gradually to assimilate the functions of the ruler themselves.

The British were able to exploit the ambiguous relationship between ruler and merchant in Indian political practice. But they were also advantaged by changes which had taken place since the Mughal heyday. The expansion of the merchant class and town-building under the successor states provided them with networks of facilities which transported their trade goods, supported their armies and underpinned their revenue systems. Without the trader–bankers of Benares or Surat, the British would have found it infinitely more difficult to succour their fragile outposts in Bombay and Madras from the surplus revenues of rich Bengal. Again, the high consumption of the new regional and local aristocracies of the Mughal decline provided capital to revitalise tracts which had fallen out of cultivation. The expansion of settled agriculture and commerce from the nodes of high farming to which they had retreated since the 1740s was beginning before the British established their Peace; and it occurred in areas where their writ did not run.

If the dynamic changes in Indian commerce and politics provided much of the force behind the British advance, they also limited its impact and formed its character. The Europeans did well enough out of India; but not as well as they intended. The relationship between trade

[10] M. N. Pearson, *Merchants and Rulers in Gujarat. The Response to the Portuguese in the Sixteenth Century* (Berkeley, 1976).

and power which tempted them into formal control of the continent also locked them out of detailed management of agrarian production. The peasant family farm and the merchant family firm were sophisticated institutions which responded vigorously to the possibility of profit. But their perception of the meaning of profit was determined by the context of institutions within which they were set, and dominated by considerations of security. They were too well adapted to be swept aside by European business methods, but they signally failed to provide the basis for a capitalist transformation or even a revolution in cash-cropping. Here there is a sharp contrast, for instance, with the case of Dutch Java. In Java, the Chinese merchant communities were outsiders rather than the oil of the petty kingdoms; dues were still paid largely in kind, and the internal market was less developed. Early experiments with cash revenue failed, so the Dutch were forced to employ a radical new means for the exploitation of Java in the Cultivation System. This gave them direct access to the labour and product of the peasant family farm. In a sense then, it was the very sophistication of the internal market and merchant institutions which sealed the British out of their Indian agrarian societies.

Historians have been preoccupied with two processes which link pre-colonial society with the colonial period and supply an internal dynamic to Indian history. First there has been much consideration of the evolution over the long term of the institutions of caste.[11] Secondly, dominant groups of landholders and peasants in various parts of the country have been traced through from Mughal times to the present.[12] This study has highlighted the evolution of two other groups. Primarily, it has traced the creation of a unified merchant class within a Vaishnavite and urban setting. But we have also isolated the development (and frustration) in parts of north India of a 'service gentry' against a largely Islamic and small town background. Both these themes seem capable of illuminating events as diverse and as separated in time as the decline of the Mughals, the rise of the Company, the 1857 Revolt and the origins of nationalism and 'communalism'.

The term service gentry emphasised the dual role of these families as state servants and *rentier* landlords. The keynote of Mughal rule had been size and centralisation. The massive army required to buttress imperial control over half South Asia and much of Central Asia created a compact bureaucratic nobility and large cities. But over time, lesser soldiers and clerical servants of the empire began to accumulate power

[11] Especially, F. Conlon, *A Caste in a changing world. The Chitrapur Saraswat Brahmins, 1700–1935* (London, 1977); K. Leonard, *The Kayasths of Hyderabad* (Berkeley, 1978).
[12] E.g., Metcalf, *Landlords*; Kessinger, *Vilayatpur*; Pradhan, *Jats of Northern India*.

and resources away from the centres of imperial pomp, in small towns which had often started life as the residences of Muslim holy men and artisans. At first the emperors set their face against such a development, but the accumulation of land-rights went ahead regardless. In later years, the rulers came to see this rurally based gentry as an important ally in their incessant battles with the Hindu clan leaders. The gentry steered an uneasy course through the shoals of eighteenth-century politics. Yet eighteenth-century changes often extended their control of land-rights and production around their small town centres. Successor states provided them with patronage and protection; in turn, they offered military and clerical expertise. Sometimes they avoided the consequence of local political decline because, like the Hindu trading or priestly corporations, their networks ran all over the country. Many of the apparently rootless families of administrators gathered in the great cities kept one foot in small centres which they called home (*watan*) and to which they remitted money.

How widely across the subcontinent did this occur? Obviously, the class of service gentry was not as fundamental to the Indian social order as it was in China. But even in those areas where Muslim influence was weak, there were other groups in an analogous position linking state to agrarian society, yet vulnerable to changes in either. Throughout Hindustan, Bihar and Central India, *qasbah* settlements of the classic sort existed; though families of Hindus who were skilled in the Persian court culture often stood alongside the aristocratic Muslim gentleman. In the Punjab the eruption of the Sikhs levelled away many *qasbahs* and their denizens, but it created in turn its own class of literate pensioners settled in small centres. In Maharashtra in the eighteenth century there is evidence of the consolidation of a kind of gentry between the substantial peasant and the state,[13] though control of village office and perquisites was more important here than *rentier* landownership. True, in the long run the fickleness of state patronage and the limited yields of agriculture in the Deccan aborted the development of a cohesive gentry of office-holders. But the point is that even within this fragile system of pre-colonial Hindu states, there developed an intermediate class between state and the substantial peasant in the form of a group of hereditary office-holders.

In Bengal, again, where the Islamic gentry was weak (outside the immediate environs of the Muslim cities of Dacca and Murshidabad) we can find analogies among the Hindu superior people – the rural

---

[13] F. Perlin, 'Of White Whale and countrymen', *Journal of Peasant Studies*, v (1978).

bhadralog.[14] By 1756, literate high caste men serving Muslim fiscal lords or Hindu rajas in the commercial tracts had established themselves as subordinate tenure-holders and had consolidated their position in semi-urban villages which they regarded as their homes. These Hindu service gentry did well out of the Permanent Settlement while at the same time they were tightening their grip on public office in colonial Calcutta. Thus, even the clerkly 'babu' of Victorian Calcutta – Macaulay's revenge as it seemed to many later administrators – did not spring fully formed from Britannia's helmet but bore witness to longer-term changes in the bazaars of rural Bengal.

The patchy emergence of this service gentry also aided the establishment of British rule and moulded the form of colonial society. The British could sweep away the rickety and 'corrupt' system of revenue-farming and turn fiscal lords into landholders. But they were only able to do this because they could recruit into their system sufficient numbers of the inferior servants of the old regimes. These provided the Europeans with skills to cut through the jungle of revenue management and with some ambivalent allies in rural society. But the perilous dominances of service gentry were also to provide an unstable element in the social politics of the later colonial period. Gentry frustration provided one of the ingredients for the combustible mixture of north Indian Muslim separatism after 1860. In Bengal, the *bhadralog* Hindu gentry, embattled in the professions and losing out in rural society, fought both the British and the rich farmers, sinking Bengali nationalism under the weight of terrorism, agrarian conflict and communal hatred. Surely, the decline of the literate gentry in the colonial period was as important a feature of colonial politics and colonial nationalism as the rise of the 'rich peasant'. Both concepts are crude, but both are capable of discovering unities in the perplexing diversity of Indian social history.

Consideration of the link between the state, the intermediate classes and agriculture suggests some new time-scales for Indian history. In the annals of events and policies, the old turning points – 1707, 1757, 1802 and 1857 – retain much of their importance. By contrast, in the slower moving agrarian economy the sea-change probably occurred after our period, in the 1890s. A widespread slowing in the pace of agricultural expansion about this time may have been related to the growing pressures of population on land. From here on the new rural elites took a bumpy ride through to the Great Depression of the 1930s when they

[14] Ratnalekha Ray, *Change in Bengal Rural Society circa 1760–1850* (Delhi, 1979), pp. 27–33.

were faced with a crisis originating outside India. But this work has argued that for large parts of urban society and for the intermediate economy of artisans, traders and service people in the countryside, it was the rapid decline of the old polity in the third and fourth decades of the nineteenth century which represented the first major break with indigenous forms.

In the Ganges valley the eighteenth-century pattern was coming under great pressure by the later 1820s. Decentralisation of power and resources gave way to a new British centralisation. The boosting up of local economies by kingly and ritual expenditure gave way to cost cutting and deflation. By coincidence, some of the *démarches* against superior landholders and large military forces came at the same time as a series of dismal harvests and the pressures on merchants and landowners were increased by a series of hiccoughs in the export trades. The 1830s saw widespread disruption, but the decline of the old order was a long-term process. In Awadh, for instance, the coup de grâce was not delivered until after the Rebellion of 1857.

Historians of colonial rule have sometimes argued that capitalism rather than modern government was the most disruptive force unleashed by the European presence. In early nineteenth-century India commercial dislocation certainly derived from external crises. These partly reflected the rhythms of the European economies. The relentless drive for higher revenue yields by colonial officials and their retreat to a resolute philosophy of laissez-faire also reflected the distant nostrums of classical political economy. However, many of the weapons being used in the battle for the redistribution of India's resources had been fashioned by indigenous rulers. The real change was that whereas these earlier despotisms had been tempered by a political culture which insisted that rulers should offer service and great expenditures in return for high revenue demand, the British acknowledged few such restraints. The crisis of early colonial rule was a moral as much as an economic one.

Peasant economies are resilient. Soldiers and unemployed servants of declining rajas could often swell the ranks of agricultural workers. In time income from external trade filled the gap left by the decline of the old regime. Yet to a greater or lesser degree, the disruption of the regional and local kingdoms which had emerged after 1720 affected the performance of agriculture. Where new export trades developed rapidly or where there existed a landowning class deeply rooted in rural production, the effects were likely to be less than in tracts where service gentry, towns and warriors had been predominant. In Hindustan, the Doab and west suffered more than the east. For similar reasons, Maharashtra's rural economy seems to have been deeply affected by political change. Sumit Guha has traced the origins of the prolonged price depression in the Deccan between 1820 and 1850 to the collapse of the Maratha aristocracy and the pressures on the institutions of rural credit unleashed by the colonial administration.[15] The contemporary price depression in Madras may have had similar origins. In Bengal also, the difficulties of the years between 1790 and 1820 appear to have arisen not only from forced land sales under the Permanent Settlement of revenue but also from the decay of the military forces which the Nawabi regime and the great landholders had placed in countless rural market places.

Changes in the theory and practice of Indian kingship were as important as the economic consequences of the demise of the old order. Indian peasant and merchant societies had their own organisations and sense of solidarity. But at the same time, the adjudication and patronage of rulers bound these units into wider groupings and mediated their conflicts. The end of royal patronage and the modification of old systems of urban and rural government sent out ripples of change which reached into even the most placid backwaters of community and religious life. Of course, this is not to say that the old regime had been unchanging. The sale of royal rights, the eruption of outside warrior rulers, the rise of the corporations, had all jarred relations between communities and changed the face of post-Mughal India in ways which brought despair to the poets and writers of the Delhi Silver Age. But the vigorous, opinionated government of the early Victorian years shook society even more aggressively with its peace than had the earlier warriors. The decline of the Muslim urban magistracy and the fading of royal and gentry power in the north exacerbated conflict between communities and economic groups. The Hindu–Muslim riots of the 1830s and the conflicts which boiled up in the Rebellion of 1857 have a common context here. But if we look to the south where royal Hindu power had been only lightly modified by Indo-Persian forms of government, similar changes can be seen. The uprooting of the *poligar* warrior chiefs in Tamilnadu and the decline of the Cochin and Travancore kingdoms along the Kerala coast exacerbated a whole range of religious and caste conflicts which helped give Madras Presidency its reputation for exotic social disorder in the later colonial era.[16]

If the decline of the old order in the middle third of the century proved a turning point in some parts of the economy and society, there

---

[15] S. Guha, 'The Bombay Deccan 1800–1930' (unpublished Cambridge Ph.D. dissertation, 1981), chs. 1–3.

[16] S. B. Kaufmann, 'Popular Christianity, caste and Hindu society in south India, 1800–1915' (unpublished Cambridge Ph.D. dissertation, 1980), ch. 5.

were continuities elsewhere. Corporate groups of service gentry and merchants also came under pressure during these years. But the broad sweep of their development reached through from the pre-colonial era to the later nineteenth century when they proved the recruiting ground for two key elements of the Indian middle classes.

In many parts of Asia and the Middle East the development of indigenous intermediate classes between the state and agrarian society provided the context for the establishment and ultimate demise of colonial rule. True, emperors, khedives, and other warlords occupied the front of the stage during the period of conquest and expansion; while towards the end of colonial rule, peasant rebellion gave a new dimension to nationalist movements. Yet the intermediate classes evolved throughout. In the early stages their form and outlook was crucial in determining the timing of European penetration. Later, the interests and ideologies of merchants and service gentry conditioned the speed with which colonial nationalists were prepared to enlist the volatile movements of the countryside in their struggles.

In Egypt, for instance, the village *sheikhs*, a class of petty landholders, office-holders and moneylenders, emerged as a key social group. Their origin lay in the interplay between a tax-gathering Muslim state and a peasant economy being drawn into the export markets in cotton and grain. From their ranks came petty officials and lower military officers. The dissidence of these rural notables gave urgency to the nationalist crises which drew Britain into Egypt in 1882 and forced her to pull out again after 1918. In China, the literate rural gentry and the merchants provided similar continuity. The picture here is more focused than it is in India. Gentry combined office-holding with landholding and even trade. They were both a class and a status group; while their grip on peasant society and local office had slowly tightened over several hundred years. 'Corrupt' gentry and merchants along the coast provided the contacts in local society which drew British opium into the interior. 'Patriotic' gentry pulled the imperial court into wars with the west after 1840. Ultimately, their successors combined with restive merchants to overthrow the regime and determine the nature of nationalist China in the twentieth century.

The complexity of the Indian subcontinent and the quirks of its historiography have made it difficult to establish such continuities in social history. There have been a few admirable studies of sections of the service or merchant classes over the long term. But these have concentrated on families, clans or castes as units, and it has been difficult to see how they relate to each other or to wider changes in the political economy. So far the sense that India had an indigenous history which persisted, albeit in a modified form, into the colonial period is much easier to grasp for rural society. We can now at least trace the slow development of some of the peasant brotherhoods of the Punjab, or the great notables of Awadh from the Mughal period into the India of the National Congress.

This work has attempted to forge a further set of links between eras which have been fractured by the history of events, and it has suggested some new approaches to the study of Indian society. The possibility that pre-colonial India could have developed an indigenous middle class, or indeed any significant intermediate group between the state and agrarian society was denied by the classical theorists. In their different ways, both Marx and Weber implied that the cellular, caste-based society of India frustrated the development of wider solidarities except the state itself; and this was largely an agency of plunder. The denial of pre-colonial 'structural change' and the emphasis on family and caste groups by recent writers has done little to challenge these views. Yet some revision is necessary. This study has suggested that from late Mughal times at least kin groups of merchant people and service gentry were bonded together in ways which strengthened their economic control and sense of identity. Moreover, the weakening of the state in the eighteenth century enhanced the significance of these wider solidarities.

Of course, gentry and merchant groups could not form in a context in any way as favourable as that provided by Roman and feudal law in Europe. But some features of the Indian social order did encourage the consolidation of intermediate classes. Privileged tenure associated with religious endowment, for instance, provided both gentry and merchant people with long-term income and association with the management of property in particular centres. Again, trading links and the institutions of the market which had to cross caste boundaries created a sense of moral community between merchant people, ascetics and Brahmins, which extended to religious and, ultimately, to political action.

By comparison with developments in the west, these were weak forces for social change. Where the disruption of trade was widespread or rulers particularly fickle and oppressive in pre-colonial regimes, intermediate classes could be uprooted. Later, the colonial state severely curtailed their power by resuming privileged revenue grants and snapping the link between the commercial classes and revenue management. Weber too was right in this sense: though corporate solidarities breached the bounds of clan and caste, it proved difficult for the intermediate elements of Indian society to meld together across the religious and historical divide which separated merchant and priest from

Islamic service gentry. All the same, many distinct characteristics and institutions of the Indian middle classes of the later nineteenth century can be traced to the pre-British past. English education or the joint-stock company wreaked their changes on developing institutions and identities, not on a stagnant and fissiparous traditional society. Many features of India's recent history seem more comprehensible against this background. Whatever the merits of the press and parliamentary government, the persistence of the capacity for self-organisation outside the ambit of the state or the army owes much to the older tradition of solidarity represented by India's commercial and religious corporations.

BIBLIOGRAPHIC NOTE

This is a book about structures and trends. It resulted from the correlation of large numbers of references from government archives with private records, interviews, travellers' accounts, gazetteer and settlement material, etc. Fully to reference every generalisation or impression would have produced a book of absurd size and cost. References should often, therefore, be taken as examples of the type of material used, rather than exhaustive indications of its whereabouts. The following sources have proved most useful:

Government records

India Office Library and Records, London

(Government of Bengal) Proceedings of the Board of Commissioners in the Conquered and Ceded Provinces, Revenue and Revenue (Customs), 1803–7
Bengal Revenue and Revenue (Customs) Consultations, for the Conquered and Ceded (later North-Western) Provinces, 1805–34
Bengal Criminal Judicial Proceedings, 1805–34
Bihar and Benares Revenue Proceedings
(India) North-Western Provinces Revenue, Revenue (Customs), Civil and Criminal Judicial Proceedings, 1834–65
Bengal Commercial Proceedings and Commercial Reports, 1800–40

Orme MSS India and various collections

Henry Wellesley Papers, Eur. MSS E 178–80
H. M. Elliot Papers, Eur. MSS D 310, F. 60
Settlement Maps, 1826–40, Map Room

National Archives of India, New Delhi

(Foreign Political Department Records) Secret Consultations, Political Branch Proceedings
Foreign Secret and Foreign Political Proceedings, 1820–40
Bharatpur and Delhi Residency Correspondence
(Public Department) Public Consultations
India Mint Proceedings, 1834–40
Bengal Mint Proceedings, 1826–34

Uttar Pradesh, Central Records Office, Allahabad

Proceedings of the Resident, Benares, 1786–96
Proceedings of the Agent to the Governor General, Benares, 1795–1834
Commissioner of Benares, Agency Records, English and Persian, 1820–40
'Duncan Records' (Miscellaneous Collection), 1772–95
Records of the Commissioner, Benares, pre- and post-Mutiny
Benares Collectorate Records, 1796–1875
Mirzapur Collectorate Records, 1800–75
Saharanpur Collectorate Records, 1806–34
Selected Oriental Records *re qasbahs* Sandila, Mallawan, 1650–1850

Records of the Commissioner of Allahabad, Commissioner's Bungalow, Allahabad

Judges' Library and Records, High Court, Allahabad

Private papers, etc.

Selections of the following records have been filmed and deposited in the Centre of South Asian Studies, Cambridge (SAS)

Papers of the 'Jangambari' Math, Madanpura, Benares, *c.* 1650–1850, last seen in the High Court, Allahabad; selections of these documents were copied into a 'Paper Book' for a pre-war legal suit, a film of which exists in SAS

Collection of the family of 'Bhartendu' Harish Chandra, with Dr Giresh Chandra, Chaukambha, Benares. The most important items are the 'Memory Book' (*Yadasht Khata*) of Lala Harrakhchand, *c.* 1820–40; the firm's *rokad khatas*, *c.* 1870–1900; correspondence regarding Sri Khirodhar Lal; fragments of proceedings of the Agarwal *panchayat* Benares, and one of Bhartendu's religious associations for the 1870s; films in SAS

Collection of Lala Sangam Lala, *mahajan*, with Sri Ram Krishna, Shiwala, Benares

Collection of Sri Devi Narayan, Sakshi Binayak, Benares; the main items are the *panda* book of the family of Sri Gajendra Nath Phatakh, covering the period, *c.* 1650–1820; miscellaneous papers of Sri Devi Narayan's family, *c.* 1800; paper book of legal documents relating to the 'Nagpuri' Math, Benares

Rokad khatas of the Hanuman Das branch of the Shah *kothis*, Benares, *c.* 1854–90, *kharach khatas*, for the 1850s and 1870s, films SAS

Rokad khata of Messrs Chunna Mal Saligram, Chandni Chowk, Delhi, covering the years 1858–61, film SAS

Collection of Sri R. S. Agarwal, Agra, includes 'Mahajanon, sarraf, bioparon khayed ka khulasat' (records composition of Agra merchant association, *c.* 1873), papers regarding boat insurance, etc. from the 1850s

Collections of letters, *madad-i-maash* grants, family histories of prominent Sayyid families of Kara, Dist. Allahabad, U.P. includes 'Tarikh-i-Kara', MSS by Fida Hussain Obeidi

Rokad khatas, c. 1880–1900, of various branches of the family of Lala Ram Charan Das, with Messrs Gappoo Mal Kandheya Lal, Ranimandi, Allahabad, and Sri G. P. Tandon, Tashkent Marg, Allahabad

Field notes of interviews, transcriptions of family histories collected 1972–80 in the main commercial centres and some *qasbah* towns of Uttar Pradesh, in author's possession

Secondary works, chronicles, selections from records

References are given in individual footnotes. Excellent bibliographies are given in:
B. R. Grover, 'An integrated pattern of commercial life in the rural society of north India during the 17th and 18th centuries', *Indian Historical Records Commission*, XXXVII (1966), 121–53
R. Barnett, *North India Between Two Empires* (Berkeley, 1980)
H. K. Naqvi, *Urban Centres and Industries in Upper India, 1556–1803* (London, 1968)

GLOSSARY

Note: the following rendering of Indian terms should not be regarded as wholly accurate or definitive. Subtle changes in the meaning of words occurred over time, and often no single English phrase can convey their full sense. Formal transliterations with diacritical marks and the Persian, Urdu or Hindi originals are to be found in W. Hunter, *A Glossary of Judicial and Revenue Terms* (London, 1885).

Abkari	revenue derived from the manufacture and sale of intoxicating liquor
Agarwal	Hindu trading caste of north India
Akhara	place where people are permanently or temporarily settled; residence of Hindu ascetics; wrestling ground
Amil (aumil)	subordinate revenue official often applied (incorrectly) to a farmer of revenue (*mustajir*)
Arethia (aurothia, etc.)	agent, broker trading on commission
Arora	Hindu trading caste of Punjabi origin
Arzi	petition or representation
Ashraf	person of rank, Muslim gentleman
Bahi khata	merchant account book
Bairagi	(lit. 'one devoid of passion'), a Hindu ascetic, most correctly a Vaishnavite ascetic
Bais	tribe of Rajputs (q.v.) in Awadh; hence Baiswara, the Bais home territory
Bakkal	inferior merchant, grocer, chandler
Bangar	high ground in the Delhi region, as opposed to *khadir*
Bangash	a tribe of Muslims of Afghan origin
Bania	trader, moneylender
Banjara	class of Hindu travelling merchant
Betel	mildly narcotic nut for chewing
Chalisa	the great famine of *Sambat* 1840, A.D. 1783
Chaudhuri	(chowdree, and many corrupt forms) headman of village, caste, market, etc.
Chaukidar	watchman in town and village, hence *chaukidari* tax, levy for the upkeep of watchmen
Chauth	tax imposed by Marathas
Chalisa	the great famine of *Sambat* 1840, A.D. 1783
Chaudhuri	(chowdree, and many corrupt forms) headman of village, caste, market, etc.
Chaukidar	watchman in town and village, hence *chaukidari* tax, levy for the upkeep of watchmen
Chauth	an extra levy made by the Marathas on areas invaded
Chela	pupil, spiritual 'descendant' in Hindu ascetic body; in Farrukhabad and Mysore a Hindu boy brought up Muslim and incorporated into a military corps
Cohong	Chinese state trading corporation
Crore (properly karor)	unit of ten million

Dacoit	robber
Dalal	agent between buyer and seller
Darbar (durbar)	royal court or levee
Dargah	in India usually a Muhammadan saint's tomb
Dasnami Naga Sannyasi	a subdivision of (usually Shaivite) Hindu ascetics
Dharma	religion, moral order
Dharna	coercion in disputes involving self-maltreatment by Brahmins to bring ill fortune on a debtor
Dhoti	garment for the lower body
Diwali	Hindu festival of light held in Oct.–Nov.
Diwan	chief minister of state particularly concerned with finance
Farman	charter (often issued by Mughal emperor)
Ganj (gunj)	small fixed market; emporium for grain
Ghat	slope, incline, especially to water, hence Burning Ghats at Benares
Ghi	clarified butter
Gosain	corruption of Goswami, lit. 'master of passion'; designation of Hindu ascetics
Gomashta	commercial agent
Guava	tree fruit
Gujar	Hindu caste of labourers and cattle keepers in western UP
Gurkha	Nepalese military caste
Hali	agriculturalist bonded by debt
Hartal	closure of market in a dispute
Hath	village market, usually periodic, bi-weekly
Holi	prominent Hindu festival held in Spring
Hundi	mercantile note of credit (hence *sahajog hundi* attests to credit of bearer and requires no endorsement; *rozahi* or *roznama hundi* stipulates payment on day of presentation)
Hundiwalla	a broker in *hundis*; comes to mean a general commission agent who arranges transport and insurance of commodities
Id	major Muslim festival (hence *Idgah* enclosure on the outskirts of town or village where Id prayers are conducted)
Imam	head of Muslims in religious matters
Inam	grant of land for service, rent-free and often hereditary (cf. *madad-i-maash* and *waqf*)
Jagir	an assignment of land-revenues (e.g. to Mughal *mansabdars*, q.v.)
Jain	religion related to but separate from Hinduism, involving the veneration of deified mortals (*tirthankaras*); its adherents often merchants in north India
Jajman	patron, originally of Brahmins, widely of all clients in caste relations; hence *jajmani* system, a general term for quasi-ritual redistribution within the caste system
Jat	the major Hindu agricultural caste in the Delhi–Agra area
Jati	kind, type; used for the endogamous, commensal group, basic unit of Hindu caste

Julaha	caste of Muslim weavers
Kaccha	rough, as opposed to *pakka*, good or well made; earthen when applied to wells, uncooked when applied to food
Kacchi	Hindu market gardener caste
Kalwar	Hindu caste of liquor distillers; became traders and landowners
Kanungo	district revenue official who recorded landed property and oversaw the working of the village accountant or *patwari*
Kayasth	Hindu writer and administrative caste
Kazi	Muslim judicial officer administering towns according to *Sharia* law (q.v.); under the British reduced to the status of an officer of registrary
Khalisa	Crown land, not made over in *inam* or *jagir* (q.v.)
Khandsari (*khandar*)	sugar manufacturer – merchant
Kharif	the autumn crop
Khattri	Hindu mercantile and administrative caste
Khudkasht	farmer cultivating his own land, cf. *paikasht* (q.v.)
Kinkhab	brocade of gold and silver thread
Koeri	Hindu market gardener caste
Kothi	establishment, usually branch agency of mercantile concern or zamindar's house
Kotwal	Muslim urban executive officer; under British town police superintendent
Kshatriya	the Warrior Order in classical Hindu 'sociology'
Kurmi (kunbi)	Hindu peasant caste renowned for success as market gardeners
Lakh	unit of 100,000
Laki	bonded servant, formerly in the Benares region
Lekha khata	merchant's account book showing individuals' accounts written out in full
Lingayat	Shaivite sectarian group, common in Mysore
Madad-i-maash	grant for charitable or religious purposes
Mahajan	lit. 'great man'; a substantial merchant; in Gujerat also used for the organising body of merchants in a town, cf. *sarrafa*
Mahal	unit of revenue; incorrectly an 'estate'
Mahant	head of religious establishment of the mendicant orders of Hindus
Maheshwari	Hindu trading caste of central India and Rajasthan
Malguzar	one with the right and duty to engage for the collection of government land-revenue
Mandi	regular market
Mansabdar	person with an official Mughal rank derived from personal status and military responsibility
Math	residence of Hindu ascetic orders
Maulvi	Muslim religious teacher
Maund (*man*)	unit of weight, in UP roughly 30lb
Mewati	caste of Hindu Rajputs (q.v.) of the province of Mewat, notorious for military and predatory character

Mohulla	urban residential neighbourhood
Mohurrum	chief festival of the Shia (q.v.) Muslim calendar; a festival of mourning for martyred early leaders of the faith
Mofussil	the countryside
Mohur	Mughal gold coin
Mouzah	village, unit of revenue management congruent with a settlement area
Muafi	land exempted from revenue-demands on grounds of service or pious donation
Mufti	leading jurist of a Muslim community responsible for expounding the law which the *kazi* (q.v.) would administer
Muhtasib	superintendent of markets, responsible also for public decency
Mulki	pertaining to the power of a raja or landowner; hence Mulki court, raja's domestic court
Munim	corruption of *munib*, a factor, agent, head clerk
Munshi	clerk
Naga	as in Dasnami Naga Sannyasi, group of mainly Shaivite Hindu ascetics
Nagar	Brahmin subdivision of Gujerati origin, often merchants or administrators
Nanakpanthi	follower of Guru Nanak, founder of the Sikh faith, though not a member of the military brotherhood (*Khalsa*), and not necessarily sharply divided from Hindus
Nath Yogi	ascetic tradition of medieval Hinduism
Naupatti (Nowputtee)	association of 'nine shares', a Benares mercantile association
Nawab	Muslim ruler; viceroy of a Mughal province
Nazrana	ritualised gift of lordship due, signifying fealty
Nullah (nala)	watercourse, drain or small river
Paisa	small coin
Paikasht	cultivator at will, cultivating another's land
Pakka	good, well-made; stone for brick or wells; cooked for food
Palanquin	litter, conveyance
Panchayat	court of arbitration
Panda	presiding priest in Hinduism, especially applied to priests in Benares who oversee oblations for the dead and compile genealogies
Pargana	subordinate unit in revenue administration
Peon	the servant or runner of an official
Puranas	collection of Hindu sacred texts generally dating from the first millennium A.D.
Prajawat (parjote)	lordship due taken from dependents on festivals, etc., taken to mean quit rent by the British
Qasbah	country town, seat of subordinate revenue administration and Muslim gentry
Rabi	the spring harvest
Radha	Hindu deity, consort of Krishna
Raj	kingdom, hence *rajwari*, royal or kingly

Rajput	great Hindu military and landholding caste of n. India
Rastogi	Hindu mercantile caste
Rohilla	(from Ruh, an area of the north-western hills), Muslim tribal group with Afghan affinities settled in Rohilkhand
Rokad khata	daily cash book of a merchant house
Sahukar (sowkar)	Hindu banker
Sambat	Hindu era roughly 57 years ahead of A.D.
Sannyasi	Hindu who has renounced the world, ascetic (cf. Gosain, Bairagi)
Sarai	hostelry (cf. *caravansarai*)
Saraswat	group of Brahmins prominent in w. India
Sarraf	gold or silver merchant, moneychanger; loosely applied to Hindu traders (hence 'shroff') and hence Sarrafa, a governing body of Hindu merchants
Sayyid (syed, saiyid, etc.)	prominent group of Muslims claiming descent from Husain, grandson of Muhammad
Seer	unit of weight, about 2 lb
Shaivite	follower of the cult of the Hindu god Shiva
Sharia	Muslim law governing both secular and religious matters
Shastra (Shasers)	from *Dharmashastra*, collective writings of the Hindus on their law, scriptures, etc.
Shia	one of the two main branches of Islam (cf. Sunni); followers of Ali, the son-in-law of Muhammad
Shraddha	oblations for the dead in Hinduism
Shudra	the labouring order in classical Hindu sociology
Sikh	follower of the Punjabi Guru Nanak and his successor; a reform movement within Hinduism which became a separate religion
Sufi	follower of a mystical path within the Muslim religion
Sunni	the majority in Indian Islam, who regard caliphs Abu Bakr, Omar and Osman as spiritual descendants of Muhammad
Takkavi	advances of money made by government to the cultivator
Taluqdar	holder of a revenue subdivision, comes to mean large landholder in Awadh
Tazia	representation of the tomb of the Shia *imams* Hasan and Husain paraded in the Mohurrum festival
Tazkira	biographical work recording the lives and works of Muslim holy men and poets
Tehsil	subdistrict revenue division, hence *tehsildar*, official in charge of *tehsil*
Teli	Hindu oil-presser caste; some became merchant–moneylenders
Thagi (thugee)	ritual murder of wayfarers carried out by *thags*
Udasi	religious mendicant, particularly among Sikhs
Ulama	the learned in Muslim law and religion
Umar	caste of Hindu traders in eastern UP
Vaishnavite	follower of the cult of the Hindu diety Vishnu
Vaishya	the merchant order in classical Hindu sociology
Vakil	representative or ambassador; ·comes to mean court pleader

Vallabhacharya	sect of Hindu Vaishnavites
Varna	an order of classical Hindu 'sociology', viz. Brahmin, Kshatriya, Vaishya, Shudra and Sannyasi
Waqf	grant of land for religious or charitable purposes
Zamindar	landholder

INDEX

Abdul Kader, 66
Abkari, *see* revenue
advances, system, 44–5, 236–7, 400
Afghanistan, 104, 160, 279
Afghans, 13, 15, 60; *see also* Pathans
Afridis, 118
Agarwals, 31, 61, 91, 162, 178–86, 217, 249, 332, 383, 445
Agency houses, 225, 232, 264, 434
Agra City, 20, 27, 56, 63–4, 85, 91, 114, 129, 332, 363, 439; Civil Court, 427; Savings Bank, 423; trade in, 63, 92, 147, 156, 159, 209–10, 372, 452–3
Agra District, 45, 80, 84–92, 273, 285–6, 297
Agra Division, 47
agriculture, 38–48, 219–26, 244–5, 427–35; depressions in, 218, 264–5, 283–98, 467; labourers, 38–45, 294–5
Ahirs, 407
Ahmed Khan Bangash, 116
Ahmed Shah Abdali ('Durrani'), 15, 56, 68–9, 87, 156, 185
Ahmedabad, 133, 423–4
Ain-i-Akbari, 77, 191
Ajmer, 142, 212, 279
Ajodhya, 116, 283, 311, 362
Akbar, emperor, 13, 52, 184, 351
Akbar, poet, 456
Akharas, 126, 140, 452
Ali Muhammad, Rohilla, 120–1
Aligarh City (Coil), 208, 335, 360–1
Aligarh, Collector of, 267
Aligarh District, 89, 220, 274
Aligarh College (University), 4, 9, 358
Allahabad City, 126–7, 129, 190, 219, 437, 439, 443; Bank, 423; Congress at, 450; Magh Mela, 127, 141, 450
Allahabad District, 83, 210, 273–4, 293, 295, 363, 400
Allahabad University, 437
Almas Ali Khan, 5, 49, 98–9, 165, 166 and n, 210, 237, 256, 277
Alwar, 136
Amir Khan, 263

Amir Khusru's Garden, Allahabad, 129, 133–4, 343, 361
Amraoti, 241
Amritsar, 157, 203–4
Amroha, 41
Aonla, 120, 270, 325
Appadurai, Arjun, 196
Arasaratnam, S., 419–20
Archaeological Survey of India, 124
Aret Ram Tiwari, 239, 254
Arethias, 179–80, 411–12
Arjunji Nathji, 68, 158, 161, 239
Armenians, 231, 239, 438
Arrah, Bihar, 57
artisans, 52, 144–8, 215, 268, 290–2, 294, 313–14, 327, 357, *see also* weavers
Asaf Jah, Nizam-ul Mulk, 25, 140
Asaf-ud Daulah, 59, 99, 117
Athar Ali, 10
Attock R., 386
Aurangabad, 397
Aurangzeb, emperor, 5, 12, 13, 15, 41, 136, 184
Ausan Singh, Babu, 319–20
Awadh (Oudh), 1, 12–14, 25–7, 205, 276–9, 436–7; nawabs of, 24, 54, 98–101; 133–4, 199; *taluqdars* of, 17–18, 436; trade in, 46–7, 96–9, 150, 173–4, 237–8, 276–7, 434, 436
Azamgarh District, 45, 66, 93, 105n., 210, 288, 435; Maulvi of, 301, 365

Babus (Benares), 182
Bacchraj, Lala, 173, 418
Bah Pargana, Agra, 223, 246, 285
Bahai Khatas, 377, 397
Bahraich District, 154, 221
Bairagis, 142, 184
Bais (Rajputs), 97–100
Baiswara, 81, 96–9, 166, 277–8
Balkrishna Bhatta, 453
Ballia District, 103, 288, 431
Balwant Singh, Raja, 93, 103–4, 178
Balwantnamah, 103
Banarsi Das, 383–4